Limited Edition
One of 350 copies

A HISTORY OF KINGSTON UPON HULL'S TRAMWAYS

by Malcolm Wells
BSc (Econ), DMA, ACIS

Published by Adam Gordon

FRONT COVER
Brush car no.37 passes through the attractively-sounding Drypool Green (officially "Square") on Hedon Road en route to Savile Street. This was the heart of a busy residential and commercial area with several timber yards and the Earle's shipyard nearby.

BACK COVER
An elaborate certificate recording a loan by the Omblers to the Hull Street Tramways Company Ltd in 1899. Note the interest payment arrangements.

ISBN 978-1-874422-90-7
Publication no. 94
Published in 2011 by Adam Gordon, Kintradwell Farm, Brora, Sutherland KW9 6LU
Tel: 01408 622660
E-mail: adam@ahg-books.com

First printing limited to 350 copies

Printed by: 4edge, 7 Eldon Way, Eldon Way Industrial Estate, Hockley, Essex SS5 4AD
Production by: Trevor Preece, 2 Sella Bank, The Banks, Seascale, Cumbria CA20 1QU
E-mail: trevor@epic-gb.com

CONTENTS

APPENDICES

Note on Sources

1. Collections
AG   Adam Gordon Collection
PM   Paul Morfitt Collection
PG   Paul Gibson Collection
MJW   Author's collection

2. Name on reverse of prints (where shown)
AF   Alf Fellowes
RFM   R.F. Mack
TL   Travel Lens
HBP   H.B. Priestley
RBP   R.B. Parr

Introduction

I am told that I rode on a tram during the last week of operation, at a tender age having been born within earshot of the Hessle Road route, but that was my only link until preparing an introductory chapter for an illustrated book published some years ago.

It dawned on me that I knew very little about the tramways and that there was no publication which drew together all the relevant events of the three systems. Anyone who looks at Hull's transport history is shackled by the loss of records during World War II when the head office and its emergency replacement were destroyed within a few weeks. Nevertheless it has been possible to undertake a fairly detailed look at the 1871-1945 period.

Hull's tramway management was, for good or bad, dominated by significant personalities. The Corporation's relationship with the horse tram company was volatile although a careful reading of the reports indicates that the company was not always at fault. The first decade of municipal operation was a golden period with expansion, cheap fares and frequent services for all, the trams seen as essential to keep residents within the city rather than migrate to the countryside. Hull was an early convert to upper deck covers and enclosed vestibules and it paid its staff well in comparison with other undertakings. Yet the unique tripartite management structure sowed its own seeds of destruction and was perhaps the reason why there seemed to be a lack of vision and policy when it was really needed after the Great War.

The tramways suffered from the need to alleviate the rate demand when its surpluses might have been better employed in re-investment in the system.

Running the tramways was a difficult task in these circumstances and management and staff alike were not given the credit that they deserved over the years. The highly effective and speedy manner in which the initial electric routes were introduced and extended was no mean achievement. To carry 118,430 passengers to and from the Yorkshire Agricultural Show over a period of three days only two weeks after the system opened is impressive, and says much for the skills of the organisation and its staff who were coping with electric traction for the first time. It says much, also. for the training that was necessary in advance of the opening

Thereafter it was largely downhill with sackings and trials of senior staff and poor industrial relations, with the advice of officials often ignored by elected representatives and at some cost. There was a liking for lengthy inquiries, there being four in 14 years. Whatever the motives, each inquiry's results had a common thread of an inefficient operation. It took the department ten years to recover (mostly) from the general strike and its aftermath.

The story is worth telling and I hope, like the author, you will find it a fascinating one.

Malcolm Wells, February 2012

Acknowledgements

There are many people without whom this book would not have been produced, as any history of transport operations in Hull is hampered by the loss of so many records in 1941, when first the head office was destroyed by bombing and immediately afterwards the temporary office adjoining Cottingham Road Depot was also destroyed.

Therefore I am indebted to Noel Proudlock for providing much detailed information about the cars both in Hull and in Leeds and for checking the various fleet lists at great length. Paul Morfitt provided much support and many photographs from his collection, as well as timetable information and the notebook of Mr Turner the former Chief Engineer. Richard Buckley contributed information used for his articles in Tramway Review and provided some very sound advice. Paul Gibson was most generous in providing photographs from his vast Hull collection. An important signpost for sources was G.A. Lee's social and economic dissertation on Hull's Tramways.

As ever David Smith and his staff at the former Local History Library in Hull were most patient and very helpful on many occasions, despite having to search the dark upper floor recesses of the former library at times. They and the staff at the new History Centre in Hull have always been very helpful. Thanks are also due to the staff at the National Archives at Kew, Susan Capes, Caroline Rhodes and Tony Diaper of the Streetlife Museum in Hull and the volunteers at the Carnegie Heritage Centre in Hull.

The late Geoff O'Connell's notes have been very useful without which the fleet details would have been sparse and I hope that I have done justice to his researches. Geoff worked for Hull Corporation Transport and became Assistant Traffic Officer whilst his father was an inspector with the Tramways Department. Some posthumous thanks should go to the Committee staff in the Town Clerk's Department from 1871 onwards whose minutes were invaluable and often (but not always) exhaustive and form the backbone of the narrative.

Thanks are also due to Mick Nicholson whose knowledge of signalling in Hull is unsurpassed and who provided the pages from the Stepney Box Occurance Book and to the intrepid group (James Wells (son), Chris Leach, Paul Simpson, Dave Burman and Adrian Gillioand) whose P4 scale model of Botanic Gardens Station set in 1915 will include a working tramway section, who provided information about the crossing and a copy of the heads of agreement.

I would also thank Adam Gordon for taking on the task of publishing this book which I hope will do justice to those men and women who managed and operated the trams in their various guises. In addition I am very pleased to thank Trevor Preece and Roger Smith for the hard work of interpreting my notes and texts and laying out the pages and translating my rough drawings into clear maps. Their forbearance when I found yet another information source was often tested.

Finally but not least, I would like to thank my wife, Andrea, whose patience and support has lasted for this, the fourth book on Hull's electric transport systems in the last twelve years.

Chapter 1

THE HORSE TRAMS

In 1870 the town of Kingston upon Hull had a population of 121,892. Residential development was increasing along the six main roads radiating from the Wilberforce Monument in the town centre. It was a compact if crowded town, where many residents lived within walking distance of their work place.

Industries such as ship building and repairing, including the large Earles yard, were naturally located alongside the River Humber, as was a large fish curing industry around the St Andrew's Dock (Fish Dock), whilst seed crushing and oil mills nestled alongside the River Hull which flowed into the Humber and bisected the town. Exceptions were the Reckitt's works in Dansom Lane, Blundell, Spence & Co.'s paint works in Spring Bank, and large flour mills on Holderness Road. Many prominent shippers and merchants lived within the Old Town. This was a virtual island bounded by the River Hull wharves in the east, the Humber to the south, and four docks (the "Town Docks") west and north. Within the Old Town was the important shopping street of Whitefriargate, a large market and associated shops, which attracted shoppers from all over the town. Many commercial firms, solicitors and banks had head offices there.

A ferry (using paddle steamers built by Earles) sailed from the Victoria Pier (opened as the Corporation Pier in 1847 but renamed after Queen Victoria's visit in 1854 although both names remained in use), across the Humber to New Holland to connect with trains for Grimsby and Cleethorpes. The ferry possessed its own "station" on the opposite side of the road. The pier and surrounding dock area were popular for "promenading" (walking) on Sundays.

Hull's boundaries at their maximum were less than two miles

from the town centre. Extending the tram routes to the boundary was often a strategic objective, but there were several extensions from 1883. Local administration was divided between the Borough and the Local Board of Health (highways and cab licensing), although they shared a common membership and the same building. They were amalgamated in 1876, Hull later becoming a County Borough, and in 1897 a city. The land within the town was entirely flat.

Although the town was compact there was a demand for local transport. The North Eastern Railway's Paragon Station was situated on the western edge of the town centre. Trains ran to Leeds and Doncaster, York, Bridlington and Scarborough, and the seaside towns of Withernsea and Hornsea. Trains to the latter travelled west from Paragon before describing an arc alongside the former town limits and running eastwards. Existing town suburban stations did not carry much local traffic. The railways crossed main roads and other streets at many locations, with consequent delays and endless complaints that lasted for another ninety years.

Public transport comprised expensive cabs and open-topped double-decker omnibuses pulled by two or even three horses, made possible in part by the flat terrain within the town. It is thought that omnibus services dated from 1858, and ran between the Victoria Pier and Beverley Road. Others included a service to Anlaby Road (Coltman Street), and a short-lived cross-town route from English Street to Holderness Road. A more successful service to the Spring Bank level crossing was started in 1864.

In 1871 the three bus routes along Spring Bank, Beverley Road (extended to Pearson Park), and Anlaby were still running usually every half hour. Fares were 3d inside, 2d outside, whilst

Car no. 4, one of the smaller cars dating from 1878 and crew pose for the camera, possibly in Temple Street. (PM)

passengers were mainly non-manual workers. Daily buses ran to nearby villages such as Hessle and Aldborough.

On 12 October 1871, the Local Board of Health received a letter from Hull solicitors representing Major Holland, CB, of London who wished to apply to the Board of Trade for a Provisional Order to construct a tramway system. The consent of the Local Board of Health as the highway authority was requested.

Six routes were proposed, all from the town centre (Wilberforce Monument) to the town boundary on Hessle Road, the first level crossing on Anlaby road, Spring Bank (Botanic Gardens), Beverley Road (town boundary), the Mile House on Holderness Road, Hedon Road (the Prison), and a loop line along Chariot Street and Carlisle Street from the Monument to Prospect Street.

A second letter omitted Hedon Road and the Chariot Street/Carlisle Street loop, but added a route to the Pier along Whitefriargate, Silver Street and the Market Place. Carr Lane was omitted in favour of Osborne Street and Waterhouse Lane. No reason was given for the omission of Hedon Road although it was less populated than other areas since once past Drypool Square the southern (river) side was lined with docks, marine industries and railway land. Given the numbers employed there, especially at Earles, it is surprising that such possible sources of income were ignored.

On 10 November Major Holland, his solicitor and engineer (Mr Kincaid), met the Board's Works Committee and, three days later, the whole Board. After discussions and the Major's agreement not to charge any fare exceeding 2d, consent was given. The Board formed a Tramways Committee of nine members with the Mayor (Alderman Jameson) appointed chairman to supervise its construction. Press opinion was favourable, emphasising the need for cheap transport to encourage workers to move to the suburbs, and to encourage the middle and professional classes to stay within the town rather than relocate to adjoining villages and towns.

Not until April 1872 was the Draft Provisional Order published. By now the Major had sold his interests (if he ever had any), to the Continental and General Tramway Company Ltd whose seven directors had no local links.

A Provisional Order (which will feature regularly in the Hull tramways story) was a method of procedure which was followed by government departments, corporations and tramway promoters and was used to authorise works under various Acts of Parliament, in this case the Tramways Act 1870. It was considered by both Houses of Parliament but in the House of Lords it could be referred to a Select Committee with witnesses called for and against the Order, which required Parliamentary approval and a confirming Bill but for convenience several orders were grouped together in a single Bill. (Further details are shown in Appendix 7)

The Board objected to certain amendments in the draft, as did the Hull Docks Company, which wanted similar powers to those of the Board for streets within its estate. The Commissioners of Trinity House opposed a double line along Whitefriargate which they considered to be too narrow. The Docks Company's claims were rejected, but the Order was amended to include a single line over Whitefriargate Bridge, along Whitefriargate and Silver Street. The Company unsuccessfully tried to have the double lines re-instated. Royal Assent to the Bill was given on 6 August 1872. Seven miles of route were approved with maximum fares set at 3d outside and 2d inside. £2,000 was to be lodged with the Board of Health to indemnify it against untoward incidents.

The Tramways Provisional Orders Confirmation (No. 4) Act of 1872 authorised the following:

1. Commencing in the parish of Sculcoates in Beverley Road at the north end of Suffolk Terrace thence in a southerly direction along Beverley Road to Prospect Street, Albion Street, Bond Street, George Street, Charlotte Street, North Street, Bridge Street, North Bridge, Witham, Holderness Road terminating at the north east corner of the Crown Inn or beerhouse in the township of Sculcoates in the parish of Drypool.
2. Commencing in Spring Bank opposite Derringham Street then along Spring Bank and Prospect Street at the junction of Pearson Street.
3. Commencing in Anlaby Road opposite St Matthew's Church, then along Anlaby Road, Midland Street, Osborne Street, Waterhouse Lane, St John Street (also called St John's Street in some documents) and Junction Street.
4. Commencing in Hessle Road sixty feet east of the south east corner of Toll Bar House of the Hessle Turnpike Trust then along Hessle Road, Porter Street to a junction with Osborne Street and St Luke Street.
5. Commencing in Nelson Street then along Queen Street, Market Place, Silver Street, Whitefriargate and over Whitefriargate Bridge to Junction Street
6. Commencing in Junction Street along Savile Street to George Street forming a junction with tramway no.1
7. From a junction with tramway no. 3 in St John Street to a junction with tramway no. 6.

Section 16 permitted cheap fares for the labouring classes with at least one carriage or more if required each way every morning and evening in the week (Christmas Day and Good Friday excepted) not later than 7am and not earlier than 5.30pm. Section 22 prohibited the running of cars on Sundays, Christmas Day or Good Friday unless the Corporation agreed. The Corporation could give six months' notice of an extension for which the Company must take all necessary steps to comply (section 23).

As can be seen some of the routes ran outside the then town boundary so the possibility of some housing development was provided for.

Whitefriargate Bridge was often (but not always), called Monument Bridge because of the adjacent monument, but the official title was Whitefriargate Bridge, and is so described in most official documents, and in the North Eastern Railway's instructions regarding freight traffic in the town docks. It separated the Queens and Princes Docks. I have used the term mentioned at the time rather than standardise on one form.

The same principle applies to Queen Victoria Square, which was also called Victoria Square and City Square, with no apparent consistency, so again I have left the names alone. Similarly, residents always referred to "going to town" when travelling to the town centre. The same holds good today, the award of city status having had no effect. Another such location was Salthouse Lane Bridge which was also known as Drypool Bridge but official records use both terms.

Royal Assent in the form of the Tramways Orders Confirmation Act was given in August 1872.

Although construction had to commence within a year (or the powers lapsed), not until August 1873 did work commence on the Beverley Road route near Queens Road at Rose Cottage, gradually moving towards the town centre. Despite many complaints and constant badgering from the Board (which never did receive its £2,000), not until December 1874 was the route ready for inspection. Despite the promise of double track in Prospect Street and the inner town, only single tracks with passing loops were laid. The standard of work was not acceptable either, since the Board's Surveyor insisted that some rails be relayed where they protruded above the pavement.

Whitefriargate in horse car days was a busy and important shopping street as seen here. The position of the tracks alongside the northern side of the road can be seen. The car is approaching Whitefriargate Bridge and is bound for Beverley Road. (PM)

Snow on 23/24 December 1874 forced a postponement of the Board of Trade inspection and opening, and not until 5 January 1875 did operations commence. No public announcement was made, and few citizens were aware of it. The *Eastern Morning News* informed readers that the car completed a round trip in less than 30 minutes. It is thought that free rides were given on 5/6 January. The inspection on 7 January by Lt Col. Hutchinson approved the installation subject to comments about some tram rails. If the local authority required it, the Company must remove the near rail at the Albion Street/Prospect Street junction to a distance of 9½ feet from the curbstone of the pavement.

Only two single-deck cars were available for the opening, although some double-deckers arrived in March 1875. It is possible that some of these were assembled in Hull having been manufactured in Belgium. They were first used on Good Friday 1875.

Teething troubles were experienced, particularly on a sharp curve in Bond Street where cars regularly parted company with the track, which required relaying to remedy this. Another problem involved the car wheels when, on at least two occasions, a wheel broke and it was decided to adopt a solid type as used by railway companies.

To local surprise construction of the rest of the system proceeded slowly, apart from short sections in Whitefriargate and Silver Street, when track was laid at the same time as street repairs to save expense and inconvenience.

The *Eastern Morning News* accused the company of making too much money elsewhere, (unspecified), to be bothered with Hull. It was no surprise when the 1872 powers lapsed and a new Hull Street Tramways Company Ltd was floated by the Continental & General Tramway Co. Ltd. in 1874. This proposed to lay single lines only with loops which, the company claimed, were more suited to the town's needs.

The revised proposals were considered by the Town's Parliamentary Bills Committee in January 1875. Among the

items considered was the principle of whether tramways should be extended throughout the Borough and after some debate the principle was approved.

The Continental and General Tramway Company Ltd were reported as being unable to carry out the works and duties and had promoted the present Bill to transfer the undertaking to Frank Farwell, James Moremont and Alexander Clunes Sheriff and other persons who might subscribe to the undertaking and who were to be incorporated as the Hull Street Tramways Company. The power to sell and purchase was merely permissive and there was nothing in the Bill to make the transfer of powers compulsory.

The proposals were considered in depth, the meeting noting the change from double to single line with passing places and also noting that the Bill, unlike the previous Provisional Order, did not define the position of the centre line in streets and this would require some action to secure such a definition. It was also pointed out that the proposed "Passing Places" tended to become "Halting Places" where cars coming in opposite directions wait and pass at such points.

The Borough Surveyor had been asked to comment on how the proposals might affect properties belonging to the Corporation along each route. There was concern that in some narrow and busy streets such as St John Street and Market Place this could create many problems. The Market Place proposal would conflict with the markets there and in Queen Street and would need careful consideration. He suggested that a clause be included to protect the monument (statue of King William III or "King Billy") in the Market Place. He also suggested that only one set of rails be laid on the curve from St John Street into Waterhouse Lane and from Junction Street into St John Street.

Several organisations in Whitefriargate and Silver Street considered that those streets were too narrow for trams, which would conflict with existing traffic (and their customers). Whitefriargate was only 25 feet wide at its widest point, whilst

Car no. 11 passes the North Eastern Railway's Stepney Station on Beverley Road. Note the knifeboard seating on the upper deck. (PM)

Silver Street was only 16 feet in places, and the position of the single track conflicted with parked vehicles. Cars travelling west would be against the traffic flow. There was no alternative route, so their objections were ignored.

A prospectus to raise £23,000 for the HST issued in November 1875 stated that the income for the completed sections exceeded £39 per week and that a year's anticipated income would be £15,210. It was calculated that working expenses would be some 60 percent of the income at £9,126 whilst interest on the Debentures would be a further £900 leaving a surplus of £5,184 over 10 per cent of the paid-up share capital of £50,000.

The Act provided for the HST to take over the tramways, but the required investment was slow to materialise, and the C&G had to commence work on the Spring Bank and Old Town routes, and not until October 1876 was the new Company operational, taking over the Beverley Road route in November.

For a time the Company had no resident engineer until R.G. Smith was appointed in 1877. The standard of track laying was still inconsistent, and part of the track in the Market Place was re-laid.

Despite the slow progress developments were already being considered, and a Provisional Order was obtained in 1876 for extensions to the Borough boundary on Hessle Road (47 yards including a short siding of 18 yards), on Beverley Road (26 yards including a siding of 24 yards) and some 450 yards beyond the Anlaby Road terminus at the Boulevard and an extension of the existing siding at the Boulevard of 24 yards. Approval was given at the Works Committee on 15 December.

The Board of Trade inspection of the Spring Bank route which took place on 11 December 1876 caused difficulties with the Company and the Corporation which was furious that the telegram from the BOT did not arrive until two hours after the inspection, particularly as the Corporation wished to point out several defects in the track between Vine Street and Prospect Street which the Company had not attended to. Major Hutchinson apologised for the delay but said that he had instructed the Company to attend to certain high and low

portions. He had not noticed that a section of track was three inches nearer the pavement than it should be but advised the Corporation to use its powers to compel the Company to remedy the work. Nevertheless the route opened on the following day, 12 December 1876. On 3 March 1877, the Board of Trade's inspector, Major-General Hutchinson, walked along the Hessle Road route before returning by tramcar. Not until 7 April 1877 did the route open using two cars on twenty minute headway. The route terminated at West Dock Avenue, but permission was obtained from the Works Committee to extend the tracks to Scarborough Street where temporary stables were provided. In the meantime the Old Town route had opened on 12 March 1877.

A. Bannister, the Chairman of HST, received agreement in January 1877 from the Streets and Lighting Sub-Committee for permission to run tram-lines (as shown in nearly all the minutes) from the present terminus on Hessle Road into the yard of stables purchased in Scarborough Street. In April approval was given to an additional line over North Bridge, this application coming from the newly appointed resident engineer, Mr R.G. Smith.

On 25 January the Company was given approval by the Streets and Lighting Sub-Committee for the erection of a car shed (but not stables) in Osborne Street. No further details were provided and it has not proved possible to discover any further information nor any map showing a location. It is not possible, either, to find out if it was ever built.

A feature of the introduction of the tramways was that many town centre stands for cabs and omnibuses had to be relocated to avoid obstructing the cars. The loss of traditional stopping places did not go down well with the proprietors who fought a running (and usually losing) battle with the Corporation and continued to obstruct the cars.

The Old Town tramway was approved by the Board of Trade for public use in March 1877. On 3 May 1877 the Works Committee agreed to the HST's request to take up and set back the curb by 30 inches at the Midland Street junction with Anlaby Road in order to provide a 14-foot radius curve provided it was at the Company's expense.

A great uproar arose on 6 May 1877 when Sunday cars were operated for the first time between 2pm and 9pm. The protests left the Company unmoved although criticism continued into electric tram days, Hull being a fervent outpost of the Lord's Day Observance Society. Sunday school teachers petitioned the Company not to run Sunday cars, and the Rural Dean said that he would rather see a smaller congregation at Holy Trinity if the cars did not run. The Company said some passengers actually went to church by tram! The House of Lords had deleted a clause giving the Corporation powers to ban operation on Sundays and Bank Holidays.

Work on the Anlaby Road route had been delayed by a large drainage programme, and it was not opened until Saturday 9 June 1877. By now Major-General Hutchinson had become very familiar with Hull as he returned on 3 July to inspect the Holderness Road route. When it opened on 7 July 1877 the original scheme had been completed in full, albeit with mainly single lines.

Of the authorised 8 miles and 50 chains of line, only 40 chains were double track, but this was gradually increased to 1 mile and 67 chains. This did not permit the operation of a speedy service. It also limited the capacity of each route so that the only way to run more cars was to provide more loops and sidings. G. A. Lee estimates that the total capacity of the system as built was only fourteen cars (four on Beverley Road and two each on the others). Additional sidings raised the capacity to eighteen but the provision of fifteen more between 1878 and 1881 gave a capacity of 35 cars. Yet more sidings and loops had been provided by 1888, and this increased capacity to forty-five cars, more than the actual fleet of thirty-one cars. Approval for additional passing places was given by the Works Committee on 13 July 1877 as follows:

1. Anlaby Road near Coltman Street
2. Hessle Road near Sir Talbot Constable's stables
3. Osborne Street near Lower Union Street
4. Beverley Road near College Street
5. Extension to the double line over North Bridge

All approvals for track additions and alterations were usually on condition that the Company executed the works to the satisfaction of the Corporation and at the Company's expense.

Initially only two town centre starting points were used: St John Street for the Pier, Anlaby Road and Hessle Road, and Savile Street for Beverley Road, Spring Bank and Holderness Road cars.

From September 1877 the HST published its weekly gross receipts in the *"Hull News"*. Until January 1878 publication was irregular but from then until 1889 there were few occasions on which the information failed to appear.

Gross income for the week ending 1 September was £282 15s 8d (the average for the four weeks to 29 September being £278). During Hull Fair week in October receipts totalled £372 6d 5d. The net profit for the second half of 1877 was £2,424, a dividend of 4% being paid out. The following six months were better with a net profit of £2,837 and a dividend of 4½% being declared.

The original bus operators had ceased to run by this time, but the success of the trams encouraged others to start up. In July 1877 a thirty-minute service on the Beverley Road route was started by the Hull General Omnibus and Carriage Company. Its buses ran to the Pier and along Spring Bank, where the HST retaliated by dividing the route into two stages of 1d each, the stage point being at Blundell's Corner. The Tramway Company attacked the bus operator by summoning them for obstructing the lines especially in Nelson Street, but this only succeeded in the bus company being given a permanent stand there!

However, the bus company had ceased trading by February 1878, and the HST bought all its property, including (apparently) the buses.

During 1877 the Company opened permanent stables and its main works and granary at the junction of Hessle Road and Regent Street, Scarborough Street being vacated. Two other temporary stables were later opened at Terry Street on Beverley Road and in Witham. Approval for the Terry Street shed (on NER land) was given when Mr Bannister attended the Works Committee on 30 May 1878 but only on condition that the temporary shed was removed within two years of the approval. Further approval for a junction from the Beverley road route into this shed was given on 30 October.

Approval for more extensions was received during 1877 (Hull Street Tramways (extension) Order 1877):

No. 1 – five furlongs and twenty-one chains in length commencing in the Hessle Road in the township of Willerby and parish of North Ferriby to a point ninety feet east of the NER's Hessle Road Junction signal box in an easterly direction into the townships of Willerby, Swanland and West Ella terminating in the parish of St Mary by a junction with existing tramway no. 4 authorised by the 1875 Act
No. 1A – a short tramway commencing at a point eight feet from and south of the commencement of tramway No. 1 in an easterly direction and terminating by a junction with Tramway No. 1 at a point three chains from its commencement
No. 1B – a short junction tramway commencing at the junction with tramway No. 4A of the 1875 Act in a westerly direction terminating by a junction with Tramway No. 1 one chain from its commencement
No. 2 – six furlongs eighty-seven yards in length commencing in the Anlaby Road in the township of Swanland and parish of North Ferriby from one hundred and twenty feet from the gate-keeper's house at the level crossing of the NER mainline and passing eastwards into the townships of Swanland and West Ella to a junction with Tramway No. 3 of the 1875 Act. Passing loops were also included as Tramways Nos 2A and 2B at the new terminus and the old terminus.
Tramway No. 3 – four furlongs five yards commencing in Beverley Road in the parish of Cottingham from Cottingham Road in a southerly direction along Beverley Road into the parish of Sculcoates in the borough terminating by a junction with the existing Tramway No. 1 of the 1875 Act. Tramways Nos 3A and 3B were passing places at both ends of the extension.

Other clauses protected the operations of the NER and defined the centre lines on each roadway and for the construction of additional passing places.

The extensions were part of the Tramways Orders Confirmation Act 1877 which also included the Barton, Eccles, Winton and Monton Local Board Tramways, Bristol Tramways (Extension), Manchester Suburban Tramways plus several others.

Construction of the extensions by Simpson and Malone was expeditious, and following the Board of Trade's inspection on 29 March 1878, they opened the following day.

By August 1878 the board of directors of the HST had been reduced to one, J.W. Maclure who became chairman, but two new directors were appointed, including the brother of Alderman Bannister (Charles Henry Bannister) and A.J. Lambert, the Liquidator of the CGTC. Another, called Bacon, joined them in 1880. Alderman Bannister's tenure was brief as he died in July 1881.

The Hull Street Tramways Act 1878 referred to the agreement

of February 1878 whereby the C&GT (which had gone into liquidation in February 1878) would sell the 1877 authorised extensions to the HST for £14,000. Also, on 11 and 18 April 1878, a formal notice appeared in the local press describing the proposed purchase and stating that objections were to reach the Board by 27 April. The Corporation did not object.

After receiving approval from the Works Committee in April 1878 The Company re-routed its Anlaby Road service on 18 October 1878 direct from Midland Street to the Monument, after the widening of Carr Lane earlier in the year. This had been delayed because the Town Clerk considered that the HST did not have the power to construct the tram-line without a Provisional Order. If it could be proved that the proposed line was a "junction" the Company could have the power under section 21 of the Act which authorised the Company to make all such crossings, passing places, sidings and junctions for the efficient working of the tramways. If not a junction there was no power to build the line. It was almost that the Town Clerk was dropping a large hint to the HST who went ahead and built the "junction" after submitting a tracing of the works and describing the powers it possessed in June!

In August following the approval given above a new service was introduced from the Pier to Paragon Station outward from St John Street along Carr Lane and Anlaby Road, returning via Midland Street, Osborne Street and Waterhouse Lane. A one penny fare was charged. This was abandoned in November, with the Anlaby Road cars running direct to the Pier (inward via Osborne Street and outward via Carr lane) until May 1885, when the Beverley Road cars were extended to the Pier.

Initially a twenty minute service had been operated on each route, with a flat fare of 2d, apart from the Old Town (1d). In July 1877, to meet growing competition, the Spring Bank route was divided into two penny stages at the Beverley Road end. With the opening of the extensions in 1878 the full distance fare became 3d.

In November 1878 the Newington Board of Health (located immediately west of the boundary) considered a request for consent to the building of a tramway from the village of Hessle in the county of York to the Dairycoates terminus of the HST which lay within the parish of Newington. When consent was forthcoming, the Hull and Hessle Tramway Co. Ltd was formed on 17 February 1879 with seven shareholders, 2 with 30 shares, 4 with 20 and 1 with 1 to lay the route, and any other tramways as it thought fit, to be worked by horse or steam. A prospectus was issued in March 1879, but by April only 276 of the required 3,000 £5 shares had been taken. Very few additional shares were taken and the Company was wound up on 16 June 1882. It had not been helped by the HST publicly disassociating itself from its scheme. Thus ended the first attempt to link Hessle by tramway with Hull.

A single sheet found in Hull's History Centre records states that the lines would become Board property should the Corporation sign up to the proposal and that the lines could be laid after the Board's approval.

By now the HST had reached its maximum size. Where there was heavy congestion, in St John Street and across Whitefriargate Bridge, across North Bridge and along Albion Street, the lines were doubled. Only one car was supposed to be on any stretch of single line unless duplicate cars were running, or cars on another route were using a common section. Despite regulations regarding the right of passage there were many recorded instances of cars meeting on single sections with the inevitable arguments about precedence!

Charles Dyson in "Fares Please!" says that the system that enabled passengers to transfer between the Pier and other routes was rather troublesome. On arrival at St John Street a passenger could obtain a transfer ticket for a Pier-bound car. Some passengers did not understand how the system worked, and tried to use the transfer ticket to change to one of the main routes. The resultant disputes with passengers who had (allegedly and sometimes actually) lost their tickets, and had picked up another in order to complete their journey, often ended in the Police Court.

Accidents were not rare. In July 1877 horses pulling car no.53 (later car no.11) knocked down a two year old child in

Savile Street was an important terminus in horse car days with three routes (Spring Bank, Holderness Road and Beverley Road) meeting there. The crooked angle of the destination board on car no. 1 was not unusual. In the distance is car no. 20. (PM)

Porter Street resulting in amputation of its left arm. A few weeks later a man was knocked down, and despite the amputation of a leg, he died. The driver claimed that he was travelling slowly and had stepped aside to let the man through. Witnesses stated the driver had refused to stop on two or three occasions. It emerged that, despite the regulations prohibiting alighting from moving cars, (and via the front entrance), it was common practice to do so. After a fatal accident in Porter Street in June 1879 the Town Clerk was instructed to write to the HST urgently requesting steps to place proper fenders or guards in front of all tram cars as then in use in Sheffield and other towns for the prevention of accidents, better protection and safety of the public. The Company replied to the effect that it had contacted the Sheffield Tramways and, if efficient, would adopt their equipment.

Charles Dyson states that he observed a car at Newland (Beverley Road) without horse or even front footboard, apparently having lost an argument with a steam roller! The two horses were seen further along the road still on the move with the front of the car!

Throughout its existence the Company received numerous complaints about the state of its horses. Between 1881 and 1883 the number of complaints rose, and the conditions of the horses deteriorated. This report in the Hull Mail during 1881 was perhaps typical. "James Rowan, driver and John Wright the manager were summoned at the Police Court on Monday the 4th inst for cruelty to a tram horse in Queen Street (on the Pier route). P.C. Banks (160) stated that his attention was drawn to the state of the horse from seeing a crowd collected around a car where the horse had fallen and seemed in a weakly state and hardly able to move. Evidence was given by a cab driver and a local tobacconist as to the unfitness of the animal." The Company received many fines but apparently did little to improve the situation. On occasions the small double-deck trams were pulled by a single horse, often in great distress, especially on sharp curves. The sale of the Company's buses in 1889 eased the situation for a while. Close inspection of some horses in the photographs in this book seem to confirm the poor condition and underweight of some horses when on the road.

There were many incidents of horses setting off with only the draw gear hanging down behind them, and legend has it that on one occasion the pair set off without both driver and conductor only to derail at the first bend!

Conductors were at risk from overhanging trees and street lights when issuing fares. On one occasion a conductor was seriously injured when a low projecting street lamp from the George public house in Whitefriargate knocked him off the car and into the road. The landlord, Mr Rose, was instructed by the Corporation to re-site it.

In order to avoid paying heavy insurance costs, the Company did not usually contest claims, paying as much as £800 to the widow of the paymaster of HMS Rupert, who fell off a car to his death, primarily because of a broken handrail. In 1889 alone, when the Company could ill afford it, the compensation bill passed £1,000!

On 11 September 1878 the Hackney Carriage Sub-Committee inspected various "Tram-carriages" as follows:

Cars 11, 12, 13 – 16 passengers inside;
Cars 5, 6, 7, 9, 10 and 14 to carry 16 inside and 16 outside (upper deck);
Cars 51 to 56 to carry 22 inside and 22 outside.

All were licensed and the Company was instructed to renumber from 1 consecutively to match the licence number. As we shall see the Company was very slow to act on this, so much so

that on 27 November the inspector, Mr Whitfield, reported that the cars had not been renumbered nor were drivers and conductors wearing their badges as required by the Bye-Laws. The Company was instructed to act on both matters at once. In addition it was told not to allow drivers or conductors to work until they had been granted a licence or face proceedings. Finally, it was told to stop overcrowding on the cars and was informed what the penalty was for this!

The first of what was to become a recurring theme during the tramway era (and beyond) was a report to the Streets and Lighting Sub-Committee on 9 January 1879 regarding the time lost to road traffic and pedestrians by the closing of railway crossings. Although not prepared in connection with tram car delays it shows that they were affected where they crossed a railway line. In this case it was the Beverley Road Line which was closed 180 times over three days between 6.30am and 7.30pm for a total of 7 hours 37 minutes, the longest period being one of 6 minutes.

In April 1879 the frequency on the Beverley Road, Spring Bank and Old Town routes was increased to fifteen minutes. The flat fare was replaced with a series of stages on 19 June 1879, with a penny fare for the densely populated central core of the town. A single stage covered the remainder of the Spring Bank route, but the others were divided into two more stages.

New cars added to stock in 1879 comprised double deck cars 1-3/16-18/20-22 and single-deck car 19.

There had been complaints about the position of the tram lines on North Bridge and its approaches in that their position in relation to the curb was such that local businesses could not load and unload rullies. The Company, in March 1879, was asked to remedy this by forming a junction on the east side of the bridge and move the southernmost line nine inches further away from the footway to enable rullies to stand on either side for the benefit of those warehouses located there.

Members of the Streets and Lighting Sub-Committee inspected the defective condition of the tram lines in several locations and criticised the method of repairs. The attention of the HST was drawn to the bad condition of the lines and the need for more permanent repairs. The Borough Engineer said that the rails were not being embedded on a sufficiently firm bearing or foundation since the rails gave way on traffic passing over them causing openings to be made into which water was able to penetrate beneath the rails.

The Company had apparently done nothing as a Mr G. Stephenson complained, in writing, that work around North Bridge had not been carried out in accordance with the Corporation instruction of 30 March and as a result his business was seriously inconvenienced. A further letter was immediately despatched to the Company ordering the works to be carried out forthwith. In July the Company had claimed that inclement weather had delayed all works and stated that it would carry out the work when settled weather was experienced. Finally, in September the Corporation lost patience and gave the HST seven days' notice under sections 17 and 33 of the Hull Street Tramways Act to repair and place in good order the rails and substructures upon which they rested and such portions of the roadway that it was bound to maintain. On 16 October the Borough Engineer was able to report that works on Beverley Road had commenced.

At 2.20pm and again at 6pm on Saturday 14 June a car was observed with persons riding on the steps and landing in contravention of the regulations. The driver refused to stop and to talk with Mr J. Whitfield, the inspector. This and other instances were drawn to the Manager's attention, but without too much success.

On 18 August 1879, workmen's cars (for artisans, mechanics

Throughout the existence of all three types of tramways Hull's many level crossings played havoc with operations and punctuality. Car no. 30 of 1882 waits at the Boulevard crossing on Anlaby Road. (PM)

and daily labourers) were introduced. A schedule laid before the Works Committee on the day of introduction gave the following information:

TOWN SERVICE
From Paragon Street Railway Station to Victoria Pier at 6.15am; returning at 6.30am.
HESSLE ROAD
From Dairycoates to the Monument at 6.15am; returning at 6.38am.
ANLABY ROAD
From the Monument to Chalk Lane at 6.15am; returning at 6.35am.
SPRING BANK
From Savile Street to Cemetery Gates at 6.15am; returning at 6.30am.
HOLDERNESS ROAD
From Mile House to Savile Street at 6.15am; returning at 6.38am.

A single fare of 1d was charged and the facility was available on all cars running between 5.30 and 6.15 in the evening for such persons returning from work

They were withdrawn in May 1880 with the cars starting at 8.15am. The last cars left at 9 pm to 9.45pm except on Saturdays when they left an hour later. On Sundays cars ran from 2pm until 9pm.

At busy times a frequency of ten minutes was provided but at certain times only a half-hour service was operated on the outer portions of the Anlaby Road and Holderness Road routes. Until 1881 it is thought that alternate cars along Holderness Road terminated at Southcoates station where there was a loop. Another fares revision took place with the maximum fare reduced to 2d (Spring Bank 1d), possibly as a result of a downturn in use due to a recession, but also due to competition from buses and waggonettes.

These initiatives came from the manager, Alexander Acheson, who had replaced Mr Constable in 1879, but he was succeeded by John Wright in April 1881, who immediately rung the changes. Services on Anlaby Road, Spring Bank and Beverley Road were increased to every ten minutes, with fifteen minutes headways on Hessle Road and Holderness Road, trams

operating from 8.15am until after 10pm. A bus service was operated to the Pier at thirty-minute intervals.

The following month the 1d fare stages were lengthened once more on Anlaby Road, Hessle Road and Beverley Road, whilst the outer stages remained more or less the same, although they did overlap the inner stages slightly.

This fares system lasted for the next six years. The majority of the town's inhabitants lived within the 1d stages of the town centre and the Pier. At approximately ½d per mile they were very cheap compared with most towns in the United Kingdom. That the fares were stable reflected the most profitable period of the horse tramways, despite bus competition.

In October 1879 the Company asked for approval of a new siding on Beverley Road between Harley Street and Providence Row, but this was deferred and following discussions the proposal was dropped and an existing siding outside the Wesleyan Chapel a short distance away was removed! Permission to reduce the minimum age for conductors from 18 to 15 years of age was denied.

Renumbering of the cars was still not complete in December 1879 and once more the Company was given a warning as eleven were still with the old numbers. The Company had been asked to alter the lines in St John Street but had done nothing so the Borough Engineer prepared his own plan which was sent to the HST also in December 1879. Not until July 1880 was the matter resolved when alterations were made to the points in St John Street to enable cars from Anlaby Road to run through Carr Lane rather than Osborne Street.

Approval was given in January 1880 for the Company to lay two lines into the car shed at a proposed building on the south side of Witham. Yet in May it was instructed to cease running its cars over the flagging into and from the shed and to make good the damage done! The HST replied that the materials for the lines had been ordered and the lines would be laid very soon. When it did so it found that some alteration to the siding in Witham was necessary and received permission to extend the siding to the westward in July.

Permission for the installation of no fewer than seven additional sidings was sought in August 1880 but, for once, a decision was deferred to permit the Committee members to inspect each location – which they did in September 1880. As a result the Committee refused to permit a siding in St John Street and asked the Company to place it in Carr Lane clear of Engine Street. This was approved in November, but was later changed at the HST's request to a location further west outside the Mariners' Alms Houses in Carr Lane. The remaining sidings: west side of Porter Street near Michael Street; south side of Hessle Road between Madeley Street and Daltry Street, the north side of Spring Bank between Peel Street and Hutt Street; the east side of Beverley road north of Stepney Lane; on the east side of Bond Street near Albion Street and on the north side of Holderness Road, west of Beeton Street, were deferred until a site inspection had been carried out.

At its height the Company employed about eighty men of whom Lee estimates that there were thirty drivers and thirty conductors. Initially wages were above average for Hull, drivers receiving 30/- per week and conductors 27/- per week. However, when a trade recession in 1879 cut its income, the Company reduced wages by seven shillings a week, taking a further shilling off in 1880, making a one-third reduction. In 1882 first class drivers received 3s 5d a day (23s 11d per seven day week) and second class drivers 3s per day (21s per week). The Company's papers do not define the duties of either class.

The pay reductions proved unpopular, and in June 1881 Mr Wright received an unsigned letter demanding a rise for all staff with a threat of strike action on Whit Monday 6 June. He rejected the demand advising the men to petition the directors.

The strike duly took place with only six cars in service at the start of the day. All the strikers (apart from some who returned to work), were dismissed and replacements were taken on so that a normal service was possible in the afternoon.

Ten double-deck cars entered service in 1882 (nos. 19/23-25 and nos. 26-31) bringing the fleet to a maximum of thirty-one cars not all of which were in continuous service depending on the results of the regular Corporation inspections. All the single-deck cars were withdrawn. It is possible but not certain that cars 23 and 24 were in service in 1880.

New permanent stables were opened in 1882 in Temple Street off Beverley Road, and in Jesmond Gardens off Holderness Road. Approval for laying the track along Temple Street was given in April 1882.

In March 1882 a new rule book was produced (54 pages!) which the men refused to accept. Strike action followed on 24 April, with a re-run of the previous year's events. The local press and passengers were supportive, providing gifts and money. The Company was resolute, but a slight softening of their stance came with the increased waggonettes' competition, including the granting of one day off in eight (apparently honoured in the breach). Appendix 7 contains a description of the rule book.

The Company countered the competition from buses by obtaining its own buses and running them immediately in front of its competitors (shades of 1986!) For a while the opposition seemed to have been vanquished, but the situation changed in July 1885 when the Alexandra Dock was opened. Some residential development had occurred nearby, mainly for dock workers, but additional transport facilities were needed. The Company had deleted the Hedon Road from its original proposal, a decision it was about to regret.

Mr W. Marsden commenced to run waggonettes for Hedon Road from Savile Street and others soon followed. The congestion in Savile Street was such that complaints about obstruction in that street from shop keepers, the HST and the Hackney Coach Sub-Committee, were sent to the Chief Constable.

On 14 April 1882 an Extraordinary General Meeting of the

HST agreed the directors' recommendation to raise the sum of £9000 through the issue of 900 shares of £10 each. These were to be offered to existing shareholders in the first instance, the shareholders to pay an initial £2 plus four quarterly instalments of £2.

Attached to the offer were the latest traffic figures which were compared with the previous year's figures:

	1881 passengers	1882 passengers	1881 receipts £ s d	1882 receipts £ s d
January	157,639	228,532	705 7 6	983 12 8
February	181,656	238,430	826 11 1	1058 1 0
March	207,664	320,296	998 17 7	1378 11 5
April	241,856	316,605	1009 14 7	1367 18 7
Total	788,815	1,103,863	3540 10 9	4788 3 8
Increase		315,048		1248 2 11

This paints a rosy picture but it hid problems. The receipts per car mile in 1882 actually fell from 10.36d in 1881 to 9.39d. The Company would never rise above 10d per car mile again. Gross income rose by £2480 but working expenses rose by £2037 whilst the number of car miles rocketed from 330.639 to 429.269. 1882 also saw the last new cars added to the fleet in the shape of small double-deck cars nos 19/23-25 and large cars 26-31.

Meanwhile waggonettes' competition on Hessle Road and Anlaby Road resulted in all tram fares being reduced to 1d (same as the competition), from the Pier or Monument to any destination. Unlike the trams, waggonettes were not popular with anyone other than their passengers. Despite being licensed (£2 guineas a year) they had no right to stop on the highway to pick up or set down passengers. Police always moved them on or fined them, and animal societies claimed that the horses were in a worse condition than the HST's horses ever were. Cab owners didn't like them either and pressed the Council for action.

When the Company applied to install more crossing places in September the Corporation challenged its power to do so, especially where doubling was proposed. The Town Clerk considered that it did not have the power and required a Provisional Order or a Parliamentary Bill, which was interesting, given his opinion when the Carr Lane extension had been considered in 1878.

On 16 March 1883 the Town Clerk was asked to report on the right of the tramway company to evade the rule of the road in passing over Whitefriargate Bridge.

At the end of 1884 the Council informed the Company that it had decided to close Albion Street for a time whilst repairs and developments were undertaken. The Company considered alternative routes and elected to run the cars along Baker Street at a cost of £1,200 to £1,400. It further decided that Baker Street would be a more convenient route and asked the Corporation if it would agree, in return for which it would surrender passing places in Bond Street and Prospect Street. This did not prove acceptable and the Corporation would approve Baker Street only as a temporary measure, the lines to be removed when Albion Street re-opened. In the event the Company decided against the expense of laying an alternative route and used buses until Albion Street re-opened.

In October 1885 the Corporation authorised a passing place covering the whole length of Albion Street and agreed that the HST could lay chilled iron blocks on each side of the rail alternately with wood or granite blocks, as had been laid in Prospect Street, in Albion Street and along Osborne Street. The Company stated that the blocks prevented ruffing and were a great advantage for vehicular traffic.

Men who wished to drive or conduct tramcars were required

to apply to the Council's Hackney Coach Sub-Committee. Thus, in December 1885 it approved licenses for seven conductors and three drivers and in May 1886 eight conductors and six drivers were successful.

An unusual accident occurred in December 1885 when a conductor on a double-deck car was injured when his head came into contact with a lamp situated outside the George Hotel in Whitefriargate! The Corporation asked the land-lord, Mr Rose, to alter its position.

The Hackney Coach Sub-Committee had asked its inspectors to carry out peri-odic examinations of the tramcars since each had to be

Overhead views of the horse cars are rare so this photograph of a car on Beverley Road is a bonus. (PG)

licensed every year. On 25 February 1887 the inspector, Mr Clarke, reported that cars 1, 2, 3, 4, 5 and 17 had been thor-oughly repaired, painted and varnished and were in good condi-tion whilst 18 and 19 were undergoing repair. In the past year twenty-two cars had been more or less overhauled and were in very fair condition.

A more detailed report was presented in August 1887 and shows where some of the cars were located. Cars 1/7/21/23/24 were at Holderness Road and were in fair condition and much cleaner than on previous occasions; nos 9/10/1/2/5/6/7/8/9/20 were very clean and in fair condition at Hessle Road whilst cars 6 and 8 were under repair; in fair condition at Beverley Road were cars 2/4/5/13/4/22/5/6/7/8/9/30/1.

The minutes of the Works Committee contain many refer-ences to the state of the track and disagreements with the HST. In April 1887 the Borough Engineer presented a long report on the condition of track throughout the town. Not all the lines were in a poor condition, despite what a reading of the minutes might infer. Osborne Street, Midland Street and Albion Street possessed lines in good condition but the track in Queen Street, Market Place and Charlotte Street was in poor condition as was the whole length of Hessle Road, Anlaby Road and most of Beverley Road and Holderness Road tracks.

As a result, on 14 April 1887, the Borough Engineer served a formal notice on the Company to put into good condition and repair the rails and pavement maintainable by them in certain streets in the borough. The directors of the Company, whose head offices were still in London, replied on 21 April. They

This calm and sylvan scene is the Beverley Road route at Lambert Street. The side destination boards on large double deck car no. 15 can be clearly seen. (PM)

respectfully submitted that the notice was uncalled for. The Company was engaged at this time of year in carrying out the necessary repairs to the lines which could not be done in the winter. It was their desire to maintain the lines and roadway in good and satisfactory condition. They asked that that the manager, Mr Wright, be allowed to meet the committee to discuss the matter.

When this was read to the Committee the Borough Engineer demurred and stated that the Company had not maintained the roadway in its care to his satisfaction and have not made good defects pointed out to the manager and his predecessor.

Mr Wright was permitted to address the Committee and read out a statement which he subsequently handed to the Committee. He started by saying "in the unavoidable absence of his directors...". How unavoidable one wonders? The Company was surprised given the "same friendly spirit which had marked all communications in the past". It was surprised to read the Engineer's report in the public press and was aggrieved at the course taken by the Committee without any previous communication. It was concerned that it would make a decided impression on the public that the Company's lines were in a dilapidated condition and that the public would think that the Company had refused to renew its lines.

In his six years as manager Mr Wright claimed that he had received no formal notice or verbal indication that was not attended to at once (not borne out by references in the minutes). The recent period of bad weather had retarded work on occasions and the severe frosts had done very considerable damage to the permanent way. Since the weather had eased a very considerable force of men had been put to work on the lines. Mr Wright, with respect to the Engineer, did not think that the lines were in as bad a state of affairs as he had alleged.

He reminded the Committee that the lines had been laid to the Board of Trade's and the Engineer's predecessor's satisfaction. The Engineer had complained that the rails were beneath the level of the pavement but had not the Board of Trade insisted that the rails be one-fourth of an inch below the setts?

During the past two years one-eighth of the system had been relaid with steel girder rails with new setts and cast iron chilled blocks on either side of the rails. These included Prospect Street to Rose Cottage on Beverley Road, most of the town centre, Wheeler Street to Thornton Street, Whitefriargate/Silver Street, Bean Street to Porter Street and Midland Street. Work was planned on the Rose Cottage to Newland section. He considered that two-thirds of the system was in a reasonable state of repair. He asked the Corporation to withdraw its notice.

His presentation split the meeting. Councillor Larard proposed that the notice be withdrawn and that the Engineer report on progress at the end of each month until the repairs were complete. This motion was defeated and the notice stood. Whilst the Company did not always respond to Corporation instructions, reading some of the correspondence one senses a certain friction between the Borough Engineer (Mr Fox Sharp) and various managers. Indeed the Works Committee did not always support its Engineer as in October 1888 when a dispute arose regarding the laying of new sidings west of Vane Street on Spring Bank. The HST refused to conform to an instruction from the Corporation to pave all macadamised spaces between the sidings and the channel of less than 8 feet at the side of the road. When Mr Wright appeared before the Committee he pointed out that the Company had paved a distance of 4' 8" between the nearest rail and the channel some 3' 2" beyond the distance prescribed by Act of Parliament. The Committee accepted his argument and decided to take no further action.

Within a month the Borough Engineer was complaining that that the Company refused to carry out work on Hessle Road at Dairycoates and Anlaby Road east of the Boulevard to the levels required by him. He and the Company differed on their interpretation of the Tramways Act. The Town Clerk was asked to report on the legal situation but the matter did not feature again in the minutes, which suggests that the Company's view prevailed – this time.

A typical complaint was made by Mr W.E. Goddard in June 1887. He stated that his dogcart had had another accident in exactly the same place as he had reported some weeks ago when the cart was smashed and his man injured. This time it was Mr Goddard who had been thrown out of his cart when his horse had slipped in the dangerous holes in the setts and touched the tram siding on the south side of Carr Lane. He stated that unless the Corporation took action he would. His cause was reinforced by a letter from nine tradesmen complaining of similar incidents in Carr lane but also in St John Street and Anlaby Road. Their complaints were forwarded to the HST.

In December 1887 the Hessle Road depot had been destroyed by fire, although no one was injured and all the cars and horses were saved. In the confusion horses were released quickly to save them and they ran free in adjoining streets until rounded up. The depot was insured, and this financed a replacement with two floors that was completed in mid-1888. The Company requested permission for the cars to stand overnight on Hessle Road until the damage was cleared sufficiently to allow the cars to be stabled in the depot area but the decision was deferred and seems not to have been raised again.

The problems with the tramways had led the Works Committee of 21 September 1888 to form a Sub-Committee to consider and report on the desirability and power of the Corporation to take over and maintain the lines of both tramway Companies upon the payment by them of an annual sum to the Corporation. Authority was given to confer as necessary with the directors of both Companies. This met for the first time on 5 October 1888 and instructed the Borough Engineer to inspect the condition of the various lines belonging to the Hull Street Tramways Company and to report what would be necessary to be done before the Corporation undertook any repairs. He was also asked to estimate what an annual payment might be made by the HST for keeping the roadways and lines in repair.

On 16 October the Sub-Committee met at short notice after hearing that two directors of the Company were in the town. Mr Maclure, Chairman, Mr Bannister, director and Mr Wright attended the meeting. The recent decision was discussed and received support for the spirit of the resolution and Mr Maclure promised to assist in any way that he could.

Acrimonious correspondence continued to flow between the two organisations during October and November, the argument raging over the levels of the rails, the Company stating that it was complying with its Act and the Corporation claiming that it did not. The Company accused the Corporation of wanting to raise the level of the lines whilst the Corporation refuted this. The Town Clerk reported that section 20 of the 1870 Act placed the duty on the Company of keeping the tramways in good repair to the satisfaction of the Corporation and section 33 provided for fines not exceeding £5 per day for every day in which the Company failed to carry this out after due notice from the Corporation. But the key section was number 19 which stated that should the road authority alter the level of any road along which any tramway was laid or authorised to be laid the Company shall from time to time alter or lay their rails so that the uppermost surface thereof shall be on a level with the surface of the road as altered.

On 20 December 1888 the Borough Engineer served formal notice regarding the tramways on the Hessle, Anlaby and Beverley Roads but not until 11 January 1889 did the manager reply to state that his instructions were to fasten loose rails and to repair defective paving. The poor weather had delayed repairs. He would forward the letter to London to arrange a meeting with the Corporation. The Works Committee was unsympathetic and decided that unless the repairs were started legal action would be taken.

As a result a director, Mr C.H. Bannister, and Mr Wright attended the Works Committee on 22 March 1889 and obtained a two month's adjournment of any proposed legal action by the Corporation.

However, although some work was carried out the dispute rumbled on. On 14 June 1889 the Works Committee considered a further report which stated that on 22 May when the two month period was up the repairs were far from complete. During the period the Company had employed about 40 men on the work and the worst of the defects on the Beverley and Hessle Roads were removed, but the rails were low along a considerable stretch of Hessle Road but when asked to raise the level, the Company refused.

The worst section of Anlaby Road between Bean Street and the Boulevard and from Wheeler Street to Walton Street had seen some attention but only the worst parts had been repaired and the rails had not been raised. Work in Witham had been completed but the Borough Engineer had taken exception to the levels to which the rails had been re-laid and he considered the rest of the route to be in a very defective condition. It would take another two months to remedy the situation. On 6 May he had written to the Company and drawn this to the manager's attention. Mr Kincaid had replied saying he had investigated the matter and as the Corporation would not agree to any alteration to the terms of section 43 of the Tramways Act he had made three recommendations to his Board.

He recommended no further alterations to the levels of the rails nor would he recommend abandonment of the tramways in Whitefriargate and Silver Street. Where the rails were worn out they should be renewed with rails of a similar section and it was not necessary in the repair to use girder rails or chilled blocks. Under the circumstances and the large expenditure incurred it was unreasonable to ask the Company to take any other course.

Meanwhile the Borough Engineer had reported to the Tramways Sub-Committee on 28 March 1889 that he thought it advisable that, before undertaking the repair of the tramways of the HST, to relay the whole of the lines with steel girder rails, to lay chilled iron blocks where these had not been laid and to relay the whole of the pavement where new rails had to be put down with new granite. The approximate cost was £31,500 whilst the annual maintenance cost thereafter would be £610.

He had discussed the matter with Mr Kincaid, the Engineer to the Tramway who had since written to the Corporation. The latter proposed that work should start on Holderness Road where the permanent way was in good order but the paving was not and the macadamised portion at the side also required repair. He suggested that he and Mr White should agree a specification for the tramway portion of the work and make an estimate of the cost after which the Company would provide the cash for the Corporation to keep the road in good repair at cost price. He considered that this work could be done better and more cheaply by the Corporation than the HST. This arrangement could be tried out on Holderness Road before agreeing the details for the whole of the system. The Sub-Committee agreed to consider the specification when it was complete.

The Town Clerk reported that the Corporation could, within six months of the expiration of the HST's Act, require the Company to sell the undertaking. Board of Trade approval was required and formal notices would need to be published and a valuation would be required. After some discussion it was

agreed merely to enter the report on the Minutes. This was surprising and did no one any favours and, importantly, the Company would usually quote the uncertain situation in future discussions and use it as a reason or excuse for not spending significant sums of money.

In July 1889 the Borough Council received its Provisional Order which gave it powers to license omnibuses and waggonettes at work or standing for hire, impose vehicle capacities, hire drivers and conductors, to suspend licences for misconduct and to fix stopping places. Bye-laws for omnibuses had been approved by the Borough Council on 6 June, and other bye-laws gave powers to regulate the numbers and fitness of the horses employed.

Nevertheless the trams still faced low-cost flexible competitors with standards of maintenance and carriage inferior to its own. Restrictions on the age of waggonette conductors were countered by abolishing conductors altogether, and a concomitant reduction in costs. The flat terrain worked in favour of the competition, whilst a deteriorating track bed adversely affected traction and put more strain on its horses. The year 1888/1889 saw a deficit recorded of £1,840 compared with the previous year's profit of £1,421.

The Borough Engineer obtained three tenders for the work in Whitefriargate and Silver Street based on a) the Company doing all the work for which it was responsible; b) the HST relaying the rail but not the paving and c) the Corporation doing all the work. He was instructed to contact the Company once more.

In September complaints were made about the unsafe practices of omnibuses stopping to take up or set down passengers on the tramlines and the Hackney Coach Sub-Committee decided to make it an offence to do so by means of a new bye-law.

September saw further exchanges of acerbic correspondence with the Company accusing the Corporation's officials of exceeding their instructions and Mr Kincaid saying very plainly that the Company would carry out the works in Whitefriargate and Silver Street but would not enhance this work nor carry out any other Council instructions. He demanded a meeting but as the Town Clerk and Borough Engineer were on holiday the Assistant Borough Engineer, Mr Bricknell, replied. He claimed that the Company had misunderstood the nature of the works that were required. They needed to rectify settlement under their rails – indeed the north rail was higher than the south rail which itself was irregular. He could arrange a meeting but saw no reason to do so as the Committee would not go back on its position.

1889 was a difficult year for the HST. Gross receipts began to slide and repairs to the track were postponed, only being done if the Corporation complained. The cost of renewing track work as we have seen was £31,000, with annual maintenance costs of £610. The Company was concerned with the high cost (given the fall in receipts), and the possibility of failure and possible sale. Instead the Company offered to give the track to the Corporation and lease it back, an idea that did not find favour with the Corporation at that time.

On 14 October 1889 the *Eastern Morning News* carried a long article which condemned the conditions of service, low wages and long hours, with many staff going for weeks without a day off. Working conditions were graphically described. Any attempt to air a grievance led to instant dismissal, as with a conductor who had spoken to the paper, the Company claiming that he was careless. The low wages were nevertheless attractive to farm labourers. The reporter was certain that waggonette competition would not have been as intense had the HST treated its employees with respect. Waggonette competition had really started with a disgruntled employee's service down Anlaby Road, and this was followed by others. It considered that more

Large horse car no. 14 looks rather neglected as it travels towards the city centre on Beverley Road. This horse tram route closed on 30 September 1899. (PG)

people travelled along Holderness Road by waggonette than by tramcar.

Each new conductor and driver had to hand over £2 (nearly two week's wages) as security, although it was unclear why drivers needed to do so. The rule book contained all kinds of situations where a conductor could forfeit part or all of his deposit (and have to pay interest!). Its fines system was a special tyranny of its own, with one conductor fined £1 for counting his takings before paying them in! By this time the rule book contained forty-one rules, including one that prevented conductors from sitting down. The manager was accuser, jury and judge and there was no appeal.

Average shifts started just before 8am and lasted until about 11pm. Men were supposed to have one day off in eight, but this occurred only if there were spare men available. A system of relief for drivers was established, but the time was so short that the men requested its withdrawal to enable them to have meals on the cars. Speaking in 1976 a former employee, Mr Reg Skelton, remembered that as a boy he had taken dinners and teas to drivers and conductors who consumed them on the cars, as they were not permitted to leave them. Men had to find their own uniforms and he used to clean their boots. He thought that the working day was 8am to 10pm without a break.

At some point (possibly in 1882) the wage system was changed so that drivers on the shorter town routes received 26s a week, those on the two "suburban" routes £24s 6d.

Initially a 78 hour week was worked, but when Sunday operation started this had risen to about 97 out of 168 hours in a week. At that time a labourer worked about 60 hours and got Sunday off. Bank Holidays were treated as normal days and there were no paid holidays. Stablemen's pay was the same as conductors, but their hours were 6am to 8pm on two days, and 6am to midnight on the third, with no days off. Crews complained to the paper that their children were in bed when they got home and when they set off in a morning. Only on Sunday mornings did they see their offspring.

The duties of the Car Shed Foreman included seeing that the horses were cared for and maintained in good healthy condition,

as well as administering any medicines, as only in extreme cases was a vet called in. Given the number of complaints and summonses one wonders what an "extreme case" was! The rule book contains no reference to calling upon the services of a vet.

A new rule was introduced to combat irregularities with the issue of tickets. Sometimes a conductor might not issue a ticket despite receiving a fare, and some conductors were known to collect used tickets and re-issue them despite the threat of prosecution. Conductors and drivers complained bitterly about the fines system for what the *Eastern Morning News* called paltry and trifling offences. A former inspector said that he was constantly blamed for not submitting enough reports against crews, and that he resigned after seven months, not having had a single day off. He was encouraged to hide in dark doorways to catch out conductors.

Another inspector picked up two tickets on a car floor which had apparently been punched together. The conductor's denial was supported by passengers, but he was reported, fined £2 and dismissed.

Conductors were given books containing 100 parcels tickets and received 10d commission for every ticket, a book lasting on average three months. One spent his receipts thinking that the sum would be deducted from his wages but he was prosecuted. However, the magistrate dismissed the case.

The *Hull Daily Mail* sent parcels by horse tram with newspapers bound for designated shops and parcels of papers for newsboys at particular street corners. Other local businesses also used the horse trams but the need to deliver so many parcels slowed the service down considerably. The rates for parcels were fixed by the Tramways Provisional Orders Confirmation (No. 4) of 1872 as follows:

Not exceeding 7 lb in weight	3d
Between 7 and 14 lb in weight	5d
Between 14 and 28 lb in weight	7d
Over 28 lb	9d

A conductor who permitted a regular passenger who had left

his wallet at home to ride for free with the promise of payment the next day, was fined £1 and had his deposit confiscated. Fines were handed out for issuing tickets on the footboard, and for allowing policemen to ride free. Conductors were instructed to keep a sharp lookout for prospective passengers, and it was not uncommon for a car that had just set off to be pulled up a few yards away to let a passenger board. Crews knew regular passengers very well, and it was said that even the horses knew where to stop for regular passengers. The editor of the *Hull Daily Mail*, a Mr Lewis who was a Spring Bank Holiday regular, always left his copy of the evening edition on the 5pm journey from Savile Street with the driver. "Christmas Boxes" from regular passengers were said to be very liberal!

Crews were fined for not completing a full complement of round trips, and for delaying other cars at loops. When a car was derailed and the crew were struggling to re-unite it with the track, another car was delayed and the director onboard reported the crew who were duly fined (the 1882 rule book stated that crews were not to leave the depot without "pieces of iron" to assist with re-railing cars). Another conductor was fined for getting off the car to speak to his driver. One conductor was accused of embezzling 2d and prosecuted although the case was dismissed.

Conductors had to pay for any fines imposed for overcrowding, a regular occurrence since the cars were often overcrowded, leading to cartoons in the press lampooning the Company. In 1882 a conductor was successfully prosecuted with nineteen seated passengers inside, eight standing inside and five on the footboard. The Company argued that the car was permitted to carry thirty-two in total, but the magistrate said this covered sixteen inside and sixteen outside otherwise the Company could carry thirty-two outside! The Company lost!

The Company's horses also received some sympathy especially when rails were wet from rain which drove more people on to the cars. Men were seen as expendable but horses were not. The granite sett paving was very bad for the horses especially in frosty weather when the track could resemble a sheet of glass whilst the use of salt was a further source of discomfort for the horses' cracked heels. Journey times in such conditions were extended and Mr Dyson remarked that payment of one's fare provided the privilege of being able to get off and push. In wintry conditions passengers tended to favour the horse cars rather than the competition. Horses were changed three times a day, the first set of horses working four turns, and the next two sets three turns.

Finally the article appealed for legislation and public opinion to do away with such excessive hours of labour, and demanded early action.

Action is what it got. The Hull Trades and Labour Council

Car no. 11, crew and onlookers watch the photographer with interest. (MJW)

expressed deep sympathy with the tramway men and decided to help them organise themselves. A meeting was held (after the day's work of course), on Sunday 3 November 1889 with many of the Trades Council present. The outcome was the formation of the Hull Tramways Employee's Union.

Its timing was good for a new manager, J.W. London, started work on 13 November. He abolished many fines and standardised working hours. Stablemen's hours were reduced, and cars were stopped at 5 pm on Christmas Day, with the union organising a celebration in the evening. Wages could not be increased because the Company's finances deteriorated. Daily hours of work on the Hessle Road route which had been 1 to 1½ more than other routes were reduced to those levels.

On 15 October 1889 the Works Committee considered a letter from Joseph Kincaid who had been instructed by his directors to deal with the Corporation as he possessed much experience with local authorities. He stated that the position of the Tramway Undertaking must be as unsatisfactory to the authority as it was to the Company. Much expenditure was needed and he stated that it seemed a pity that the Corporation should not have full control over its own streets, the more so that when special works were needed on the roads the Tramways Company always seemed to lose the goodwill of the Corporation. (He might have mentioned that the area outside the lines which the Company had to provide and maintain was used by all other road vehicles including waggonnettes and buses for which the Company received no income, and suggested that the Corporation make a payment for this.)

The Company had suggested a contract with the Corporation but the sticking point was the amount to be spent on the tramways before such an agreement could be instituted. The powers of the Corporation under the 43rd section of the 1870 Act were such that the Company had to give serious consideration to any cost involved in reconstructing the tramways at that time. He suggested that the Corporation obtain a loan for doing the reconstruction works with the Tramways Company providing for the repayment of the loan, with interest, and the cost of maintaining the lines for 21 years as made possible by the 1870 Act and as in place in many other towns.

Both Mr Kincaid and Mr Bannister attended the meeting. Mr Kincaid that experience showed that it was better and cheaper for the Corporation to maintain the lines. Mr Bannister hoped that direct discussions would avoid the friction that was constantly occurring regarding the repair of the roads, especially the differences that arose between the Engineers.

The Corporation's Engineer had mentioned a very large sum for the reconstruction before any purchase, but the Committee was asked to remember that as the Corporation possessed the right to buy the tramways, in a very short time the expenditure of a large sum with this purchase hanging over it was a serious matter for the Company. The result was agreement that the Engineers should discuss the matter further and that the Tramways Sub-Committee should consider any proposals.

This proved abortive. The Company wrote to the Corporation stating that if the Corporation would accept the surrender of the tramways at a price to be agreed, an application to Parliament during the next session would be required, and a notice in the newspapers would need to be inserted before the 17 November in order to expedite matters. However, The Borough Engineer, Mr A.E. White, still questioned whether the Corporation should pay for putting the tramways in order and the proposals were refused.

In October 1889 the Company had raised all fares to 2d for inside passengers. The effect was catastrophic for receipts, for the week ending 21 October they were £156 compared with the previous year's total of £285. Trams were half-empty with middle class passengers opting for waggonettes. On 1 November

A Pier-bound car negotiates the busy Market Place and skirts "King Billy". (MJW)

the inside fares reverted to 1d for short sections from the town centre (usually within the confines of the level crossings). 1½d was charged for two sections with a 2d fare from the pier to any outer terminus. Outside passengers continued to pay the flat fare of 1d.

Receipts began to recover slowly. Mr London restored 1d fares for inside passengers on 15 November. The last published figures for week ending 23 November saw increased receipts of £193 9s 11d, still short of the £272 of the previous year.

It mattered little, for on 16 November 1889 G.&T. Earle, a local cement manufacturer, presented a creditors' winding up petition for the sum of £1026 7s 10d to the Chancery Division of the High Court of Justice. Weekly receipts were said to be £150 or thereabouts whilst expenses amounted to £100 or thereabouts. William Parker Burkinshaw, a local chartered accountant, was appointed as the Provisional Official Liquidator on 18 November and charged with carrying on with the tramway to ensure collection of tolls (fares) etc. By 22 November he had compiled a list of the Company's assets:

	£	s	d
156 horses at £12 each	1872	-	-
33 sets of double harnesses at 10/-	16	10	-
33 cars	1019	-	-
Stable fittings/tools	25	-	-
Provender & litter	30	-	-
Blacksmith's stores	12	-	-
Office furniture	15	-	-
Other	21	5	-
	3010	15	-

The total of 33 cars is interesting since most sources have tended to agree that the maximum number of cars owned was 31 and this seems to be confirmed by various Corporation inspection reports, except that an inspection report to the Hackney Carriage Committee in August 1891 includes references to cars 32 and 33. Were some older cars retained (which is unlikely as they would have been picked up by the regular inspections) or were the additional cars actually horse buses?

On 3 December he was authorised to open a bank account for the Company and instructed that whenever the balance exceeded

£200 to transfer such excess to his account as the Provisional Official Liquidator of the HST.

Before the Company went into liquidation one car had been damaged by fire and an insurance claim of £55 lodged. The Guardian Insurance Company had offered £50 which he accepted. It is not clear which car was involved or if it was repaired.

What had brought about this demise? It had initial high capital costs of over £100,000, and had not made good enough provision for depreciation. After Anthony Bannister's death there was no local champion or stakeholder with the desire to succeed. Despite the presence of a manager, the Company's board was remote and seemingly insensitive to local opinion, with a lack of understanding of local transport issues (hence why would it have instituted the suicidal fares increases?) and gave local staff little room to manoeuvre.

Waggonettes were more flexible and much quicker than the trams. Most were very small concerns or mainly owner-drivers with few fixed overheads. Many were traders of one sort and this defrayed the costs of horse operation. The flat terrain helped, and it was relatively easy to start up. By the mid 1890s it is estimated that some 300 were in operation against 31 horse trams and seven steam trams. Another estimate had them carrying eight million passengers a year compared with the trams' three million.

Under Mr London receipts grew modestly without reaching pre-1889 levels. There was a slight drop in its last two years of existence. However, after 1892-3 it did not break even, and was faced with an increasing expenditure on track and cars. Mr London, who stayed until 1896, had little freedom of action, everything being controlled by the Liquidator. He could not increase fares, increase wages or change hours of work. Forces were at work to reduce his empire, as discussions were held to sell the Holderness Road line to the new Drypool and Marfleet Steam Tramway Co. Ltd, full details of which are in the following chapter.

However, there was little money for repairs to roads at least according to the manager when replying to yet another letter from the Corporation in April 1890. The money allocated after paying off part of the debt was insufficient for him to employ

Horse car no. 25 leaves the St John Street terminus. Of the buildings in view only the Punch Hotel survives despite a proposal to demolish it to allow double track to be laid in Waterhouse Lane for the Hessle Road electric trams. (MJW)

additional men. This was confirmed by the Receiver who met the Borough Engineer later that month. No more than six men could be funded from the limited resources at his disposal. Nevertheless the Corporation once more threatened to take legal action.

Despite the failure of discussions with the Hull Street Tramways Company the Corporation continued to consider purchase and rentals. The Borough Engineer obtained information from sixteen towns regarding their arrangements and relationships with the local companies. Half including Newcastle-on-Tyne, Manchester, Bradford and Sheffield owned the tracks (Huddersfield of course uniquely owned and operated the trams). In the other half, including Plymouth, Dewsbury, Rochdale and Leicester, the Company owned the tracks. In ten cases the Corporation undertook repairs to the track. In Manchester the Corporation carried out the work at the expense of the Company and in Plymouth the Corporation received a quarterly deposit and used this to carry out any repairs that were not done or were not done adequately. In the road 18 inches on either side of the tracks was undertaken by the Corporation at the Company's expense. Of the Corporations where the Company owned the tracks only Birkenhead was applying for powers of purchase.

Unlike Hull very few had had serious disputes with the Company. Plymouth had experienced severe problems with the previous Company but another had purchased the lines. Bradford had had problems but the Company had given way in the end. Nor had many disputes arisen regarding the extent of necessary repairs and one wonders why there were so many disputes in Hull and were these always the Company's fault?

In Bradford the rental was £290 per annum per single line for the first 10 years, thereafter £300 for one Company and £400 for the other. The rental in Sheffield was £100 per mile per annum.

The failure of the horse tramways involved the Corporation in a decade of discussions, proposals and counter-proposals. In June 1891 Alderman Frederick Larard, who was elected chairman of the Works Committee, was to shape the future of public transport in Hull for the next two decades.

In October 1891 the Liquidator, Mr Burkinshaw, offered to sell the system (tracks and depots only), minus the Holderness Road route to the Corporation for £15,000. He enclosed a letter from Mr Kincaid showing "the terms on which he and his friends were prepared to take a lease of the Tramways and Undertaking from the Corporation". Mr Kincaid, the original Company's engineer, required a 21-year lease once the Corporation had rebuilt the depots and tracks to enable a four minute frequency to be operated on all routes. He wanted a lease that was fair and reasonable security to both parties. The Company would pay a rental representing the annual payments made by the Corporation for interest on the capital required and maintenance of the property, and an additional ½ per cent for the sinking fund representing the redemption in sixty years of the Corporation's expenditure. Six meetings had taken place between the Promoters, Liquidator and the Corporation.

The Tramways Sub-Committee was not impressed, and wanted the capital paid off within 21 years, and a further nine year lease to cover maintenance costs. It also wanted two years' rent in advance and a charge on its assets.

Plans and associated details were deposited at the Town Hall on 30 November 1891. These had been prepared by Joseph Kincaid (MICE) for the Hull Street Tramways Company. This gave notice that an application for a Provisional Order would be lodged with the Board of Trade on or before 23 December 1891which would seek the sale of certain tramways in Hull to the Corporation, construction of tramways, power to use steam or some other mechanical power, power to Hull Corporation to lay such tramways and to lease them to a private company. Authority was sought for no fewer than forty-three (43) sections of double line tramway which, in effect, covered the single lines between the passing places!

For instance, Tramway No. 2 (double line) commenced in the parish of Newington by a junction with the existing tramway in Hessle Road at a point 1.63 chains or thereabouts westward from the intersection of St George's Road and Hessle Road and terminating by a junction with the existing tramway at a point 1.40 chains eastward from the intersection of Hessle Road and West

Some of the horse tram routes ran beyond the then town boundary. The Beverley Road terminus at Newland lay within the township of Sculcoates. (MJW)

Dock Avenue. Why such an approach was utilised is unclear but it was not the last occasion on which it was used.

The centre lines of each tramway were clearly marked together with an imaginary centre line of the road. It was proposed, except where otherwise indicated on the plans, to lay tramways along the centre of any such road. In places (marked A......A on the sheets) there would be less than 9' 6" between the edge of the footpath and the nearest rail of tramway on the side of the roadway where this occurred. In fact there were twenty-six (26) such places described including most of the town centre tramways.

Whilst the sale of the steam tramway was included in the wording the plans and sections did not make reference to any lines along Hedon Road or the Old Town.

In December 1891 a driver (Knaggs) was reported for driving whilst under the influence of drink, having been found asleep on duty sitting on his stool on a car whilst it was in motion. He was discharged and later became a cab driver despite his record!

A new Hull Tramways Company was incorporated on 23 December 1891, but Kincaid was not among the directors. Three directors were from Bristol one of whom was a director of the Imperial Tramways, which also ran the Bristol and York tramways. The aim was to buy and rebuild as well as operate the Hull tramways, and provision was made for agreements with the existing Company and the Corporation.

Local opinion was supportive, but the Company wanted to abandon the Old Town line (a reasonable financial move but not politically sound), since it was of doubtful value. After pressure from Old Town interests, who were vocal throughout the life of the tramways in Hull, and discussions with the Corporation, it agreed to double the line despite the unlikelihood of any consent for double lines in Whitefriargate and Silver Street. The promoters estimated that an increase of between fifty and one hundred per cent in passengers was required to enable it to pay the Corporation and make a realistic profit, something which it considered was possible.

The HTC wanted the Corporation to restrict the number of waggonettes to which the Corporation concurred. This did not

prove popular either. A final straw was the Sub-Committee being told by the Company that it couldn't afford the rental payments unless the lease could be for thirty years. It also asked for the deposit to be reduced to a single year's rental. Discussions lapsed and the ageing cars continued to run and began to deteriorate.

Back came Mr Kincaid, this time representing a London syndicate. This had more success, for in April 1892 the Works Committee accepted the proposals. It referred to the agreement for the Hull Street Tramways Company to sell the Holderness road line to the Steam Tramway Company (agreed in 1891), and the agreement by which the Hull Street Tramways Company was to sell the remaining lines to the Hull Tramways Company for £15,000 (agreed in 1892). Also involved was the 1892 agreement of the Drypool and Marfleet Steam Tramways Company to sell both its lines to the new Company for £15,500 plus £72 per annum rent.

The new Hull Tramways Company would then sell the lot to the Corporation (for £30,500!) which would rebuild the lines within one year, and give the Company a thirty-year lease for which it would receive an advance rent of £3,000 (later altered to 5% of the annual Corporation expenditure). Maintenance costs would be £160 a mile for single track, and £240 for double track, plus £200 for depots. A further sum of £110 would be contributed to the sinking fund, and 10 per cent of a year's profits would also accrue to the Corporation, which would have a seat on the Board of Directors. A deposit of £10,000 would be placed with the Corporation. Buses would replace trams in the Old Town. Maximum fares were set at 1d for trams and ½d for buses. A 12 hour day would be worked (including meal times). The overall cost was estimated at £112,000. The Company was prepared to work the lines by electricity.

Old Town agitation which was backed by the Manchester, Sheffield and Lincolnshire Railway Co. was concerned about possible effects on its ferry service, continued. Questions were raised about the motives of the unknown syndicate, and on 30 May 1892 the Town Council rejected the scheme. The Bill was dropped despite pressure from the Works Committee to keep the scheme alive.

Meanwhile the 1892 Tramways Order had been withdrawn, so that Kincaid could submit a Hull Tramways Bill to dissolve the Hull Tramways Company Ltd and replace with a new Hull Tramways Company. Tracks were to be double, Spring Bank excepted, but there was no mention of steam tram operation.

The Committee could be forgiven for having "tramway fatigue" when along came another proposal which involved retention of the Old Town route, and double track apart from Silver Street. The deposit was to be £20,000, whilst the Corporation would have powers to make the Company construct and operate extensions.

For five hours on 6 October the Town Council considered the issue, refusing any attempt to adjourn. The debate was animated with nine motions, and amendments flew including a double line in Whitefriargate (with crossovers to enable cars in either direction to take either line for any portion of the length of the street!), doubling of all tracks wherever practical, and a six-day working week for tramway men. Other rejected proposals were to shorten the lease, and for the Corporation to take over and operate the whole tramways.

Local opinion had swung against the involvement of a remote London-based company, partly due to experiences with the existing Company, and partly due to the realisation that it might not be prudent to rebuild the system and hand it and profits to a private company.

The 1870 Tramways Act permitted local authorities only to construct tramways, not to operate them. The only exception was Huddersfield, which could not attract anyone to take on a lease, and was allowed to operate its system on condition that it would hand it over to anyone wanting to run it. Alderman Larard and some traditional Liberal colleagues were against any municipal operation of tramways, whilst a small number of councillors were beginning to consider that to be the best way out of the morass that Hull tramway operation had become. The latter were given a boost when in 1892 Parliamentary Standing Orders placed all local authorities in the same category as Huddersfield.

The Hull Tramways Co. Ltd gave Parliamentary notice in November 1892 for a Hull Tramways Order 1893, which would enable the two systems to become one, and for most of the tracks to be doubled, and awaited the final decision from the Corporation, probably with some trepidation, for there had been a very strong anti-leasing vote on 6 October.

Plans for this were deposited at the Town Hall on 30 November 1892. Prepared again by Mr Kincaid (whose fees must have been very satisfactory) they had the same objectives but the number of sections of tramways had risen to forty-eight to include Hedon Road as far as Lee Smith Street and a double line

from Silver Street to the Pier. Clarence Street was not mentioned. The contents of the plans and the intentions were much the same as the previous year although the number of places with less than 9' 6" clearance had risen to twenty-eight (28).

A special meeting of the Town Council in accordance with the provisions of the 1870 Act was held on 1 December 1892. As a minimum two-thirds of council members were required to vote, but a simple majority in favour was all that was needed (in practice just 20 members of the 56 strong Council had to approve the scheme). Conversely, 19 abstentions would mean the scheme would fail. Three members could not vote because they were interested parties.

Alderman Larard and colleagues supported the scheme, but the majority of speakers were against it. The thirty year lease was too long, and some members wanted the Corporation to run the tramways for the benefit of its citizens. The result was 23 in favour (probably a higher number than might have been anticipated), but this was not enough, for in addition to 5 who opposed the scheme no fewer than 16 abstained, thus rejecting it.

The promoters tried again in January 1893 with a revised scheme in which they would acquire the steam tramways before sale to the Corporation, but nothing came of it and the Hull Tramways Company was dissolved in 1896.

There was still time for another attempt by the steam tramway to reach the town centre. A Parliamentary notice appeared in November 1893 whereby a proposed West and East Hull Tramways Order 1894 would permit the steam tramway Company to finalise the acquisition of the Holderness Road tramway (including the depot), before all lines were doubled, and the Holderness Road route would be extended to East Park. It would authorise the Corporation to acquire the entire system and lease the lines to the two existing companies or a new one for a period not exceeding thirty years.

Neither Company could reach an agreement for the sale of the Holderness Road line so that references were deleted from the Order which now became the East Hull Tramways Order 1894. The Corporation would be able to appoint two directors to the Board. It would buy the system for £15,000 before rebuilding and leasing back for 21 years. The cost of rebuilding was £41,000 and the annual rent was £3,370 plus half of the profits. This, too, was rejected, and a tiring and frustrating period came to an end.

Thus ended serious discussions about a private solution. Had an agreement been reached at any time, it would have been interesting to see how the inevitable push for electrification would have been handled, and who would have paid for what. The cars, the newest of which were now twelve years old, continued to run amid mounting pressure for firm action by the Corporation.

According to Charles Dyson the date of this last horse car is early November 1899 but the Tramways Committee was informed that the closure date was 30 September 1899. Car no. 23 carries a black flag (affixed by Mr Dyson) to mark the occasion as it prepares to enter Temple Street depot. (PM)

Chapter 2

THE STEAM TRAMWAY

The first proposal for horse tramways had included a short line along Hedon Road on the eastern side of the town, but this was subsequently deleted. The opening of the new Alexandra Dock in July 1885 changed everything. Some form of public transport was needed to import workers from other areas of the town and to take residents to town.

Waggonette owners were quick to exploit the gap in the market, but it was not long before there were proposals for additional public transport. Four local businessmen including Alderman James Stuart, J. Fisher, F.B. Grotrian and Councillor H.H. Briggs, proposed to construct a steam tramway along Hedon Road. Plans and sections were deposited with the Borough Council on 20 November having been prepared by William H. Wellsted (AMICE), Engineer.

The promoters asked the Works Committee for permission to obtain the Provisional Order. Consideration was deferred to allow the Borough Engineer to report to the December meeting. He pointed out that the position of the tram tracks from the kerbs (mostly passing loops) would be less than the statutory 9' 6". Until the Corporation widened the Hedon Road from 15 feet to 24 feet the tramway could not be laid. There remained many matters to be agreed with the company such as materials with which the surface of roads occupied by the tramway would be paved, the mode of construction of the tramways, and what limits could be placed on the time cars or engines could stand on any tramway or siding (ie loop). Other points concerned the construction of engines and boilers to avoid steam being

discharged so as to frighten the horses, and how much of the working parts of each engine could be concealed, and how emission of smoke could be controlled.

The proposers attended the Works Committee on 1 January 1886 (no holiday in those days) where they emphasised that their motivation was for the public good rather than personal gain. They also wanted powers to carry goods, cattle and merchandise as a fall-back rather than out of a desire to introduce such services. The Committee was not keen on this and both parties settled for a more prosaic "Carriage of passengers and parcels". The Corporation also agreed to reduce the deposit from the Company from £1,000 to £500 per mile, but insisted that a clause be inserted in the Provisional Order that the company pay half the cost of widening bridges over the Holderness and Marfleet drains.

The Company opposed this to the extent that it threatened to abandon the scheme altogether unless the clause was waived. Messrs Fisher, Stuart and Birks represented the Company at the next Committee meeting on 5 January to plead their cases and ask for a fixed sum. It was (on an 8-4 vote) agreed to contribute to the cost of widening the Holderness and Marfleet Drain bridges subject to a £500 maximum.

Formally incorporated on 15 January 1886, the objectives of the Drypool and Marfleet Steam Tramways Company Ltd were to build and operate tramways in East Hull, elsewhere in Hull and in the East Riding, and to operate omnibuses to connect with the tramways. The four promoters became the first directors, Mr

Steam tram no. 4 of 1889 and an imposing trailer pose with their crew probably in Hotham Street. The date is unknown but may be shortly after the opening of the system. (PM)

A similar scene shows the large amount of advertising that was carried on both locomotives and trailers in later years. (PM)

Fisher becoming chairman. He was also chairman of the Hull and Barnsley Railway, and it was said that both his concerns went from "nowhere to nowhere"!

The proposed route ran from Great Union Street at the west end of North Bridge (near the Holderness Road line), along Hedon Road to the village of Marfleet. A short spur was also authorised along Clarence Street. A new bridge (Drypool Bridge but also called Salthouse Lane Bridge) was not opened until 1888. A glance at any contemporary map for that time would raise doubts about the line ever reaching Marfleet, since there was only a prison, a sanatorium and a cemetery beyond Lee Smith Street. Local press comment was favourable, and one writer wondered if the small borough of Hedon some distance east of Marfleet (and served by the NER's Withernsea branch) might enjoy trams one day.

Another unknown was the reaction of the travelling public to the necessity of daily transfers between horse and steam trams near North Bridge, and whether the workmen might settle for waggonette transport to avoid the need for change. The inability of the steam trams to reach the town centre remained a serious weakness.

Royal Assent was given on 25 September 1886 to the Tramways Orders Confirmation (No. 2) Act 1886 that authorised three tramways: from Witham to Marfleet, from a point near the River Hull (Salthouse Lane Bridge) and along Hotham Street.

Tramway No. 1 was two miles four furlongs and one chain long of which two miles one furlong and four point two chains were single line. It commenced in Great Union Street at the junction with Witham and ran in a south easterly direction along the centre of Great Union Street, Popple Street along the Hedon Road, terminating at a point one chain west of Marfleet Drain. Double lines or passing places were to be provided in Great Union Street for a distance of three chains and along Hedon Road at the following points (all three chains long and running in an easterly direction) comprising Popple Street, Seward Street, Woodhouse Street and the Sculcoates town boundary.

Two further locations were the eastern boundary of the New Cemetery (5.80 chains easterly) and 3.50 chains west of the terminus the double track being 3 chains in length.

The tramway was not to be opened for public traffic unless and until the paved road or macadamised roadway of such road was of a clear width of not less than 24 feet. Corporation approval was required for the installation of additional sidings.

Tramway No. 2 was 4.87 chains in length of which 1.87 chains were to be single line. It commenced in Clarence Street, some two chains from the landing steps leading down to the River Hull, and ran easterly and terminated at a point on Tramway No. 1 some one furlong and four chains from the start of that tramway.

Finally, Tramway No. 3 was 1.50 chains long and formed a west to north single line curve linking Clarence Street with the Witham tramway.

Various provisions protected the interest of the North Eastern Railway's level crossing on Hedon Road, and gave the company the power to insist on the provision of signals to control the trams' crossing of the railway line and the local highways authorities. The line as proposed went beyond the town boundary into the Sculcoates "township".

Design of engines and carriages were to have prior approval from the Board of Trade and the local authorities. Were it to be necessary for the widening or rebuilding of bridges over the Holderness and Marfleet Drains, the company must pay half the costs.

The use of steam power would be authorised for an initial seven years renewable for a further seven years thereafter. If so required, local authority approval would be needed for any conversion to electrical operation.

Tolls for passengers should not exceed one penny per mile, but the company could fix stages of not less than one mile in length and could charge not more than one penny for this stage. Two workmen's cars were to be provided in each direction on weekdays before 7am and after 6pm except on Sundays,

Christmas Day and Good Friday. Workmen's fares were not to exceed 1d. Proposals for the revision of fares were to be sent to the Board within three years of its opening. The Board had the power to conduct an inquiry before making any decision regarding any revisions.

Section 44 provided for leasing the steam tramway to the Hull Street Tramways Company subject to BOT approval, whilst section 45 provided for agreements for joint working, traffic arrangements and tolls sharing between the two companies. The possibility of a connection between the two tramways in Witham was covered subject to Corporation and BOT approval.

Finally, if required by the Postmaster-General, the company could provide mail services, parcels not to exceed in weight the personal luggage of ordinary passengers (twenty-eight pounds in weight). It could run a carriage for the conveyance of parcels only for which agreement with the P-G was required. Mails on passenger carriages must not inconvenience passengers nor must they interfere with company staff or postal staff.

The company's prospectus (of April 1888) emphasised the good prospects for traffic on Hedon Road which served two docks, a shipyard and a growing residential area. It highlighted the connection with the new bridge (Salthouse Lane) that would give its passengers (if not its cars) access to the Old Town. At first it intended to lay track only as far as Lee Smith Street (near Alexandra Dock). The prospectus proved less than attractive to local investors with only £9,590 of the required £12,000 being raised.

The use of steam power was not universally accepted. Alderman Rollit campaigned against these "hideous things which were a danger to life and limb", or so he claimed. Elements within the Council did not favour steam either, but the Town Clerk pointed out that the Provisional Order had approved its use so the Committee was powerless.

Many details still required agreement, particularly with regard to track plans, and a dispute arose over the position of lines in Great Union Street in relation to Witham. The Corporation wanted the tracks set back from Witham (the company wanted to run the tracks into Witham and make possible a connection with the horse tramway lines at some time and said a further costly Provisional Order would be required if this were not permitted). A compromise located a passing (terminal) loop some 155ft from Witham but the single line ended just short (two chains) of it. Other amendments involved the location of the centre lines in loops, including that on the Holderness Drain Bridge. Provision was made for the lines to be leased to the Hull Street Tramways Company, and an agreement between the two companies regarding working arrangements and for a physical link between the two companies.

Construction began in July 1888, despite the original intention of completing track laying by September 1887. This was the result, in part, of a lack of serious negotiation about road widening costs. The line was complete to Lee Smith Street by May 1889 at a cost of £6,800 per mile, lower than the estimated cost of £8,000 and much lower than contemporary lines elsewhere. It was the responsibility of Mr William Wellsted, a local man, who had prepared the scheme, and who was fortunate to have a street named after him off Hessle Road, who was called before the House of Lords in 1900 as a Corporation witness when a dispute arose with the NER regarding the Hedon Road level crossing. The Board of Trade inspection on 18 May was carried out by Major-General Hutchinson accompanied by Mr W. Penrose Green representing the engine builders.

When the company provided the Board of Trade with a set of plans of the route before the inspection, any variation from the authorised plan had to be shown in red. These were those deposited on 20 November 1885. One plan showed the original proposal for a double track terminus in Witham between Great Union Street and North Bridge. A new loop was shown between Hyperion Street and Coleus Street, and a single line ending just short of Witham.

On 21 May 1889 Corporation dignitaries and guests, including the manager of the horse tramways, walked from the Town Hall to Drypool Bridge to transfer to two cars which departed just after noon, and took them to the terminus at Lee Smith Street, and thence to luncheon at the depot in Hotham Street before returning by car to the town. The company reaffirmed its commitment to complete the line to the Holderness Drain and then to Marfleet. Mr Grotrian described the carriages as "luxurious" and said that workers could enjoy them at 1d per mile. The Hull News report pondered on the possibility of running as far as Hedon, despite the fact that no such powers existed.

After the official opening the cars started operations and carried many passengers eager to sample the new trams. The public service began on the next day (22 May). In 1923 Mr Rayner, the City Tramways Manager, stated that the public service began on 1 August, but this is contradicted by the company's own traffic receipts. Four steam trams and four cars provided a 7½-minute service from 8am until 10.15pm from Lee Smith Street, each car working alternately to each bridge. In addition a fifteen-minute service for workmen ran from North Bridge between 5.30am and 8am on weekdays. Sunday operation was half-hourly between 1pm and 9pm. In January 1890 the weekday headway was increased to five minutes. Fares were 1d for any distance, workmen's fare being ½d.

A reporter in the *Hull Times* on 17 November 1923 recalled the early days of the steam trams when he was a young boy. He remembered paying a humble "meg" (half-penny) for the ride on the very tall trailer cars which seemed to reach to the sky. He considered the "boiler house" and the car to be out of all proportion, but he lived near the trams and enjoyed their coming and going.

The appearance of steam traction frightened many horses at first, but this could not detract from the smooth ride that made the *Hull News* very enthusiastic about the trailer cars, stating that they were as good as they could possibly be, as they were handsome and furnished to a high standard. They appeared to passengers to be much higher than horse cars, possibly a result of being fully enclosed. Entrance to and exit from the cars was, under Bye-Law IV, to be by the hindermost or conductor's platform.

Hedon Road was crossed by two railway lines – the Hull and Barnsley Railway's line crossed on a bridge over the road, and the North Eastern Railway's line used a level crossing. Cars had to make a compulsory stop at the crossing. Although the Provisional Order allowed for signalling to be installed at the crossing, it was never provided. Other compulsory stops had to be observed at the Clarence Street/Great Union Street junction, the Williamson Street junction with Hedon Road, and a point near the HBR bridge. Drivers were asked to sound their bell when approaching Popple Street.

Engines and cars were serviced at a depot in Hotham Street alongside which the manager's home was built. Four engines and five cars were available for the opening of the route. The four-coupled engines came from Thomas Green & Sons of Leeds, and the cars which seated seventy-four were built by G.F. Milnes of Birkenhead.

The engines burnt coke, the fire being kept in good condition by a forced draught, and on the top of each engine steam could be condensed through a system of copper pipes. It was claimed that the locomotives could achieve a speed of 24mph, but an automatic regulator was fitted which brought the locomotive to a halt if speed exceeded 10mph. Cars were allowed a ten-minute layover at each terminus to enable crews to attend to the fire, carry out any oiling required, and to replenish water supplies (how is not recorded). However, this was often eroded by delays incurred at the North Eastern Railway's crossing, which could amount to as much as fifteen minutes.

Engines, cars and crews could be very dirty and smoky if a locomotive was steaming badly and the wind was from the wrong direction! Both driver and fireman became more begrimed as the shift progressed! Drivers were encouraged to become mechanically proficient, so as to carry out ordinary running repairs to avoid "running in" to the depot. Unless there was a serious defect management did not encourage "running in"!

Despite low fares the anticipated traffic did not materialise since passengers preferred to travel into the town centre by waggonette for 1d, whereas steam car users faced a walk or the expenditure of another 1d on the Holderness Road trams. It was imperative to reach the town centre. Some informal arrangement appears to have been made with the Hull Street Tramways Co. for transfer at Witham, but no through fares were available.

In 1889 the DMST in full agreed to buy the Holderness Road line from George Street and the depot, and to promote two Provisional Orders. The first was to upgrade the remainder of the horse system as a preliminary for conversion to steam traction, but this was withdrawn when the Hull Street Tramways Company collapsed whilst the other, with an amendment giving the Corporation the power to repair the steam tracks and charge the DMST, went ahead. In March 1889 approval had been obtained by Major Wellsted from the Streets and Lighting Sub-Committee for its proposal to connect its lines with those of the HST at the junction of Great Union Street and Witham.

The Regulations and Bye-Laws approved by the Board of Trade were reported to the Hackney Coach Etc. Sub-Committee on 29 May 1889.

The Tramways Orders Confirmation (No 1) Act of 1890 gave the DMST the power to buy the Holderness Road line, after which the company's title would change to East Hull Tramways Co. Ltd. Should the purchase not be completed the DMST would have the power, with the HST and Corporation consent, to run steam trams over the existing tracks.

Agreement to purchase at a cost of £6,500 with a deposit of £650 was concluded in May 1891. Both companies were to obtain permission for steam power from the Corporation, whilst the Corporation would waive its right to purchase in 1893/4. The agreement could be rescinded if all this did not come about within two months.

But the Works Committee surprisingly rejected, at first, the use of steam trams within the town centre, on the grounds of danger, but the Town Council overturned this so that consent was given in August 1891, provided that the rails were re-laid to the Corporation's satisfaction, a 4mph limit imposed on North Bridge, and 6mph on its approaches. Some Holderness Road traders also opposed any attempt to run steam trams along that road, citing the usual reasons of loss of property values and loss of trade. Double lines were to be laid throughout.

The agreement was not confirmed and the DMST continued with its truncated line, extension to Marfleet being seen as increasingly unlikely. With the failure of another attempt to extend its running powers, the DMST promoted another Provisional Order to obtain the power to sell to the Corporation and, with the Corporation's consent, sell to the HST or its successors. It also obtained the authority to abandon construction of the line beyond Lee Smith Street, thus relieving it of the liability to contribute towards the widening of Hedon Road beyond Holderness Drain. All this was included in the DMST Order 1892 and the Tramways Order Confirmation Act 1992.

Until 1894/5 the steam tramways operated at a loss (the first

six weeks apart). It was adversely affected by the Hull Dock Strike of 1893. Although the trams never stopped running, there were incidents and fights on the cars between strikers and imported labour. A reversion to the 7½-minute frequency, and an upturn in the fortunes of the docks and shipyard, increased its revenue so that it broke even. Initially, the capacity of the system was four trains with two in each direction, operating alternately from Lee Smith Street to North Bridge or Clarence Street. Later track alterations permitted six trains. These included additional loops at Drypool Square (Ripon Street), and the Alexandra Dock entrance, whilst the Williamson Street loop was extended. A general speed limit of 8mph was imposed except for facing points, when it was 4mph.

The line seemed to be fairly accident-free, although a locomotive demolished an aerated water cart, cascading the contents over the highway. According to a former employee, James Brewis, who later became a motorman and later Inspector Timekeeper at Hedon Road depot, there was a collision with a funeral cortege at Hotham Street! However there is some doubt about this. Mr Brewis, who lived in France during the Franco-Prussian War and experienced the siege of Paris, worked for all three tramway undertakings. He started driving in 1892 without much instruction, being given engine no. 1 and car no. 8 and sent on to the road.

The steam trams required far fewer employees than the horse trams. In December 1892 it employed 12 drivers and 12 conductors, but later service reductions saw this fall to 8 drivers and 9 conductors. The whole staff probably did not exceed 30. Working conditions were better than on the horse trams, there being no fines for staff's misdemeanours in the same manner as with the horse tramways, and the hours worked were less. From 1890 crews were given meal breaks for dinner and tea which could be taken at home. In addition to alternate Sundays being free they had one free evening a week. Commencing wages were 30s a week, but this could be increased by extra duties. The early car service which was in the charge of the night staff started at 5am whilst the day shift commenced at 8am and finished at 10pm.

The Company used to offer a prize for the most competent driver. One recipient was Driver Baldam who received a gold watch and a purse of gold. He had also worked on the horse cars and became an instructor with the steam trams, it being his decision to "pass out" new drivers and firemen after he had put them through a period of instruction. Mr Baldam considered the Green's locomotives to be most reliable.

Another former DMST employee was Mr David Tarbert, later assistant manager and chief cashier of the electric tramways, and in temporary charge during the managerial upheavals of 1919.

No tickets were issued in the first years of operation, with conductors putting fares direct into a small brass box supplied by Kaye's. This had a glass compartment at the top to show the coins which were only sent into the lower and locked part when the correct change had been given. The cash box registered when it was unlocked, a security device to deter interference with the cash. Not until 1894/5 were tickets introduced.

On commencing work conductors were given 15s which had to be present in the bag at all times, usually comprising three half-crowns, two florins, two shillings and three sixpences. There were regular inspections of the bag, but one clerk would "tip off" men on the day before this was due, and between them they ensured that the bags had the correct money. Cash flow was a constant problem, and when an unpaid bill led to the Eastern Gas Works refusing to supply further coke the director, Mr Grotrian, paid the bill himself!

There was a time clock near the Rank's flour mill which gave notice of the starting time of the next car. The time was fixed by

This shows the North Eastern Railway level crossing on Hedon Road that was negotiated by the single track of the steam trams and that caused so much trouble when electrification was proposed. (MJW)

a conductor who used his finger to move the hands on the clock to the departure time of the next car!

In April 1896 the DMST asked the Board of Trade to renew its licence for steam operation. Colonel Yorke's inspection revealed the permanent way to be mostly in good order, but recent repairs were not of a good standard. None of the engines, contrary to regulations issued by the Board of Trade, retained governors, which meant that speed indicators did not work either. Drivers did not invariably connect the emergency break (spelt this way in BOT reports), between engine and carriage. Engine boilers were in good condition. The company was instructed to put the steam breaks in proper order and refit governors and indicators. The licence was renewed for one year only. The company protested, blaming a previous manager (Mr Rae), and said in Hull the hand brake was sufficient. The Board was unmoved, and the year's extension stood. The subsequent annual inspection in 1897 by Colonel Marindin found only four engines in use, but all was well and a seven year extension was approved.

G.A. Lee carried out an analysis of the company's traffic but was frustrated by some inaccurate/non-existent records and the fact that no tickets were issued in its early years. Accurate counting of passengers did not commence until 1895.

The years 1890/1 to 1894/5 all recorded deficits with a maximum loss of £467 in 1890/1. The preponderance of workmen's half-penny fares was such that they accounted for ninety-five per cent of all fares. The wonder is that there were so many, although not all workmen wanted to travel to and from the town centre and beyond. Many transferred to the Holderness Road horse trams.

Costs fluctuated greatly over the decade. Its total working expenses fell in the middle of the decade, but had risen by 25 per cent between 1896 and 1899. Engine repairs and renewals rose from £176 in 1895 to £536 in 1899. Repairs to the cars showed a similar increase (around 60 per cent), from £104 to £196. Expenditure on the permanent way also fluctuated, peaking at £403 in 1897. Yet the highest running costs were in the period 1891 to 1894 with a peak of £3242 in 1892.

Although the residential population along Hedon Road grew slowly it had little effect on the company's fortunes. Without access to the town centre and a greater number of the public travelling at the one penny fare, the line beyond the confines of Drypool itself remained a basic workmen's service for the two docks and the shipyards, whose use fluctuated according to economic conditions. When Corporation ownership became a real possibility at the close of the century the company was struggling, and it seemed that salvation lay in a municipal takeover in the same manner as the horse tram system.

On 9 June 1898 Alderman F. Larard and various civic dignitaries laid the first rails for the new electric tramways with due ceremony in Porter Street watched by a sizeable crowd. Alderman Larard was the "father" of the electric tramway system and would chair the Tramways Committee with a great deal of passion for 12 years. (PM)

Mr A.E. White, the Borough Engineer who was responsible for the construction of the original electric tramway system, inspects the first length of track, also on 9 June 1898. (MJW/HC)

28

Chapter 3

THE CORPORATION TAKES OVER

Discontent with the performance of the Hull Street Tramways Company continued throughout 1894 and received added impetus when, in August 1894, the Receiver obtained High Court approval to sell the horse tramways to the highest bidder, and placed an advertisement in local papers offering it as a going concern with tenders due back by 20 November. On 21 November the Court considered the only tender received and adjourned, leaving everything confused or giving every party time to resolve the situation, (depending on one's viewpoint),

On 14 November the Works Committee considered a motion from the Town Council and letters from ratepayers associations calling upon the Corporation "to take the necessary steps to compel the Hull Tramways Company to place the roads of the town in a proper repair". The Town Clerk was instructed to invite comments from the company.

Before a reply was received a letter dated 23 November arrived from Messrs Holden, Sons and Hodgson acting on behalf of the Receiver. He offered the existing lines and depots for sale to the Corporation at a valuation, based on the present value of the materials in situ, less an allowance for the value of the materials on the roads at the time of construction of the tramways, and the valuation of the depots on the basis of the present value thereof for the purpose of the undertaking. He also threatened to sell the system for scrap if need be, clearly designed to concentrate the Corporation mind.

Consideration was deferred to permit the Borough Engineer to prepare an estimate of the value of the tramway's permanent way and depots, after deducting the value of the materials on the roads at the time of their construction.

On 19 December the Works Committee received a letter from Mr Francis J.R. Hopwood, Railway Department of the Board of Trade. He enclosed a letter from Mr F.C. Manley, solicitor of Hull, and a petition complaining about the state of the tramways. Mr Hopwood sought the Corporation's observations.

All the letters and proposals were considered at the Tramways Sub-Committee on 3 January 1895. After a long discussion it was agreed that the Chairman, Deputy-Chairman, Councillor Skinner, the Town Clerk and the Borough Engineer endeavour to negotiate the purchase of the undertaking and depots.

Their discussions with the Liquidator and the solicitor were unsuccessful. There was a difference in the estimated value of the undertaking so great that no agreement could be reached. It was agreed to appoint an independent valuer.

However, the valuation from Mr W. Botterill for the stables, and Mr W.H. Wellstead for the permanent way, did not meet with the Liquidator's favour, and the deputation suspended negotiations pending further instructions. The Town Clerk was instructed to take such action as he may be advised to terminate the nuisance caused by the extremely defective condition of the tramways, thereby increasing the pressure on the company

The Town Clerk wrote to the Board of Trade in accordance with section 42 of the Tramways Act 1870, and the Board in turn wrote to the company's solicitors and forwarded their reply to the Corporation. The HSTC denied that it was insolvent and unable to maintain and work the tramways with advantage to the public. Roads were at their worst at this time of year with more repairs needed after an exceptionally severe winter, and that these were being attended to. Whenever the Borough Engineer had drawn the company's attention to any defects, repairs had always been immediately executed (thereby inferring that there had been several such cases).

This letter was considered by the Works Committee on 26 April 1895 which asked the Council to adopt the following resolution "That it appears to the Mayor, Aldermen and Burgesses of Kingston upon Hull who are the Local Authority and the Road Authority of the said Borough that the Tramways Company are insolvent so that they are unable to maintain their tramways and work the same with advantage to the public and that, in pursuance of section 42 of the Tramways Act 1870 the said Mayor, Aldermen and Burgesses acting by the Council, hereby make a representation to that effect to the Board of Trade and request the Board of Trade to direct an inquiry by a referee into the truth of the aforesaid representation".

The Town Clerk had stated that if the tramway became insolvent, the Board of Trade could make an Order terminating the company's powers after a period of six months, and awarding the highway authority power to remove the tracks at the company's expense.

Within a week the company's solicitors tried again to persuade the Corporation to buy. As the difference was now a comparatively small sum their clients had instructed them "to make an offer, the price to be fixed by Sir James Woodhouse, on the condition that the amount awarded by him did not exceed that asked by the Liquidator, nor be less than that offered by the Corporation at its last meeting." This offer was rejected because the Corporation's offer already exceeded the Corporation's true valuation of the company.

Three weeks later the company capitulated. In order to end the deadlock, and although the Receiver and the debenture holders considered the offer totally inadequate, it wished to accept the offer of £12,500. The Tramways Sub-Committee recommended to the Council that the offer be accepted, subject to satisfactory arrangements for the temporary continuing of the undertaking in accordance with a contract prepared by the Corporation. This was approved by the Council subject to Board of Trade approval, and a temporary contract was agreed in July.

Whilst the decision was welcomed by many residents, not everyone was impressed. The Hull and District Chamber of Trade told the Council on 31 July it didn't think that tramways could be operated at a profit. It deplored the effect on the local ratepayers who were already having to pay for public education and libraries (of which it did not approve!) and hoped that the Council would resist further municipalisation!

In the midst of all the negotiations the possibility of battery tramcar operation was considered by the Corporation! This arose from a proposal to use heat generated by new refuse destructors to produce electricity, which could be used to charge accumulators to drive trams in the same manner as was already in operation in Birmingham. The chairmen of the Sanitary and Electric Lighting Committees and Alderman Larard visited Birmingham to investigate. The operation was not considered to be economic and the Corporation dropped the idea.

The acquisition of the HSTC required a Provisional Order, and on 27 September the Works Committee asked the

Cars and trailers were assembled by the City Engineer's staff in Liverpool Street Workshops and in Wheeler Street Depot, the first fifteen in 1898, the next fifteen in 1899. Milnes car (no. 12) and Brill car (no. 29) are in view. (PM)

Parliamentary Committee to take the necessary steps to obtain powers for the construction of double lines in the streets in which the HSTC tramways existed.

Some members raised the question of tramway operation outside the borough limits but the Tramways Sub-Committee declined, possibly not wanting to complicate matters, since the East Riding County Council was likely to object to any possible incursion by the town council. At the same meeting, on 30 October 1895, the Borough Engineer's proposals with the addition of an extension of the Spring Bank route along Princes Avenue to Queens Road, and an extension along Holderness Road to East Park, were approved. All lines would be double-track, apart from single lines in Waterhouse Lane and Osborne Street for turning cars on the Hessle Road route. The Hessle Road route terminus arrangement was to comprise a loop around Osborne Street and Waterhouse Lane. This was later changed to run via a single line along Midland Street following receipt of advice from the Board of Trade.

As ever the Old Town proved to be controversial. After ignoring a memorial against double-track from various parties in Whitefriargate and Silver Street, the Corporation changed its mind in January 1896 and deleted all Old Town lines, only to rescind that decision after another deputation supported the proposal!

Alderman Larard, the Town Clerk and Borough Engineer, visited the Board of Trade's offices on 20 January 1896 to discuss the tramway proposals. As a result the full scheme was despatched to the Board on 1 February together with a breakdown of the estimated cost of £270,000.

In April 1896 the Tramways Sub-Committee asked the Borough Engineer to prepare a report on various systems of electric traction in use, places where they were in use and, as far as possible, the results obtained.

The Provisional Order passed through Parliament on 9 July. Whilst it was in Parliament municipalities were given the power to operate tramways in their own right, and the clause which had permitted operation by the Corporation only if no one else expressed a wish to do so was amended accordingly.

As a result the question of direct operation of the tramways by the Corporation, or the system being leased was discussed on 10 July, but the meeting proved inconclusive as there were wide differences between members, the Chairman and other Liberal members being in favour of leasing the system to a private company. Four days later the Sub-Committee resolved (not unanimously) to lease the tramways to a private operator. The Borough Engineer was authorised to prepare terms and conditions upon which a lease might be granted.

July 1896 was blessed with two meetings of the Works Committee, which endorsed the decision to adopt electric traction, but a motion to ascertain information from towns and cities which owned and worked tramways was lost. A similar motion was defeated at the next meeting, which also instructed the Borough Engineer to make arrangements with the Official Liquidator, or HSTC, or any other person, for the working of the tramways until the reconstruction of the tramways commenced.

On 14 August the Drypool and Marfleet Steam Tramways' request for a further two year agreement for the use and repair of roads along which their tracks ran was approved with effect from 1 October, and it was agreed to invite tenders for the temporary working of the horse tramways for a period not exceeding twelve months.

Three tenders for the temporary operation of the horse tramways were received from Mr W. Nettleton (£100 as per the draft agreement), Mr W.S. Graff Baker (£105 per mile of single-track), and the New General Traction Company Limited (£50 per single line and £75 per double line per mile), and were considered on 21 September 1896. Both the Baker and NGTC tenders tried to impose conditions on the lease which gave them preference at the end of the lease, or wanted the Corporation to purchase all plant used by the lessee. The meeting awarded the lease to Mr Nettleton, with effect from 15 October 1896.

According to Charles Dyson in his short book (published in 1920) about his experiences as an employee of the company the new regime sold off many old horses and brought in fresh and fit ones, to the dismay of older drivers who had to break in the new arrivals. The older cars which had not seen the best of maintenance did not cope with new and stronger horses and gradually fell to bits! Mr Dyson considered that the cars seemed to be held together only by the advertising boards all over the cars!

The Tramways Sub-Committee on 23 October 1896 considered the report about towns where operation of tramways by the Corporation had been under consideration. The Chairman's

Trailers and motorcars can be seen being assembled in this view in Liverpool Street depot. (PM)

report of thirteen pages covered operations in eight towns (Huddersfield, Birmingham, Leeds, Manchester, Plymouth, Glasgow, Sheffield and Blackpool).

A diverse set of circumstances and experiences was discovered. Huddersfield had wanted to lease the tramways, but no bona fide offer had been forthcoming. It had obtained powers to work the tramways and had subsequently constructed extensions. Between 31 August 1892 and 31 March 1895 the total income was £212,517 against an expenditure of £276,700. Various portions of the Birmingham system were granted to the Central Tramways Company which were to be transferred to a new company for twenty-one years. Birmingham Corporation did not consider that there was sufficient evidence of municipal operation to form a view about operation of the tramways by the Corporation. In any case, experiments with electric traction and auto cars made it prudent not to acquire the tramways at that time.

In Manchester the tramways were owned partly by the Corporation and partly by the Manchester Carriage and Tramways Company, but were not worked by the City. From 1877 to 1895, £70,911 had been transferred to the City Fund for rates relief. It intended to obtain powers to work the tramways itself. Plymouth's tramways were owned and worked by the Corporation. The third year's operation had yielded sufficient funds to cover working expenses, depreciation fund and interest (at three per cent) on capital, but not enough to pay the sinking fund. A deficit of £923 had resulted in 1895-1896. Glasgow had worked the tramways for only a single year but had made a profit of £86,267 of which £16,259 had been allocated to the general reserve fund. Blackpool had made a small working profit of £524.

As not all members were present it was decided to re-convene seven days later. It was decided (not unanimously) that the tramways should be leased for a period of twenty-one years, and that the lessees should pay a rent that was satisfactory to the Council. The Chairman, Alderman Larard, was in favour of a lease, and no doubt members were impressed by the sums paid to offset rates by the companies in some cities.

In December the Committee approved the draft lease agreement and authorised the Borough Engineer to obtain tenders. The lessees would be expected to reconstruct (or pay for the reconstruction of) the tramways to the satisfaction of the whole of the Tramways Committee, the portions of the road referred to

in the 1870 Tramways Act (section 28) and materials to be used in the construction of the tramways, and would pay for the removal of the existing track. The Corporation would maintain the line and the lessees would maintain and insure the depots. Persons who submitted tenders were to state:

1. the period of lease required
2. the rent offered
3. the mode of traction to be employed with full particulars of the system (the Corporation was prepared to supply any necessary electric current)
4. the service on each route
5. proposed fares
6. hours of labour for employees

The existing depots could be included in the lease but not the existing tenant's fixtures and fittings.

The specification then listed the routes which comprised the present tramways with the addition of Princes Avenue as far as Queens Road. It covered in great detail the track foundations and construction which was to contain double lines as far as possible. Lessees were to pay 2½ per cent for the Corporation's supervision and office costs as well as the cost of taking up the existing tramways. Tenders were to be returned by 1 February 1897.

After six tenders had been opened by the Chairman and deputy Chairman together with the Town Clerk and Borough Engineer, the Tramways Sub-Committee considered the tenders on 8 February 1897. Mr W. Nettleton (the horse tramway operator) wished to continue with horse traction for fifteen years, but wanted the Corporation to lay and maintain the lines and to provide stabling for 300 horses and sixty cars (double the existing number). The Corporation would pay all rates except water, and he would pay an annual rent of £3000. Fares would be unchanged and a six minute service would be provided.

The Gas Traction Company Ltd wanted a twenty-one year lease at a rent of £300 per single mile of line. Gas motors would provide a 5 to 10-minute service at fares of 1d per mile. Hours would total 10 per day. The bid failed to mention anything about construction and laying of track and it was assumed the Corporation would do this,

Construction of the permanent way was required by the New

General Traction Company as was the supply of electricity. A twenty-one year lease was proposed at an annual rent of £500. A five-minute service was offered whilst hours of labour were to be 70 per week.

British Thomson-Houston declined to tender for the system as a whole but would be interested in providing any electrical equipment.

Alfred Dickinson and Co. wanted a twenty-one year lease at a minimum of £100 per annum per single mile of track, plus a bonus for the Corporation if the company paid a dividend in excess of six percent. A minimum ten-minute service would be provided by electric cars using side collection. Ten hours a day would be worked.

Finally, the British Electric Traction Company Ltd would construct the track and charge the Corporation 10 per cent for doing so. A five-minute service would be provided by electric cars, but fares and other charges were based on a complicated set of conditions.

Faced with such a variation of proposals the Sub-Committee was unable to recommend the acceptance of any tender, and instead recommended the formation of a Sub-Committee to visit such towns as necessary before deciding on the most suitable tramway system. This was accepted.

On 30 April 1897 the Works Committee considered the Special Sub-Committee's report regarding the most suitable tramway system for the Borough. Members had inspected the electric tramways in Bristol (where 21 motor cars and 12 trailers operated on two routes to Kingswood and Eastville); South Staffordshire (whose overhead was considered to be lighter and cheaper with no attempt at ornamentation, and whose track was not in good condition); Coventry (which made greater use of span wires across the entire road than did other operators – its track was also poor, and both this and the South Staffordshire condition was laid at the door of previous steam tram operation); Dublin (30 motor cars and 30 trailers but whose overhead did not match the standard of Bristol) and Hartlepool (5 motor cars and two trailers operated by the General Traction Company whose track also did not impress the Hull party!).

In Dublin the delegation was addressed by Mr William Anderson the secretary and manager of the Dublin United Tramways Company. He told them that he and four directors had visited America spending four weeks there, an excursion that had convinced the company that the overhead electric system was the most suitable for Dublin, even though Dublin Corporation had not then sanctioned the adoption of overhead within the city.

The comprehensive twenty-five page report also contained references to other reports submitted to the Corporations of Leeds (which wanted conduit operation in the city centre and overhead elsewhere), Belfast, Glasgow (which at first would have preferred a system without any overhead construction), Sheffield and Birmingham (where the City of Birmingham Tramway Company had sent officials to visit Continental and British systems resulting in its favouring the conduit system, and recommending that no consent be given for overhead wires within the city) and, taken from the Glasgow and Sheffield reports and Duncan's Tramway Manual, the working expenses and receipts per car mile of eight American and two Canadian systems covering horse, electric (overhead and conduit) and cable systems.

American and Canadian Comparative Statistics (Glasgow Corporation)

Location	Type	Expenses (pcm)	Receipts (pcm)
New York			
Third Avenue	Cable	7d	54% of receipts
Jersey City	Trolley	53% of receipts	
	Horse	75% of receipts	
Philadelphia	Trolley	53% of receipts	
	Horse	80% of receipts	
Washington	Cable	50-60% of receipts	
Cincinnati	Trolley	58% of receipts	
Cleveland	Trolley	60% of receipts	
Buffalo	Trolley	5.55d	10.8d
	Horse	8.50d (estimated)	
Toronto	Trolley	49.3% of receipts	
Montreal	Trolley	5.25d	56.48% of receipts
	Horse	82.68% of receipts (1892)	
Boston	Trolley	13.46d	17.46d (77.7%)

British and Continental Comparative Statistics (Sheffield Corporation)

Location	Type	Expenses (pcm)	Receipts (pcm)
Birmingham	Cable	5.43d	11.86d
	Accumulator	18.43d	15.70d
Blackpool	Gas	4.50d	
	Conduit	Not given	
Bristol	Electric	5½d	
	Horse	9½d	
Brussels	Electric	4½d	
Dresden	Elec/horse	6d	10.8d
Edinburgh	Cable	5½d to 6d	10.53d
	Horse	10.39d	15d to 16d
Milan	Electric	3.8d	6d
	Horse	4.5d	6d
Remschied	Electric	4d	5½d
Rouen	Electric		9d
Sheffield	Horse	10.34d	13.88d
Walsall		8½d paid to the company who work the line	

The General Manager and Engineer of the Glasgow tramways estimated that with overhead electric tramways the percentage of operating expenses to receipts were at least 15 per cent less than horse traction in America, and that operating expenses were on average 2d per mile less than horse traction. Electric cars in America tended to run at faster speeds than in the UK due in part to wide straight roads.

Comparative Statistics – Duncan's Tramway Manual

Location	Type	Expenses	Receipts	Expenses in relation to receipts
Edinburgh Northern	Cable	5.68d	9.76d	58.2%
Twin City	Trolley	8.19 cents	19.01 cents	42.56%
Belfast	Horse	8.42d	11.35d	
Dublin United	Horse	9.52d	12.84d	76.06%
North Metropolitan	Horse	9.99d	12.53d	
Birmingham & Midland	Steam	9.08d	14.27d	
Burnley	Steam	12.43d	19.38d	63.64%
North Staffordshire	Steam	9.03d	15.27d	

Hull's electric tramway system was formally opened on the afternoon of 5 June 1899. After opening the power station and turning on the power the Civic party rode in five cars along Anlaby Road and Hessle Road. Cars nos 4 and 26 are ready to convey the official party and guests in St John Street. (PM)

Three other means of mechanical traction were referred to which were the gas motor, the Serpollet Motor (a form of steam motor) and the compressed air motor, but as these were comparatively untried they were discounted. Various forms of conduit systems were described and discounted, as was the accumulator system which lost out owing to the expense and inconvenience incurred by the labour needed to change the batteries. The Sub-Committee were strongly and unanimously of the opinion that the overhead system of electrical traction was the most suitable for Hull. It was agreed to proceed with the re-construction and extension of the tramways, as authorised by the Hull Corporation Tramways Order 1896, and to adopt the overhead electrical traction as early as circumstances permitted.

In the meantime, despite Alderman Larard's views, it was decided that the Corporation would operate the system. Opinion had swung away from allowing an external organisation to make profits; instead the Corporation was to retain any profits within Hull.

It decided that the Corporation did not have sufficient information to take a decision about the construction of a separate generating station for the tramways, or the extension of the existing electric lighting station at Sculcoates. It considered that by allowing prospective contractors to quote for either would help with the decision making. The Borough Engineer felt unable to prepare a detailed estimate of the proposed works, but an approximate estimate including equipping the tramways for a four minutes service over the entire system was £225,000, which did not include money already spent on the purchase and maintenance of the tramways.

Rumblings about the expense and other consequences connected with the electrification of the tramways continued. The Sailors Institute urged the Tramways Sub-Committee in May to reconsider the proposals, stating that this would deprive a number of workers connected with the present system of their livelihood, and would throw out of employment some hundreds of workers in the town, all as a result of the extravagant electric tramways proposal.

On 6 July 1897 the status of Kingston upon Hull changed

when, by Charter from Queen Victoria, it became a City. Its Chief Officers gained new titles, the Borough Engineer, for example, becoming the City Engineer, although the Town Clerk retained his title.

The plans for the tramways and the NER dock proposals had not gone unnoticed. The United States Consul in Hull, Mr Miller, wrote to the State Department in May to acquaint it of the schemes, and a short piece appeared in the *New York Times* on 18 July 1897. It commended the two schemes (including the ten miles of double-track tramways), to American firms and provided details of persons to contact. This would not be the last time when the Hull system featured in the *NYT*. Perhaps the bids from Brill, the St Louis Car Company and other American companies for supplying tramcars were the result of Mr Miller's interest.

A draft specification, prepared in conjunction with the Electrical Engineer for the electrical equipment of the tramways, including engines, generators, switchboards, feeders and other conductors, trolley wire with posts and other supports, switches and sundries and rail bonding, was submitted by the City Engineer to the Tramways (Deputation) Sub-Committee on 17 August 1897. The specification was written to enable prospective contractors to propose their own schemes and include transformers were current to be generated at high tension.

Other works formed part of contracts or were to be carried out by the Corporation itself. These comprised permanent way and paving, station buildings (and transformer station buildings if required), boilers and main steam pipes, trench work for feeders, access boxes for these and concrete work for posts. This gives a good idea of the infrastructure required to construct a new tramway system (for that is what it was), and the amount of usually unrecorded work needed to bring that system into being. The number of items considered by the Sub-Committee more than tripled as a result.

Quotations were required for 15 motor cars complete, 10 with motors sufficiently powerful to enable them to be used with trailers, and 5 for self-propulsion only. Five trailers were also required. No reason was given regarding the choice of "trail"

33

An overhead view of car no. 26 shows the treatment of the upper deck sides on the earlier cars – doesn't look very safe! Nor does the person watching from the first floor window ledge! (MJW/HC)

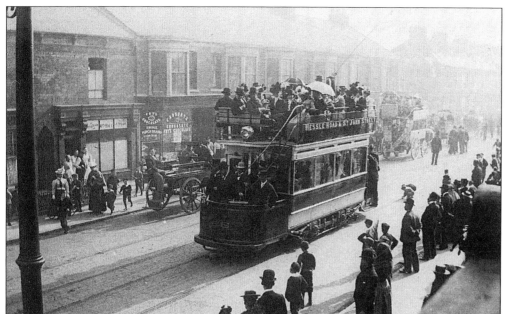

cars and the minutes contain no clue. Bristol possessed 21 motor cars and 12 trailers, Coventry 8 motor and 2 trailer cars, Dublin 30 motor and 30 trailer cars and Hartlepool 5 motor and two trailer cars. It was, presumably, this experience that led Hull to follow suit. The City Engineer said that the twenty units would be sufficient for one road only, as he did not consider it advisable for the Corporation to commit itself at present to a particular type of car for the whole system. They would be sufficient to maintain a three-minute service for most of the day, although the feeders would permit a more frequent service. Some 60 motor cars would be eventually required. All should seat about fifty passengers. Seats should be comfortable but without elaborate upholstery. Cars with roller bearings would be favourably considered. The specification provided for current generation at the Electric Light Station in Sculcoates Lane, or at a site to be selected on the north side of Queen's Dock or the west side of Prince's Dock.

The type of rail was not specified at that time since he was awaiting a consultant's report, but the City Engineer had assumed that steel girder rails with cast welded joints would be used. If another type were adopted he would inform prospective contractors of that fact. The consultant was Mr G.F. Deacon, the former City Engineer of Liverpool, who had adopted an alternative method of laying tramways which claimed to save 375% on the life of a rail. Mr Deacon agreed by letter on 17 July to report on the best system of permanent way for tramways in Hull at a cost of 60 guineas (£63 equivalent to £4980 in 2009 terms).

The City Engineer was authorised to advertise for tenders as described in the specification, as well as advertising for Australian hardwood planks for paving, for cutting such planks into blocks, for Australian hardwood blocks and tenders for paving the streets along which the tramways were to be constructed.

On 3 September Mr Nettleton reminded the Corporation that his lease would terminate on 15 October 1897, and enquired if he could continue to run the cars and, if so, for how long. His lease was renewed subject to three months' notice on either side. Any amendment could be made at one month's notice on either side. Mr Nettleton had fallen foul of the Hackney Carriage Committee which compelled him to provide both smoking and non-smoking cars.

In November consideration of the tenders for the electrical works was deferred because the City Engineer wished to modify them to be more advantageous to the Corporation, and to allow the Electrical Engineer to advise the Sub-Committee regarding the question of the generating plant and associated matters.

The question of the supplier of rails for the tramways was resolved in December 1897 when, after perusing seven tenders, it was decided to utilise long rails rather than short ones. The City Engineer was instructed to discuss delivery arrangements with the Societé Anonyme des Acieries d'Angleur. Board of Trade approval for the type of tramway rail and the mode of laying was received on 3 November, a decision which took a remarkably short time since the City Engineer had only submitted it after the Sub-Committee's meeting on 27 October! The City Engineer was authorised to obtain prices for points and crossings required for the first tramways. The lowest tender received, that of Messrs Askham Brothers and Wilson amounting to £482, was accepted in February 1898.

Arrangements for street works were also considered in December 1897. Work in Carr Lane and Hessle Road would be dealt with first and split into two contracts. Work on other roads would be split into various lengths where work would be carried out day and night between 1 May and 1 December 1898. Each length would be closed to traffic until work was complete. No mention was made of how existing horse tram services would be affected, whether passengers would walk between tracks on either side of the work, or whether the service would be suspended or withdrawn permanently.

It was also decided to construct a central power station for the tramways. In January 1898 twelve tenders for electrical equipment for the tramway system were considered. Two tenders stood out – those from Siemens and R.W. Blackwell. There was very little to choose between them, the only major point being the question of feeders where Siemens opted for a more extensive system which found favour with the Electrical Engineer,

Both companies proposed the same bodies by Milnes, but Blackwell specified Peckham trucks and Thomson-Houston motors, whilst Siemens specified Brill trucks and their own motors which were slightly more powerful, both of which were comparable and acceptable to the Corporation. The City Engineer and the Electrical Engineer both considered that roller bearings should be provided at an additional cost of £20 per car. Eventually, the tender submitted by Messrs Siemens Brothers amounting to £42,228 1s 5d was accepted.

On 11 March 1898 tenders for street works on the Hessle Road route were re-considered after the City Engineer had pointed out some errors of calculation to the firm whose lowest tender had been accepted. The latter submitted a revised one which put his price above the next lowest. The Sub-Committee then awarded the work to Mr Nicholls of Morecombe for both divisions of the Hessle Road route, and also the Anlaby Road route. Mr Nicholls would lay the paving, the City Engineer the tracks.

Traction pole positions for the Holderness Road route were

discussed by the Tramways Sub-Committee on 16 May. The question concerned whether the poles should be placed on the north side or the south side of the road. It was being arranged to place the poles on the right hand side going out of the town, on the Hessle Road, Anlaby Road, Spring Bank and Beverley Road routes, and on the right hand side of the Market Place and Lowgate (from the Pier direction). If it was not for the fact that through cars could be run from either Hessle Road or Anlaby Road to the Holderness Road route, the City Engineer considered it desirable to adopt the left hand side for the route.

It was necessary that on any one line the side poles should be fixed at the same side of the road throughout, so as to correspond with the side of the car on which the trolley standard was fixed. The only disadvantage which could arise from using the north side of the route appeared to be that, unless the lines were arranged so that cars would run straight through by connecting Savile Street to St John Street or otherwise, a car could not, in an emergency, be transferred to or from the Holderness Road without turning it round. If a double junction were provided at some suitable point on the system, a car could be turned if necessary. It was agreed to locate the poles on the north side of the road.

At the same meeting a request from Messrs Siemens to replace the 4D 15/12 motors in the tramcars with the smaller 4D 15/8 motors which were more suitable, and £100 cheaper, was agreed. Finally, it was decided to hold a ceremony on the occasion of the laying of the first rail for the electric tramways.

This took place on 9 June 1898 when Alderman Larard laid the first length of rail in Porter Street. He forecast that Hessle Road would be complete within five months, a prediction that was to be very optimistic. In anticipation of the reconstruction the Hessle Road horse trams had ceased to run in May 1898.

The plan of the Hessle Road route showing location of the poles and overhead was sent to the BOT for approval on 2 June 1898. However, the Board, on 7 June 1898, questioned the desirability of side running, and asked the Corporation to consider centre poles and/or span wires. Mr White stated that some curb lines were 40' or less apart, and that side running was essential at such places. Wherever practicable, centre poles and span wires would be used on other routes. The Board remained unconvinced and asked the Corporation to reconsider. On 30 July Mr White said that the Corporation would adopt centre poles on the widest part of Hessle Road from Wellstead Street to West Dock Avenue, some 550 yards, and that here tracks would be 10' 6" apart. This seemed to satisfy the Board.

The Tramways (Deputation) Sub-Committee on 18 August expressed concern about slow progress on the tramway works, and decided to write to the contractor to remind him that he was not completing the agreed quantity of work on each day, and informing him that the Corporation would insist on him working at a greater speed.

In late September he stated that the first month of any contract counted for nothing and, in any case, nothing much could be done until after the rail laying ceremony. Delivery of concrete and paving had been delayed but, at the time of writing, actual work completed was much more than that in the Corporation's letter. However, he did say that his estimate of what could be achieved each day had been too high given the high standard of precision required. He would try to complete the work on time but if he failed to do so he would not complain if the Corporation imposed a penalty. The Corporation wrote to re-emphasise the necessity to complete all works on time.

On 6 September 1898 the Tramways (Deputation) Sub-Committee discussed a letter from a local solicitor A.M. Jackson who had influential London clients, with a plan for building an electric tramway from Hessle (to the west of the city) to connect with the new electric tramways in Hull. They had ample capital available to build the line quickly, but did not wish to commit themselves without an indication of the Corporation's views. They sought a meeting to explain their proposals which would require an application for a Provisional Order in the next session of Parliament. Members decided that they could not see their way to entertain the proposal, and that no useful purpose would be served by an interview.

After much discussion land for the central generating station for the tramways was purchased in September 1898. The site in Osborne Street, just west of Princes Dock, in the town centre comprised 2207 square yards and cost £7640. A revised scheme was agreed with Siemens in May, a contract for the foundations was placed with Mr J. Sangwin in July, and the supply of boilers with Vickers stokers was awarded to Messrs E. Danks in September. Subsequently, further adjoining properties were purchased at a cost of £1150. (According to G.A. Lee, Alderman Larard bought a site in Osborne Street through an intermediary in order to save the Corporation the cost of re-housing tenants when the houses were demolished!)

At the same meeting the Works Committee considered a letter from Mr Nettleton asking when the Corporation would take possession of the Anlaby Road route for reconstruction. He expected the Committee would allow him to put his cars on Hessle Road until the electric cars started running. The Committee could not provide a date, nor would they permit him to use the Hessle Road line.

The Chairman had reconsidered the Hessle tramway proposal, and thought it advisable that the Committee meet Messrs A.M. Jackson's clients. Dr Jackson (Messrs A.M.

Jackson and Co.), Mr J.F. Albright (Managing Director of the Drake and Gorham Electric Power and Traction Company Ltd), and Mr Stewart submitted proposals for the scheme. It was agreed to circulate these to members of the Sub-Committee for consideration at a meeting on 10 October 1898.

To connect with the Hull Tramways, at Dairycoates, a mile of line would be constructed inside the Hull boundary. The promoters would have preferred for this to be constructed by the Corporation, but as Parliamentary powers did not exist for the construction of this line the promoters were willing to include it in their Provisional Order and at any time sell the short line to Hull Corporation at its fair cost price, the object being solely to get a through connection. It would be possible to construct the whole line during the summer of 1899. The portion of line outside the boundary could also be acquired by the Corporation at some future date after a period of ten years. The proposed line would be of no practical value to either Hull or Hessle if a transfer of passengers had to be made at the Hull boundary. Both organisations would have running powers over the whole line from Hessle to Monument Bridge in order to avoid a change of car at the boundary. Shared costs would include electric power used, interest and depreciation, superintendence etc. The promoters also pointed out that the NER and private conveyances provided very little revenue to the Corporation whereas its scheme would afford a steady income stream to it.

Cars would run every 15 minutes morning and evening, and half-hourly at other times, at a fare of 3d for the whole distance with season tickets at £4. A single-track line with passing points would be provided. After due consideration, the unanimous decision was to reject the proposals, since it was not considered advisable to allow anyone to have running powers over the roads of the city. In any case, the Corporation might seek its own powers for a

service to Hessle.

No mention was made of any undoubted opposition from the East Riding County Council, which always regarded Hull Corporation's activities with deep suspicion, and the North Eastern Railway whose trains served Hessle already, admittedly with a station some distance from the centre and with an infrequent service.

And yet was it a lost opportunity? Would a successful Hessle venture have seen a desire for other places such as Anlaby, Cottingham or Hedon to have a service? Would housing have developed along the line? How would the tram network have then looked and developed?

On 19 October the Tramways (Deputation) Sub-Committee considered tenders for rolling stock. The tenders are shown in full to illustrate the keen competition in what was a new industry and to provide an idea of the wide range of options available. Nine companies, some familiar some not so well known, had submitted tenders for forty-five double deck cars seating fifty one passengers with prices ranging from £522 to £734 per car. Seven separate body makers were mentioned as were nine different motor suppliers.

Here is the full set:

Name of firm	Cost per car			Motors Supplier	Bodymaker
	£	s	d		
Westinghouse Company	522	10	0	Westinghouse	Brush Co.
	536	0	0		Milnes
	582	0	0		Brill
Warburg, Dymond & Co.	531	0	0	Johnson	St Louis Car Co.
Blackwell & Co.	588	1	9	G E 52	Milnes
Crompton Co.	598	5	0	Crompton	Electric Railway
					& Tramway Carriage Co.
Brush – if 40 cars	640	0	0	Brush	Brush Co.
– if 20 cars	645	0	0		
– if 10 cars	650	0	0		
Hurst, Nelson & Co.	650	0	0	American type	Hurst, Nelson & Co.
	656	0	0		
Laing, Wharton and Down				Steel	Brill
if 40 cars	656	10	0		
if 20 cars	659	0	0		
if 10 cars	661	10	0		
Siemens Bros & Co.	688	0	0	Siemens	Ashbury
	695	0	0		E.R. & T.C. Co.
	706	0	0		Milnes
Witting Bros	708	0	0	Helios	Not stated
If 40 cars	692	0	0	Belgian	Not stated
If 20 cars	714	0	0	Belgian	Not stated
If 10 cars	734	0	0	Belgian	Not stated

This is a fine view of Milnes car no. 5 which shows how precarious riding on the upper deck must have been. Also in view are the soon to be removed curtains and the side destination boards. The total lack of protection from the elements for motormen can also be seen. (PM)

The Warburg tender failed because it submitted no specification, and neither the motors nor the cars as offered were in use in the United Kingdom, and very little information about them was available. Those specifications that were submitted had little to choose between them but the City Engineer stated that the reputation of Brill and Milnes cars "was somewhat better than that of Brush cars".

The tender from the Westinghouse Company was approved subject to the provision of an improved design of trolley, and subject to the fitting of chilled iron wheels at a reduction of £10 per car. Brill trucks would be fitted and Westinghouse's own motors would also be fitted. Bodies would be supplied by Brush (30), Milnes (10) and Brill (5). The choice of Brush was surprising given the comments by the City Engineer.

Twenty double-deck trail cars were also required. No reason for this increased requirement was ever recorded in the minutes, and it is possible that the decision reflected the results of the previous year's visits. Nine companies had submitted quotes of between £195 and £372 per car.

The City Engineer stated that there was nothing to choose between the designs of the lower priced cars offered. Provided that Messrs Siemens would provide trail cars without motors, their tender for ten cars with bodies by the Electric Railway and Tramway Carriage Co., and ten cars with bodies by Messrs Milnes and Co. was accepted. Failing that, the tender from the Westinghouse Co. would be accepted with all the cars bearing Milnes bodies.

The third requirement was for five open trail cars carrying not less than 36 passengers. Although many companies had submitted tenders, only those for cars seating 36 or more or costing less than £225 per car were placed before members. The City Engineer considered that none of the designs, which included large bogey cars from Hurst, Nelson & Company, seemed to meet the specification, and recommended that the matter be deferred. The question did not arise again and the proposal was dropped. For the record the bids that were considered were:

Name of firm	Price			Builders
	£	s	d	
Siemens Bros & Co.	195	0	0	Electric Railway & Tramway Carriage Co.
	210	0	0	Milnes
Crompton & Co.	210	0	0	E.R.T.C Co.
Westinghouse Co.	215	0	0	Milnes
	225	0	0	Brush
Brush Co.	216	0	0	Brush
Hurst, Nelson & Co.	234	0	0	Hurst, Nelson & Co.
	294	0	0	Hurst, Nelson & Co.
Warburg, Dymond & Co.	254	0	0	St Louis Car Co.
Witting Bros	319	0	0	Industrie of Louvani (Louvain?)
	340	0	0	Herbrandt
Blackwell & Co.	345	15	3	Milnes
Laing, Wharton & Down	372	0	0	Brill

Name of Firm	Price			Passengers	Builders
	£	s	d		
Siemens Bros & Co.	128	0	0	43	Milnes
	144	0	0	36	E.R.& T.C. Co.
Westinghouse Co.	131	8	9	43	Milnes
	134	0	0	40	Brush
Brush Co.	130	0	0	40	Brush
Crompton & Co.	152	10	0	36	E.R.& T.C. Co.
Warburg, Dymond & Co.	211	10	0	40	St Louis Car Co.
Hurst, Nelson & Co.					
(Bogey car)	220	0	0	48	Hurst, Nelson & Co.
(Bogey car)	225	10	0	56	Hurst, Nelson & Co.

In addition, the Sub-Committee accepted the Westinghouse Co.'s tender of £672 for two sprinkling (the City Engineer's words) cars, but deferred a decision about the supply of travers-

Views of electric cars with trailers are almost non-existent. This rare view shows an electric car and trailer no. 114 in St John Street near the Punch Hotel (AG)

and the manner in which the work was being carried out (ignoring the delays arising from a re-tendering exercise).

The Town Clerk had requested evidence in support of their allegations but had received no reply. He then asked the Association to send a deputation to a meeting of the Committee. Not until January 1899 did that deputation, which included several contractors who were already carrying out work in connection with the tramways (Mr J. Sangwin being one) attend the Committee. Resolution of the complaint was passed to the Streets and Lighting Committee which inspected the works on 16 January.

No overall project plan and timescale was ever submitted to the Works Committee regarding the construction of the tramway system. Having ordered all manner of equipment and even cars, only in November 1898 was the City Engineer empowered to purchase suitable sites for the erection of car sheds for the Anlaby Road and Hessle Road routes. As events would show, there was insufficient time for their purchase and erection before public service began, even though a tender from Mr G. Houlton of £4180 for the construction of the Hessle Road shed was accepted in January 1899. He was also appointed to construct the Anlaby Road sheds at the same rates described in his Hessle Road tender but no actual cost was quoted.

Difficulties arose over the purchase of the land for the depot on the south side of Anlaby Road alongside the NER's Cottingham Road branch near the Anlaby Road terminus. Further negotiations were necessary to buy another adjoining piece from the same landowner. Some tenanted cottages were included in the deal and its occupants were allowed to remain on a temporary basis, but when they failed to demolish outbuildings on the site the Corporation did it for them and charged them for doing it!

As further evidence of the pace of work involved in the new tramways system, an Electrical Assistant, Mr T.D. Clothier, was appointed to supervise the electrical works at the salary of £150 per annum.

The Tramways (Deputation) Sub-Committee received a letter from The Westinghouse Electric Co. regarding the livery of the cars and the provision of a screen or boards for advertising purposes. Members decided that it was undesirable at present to allow advertisements on or in the tramcars, and also decided to paint the cars in different colours for each route. The question of lettering on the cars was delegated to the Chairman, Deputy-Chairman and the City Engineer.

Messrs Milnes informed the Corporation that nearly all the Corporations so far were painting their cars in a uniform colour, and that they were also fixing moveable distinctive route boards so that cars could be run over any route. The Works Committee delegated the decision to the City Engineer. It appears that no decision was ever reported to the Committee regarding the livery to be adopted.

ing platforms since it was considered that these would not be required.

Finally, the Sub-Committee accepted a recommendation to use centre poles along Anlaby Road between Park Street and Regent's Terrace following the widening of the main road.

The first major problem that arose concerned the contractor for the Hessle Road and Anlaby Road routes. Having seen that construction work had stopped, the City Engineer wrote to Mr E. Nicholls on 25 October. The reply of 26 October 1898 was presented to a hastily-called Tramways (Deputation) Sub-Committee on the 27th.

Mr Nicholls stated that he had stopped work because it was clear that there was something radically wrong with the measurement of work, as payments to him were less that his outgoings in wages alone. He asked the Corporation to arrange for a thoroughly reliable measurement of work done in order to address the problem.

The Sub-Committee asked the City Council (meeting that afternoon) to empower the Works Committee to take any action desirable for securing the completion of the tramway works and paving on Hessle Road. It also instructed the City Engineer to give notice to the contractor and his sureties to proceed with and complete the works on Hessle Road in accordance with the contract, and that if the contractor failed to proceed to the satisfaction of the City Engineer before Monday next, 31 October, the contract would be terminated. Mr Nicholls was subsequently declared bankrupt and the City Engineer's Department took over the contract, a move that caused outrage among private companies in the City and eventually led to an official complaint from the Hull Master Builders' Association on 19 December.

Because the work had been taken over by the Corporation instead of being relet, it was seen as a great injustice. The Association alleged that the work was not undertaken in accordance with the rigid conditions placed on the late contractor, and had voted unanimously to enter a strong protest against the action of the Works Committee in not re-advertising the work,

Further discussion involved whether the Corporation had the power to provide for a siding off the Anlaby Road route down the Boulevard, which was located near the railway crossing at Selby Street. No reason was given, although the Hull Rugby Club's ground at Airlie Street was located down the Boulevard. The Town Clerk was asked to report further about the powers for the siding but there appears to be no other reference to this siding, which does not appear on any contemporary maps.

In December the Sub-Committee decided to order five enclosed trail cars in place of the five open trail cars previously considered. A price of £195 per car from the Electric Tramway and Carriage Company Limited was accepted in January 1899.

To date all work involving the reconstruction of the tramways had involved the City Engineer and the Electrical Engineer, but in January it was decided to advertise for a Tramway (not Tramways) Manager at an annual salary of £300. Sixteen applications were received from which five candidates were selected, being granted third class rail fare and one guinea for expenses! Interviews took place on 17 March 1899, and Mr William J. M'Combe of Belfast (at 30 years old the youngest candidate) was appointed as Tramway Manager.

The crew of Milnes car no. 10 display their uniforms for the camera also on the opening day. Crews on the cars could, it was claimed, be mistaken for French Railway Officials! (PM)

When the Spring Bank and Beverley Road routes opened in 1900 the terminus was located in Savile Street and cars ran from Prospect Street via Albion Street and Bond Street. This car is turning into Albion Street from Prospect Street. None of the buildings shown here exist today. (PM)

Subsequently, certain officials were granted an honorarium in recognition of the extra work that they had performed. These comprised the City Engineer (£200 guineas and a salary increase of £100), the Electrical Engineer (£100 guineas plus £100 for acting in a consultancy capacity), and Mr Bricknell (the Deputy City Engineer), later to become the City Engineer, was awarded £50 guineas and an increase of £50 per annum in salary.

The management arrangements were unique to Hull. The Chairman, Alderman Larard, a passionate advocate of the tramways, acted as a de facto Chief Executive. He conducted his council business from his office in the Old Town and Council officials were allocated specific times each day for consulting him, Mr M'Combe's time being 11am! The Chairman was "hands on" apparently resolving a dispute involving a wife-sharing arrangement that involved five tramway men! He was also a Corporation Director of the Hull and Barnsley Railway, a role that would not endear him to the North Eastern Railway.

Responsibilities were divided between the City Engineer

(tracks, paving and car bodies), the Tramway Electrical Engineer (electrical equipment power, and motors), and the Tramway Manager (operation and general administration). In addition the Tramway Electrical Engineer was responsible for the Liverpool Street Workshops whose joiners and painters were controlled by the City Engineer! A unified approach was difficult but not impossible, although on occasions Mr M'Combe and the City Engineer disagreed in Committee about the desirability of a particular extension (to Inglemire Lane on Beverley Road).

The City Engineer informed the Tramways (Special) Sub-Committee on 11 January 1899 that it would be necessary to install signalling apparatus at the Midland Street/Anlaby Road junction, to regulate cars to and from Hessle Road. Midland Street was a narrow street and only a single line was proposed. He was given approval to ask the North Eastern Railway Company for permission to fix a signal box on the west side of the large gate-way at the Anlaby Road entrance to Paragon Station. Agreement was forthcoming, but details are not known about any agreement with the NER. He was also authorised to obtain tenders for the required signalling and interlocking gear, the cost of which was £107, by the Railway Signalling Company Limited.

In May 1899 the City Engineer reported that he had obtained prices for a sample motor car with double bogey (the Hull spelling) trucks from Messrs Geo F. Milnes & Co. and the Westinghouse Electric Co. It would seat 30 passengers inside and 39 outside with a roof similar to that of Edinburgh Tramways, which the Sub-Committee had inspected at Birkenhead. The cost including the provision of electric braking system and roller bearings was £685, and the City Engineer was authorised to order a sample car. He was also authorised to purchase three spare motors for Siemens cars and nine for Westinghouse cars and 60 car jacks, about £1500 in cost.

Plans for the improvement of Regent Street involved a new junction with Hessle Road. The City Engineer recommended pulling down the building on the corner including the gable end of the former tramway stables, re-building the wall to the new street line, and boarding up that part not affected.

With the opening of the system not far away the questions of working hours, wages, appointments, uniforms, stopping places, punches, tickets (at 4d per 1000 from the Glasgow Numerical Printing Company), advertising on the back of the tickets, badges (1s 3d per dozen), rules and regulations, carriage of parcels and other matters were agreed on 29 May. Timetables for the new routes were also approved, but no details were recorded in the minutes.

In April several members and officers visited the power station site and the car shed at Liverpool Street to inspect some of the new cars at the Hessle Road tramway depot. Progress on the track work on both Anlaby and Hessle Roads was also inspected and they were told that the opening was not far off.

On 9 May 1899 the City Engineer said that the Hessle Road car shed alone would not hold the number of cars which would be delivered by the date of the Yorkshire Agricultural Show, and since Anlaby Road depot would not be completed by that time he obtained approval to construct an additional temporary car shed alongside the Hessle Road shed. The cost would be £300, and the shed would hold 24 cars.

Also in May (on 12th) the City Engineer informed the Board of Trade that most of the widening of Anlaby Road had been carried out, but that not all owners had voluntarily agreed with the acquisition of part of their frontages for the scheme. The Corporation would require a Compulsory Purchase Order to acquire the land, which would mean that the works could not be completed in time for the opening of the tramways. Therefore he intended to provide a short section of single line from a point 190 yards west of South Street near the College of Art, and a point 70 yards west of South Street.

The outward track would be laid in the agreed position, as would the inward track, apart from the 120-yard gap. Temporary points would be installed to enable cars bound for St John Street to cross from the inward line to the outward line and then back again. Outward bound cars would remain on the outward track. This was agreed. There was no indication of how the single line would be worked, but special arrangements were surely needed as the westernmost points were situated near the junction with Midland Street.

There was more opposition to the provision of tramways in the Old Town, particularly with reference to Whitefriargate, and deputations attended a meeting on 30 June to discuss the proposal with Committee members. The decision to run the tramway in the Old Town was confirmed.

One of the features of Hull's correspondence with the Board of Trade is the prompt response by the Board's officers, sometimes by return or within a few days although the reply was not always welcome, as we shall see. Even more remarkable is the number of internal consultations undertaken (recorded in highly stylised pen and ink copperplate writing) in such a short time.

On 31 May 1899 the City Engineer informed the Board of Trade that he wanted to run experimental cars on the Hessle Road section during the following week. He wanted to know if he could run the cars without formal BOT inspection or whether the Board would sanction the running first. If he could run the cars, were there any special requirements to be met? In any case he considered it desirable to run the cars before any official inspection.

The reply on 2 June merely said that Board inspection was necessary before the lines opened for public traffic, which didn't really help much since Mr White (the City Engineer) wanted to gain running experience before any inspection or public running. So he tried again, asking how much notice would be required for an inspection. Fourteen days later came the reply. When Mr White enquired if sanction for public running would be given immediately after the inspection he was assured that, subject to everything being satisfactory, the answer was yes. "Right" said Mr White. "Can you inspect on 4 July?" Two days later came a letter from the BOT stating that Lt-Colonel Sir Francis Marindin would carry out the inspection but no date was given.

The following day Mr White informed the Board that the Corporation wanted to run trams for the Yorkshire Agricultural Show which would open on 19 July, and that he wanted several days' experience of operation before dealing with the large number of expected passengers. The Board's internal notes recognised the need for this, and the desire to make arrangements for the public opening of the tramways, and the Lt-Colonel was advised to contact the Corporation. He sent his

Milnes cars nos 8 and 16 are caught in Carr Lane shortly after the opening of the system. No. 16 carries a route letter board. (PM)

Brush car no 33 stands at the original St John Street terminus in 1900. Passengers appear to be boarding at both ends, contrary to regulations. (PG)

badge at 7s each and for drivers and conductors at 4s 6d each).

It had been decided to open the Hessle and Anlaby Road routes at the same time, and accordingly 5 July 1899 was chosen as the inauguration day. At 2.30pm the Lord Mayor (Alderman Gelder) and Corporation assembled in Osborne Street, where Alderman Gelder opened the power station door with a golden key. Alderman Wilde started the first engine, after which the Mayor presented Mrs Larard with a commemoration (a solid silver salver suitably inscribed) of the opening of the Electric Tramways, and "as an acknowledgement of the able and devoted services of Alderman Larard in promoting the establishment of a system of electric traction for the City".

The assembled group walked down Osborne Street and Waterworks Street to St John Street, where a large crowd had gathered before boarding five tramcars, including Milnes car no. 4 and Brill car no. 26. They travelled along Anlaby Road to the terminus before returning to Midland Street for the journey along Hessle Road. Both roads were lined with the local citizenry eager to see this new mode of transport. Refreshments were taken in Liverpool Street Workshops before returning by car to the city centre.

The first fares were taken on car no. 26 which was driven by motorman G. Crawford (who later became an inspector). A souvenir collector offered half-a-crown for the first ticket punched and numbered "0000"! A councillor tendered three pence for the first two tickets issued and told the conductor (a former horse car employee) to keep the change!

Meanwhile the public service had begun (and lasted until midnight) with 8763 passengers being carried for the sum of £36 10s 3d, and on the following day 17,261 passengers paying £71 18s 5d were carried. Alderman Larard must have thoroughly enjoyed the day, having seen his vision come to fruition.

Thirty motor cars were available for the opening (Milnes nos. 1 to 25 and Brill nos. 26 to 30) together with trailer cars nos 101 to 125.

The initial timetable started at 5.30am with a fifteen-minute workman's service until 7am when cars ran at six-minute intervals until 5pm. A two-minute headway was then provided until 8pm when a four-minute service was operated until 10pm when a six-minute frequency was run until the last departure from the city terminus at 10.36pm.

report to the Board on 12 July and the Board despatched it with a certificate of operation to the Corporation on 17 July.

On 16 June 1899 tenders for uniforms were considered. Six tenders complete with samples were examined by the Tramways Sub-Committee and Messrs Hall and Cohen (described as experts). Sample D41 was chosen for inspector this being from Messrs G. Dimbleby & Son, Market Place (cost £3 7s per uniform) whilst sample number 1(4) was selected for drivers and conductors at £1 15s 2d each from Messrs Burn & Co, Porter Street, and sample number 1 for caps from Mr T.A. Gillet, Market Place, was chosen for caps (inspectors complete with

Car no. 17 passes Albert Avenue en route for St John Street with the conductor regarding the photographer with suspicion. (MJW)

Chapter 4

THE SYSTEM EXPANDS

The first traffic returns were submitted to the Tramways (Special) Sub-Committee on 27 July 1899. During twenty two days of operation (5 to 26 July) 473,972 passengers had been carried with receipts of £1974 17s 8d, the daily average being 21,544 and approximately £89. The "normal" averages were much lower since the Agricultural Show (whose ground was situated just beyond the Anlaby Road terminus) had attracted 118,430 passengers over three days, the greatest number being 52,780 on 20 July, bringing receipts of over £219. As this traffic used the Anlaby Road route the organisation that coped with such numbers within three weeks of opening must have been very impressive. For all that effort the report was merely entered on the minutes! However, in August the tram Inspectors were awarded £2 in respect of their extra duties.

Board of Trade regulations required operators to maintain a series of records to be forwarded, if required, to its offices. These were:

Daily Records
Number of cars running
Maximum working current
Maximum working pressure
Maximum current from the earth connexion
Leakage of current
Fall of potential in return

Monthly Records
Condition of earth connexions
Insulation resistance of insulated cables

Quarterly Records
Conductance of joints to pipes

Occasional Records
Tests made under regulation 6(ii) of the Board of Trade's Statutory Rules and Orders 1897 as they applied to Hull Corporation. This referred to the arrangements for testing any uninsulated earth return.
Localization and removal of leakages
Particulars of abnormal occurrences affecting the electric working of the tramway

The City Engineer was authorised to order 80 route boards lettered "A" and "D", similar to the boards already in use on some of the Anlaby Road cars at 14s each, including the requisite ironwork for fixing, from Messrs G.F. Milnes & Co. Clearly these boards were in use some three years earlier than had been thought. The City Engineer stated that the boards were needed to show from a distance which route respective cars were taking.

Authority was given to the City Engineer to negotiate with the NER regarding the arrangements for the Holderness Road level crossing on the same terms as the Anlaby Road crossing. He was also authorised to stop up the entire width of Savile Street while reconstructing the tramways.

On 18 July the Board of Trade despatched the inspection reports for the two routes. Both were passed as fit for public use (thirteen days after their inauguration!) and the use of electric traction was also approved, subject to inspection requirements (not specified in the minutes) being completed.

The local brewery, Messrs Moors & Robson were castigated for one of its rullymen obstructing car no. 2 on 5 August. A director, Mr Peter Robson, expressed his regret at the meeting and assured members that all rullymen had been instructed not to obstruct the tramcars. (Another director was member of the Committee, later succeeding Alderman Larard as chairman). It should be mentioned that a rully (sometimes spelled "rulley") was a cart that carried goods and was pulled by a horse. In later years the term also applied to motor transport – the driver was often called a "rullyman".

Problems had been experienced with the overhead line at the Midland Street junction. For safety reasons conductors had to ascend the car, take hold of the trolley rope and stand by the trolley pole while the cars negotiated the junction, which the Tramway Manager considered unsafe. The Town Clerk informed Messrs Siemens Bros & Co. Ltd of the very serious nature of the matter and instructed them to remove the cause of complaint. He also requested them to expedite the delayed erection of overhead equipment at the Liverpool Street Car Shed. Were all or part of the car sheds not in use and, if so, how were trams being operated or stabled for the night?

Siemens replied on 19 August stating their intention to erect straight hangers at the Midland Street junction, which would remedy all complaints in a fortnight's time. A more short term solution was proposed for the tram sheds, in that it would erect the trolley wire in a temporary manner by means of the pull-offs until delivery of the required equipment.

One surprising omission in equipping the tramways had been the provision of ticket boxes for conductors. This was remedied by the purchase of 100 tin boxes in August 1899.

Meanwhile discussions had taken place between the Corporation and Mr John Fisher, J.P. and Colonel Wellsted of the Drypool and Marfleet Steam Tramways Company who attended the Tramways (Special) Sub-Committee on 28 September. It was agreed to purchase the company for £15,500 subject to satisfactory arrangements for the temporary operation of the line to a contract prepared by the Town Clerk and the approval of the Board of Trade.

Concern was expressed about the slow construction of the Holderness Road route. Delays in acquiring property west of Thomas Street had, in turn, delayed road widening and made it impractical to lay the tramway along the intended line. The City Engineer who had taken on the contract as second highest bidder when the original contractor had declined to undertake the work, said that if the question was still unresolved when track laying was in progress, he would lay a single line (as had occurred on the Anlaby Road route) or lay the track on a diverted line until the road was available.

The same meeting approved work on the Spring Bank route in advance of the Beverley Road route as the necessary widening at various locations on Beverley Road had not been arranged.

On 21 August 1899 the tramway carried its one millionth passenger, and by 29 August the total had risen to 1,117,612, with receipts of £4881 14s 4d, rising to 1.8 million on 30 September and £7744 15s 6d respectively.

Car no. 92 (Hurst Nelson of 1901) is framed by the Hull and Barnsley Railway bridge near Fitzroy Street on Beverley Road as it returns to the city centre. Note the almost complete lack of traffic in this pre-1904 view. (PM)

Overcrowding was chronic, according to contemporary sources, with overloaded cars "shuttling about". Byelaws introduced in 1900 prohibited riding on the steps or platform and standing outside or inside, were generally unenforced. Cartoons depicting the extent of overcrowding appeared in the local press.

To assist with tramway overhead maintenance and repairs, an emergency tower wagon was purchased from Messrs Macartney, McElroy and Co. Ltd. for £110 in August 1899.

The first recorded instance of an assault of a conductor was reported to the October Works Committee. Robert Kirman, the conductor, was assaulted by a Charles Lowe who had struck him in the face on 16 September. The Town Clerk thought it right that Kirman should have legal assistance, and he obtained a summons and represented the conductor before the magistrate who found Lowe guilty and fined him 10 shillings and costs.

In September and October 1899 the Corporation and the Board of Trade argued about the provision of speed indicators. The Board's Regulations (No.1) stated that cars should be fitted, if and when required by the Board, with an apparatus to indicate to the driver the speed at which a car was running. It had recently insisted that these be fitted, but the City Engineer had contacted every tramway operator, and none knew of one type that worked. The Board's internal consultations insisted that some were available, but the matter was not resolved, especially when the Town Clerk's legal opinion was that the Board's regulations referred only to steam trams.

The Board also insisted on second couplings between motor cars and trailers, but the Corporation said it was unnecessary given the flat nature of the terrain.

Colonel Marindin, the Inspector, had instructed that all cars should be brought to a standstill before reaching the point on Anlaby Road at the junction with Midland Street. The City Engineer thought this unsafe to stop cars on all routes, and said that this should refer only to cars about to turn into Midland Street.

When authority was given to negotiate for a suitable site for a depot on Holderness Road a site was found on the south side of Holderness Road beyond East Park. It was 400 feet long with a road frontage of 100 feet.

The City Engineer was also authorised to submit plans to the Board of Trade for the temporary tramways in Bond Street and Albion Street for the Beverley Road and Spring Bank routes, pending construction of the new street between Prospect Street and Junction Street. The new street would be King Edward Street, whilst Junction Street would disappear with the construction of Queen Victoria Square.

Mr Nettleton ceased to run horse trams on 1 October 1899, according to a report by the Town Clerk in the Committee minutes. Mr Dyson in his recollections states that this occurred in November and he included a photograph taken, with the car concerned carrying a black flag provided by him. Mr Dyson transferred to the electric tramways and in the early 1920s was still employed as a motorman on the Beverley Road route.

Passenger numbers passed the two million mark on 7 October. On 11 October, with the annual Hull Fair in full swing, no fewer than 72,500 passengers were carried, the majority on the Anlaby Road route.

As construction of the Holderness Road and the other routes continued, it was decided that in order to permit cars to be transferred between routes, a temporary single line should be laid linking St John Street and Savile Street. With no suitable depot available, another temporary solution was required, and the Parks Committee approved the erection of a temporary shed behind old farm buildings at East Park.

On 20 October the Committee received a letter and drawings from the North Eastern Railway Company, suggesting that signals be fixed on trolley poles each side of the Anlaby Road crossing for the purpose of regulating tram traffic, such signals to be worked by overhead wires from the railway signal box. For some reason this work was never carried out.

On 17 November 1899 the Hull and District Chamber of Trade wrote to the Works Committee to complain about excess speeds of the tramcars which was putting its members at great risk, loss and inconvenience. Speeds, it claimed, were in excess of those permitted by the Provisional Order.

Another complaint, dated 28 November was received from the Waggonette Proprietors Protection Society. This called attention to the Schedule "A" of the Provisional Order with regard to speed indicators being fixed on the cars and also to the excessive speed. This read "cars shall be fitted, if and when required by the Board of Trade, with an apparatus to indicate to the driver the speed at which a car is running". The Society asked when Schedule "A" provisions were to be carried out.

At first, smoking was permitted in the trailer cars but not in motor cars. The question was discussed by the Sub-Committee, and it was decided that the use of trailers as smoking cars should cease and that smoking be permitted in ordinary cars at certain times of the day, it being left to the Chairman and the Tramway Manager to decide.

Trailer cars were not provided with interior lights when first designed. Tenders from Messrs Siemens (£15 per car and £3 15s for each motor car) and Westinghouse (£12 19s 6d per car and £3 5s per motor car) were accepted in early 1899.

A special meeting of the City Council was held on 9 November 1899 where, by 50 votes to 4 it was agreed to purchase the Drypool and Marfleet Steam Tramways Co. Ltd., comprising 1¼ miles of track, a depot and rolling stock. The cost of the sale was £15,500.

As a result the company held an Extraordinary General Meeting at 12 noon on Monday 27 November 1899 where a resolution proposed by Mr F.B. Grotrian and seconded by Mr J. Fisher to sell the company to Hull Corporation was approved.

On 1 December 1899 the Corporation forwarded to the Board of Trade a conditional contract of the sale of the DMST and stated that the sale would take place, subject to the Board's approval, on 31 January 1900. In addition to the terms of Section 44 of the Tramways Act 1870, the Board's approval was also required under Section 53 of the Company's Order of 1886 confirmed by the Tramways Orders Confirmation (No. 2) Act 1886, as well as Section 5 of the Tramways Orders Confirmation Act 1892 (which indicated that a sale would probably be made to the Corporation). The Town Clerk pointed out that the Corporation were now the owners of all the tramways within the City. The contract contained the following list of major items:

Seven tramway engines
Eight bogie saloon double deck cars
One set spare engine wheels and axles
Twelve pairs spare car wheels and axles
Five pairs spare engine springs
Three pairs spare car springs
Two engine axle boxes
Four car axle boxes
One gas engine
One bogie each for bringing in disabled engines, for road repairs and for salting purposes [sic].
All other items being more or less fixed equipment

The contract was signed by the Town Clerk (E. Laverack), two DMST directors (F.B. Grotrian and J.N.O. Fisher) and the Company Secretary, J. Barker Butterill. The Board of Trade sent its approval on 11 December. Final confirmation of the sale was sent to the Board by the Town Clerk on 31 January 1900.

The same meeting agreed to maintain the Hedon Road steam tram service until the Corporation were in a position to reconstruct the tramway. Its employees were to be taken over by the Corporation upon terms to be agreed by the Chairman. The company's manager, Mr Entwisle, had been allowed to run a business of his own, and he claimed that the Corporation's decision to take on all the staff on the same terms would permit him to continue as before. He described his arrangement at a subsequent meeting, after which the Committee gave him a week's notice! Approval was given at the December meeting of the

Tramways (Special) Sub-Committee for the two sprinkler cars to be equipped with snowploughs (made by the City Engineer's Workshops). This meant that the cars had to be fitted with an additional motor (from Westinghouse) and headlights at a cost of £135 10s per car.

Also in December 1899 the Board of Trade expressed concern about the overhead at bridges on Beverley Road and Holderness Road, and Mr Trotter (its electrical expert) suggested improvements. The City Engineer was willing to comply, but the inner trolley wire would be nearer the side at which the side poles and bracket arms were located. The wire would be four feet from the handrail, but his alternative was to take the wire more out of the direct line than intended. The trolley arm would never be directly over a car at its lowest position, and it would be almost impossible for a passenger to come into contact with it unless done deliberately. The Board concurred. Interestingly the Board's internal memo said that Hull's original submission had shown only single deck cars! Unfortunately, the plan has not survived and the mystery is unsolved.

On 19 January 1900 the City Engineer submitted an offer from the Electric Railway and Tramway Carriage works Co. Ltd for the conversion of five trailers into electric cars that were to have been supplied under their contract. The cost, which was £300 each plus £281 5s per car for electrical equipment from the British Westinghouse Electric and Manufacturing Co Ltd., was accepted by the Cars Sub-Committee. Brill trucks with ordinary bearings would also be supplied.

The City Engineer and Tramway Manager then proceeded to inform the Sub-Committee that 100 (not 60 as stated in the original tender document) motor cars would be required for working the five tramway routes at present in hand. The number which had been delivered and on order, excluding the sample "bogey" car was 60, and the five "Preston" cars just approved, would give a total of 65.

If it was decided not to continue using trail cars the twenty-five on hand could be converted into motor cars, leaving only 10 additional motor cars required. This implies that the question of trailer operation had been previously discussed but no reference has been found. The City Engineer had asked Messrs G.F. Milnes & Co. if they could convert 10 cars in four months, and the remaining 15 in seven months, but the reply had indicated that the work could not be achieved in that time. It was possible that the cars might be converted by the Corporation's own workmen. 35 pieces of equipment and trucks would be required for the conversion of the twenty-five trailers and the ten additional cars. He sought authority to advertise for these but was given approval to convert only five trailer cars in the first instance, but he was authorised to order all equipment for all 35 cars and the ten bodies.

The City Engineer had asked the British Thomson-Houston Company to ensure that the interior roof of the cars on order should correspond with the roof of the bogie (from this point the minutes use the word "bogie" rather than "bogey") car on order. BTH said that this could be done but it would cost an additional £11 10s per car. To fit an additional two lengths of top deck railing as fitted to the Preston Cars would cost £2 12s per car. Approval was given.

What was to become a long drawn out affair had started with the November 1899 decision to seek a Provisional Order to construct an electric tramway along Hedon Road, and to extend it beyond the steam tram terminus to Marfleet Lane. The Parliamentary Bill negotiated the Commons unopposed, but when it (Tramways Orders (Confirmation) (No.3) Act) reached the Lords in June 1900 it was opposed by the NER who submitted a petition to stop the Order. This was heard under the chairmanship of his Grace, the Duke of Northumberland, and the record of the proceedings ran to 143 pages and 18 witnesses were called, all subject to cross-examination!

The scheme for Hedon Road involved laying a double line across the NER's railway crossing in place of the single-line steam track. Straightforward and no different to the four already in operation you might think. But the Company said it would be prejudicial to its interests and the public's and asked for it to be disallowed.

Counsel for the NER pointed out that when the Corporation objected to its Bill for the amalgamation with the Hull Docks Company, the result was a clause inserted in the Act which gave the Corporation the power, by notice in writing, to require the NER to apply to Parliament for the power to stop up and abolish (or both) the existing level crossings at Hedon Road and at Hessle Road. A bridge was proposed for Hedon Road but a subway under the Hessle Road crossing was envisaged. In each case the Corporation would pay one-third, the Company two-thirds. The NER was still willing to abolish the Hedon Road crossing but the Corporation had never bothered to exercise its powers.

There was, therefore, no local or public necessity to justify the interference and injury which would result to the Company and the Lords were asked not to pass the Bill and confirm the Orders.

The Corporation's Counsel stated that all that the Corporation wished was to double and extend the tramway along Hedon Road to cater for anticipated additional traffic when the new dock opened east of Alexandra Dock. Double lines of electric tramway already crossed other NER lines in the city. The NER's rights were already protected by the excessive legislation (forced on a small company without the resources to challenge it by a large company) that permitted the steam line to be built. It was "monstrous" that the railway's traffic (all goods, no passenger) should have precedence over tramway traffic.

The Corporation had not exercised its power to build a bridge since it saw no danger at the crossing despite the Company's accusations. A bridge over the railway line would be very inconvenient to tramway, road and foot traffic alike. An extra horse known as a "Trace" horse and worker would be needed to be stationed there by users to assist horse traffic over the bridge. Traffic would be delayed whilst horses were attached and unharnessed. He reminded everyone that most of the traffic originated in the NER's good yards.

Any reference to Hessle Road was irrelevant since given the nature of land there and experiences with the subway under the railway at St Andrew's Dock (Hull's Fish Dock) it would be mostly filled with water. The Corporation was unlikely to build it.

Both sides wanted to abolish the level crossing so why not build a railway bridge over the road? This would eliminate all inconveniences to everyone. Why did the NER consider that increasing traffic on road and railway would result in a more dangerous situation? The Chairman also wondered this and asked the NER to comment which it did but without conviction. Why would the double line mean an extra man would be needed at the crossing? Mr Moon (NER) had claimed that there had been a great many mishaps but there were only two cases of trams touching the gates with subsequent repair costs of 16 shillings! Under questioning the NER admitted that some mishaps (with other road users?) were the result of its employees' errors.

Nevertheless the NER claimed that it was only a matter of time before a life was lost. (Curiously, no-one appeared to mention the existence of signalling and catch points at the other crossings). Its witnesses even claimed that tram drivers played tricks with the cars which were thus not under control! One

horse was perfectly capable of pulling 2½ tons up and down a bridge of a 1 in 40 gradient. It claimed that possible additional cartage costs had resulted in local pressure on the Corporation to resist the road bridge.

Both sides called a number of witnesses. The Town Clerk, Mr Laverack, confirmed that there had been only two accidents to date and confirmed that the Corporation wanted a railway bridge over the road. He also warned the NER that if the safety issue was as bad as it stated the BOT had the power to force it to build the bridge at its own total cost! Alderman Larard stated that only the NER objected to the double line. The steam tram service under the Corporation was faster but a six-minute service was run without mishaps. A road bridge would be disastrous. Horse and cart traffic (and some cabs) avoided the bridge in Park Street (which ran from Anlaby Road to Spring Bank) over the railway and went through the city centre along Brook Street causing congestion. He was aware that on occasion the NER's own engines had run into the gates and caused more damage than the rest of the city combined!

William Wellsted had constructed the steam tramway and stated that there had been no accident of any kind caused by road traffic, but he conceded that the presence of a passing loop at one side of the crossing slowed cars down. In his experience the delays were down to engines shunting the yards of timber, coal and salt since there were only two goods trains a day using it. The NER would benefit from electric trams over the crossing because electric trams would be lighter and cause less wear and tear. The NER had no cause to complain about safety when the foot gates were not locked even when the road gates were closed to road traffic. Under pressure from the Chairman the NER admitted that the crossing was not controlled by a signal box but by the gate staff and shunters.

Mr Joseph Pearson of Messrs Bencroft and Whiteman which had saw mills in Hull and in Bradford said his rullys already took a circuitous route to avoid the Craven Street bridge, and the same would happen with Hedon Road. In Hull one horse was used, in Bradford two. Any deviation from the normal route would cost time and money. The NER dismissed the Craven Street situation as being steeper than Hedon Road would be. Its witnesses dismissed claims that one horse could not cope with a bridge, and used its experience at Stockton where it was claimed there were several mishaps after electric cars took over from steam trams to justify its stance.

The Corporation didn't want the road bridge, which would block side roads and force road traffic to use an extra horse. However, it was prepared to contribute to a bridge over the road. An adjournment was granted so that the Corporation could reconsider it. Council members were divided and after a long debate voted against the road bridge. The NER decided to build a four-track railway bridge, but would not allow electric trams over the crossing, and in addition to the Corporation's one-third contribution it wanted compensation for any land taken for road widening. It also proposed a second bridge forty feet further east to carry two more tracks, with the road lowered seven feet, for which the Corporation was expected to contribute one-third. It prepared its own Bill to enact this but the Corporation opposed it. Not until April 1901 did the parties agree a compromise. The Corporation would not be required to pay for the second bridge; the NER would restore the road at the crossing, undertake the works within two years, and give land to road widening. Did the NER want rid of the crossing far more than the Corporation and see its opposition to the doubling of the tramway as a means of forcing the issue? If so it was an expensive and avoidable exercise for both parties.

By January 1900 agreement had been reached with the NER for the work required to enable the tramways to cross the line at

Southcoates on Holderness Road in a less expensive and quicker manner. Approval was given for similar negotiations regarding the crossing at Botanic Gardens on the Spring Bank route, including the installation of larger gates, if required.

The question of a tramway service to the Old Town was complicated by the Corporation's opinion that Whitefriargate was unsuitable for electric cars. It wanted to use a new street from Whitefriargate Bridge, over the entrance to Queens Dock, to Lowgate. However, the bridge required widening to make it suitable for tramcars, and negotiations were initiated with the NER in January 1900.

Two would-be suppliers attended the January Works Committee. The secretary of Mackenzie's Patents Company Ltd. demonstrated electric lights for tramways, whilst Mr Pennington exhibited an invention for the purpose of facilitating the replacing of the trolley pole on the overhead line. Messrs Mackenzie's were turned down but Mr Pennington was referred to the Electrical Engineer who was authorised to deal with the matter. No further reference has come to light.

A number of organisations had requested the issue of free passes for their staff, the latest being the Hull Jubilee District Nurses' Union. They were informed that no free passes would be issued to any organisation.

Eleven tenders for further cars were considered on 23 February 1900. That of British Thomson Houston Co., Ltd was the lowest although BTH had raised some questions about the Corporation's terms and conditions. It was agreed to order 10 cars and 25 equipments for the cars and the trailers. The cars became nos 91-100 with bodies by Hurst Nelson.

Postmen on duty had been carried by the former tramways company at contract rates, and the Tramway Manager's suggestion that he approach the Postmaster-General to arrange a similar scheme was approved by the March meeting of the Tramways (Special) Sub-Committee. The Chairman and the Tramway Manager subsequently met the local postmaster and agreed that the Post Office would pay an annual sum of £350 (equal to three-fifths of a penny per journey) for use of the tramways by postmen and telegraph boys on duty.

A significant aspect of public transport in Hull has always been the delays suffered from the closure of one or more of several level crossing gates to road traffic. Long delays were a feature in tramway days, and the conductor of car no. 38 reported that on 10 March 1900 a delay of eight minutes from 5.25am and 10 minutes from 6.40am had taken place at the Anlaby Road (Boulevard) crossing. The Town Clerk was instructed to write to the NER for an explanation.

The same meeting received a request from Mr Cudworth, the NER's Engineer, for the Corporation to install catch points at the Anlaby Road crossing. Whilst other crossings were protected by

47

Another ex-trailer car is no. 88 which is unloading passengers in Princes Avenue near Queens Road. This was the "S" terminus from 8 October 1900 until 19 January 1903 when the route was extended to Newland Avenue. Both the Queens Hotel public house and church are still there today. (PM/Travel Lens)

a catch point, photographic evidence seems to indicate that such points were never provided here.

With the opening of the Holderness Road and Spring Bank routes approaching, a further 75 punches were ordered for conductors on those routes. The Board of Trade carried out its official inspection of the Holderness Road route on 9 April and

it opened on 10 April 1900. It is reported that a civic party travelled on the new bogie car, no. 101 to inaugurate the route. Another thirty cars entered service in March and April 1900, these being nos 31-60 of Brush manufacture with 29/22 seating.

A recurring theme throughout the first phase of the electrical tramways system was the number of bankruptcies suffered by

Snow rarely seemed to bother the trams which could maintain the service as shown by two unidentified cars braving the snow at the Beverley Road (Newland) terminus on 16 January 1902. Note that the motorman wears a cape to minimise the effects of clinging snow and that someone has drawn a "B" in the snow on the front of the car. Upper deck travel seems not be popular on either car! (AG)

the Corporation's chosen contractors, and the delays in providing often vital equipment, not to mention the unreliability of the equipment when it was in operation. We have seen that the contractor for laying parts of the Anlaby Road and Hessle Road tramways had suffered bankruptcy, and a main contractor for the power station also went into receivership. Messrs Siemens' name seems to crop up in the minutes on several occasions with reference to delays and/or faulty equipment.

At the March Sub-Committee meeting, the Electrical Engineer and the City Engineer reported that satisfactory tests had not yet been obtained on the two generating sets which had been fixed at the Power Station. Messrs Siemens had been making certain alterations to the dynamo of the third set, and this was to be tested at the Birmingham works of Messrs Belliss at an early date. The engineers had complained strongly to Messrs Siemens about the delay in completing the generating sets for the Power Station and pointing out (prophetic words) the inadequacy of the two sets in operation. With the opening of the Holderness Road route the Corporation would have no stand-by set, leaving it in an unenviable situation. The Town Clerk wrote to the company to call their attention to the problem and to defects which from time to time occurred in the overhead equipment, particularly the breakage of the tramway wire at the ears. Not until April could the Electrical Engineer report that the final trial of the third set had been successful, although it still did not conform to the tender specification.

Messrs Siemens said that the outstanding set would be ready in mid-April and that it was already attending to the wire defects. Its staff had noticed these in February, and had discovered that they came from a design defect in the section insulators. Replacement of the insulators had been completed.

A further delay to completion of the Anlaby Road car shed (seven months after the Anlaby Road route had opened!) arose when the painting contractor informed the builder, Mr George Houlton, that he declined to carry out the work at the same rate as the Hessle Road shed and required a further £12 to complete the work. To give an idea of the value of this sum in 1900 the Tramway Manager had recently taken on an office boy at the sum of £13 per annum! It was left to the Chairman and the City Engineer to sort it out.

With the demise of trailer operation, draw bars were no longer needed so the City Engineer accepted an offer from Westinghouse of £3 per set for 12 sets.

The City Engineer was authorised to negotiate with the NER to widen the level crossing gates to align them with the road width at Stepney on Beverley Road. He was authorised to construct a line from Beverley Road down Stepney Lane to the proposed depot, and to widen both carriageway and pavement, and to use granite setts paving as far as Nicholson Street.

A major failure took place at the Power Station on 27 April. The tramway service was suspended at 9.35am after four hours of problems, which included a seized dynamo-bearing, a burnt out armature and a short circuit. When the Tramways (Special) Sub-Committee met later that day engineers from Siemens were still working on the machinery. The Sub-Committee decided that the company should be interviewed by three members, the Town Clerk and the Electrical Engineer, and that they should report on the causes of the breakdown and what steps (if any) should be taken to avoid future breakdowns.

This interview was seen as satisfactory, particularly as the company was given permission to install the third set at their own risk, and the responsibility of having to alter the dynamos to conform to the specification subject to the approval of the Corporation Engineers.

The three members had interviewed the driver in charge of the engine, the station foreman, the Siemens Brothers' representative at the power station, the switchboard attendant and the Electrical Engineer. They reluctantly concluded that the statements made by the driver were not satisfactory and could not be relied upon. They believed that the first breakdown was caused by his inattention in allowing the bearings to get heated and that, under the circumstances, his services should no longer be retained. However, the remaining failures were attributed to a design fault in the dynamo for which the contractors were solely responsible.

A by-product of the inquiry was that the wage of the Station Foreman, Mr Elliot, was increased from £2 per week to £2 5s per week and the engine drivers' suggestion that their hours of duty be altered to three shifts of eight hours was agreed, as was the appointment of another engine driver and switchboard attendant.

The City Engineer reported that conversion of four trailer cars was completed and that a fifth was in hand. It had now been determined what method was best to carry out the conversion of some or all of the remaining cars and he was given authority to obtain alternative prices for these conversions.

Two companies were asked to quote for the conversion of the remaining trailer cars, but one, Messrs Dales and Mr Annison had too much work in hand and would not quote, whilst Mr Dale could not carry out the conversion in the time required. Therefore, the recommendation that the Corporation workmen should carry out the remaining conversion was approved.

In 1899-1900 the Boer War was still raging and the whole country celebrated the relief of Mafeking on Monday 21 May 1900. In recognition of tramway staff working during the half day's holiday that was granted to everyone, drivers and conductors were awarded an additional half day's pay in lieu of their lost holiday.

Routine insurance inspection of the steam tram engines continued to be made and nos. 1-3 were found to be satisfactory in March and April although all had minor defects.

The old tramway depot on Hessle Road was still owned by the Corporation, but when the London and North Western Railway asked to lease part of it, it was informed that the Corporation was not prepared to let it at the present time.

A dispute with the Board of Trade broke out in May 1900. The Board wanted to limit tramcar speeds on the Holderness Road route to 6 miles per hour, whilst the Corporation wanted 8 because the highway was straight and wide. Colonel Yorke for the Board also said that only one car should be worked over North Bridge at any one time and that a car approaching the bridge should wait until the car in front or a car going in the opposite direction had cleared the bridge. The Corporation argued that this would cause congestion on the approaches to the bridge and that the clearance between trams of 8 feet 8 inches was sufficient. After an exchange of letters the Board would not press further the Colonel's recommendations, and 8mph was allowed.

The Spring Bank route opened as far as the Botanic Gardens crossing on 2 June 1900. The City Engineer reported in July 1900 that a great deal of delay had arisen with the NER regarding conditions for carrying the Princes Avenue tram track over the Botanic Gardens crossing. Despite heads of agreement being in hand in April, nothing had been received from the company. However, the Town Clerk and the City Engineer had been to London with regard to the Tramways Order, and had raised this with the NER's Solicitor and Engineer who had promised to expedite the matter. The extension to Queen's Road was opened on 8 October 1900, but as the necessary pointwork and signalling had not been installed passengers had to alight at the crossing, walk over it and re-join a tram on the other side until the equipment was in place on 26 October 1900.

In July 1900 the first annual report was submitted by the

Tramway Manager. This covered the period from 5 July 1899 to 31 March 1900 and took the following form:

		£	s	d	
Length of route open					4 miles
Miles run					573,420
Passengers carried					
Total					6,218,971
Daily average					23,033
Highest number in one day (11 October 1899)					72,500
Average number of cars running daily					23.70
Average number of passengers per car week					6,803.06
Average number of receipts per car per week					£28 6s 11d
Fare receipts		25,912	7	7	
Other receipts		393	12	10	
		26,306	0	5	
Receipts per mile					11.01d
Cost per mile (d)					
Power Station building repairs		7	11	10	
Machinery repairs		67	16	3	
Generation of electricity		2,069	1	6	
		2,144	9	7	0.90
Working expenses					
Depot building repairs		10	16	10	
Permanent way repairs		27	0	0	
Overhead equipment repairs		24	18	5	
Rolling stock repairs		569	16	9	
Traffic expenses		6313	17	4	
General charges		1595	16	9	
		8542	6	1	3.57
Total		10686	15	8	4.47
Interest		2402	19	7	1.01
Sinking Fund		3225	10	10	1.35
		16315	6	1	6.83
Balance on year		9990	14	4	4.18
		26306	0	5	11.01

In July 1900 the City Engineer reported that the rail supplier, the Angleur Co., had failed to maintain a sufficient supply and had delivered a number of slightly defective rails which were suitable for car sheds, but not for street running, and had only been accepted for the sheds at a reduction in price of 5% to 10%. The company had suffered a breakdown in rail production machinery, and between 5 May and 16 July only a small quantity had been received, and none at all from then until 20 July. The City Engineer had complained very strongly and had requested a double quantity of rails each week for the present.

An inspection of the generating station by the Insurance Company revealed leakages from eight rivets at the top of the furnace opening and some plate cracks, although overall the boiler was in a sound condition. The economiser was also inspected and a number of corroded pipes were discovered. The company made a number of recommendations regarding remedial work which was carried out.

The City Engineer reported that construction of the Hessle Road and Anlaby Road routes had cost an additional £1311 and the work had taken three months longer, due in part to the need to obtain men and materials when it was taken over.

More trouble occurred at the power station on 30 August when cleaning no.3 boiler – it had been discovered that one of the flues was depressed on the crown. The Insurance Company's representative inspected the boiler and repairs were soon under way. It was suggested that the depression might be due to the presence of oil in the feed water, and the use of condensed water had been temporarily discontinued.

The question of the costs of seating for tramcar upper decks had been raised by members, and in September the City Engineer submitted a quotation from Mr Peter Burns for "New London" dry seats for car tops, 27s for double seats and 21s for each single seat, and an alternative offer which would permit the Corporation to construct the seats, paying a royalty for each seat. It was decided that the Corporation would construct the seats, and to omit seats in each car being built by British Thomson Houston, a saving of £8 10s.

Reports of accidents and claims for compensation by individuals and organisations (usually refused) were, by now, a routine feature of each Committee meeting, the August 1900 meeting being no exception. The reports included a collision involving a steam tram engine and a fall from an electric car. However, the third report was untypical in that Mrs Green of 54 Liverpool Street fell from a car on Hessle Road as she was alighting through another car striking it. Mrs Green was offered £5 compensation for her injuries and the motorman was suspended for a week. Eventually a Claims Sub-Committee was formed to consider the increasing number of cases.

Five more cars entered service in August and September 1900 (nos. 61-65 built by ER&TCW with 31/22 seating).

In September 1900 the Hull Progressive Party drew the Works Committee's attention to the fact that no workmen's cars were run at half fares in accordance with the Act of Parliament, and asked the Committee to comply with the Act. The matter was referred to the Town Clerk.

Serious concerns about the continuing breakdowns and defective equipment on the tramcars and the overhead line were considered by the Tramways (Special) Sub-Committee in September 1900. The Electrical Engineer submitted a long list of day to day operational defects. Three principal defects were identified:

1. Siemens Bros' controllers and trolley heads had never been satisfactory.
2. All cars and car equipments had suffered considerable wear and tear during the previous fifteen months.
3. Breakages of overhead line had become much more frequent of late.

Messrs Siemens had acknowledged that their controllers and

This is the same location seen from the opposite direction. Cars 72 and 92 (both former trailer cars) are in sight along with a third behind no. 92. The buildings behind the cars were demolished when Beverley Road was extended northwards in the 1920s and a new Haworth (pronounced locally as "Hayworth") Arms public house was built. (MJW)

trolley heads were unsatisfactory, and in May 1900 had submitted new designs which the engineers had approved before fitting to all their fifteen cars, and it would be another month before the work would be completed. Meanwhile Siemens were maintaining the equipment on their cars at their own cost.

With regard to wear and tear on the car equipments on all types the Electrical Engineer considered it necessary to give each car a complete overhaul one by one. Whilst the existing staff could keep the cars running in normal daily service, it would be necessary to employ a fitter and two labourers who would work on these cars alone.

Many overhead line breakages were the result of faulty workmanship and had been replaced by the contractors at their own expense. Some resulted from carelessness by Corporation employees, and some were the result of wear and tear. The first two causes had been reduced, but the wear and tear on the line was increasing. The Electrical Engineer reminded members that when comparing the Hull system with other towns, owing to the quick service over short lines, the car miles run on any one piece of line were very heavy indeed with a corresponding higher wear and tear.

During the past year, with seven miles of track in use, the car miles run were approximately 15,100 per week, or each fixture on the overhead line had 2157 trolleys running over it every week. The only way to avoid accidents from wear and tear was to adopt a rigid system of inspection of the lines with every hanger and fitting being gone over at least once a fortnight. Indeed, Messrs Siemens Bros. & Co. had been doing this on their behalf to a certain extent, but the Electrical Engineer considered that it was now time for the Corporation to undertake the work. He recommended the employment of a competent linesman and labourer to maintain the trolley wires and mains, and that a horse and driver be hired to take the tower wagon over the lines every Sunday morning.

He did not consider that the Hull system was seriously defective and said that the number of defects was certainly not more in proportion to the car miles run in Hull than in any other town. His report illustrates the struggle that operating staff experienced when trying to keep the system running. Electric tramway operation was still in its infancy and there was much to be learned about new types of equipment. It also suggests that towns using the same supplier would have experienced similar problems, and that Siemens were expending a great deal of time, effort and expense to ensure that their fittings and equipment were operational in Hull.

More extensions were being planned, and the Town Clerk was instructed to insert in the proposed Parliamentary Bill powers for extending the Spring Bank route along Queens Road and Newland Avenue to Cottingham Road. Another proposal was added at the next meeting in that powers for tramways would be sought for the new road (later Alfred Gelder Street) from Whitefriargate Bridge to Lowgate, and along Lowgate to the north end of the Market Place.

The Tramway Manager submitted a report on the steam tram service in October 1900. Seven engines and eight cars were in stock. Four were in service every day, one engine was spare being fit to run, one was being overhauled and one was not fit to run as part of the internal mechanism was defective. Six cars were in running order and two were useless (his words). One was in that condition when the line was purchased and the wheels were in bad order.

The early service ran every ten minutes from 5.10am until

8pm. To accommodate dock men an engine with two cars attached ran at 5.45am from Witham during the busy season. This was a very unusual occurrence in Britain. A regular service of four cars began at 8am and continued at every seven or eight minute intervals until 6.30pm, after which cars ran every 15 minutes until 10.12pm from Witham (Mondays to Fridays) and until 11.19pm on Saturdays. The Sunday service began at 12.30pm from Lee Smith Street and ended at 10.15pm from Witham. When the Corporation bought the line five cars per day were running to give a six-minute service, but in the past three weeks the manager had taken one car off without detriment to the service.

A more expeditious service was now provided, but the main barrier to an efficient service was the Hedon Road level crossing, which typically delayed cars by between five and fifteen minutes. Cars no longer waited for a long time at the termini, but the combination of defective plant, faulty permanent way, and the stoppages from the level crossing made it impossible to maintain a satisfactory service. All employees had the same conditions as the electric car employees. Receipts averaged £50 per week compared with a daily average of £60 for electric routes.

On Friday 26 October 1900 the Town Clerk informed members that there was no statutory provision requiring that cars be run for workmen at half fares. The present obligation on the Corporation was to run "a proper and sufficient service of carriages at such hours not being later than eight in the morning and five in the evening (two o'clock on Saturdays) as being convenient for such workmen going to and returning from their work at fares not exceeding one half penny per mile for every mile or fraction of that distance". Consideration of the implications of this clause was deferred to another meeting.

The same Committee authorised the erection of a temporary car shed on land at Stepney Lane, and approved Mr Nettleton's request to give up possession of the Hessle Road and Beverley Road tram stables when he had finished, rather than give one month's notice.

Members also agreed alterations to the signals at the Holderness Road level crossing which had been suggested by the NER as being advantageous to tramway traffic. The work involved providing two special poles and signals of an increased size at a cost of £78 10s.

In November the City Engineer reported that a large number of roller bearings would have to be renewed, using especially hardened parts from the Cooper Co. of Kings Lynn at a cost of £6 per bearing less 30s for the old bearings. He had ordered 12 for immediate use but a further number would be required almost immediately. Also ordered, as an experiment, had been one set of old roller bearing cases to be fitted by Messrs Amos and Smith with ordinary gunmetal liners, with a view to using some of the worn-out bearings.

Also approved were two tarpaulin coats for the Linesmen for use on the Tower Wagon. On a lighter note the Chairman, three other members and the Tramway Manager were given the delegated authority to arrange the usual Social Meeting of the Tramway Employees for Christmas.

Lt-Col von Donop RE and Mr A.P. Trotter had inspected the Spring Bank route and passed it fit for public traffic. Pending receipt of regulations from the BOT for the Spring Bank route, all speed restrictions and recommendations about stopping places would be observed strictly.

The Beverley Road route opened on Saturday 8 December 1900. The Stepney signal box's Occurance (the signalman's spelling!) Book recorded that trams ran to either side of the crossing and transferred passengers between them. Later that month the NER installed new cables over the tram overhead, and

between 20 January and 28 January 1901 a new level crossing with a double set of tram lines was laid. A new frame and gate was installed on 10 February, and the new gates were connected on 14 February. Finally on 25 February at 12.42pm the trams commenced to operate over the crossing whilst carrying passengers, and the book records that trams were stabled overnight in Stepney Lane Depot for the first time on the 25th.

An early casualty was a tram from Newland (the Beverley Road terminus) which came off the track and ran halfway across the crossing at 9.01pm. Staff were able to get it back on the rails and it returned to Newland.

The decision to continue with the Old Town route caused great controversy. Some businesses wanted the tramway to go down Whitefriargate rather than the new road, whilst others did not want the route at all. Some businesses there feared that the new streets around the Queen Victoria Square would take trade from them, and claimed it was essential to install the line as that part of the Old Town was becoming isolated, and without the tramcar service it would become more so, and property would deteriorate in value more than it had already done.

In January 1901 a deputation attended the Tramways (Special) Sub-Committee and suggested that the fourteen lamp posts in Whitefriargate as far as Scale Lane should be replaced with tramway poles on which electric lights could be placed. It was suggested that smaller tramcars could be used on this section! Alderman Larard blamed the delay in building the tramway along the new street on the NER (as dock owners). He assured the deputation that their points would be fully and fairly considered.

Two conflicting reports were considered at the 9 January 1901 meeting. The City Engineer said that an insurance report of 14 December 1900 found the steam engines to be generally satisfactory, but that nos 4 and 5 were due a thorough examination. Mr McCombe stated that the service had been reduced because engines were out of order and only two cars and two engines were operational. As the service was quite inadequate he recommended that it be discontinued and it ceased on 13 January.

A tramway map was prepared early in 1901 showing routes in operation and those approved but not yet open. It is too fragile to reproduce but it also gave a good indication of the housing density on each route. Hessle Road was the most heavily populated with housing the full length of the route. On Anlaby Road there was little housing west of Alliance Avenue. The Spring Bank route was built up as far as Queens Road but there were few houses north of there and along Newland Avenue. Beverley Road was built up to Newland. Housing was densely featured as far as Jalland Street on Holderness Road but it was sparse east of that point. There were few houses east of Lee Smith Street on Hedon Road.

Meanwhile a decision had been taken to build a car shed (400 feet long by 100 feet wide) for the Beverley Road and Spring Bank routes adjoining the Sailors Orphan Homes on the north side of Cottingham Road. Several discussions took place with the land owner, Mr Foster, regarding price). Mr Foster was unwilling to lower his price but had agreed to widen the entrance strip from 15 feet to 20 feet.

Entry into service of the converted trailer cars was well under way. Nos. 101-125 were now numbered 66 to 90. The first fifteen (nos. 66-74/6-81) commenced work on 8 December 1900, whilst the last into service was no. 88 on 8 April 1901. A further ten cars entered service between 4 April 1901 and 24 May 1901, having been built by Hurst Nelson and having 31/22 seating.

At the Tramways (Special) Sub-Committee meeting on 13 February 1901 the Chairman reported on a meeting with the

The former trailer cars seemed to have been allocated to the northern routes when they entered service from December 1900. No. 71 has entered Prospect Street from Beverley Road whose tracks are on the left. Those on the right lead from Spring Bank. (PM)

Mayor, Chairman of the Finance Committee, the Town Clerk and the City Treasurer. They informed him that the expenditure for the Corporation departments for 1901/2 would result in a high rate increase. He was asked to recommend to his Committee to hand over some of the undertaking's balance to the Finance Committee. He agreed, as a special matter for this year only, subject to confirmation, to contribute £23,000.

The estimated surplus for 1901/2 was £27,000 which added to the £9,900 surplus for 1900/1 totalled £36,900. After deducting the £23,000 a sum of £13,900 remained, and the chairman recommended that this should be set apart as a Reserve Fund, although it must not be taken as a precedent. He added that a larger sum another year would probably have to be added to the Reserve Fund. This would not be the last occasion on which the tramway undertaking funds would be "raided". Alderman Larard must have been under considerable pressure since recent reports regarding car overhauls, more frequent inspections of the overhead line (and a lines man and labourer), seemed to indicate that running costs would rise. Indeed, the same meeting authorised the fitting of compression stays to the trucks of those cars that did not possess them.

The Town Clerk informed the Board of Trade on 27 March 1901 that the use of trailers was being discontinued, since they could not be used without inconvenience and loss of time at termini. Instead of trailer cars additional double-deck cars would be purchased

On 18 April 1901 the Sub-Committee again considered the Old Town tramway. It concluded that the restrictions in Whitefriargate and Silver Street would prevent an efficient service to be operated, and that the expense in reconstructing those streets would be too great. It would not be possible to construct a double line, and the Tramways Order of 1896 prohibited "more than one tramway car being between the west end of Whitefriargate and the east end of Silver Street at one and the same time".

The cars would cause considerable obstruction at the west end of Whitefriargate while standing for passengers to alight and for the trolley to be turned round. Further obstruction would emanate from cars standing at the north end of the Market Place to await passage of the Pier bound car. Nothing was mentioned as to how cars in Lowgate and Market Place would be aware of any car in the two streets; presumably some kind of signalling as with Midland Street? Their recommendation that no service be provided along Whitefriargate was accepted.

The Committee's day was a busy one for it began with a visit to Liverpool Street workshops to inspect three devices. The first was Bostock and Cheetham's automatic device for disconnecting current from a broken trolley wire; the second being Wilkinson's device for automatically checking the tension on the trolley springs every time a car left or entered the sheds, and the third was Bundy's patent time records. Annoyingly there are no more references to these in the minutes.

A recommendation from the Board of Trade that the curbing of the centre poles along Beverley Road be rounded off in accordance with BOT standards to prevent their being used as a refuge for people crossing the road was accepted.

A change of heart regarding roller bearings was reported to the Committee. Although the latest purchases were working much more satisfactorily than previous purchases, they were causing much more rapid wear on the axles. The advantage gained from the use of roller bearings was no longer sufficient to warrant the extra expense (£6 against £1 16s 8d for plain bearings) and it was recommended to change to plain bearings and to order 24 from the Brill Company.

Expenditure of £216 on the City centre electrical supply system was approved. This resulted from the construction of the new streets in the centre, and covered alterations to the overhead equipment at the junction of Albion Street and Prospect Street, and the conversion of the existing section pillar near the Dock Offices into a feeding point.

The Annual Accounts for 1900/1901 showed a working balance of £27,680. An average of 47,298 passengers was carried each day (23,033 in the previous year) the highest being 123,946 on 13 October 1900 for Hull Fair. Revenue per mile was down from 11.01d to 10.54d whilst running costs had risen from 3.57d per mile to 3.84d per mile, and the percentage of working expenses to Gross Receipts (Operating Ratio) had risen from 40.62 to 44.79. The busiest route was the Hessle Road route (a situation that was to last into trolleybus days), whilst the least used was the Spring Bank route, although its weekly receipts for 6 April to 25 May 1901 showed a remarkable stability with a low of £258 18s 4d and a high of £281 5s 8d.

More problems with the power station boilers were reported to the July Committee. Remedial action had been taken regarding a crack in no.1 boiler in order to avoid further leaks, and the City Engineer informed the Committee that Siemens Brothers had written to state that an improved design standard for a bedplate to make the new dynamo suitable for coupling with existing engines would result in the delivery period of five and a half months being extended by one month.

The City Engineer considered that the steam tramway depot at Hotham Street was unsuitable for conversion as costs would be too great to be value for money. His recommendation that a site for a new depot be found further eastward along Hedon Road was accepted. Not until April 1902 was a new site east of Hedon Road Cemetery approved, with the proviso that the tramway be not extended beyond that shed at that time.

On 22 August 1901 trams had to resort to transferring passengers over the Stepney crossing, as following the passage of a Withernsea train at 6.38am the signalman was unable to replace the starting signals and thus release the tram signals. Not until 8am was the signal cleared, but in the meantime a ganger disconnected the catch points and wedged them to enable trams to pass over the crossing.

The Tramways Sub-Committee meeting on 4 December 1901 proved a busy one. Approval to operate electric trams in the newly constructed King Edward Street was given by the Board of Trade in a letter dated 5 November submitted to the Committee. This was only to be expected for the new street had been officially opened by the Right Honourable W.H. Long MP, President of the Board of Trade! Speed of tram cars was not to exceed 8 miles per hour. All was now ready to transfer the Spring Bank and Beverley Road termini into that street.

These proposals were opposed by the traders of Bond Street and Savile Street, (despite the fact that Savile Street was linked with the new street and the new termini would be a mere fifty yards away at the most). A deputation of Savile Street traders (with a combined rateable value of £17,400) addressed the meeting, but the Sub-Committee decided to discontinue the Albion Street, Bond Street and Savile Street section of the Spring Bank and Beverley Road routes for a month. Clearly the traders had not made much of an impression! It is not known when the routes were transferred to King Edward Street, but when the matter was discussed once more in February 1902, consideration was deferred.

Back came a stronger deputation which included traders from streets adjoining Bond Street and Albion Street, all claiming that takings had been reduced considerably by the diversion of the routes. They submitted three petitions, one containing 1226 signatures from Spring Bank and Beverley Road residents, the second by a large number of ladies from Beverley Road, and a third representing practically all the residents in the streets adjoining the routes. Again, no decision was taken and the matter was referred to the Tramways Sub-Committee, frustrating for the traders as the Sub-Committee comprised members from the Works Committee!

Although not mentioned in contemporary minutes a report to the February 1912 Tramways Committee stated that for a time cars did run alternately to either terminus, but there were difficulties in maintaining a regular headway, and all cars were returned to King Edward Street.

A special meeting of the Works Committee on 11 December 1901 considered action taken by the North Eastern Railway in laying an additional line of rails on the site of the new street on the south side of Queen's Dock. This street would be a continuation of Alfred Gelder Street and would carry the Old Town tram route rails. Relations with the NER were usually that of an "armed truce" nature, but often spilled over into outright war as the Corporation had encouraged the construction of the Hull and Barnsley Railway to thwart the NER's monopoly of rail and sea trade.

Five pages of correspondence were considered by members, and it was clear the company had ignored letters from the Town Clerk and started to excavate for the line. The dispute revolved around who had the right to approve construction, the Town Clerk being of the opinion, backed by clauses in the Hull Docks Act 1846, that Corporation consent was required before any railway company could lay tracks over any road or bridge. Indeed, on previous occasions the company had adhered to this provision and sought consent. The Corporation had planned to commence construction of the new street and tramway, and it was unhappy with the prospect of further delays to the Old Town tram route and the link between Lowgate and Holderness Road. Authority was given to certain members, the Town Clerk and the City Engineer to take any necessary action to protect the interests of the Corporation.

A cascade of meetings and correspondence ensued during which time work on the tracks was suspended. The company insisted that it did not require permission to lay the tracks alongside the dock, but reluctantly conceded that it should have sought consent to cross Mytongate (to the south of Whitefriargate). Eventually sanity prevailed and it was agreed to coordinate plans so that both tram and railway lines could be laid at the same time. On 30 December 1901 The NER submitted a formal request for the track laying. The whole question was then referred to the Whitefriargate Bridge Sub-Committee, with further exchanges of acerbic letters until 16 April 1902, when the Sub-Committee finally acceded to the laying of the rails subject to various conditions.

The Works Committee on 13 December 1901 received a letter from the Hull and District Chamber of Trade asking the Corporation to discontinue the running of smoking cars in the interests of the public. The Town Clerk's reply, although couched in diplomatic and polite terms, more or less said it was none of their business and suggested they dealt with trade interests only!

The Electrical Engineer received a set of regulations and requirements from the Superintending Engineer of the Post Office in respect of guide wires. Any certificate issued by the Board of Trade approved the use of tramways subject to all the Postmaster's requirements being met. Most of the Hull installation met these except that the posts would have to be bonded to the rails and the guide wires raised 3 inches higher above the trolley wire than at present. The alterations were very slight and inexpensive and he recommended that they be carried out. A request to the Post Office to lay wires underground at the Stepney Lane crossing had been turned down.

Initially, tramway crews worked a seventy hour week at first with appropriate meal breaks. Motormen received between 28 shillings and thirty five shillings a week, conductors between 18 shillings and twenty five shillings, and inspectors between thirty and forty shillings a week, the increase being paid at one shilling per year. Uniforms were provided.

The Great Central Railway had a "station" at the Corporation Pier from where paddle steamers crossed the River Humber to New Holland (for Grimsby and Cleethorpes). The station is the backdrop for ex-trailer car no. 66. Its side route board informs passengers that it is running between Whitefriargate Bridge and the Pier. (PM)

Power station wages ranged from twenty five shillings a week to fifty shillings a week, whilst car washers and depot men received twenty-one to twenty-five shillings a week. This compares with 3/9d a week for an office boy, to Mr M'Combe's one hundred and fifteen shillings a week. Overtime was paid at 4d an hour (4½d after three years' service). Conductors' pay compared unfavourably with local wages even in Hull's low wage economy, yet the pay was much greater than the horse tramway rates and the conditions of service were better.

Following a national award in 1901 the working week was reduced to six by ten-hour days with one day's rest in seven, but demands to eliminate the split shifts were rejected; conductors' wages were increased to twenty seven shillings a week and the

overtime rate increased to 7d for motormen and 5d for conductors.

In January 1902 after a comparison with other undertakings, the hours worked by inspectors were reduced to sixty per week. Later that month (on the 30th) members inspected Anlaby Road, Liverpool Street and Holderness car sheds, and the new Holderness Road tramway extension.

Differences of opinion between the Corporation and the NER surfaced once more on 23 January 1902 at the Tramways Sub-Committee meeting. The City Engineer drew members' attention to a previous decision, whereby the Corporation had rejected the company's request for the installation of signals and catch points at the Anlaby Road crossing, to bring this crossing

Although this postcard is not in good condition it illustrates the semaphore signals (operated from a cabin in the station entrance to the right of the photographer) which controlled the Anlaby Road/Midland Street junction. (MJW)

This is Prospect Street in 1903 with car no. 78 which seems to have few passengers on board. (PG)

into line with the others in the city. Another request, dated 17 January, had been received asking for this work to be done. Once again, the request was turned down. It is difficult to see why, if they were essential at the other crossings, the work was never undertaken. Nor can it be understood why the Board of Trade did not order the work to be carried out.

The Tramway Manager had considered arrangements for transporting large numbers of workmen that worked on the Alexandra Dock and at the nearby Earles Shipyard, and successfully recommended to the April Committee meeting the provision of a siding on the Hedon Road route immediately east of the Hull and Barnsley Railway bridge on the southern side of the road near the gates. Several cars could wait here in order to be ready for the exodus of workers.

Between Saturday evening 24 May and Sunday afternoon 25 May 1902 the Tramways Office in Osborne Street was broken into and a sum of £137 4s in gold, silver and copper stolen. A small safe had been broken open and the key to a large safe had been taken and used to open it. It was normal practice for the cashier to collect the keys on Saturday afternoons and take it home, but this had been the only occasion on which this had not occurred. The perpetrator was not discovered.

The Corporation's plans to celebrate the Coronation of King Edward VII included the decoration of some tram cars, and it was left to the Tramway Manager and the Chairman to make the necessary arrangements. Staff who worked through the celebrations were awarded two day's extra pay in lieu of the holidays.

Concern had been expressed regarding the effectiveness of the lifeguards in use on the tram cars. The Electrical Engineer had designed a replacement which was manufactured at Liverpool Street Car Sheds where the Sub-Committee inspected it. Another two types of lifeguard were tested and the one designed by Mr R.S. Burns was considered most suitable. He was asked to provide estimates for their supply, and the Board of Trade was asked to inspect it.

On 10 July 1902 the *Tramway and Railway World* carried an article about the Hull Tramways. It stated that Mr Nettleton who had operated the horse trams in their final years had been fairly successful in catering for the needs of the public. During the

interval between the horse tramway service and the start of electric tramcar operation, an irregular and intermittent service was provided by waggonettes or traps as they were indifferently called (the magazine's words), also known as "town way ups". An advantage of the Hull Tramways was that the rails had been laid in streets the whole extent of which from curb to curb had been paved with wood in the best method.

The frequency on all sections was every three minutes all day with a ten-minute service for workmen in the morning. There were one hundred and one cars in stock, of which seventy-one were run every day and forty on Sundays. Of the four depots in use, two were temporary structures. Daily, weekly and monthly journals as well as games were supplied for employees in the mess rooms.

Inspectors and car depot foremen wore a handsome uniform of blue cloth piped with red with caps to match, bearing silver badges on which their status was designated in silver thread. The 120 motormen and conductors had a smart tunic and trousers of blue serge piped with red with a cap to match. They also wore an official number with the letters HCT above. Uniforms were to be renewed every year, overcoats every two years. It did not mention that crews felt that they looked like "French Railway Officials" and inspectors like "naval officers"!

A ten-hour day was general, each week averaging 60 hours, one day being allowed off duty for every six days worked. The men were relieved for meals, ample time being given for this, and they were not allowed to take food on duty. A day's work of each car was called a "regular duty", and a special duty called a "relief duty" was set apart to relieve two "regular duties". Hours were so arranged that a relief duty (motorman and conductor) was at work in the mornings, off work in the afternoons and at work in the evenings. One of the regular duties started work after dinner and remained until the finish, with the exception of a period for tea. The other regular duty was at work from morning until tea-time with a break for dinner. Men changed duties each week. The day off was arranged to be a Sunday as far as possible every fortnight. The system appeared to work well. However, some duties were spread over 15 or 16 hours with only 8 hours rest overnight, whilst two Saturday shifts comprised spreadovers of 19 hours. Of this less than three hours were allocated for meals.

Plans for tram lines in Queen Victoria Square were submitted to the Tramways Sub-Committee on 18 July 1902. The City Engineer stated that they were complicated and expensive, and might need some modification when they had been in use for some time. The genesis of what became known as the "tramway station" was approved. No plan is attached to the minutes, and it is not known what the configuration was at this time.

The Newland Avenue extension was under way, and the City Engineer obtained a quotation of £513 10s for poles and bracket arms similar to those already in use. Messrs James Russell and Sons Ltd's tender was lower than that previously paid and was considered "reasonable".

A major dispute arose between the Board of Trade and local authorities who owned and worked tramways. The local authorities wanted to eliminate the statutory need for a red light to be displayed at the rear of tram cars when in motion. BOT rules stated that each carriage (tramcar) had, during the period between one hour after sunset and one hour after sunrise (or during fog) to carry a white light at the front and a red at the rear in such a fashion to be seen within a reasonable distance. Following a conference the Board of Trade had reviewed the regulation but concluded that the need for a rear red light should be maintained. Local authorities were still opposed, and the Chairman was authorised to attend any further conferences dealing with the subject.

When the City Engineer applied to Mr Pawley, Engineer to the Hull and Barnsley Railway for permission to attach trolley and guard wires to its bridge in Newland Avenue, permission was granted on the same lines as that for the Beverley Road and Holderness Road bridges with one proviso. On one or two occasions the trolley had left the overhead at the Beverley Road Bridge and had made contact with the girders, with the result that the current working the Company's block instruments was reversed and showed "Line clear" instead of "Line blocked". The Corporation agreed to fix, at all three bridges, inverted wooden troughs with an earth wire connecting the insulators with one of the posts.

In October 1902 the City Engineer informed the Tramways Sub-Committee that the Hedon Road car shed would be of a similar design to that of the Holderness Road shed, but was sixty feet longer and would hold eight more cars. Quite why this was so much larger is unclear, as apart from works and docks traffic the passenger potential on Hedon Road was much less. It is possible that workers' cars were stabled there during the day to prevent excessive "dead" mileage, but it has not been possible to confirm this.

Following discussions about roof coverings for tram cars two Committee members, the Tramway Manager, the City Engineer and the Electrical Engineer, visited Liverpool on 16 October to inspect the type of top covering which had been devised by Mr Bellamy, the General Manager of Liverpool Corporation Tramways. They had discussed the top coverings and other tramway matters (not specified) with Mr Bellamy.

The cover enclosed the top of the car from a point at each end a little outside the end of the car body, but left uncovered the staircase opening and some seats on the canopy. It was carried by curved steel angle bars fixed to each edge of the upper deck. The central part of the roofing comprised permanent boarding about 2ft 6in. wide running from end to end of the covering. This boarding carried the trolley standard which was fixed over the centre of the car. The ends of the enclosed space comprised fixed wood framing and glass with sliding doors. The parts of the roof not covered by the boarding were enclosed by waterproof spring blinds, which could be pulled down at will by passengers or

conductor. The sides of the cover could also be enclosed by spring blinds of canvas pulled down in like manner.

The visitors rode on one of the cars in service in inclement conditions (strong wind and rain) and they inspected some under construction at the tramway workshops. They considered it somewhat unsightly despite every attempt to reduce this to a minimum. Mr Bellamy emphasised that the covering afforded considerable additional comfort for passengers and that it would materially increase the average number of passengers carried during wet weather, something which the deputation endorsed fully.

When the deputation reported to the Tramways Sub-Committee Committee on 31 October they considered Mr Bellamy's invention to be the best form of top covering currently available. It had been patented, and the Electric Railway and Tramway Carriage Works Limited of Preston were authorised to construct it, although other car builders could also build it on payment of a royalty thought to be £15 per car.

The report stated that cars with the trolley pole fixed in the centre as with the Bellamy design would not run with the existing overhead equipment in Hull, as the trolleys would not reach the trolley wires where side poles are used with bracket arms of the present length. However, the overhead equipment on the Hedon Road route could be erected so that such cars could be used there and so that the existing cars in use in the city could also be used there. If, after experience with the top covers on the Hedon Road route, it was thought desirable to use such cars on other routes, the cost of altering the overhead to make it suitable for the centre trolley would not be great, and if such alterations were carried out some other improvements could also be carried out to the overhead at the same time. The Sub-Committee decided that, subject to the royalty fee being reasonable, to purchase fifteen cars similar to previous cars but with enclosed tops.

It was also decided that one of the lifeguards seen at Liverpool be fitted to one of the tram cars to be tried and examined by the Sub-Committee. Subsequently the Board of Trade approved the Tidswell form of lifeguard. It was adopted by the Corporation at a royalty cost of £1 10s per car, subject to this applying to the remaining cars and the fifteen on order. A royalty of £2 per car was paid for the twenty-one cars already fitted.

Finally, the Sub-Committee decided to apply for powers along Cottingham Road from Beverley Road to Newland Avenue, along Alfred Gelder Street from Lowgate (the Old Town route), to and over Drypool Bridge and along Clarence Street and the new street to the intersection of Dansom Lane and Holderness Road. G.A. Lee mentions suggestions for a line along Charles Street, but no details were given.

The Beverley Road Baptist Church Mutual Improvement Society asked the Corporation to regulate the speed of trams and other public vehicles when passing places of worship on the main roads during the hours of divine service on Sunday evenings and also prohibit, as far as possible, the ringing of bells and gongs.

The first major industrial relations problem arose in November 1902. The National Amalgamated Union of Motormen and Conductors, following a mass meeting of the Corporation tramway employees on 9 November, had submitted a letter requesting the Corporation to consider three areas of grievance. These were:

1. The split shift did not permit proper rest
2. The other regular duties did not allow sufficient nights off
3. Saturday duties on the workmen's cars were excessively heavy

They respectfully asked to be granted double shifts of eight hours per day, each day to stand by itself with every other

Sunday off, as they considered that the best possible solution to the difficulty. Resolution of the problem was delegated to the Tramways Sub-Committee which met with the two union representatives and six motormen the same night!

A similar situation had arisen in August 1900. No change in hours was made although conductors' wages had been increased and duties so arranged as to allow one day off in seven. The Sub-Committee at that time had expressed a wish to meet the men to discuss the matter, but the Chairman would not permit it and the matter was dropped.

This time members felt unable to grant items 1 and 2, but were prepared to listen to any proposal from the men which might meet their wishes, without interfering with the services to the public but would meet their wishes and their convenience.

Information was obtained from 22 tramway undertakings which revealed that 12 were working the same 60 hours per week, 4 were working more than 60 hours, one 56 hours, four 56 hours and one was working 48 hours. An interesting table was included in the report as follows:

	Hours	Rate per hour	Drivers' wages (max)
Glasgow	54	6.75d	24s to 30s
Halifax	54	7.00d	27s to 31s 6d
Cardiff	54	6.50d	24s 9d to 29s 3d
Newcastle	54	6.50d	26s to 29s
Huddersfield	48	7.00d	27s to 28s
Salford	56	6.50d	28s to 30s 4d
Hull	60	7.00d	28s to 35s

In only one place was the maximum wage of drivers more than in Hull, but as that undertaking worked longer hours the hourly rate was smaller. The Sub-Committee considered that the conditions in those towns that worked less hours made the work more laborious and imposed a greater strain than in Hull

With regard to the double shift or the full day's work being worked in one spell, the members were of the opinion that the valuable machinery and safety of the public were their first considerations, and that it was not wise to allow the men to work it without relief for meals and other easements.

Members were not against change, and they recommended that motormen and conductors should be allowed to run early morning workmen's cars in turn, rather than by special men chosen for the duty. This should give ordinary men extra turns off in afternoons, evenings and Sundays. They would consider with the Manager if any alterations to duty shifts could be made without inconvenience to the men and the public.

On 19 January 1903 the Spring Bank route was extended to the junction of Newland Avenue and Cottingham Road. The *Hull Daily Mail* carried an article on the opening and stated that two additional cars were required to maintain the three-minute service. It also referred to speculation that a circular service linked with the Beverley Road service would follow. Mr M'Combe said that such services were for those who were "pleasure bent", and were not envisaged as the tramways services were primarily for those on business purposes!

The Tramways Sub-Committee on 20 February 1903 considered the tenders for the Hedon Road route from no fewer than ten firms for cars with and without top covers, and six types of electrical equipment, not to mention four different types of top cover! Prices ranged from £6888 (without covers) to £8744 (with covers).The City Engineer and Electrical Engineer concluded that the most advantageous was the tender of the British Westinghouse Company, with car bodies by G.F. Milnes and Company, both of whom were willing to accept a delay regarding a decision about the type of top cover to be fitted until

two months before the projected delivery date. This would enable the Corporation to test one or two coverings fitted on to existing cars before coming to a decision. They were prepared to supply any type of other covering providing all fifteen cars were so fitted.

The Sub-Committee also considered a tender from Messrs G.C. Milnes, Voss and Company for the fixing of "Kennington" top covers to one of the existing cars at the sum of £110, and an offer of £76 for the fitting of a "Magrini" type as fitted to a Huddersfield car, but with certain modifications. A decision was left to the City Engineer and the Chairman, as the City Engineer thought that some modification was needed to the "Kennington" design and wanted to examine further the "Magrini "proposal.

In March 1903 the Tramways Sub-Committee approved the purchase of the point work and associated equipment for the proposed junction at the intersection of Clarence Street and Great Union Street, which would enable Hedon Road cars to travel by North Bridge or Drypool Bridge. The equipment comprised two moveable points, six open points each thirteen feet long, and twenty eight crossings, all made of Hadfield's Patent Manganese Steel. A quotation from Messrs James Russell & Sons, Limited for poles for the Hedon Road route was also approved. This comprised 10 A Poles at 127/6 each, 67 B Poles at 165/- each and 5 C Poles at 245/- each and 80 bracket arms with scrolls, clips, stay rods etc. of varying length from 15ft 6in. to 21 ft were also bought at prices ranging from 72/- to 92/6 each. Both poles and bracket arms were similar to those already in use, but the poles were slightly longer and the bracket arms heavier to make them more suitable for the form of elastic suspension of trolley wires then being adopted. The prices, despite the increase in length and in weight were slightly lower than those previously quoted by the company.

The City Engineer recommended the purchase of portable crossover roads to enable tramway traffic to be turned back at points where there was an obstruction, or because an event such as the recent visit of The Prince of Wales required certain streets to be blocked off for a while. They could also be used to turn back trams when certain lengths of track were being prepared.

The Holderness Road extension to Aberdeen Street was opened on 27 March 1903. The new Holderness Road sheds were opened at the same time.

When the Yorkshire Tramways Parcel Express Syndicate wrote to the Corporation in April 1903 offering an annual rental of £150 for permission to carry parcel traffic on the trams, the Committee rejected the application without giving any reasons.

Top covers for tram cars appeared on the agenda of the Tramways Sub-Committee meeting on 14 July 1903. Members had inspected the sample "Kennington" and "Magrini" top coverings erected by Messrs Milnes, Voss & Company on two cars, and decided that the "Magrini" type be fitted to the fifteen cars to be supplied by the Westinghouse Company, which became nos 102-116. The City Engineer was instructed to arrange with the company either for them to alter the "Kennington" covering which was unsatisfactory, or to take it over in its present condition, subject to a deduction from the payment, and to have the covering altered by Corporation workmen. It was considered that the seats in the two covered tops were not satisfactory, and the City Engineer recommended that two sets of seats similar to those on the new cars be fitted at a cost of 19s per seat. This was approved.

The Pier route finally opened on 20 October 1903 (route "P") – this ran only between the east side of Whitefriargate Bridge and the Pier until 1906, but there is no indication where cars were housed, how they reached the tracks or how power was provided. Passengers had to cross a temporary bridge between Alfred Gelder Street and New Cross Street. On 17 October the

A busy scene at Blundell's Corner in 1903 with two well patronised cars. No. 81 has just entered Prospect Street from Spring Bank on the left whilst car no. 100 will swing right into Beverley Road. (PG)

Town Clerk had informed the BOT that the route was ready but suggested that, as the Hedon Road route would be ready in December, both routes might be inspected at the same time, a suggestion that was accepted.

Is it possible that the lines between Lowgate and Great Union Street via Drypool Bridge were in situ and used? The Annual report for 1903/4 shows the Old Town service in operation with a route mileage of 5 furlongs and five chains (increased to 5 furlongs and 9.62 chains when the trams were able to cross the new bridge). I can find no mention of any official inspection, which is unusual. The full route between Alfred Gelder Street and Witham was not authorised until 18 December 1906, but Lt-Col. von Donop also authorised the use of two curves (not described) which had been constructed under general powers rather than tramway powers. Which curves – Great Union Street into Alfred Gelder Street or Lowgate into Alfred Gelder Street? Remember that in March 1903 authority had been given to purchase equipment for the former junction, so was this used by the Pier cars?

Delivery of the fifteen cars by Westinghouse and G.F. Milnes had fallen behind schedule and the companies asked the Corporation to consider not to enforce the forfeiture sum (a financial penalty for not meeting the delivery date). The Corporation declined to make a decision, but informed the company that any sum would depend on the actual lateness of delivery. The first cars were apparently received in December 1903, for the City Engineer reported that the car tops were higher than specified. When Westinghouse was approached it altered the design to bring the cars within the required height. After discussions the original forfeiture sum of £896 10s was reduced to £500, subject to certain defects in the roof blinds being remedied by the contractors.

A consequence of their delivery and the proposed fitting of covered tops to other cars was an inspection of bridges under which the trams passed. As a result the City Engineer was autho-

rised to lower the road under the Hull and Barnsley Railway bridge on Holderness Road by five inches.

On 9 December the Sub-Committee, the City Engineer and the Tramway Manager visited Liverpool Street to inspect the Kennington and the Magrini top covers on cars nos. 61 and 64. Two days later the Sub-Committee re-convened to consider which type to adopt. The City Engineer submitted a letter from Mr G.A. Throp of A. Lackenby's Shop Fitting Works dated 11 November, which offered to supply 15 patent Kennington Collapsible Car Covers fixed to complete cars as per the sample, one patent Kennington trolley base for the sum of £80 per car provided the Corporation had cleared the car decks, removed existing screen boards and railings as well as the trolley standard and other electrical work. It was decided to order 14 (including the sample) with the first top being delivered within one month of the receipt of the order, and thereafter at fortnightly intervals. Leckonbys were also to provide and fix an additional two interior end seats.

On 16 December 1903 the Board of Trade was informed that the Hedon Road route was ready for inspection. The total length of the new track was 1 mile 6 furlongs and 2.55 chains. Curves at the corner of Great Union Street and Witham had a radius of 30ft on the inner line and 37ft on the outer line. Although the level crossing had been abolished all the street works were not completed, but were sufficiently far advanced to allow the tramway to open. The Town Clerk asked for authority to open it at once as the Corporation was anxious to capture the additional Christmas traffic. The line opened on 17 December 1903, designated route M, and worked to the depot on Hedon Road.

The inspection report is dated 18 January 1904 but does not give an inspection date. Lt-Colonel von Donop had received objections from a Mr Walker and a Mr Colbeck stating that excessive timber traffic from timber companies along Hedon Road would cause danger to the working of the trams. He did not agree with them and certified the line as fit for public use.

Brush car, no. 38, and several employees pose in front of the impressive front elevation of Holderness Road Depot which opened on 27 March.

Milnes car no. 116 waits for the Botanic Gardens level crossing to open for road traffic. The semaphore that controlled tram access to the crossing is "on" and the traction pole possesses red and white hoops to indicate an official stopping place. (PM)

60

Chapter 5

CONSOLIDATION

On 22 January 1904 the Works Committee received a deputation from seven local Ratepayers Associations asking the Corporation to bring to the attention of the North Eastern Railway Company the extent of the obstruction caused on all the main roads in the city by the level crossings. They also suggested that the Corporation carry out a new census to determine the number of trains passing over the crossings and the times the gates were closed to the public.

The meeting proved to be a busy one, although as the system grew and matured the number of items for consideration actually dropped. Mr M'Combe's salary was increased from £350 to £400 per annum from 1 January 1904 with a further two annual increments of £25.

In March a deputation from the Ratepayers Association of the Myton Ward asked the Corporation to divert the Hessle Road tram service via Osborne Street and Waterhouse Lane to Queen Victoria Square. This would relieve congestion (that word and in 1904 too!) in Carr Lane, and would enable the signal box at Midland Street to be abolished. The Traffic Sub-Committee subsequently received a 600-name petition of the largest ward ratepayers. The cost of laying a single track in Osborne Street and Waterhouse Lane would be £3200, exclusive of the widening of Waterhouse Lane and the acquisition of property. The City Engineer didn't think a single track would be of any use since it would have to be used for outward traffic. It was decided not to proceed with the line.

Approval was given in April to buy an additional tower wagon from Messrs R.W. Blackwell & Co. of London at a cost of £75.

In April a letter from the Chairmen of the Glasgow and Manchester Tramway Undertakings referred to a recent House of Lords decision to award compulsory running powers over the whole Newcastle municipal tramway system to a private tramway company. The Town Clerk and the Chairman were authorised to attend a meeting at the Westminster Palace Hotel, London on 10 April. Had the Hessle tramway scheme been constructed, the Lords decision would permit the promoters to run into Hull over the Corporation tracks.

Fifty-eight Corporations and the London County Council attended, and they decided (unanimously) to contest the decision which would prove detrimental to the working of large central tramway systems. The House of Commons Select Committee confirmed the House of Lords ruling, but the local authorities aided by their members of Parliament and "friendly" peers continued to press for its rescindment; so much so that later in the year the bill was defeated on its third reading. The cost to the Corporation was a mere £2 12s 4d!

In June the City Engineer informed the Committee that Messrs Lackenby's would shortly complete its contract for top coverings, and it had asked if any further "Kennington" top covers were required. The contract provided for fitting covers to all the cars fitted with reversed staircases not already fitted, but he considered that the "Kennington" would not be suitable for cars with ordinary staircases without some modification. He was given authority to arrange with the company to fit a modified cover to a car with an ordinary staircase.

On 6 July 1904 the New York Times carried a report on the Hull Tramways that had been submitted to the United States Department of Commerce and Labor by its consul in Hull, Mr Walter C. Hamm. The Department had published his six-page report which contained photographs of open top car no. 41 and no. 103 with a covered top on 5 July 1904 (report no. 1995). Mr Hamm compared the slow development of Hull with other British municipalities which had changed when Sir Alfred Gelder became mayor. The result included new broad and well kept avenues, a modern water supply system and an excellent municipal street car system.

Hull was regarded as one of the most uninviting towns in the United Kingdom. Despite being the third port little was known about it and the Humber, which offered unrivalled facilities for shipping, had shut it off from the direct line of railroad travel to London or Edinburgh, a view that probably still holds good today. Its system of city transit was antiquated and inadequate.

Hull had begun municipalisation of the street cars at an unusually favourable time, with the old tram companies about to expire, so that there were few rights and privileges to be acquired. New streets were being built and it was possible to lay tracks at the same time. The new paving had the most enduring character and afforded a foundation unequalled to anything that he knew in the United States

A layer of chalk ten inches thick was laid first, followed by an eight-inch layer of broken stone and cement in which the ties for the stringers were laid. On this layer were superimposed the blocks of wood or stone which formed the pavement. Rails were of the centre groove girder pattern weighing 96 pounds to the yard, which formed a track which for solidity and evenness could not be surpassed.

Mr Hamm mentioned the resistance to double-deck cars (presumably in the United States), but said the cars in service in Hull were usual for Britain where 90 per cent of the 6,500 cars in service were double-deck. Seating capacity was more than double that of smaller cars, with 22 below and 35 on top. This made the cars heavier than in the US and more expensive, costing some $3,000 (£600) each without a top cover, but those were now being added to each car. From first-hand experience double-deck cars could be filled and emptied as quickly as single-deck cars. Covered tops offered sufficient protection from the weather. The extra weight did not prevent rapid and easy handling on ordinary grades. The upper deck also acted as an observation deck with an extended outlook over the city. Additionally, it enabled gentlemen to smoke freely since men invariably used the upper deck more than did women passengers.

Fares were cheap at one penny (2 cents) for every journey. A net profit of $122,000 (£25,000) was achieved in 1903 some $12,000 (£2,500) per mile of double track. Wages were low compared with the United States at $6.70 (25 shillings) to $8.50 (35 shillings) per week for motormen and $5.00 (21 shillings) to $6.59 (24 shillings) for conductors, some $2 (10 shillings) per week less than equivalent US wages. However, he thought that rents were much cheaper in Hull. He was impressed with the employees whom he considered as smart and efficient as any other systems. They worked ten hours a day and cars were operated from 5.00am to 11.30pm with a maximum speed of 12mph.

He lamented that so many American towns and cities had given the transit systems to companies who operated them for

This is a fine photograph of trams and employees outside the car shed in Temple Street sometime after 1905 but before closure in 1909. (MJW)

private gain, and often to the detriment of the travelling public.

It is interesting to read a contemporary account from someone who had experience of cars outside Hull and Great Britain. It gives us a valuable and independent sense of the system's worth. Mr Hamm submitted a further report at the end of 1904 about all the municipal services, which was also reported in the New York Times.

Mr J.E. Walker, who was selling advertising on the backs of tramway tickets, advised the Corporation that with the increase in the number of tickets being sold and the "slackness of trade" it was impossible to provide sufficient advertisers to meet his obligations. He was likely to give up the task unless the Corporation were to permit advertising on the tramcars themselves. A small group was given the task of resolving the issue.

A profit of £18,985 3s 6d was made in 1903/4. Total income was £100,642 5s 1d made up of the following:

Route	Passengers	Income		
		£	s	d
Anlaby Road	5,225,826	21,774	5	6
Hessle Road	5,098,985	21,245	15	5
Holderness Road	4,547,120	18,946	6	8
Spring Bank	4.659,970	19,416	10	10
Beverley Road	3,638,555	15,160	12	11
Hedon Road	624,507	2,602	2	3
Old Town	425.755	1,773	19	7
	24, 220,718	100,919	13	2

less discount on passes issued
by HM Postmaster   277   8   1

                            100,642   5   1

64 cars were in service throughout every day (from a stock of

116!) whilst the operating ratio had risen from 52.56 to 62.18. The Tramways Department now employed 368 staff.

In October the City Engineer reported that Messrs Lackenby & Co. had now fitted a "Kennington" cover to a car with an ordinary staircase at a cost of £80, to which must be added the work carried out by City Engineer's staff to alter canopies and staircases and re-arranging the seating and lighting. It was agreed to fit a further twenty cars with top covers at a cost of £79 per car to be delivered at a rate of one per fortnight.

From November 1904 a full and independent Tramways Committee with Alderman Larard as chairman was formed with three Sub-Committees to cover accounts, labour and day to day operational matters.

Cars 102-116 which had recently entered service were the first to be fitted with double sand hoppers. Staff asked for these to be fitted to all cars to make it less difficult to pull up, and to add to the safety of the public. The December Committee agreed to fit all cars with this equipment, and to amend the contents of the tool kit on each car with one combination tool comprising hammer, adjusting spanner, pinch bar and pick.

In December 1904 the Tramways Sub-Committee considered safety arrangements in connection with the tramway over Drypool Bridge. The City Engineer proposed to install two movable pillars to act as buffer stops, one at each side of the river, between the rails of the line approaching the bridge. They would be operated by hydraulic power and would be raised whenever the bridge was about to be opened for river traffic. When the bridge was closed they would sink into the roadway, the tops of the pillars being flush with the paving. For working the buffer pillar at the east side of the bridge hydraulic power would be taken to that side by means of a pipe laid in the river bed.

Additional steel supports would be required for the rails and the planking between the existing cross girders of the bridge. The carriageway would be paved with wood, and the carriageway of the fixed span would be dealt with in a similar way. It was

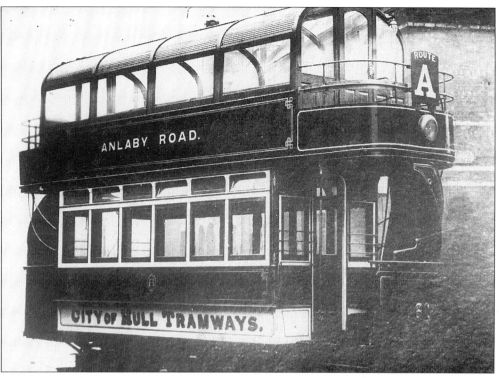

The first tram to receive a top cover was car no. 61 which is seen with its new prototype Kennington adjustable top in September 1903. It is thought that the location is Liverpool Street Workshops. (PM)

agreed to submit the scheme to the Board of Trade, and to ask the Bridges Committee to obtain prices for the work.

In January 1905 the Tramways Committee considered proposals for a single-line tramway in Osborne Street (which the reader will remember had enjoyed a horse tram service).The cost of work exclusive of any widening of Waterhouse Lane was £3200. The City Engineer pointed out that the tramway would have to be used for outward traffic because an inward car would have to cross the inward traffic in two places. He did not think that Osborne Street traders would benefit from an outward service in the same manner as an inward service. A schedule of property on the west side of Waterhouse lane between Osborne Street and St John Street (which included two public houses) accompanied the report. The cost of this was deemed prohibitive and the proposal was rejected.

The roller shutters on the "Kennington" covers had proved troublesome, and in March 1905 the City Engineer reported that the zinc casing of the rollers had not proved very satisfactory, and submitted a letter from Messrs Lackenby & Co. offering to provide copper casings for the remaining covers to be supplied at £2 14s 6d per covering. This was agreed.

Work on the Drypool Bridge was to have been completed by the time that Whitefriargate Bridge would have been closed for reconstruction. However, the work on the latter bridge was in advance of schedule, and it would be necessary to postpone the Drypool Bridge work until October. This may have changed because there was considerable correspondence between the Corporation and the North Eastern Railway about the time being taken to complete the bridge which ended when an exasperated NER Dock Engineer accused the Corporation of taking longer to build smaller bridges. He also said that the same

reasons for delay in the Corporation's new public hall applied to the Whitefriargate Bridge. The contractor, the Motherwell Bridge Co. was agreeable, but stated that additional cost would be incurred but could not say how much at present. It was agreed to postpone the work until October. The reconstruction of Whitefriargate Bridge took place during 1905/6, but it is not known what arrangements were made for the Pier service.

In June the Committee agreed to pay a bonus of 10 shillings to any youth in the employ of the department who passed an examination at the Technical School in an approved subject or subjects. Bearing in mind that a junior office boy's salary was £15 or less per annum this was a significant amount (around two weeks' wages).

Proposals for larger rented office accommodation for the Tramway Manager and his staff were considered in June 1905. A building in Alfred Gelder Street alongside the Empress Hotel (public house) had been identified as being suitable.

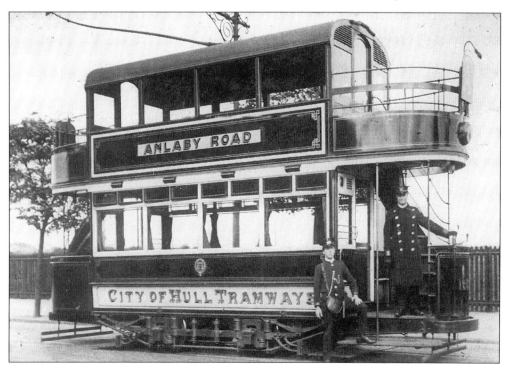

Car no. 125 was one of fourteen built by the Corporation in 1909/10. It is seen here near Wheeler Street. After much modification it was sold to Leeds (along with the rest of the batch) in February 1942 where it became no. 456. (PM)

A verdant Beverley Road sees car no. 80 with a modified Kennington top cover approaching a stopping place near Queens Road. A crossover was installed just behind the photographer for peak journeys and specials. It is bound for "Town" by which name the city centre was (and still is) known, the change to city status being totally ignored. (PM)

On 27 October the City Engineer reported that car no. 48 had been fitted with a top covering with a fixed roof and this had proved very satisfactory. It had been fitted by the City Engineer's staff in a manner similar to that carried out by Messrs Lackenby at a cost of £67 6s 5d. He considered that this price would be reduced by about £5 per car if a large number of cars were dealt with at one time. Messrs Lackenby had submitted a quote of £74 per car for a similar covering. Of the total fleet of 116, some 64 were without top coverings. His men could complete a top covering every ten days. It was agreed that the City Engineer would fit 30 coverings to existing cars and that prices be obtained for the remaining 34. In January 1906 it was decided that the City Engineer should do the work on all the remaining open top cars. Thirty-five cars had been fitted with moveable covers between September 1903 and April 1905, before work started on fixed top covers in November 1905.

The October meeting also agreed to fit, as an experiment, a Westinghouse magnetic brake to one tramcar at a cost of £50, and it agreed to seek Parliamentary powers to construct a

tramway from Witham (just east of North Bridge on the Holderness Road route) along Cleveland Street and Stoneferry Road to its junction with Leads Road, the first reference to what was to become a battleground between ratepayers, local companies and the Corporation. Quite why this proposal was agreed is a mystery, since the concentration of housing lay at the southern end of New Cleveland Street, much of it within reach of the Holderness Road trams. To the north were several industrial works with very few houses. Whilst peak traffic could have been high, the rest of the day would have seen little traffic, some of which would have been abstracted from existing services.

Another possible extension was agreed on 10 November 1905, it being the intention to seek powers to construct a tramway from Anlaby Road through a proposed street, forming a continuation of Brook Street through to Osborne Street and

Cars 79 and 96 are pictured in the still new King Edward Street. Both possess adjustable top covers putting the date between 1904 and 1906. No. 96 would have a long and varied life being withdrawn from passenger service in 1933 for conversion to a single deck works car. It was eventually sold to Leeds after which it was preserved and now carries passengers at Heaton Park in Manchester. (MJW)

Cars 85 and 89 are on Spring Bank near the Botanic Gardens crossing. This was the original terminus of route "S" and the crossover can be seen. It was still used at peak times and for additional cars provided to cover gaps in the service due to delays at this crossing. (PM)

connection with the Corporation tramways when the running of the carriages thereon was impracticable during the construction, alteration or repair thereof, or in the prolongation of any tramway route the extension of which may be contemplated by the Corporation which may demand and take tolls (fares) for the use of such omnibuses.

along Osborne Street to Porter Street. It was hoped that this would eliminate the use of Midland Street. The new road would eventually be called Ferensway. Powers were obtained in the 1906 Act (cost £2,606 for track and £608 for the electrical equipment) but the road extension was not carried out because of the expense of property acquisition. (The section between Anlaby Road and Osborne Street had to wait until 1958 to open).

The 1906 Act also contained powers for the Stoneferry tram route which was to be 1 mile 4 furlongs and 7.90 chains long and double-track throughout. The total cost was £21,393 for permanent way, £5595 for electrical work (£26,988) and £8,400 for 12 cars. Clause 53(1) empowered the Corporation to provide and run omnibuses (whether by animal or mechanical power) in

A modification to the track layout in Queen Victoria Square was agreed on 22 January 1906, when the City Engineer was instructed to provide a crossover opposite the dock office to enable cars running between the Pier and the Square to turn back at that point. This would reduce the route by a few feet only and presumably was to relieve the congestion in that area.

Readers will recall that the equipment of the first cars had caused some concern in the Tramway Department. To redress this, the City Engineer and the Tramways Electrical Engineer recommended the purchase of eight sets of controllers from the British Thomson-Houston Company at a cost of £33 per set for use on the Siemens cars.

Since the opening of the electric tramways, conductors had

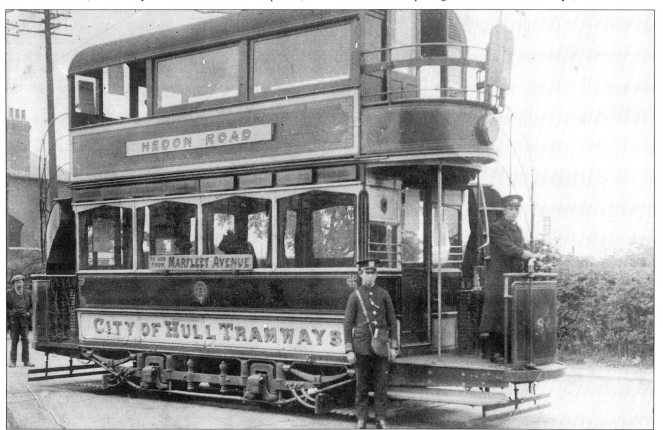

Former trailer car no. 84 is pictured on Hedon Road with route board "MA" which was used for the extension to Marfleet Avenue to distinguish between it and cars showing "M" which ran only as far as Hedon Road Depot. No. 84 has a modified fixed Kennington top cover dating from 1908. Note that it carried two side route boards at waist level and on the upper deck. (PM)

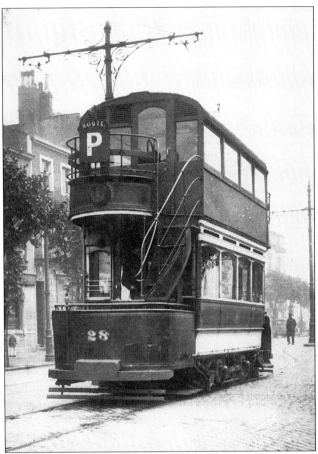

American-built Brill car no. 28 rests outside the Pier "station". The block fitted above the bumper in the centre of the end of the car can be seen. It is thought that this was fixed to prevent other cars from riding above the bumper as the Brill cars may have had 28in. diameter wheels rather than the 32in. ones fitted to the rest of the fleet. The Brill cars were never fitted with canopies or vestibules and no. 28 was withdrawn in 1931 in substantially this form. (PM)

Brill car no. 30, in original condition, leads former Milnes trailer car no. 71 with Kennington top deck cover through the junction at Blundells Corner whilst Milnes car no. 104 with Magrini top cover awaits their passage. The route letter board on no. 30 is unusual. Date is 1905. (PG)

used Bell punches which were hired by the Corporation at 12s 6d per annum. The Bell Punch and Printing Co. paid for any repairs and half the carriage, the total yearly hire cost being £189 2s 6d. The Tramway Manger obtained quotations for the purchase of suitable punches, breast and hand punches from Bell, hand punches from the Ticket, Punch and Register Co. Ltd, and Mr Alfred Williamson of Ashton–under-Lyne. He preferred hand punches for ordinary use, and recommended that the Committee accept the offer of Bell to sell the 300 punches in use at £1 10s each and to carry out repairs and provide spare parts at £30 per annum. The punches were of an old type but were quite satisfactory for all practical purposes.

After representations from the employee's Union it was agreed to discontinue the practice whereby conductors paid a deposit at the commencement of their shift. Existing deposits would be repaid to staff by the City Treasurer. The Committee also agreed to look at the hours of duty for motormen and conductors on Saturdays, some of whom commenced work at 5am and worked through to midnight.

On 31 May 1906 Lt-Col. von Donop submitted his inspection report for "Whitefriargate and West End of Alfred Gelder Street" and duly authorised public services to commence. Note that this covers only the lines over the rebuilt bridge and affected only the Old Town route.

Services were interrupted on 5 September 1906 when several main feeders supplying the Beverley Road and Spring Bank routes failed. The fault occurred on underground cables just 25 feet from the Power Station in Mr Lockey's yard. Temporary repairs were carried out to permit operation to recommence. The cause was traced to the yard where drainage matter had saturated the cables, which had rapidly eaten through the lead sheathing. New cables were installed the following weekend although another fault occurred on Spring Bank. As a result the City Engineer and the Tramway Electrical Engineer recommended three additional feeder boxes at both ends of Park Street on Anlaby Road and Spring Bank, and another near North Bridge, as the traffic on these three routes was much heavier than originally envisaged and the feeders at times carried a heavy overload.

The full Council meeting on 4 October 1906 asked Committees to present a return showing the rates of pay and conditions of any men over 21 years of age who were receiving less than 6d per hour, which the Council wished to be a minimum. Of 130 non-platform staff only seven men received less than 6d but all would eventually be paid the 6d. Some 104 conductors over the age of 21 were in receipt of a wage below this level, whilst a further 21 who were under that age were below the level. In addition, there were 46 car washers, depot men and signalmen who received less than that amount. To raise the wages to 6d per hour would incur an additional £21 1s per week for conductors, and £6 10s for the other staff.

The North Eastern Railway Company wished to redevelop the area around the Paragon Railway Station gates on Anlaby Road, and informed the Corporation that it would abolish the recess where the signal cabin for Midland Street stood. The new plan envisaged a new kiosk with the signal cabin on the first floor, for which it would charge the Corporation £10 a year for five years. The offer was accepted in November 1906, subject to satisfactory arrangements for the lever connections in the cabin.

On 28 November 1906 at 5.41am car no. 53 (5.35am from King Edward Street) was brought to a stand by an adverse signal at the Spring Bank level crossing. Not until 5.47am was it able to proceed, but in the intervening time no train passed through! The Town Clerk was instructed to ask the NER to explain.

There had been some inconclusive discussions about early morning fares especially for workmen. Mr M'Combe obtained information from other undertakings regarding the adoption of a

The complete lack of traffic can be seen as Milnes car no. 76 passes along Spring Bank near the Park Street stop. A good view can be had of the paving used on the tramways. (MJW)

half-penny fare, and reported to the Tramways Committee on 2 January 1907. The Committee declined to adopt the fare but decided, instead, to sell books containing 12 tickets at 9d each. These could be used on any route between 5am and 9am. The arrangement would be reviewed after operation for six months.

It is known that point boys were employed, but no evidence

of numbers and locations have come to light. They were at the mercy of all types of inclement weather, and the Committee considered providing some form of shelter. The City Engineer thought it impractical to provide a shelter to be of much service and, although a roof on a tramway pole could be provided it would be of little value since it would not protect staff to any

Cottingham Road Depot opened in 1909. This view dates from September (31st according to the back of the photograph!) and shows cars 57/30/67/70/87 together with Water car no. 2. (MJW)

This 1910 scene at the end of Walton Street on Anlaby Road shows the change from centre poles to side bracket arms. Extra trams operated to this point when the week long Hull Fair was held in October. (MJW)

degree and would look unsightly. In any case automatic point controllers were now being introduced in several towns, and Hull would probably introduce them in the near future. In that event, point boys could be disposed of. The City Engineer and the Tramway Electrical Engineer were asked to consider the use of such controllers.

A price of £80 15s for each automatic point controller was obtained from Messrs Bracknell, Munro and Rodgers Ltd complete with a three months' guarantee. Points were controlled by the motorman keeping the electric controller either on or off while passing over the point, according to whether he desired to take the straight line or the branch line. It was agreed to install a set at the Dansom Lane/Holderness Road junction, and this commenced operation on 27 November 1907. The trial was successful, and it was subsequently decided to install a further four at Queen Victoria Square at £62 15s 9d each. The system

This early view of Queen Victoria square shows the original track work for the Hessle Road and Anlaby Road routes. The car is probably no. 103 of 1904. (MJW)

was extended to other parts of the system but it is possible that Weenen Automatic Point and Signal Control apparatus was used as drawings exist dated 25 September 1913 showing the general arrangements of the automatic points for Hull Corporation.

Previously the committee had rejected several requests for free travel or reduced fares. The Education Committee, who in turn had been asked by parents for some contribution towards travel costs, asked for free travel for deaf children who attended daily the Osborne Street Centre. The cost for 27 children was £48 7s 6d a year and the Education Committee wanted free passes to be used on schooldays between 8 and 9am and 4 and 5pm. The Committee said no to free travel, but were prepared to carry them at the same discounted rate (three-fifths of a penny per journey) as postmen, provided that the Education Committee supplied the tokens. It would appear that this was introduced.

After experiencing a number of rail breakages at level crossings, the NER suggested an alternative method of construction, and recommended that one crossing be reconstructed with manganese steel at a cost (including paving and decking) of £320. However, the City Engineer did not consider this to be the best method and devised his own proposals which were sent to the NER.

In February 1907 the Hull trams again featured in the *New York Times*. The National Civic Federation visited the United Kingdom to investigate the performance of municipal owned utilities. An argument was raging in the USA about the desirability of municipal ownership and the delegation was in favour of it. Amongst the examples of good practice were Glasgow, Manchester, Liverpool and Hull where a surplus of $136,120 (£28,000) on the trams was quoted along with a surplus of $31,165 (£13,000) by the Tramways Electricity Department. A later piece attacked the conclusions.

On 12 February 1907 Lt-Colonel von Donop submitted his inspection report for

the Alfred Gelder Street – Drypool Bridge – Clarence Street line. He was happy with the construction, but asked for additional guard rails to be installed on the bridge in the places he had indicated to the Corporation. The new section opened on 27 July 1907 when route TH to Holderness Road commenced. A triangular junction was installed at Lowgate but there is no evidence to show that trams from East Hull ever ran direct to the Pier despite much agitation to do so.

Early morning fares were considered again on 24 April 1907. In an about-turn it was agreed to charge half-penny fares between 5 and 9am in the morning. Not all members agreed, and an amendment moved by Councillor Hall and seconded by Councillor Bentham advocating the issue of return 1d tickets between 5 and 9am with a return at any time of the day was rejected. They tried again at the next meeting in May and suggested a census between 9. 30 am and 11. 30am. When this was defeated they tried again on 31 May but once more were rejected.

The Old Town route generated around two per cent of the annual passenger numbers with an equivalent revenue contribution. Fewer people lived there, but it still retained a strong open

Both semaphore signals can be seen as Brush car no. 46 prepares to negotiate the Southcoates level crossing en route to Aberdeen Street. (MJW)

market and the pier terminal for the paddle steamers service to New Holland. Local ratepayers and businesses were convinced that the tram service did not give proper access to the Old Town, and advocated a direct service from the eastern tram routes to the Pier. Various ratepayers' organisations and the Hull and District Chamber of Trade considered that alternate cars over the Saltshouse Lane Bridge from Holderness Road and Hedon Road should be diverted to the Pier rather than Savile Street. The matter was referred to the Chairman, Deputy Chairman and the Tramway Manager but no action seems to have been taken.

Finally, the Committee asked the Tramway Manager to examine extending the tramway or "other modes of traffic", and report as to the districts where such extensions were to be carried out. There is no clue as to what other modes should be considered, be they motor bus or even trackless trolleybuses. Mr McCombe (note the change in spelling of his name which was used from now on), had in 1906 told a local ratepayers' meeting that the trackless vehicle might have a future to develop traffic.

The report was submitted to the Tramways Sub-Committee on 24 July 1907. No mention was made of other modes, but certain tramway extensions were recommended as follows:

1. Beverley Road from the existing terminus to Igglemire (Inglemire) Lane
2. Cottingham Road from Newland Avenue to the first entrance to Newland Park
3. From Cemetery Gates (Botanic Gardens) along Spring Bank West to a point near Chanterlands Avenue
4. Queen Victoria Square to Paragon Station. The object was to enable the Old Town cars to provide a through service between the station and the Pier, although given the low number of passengers one wonders why. A further report would be submitted.

This (no. 4) could be one of three possibilities, with a single line from the Square along King Edward Street, then Jameson Street to the station returning via Paragon Street and Waterworks Street. An alternative would be to continue from the station along the Brook Street extension (see previous reference), Anlaby Road and Carr Lane. A third possibility was to run the cars in the opposite direction.

After discussion it was decided to construct a clockwise loop, even though it would be necessary to alter the crossovers in King Edward Street, to enable Spring Bank and Beverley road trams to run on the down line at the terminus to clear the line for cars from the station.

Thoughts were turning to the construction of a new car depot on the north side of Cottingham Road, a few hundred yards from Newland Avenue. On 17 August 1907 the City Engineer forwarded a small sketch of the

Another view of Brush car no. 46 which is bound for the city centre sometime before February 1906 when it acquired a top cover. (MJW)

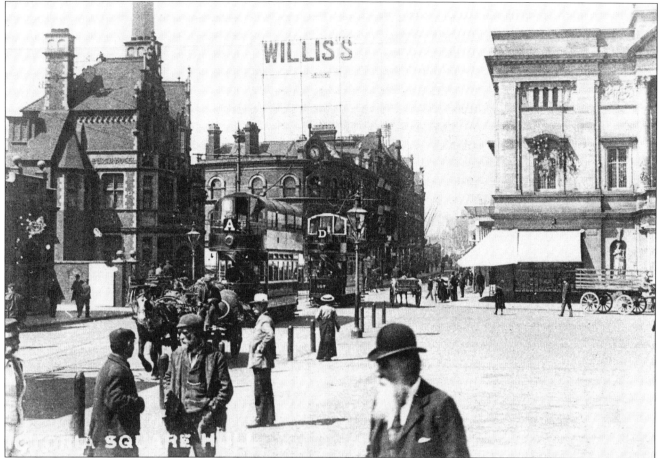

These two cars are standing at the original terminus of the two western routes in St John Street. (MJW)

proposed car shed to Mr McCombe and invited his comments.

The latter thought the design to meet his requirements very well. However, he considered that the water supply could be improved and he wanted an improved lighting system whereby pendant lights could be lowered at will between the cars and improve the work of maintenance staff. Additionally, Mr McCombe asked for a fixed platform suspended from the roof to permit cleaners to carry out their work more easily. The platform would not interfere with normal daily running.

On 30 September 1907 Milnes car no. 114 driven by Motorman Bishop stopped at Grimston Street on Holderness Road to set down passengers. He found that the car would not start because of an accumulation of sand on the rail. He switched off the lights to see if the current was on the line and went round the outside of the car to look at the wheels.

An elderly person, Thomas Stokes, got off the car at the driver's end and owing to the wheels being insulated from the rails by the sand he received a shock and fell back against the platform. As it happened the Overhead Line Foreman, Mr Tarr, was in the area and saw the incident. He went to the aid of Mr Stokes and took him to the Infirmary where he was treated and given an Outpatients Certificate before Mr Tarr saw him home.

Mr Wilkinson, the Tramways Electrical Engineer, said it was a most singular incident and could not happen without the car being entirely insulated from the rails. No. 114 was undamaged and continued in service.

However, there were other instances and Alderman Larard asked for an explanation. Mr Wilkinson, the Tramway Electrical Engineer, stated that the trouble was due to a combination of three things: the depth of the rail groove, unsatisfactory cleaning of rails and unnecessary sanding of rails by motormen. He reminded the Chairman that the Tramways Committee had, in December 1904, authorised the fitting of double sand hoppers to all cars.

At that time rails were in near perfect condition and the tread of the wheel made the maximum contact. Since then a considerable amount of wear had taken place in addition to necessary grinding of rail surfaces from time to time so there were a number of places where the position of tread and wheel flange were irregular.

Any dry dirt in the groove of the rail would lift the wheel from electric contact with the rail even when the rails were kept perfectly clean at these places. The only contact made between the rail and wheel was at the bottom of the centre flange of the wheel so that any excess sand distributed by motormen from the double sanders tended to insulate from the rails some of the cars following.

He considered that the best means of keeping rails perfectly clean was by watering and cleaning the rails and doing away with one sander. Both Mr McCombe and Mr White agreed with him.

Workers' rates of pay were considered in December 1907. Several members of staff over 21 years of age were now paid above 6d per hour, including every motorman, although a large number of conductors remained below it as did many signalmen, car washers and depot men. Conductors, motormen and signalmen received a uniform which was costed at 1s per week. The times and hours of night washer staff were also discussed. They still worked a sixty-hour week, and to reduce this to fifty-four would entail the employment of four additional staff costing £5 per week. Their hours had not changed when those of the motormen and conductors had been reduced to fifty-four. It was agreed that the hours be reduced to fifty-six per week and that all washers be paid at 6d per hour and that chargemen at the five depots be paid 1s per week extra, all increases to take effect on 1 January 1908. It was also agreed to increase the wages of all conductors over the age of 21 to 6d per hour.

The Stoneferry proposals were discussed at the same meeting

These two cars are outward bound from the city centre on the lower part of Anlaby Road. The semaphore signals for the Midland Street junction can be seen in front of the cars. (MJW)

One of the original Milnes cars of 1898 (no.4) passes the Circus Theatre on the lower part of Anlaby Road. (PG)

Victoria Square reported in February. A plan was submitted showing the lines carried across the square from Savile Street to St John Street, and branching out in the centre of the square to four lines, enabling eight cars to stand at one time clear of the lines of traffic in Junction Street and St John Street. The arrangement would be suitable for either through running or for creating a terminus for the Hessle Road, Anlaby Road, Holderness Road and Hedon Road routes. Through running was not recommended owing to delays from stoppages at North Bridge and railway crossings. The plan also shows lines carried into the square from Whitefriargate Bridge, which would enable cars to stand in the Square. The report was adopted.

Agitation about the Old Town trams was unabated. Several organisations including the Hull and District Chamber of Trade, the Hull Drapers Association and the Whitefriars Ward Ratepayers Association again urged the Corporation to run through cars from Holderness Road and Hedon Road to the Pier. (It should be noted that Holderness Road (TH) route cars passed the top of Lowgate, and the distance to the Market Place was less than that from Queen Victoria Square from where there was no through service.)

Another deputation in March, with support from the Great Central Railway, which received a deputation of merchants, shopkeepers and inhabitants of Stoneferry, and a petition stating that a tramcar service might not be profitable initially but would be a great boon to the district. The Chairman was as anxious to get the tramway system carried to Stoneferry, and said that as soon as the land was obtained for the necessary widening they would get on with the work as quickly as possible.

Differences of opinion existed amongst Corporation's officers about paying for the widening of Midland Street, but the City Treasurer's view prevailed. It was accepted that the Committee would have to pay for the acquisition of the properties at a cost of £25,000. However, a Town's Meeting rejected the proposal to widen the street and other schemes as too expensive. The Sub-Committee persevered and won over the full Council by four votes, but a Local Government Board inquiry in November rejected it and Midland Street was never widened.

The Sub-Committee considering the layout for Queen repeated the plea for a direct service from Holderness Road and from Hedon Road. After much debate it was decided to run two extra cars on the "P" route and to allow passengers on the "M" route to transfer to "TH" cars at Clarence Street, to ride to the Town Hall and from thence to the Pier. The situation would be reviewed after six months.

In 1906 the Corporation and the NER had agreed a scheme to replace a level crossing in Stoneferry Road with a railway bridge. The NER had submitted the draft plans and specification for the work, and had asked if it was still the intention to construct the tramway. The Committee confirmed its intention to build it, and asked the City Engineer to make the necessary arrangements with the NER.

When the half-penny fare was introduced it was anticipated that a significant increase in passengers would occur. Therefore, the Tramway Manager received authority to appoint additional inspectors for a six-month trial period, and a junior clerk and an

At the town end of Beverley Road a former trailer car no. 68 is passing College Street sometime in 1905 on what has the feel of a Sunday given the dress of the people on the right. (PG)

office boy. Three hundred larger tin boxes for conductors were purchased for the same reason.

On 1 July 1907 early morning transfer tickets covering two separate routes were introduced on a trial basis, and the Tramway Manager compared results from the last three months in 1907 with the last three months in 1906 when there were no transfers. In 1906 the receipts from the 5 to 9am period were 10.3 percent of the whole, whilst in 1907 they were 10.7 percent of the whole. The early morning transfer tickets issued in 1907 were 25.5 per cent of all tickets issued between 5 and 9am. Receipts had increased by 12 per cent. The extra cost of running the scheme amounted to £19 15s 9d for additional car miles, current used and track maintenance whilst staff costs were £17 14s. Given these results it was decided to continue with early morning transfer tickets.

Alterations to the design for the tramway in Cottingham Road and the new car shed were reported to the May 1908 Committee. The layout at the junction with Beverley Road had been altered

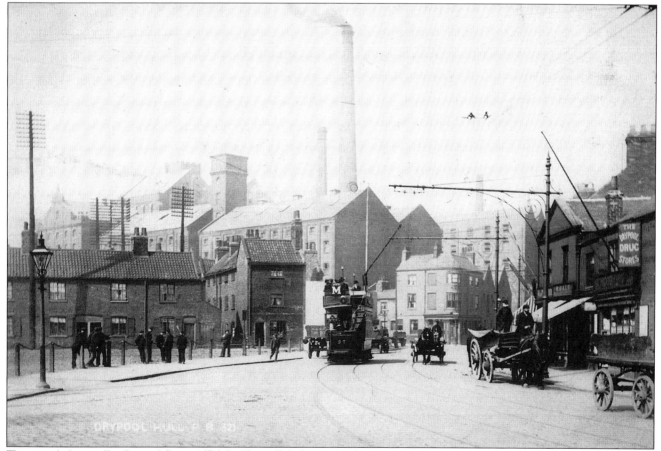

The attractively sounding Drypool Green (officially "Square") is the location for this view of Brush car no. 37 which is en route for Savile Street. Despite the name this was a very busy commercial area with many timber yards and the Earle's shipyard nearby. (PG)

The City Engineer said that the design of the cars was on the general lines of those now in use by the Corporation with top covers, although there were detail differences in each design. Detailed drawings and specification required to be finalised.

The tender proved to be very advantageous to both parties, for the Corporation was sufficiently impressed by the extract ventilators for the cars, that it obtained the company's permission to fit them to the cars that the Corporation intended to produce at a cost of £5 per car. Tenders for trucks, resistances, controllers and cable bundles were also considered.

The motorman of Milnes car no. 21 appears to be conversing with the driver of the rully in this pre-1906 scene on Hedon Road. (PG)

to enable the line to be extended northward along Beverley Road if required, and to permit the extension along Cottingham Road and a turnout to permit cars to stand at that point. Also shown were a double junction at Newland Avenue and two lines into the car shed. The position of the line into Cottingham Road was altered in July 1908 to avoid the destruction of trees on the north side of Cottingham Road.

Tenders for the work were received in June, and the quotation from Messrs Hadfield's was accepted, comprising £373 11s 3d for the Beverley Road junction, £252 17s 6d for the lines into the car shed, and £495 7s 6d for the Newland Avenue junction, a total cost of £1121 16s 3d.

The City Engineer recommended the purchase of further cars. He sought to have cars built by an outside contractor and by his own department. An attempt by members to have him build all the cars was defeated. In October it was decided that the City Engineer would construct fourteen cars and that a private company would supply six. Mr McCombe's views are not recorded!

Increased traffic levels on the Holderness Road route resulted in an increased frequency from six minutes to four minutes, for which three additional cars were needed. The "TH" route was unaltered.

On 16 December 1908 the Tramways Sub-Committee accepted a tender from the United Electric Car Company for six car bodies at a total cost of £1800. This was not the cheapest, but the City Engineer considered it the most advantageous. The full list was:

Company	Delivery time	Cost £
Metropolitan Amalgamated Railway Carriage and Wagon Co.	16 to 18 weeks	2100
Milnes-Voss & Co. Ltd	8 weeks	2070
Brush Electrical Engineering Co. Ltd	10 weeks after settlement of details	1800
United Electric Car Co. Ltd	10 weeks after settlement of details	1800
Hurst, Nelson & Co. Ltd	16 weeks	1770

In the first instance the contractors were able to specify their own designs, but none of the designs appeared to be suitable in certain respects (unspecified). Therefore, the two firms who had submitted the lowest prices for trucks with forged side frames, namely the United Electric Car Company Limited and Messrs Mountain and Gibson Limited, were asked to submit amended prices for twenty trucks embodying certain specified details. The amended tender from Mountain and Gibson for twenty trucks at £43 per truck was accepted. The full list was:

Firm	Truck	Side frame	With wheels & axles £ s d			Without wheels & axles £ s d		
United Electric Car Co (amended)	Brill No. 21E	Forged steel	65	0	0	41	0	0
						46	0	0
Preston Compensating	Cast steel		72	0	0	48	0	0
J G Brill Company	Brill No, 21E	Forged steel	72	10	0	48	10	0
Brush Electrical Engineering Co. Ltd	Brill No. 21E	Forged steel	65	10	0	45	10	0
Hurst, Nelson & Co Ltd	HN Standard 21E	Cast steel	61	12	0	37	12	6
	HN Standard 21E	Forged steel	68	2	6	44	2	6
Mountain & Gibson Ltd (amended)	No. 21 EM	Forged steel				41	0	0
	No, 21 EM	Forged steel				43	0	0

Tenders from six companies for motors were considered together with one from Messrs Raworth's Traction Patents Limited for regenerative equipment, one equipment erected complete on a car £350, one delivered to a car shed £326 10s, and one erected complete on a car (with the guarantee of an order for ten additional equipments). The first two were subject to the Company supplying nine additional equipments to a car shed if testing proved suitable and it was decided to order more.

The City Engineer and Tramway Electrical Engineer had visited the Yorkshire (Woollen District) Tramways Company where the Raworth equipments were in use, and concluded that it was desirable to test one before committing the Corporation to a large purchase. So the offer costing £326 10s was accepted. It was also decided to order five pairs of 40hp interpole motors from Dick Kerr, and five pairs of 38hp interpole motors from Siemens, and that the equipment for the remaining nine cars could be left over until the Raworth trial was concluded.

The Tramways Committee decided not to extend tramway operations for the time being. As a result the City Engineer had

All three employees watch the cameraman taking this photograph of car no. 16 which is outside Hedon Road depot entrance. The date is pre-1907 and the extension to Marfleet has not yet been constructed. The similarity with Holderness Road Depot can be seen. (PG)

considered the need for replacement rails was so small (100 tons) to secure an advantageous price. He contacted Doncaster Corporation which used the identical sections of rail and discovered that it required 200 tons. It would be useless (his word) to ask a number of companies to tender since they would not supply small amounts, 500 tons being the minimum order. Therefore, a joint approach to the previous supplier (Angleur Company of Liège) had produced prices for 300 tons (£6 7s 6d)

and 350 tons (£6 11s) of rails and accessories. If Sandberg steel rails were adopted in place of ordinary steel rails the cost per ton would increase by 15s per ton. It was left to the Corporation's officers to decide which type of rail to obtain. Subsequently, prices were obtained from British manufacturers and an order for 350 Sandberg rails was given to Messrs Walter Scott Limited at £7 5s per ton.

Readers may recall the correspondence between the

Original Milnes car no. 1 passes St George's Road on Hessle Road in 1903 on its way to "Town". (PG)

This is the same location at a later date with Milnes car no. 114 which received a Magrini cover in February 1904 centre stage. (PG)

Corporation and the Board of Trade regarding a suitable speed indicator, but that no resolution had been reached. The matter was raised once more by the Board of Trade in a letter dated 13 January 1909, stating that it appeared from the circumstances of certain accidents occurring on tramways, and from other evidence, that the Board's maximum speeds were frequently exceeded in practice.

Many operators had asked the Board to make it mandatory to fit indicators since it was difficult for motormen to estimate speeds accurately without them. It could not make it mandatory (a change from its previous stance) but did want a certain proportion of cars on all systems to be so fitted to enable motormen to be trained in estimating speeds. The Board would be glad to learn when this would be adopted in Hull and to learn, in due course, the precise steps taken and the particular form of indicator adopted. There were from time to time references to high

Even in the early part of the 20th Century roads could be very busy as shown here with two cars led by no. 58 together with examples of contemporary traffic. The location is Holderness Road near Kent Street. (PG)

Another busy scene on Holderness Road with Milnes car no. 103 in view possibly in 1910. (PG)

speeds in the Committee minutes with complaints from other users and passengers, but no action resulted. The earliest reference was as far back as November 1899.

The matter was referred to the three officers, the Chairman and the Town Clerk, and in the infuriating way of things no further reference regarding the Hull situation to this was recorded in the minutes, nor can anything be found in the Board of Trade records at Kew!

However, the letter had been sent to 173 tramway undertakings most of whom responded but not very positively. The Tramways and Light Railways Association had discussed this issue at a special meeting and informed the BOT that there was not at present a speed indicator on the market which would satisfy practical conditions, and it was extremely doubtful if considering the varying speeds and different services required any indicator could fulfil a useful function. Its members were of the opinion that the question of speeds could be adequately dealt with without resort to indicators. In any case the fitting of an additional device occupying the attention of drivers was undesirable in the interests of the safety of the public!

There were even questions in Parliament about the fitting of indicators. Opinion within the Board was divided as some inspectors were sceptical about the accuracy of any device. But the pressure mounted with the Metropolitan Police wanting all road traffic to be fitted with a hooter that would sound when speed reached a given limit! The Board was opposed to this and its extension to cars throughout the country so there was some fairly acerbic correspondence between the two organisations.

Eventually the Tramways and Light Railways Association persuaded its members to test ten indicators and devoted its April 1911 journal to the results. The final report which was written by six members including the manager of Liverpool Corporation Tramways, the Chief Engineer of the Metropolitan Electric Tramways Ltd and the Rolling Stock Superintendent of London County Council Tramways, was unenthusiastic. Several indicators worked satisfactorily during the tests but it was impossible to estimate what life they would have when fitted to a tramcar. Transmission gears able to stand the rough conditions

under a tramcar would be costly for purchase and maintenance. Tramcar undertakings did not want another piece of equipment to have to maintain in the short time cars were present in sheds. If indicators did become mandatory they should be fitted only for instruction and test purposes. Indicators showing the maximum speed attained were of little value as the authorised speeds on tramways were many, and varied widely between locations. It was safe to go at 16 miles an hour on some parts of the route but it could be dangerous to exceed four miles an hour on others. Everyone was none the wiser for the study and the dispute rumbled on.

The new Cottingham Road car shed opened on 13 March 1909, and the Stepney Lane premises were vacated. The new shed was lit by electricity, and so impressed were management that it recommended that the less than satisfactory gas lighting at Liverpool Street be replaced with arc lighting supplied from the tramway current using lamps from The Jandus Arc Lamp Co at £7 6s 3d each.

The new shed's foreman, Mr Ernest Firth, obtained a house in Haworth Street alongside the eastern wall of the new shed. He asked for a door to be made into the shed from the rear of his house and offered £1 to rent adjacent land. The Committee agreed to this. Subsequently, in March 1911 he informed people that he was leaving the city to visit a sick brother but was never seen again despite having uncollected wages!

Another deputation from the Stoneferry and Wilmington Ratepayers' Association attended the Tramways Committee on 24 March 1909. It stated that the Stoneferry community was isolated, with the only means of conveyance being a Waggonette, and deplored the decision of the Corporation to postpone indefinitely the Stoneferry tramway. The district was the wealth earning district of the city and a more satisfactory means of transit was essential.

Officers and councillors were convinced that a tramways solution was not possible at present because of the very high cost of road widening. They were attracted by the "trackless trolley", but thought the costs of overhead outweighed the low running costs. They may have been influenced by Mr McCombe's

A city-bound tram squeezes past the "King Billy" (King William III) statue in the Market Place in 1910. (PG)

address to the Myton Ward, Botanic and Park Ward Ratepayers Associations in January, and on 2 February when he expressed support for trackless trolleys where roads were too narrow for tramways.

Committee members made various visits and recommended that six motor omnibuses be purchased from the Mersey Railway Company to provide a service to Stoneferry. It was acknowledged that a 15-minute service would result in a loss of £1,200 per annum, since the average receipts of 5d per mile would be only half the estimated running cost of 10d per mile. Tramway running costs were 5.08d per mile with receipts of 9.14d per mile. The recommendation for motorbuses was accepted.

Representatives of Hessle Urban District Council asked the

Corporation for a meeting to discuss the extension of the Hessle Road tram service to Hessle. This took place on 12 January 1909. The Corporation had already widened the road to Priory Farm near the city boundary. A number of Hessle residents already travelled regularly by rail and horse bus to and from Hull, and the Urban District now had a population of 5000. The Town Clerk was instructed to report on the legal situation, and, unusually, the City Engineer and Tramway Manager were asked to report separately on construction costs and working expenses.

The Town Clerk stated that the distance from the Dairycoates terminus to the city boundary was one and a quarter miles, which was about the same distance from there to the centre of Hessle. Road works and the laying of track within the Urban District would be supervised by the district, for which Hull

Former trailer car no. 82 has just entered Newland Avenue from Queens Road in 1904. It is approaching the Hull and Barnsley Railway bridge which crossed all seven main roads traversed by trams. (PG)

In this 1905 view of Prospect Street car no. 73 is overtaking a horse bus. (PG)

Corporation would have to pay. Additionally the Corporation would have to maintain the road within the track and eighteen inches on either side. The Urban District Council would, after 21 years and every subsequent seven years, have the right to purchase that part within their district. It would also regulate speeds and have the power to grant licences with respect to tramcars, their drivers and conductors. In one sense this did not trouble him since he assumed that, in due course, the city boundary would be extended to include Hessle (it never was).

The district should contribute towards the cost of the extension or to make up any loss that might be involved. It was only equitable that as the extension would be of principal benefit to the district, they should bear a significant part of the financial burden. He quoted examples from Leeds involving the districts of Rawdon, Yeadon and Guiseley, which required them to pay £400 per annum in advance for a period of twelve years from the date of the opening of the extension. A particular problem lay with the need to widen the road into the village of Hessle where within the village itself the road was built up on both sides.

He anticipated that there may be losses incurred at first on the extension of service and he proposed that a separate account be kept for the section between Dairycoates and Hessle to calculate any loss to which the Urban District might contribute. He did not say what might happen with any profits!

Construction of a double line throughout would, according to the City Engineer, cost £30,000 inclusive of road widening costs. A single line with loops would save £8,000. The cost of additional cars and electrical supply was not included, as it was assumed that the present fleet and supply would be sufficient.

The Tramway Manager considered that if the line was built housing construction would follow which would lead to a steady increase in the possible revenue. The distance from Queen Victoria Square to the existing Hessle Road terminus was 2 miles and from there to the Granby public house in the centre of Hessle a further 2¼ miles. There would be potential for summer evening, Saturday afternoon and Sunday afternoon traffic from Hull into the countryside around Hessle. He forecast that many additional cars would need to be provided on such occasions. A 10-minute service would suffice for ordinary traffic but this would be supplemented for any pleasure traffic. The service would incorporate the existing one to Dairycoates, the whole journey taking 30 minutes. (The 1912 NER timetable shows trains taking between nine and thirteen minutes, although the frequency was irregular and the station not very convenient for parts of Hessle itself.) This would require three cars to maintain the 10-minute service.

Some 400 to 500 passes were issued by the North Eastern Railway between Hull and Hessle. Not all the train passengers would transfer to the tramways, only those who considered it more convenient to board a regular tramcar that passed their door and took them right into the city centre. Working expenses on the new section would exceed the existing costs per mile run of 5.80d. He assumed that this would reach 6d per mile. There the matter petered out as the Committee decided that the three reports be printed and circulated to all members of the Committee. There was support within the city, and the Coltman

Car 73, returning from the Pier to Queen Victoria Square is about to enter the Market Place from Queen Street. (PG)

A fine (1905) view of no. 111 which has just crossed from North Bridge into Witham. The Hedon Road route diverges to the right into Great Union Street. Had proposals borne fruit the Stoneferry route would have turned left at Tailors World along Cleveland Street. The motorman of a car in Great Union Street can be just seen on the right. (PG)

and Albert Wards, through which the Hessle Road route ran, urged the Corporation to proceed as soon as possible.

On 18 October 1909 the Hull and District Chamber of Trade condemned the running of cars into the City Square where the tramway station had opened on 30 September, and asked the Tramways Committee to withdraw all the cars from the Square excepting the "TH" and "P" routes. When the Committee considered the resolution, it was decided that the Holderness Road (H) and the Hedon Road cars would terminate in Savile Street rather than the Square.

The same Committee authorised the City Engineer to remove the old horse tram tracks in Waterhouse Lane, and to re-upholster the seats in the Brill cars at £2 19s 6d per car.

In October 1909 the International Order of Good Templars held its annual Yorkshire Conference in Hull, and passed a resolution which strongly protested against the action of the Tramways Committee in allowing tram tickets to be used for the purpose of advertising intoxicating drinks. It called upon the City Council to take measures to stop such use! The ensuing letter was read out at the November Tramways Sub-Committee and merely entered on the minutes.

As a result of a fatal accident on 21 May 1909 on the Wolverhampton District Electric Tramways, the Board of Trade asked all tramway operators to review their procedures for checking trolley poles. A man had been found dead on the top deck of a tramcar with his feet (on which he wore nailed boots) resting on the base of the trolley standard and the upper part of his body against the hand rail. Death was due to an electric shock, and it was discovered that arcing had taken place between the main cable bolt and the trolley boom. Additionally, the red warning lamp had failed. The Board wanted an audible signal, and the company had instituted a daily test to ensure that all standards were properly insulated, and was about to equip all cars with a magnetic blow out fuse which gave a distinctly audible signal.

The City Engineer and the Tramway Electrical Engineer stated that such an accident was impossible in Hull, where the trolley was insulated and carried on all cars above the top cover. The base was earthed direct to the car truck and rail by a cable of sufficient current-carrying capacity, which in the event of leakage would blow the fuse at the feeder point, or bring the automatic switch out at the power station. Before the current could be replaced on that particular section it would be necessary to remove the trolley of the defective car from the wire. The trolleys were tested periodically.

The first new cars with fixed top covers entered service in May and June 1909 (nos 117-122 with 43/22 bodies by U.E.C).

A joint report was submitted by the City Engineer and the Tramway Electrical Engineer, (not Mr McCombe), regarding the turning round of tramcars. The arrangement of trolley poles above the top covers of tram cars did not prevent cars from being turned round from time to time as the previous arrangement had. There was great advantage to be gained from turning cars at times.

Cars 74 and 87 pass either side of the Andrew Marvell statue at the junction of Jameson Street and King Edward Street. Passengers on no.87 are still ascending the staircase, which looks a hazardous exercise. (PG)

This was borne out from experience on the Beverley Road route, since the opening of the new Cottingham Road sheds where the triangular arrangement outside the shed permitted cars to be turned each time that they went to the shed, wear on the wheels of the Beverley Road and Spring Bank cars was much more even than on other routes.

It was possible to turn cars at Hedon Road, but this involved additional labour and it had been decided to turn cars here on a weekly basis. A similar arrangement could be made at Holderness Road by installing one line of track and an additional curve in from the shed. It was not possible to do this at Liverpool Street and Wheeler Street, and their recommendation that their cars be turned once a week at Queen Victoria Square was approved.

Car no. 104 had been fitted with Messrs Raworth's regenerative equipment despite considerable delay in obtaining it and current recording equipment. After some time in service it was found necessary to alter the gearing so that the car was not as quick to run in conjunction with other cars.

Tests during the previous month with this equipment and Siemens equipment using a new type of controller which shunted the field of the motors, had revealed the temperature of the regenerative equipment to be much higher than the Siemens product. Raworths were informed and its employees visited Hull to make alterations to the equipment. This did improve current consumption, but took the electric brake out of operation, and when the car was taken out on test a slight collision occurred, no notice being given by Raworths that the electric brake was inoperative. The City Engineer's recommendation that it be removed, and ten sets of Siemens equipment be obtained, was approved.

These turned out to be 33hp motors at £180 per pair, together with ten pairs of controllers at £52 per pair. Siemens had also suggested 38 hp motors but this was rejected, although some were already in use, but no reason was given. The company had also given a price of £15 per set of resistances, but these were suitable only for being fixed underneath the car whereas the City

Engineer and Tramway Electrical Engineer preferred the platform type in use in most of the cars. Ten sets of resistances were ordered from Messrs Boydell & Sons, who had supplied these previously, at £6 16s 6d per pair. The City Engineer and the Tramway Electrical Engineer were authorised to mount the equipment on cars when supplied, and to make up the necessary cable bundles using the Corporation's own workmen.

Fourteen new cars (nos 123-136) entered service between November 1909 and November 1910, having been assembled by the City Engineer's staff at Liverpool Street, although it is thought that some work was undertaken in its own workshops,

Mr Fearnley, secretary of the Municipal Tramways Association wrote to state that a Special Committee had been formed to investigate the cause of corrugation on tramway rails. A number of towns including Bradford, Leeds, Glasgow, London and Sheffield, had agreed to help and he wondered if Hull would also assist with any experiments. The City Engineer and Tramway Electrical Engineer were authorised to make any necessary arrangements.

The increase in the size of the tram fleet, and the increased frequency employed on the Anlaby Road route, plus the use of the Anlaby Road car shed by Old Town tram cars, meant that the shed was now too small. It was also used by cars operating Hull Fair services and Football Specials. It was agreed to extend the depot to accommodate twenty-four cars at a cost of £7,500.

The Tramway Manager reported that an improved coat of arms was required for the side of tram cars, and suggested that the School of Art should ask its students to design possible solutions, and that a fee of £1 10s be offered. This was approved but is not mentioned again in the minutes.

On 21 October 1910 five possible tramway extensions were discussed comprising the Beverley Road extension to Igglemire Lane; from Botanic Gardens along Spring Bank West to a point near the Walton Street crossing; a single line along Wheeler Street from Anlaby Road to the car shed extension; from Dairycoates to the Pickering Park entrance and the Paragon

Awaiting departure in St John Street is car no. 114. (MJW)

Station tramway. Proposals for the latter had envisaged an anti-clockwise loop but the new proposal saw a clockwise loop over the same streets to be used by the Pier cars. There was no mention of running cars from Anlaby Road to Osborne Street over an extended Brook Street.

Subsequently, two further extensions were included in the bid for Parliamentary powers. These comprised the continuation of the Cottingham Road service to the second entrance to Newland Park, and the continuation of the Spring Bank West scheme over the Walton Street level crossing along Spring Bank West to Alliance Avenue. The latter would have seemed the more profitable since the Cottingham Road service would be extended into a low density but affluent area. A proposal by Alderman Hanger for a line from George Street along Jameson Street to Paragon

Milnes car no. 18 passes the entrance to West Park on Anlaby Road with another car in the distance. (MJW)

Milnes car no. 16 is shown on Anlaby Road after it had received its Hull-built top cover in January 1907. (MJW)

82

Square, which would have required a double line in place of the single track loop in Jameson Street from Paragon Square to King Edward Street, was defeated.

Many attempts to secure free or reduced travel had proved unsuccessful but the Hull Teachers' Association succeeded. An Oriental Missionary Exhibition was held at the City Hall, and because it was of an educational character the Education Committee had allowed those teachers and children who wished to attend to do so. A deputation from the HTA suggested that scholars might be carried at reduced rates. To this the Committee agreed provided that groups of ten children were supervised by a teacher, they would be carried at a half-penny fare.

Car no. 56 is travelling south along Newland Avenue and is near the Monica Cinema. However it is carrying a "B" route letter so it is possible that this may have been taken when the circular service linking routes "S" and "B" was in operation between 1919 and 1923. (PM)

From 11 October 1910 the Tramways Committee had a new chairman, Alderman Robson, since a new Council policy prevented Alderman Larard who had championed the electric system so well from holding the chair of more than one Committee. Alderman Larard had acted as a de facto Managing Director with three departmental heads under him so his influence would be missed.

Public concern about delays caused by river traffic had been debated on previous occasions. It was suggested that cars held up at the bridge on the Holderness Road and Hedon Road routes should turn back, and that passengers should cross the bridge to other tram cars. This would, it was claimed, ensure a regular service on these routes.

Mr McCombe was not keen. Inward "H" cars would have to stop on the eastern side of the bridge near Great Union Street, and the inward "M" cars opposite Wincolmlee. Outward cars would stop in Charlotte Street. Additionally, at least two cars would have to wait for passengers to cross the bridge, whilst passengers would be at risk of being caught up in heavy traffic near the narrow bridge. He doubted that passengers would consent to such a transfer, especially in inclement weather. At peak times cars would be carrying full loads, and it would be difficult to ensure that only legitimate passengers boarded the waiting cars. Two inspectors, who would have total discretion regarding the turning of cars, would be required to regulate the cars. There was also the question of relieving men for breaks and meals not changing shifts. Turning of cars would interfere with this and the men would have to put up with it since no alternative could be found.

He was willing to try an experiment but only if he could have the two inspectors. Finally he asked members if anything could be done to shorten the North Bridge opening times. A six-month trial period was agreed but it is not known if it was introduced.

On the night of 8/9 February 1911 the Foreman Car Washer at the Holderness Road Car Shed, Mr William Chambers, died from injuries received through being crushed between two tram cars in the depot. A Coroner's Inquest was held on 15 February 1911 before which the Coroner and Jury went by tram to view the shed and the mechanisms.

Mr Chambers was passing between the ends of two cars and brought the trolley, which was off the overhead, momentarily into contact with the trolley wire by means of the trolley stick. Another employee, Mr Harry Kaye was cleaning and adjusting the controller of car no. 115 and had, unfortunately on this occasion, omitted to turn off the canopy switches. The other car was two or three feet in front. One of the car washers had taken the trolley off the wire, and the bamboo pole was hanging from the trolley. As long as the trolley did not touch the wire it did not matter if the switches were on.

The first indication that something was wrong was a flash from the controller which affected his eyes and dazzled him. The car moved forward at full speed and struck the car in front. Under cross examination he stated that there were printed instructions in the shed for the cleaners, and the first clause instructed them always to shut off the controllers. He had noticed that men when crossing the plank across the pit caught hold of the trolley sticks to steady themselves, even though there was no reason to do so. The Jury brought in a verdict of "Accidental Death".

A Notice of Accident under the Factory and Workshop Acts of 1901 and 1907 had to be forwarded to the Board of Trade and the Inspector of Factories.

Solicitors acting on behalf of the widow of Mr Chambers (who had ten years of service with the Corporation) submitted a request for an ex gratia payment and for compensation under the Workman's Compensation Act 1906, pointing out that the death was caused by negligence by a servant of the Corporation but that, owing to the doctrine of common employment, damages could not be claimed from the Corporation. The Tramways Committee decided against an ex gratia payment, but left the compensation decision to the Chairman, Deputy-Chairman and Town Clerk.

On 7 March the Tramways Sub-Committee inspected the route of the proposed extension to Marfleet Avenue and decided to authorise it, but to leave the question of any additional fare to be charged until a later date. The North Eastern Railway objected to the proposed arrangement of tramways in Paragon Square, and to the proposed junction at Botanic Gardens for the Spring Bank West line, and the matter was delegated to the Chairman and Deputy-Chairman in conjunction with the Parliamentary Sub-Committee.

Requests for free or reduced fare travel were increasing and the March Committee considered several. It had to respond to a Council resolution that blind persons be allowed to travel without payment. Information obtained revealed that only 12 of 42 municipal tramway systems carried such persons free of charge.

It was decided that an application form be sent to each blind person for his/her signature, and that of an Ophthalmic Surgeon practising in Hull. Blind persons would then apply to the Tramway Manager for a pass which would need to be renewed annually. It must be shown to conductors and inspectors, and was not transferable. Pass holders were allowed to travel only when seating accommodation was available in the lower saloon. Riding on the upper deck was not permitted.

The City Council had also asked the Tramways Committee to consider issuing tickets to school children at one half-penny each. Research by Mr McCombe revealed that it was common practice to give special facilities for young persons, and it was agreed that Hull should fall in line.

Children under the age of three would still be carried free, and those between the ages of three and fourteen would be carried at half-fare, and would be able to transfer to and from the Old Town section. Every person over the age of fourteen would pay the ordinary fare. The ordinary half-penny fare would be

Quite why car no. 125 was decorated has been lost in the mist of time, possibly the Coronation of King George V? It is seen outside Cottingham Road Depot. (PM)

charged to such children as travelled between 5am and 9am. Subsequently the Honorary Secretary of the Hull Head Teachers' Association, Mr Percy J. Bigford, wrote to express the Association's gratitude for the concession and for the tram facilities in connection with the Orient Exhibition. A letter of thanks also came from the Hull and District Chamber of Trades. Even in those days a "thank you" in the Committee minutes was a rare event!

With the new Pickering Park due to open on 13 July 1911, the Pickering Park Sub-Committee asked the Tramways Committee to provide a public service of motor buses from the Dairycoates tram terminus and the Park Gates on the opening day. It was left to the Tramway Manager to arrange this.

Next to seek a concessionary fare were the commanders of

Car no. 37 is pictured near the Botanic Gardens (formerly Cemetery Gates) level crossing. (PM)

Car no 85 is in company with no. 148 at the Newland Avenue terminus. The date is problematical since it looks pre-1914 but the curve into the western side of Cottingham Road is in place ready for the extension to Newland Park. Work had started on this in 1914 before the Great War started so it is possible that this was in place by that time. (PM)

six Territorial Army units. Their headquarters had been moved from the town centre to the Wenlock Barracks on Anlaby Road near Walton Street. This was an extra travelling cost to soldiers, and the commanders asked that they be given a transfer ticket by the conductor of the car on which they were travelling to enable them to continue their journey. This would maintain revenue for the trams and they hoped that more would join and increase revenue even further. They were, however, unsuccessful.

The increased size of the fleet was imposing strains on the workshops at Liverpool Street. The City Engineer described them as much too small and overcrowded to carry out car maintenance and repair work on anything like a profitable basis. It was impossible to get a sufficient number of cars into the works without crowding out the Hessle Road running cars, and in order to make room for these a number of cars had to be shunted into the temporary shed each night, entailing a considerable waste of time. The Armature Shop was not large enough, and the temporary wooden shed was dark and draughty requiring to be lit for the whole day. A brass finishers shop was required along with a test room. The mess room could no longer accommodate all the workmen. After considering the report and the question of having one central shop at Stepney Lane, further consideration was delegated to the Chairman, Deputy-Chairman, City Engineer and Tramway Electrical Engineer (again not the Tramway Manager).

Recording clocks which had been installed at the power station, Liverpool Street car shed and the Cottingham Road car shed had been most satisfactory and had effected a saving in time checking. Authority was given to fit these at the remaining sheds.

The Tramway Manager stated that in view of the increase in traffic, the needs of projected extensions and the probabilities of the future 24 new cars were required. He was asked to submit a joint report about this with the City Engineer. Authority was given for the purchase of 18 cars with the proviso that this would be increased by six if the Corporation decided within six months to order them.

Arrangements to celebrate the Coronation of King George V were delegated to the usual members and officers. These included painting the trolley booms on a number of cars red, white and blue. Arrangements went very smoothly, so much so that all the men who worked during Coronation week and did not receive any recognition were given an extra day's pay!

In May the Corporation agreed, in response to a request from the Municipal Employees Association, to grant six days' leave per annum to all staff who had been employed for not less than six months. The cost to the Tramways Department was £1470 10s 3d per annum.

In May 1911 the Committee agreed changes to the rules for drivers and conductors, but the subsequent City Council meeting suggested that a draft be submitted to the tramway men for their observations and that, if necessary, a deputation from the men be received by the Committee. A meeting between the deputation and various members and officers took place on 26 June. It was agreed to substitute black buttons for silver ones on overcoats. The payment of time and a half on Bank Holidays for men at work as usual was rejected, but those who were asked to work a rest day would receive double pay. The men's suggestion that rule 39, the closing of the top front door on leaving the terminus be carried out by conductors instead of drivers was agreed. A plea to install double sanders instead of single sanders was rejected. Interestingly, the use of single sanders had been questioned within the Board of Trade at an early date, but had been agreed only because Hull possessed no gradients of any note. Conductors asked for mirrors to be provided so that, when off the platform, they could clearly see passengers getting on and off and so avoid accidents. This was deferred for further consideration.

Two cars (the second being ERTCW no. 64 of 1900) approach the tramway station in Queen Victoria Square from Carr Lane. No.64 was given the prototype Magrini top cover in September 1903 but, in 1907, this was altered to a fixed top cover retaining the Magrini higher roof profile seen here. (PM)

The Tramways Committee on 28 June ratified these decisions. It also agreed to the Tramway Manager's suggestion that cars be provided with two boxes into which passengers could place used tickets as they alighted. This was to avoid the large number of tickets that were thrown away in the city centre, and would also do away with the practice of children begging for used tickets from passengers at termini. Committee members also approved the installation of clocks at each terminus (as provided at the Stoneferry motor bus terminus) at a cost of £26. This was to counter the lack of consistency of clocks in the city centre.

The minutes are full of accident reports and complaints from

This is a fine view of the tramway station with cars from four different routes in sight. There is an "M" car in Savile Street and a Pier car outside the Docks Offices. (PM)

The hire of trams for social and recreational outings was a popular and regular event before the First World War as shown by these two well loaded cars on hire to the Olive Branch Lodge of the Free Gardeners from East Hull. The location appears to be Newland Avenue. (PM)

the public about the conduct of staff, mostly unfounded. On 28 June 1911 the Tramways Committee were informed about the "meritorious conduct of two employees". Motorman William Trowill was driving his car from Savile Street to Hedon Road when a child aged three ran in front of the car. He applied the emergency brake and leaned over the dasher, caught the child by its clothing and swung it out of the way with no injury to the child. An eye-witness called at the office to inform the authorities of his smartness and presence of mind.

Three days later Conductor James Wright was on a Beverley Road car near Queen's Road when he observed a lady on a cycle try to ride between the car and a coal rully. She was in difficulties and grabbed the side of the rully to save herself. The back wheel of the rully would have probably have gone over her had not Mr Wright jumped off the car which was going at a good speed (and probably against the regulation which everyone ignored) and dragged her and her cycle out of danger. This was seen by a Tramway Inspector who reported it to the authorities.

The Committee expressed its appreciation and awarded a gratuity of one guinea (21 shillings) to Mr Trowill and half a guinea (10s 6d) to Mr Wright.

The City Engineer submitted duplicate prints of new cars of which eighteen were to be ordered initially, with an option to order a further six, to the Board of Trade on 30 June 1911. They would have side running trolleys of Brecknell, Munro & Rogers manufacture similar to those already in service. He proposed to provide sanding gear for one rail only unlike previous cars which had the gear for both rails. Passengers had received shocks due to a car being charged with electricity, apparently owing to the wheels being insulated from the rails through the sanding of both rails. In consequence two sets of sand gear were removed from each car, leaving the one set. There was some discussion about this in the BOT but it was accepted because Hull was "free from gradients".

On 3 July 1911 the tenders for the new cars were examined. Only three companies had tendered for the bodies, whilst only four (including these three, had quoted for trucks). After careful

consideration, the tender for 18 bodies and Brush's own trucks from the Brush Engineering Company was accepted, the costs for bodies being £347 and trucks being £37 10s each. The contract for 33hp motors (£180 per pair) and controllers (£49 10s per pair) was awarded to Siemens. Wheels and axles would be supplied by John Baker & Co. of Rotherham at £10 10s per pair of wheels with one axle and Brecknell, Munro and Rogers of Bristol were to provide trolleys at £6 5s each. Resistances would again be supplied by W. Boydell and Son at £9 5s per pair. The City Engineer and the Tramway Electrical Engineer were authorised to make up the cable bundles required for the cars, as well as to provide life guards and lighting fittings.

Readers may recall that the School of Art had been invited to submit a new design for the Coat of Arms, but that nothing more had been heard of this. Two tramway staff, Mr A.J. Boynton (Foreman Painter) and Mr Bray, had prepared a design which the City Engineer submitted to the Tramways Committee. This was approved and a sum of one guinea each was awarded to both men.

A long railway strike took place in the summer of 1911 along with many industrial disputes in the city. There was some unrest and the overhead at Whitefriargate Bridge was damaged in mid-August.

In October 1911 the Tramways Committee confirmed its intention to provide a tramway to Stoneferry, and resolved to seek the necessary powers, an interesting decision given the dire financial status of the motor bus service. Indeed, rails were laid under the new railway bridge at Wilmington after the road had been widened, following the removal of the level crossing.

On 27 December 1911 the Tramway Manager submitted a report regarding delays to tramway traffic resulting from the closure of the river bridges and level crossings. This was in response to a request from Councillor Ombler at the previous Tramways Committee meeting to consider the provision of short workings to minimise delays.

Mr McCombe thought the risk of considerable delay in the city was high, and that any system of communication between

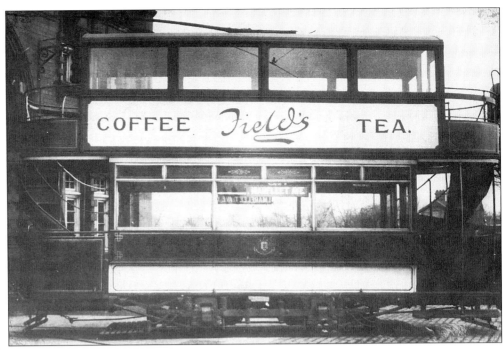

cars held at railway crossings and a tramway official in the city centre, would not be of any practical help since the situation could only be adequately dealt with when cars arrived back at the terminus. (The Occurrence Books of signal boxes, including that at Stepney on Beverley Road, show that a single long freight train of seventy wagons could take six or seven minutes to cross the road, by which time at least two cars in each direction would be affected and running six minutes late.)

Staff had instructions that after having been delayed at crossings to use their discretion about going past passengers without stopping to pick them up unless they had passengers to set down. The first man would, as a rule, get up speed and pass at least three stopping places without halting to pick up, thereby gaining a minute. When cars arrived at the city centre they had, of course, become bunched and the policy was to get them away as quickly as possible. The men did not, as a rule, waste time in this operation but they had to pick up waiting passengers. A tramway official at this point would be useful to grasp the situation and direct cars accordingly. It would be still better if a timekeeper could be stationed at each outlying terminus to avoid losing time

there, but the cost of £800-£900 a year was prohibitive. Nevertheless such provision would pick up lost traffic in these situations since passengers preferred to walk rather than await late running cars.

Mr McCombe stated that a system of signals between North Bridge and Saltshouse Lane (Drypool) Bridge, and at Queen Victoria Square and Dansom Lane, had been considered previously, but it was not considered practicable, because bridges were only open for short periods of time, and on occasions were open at the same time, so giving no alternative route. Such rerouteing would cause inconvenience to passengers on the Holderness Road and Hedon Road trams who would be diverted from their destinations. However, he recommended that two inspectors be employed at £160 per annum to regulate traffic and react to delays as they occurred.

The same Committee received a 682-name petition from resi-

Spring Bank near Park Street is the location for this pre-World War One view. Of the buildings in the picture only the church is no more having been replaced with a more modern building. (MJW)

dents requesting the Corporation to consider extending the proposed Hedon Road extension for another 633 yards to the end of Marfleet Avenue. It was referred to the Tramways Sub-Committee but did not feature when extensions were considered in February 1912.

Authorisation for the additional six cars was given on 3 January 1912, thus increasing the Brush order to twenty-four. The whole batch, delivery of which was two months behind schedule, entered service during 1912 numbered 137-160 with 42/22 bodies.

The Tramways Committee also agreed to the provision of telephone facilities at the Boulevard on Anlaby Road to assist with dealing with heavy football and cricket traffic at various times of the year.

The Tramway Manager had prepared a complete set of revised duties to provide additional services and meet claims for a reduced working week. In January 1912 the Hull Branch of the Amalgamated Association of Tramway and Vehicle Workers agreed to work the new duties, after some negotiation, for a seven month period, after which they would inform the Corporation of any weaknesses that were discovered.

An embarrassing letter was sent by the Town Clerk to the Board of Trade on 30 January 1912. He ruefully admitted that his department had lost the sealed copy of its Tramways Byelaws and he asked if another sealed copy could be provided. BOT internal memos veered between a "true copy" and a certified copy before a classic compromise resulted in a "true copy" and a certified copy being sent to the Corporation on 16 February 1912.

On 19 February 1912 when the Tramway Manager submitted his annual report to the Tramways Committee, the increasing losses from the Stoneferry motor bus service resulted in a decision to discontinue it on 31 March. Subsequently the City Engineer was authorised to convert one into a tower wagon and another into a rully.

At the same meeting Mr McCombe, the Chairman and Deputy Chairman in view of the extensions to the tramway system submitted proposals for a revised fare system, the first major review since the inauguration of the electric system in 1899. Several recommendations were made. The one penny fare as far as the cars went should be continued and that this fare should apply for the whole distance even after the new extensions were introduced. The original one penny fare had been very successful but they thought that the time had come for adjustment to meet modern requirements. Those passengers who resided at the ends of the extended routes were at an advantage when compared with those who lived nearer the city centre, in that they both paid the same fare. Similarly, short distance passengers, or those who travelled between points other than the terminus, also paid the same fare irrespective of that distance.

They proposed to replace the Old Town transfer system with an all day half-penny fare on the Old Town route, which would also apply to the Paragon Railway Station extension. The half-penny fare between 5am and 9am would continue, after which half-penny fixed stages would be instituted with three such stages on every route except for the Old Town and Spring Bank West.

This would ensure that passengers paid a fare commensurate with the length of ride and a more equitable return for their fare. It would mean a large increase in tramway passengers without materially affecting the financial standing of the undertaking.

A decision was deferred until the next meeting when the recommendations were accepted with a starting date of 1 April 1912. However the report was rejected at the subsequent council meeting and the fare structure was unaltered.

Tramway extensions were considered again on 28 February 1912. Mr McCombe was not in favour of connecting The King Edward Street/Jameson Street junction with the George Street/Savile Street junction, and running alternate cars on the H and M routes to the station. It would be impractical to maintain a regular service over the two routes from two separate city termini, as had proved the case when for a short time the B and S cars had alternated between Savile Street and King Edward Street. This was deferred for further consideration. The extension to Igglemire (Inglemire) Lane revealed a difference of opinion between the City Engineer who saw no demand for it, and the Tramway Manager who wanted to build it. Members decided to adopt it, although the distance was very short and would attract passengers that already used the trams.

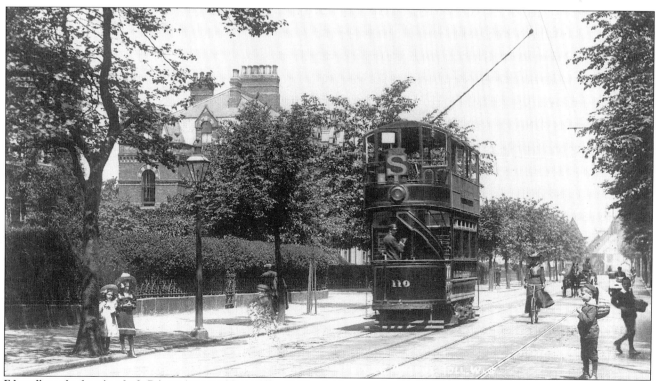

Edwardian splendour in a leafy Princes Avenue with car 110 with Magrini top cover bound for Newland Avenue. Pearson Park is to the left of the car. (MJW)

General Post Office, Hull

This is a commercial post card which shows cars on routes "P" and "TH" outside the fairly new General Post Office at the corner of Alfred Gelder Street and Lowgate. The date is probably pre-1914. (MJW)

Also approved were the Hessle Road extension to Pickering Park, despite some reservations by Mr McCombe, and the Cottingham Road route to the second entrance of Newland Park. The latter was included partly because the road was to be widened, and it was considered prudent to carry out the tramway works at the same time. Presumably, Mr McCombe was thinking about future extensions along Cottingham Road towards Cottingham, since the extension would attract little if any additional traffic. Subsequently the Chairman and Deputy Chairman were empowered to make arrangements with the NER regarding safety devices at the Botanic Gardens and Dairycoates level crossings.

Following a complaint in the local press the Tramway Manager was asked to report on the system in use for conductors paying in fare receipts after their shift. The issue revolved around whether a conductor had or had not deposited his money bag. The matter was to rumble on for some time.

During the day conductors, having entered details on a cash card, placed the money in a canvas bag and took it to the ticket lobby in Queen Victoria Square, and dropped the bag in a strong box. At frequent intervals the bags were removed and taken to the Tramway office. After office hours the money was deposited at each depot in a strong box by the conductor putting his hand through an aperture in the wall and dropping the bag in. This enabled the conductor to go home without delay although there was no receipt for the money, and no proof that it had been deposited. The Depot Foreman had the strong box key and the room was locked overnight. In the morning at about 8am the foreman and one other opened the box, and checked that the number of bags actually deposited matched what should have been paid in, and the bags were then taken to the Tramway offices.

This view shows a Milnes car (from the 102-116 batch) as provided with a Magrini top cover, possibly in 1904. (PM)

In twelve years of operation no bag had gone missing after being deposited in the depot box. However, some conductors left the bag on the tramcar overnight, whilst a few forgot to deposit the bag, which was subsequently found in the depot. Whenever they were challenged all usually maintained that they had deposited the bag!

In the case in question no bag had been found and the conductor had not deposited the money. At first he was unclear about whether he had deposited, but later claimed that he had definitely done so. Mr McCombe was adamant that it had not been paid in and that the system was being blamed for someone's own shortcomings. The conductor concerned had been suspended.

On 12 March 1912 the Committee visited Liverpool Street Depot and viewed the paying in arrangements, finding them to be exactly in accordance with the Tramway Manager's description, and stating that they were impressed with the ingenious arrangement.

On returning to the Guildhall two deputations of three conductors were interviewed. Their opinions varied, the first considering that the present system was not fair to conductors, and requesting that someone should count out the money when it was paid in. The second thought that the system was satisfactory, but that someone within the depot should record which conductors paid money in. They were not in favour of the contents being counted out before a man left the depot, since much valuable time would be wasted. Any shorts were usually the result of carelessness when conductors were in a hurry to leave.

Members decided that overall the system was efficient, but that some responsible person should be deputed to see the money deposited and to issue a receipt or ticket to the conductor. The practice of depot foreman and one other opening the box with two keys should be discontinued, and only one key should be kept at the depot with the foreman, and a traffic clerk should visit each depot in a morning and open the box in conjunction with the foreman. The bags in which money was conveyed from the depots should be locked in the depots and opened by a responsible person in the Tramway Office. Its final recommendation was that fares taken on the cars at night should be counted in the depot and not on the cars.

The local branch of the Amalgamated Association of Tramway and Vehicle Workers stated that the conductor was the victim of a very unbusinesslike system, and that he should be reinstated without delay and his wages paid from the time of his suspension. The Committee declined to meet a deputation, and would not agree to his reinstatement unless he refunded that money that should have been paid in within seven days, after which he must hand in his uniform.

An animated discussion took place at the following City Council and the matter was sent back for reconsideration. The main issue was that of providing receipts for all conductors who paid in cash. Those on early morning duties began to pay in from about 9.30am, with later men starting about 11.30am and continuing until 5.40pm. All such payments were made at the Tramway Lobby in Queen Victoria Square from where the bags were taken to the Tramways Office. If a system of giving receipts and counting out the money were introduced, it would have to apply to the Tramway Lobby as well, which could cause serious delay to services.

Seven traffic clerks would be required to be on duty from 1pm until midnight at a wage of 30 shillings a week costing £546 annually, and money would have to be spent on converting existing rooms for the new system, a total cost of £50. Having regard to the small amount of shortages on the cars and the costs involved, the Tramways Committee refused to depart from their previous recommendations. This time their decision was accepted. A quotation for transporting the money bags from depots to the Tramway Offices on a daily basis was obtained, the cost being £136 17s 6d a year, but it was decided to buy a motor car instead as being cheaper and more convenient!

On 29 April 1912 the Hedon Road extension opened for

The Beverley Road (Newland) terminus once more with a car turning right from Cottingham Road into Beverley Road. (MJW)

The first North Bridge was a simple unimpressive structure as can be seen here in the early 1900s as a Holderness Road car makes its way gingerly over the bridge. It lasted until a new bridge was opened in 1931. (MJW)

traffic. Alternate cars designated "MA" ran to Marfleet Avenue. Board of Trade authority had been received two days previously.

A curious incident was reported to the Committee whereby the captain of a vessel in the General Steam Navigation Company, T.W. Dyer, who had alighted from the wrong platform on a Hessle Road car on 9 May 1912, was fined £1 including costs at the City Police Courts!

In May 1912 His Majesty's Inspector of Factories visited Liverpool Street Works and criticised the lack of warming arrangements, and asking for this to be remedied before winter. The City Engineer had discussed the matter with the Inspector who, in view of impending extensions and alterations, was agreeable to the provision of low combustion stoves at certain points. The Committee also agreed to provide additional toilet accommodation at the works to reflect the increase in staff. The increase in the number of staff and tramcars led to approval to extend the inspection pits at Holderness Road.

Discussions for the Hessle Road extension were under way with the NER, but when the City Engineer suggested a new foot-bridge the company wondered if a subway might not be prefer-able, despite this costing £1500 against £500 for a footbridge. The NER wished to double the number of railway lines from two to four, with an effect on the tramway crossing as well as the length of the footbridge.

In view of this the Corporation decided to approach the NER to see if it would be prepared to abolish the level crossing and provide a bridge, a solution not helped by the presence of the Hull and Barnsley Railway bridge immediately west of the crossing. A meeting was held at York to discuss possibilities

without any financial commitment at this stage. Subsequently, the City Engineer persuaded the Committee and the NER to go ahead with the proposed crossing of two lines since work involved in agreeing costs, obtaining tenders, and purchasing any necessary land would take considerable time.

On 25 June 1912 a tramcar arrived at the Newland terminus of the Beverley Road route and its passengers alighted. Nothing unusual in that except that a Mr Walter Herbert Stickley left the car by the end nearest the terminus when, the Corporation claimed, he should have used the other end of the car, the conductor's end. The result was a prosecution, conviction in the Police Court and a series of court cases that ended in the King's Bench Division in April 1913.

Mr Stickley was convicted on 3 July 1912 of contravening byelaw no. 2. Mr Stickley and his brother Mr J.E.D. Stickley were prosecuted for the same offence on 10 August when there were six alleged offences, and again on 18 August.

The affair started with the posting in all cars of the bye-law that stated that passengers must enter or leave by the "hinder-most" or conductor's end of any tramcar. According to the local press this irritated the travelling public, but most people complied. But the difficulty arose at termini as to when one end of a car ceased to be the hindermost and became the driver's end.

It appears that after his conviction Mr Stickley wrote to Mr McCombe asking several questions. When a tram was stationary at the Beverley Road terminus, which was the hindermost plat-form, the one nearest Beverley or the one nearest Hull? Mr McCombe said that he could not answer as there were two inter-

St Mary's Church in Lowgate dwarfs this car which is bound for the Pier. Most of the buildings in view have survived into the 21st Century. (MJW)

pretations, something he repeated in the witness box. For passengers getting on a car the hindmost end was near Beverley, whilst for those alighting the rearmost was nearer Hull. He conceded that much depended upon the interpretation by individual passengers.

The *Hull Daily Mail* suggested that the fault lay with the design of the cars. In the absence of any notices, why not employ a figurehead on each car which would show which was the front end and which was the hindmost! The driver could take this with him when he changed ends!

The article criticised the Corporation for not enforcing its own overcrowding byelaws, and said that it couldn't enforce one law one day and not another. It hoped that a free-for-all would not result, and considered that in City Square it would be better

The extension from the Mile House (near the Crown Inn) to Aberdeen Street opened on 27 March 1903. It was on a central reservation and the car in view is just passing East Park (on its right) en route for Savile Street. (MJW)

for alighting passengers to leave by the front and new passengers board by the rear.

Six months after the first case it was realised that a Board of Trade bye-law existed to cover similar situations, and in November 1912 when both brothers appealed, the Stipendiary Magistrate upheld the appeals stating that the Board of Trade bye-law took precedence above the Corporation's bye-laws.

The Board's version stated that when cars were "in transit", passengers must leave by the "hindermost" end, which the defendants contended gave them the right to leave the car at a terminus from either end. There was a heated exchange at the hearing with the Corporation promoting their bye-laws as the ones that were relevant, and the defendants supporting the BOT version. The Stipendiary Magistrate was in no doubt. The BOT version overrode the Corporation's version and he granted their appeal. He also stated that if the BOT regulations had been made public previously, there would have been no cases to answer.

The *Eastern Morning News* was very supportive of the Stickleys, and it considered that they had rendered a distinct service to the travelling public of Hull. They should not have been prosecuted and been "martyred". The dispute between the public and the Corporation was now ended (how wrong he was on this point) and everyone could get on with their lives.

Yet it had some sympathy for Mr McCombe and the difficult position in which he found himself. For many years there had been great confusion at the city terminus when cars had come to a standstill, with alighting passengers fighting against a tide of passengers attempting to board. This would now return unless an answer could be found. It did not think that the brothers would offend again since their case was one of a point of law alone.

A full report of the Council's decision to appeal appeared in the following day's Hull News, and Mr Stickley was incensed when the Corporation posted details of his conviction in every car. He subsequently sent a circular to council members which further inflamed the situation, since the Town Clerk saw it as an attack on his person and his own professional competence.

Mr Stickley's solicitor had visited his office and seen the Deputy Town Clerk who had given him a copy of the Corporation's bye-laws. He had not asked for the Board of Trade's bye-laws nor had he (the Deputy Town Clerk) thought about giving him one, since he considered (and the Town Clerk agreed with him) that the Board's model did not override the Corporation's bye-laws.

At a subsequent meeting the Town Clerk had asked him if it was worth £150 to find out if the bye-laws were valid, and clearly Mr Stickley did so. His brother consulted another solicitor, and although the Corporation had contacted him it had not received a reply. Mr Stickley then wrote his circular to the Council, a circular from which the solicitors disassociated themselves. Mr Stickley accused the Town Clerk of deliberately delaying the case, an accusation cut to shreds by the information that

This enlargement from a postcard shows a car with advertisements crossing Whitefriargate Bridge. The advert is different from the one previously shown. It is not known how many cars were so treated. (MJW)

A rare view showing the tram track that was laid in Stoneferry Road but never used. The date is unknown. (MJW)

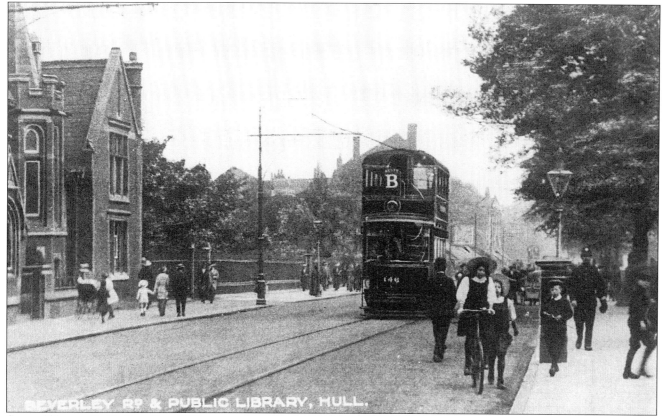

Car no. 146 passes the Northern Branch Library on a busy Beverley Road; the building survives but not as a library. (MJW)

Mr Stickley had declined to return the statement of facts for the case sent some 105 days previously. He had also undertaken in front of witnesses not to break the bye-law until the case was resolved, but it appeared that this had been broken.

Whilst some council members thought the bye-laws to be valid, others did not, and some members who had previously supported Mr Stickley had been unaware of the meetings with the Town Clerk and subsequent events, withdrew that support. Mr Stickley also claimed that the delay with the conviction hanging over his head had prevented his standing at the municipal elections. By a large majority the Council decided to appeal. This was heard at the King's Bench Division in April 1913. After considering the evidence the three judges decided that the previous appeal decision to overturn the conviction was not correct,

Views of "TH" trams on Holderness Road are not as numerous as "H" cars. This car is near Laburnum Avenue. (MJW)

"Old Preston" Car no. 61 is also travelling along Holderness Road. (MJW)

This photograph shows the construction work for the Spring Bank West extension in 1911. (MJW/HDM)

and that the case should be sent back to the lower court with a direction to convict. The Court was of the opinion that the Corporation bye-law which said that passengers must leave by the hindermost, or conductor's end, meant that end that had been the conductor's during the journey. Their lordships found it impossible to say that the Board of Trade regulations conflicted with the Corporation bye-laws. The appeal was allowed with costs.

Mr Stickley had become obsessed with the question of which end was to be used for alighting, and was willing to take any action that he thought fit to win. The wording of the bye-laws could have been improved so that the confusion might not have arisen. Mr McCombe's two interpretations had not helped matters and if he had produced the definition that the judges produced, the situation might not have got out of hand.

On 30 January 1913 meanwhile, a Mr Richard Bowers of 32 Spring Street (off Spring Bank) wrote to the Board of Trade and drew its attention to the "shameful overcrowding and flagrant disregard by Hull Corporation of its own byelaws" (section 48 prohibiting the carriage of excess passengers either inside or outside) with regard to the numbers permitted on tramcars. He had drawn the attention of local councillors to the situation. They had promised to look into it but no action had ensued. He understood that the Corporation were seeking alterations to these byelaws (partly thanks to Mr Stickley!) and he asked the Board to ensure that the Corporation enforced its own byelaws as a condition of any changes.

Following much internal consultation the Board concluded it possessed no powers to impose penalties on tramway operators who did not enforce their own byelaws! Given the fracas with Mr Stickley it is surprising that this did not receive more publicity!

The question of trams in the eastern part of Jameson Street was raised by officers in December 1912. They requested a final decision before commencing work on the Paragon Station loop, since the construction of a double line in that part of Jameson Street would require additional pointwork at the junction with King Edward Street, and alterations might be required to the crossovers as planned in King Edward Street. It was decided not to construct lines between King Edward Street and George Street, but it was agreed to provide three lines in King Edward Street between the De La Pole Monument and Queen Victoria Square, whereby the centre line could be used as a siding for waiting cars to leave the northeast side clear for cars to return from the station, and the southwest side clear for the "S" and "B" cars to run on when starting their outward journeys. King Edward Street was 51ft wide, of which the tree lines would take up 28ft. However, as with so many of the Committee's decisions, it was not ratified by the Council and it was never implemented.

Although the fares policy had been rejected, the agitation for a change continued, culminating in an article in the *Hull Daily Mail* on 14 November 1912. The writer mentioned opposition from the Old Town businesses who feared that they would lose out. However, he had discussed the half-penny stages with the riding public who were wholeheartedly in favour since the majority did not travel the full distance over a route.

The author of the article stated that in September Mr McCombe had submitted a paper to the Municipal Tramways Association claiming that the question was one of swings and roundabouts, since the loss of individual fares would be more than made up by the increased numbers of passengers. Mr Dalrymple of Glasgow was a recent convert to the half penny fare. The results were an unqualified success with an additional income of £2000 a week and an increased ridership of one million.

Mr McCombe included an analogy to the half-penny newspaper which had succeeded against all odds and like the half penny fare

An end view of Milnes car no. 22 complete with motorman near Dairycoates on Hessle Road. (PM)

The article did not think that those who rode the full distance would be against the half-penny stage, but he wondered if the proposed three-fifths of a mile stage was the correct distance as in Glasgow it was one mile, and in Sheffield and Leeds it was half a mile. Of 80 municipal tramway undertakings some 28 had adopted the half-penny fare with success and only one (Darlington) had not succeeded owing to a low density of traffic. Between 10am and 12 noon no tramway paid its way. It was anticipated that the fare would enable less well-off passengers to ride more often and he called upon the Corporation to introduce it.

In January 1913 the Chairman, City Engineer and Tramway Manager visited London, Huddersfield, Birmingham, Leeds, Bradford, Liverpool and the United Electric Car Works at Preston in connection with an order for additional cars.

They inspected London County Council bogie cars with two maximum traction trucks built by the Brush Company and Messrs Hurst, Nelson and Co., and similar cars of the Metropolitan Electric Tramways Ltd. built by Brush, who had recommended they examine the bogie cars as being suitable for Hull. However, the visitors were unimpressed.

They examined four-wheel trams built by the United Electric Car Company in Birmingham to a length of 18 feet instead of the usual 16 feet, with a longer wheelbase of 7ft 6in., and enclosed vestibules with a platform length of 5ft 9in.

Kirkstall Road Depot was

Another end view, this time of car no. 54 on Hedon Road (route M/A) in 1915. (PM)

produced the "greatest good for the greatest number" (a tenet of contemporary philosopher Jeremy Bentham). The tramway Manager ventured to say that large profits from a single fare were tantamount to an over-taxation of passengers!

Many people saw the penny fare as the "natural" fare but horse tramways had seen their "natural" fare as the tuppenny fare, but they had been forced to change to meet altered circumstances. He did not consider that the half-penny fare would remove the financial backbone of the undertaking, but rather would enable more people to ride more often and thus increase income.

visited in Leeds where more conventional cars were inspected albeit with enclosed vestibules and vertical movable screens to close the staircase opening. They were informed that Leeds had tried 18ft-long cars but had returned to the 16ft version. A "Cavena" car with enclosed vestibules was inspected in Huddersfield. It possessed folding doors over the entrance steps to prevent draughts due to the enclosed vestibules.

Enclosed vestibules were also inspected in Bradford. Nearly new cars were examined in Liverpool. They were four wheeled cars with a 17ft body and 7ft 6in. wheelbase. The General Manager, Mr Mallins, showed the drawings of two experimental cars, one of which was a bogie car. The four wheeled car on a 16ft body had cross seats on both decks with platforms considerably greater in length than usual, with separate entrance and exit and two staircases on each platform, one for ascending and one for descending. Neither car had vestibules, but both could be arranged for a "pay as you enter system" if required. They were impressed with the greater number of seats on the Liverpool cars, but as this would reduce the number of standing passengers they were not recommended for Hull. The increased wheelbase had advantages, but the City Engineer had experimented with a truck whose wheel base had been temporarily increased to 7ft 6in., but found the sharp curves in Hull did not favour them. The City Engineer had also visited Southend to inspect radial trucks but did not recommend them for Hull.

Opinions of towns visited regarding closed vestibules differed, with the majority agreeing that the draughts caused by ordinary enclosed vestibules were a greater disadvantage to the driver than other protection afforded to him. To prevent these draughts it was necessary to have a means of closing either the staircase opening or the space over the platform entrance step. These added considerably to the construction costs, and created more work for the crew, in that they were required at termini to open and close the doors. The deputation recommended that closed vestibules be not adopted, and that Hull should wait and see what further developments arose from experiments being carried out. However, they did suggest that the upper roof be carried forward over the canopy at each end. They further recommended not to purchase any new cars at that time as the existing fleet was coping with additional passengers carried as a result of the half-penny fare introduction. Closed vestibules had been considered previously. A discussion had been reported by the *Hull Daily Mail* on 2 November 1906, but no action had ensued. One councillor was quoted as saying it would be like putting the men in glass cages, a comment that did not endear him to the men!

On 12 March 1913 a letter from the various Ratepayers Associations again pleaded for a tram service to Stoneferry which would be more suitable than the defunct motorbus service. This was followed by a deputation on 28 March, which was informed that the Committee would give its most serious consideration to the matter (without specifying what might transpire).

In April Mr McCombe

reported on the proposed operation of the Spring Bank West extension. One method was to run between the Chanterlands Avenue terminus and the Cemetery Gates (Botanic Gardens), with the consequent transfer of passengers. He recommended, however, running cars all the way to Queen Victoria Square, partly because no crossover had been provided at the Cemetery Gates. Four cars could provide a six-minute frequency and relieve the strain on the Spring Bank route, and eliminate additional morning cars operated between Botanic Gardens and King Edward Street. The statement that no crossover had been provided at Cemetery Gates is interesting because contemporary NER plans show one such in Princes Avenue opposite the station entrance as do some (but not all) track plans that have been published. It is thought that the crossover at Derringham Street on Spring Bank was still in situ. It has not been possible to determine whether the Princes Avenue crossover was ever provided although a John Gillham plan had this near Welbeck Street. Photographs have proved inconclusive.

Final approval for the Paragon Station loop was given on 16 May 1913. The plan considered also showed the two most easterly sidings in Queen Victoria Square connected to the tramway

This confirms how straight were the majority of Hull's tracks. This is near Saner Street on Anlaby Road. (MJW)

Car no. 68 negotiates one of the fountains in Princes Avenue. (MJW)

in St John Street, to enable them to be used by the Hessle Road and Anlaby Road cars. This layout was amended at the June meeting, when the City Engineer was authorised to install an additional crossover in St John Street to enable the Hessle Road and Anlaby Road cars to use the sidings without alterations.

Delays caused by the river bridges continued to disrupt services, and in May 1913 the City Engineer obtained the agreement of the Bridges Committee and the Tramways Committee to the installation of a scheme of signalling which would obviate, to some extent, those delays.

The question of split shifts was raised once more at the May 1913 meeting. The local branch of the Amalgamated Association of Tramways and Vehicle Workers threatened drastic measures unless a 51 hour week was introduced and the split shift abandoned. Mr McCombe had some sympathy with the aversion to the split shift since they were, in Hull, 8am to 1pm and 6pm to 11pm, but no undertaking had managed to abolish it. In compiling a new timetable he had tried to solve the problem by suggesting that two new types of employee be adopted. One would combine the duties of car washer at night in the depot and a motorman during the day, and the other to combine the duties of car washer at night and conductor during the day. The split shift work could be divided amongst men who could work outside and inside. In both cases men would be paid at the higher rate. Consideration was deferred whilst a copy of the report was issued to the Union.

Members expressed concern about the rising cost of maintaining the tram car fleet. On 30 July 1913 the Tramways Sub-Committee visited the Liverpool Street Car Shed to inspect facilities. The City Engineer and Tramway Electrical Engineer (but not the Tramway Manager) were instructed to report in detail on the wages paid to the different classes of workmen employed at the several depots over the last five years, costs of material used, and the number of cars running from each depot during that period, and to make any recommendations that they wished concerning this matter.

At the same meeting the sub-Committee agreed to introduce

a transfer ticket system between the Spring Bank West and Newland Avenue routes, to be reviewed when half-penny stages came into operation.

On 9 October 1913 the Spring Bank West extension to Walton Street opened and the first car from the new terminus was observed by Mr McCombe, Councillor Hargreave (Lord Mayor designate and a Tramways Committee member), and a *Hull Daily Mail* reporter. The latter reported that the route letter "SW" was carried together with a glass sign "Chanterlands Avenue" in the windows. A ten minute service was provided until 7.30am, and a six-minute one thereafter. On the basis of the first day's takings the reporter didn't think that receipts would be greatly augmented! He thought that the Committee saw it as an accommodation route.

It is thought that the triangular junction at Botanic Gardens was brought into use at this time. No mention of it seems to have been recorded. Whilst it was used for Hull Fair Specials its primary use may have been for depot workings, since it avoided the necessity for cars to negotiate the level crossing and reverse in Spring Bank. A contemporary NER drawing of the area shows a crossover in Princes Avenue outside the station entrance.

His report was adopted and he was authorised to arrange an experimental trial of the new system on the Hessle Road route.

Also in October the North Eastern Railway asked for clarification about the Paragon Square tramway. The Committee confirmed the intention to build the anti-clockwise line but also informed the NER that at some point it may wish to make this a double line and put in two crossovers to enable cars to turn back at Paragon Station. No such proposal was ever placed before the Committee.

On 12 November 1913 the Chairman, Councillor Robson, resigned due to ill health and the Mayor (Councillor Hagan) took the chair until the annual appointments in late 1914.

On 6 January 1914 Mr McCombe submitted a long report regarding a possible revision to the existing fares system. He stated that the universal penny fare had been in existence since the opening of the electric tramways in July 1899, the only variant being the "halfpenny-all-the-way" fare before 9 o'clock in the morning which started in July 1908. There was no doubt that the uniform one penny fare had proved popular with tramway riders but in recent times there had arisen a feeling that short distance riders should be specially catered for and that fares should be more equitably adjusted to the distances which people might wish to travel, especially with the recent and proposed extensions.

The Tramways Committee had recently decided against charging an additional half-penny on the Hedon Road extension to Marfleet. Mr McCombe considered it advisable to refer back to the Tramways Committee decision of 28 February 1912 which were subsequently rejected by the full Council:

1. that the policy of charging one penny as far as the car goes should be continued and that this should include any subsequent extensions
2. that the transfer system should discontinued and a half-penny fare be charged on the Old Town route
3. that the half-penny fare be continued between 5 o'clock and 9 o'clock in the mornings, the same fare to be charged independently on the Old Town route
4. that half-penny fixed stages be instituted on the suburban routes after 9 o'clock
5. that three half-penny stages cover each route and that one penny be the fare over the whole route.

The changes were suggested to meet the modern passenger demand for a ride to give as nearly as possible value for the fare paid. Of the two ways of meeting this demand, namely by half-penny stages or transfer tickets, tramway practice was almost unanimously against transfer tickets which were complicated to issue, difficult to control and open to much abuse.

Although the penny uniform fare had been exceedingly popular in Hull it was necessary to move with the times and adjust the fares to more modern requirements. These would meet the wishes of the travelling public and would result in a large increase of passengers carried without affecting the financial stability of the undertaking. He listed twenty one stages (see appendix 2 for the full list). His recommendations were accepted but he was instructed to arrange for a trial period on the Hessle Road route. This commenced on 15 February 1914.

In March 1914 Mr McCombe informed the Tramways Committee that the new half-penny fare stages on the Hessle Road route had seen an increase of 377,715 passengers compared with a decrease of 189,693 paying the penny fare (a net increase of 188,022). Receipts for the five week period had fallen from £3087 11s 11½d to £3084 2s 4d, a reduction of just £3 9s 7½d! It was agreed to institute the new system over the whole system, the actual stages on each route to be fixed in consultation with the representatives of the several wards concerned.

Before it could be introduced the Board of Trade advised the Corporation no half-penny stage could be under a half mile distance. The Mayor and Town Clerk visited the Board of Trade and this was confirmed, although it approved the general policy of stages. The Chairman and Deputy Chairman consulted representatives of several wards through which the routes ran, and a revised scheme was submitted to the Tramways Committee on 6 May. It was agreed to continue the Old Town transfer system and to apply a half-penny fare between Victoria Pier and Paragon Station. The first full week of operation from 18 May saw an increase of 97,311 passengers but a reduction of £10 12s 3½d in receipts.

The Hessle Road extension to Pickering Park gates opened on 16 February 1914. Owing to protracted negotiations about the

A busy scene at Whitefriargate Bridge with a car entering Queen Victoria Square after negotiating the bridge in 1913. (MJW)

abolition of the crossing, the installation of equipment was delayed, and passengers had to transfer between both sides of the crossing. Not until 6 June 1915 were through cars introduced.

In March 1914 the issue of vestibules for tram cars was considered again. The Chairman, Deputy Chairman, the City Engineer and the Tramway Manager had been on their travels once more, this time to Leeds, Leicester, Burnley and Bradford as well as the UEC's works at Preston and Brush at Loughborough. They inspected several types of vestibule cars including a "wind-screen" in Leicester which was rejected. The cars at Burnley particularly impressed them, as they considered that they provided adequate protection for motormen without interfering with their hearing or sight. The Burnley manager estimated that the cost was £25 per car. They were also convinced that short cars rather than long bogie cars were best suited for Hull, and recommended that the City Engineer invite tenders for twenty cars and equipments, and that these be fitted with vestibules of the type mentioned.

On 20 April 1914 prints of the new cars were submitted to the Board of Trade. The design followed previous deliveries but had enclosed vestibules and platforms, and canopies six inches longer to provide room for a working brake handle and controller inside the vestibule. The roof at the top was to be carried over the canopy and a means of closing the staircase opening was to be provided to prevent draughts. Additional seating would be provided on the canopy. The Board approved the design but added the provision of side guards, but not until 5 August 1914 did the City Engineer state that he proposed to fix Philipson's Patent Automatic Side Lifeguards manufactured by Philips & Co of Astley Bridge, Bolton.

An information (promotional) brochure accompanied the letter from the City Engineer. This claimed that the only lifeguard that had proved worthy of the name was the Philipson's Patent Flexible Cradle and Patent Side Lifeguard combined. Unlike the "dangerous and unsafe "gate and cradle" type with wood or iron cradles" the Philipson's version "was entirely automatic and free from complication" and "met the requirements of the Board of Trade Inspectors".

It was claimed that it was the only appliance for safeguarding anyone from falling under the platform of a tramcar, between the gap, caused by the distance between the front gate and the cradle. It was hinged to the framework of the car and was free to move lengthwise backward or forward yet was rigid to resist side shock.

An adjunct to the visits to other operators was that members recommended that new applicants for the tramway service be medically examined before entering the service. Much useful information had been gathered on their travels which would be used to improve various parts of the service, but overall they considered that they had little to learn from other undertakings.

The question of congestion and delays was raised by two correspondents in May 1914 and October 1914. The first suggested that outward bound tram cars on the northern routes should use the proposed new road from Paragon Station to Beverley Road to eliminate the need to turn out of Brook Street in peak times. This road was not opened until twenty years later, and no tram ventured along it. The second suggested that the "P" and "TH" trams should use the proposed line in Waterworks Street to eliminate the conflict with the Anlaby Road and Hessle Road cars.

On 15 May the Committee decided to order twenty car bodies from the Brush Electrical Engineering Company Ltd at a cost of £481 each, together with ordinary parallel control motors from Siemens (£181 per pair and latest pattern controllers at £43 per pair). The City Engineer did not recommend the trucks of Brill manufacture proposed by Siemens, and opted for trucks from the M and G Truck and Engineering Company Ltd at a cost of £49 17s 6d. Other equipment included resistances from the Electro-Mechanical Brake Co Ltd, trolley standards from Brecknell, Munro and Rogers, trolley booms from The Equipment and Engineering Co., and trolley heads from William Wood & Co.

Messrs Siemens Brothers had written to the Corporation stating that they were prepared to provide 24 car sets of gear wheels and pinions of material on which they had now standardised. These would be free of charge if they received the present order for equipments and would replace equipments previously supplied. The City Engineer had contacted the company to ascertain if a superior type of gear known as the "Scholey" gear could be supplied. Siemens were prepared to do so but at an extra cost of £9 5s per equipment. As it had not been decided which form of "Scholey" gear to adopt the matter was delegated to the Mayor, Deputy-Chairman, City Engineer and Tramway Electrical Engineer.

A report from the Board of Trade dated 12 May 1914 approving public operation of the Paragon Station line was submitted to the Committee. Speeds were restricted to 12 miles an hour in Jameson Street, Paragon Square and Anlaby Road, and four miles an hour around the curve between Brook Street and Anlaby Road. The extension was 2 furlongs 0.50 chains long, the sharpest curve had a radius of 40' and the steepest gradient was 1 in 143!

In May the Tramway Manager received approval to ask the Chief Constable to provide point duty policemen at the junctions of King Edward Street/Jameson Street, Brook Street/Anlaby Road and Park Street/Spring Bank. Authority was given to provide enclosed vestibules for some of the existing tramway cars.

The experience of riding on Hull's tramcars when a boy was recalled by Mr Laurie Coulson in a Manpower Services Commission publication in 1988. His family used to catch the "S" tram, and he mentions the treat when going along Princes Avenue of the trams grinding round the fountains in the middle of the road. There was a very acute curve involved and the trams made awful noises. Small boys would grab at the trees when open top cars were used. He enjoyed open trams in fine weather but not in worse weather. Also he enjoyed the sight of the conductor pulling the trolley boom down with a hook and turning it round, not always succeeding to place it on the overhead at the first attempt. A shower of sparks was the result. He also remembered the conductor going along the car to change direction of the seating.

He stated that the tramways employed boys called orderlies who had a little barrow and equipment with which they used to sweep the road, going along the tramlines with a metal rod in front of the sweeping brush to scrape all the dirt out of the gap between the rails, and then sweeping up the accumulated dirt. All this in the middle of the road!

The financial year 1913/1914 saw a net surplus of £14526 2s 0d of which £7,000 was allocated to the relief of rates. 45,679,094 passengers were carried who paid £165,893 in fares. Car mileage was 4,229,625 and route mileage was 18 miles 6 chains and 2.28 furlongs.

A royal visit took place on 26 June 1914 in order to officially open the King George Dock at Marfleet. Additional pay was granted to those who were working on that day, and approximately seven thousand school children were conveyed to and from Hedon Road free of charge on the morning of the visit.

However, the assassination of Archduke Franz Ferdinand at Sarajevo on 28 June 1914 led to the outbreak of war with Germany in August 1914, and the deferment of any developments for the next few years. The Tramways Sub-Committee had resolved on 15 July to seek powers to extend the Anlaby Road route to the city boundary at Calvert Lane, for a single line down Paragon Street and from Carr Lane through Chariot Street to Victoria Square and double lines from Witham along Cleveland Street and Stoneferry Road as far as the corner of Leads Road and Stoneferry Road.

The increased number of cars using the Cottingham Road Car Shed led to a serious complaint from the owner of no. 60 Cottingham Road who claimed that the vibration when cars left the depot in the morning and returned at night was causing great damage to his property. He asked the Corporation to buy it from him at the same price (£325) that he had paid for it. The matter was left to various officials and the purchase subsequently took place.

Notwithstanding the imminence of war a major re-equipment of Liverpool Street Workshops was instituted. An overhead travelling crane was purchased from Messrs Herbert Morris at a cost of £489 and a traverser from Messrs Cowans, Sheldon & Co. for £245. The quotation of £194 10s from Messrs W.G. Bagnell Ltd for two turntables at the workshops was accepted and three roller shutters were bought from Messrs A.L. Gibson & Co. for £167 8s despite a lower quote from The Wilson Roller Shutter Co. The City Engineer said that the Gibson bid was more advantageous to the Corporation. Two additional sets, together with the required power pump, of Quadruple Hydraulic Jacks for lifting cars bodies were purchased from Messrs Youngs of Birmingham.

Chapter 6

THE FIRST WORLD WAR

The effects were felt immediately within the Tramways Department. In August ninety men joined the colours including 30 motormen and 50 conductors. Some were Reservists or Territorials. Steps were taken to fill the vacancies on a temporary basis, and the wages of absent men were paid in accordance with the Corporation's agreed scale.

The Automatic Ticket Printing Company Ltd. informed the Corporation that they were unable to obtain the special paper used for printing tickets, and a new agreement was concluded at a price increase of 1d per 1000 tickets.

On 28 October 1914 Mr McCombe reported the death in action on 28 September of a former conductor, Private Albert Haldenby (2nd Coldstream Guards). He left a widow and it was agreed to pay wages to his widow for the time being. This was the first of what was to become a monthly report of deaths or "missing in action", usually of army personnel but not exclusively so. Formal condolences were conveyed to the family of the men concerned. Dependant upon circumstances, wages were usually paid for a while until the army pension started, or a pension was provided under the terms of the Kingston upon Hull Local Government Act 1903. Acts of bravery including the award of a decoration were also reported, as were promotions or recommendations for a Commission.

When the Town Clerk informed the Committee that the Parliamentary Bill which included tramway proposals had been abandoned, he was asked to seek a Provisional Order for the Anlaby Road and Waterworks Street proposals. This duly became the Kingston upon Hull Tramways Order 1915, and provided for a westward extension from the existing Anlaby Road tramway 0.70 chains west of Wheeler Street along Anlaby Road to the city boundary, some 0.15 of a chain south east of the Calvert Lane intersection with Anlaby Road. The double line extension named Tramway No. 1 would be 2 furlongs 0.40 chains long. The other, Tramway No. 2, was just over 1 furlong in length from the intersection of Chariot Street and Carr Lane, running north along Chariot Street and east along Waterworks Street, to form a junction with the existing tramway in Queen Victoria Square at a point 1.20 chains south of the New Cross Street/King Edward Street intersection.

Note that the Anlaby Road extension was to Calvert Lane only and not as is usually thought to Pickering Lane (Road). That came later.

Equipment ordered from Messrs Siemens had been considerably delayed, which the company attributed to war conditions. The Acting City Engineer disagreed, as the first six should have been delivered before 24 August, and said that other factors must be involved. He refused to sanction a payment until this had been resolved to his satisfaction. Members of the Committee visited Anlaby Road Depot to see the work on the assembly of

The employment of female conductors in the Great War caused much friction between the Corporation and the labour organisations. They were given smart uniforms as shown here. Also on show are the cash bag and ticket punch. (PG)

the new cars, and to Liverpool Street to view similar work, and the new workshops under construction.

It has always been assumed that new car building and assembly work had been undertaken at Liverpool Street Works, but clearly this was not the case, although it is unclear how much work was undertaken at Anlaby Road, and whether this was occurring due to the shortage of space at Liverpool Street. All twenty cars (numbered 161 to 180), the first with vestibules, entered service between February and June 1915.

The Tramwaymen's Union asked that drivers and conductors in uniform should have free travel at all times, but the Committee refused and reminded the Union that travel to and from duty in uniform was free of charge.

Two cars were decorated for recruiting purposes, and ran at selective times on individual routes from October 1914, but had apparently ceased to run because Lord Nunburnholme wrote to the Committee in December asking that they be re-started at the beginning of January 1915. The matter was left to the Chairman,

These two cars are near Boulevard where the memorial to the Hull fisherman killed by the Russian Fleet can be seen. (MJW)

Deputy-Chairman and the Tramway Manager to resolve. Twelve recruits per car were able to ride free of charge.

In January 1915 the head of the West Division of the Local Emergency Committee informed the Corporation that Liverpool Street Works had been selected as a first aid post in the event of an air raid, and in the event of an invasion, a concentration point. Holderness Road Depot had been selected for a similar role for the eastern part of the city.

The first of several pay claims that were received with some regularity during the war years was deferred on 24 February 1915. An increase of 5s per week, taking the motormen's maximum wage to 40s per week, and 3s per week for conductors, taking their maximum to 35s per week, was sought. The minimum wage for conductors under the age of 21 was to be 24s a week. Two main reasons were advanced, the extra work from the fare stage system and the increased cost of living due to the war.

Workshop staff employed in private industry were already paid an extra 3s per week, and this had been extended to Corporation employees of a similar nature. After receiving a deputation from the platform staff union it was decided to pay a "war bonus" of 3s per week to those men receiving over 30s per week and 2s to those under 30s per week.

The new cars finally began to enter service in March 1915. Nos 161/2/5/9/70/2 commenced work in March, with the last cars nos 178 and 180 entering service in June 1915.

The Works Committee on 26 March 1915 resolved that all architectural work formerly handled by the City Engineer should transfer to the City Architect's Department, and that all tramway matters apart from laying and maintaining track would transfer to the Tramway Manager. The exact nature of the work involved was not described nor was the matter raised at the Tramways Committee.

On 8 April 1915 the *Hull Daily Mail* contained a photograph (in Queen Victoria Square) of the new indicators that would inform motormen which of North Bridge and Drypool Bridge was open or shut. The indicators were located in the Square and at

In 1914 two unidentified cars were decorated as recruiting cars and ran on each route in turn. The first twelve recruits travelled free. Note the unique route board. (PM)

Dansom Lane just before the junction of Witham and Clarence Street. This gave motormen clear information regarding the bridges (except for Whitefriargate Bridge which was also opened but with less regularity). It was accepted that the arrangement might inconvenience some passengers but it was thought that only a small majority were involved and that the time saving outweighed this inconvenience. A full description of the system can be found in Appendix 3.

With the loss of so many experienced men the Tramways Department found it very difficult to maintain a service with untrained men. After discussions with Mr McCombe, the Chairman's recommendation that the TH service be discontinued for the period of the war was accepted by the Committee.

Mr McCombe reported that to maintain services men had been asked to work a certain amount of overtime, and the local branch of the Amalgamated Vehicle Workers had agreed provided it did not exceed 12 hours per week. It was also willing to forego the week's holiday provided the week was worked at overtime rates. The Tramways Committee agreed to pay a week's wages in lieu of holiday in addition to the week's pay.

The cost of obtaining new rails had also risen and the City Engineer had considered alternative methods of repairing lengths of track that had been hammered (his word) by heavy traffic. In some places the wheel flange pressed on the bottom of the groove and in one or two cases the rail had split at the bottom of the groove.

In many cases the full length of rail was in good condition with only a small portion being defective. He had made enquiries about modern methods of repair, and had arranged a demonstration by the Acetylene Illuminating Company to build up some worn places by the high pressure oxy-acetylene process, using a particularly bad example in Prospect Street. The result proved very satisfactory and he recommended the purchase of an outfit for £40. The work had cost about £1 per joint – much less than cutting out and replacing a length of rail.

The same meeting authorised the Tramway Manager to make such arrangements about the Spring Bank West service as he thought fit.

Following the decision to suspend the TH service, the East Hull Progressive Party urged the Corporation to reinstate the service as soon as possible after the war. It suggested that the cars should cease running to Paragon Station and terminate in Queen Victoria Square as previously, and to introduce a transfer system for the Pier or Station.

Previous references have referred to the Pier service only as running to the station. The TH service would have been very convenient for Holderness Road residents who wished to travel to the station or the shops nearby, more useful than the main H service.

The Tramway Manager reported on the continuing lack of suitable staff, and suggested withdrawing the Old Town route, thus leaving the station without a direct service from the east. This question and that of restrictions of frequencies on several routes was left to the Chairman, Deputy-Chairman and the Tramway Manager to take such steps as they deemed necessary.

Difficulties had arisen at the Dairycoates terminus since the space between the crossover and the catch points was sufficient for one car only. When a Pickering Park car was held up at the railway gates, D cars were unable to use the crossover, with a consequent delay to the service. The old crossover at Carlton Street could not be used as it required extensive repair, and his suggestion that this be abolished and a new crossover installed nearer the railway crossing was approved.

A Zeppelin raid occurred on 7 June 1915 and caused damage in the Old Town so that the Pier service terminated at Church Lane for a time.

A profit of £14574 11s 11d was achieved in 1914-1915.

In June 1915 the Departmental Inquiry (Special) Committee submitted its report on the management of the tramways. It considered that the staff were generally efficient and experienced, but the present system of divided control was not in the best interest of the undertaking. It revealed that the charge for the City Engineer's staff employed in the Liverpool Street workshops included an additional ten per cent for overheads. This forced up the repair and overall running costs to an artificial level. Persons responsible for the upkeep of cars and equipment, electricity generation and all other engineering costs, had no control over speeds, loading and driving of cars. There was general acceptance that cars were heavily overloaded, which led to heavy repair costs and a higher level of electricity consumption than it should have been. The meters on the cars were read regularly by the Tramway Electrical Engineer's staff, but no action was taken by anyone.

On 9 June 1915 a special meeting of the Tramways Committee considered the employment of women conductors. These were being employed all over the country, and the Chairman suggested that Glasgow (with the longest experience) and Newcastle be visited to obtain information, and that a register be opened for suitable women over the age of 25 to indicate their interest.

Two weeks later the Committee considered the results of the visits, and letters strongly criticising any decision to employ women. Various trade organisations strongly protested and considered that there were many tradesmen without work due to the war who could be employed. Predictably the Amalgamated Association of Tramway and Vehicle Drivers (AATVW) thought it a dangerous and unwise decision. If the Corporation relaxed its probation regulations it would be easier to find more conductors. The Hull Labour Party considered it not essential to the moral and material welfare of the public, and thought that the male labour supply was not exhausted.

All in vain, as the Committee was impressed by the results of both visits. Newcastle saw the experiment as a quite a success, with women carrying out their fair share of the work apart from early workmen's cars, although they were assisted in that a number of cars were single-deckers.

Glasgow employed 300 women and expected to employ one hundred more. A parade of sixty women who had just completed their training and were preparing to take up their duties was observed. They wore uniforms of the same material as the men, although it was planned to provide a lighter skirt. They received 27s a week which was the usual minimum rate. The innovation was exceedingly popular in the city and had justified all expectations.

Employment of women in Hull was necessary because of the shortage of suitable men, and would be successful given the evidence of the two visits. The report recommended that women be employed during the emergency created by the war, and that proper training should be provided for them and their personal accommodation. It was suggested that the recently purchased dwelling house adjoining Cottingham Road Depot should be set apart for them.

In Glasgow members had observed a small mirror placed on the front side of a car to enable the motorman to keep the rear step in view, and so avoid starting the car when persons were alighting in the absence of a conductor. Mr Dalrymple, the Glasgow manager, had provided an example to bring back with them, and their strong recommendation that all cars be fitted without delay was agreed.

On 9 June 1915 the Board of Trade wrote to the Corporation to confirm that the Hessle Road extension was fit for public traffic and that electric traction could be used. Maximum speed was 16mph and compulsory stops were necessary in both directions at the Dairycoates railway crossing. Operation over the crossing had commenced on 6 June.

The argument about women conductors rumbled on. Unions still claimed that sufficient men were available, who were ineligible for military service, to meet the requirements of the tramway service. It was seen as a ruse to introduce casual labour. Had the Corporation listened to them and reorganised duties there would be no problem. Unless the scheme was withdrawn they would refuse absolutely to work with women conductors on and after Monday 12 July. Not only did the Committee confirm their decision but they approved a letter drafted by the Town Clerk for submission to the Press to inform the public of their intention.

Support for the decision came from the Hull and District Chamber of Trade on 8 July, but a meeting of the Joint Committee of the Hull Trades and Labour and the AATVW rescinded the previous resolution, and agreed to leave the matter in the hands of a joint deputation to negotiate with the Tramways Committee.

The ten man deputation met the Tramways Committee on 14 July. It contained one local councillor as president of the Council, and a Salford Alderman. They asked for several assurances in that men would be employed in preference to women, applications being made to the Union for suitable men before the employment of women, an assurance that all women would be dispensed with when the war ended (thereby giving a tacit acceptance of their employment), and a formal agreement between the Corporation and the Local Trades Council. Their case was not helped by Motorman Knight and Conductor Close who also attended the meeting and supported the employment of women conductors.

The Committee assured them that suitable men would be given preference (no definition of "suitable"), that applications submitted by the Union would be considered, that women conductors would be dispensed with when the war ended, and when Corporation employees returned. The Committee was not prepared to enter into a formal agreement but their assurances were accepted by the Local Trades and Labour Council on 18 July.

In October 1915 the Tramways Committee received a letter from Messrs Feldman and Gosschalks, Solicitors complaining about large sums of money being spent vestibuling a number of cars at the Liverpool Street Depot. They considered it absolutely unnecessary, as they understood that cars in question were only purchased twelve months ago. The Chairman reminded members that they had agreed to set aside a sum of money to provide vestibules for certain cars some time ago, and that the work was proceeding steadily using funds specially set aside. The cars involved were not those purchased twelve months ago.

On 4 August The Local Government Board asked local authorities to consider what economies could be made. The Tramways Electrical Engineer stated that no less than 78 men had already joined the Forces, whilst 14 had been seconded to munitions work. Any further reduction in staff or materials would make it impossible to maintain the present service level of cars. Twenty additional cars were helping to convey men engaged in various parts of the city on munitions work, and any further economies or staff reductions would seriously affect these workers. The Committee was informed that the only work being carried out on the track was the turning of wood blocks and the overhauling of rail joints in those cases where it was absolutely necessary.

Indeed, difficulties were being experienced in obtaining tyres, and the City Engineer, the Chairman and Deputy-Chairman were empowered to order any tyres as they considered suitable.

Complaints were received about lights in the lower saloons showing through the curtains, many of which had shrunk considerably. The City Engineer said that replacement would cost about 15s per car. At a further meeting it was decided to approach the military authorities and, if necessary, visit Newcastle to inspect the system of lighting adopted.

In March 1916 Hull was subjected to another air raid which led to some track damage at the junction of Alfred Gelder Street and Lowgate.

The Tramway Electrical Engineer had made enquiries about two emergency tower wagons that were electrically driven by means of storage batteries which he considered to be both efficient and economical in use. He was authorised to obtain process for both petrol and battery driven wagons.

The profit for 1915/6 was £12,468 of which £10,000 was given to rate relief. Of the 180 cars in stock an average of 90 were employed during the 16 hour day compared with 97 in the previous year. Car mileage was down by some 48,000 miles whilst passenger numbers had increased by 165,000, raising the average fare per car mile to 9.54 compared with 8.53.

Hull's economy suffered greatly during the war. Wilson Line lost 47 ships, and many trawlers were requisitioned by the Admiralty. There were reductions in fishing and foreign trade since Hull's traditional Baltic markets were largely closed. Shipbuilding fell by 75% until 1917, when it began to rise once more. Some factories were converted to munitions making, often staffed by women at lower wages as 70,000 men from a population of 291,118 were ultimately in the Armed Forces. By March 1915 160 tramway men were serving the colours, 27% of the work force.

The Tramways Committee had not attempted to obtain exemptions for staff from military service. However, the Tramway Manager was concerned at the potential loss of further staff, the Tramway Electrical Engineer had already lost 92 staff, and it was possible that a further 68 might be called up within the next few days. The matter was left to the Chairman, Deputy-Chairman and the officers concerned.

Subsequently, in October 1916, a deputation attended the Committee meeting and requested a definite statement regarding action about the position of tram drivers under the latest Military Service Act developments. The Committee refused to change its position and re-affirmed that no appeals would be made in respect of any tramway employee.

In another effort to alleviate the strain caused by the loss of staff to the armed services, men in power station engine rooms (cleaners and storekeepers) had been replaced with female employees.

Another request for free travel came from the Hull and District United Purity Campaign asking that Woman Patrols be allowed to ride free on tramcars when on duty. Only six to eight women were involved. The Rev A.T. Greenwood attended the June meeting of the Tramways Committee to press the case, but the Committee neatly side-stepped the issue by pointing out that the work of the women patrols was carried out in conjunction with local constabulary, and it might be more appropriate if they applied to the Watch Committee for assistance!

When the Tramway Manager suggested that women conductors be given a seat on the tramcars, the matter was delegated to the Chairman, his Deputy, the City Engineer and himself to consider it. No further mention appears in the minutes so we do not know if they were provided.

In October the double bogie car no. 101 was sold to Erith Urban District Council for the sum of £400. It was transported by sea arriving at Erith Pier not far from the depot. It was renumbered 19 and remained in service until the London Passenger Transport Board took over and promptly withdrew the open top cars. It is believed that it was scrapped at Brixton Hill depot.

A view of another recruiting car this time on Holderness Road. (MJW)

When the Traffic Charge-Man at Anlaby Road Depot was found guilty of allowing lights to be shown at the depot he was fined £10 by the Justices of the Peace. The Committee agreed to pay him an extra £10 in respect of paying the fine.

The City Engineer reminded the Tramways Sub-Committee on 28 November 1916 of projects that were still outstanding. These included the Anlaby Road and Beverley Road extensions, the Waterworks Street line, completion of the workshops at Liverpool Street, and additional power and provision of coal storage at the Power Station.

The situation at the Power Station was the most critical. With the generating capacity almost used up, power was already being taken from the Corporation's station at Sculcoates. Additional coal storage could be put in hand fairly quickly, but he did not think that tenders for new machinery would be answered, except at a very high cost. The work at Liverpool Street could be completed without much delay. Not enough rails were in stock for all three extensions, and he would recommend the Waterworks Street scheme if one were to be approved. However, there was only enough paving in stock for a few months, and he was loath to use this. The Sub-Committee made no immediate decision but referred the report to the Parliamentary Committee.

The Tramways Committee on 29 November considered a letter from the Ministry of Munitions of War requesting (i.e. ordering) the release of fifteen bodymakers and two wiremen for work of greater importance elsewhere. It was left to the Chairman, Deputy-Chairman and Town Clerk to sort it out.

The same Committee received a deputation of motormen who stated that a motorman rated fit for home service had left to take up munitions work. However, he had retained his uniform, and when not working at Priestman's Works he was driving cars on a Saturday afternoon and on a Sunday, and in his spare time worked overtime at 1s per hour. The deputation wanted to know if this privilege could be extended to other former motormen.

The Committee thought this must stop and wrote to the person concerned, asking him to decide for whom he wished to work as he could not have the two jobs.

The Hull and District Chamber of Trade urged the Committee to cease running at the earlier time of 11pm on week nights and 10.30pm on Sundays to secure some economy whilst the war continued. Discussion had taken place at the previous meeting with some members suggesting weekday cessation at 10.45pm and 10.30pm on Sundays.

Mr McCombe said that some undertakings had already curtailed evening services owing to the dark streets, the earlier closing of shops and the consequential diminution of tramway traffic. Changes had been accepted in good spirit by the travelling public. Many factors needed to be taken into account, especially the convenience of the travelling public. Most places of amusement closed at 10.30pm the latest being 11pm. There was also the question of workpeople whose shifts started and finished at those times such as the Post Office staff. The floating traffic between 10.30pm and 11.30pm was not sufficient to pay for the service, but revenue matters alone should not always determine the level of service.

On the other hand there was the constant heavy strain upon crews, and with the dark streets came an increased risk of accidents. There would undoubtedly be a saving in wear and tear, but there would be no real saving in staff time unless the cars were taken off the road much earlier in the night. He recommended that cars cease running at 11pm from Queen Victoria Square (instead of 11.24pm on ordinary nights and 11. 40pm on Saturdays) and at 10pm on Sundays (formerly 10.48pm). The recommendations were adopted but not after some heated discussion and a number of motions.

When the Tramwaymen's Union suggested that no cars be run on Christmas Day but that the men be paid for a normal day it was rejected and cars were to run as usual.

In an effort to increase income, commissioned officers in the forces had to pay fares from 5 June 1916. In November 1916 it was decided that all non-commissioned officers and men should pay a flat rate of one-half-penny on the cars. However, the full Council meeting referred this back for further consideration and the matter was re-examined on 13 December.

The Chairman (Councillor Wheatley) was not pleased with the Council's decision. He didn't think that the seriousness of the Tramways Committee's situation in terms of revenue and numbers riding on the cars had been understood by Council members. He felt that the flat fare should be introduced partly to remove the situation where riding to music halls, cinemas, clubs and football matches was free, but Sunday travel to church or chapel was not. The original intention was to provide free travel to and from places where drill was performed. By 1915, however, Hull was alone in providing free travel for the armed forces.

Not twenty per cent of the men in khaki were Hull men, and they were incredulous when told that travel was free, as it was unknown elsewhere. The number of military men travelling had risen greatly at the expense and inconvenience of the daily users who were faced with full cars. In his opinion cars were provided for workers and shoppers and, given the Department's inability to provide a full service due to a shortage of skilled men, promiscuous travel must be discouraged.

Therefore he recommended the following:

Although there was much opposition to the use of women to take fares everything seems amicable in this shot of no. 106. (PM)

1. All soldiers and sailors and non-commissioned officers be charged a flat rate of one half-penny
2. Morning fares from 5am to 9am be raised to the full stage tariff in operation after 9am
3. The Old Town route be treated as a stage, and the transfer system be abolished.

If these were to be adopted the Corporation would be better placed to meet the growing level of expenditure in which the war had involved them, namely:

1. War bonuses
2. Allowances to our brave boys in His Majesty's Service
3. Increased cost generally of maintenance
4. The recognition that at the conclusion of the war increased expenditure would have to be faced in the direction of extra repairs, renewals, alterations and essential improvements to the cars. (He didn't say so, but the oldest cars were now 18 years old).

He recommended a reduction in the number of stopping places to save current and eliminate wear and tear on the equipment. This was agreed although there were many objectors.

He did not get all his own way. It was agreed that no alteration be made to the arrangements for carrying military personnel, the Old Town route was to continue complete with transfer system, and the early morning fares were to continue. A flat rate fare of one penny was to be charged on all routes after 9am. The Committee called for a further report regarding curtailing the service on every route.

Once again the Council referred the matter back to the Committee which met again on 3 January 1917. Nine motions were tabled and the discussion became animated to say the least! The results were that it was agreed that all non-commissioned officers and men were to be charged a half-penny fare, early morning fares to be unaltered, the Old Town route was to be half-penny stage, and a penny fare be charged on all routes (except the Old Town route) after 9am. A further report on the length of fare stages was requested. Finally, it was agreed, subject to Council approval, the new arrangements to be introduced on 15 January 1917.

As if to emphasise the department's fragile situation there was a short breakdown at the Power Station on the day of the Committee meeting. No apparent reason could be discerned, but the accident left the undertaking without any reserve power.

Fares were considered once more at the next meeting on 24

January 1917, when a letter from the Amalgamated Society of Smiths and Strikers protesting at the decision to abolish the ½d fare was read out. The Tramway Manager submitted the following statistics:

Week Ending	½d passes	1d passes	Total	£	s	d
20 January 1917	327,507	652,796	980,303	3402	5	9
13 January 1917	588,945	467,667	1,056,612	3175	11	8
22 January 1916	588,065	478,637	1,066,702	3219	9	1

	Under new conditions				
	Decrease ½d	Increase 1d	Revenue increase		
			£	s	d
Compare with previous week	261,438	185,129	226	14	2
Compare previous year	260,558	174,159	182	16	8

These figures persuaded the Committee to take no action on the letter.

On 22 January 1917 at 4.10pm Motorman Frederick William Jackson who belonged to the Spring Bank route was working a relief car on the Hedon Road route and had stopped at the town side of North Bridge to let ingoing cars to pass him. When he was free to continue he started on the double line, entered the single line and when taking the points to the double line the car left the track ran across the pavement, mounted the flags and collided with a wall between two stops.

At some point he lost his balance and fell off the car and rolled under the front. When the car stopped he was found pinned beneath the step. He was extricated as soon as possible and taken to the Infirmary.

Mr McCombe reported that he was still there in a dangerous condition and recollected nothing about the accident. Mr McCombe surmised that he put more power on instead of shutting it off, and the consequent rocking of the car caused him to lose his balance and fall off. Mr Jackson had started as a conductor on 14 September 1914 and had become a motorman on 17 September 1915. The damage to the car and shop fronts was, he said, immaterial.

The incident was even reported in *Punch*, the well known satirical magazine, as follows "At Hull, the other day, a tram-car dashed into a grocer's shop. No blame attaches, we understand, to the driver, who sounded his gong three times."

By this time between 70 and 80 conductresses were employed.

The fares question still wouldn't go away and on 1 February the full Council intervened again and rescinded its original resolution, suspending the ½d stages and charging a flat rate of 1d on all routes (Old Town excepted). On 7 February the Tramways Committee decided to reinstate the half-penny stages system, and to ask Mr McCombe to report on short running and stopping places. Five days later the Tramways Sub-Committee met again and decided to discontinue no fewer than forty-nine stopping places. It also considered the possibility of employing women inspectors and short journey cars.

Four days (19 February 1917) later the Tramways Sub-Committee considered a long report from Mr McCombe (who must have burnt the midnight oil!). Short running was already employed on the Hessle Road route to Dairycoates, whilst alternate cars on the Hedon Road route ran only as far as the depot. The needs of the travelling public must be taken into account. There was no point in stopping cars short if demand warranted a full service. To turn short running cars required a crossover and a siding in which the car could wait to allow normal service cars past, or the car must return to the city centre as soon as possible,

with a consequent effect on the frequency over the short part of the route. Add to this the delays from railway crossings and the maintenance of a regular service was almost impossible.

On Hessle Road certain cars turned at Dairycoates despite the fare stage being Hawthorne Avenue, causing some "dead" running between the two points. On Anlaby Road the crossover and stage point coincided at Walton Street, so there would be no problem. It was desirable to continue running to Chanterlands Avenue on the Spring Bank West route. A suitable place for turning cars on the Spring Bank route existed at Queens Road, but the stage point was at Ella Street in Newland Avenue, which meant that passengers would have to alight at Queens Road, or cars must continue to Ella Street and return on the "wrong" line to Queens Road, which was unworkable. The stage point could be relocated to Queens Road. On Beverley Road the crossover was at Stepney but the stage was at Fitzroy Street (down which lay a Hull and Barnsley railway station), so some change would be required. Cars already turned short at the depot on Hedon Road. The crossover on Holderness Road was located at Mile House but the stage was at Jalland Street.

Other constraints included turning the trolley pole in the dark. At the present termini there was a screened overhead light to enable men to turn the pole with little trouble. Even so the light was minimal. There would be no such light at short turning crossovers, with a consequent difficulty in reuniting the pole with the overhead and possible consequent delays to the through

These two employees, status and date unknown (possibly 1915) show off their uniforms" (PG)

This is the only view of a tram outside the Station Hotel which adjoined Paragon Station. (MJW)

cars. An experiment might be worthwhile, and the report suggested that the Holderness Road should, for a short period, act as a trial with cars turning at Jalland Street as there was heavy congestion of traffic at certain times of the day. This suggestion was agreed.

Mr McCombe had considered another suggestion whereby some journeys to Pickering Park would operate from Dairycoates only, and that passengers would transfer across the railway crossing. He didn't like the idea of interrupting the service and considered that passengers would abuse the system.

Most women conductors took fares on the platform before passengers ascended, and he proposed to instruct all conductors to do the same. The employment of women inspectors to supervise women conductors was also discussed, and he suggested meeting with the local union branch first in order to avoid a repetition of recent trouble at Salford. He had ten inspectors at present, and had four vacancies, and he considered it impossible to appoint any more. Another way to eliminate fares "leakage" (ie, fare avoidance) might be to impose a compulsory stop before all stage points after 9 am to enable all fares to be collected.

Absenteeism was a great problem, with 12 motormen and conductors not turning up for work on the previous Saturday, not all with genuine reasons. Many cars did not run at all. Recruitment was falling behind the call-up rate, and it was taking longer to train new employees to the standard required. War industries which were short of

manpower were attracting would-be staff. He admitted that the service was inefficient when compared with pre-war times. Because Hull had never attempted to obtain exemptions it could not release such men and take "general service" (lower grade military men) men in their place in order to maintain numbers.

A complete revision of fare stages was agreed, as was a reduction in the frequency on the Spring Bank West route by half. No action was taken regarding early morning cars, despite the Tramway Manager reporting on fare and revenue levels. For the four weeks in July 1914, revenue was 0.25d below working expenses and for the four weeks commencing 24 November 1916 working expenses were 0.08d below revenue costs. It was also agreed that the summer time service of cars would be the same as the winter service.

The fare stages and fares were the subject of a heated discussion at the full Tramways Committee on 21 February. Argument raged about the adoption of a single flat or through fare of one and a half pence, which was agreed by a small majority. This didn't solve anything, for the Council on 1 March referred back most of the matters for further consideration.

A letter was received from the Transport Officer, Ministry of

This is an April 1915 photograph of one of the new signs recently erected in the city centre to inform crews which bridge was available for use. Cars on the eastern routes (H, M and TH) could use Drypool Bridge if North Bridge was open for river traffic and vice versa. Presumably they were useful for crews operating works journeys along Hedon Road. (MJW)

Munitions, asking how many cars the Corporation possessed, and what number they were prepared to sell or let out on hire. The matter was delegated to two members and two officers, and no more was heard of it.

Notwithstanding the shortage of staff the Department was able to provide ten tram cars for the transport of soldiers to the opening by Lord French of the new V.A.D Hospital at the rear of the Training College on 15 April 1915.

The thorny question of the National Service Scheme arose again in April. The Local Government Board had written to all local authorities to encourage them to release men. The Committee could not really object, and offered to keep the jobs open for permanent staff but not temporary staff. At a subsequent meeting they did change their policy, and agreed to appeal for all men except for grade B1 military men, but in all cases for power station staff and repair shops men.

On 25 April it was agreed to operate all Hedon Road tramcars through to Marfleet as an experiment, instead of alternate cars terminating at the depot. No reason was given, and it is not readily discernible why this change was necessary.

The first deficit was recorded for 1916/17, this amounting to £2,449, being met from the reserve fund. Costs per mile increased from 8.56d to 9.20d. In addition some £2,503 spent on canopies for tram cars and £1,183 for renewals was also charged to the reserve fund. Also some £8,759 was paid to employees on war service.

Following the refusal of a V.A.D nurse to pay a fare when travelling on the Anlaby Road route, the Tramways Committee rescinded its previous decision to allow the St John Ambulance nurses free travel when on duty. This resulted in some expeditious discussions between the two organisations, and an agreement that V.A.D nurses could use tokens when travelling to and from work, the tokens being purchased at 9d a dozen and distribution in the hands of the Association's Colonel Easton.

Having employed women conductors, the Tramway Committee considered their employment as drivers and authorised a visit to such towns where they were employed and to report on the matter. It was also decided to appoint two women as inspectors or supervisors for duties in connection with women employees. Not until December 1917 was the decision taken to train suitable women as drivers.

On 23 May the Tramways Committee reversed its former policy of not appealing against the call up of any of its men, and decided to appeal for all but A and B1 men and also, where absolutely necessary, for staff in the Power Station and repair Shops. In April 1918 Mr McCombe's assistant, Mr Bruce, was called up and the Committee agreed to appeal but to what effect is not known.

In July 1917 the City Engineer asked the Board of Trade for permission to replace the short length of single line, including the points and crossings, at the intersection of Charlotte Street and Wincolmlee, which was in urgent need of renewal. He wished to replace it with an interlacing length of track in order to speed up traffic on two very busy routes to Hedon Road and Holderness Road, each with a three-minute service and the additional docks and works traffic on Hedon Road.

He wanted to install a double line, but the owner of the frontage on Dock Office Row would not consent to it. The Board approved subject to at least 9' 6" clearance between the kerb and the nearest rail on each side.

Predictably there was opposition to the employment of women drivers from the Hull and District Trades and Labour Council, claiming that they would be a danger to the travelling public. They wanted the Corporation to employ discharged soldiers and sailors who were unfit for laborious work instead. The Committee replied that it had not yet taken a decision, and

discharged personnel were already being employed in preference to others. However, the Tramways Sub-Committee decided to go ahead with the employment of women tram drivers. Equal payments for women and men cleaners were agreed subject to the women providing their own overalls.

It was agreed to provide a third line at the Dairycoates terminus, so that cars bound for Pickering Park would not be delayed by the shorter working cars which were themselves subject to delays from the level crossing. The Board of Trade approved the line on 28 November 1917, subject to a minimum clearance of 15 inches between the side of a car in the new loop and the nearest kerb.

Renewal of the Anlaby Road railway crossing at a cost of £675 by the NER was approved as a matter of urgency. The NER Engineer had deferred the renewal until 1918 but thought it essential to do the work as soon as possible.

The City Engineer again raised the question of difficulties in maintaining operation of the Power Station. There is a sense of exasperation in his report which followed a series of breakdowns. He had raised the matter of additional equipment several times in the previous years, and each time the expenditure had been deferred. Even if the war was to end suddenly the position would still be serious since the purchase of new machinery was very remote. At the very least he wanted either a new 900kW set, or a rotary transformer to take power from the Corporation's Power Station. He pointed out that power from this source cost about twenty per cent more that the Tramways' own station. Predictably, a decision was deferred. If that were not enough, the Ministry of Munitions had refused him a priority certificate to purchase a new armature, although he was authorised to carry out urgent repairs to existing equipment. Subsequently a report was called for to examine the terms of obtaining power from Sculcoates. On 20 October the number six generator broke down.

Other problems concerned the repair and maintenance of rails which was held up owing to difficulty in obtaining supplies of acetylene. The City Engineer recommended the purchase of a light trolley and portable plant to enable repairs to be carried out at night.

Only nine inspectors remained in service, and all of them received a pay rise in December subject to their undertaking more responsible duties. A maximum of £3 per week was now to be paid

During 1917 the first doubts were raised about the continued ownership of the Power Station in Osborne Street. The station was operating below capacity and the machinery was becoming obsolete and costly to run. Additional costs were incurred in having to move coal by road from Cannon Street Goods Depot. Negotiations were opened with the Electricity Committee, and a Joint Committee was created in May 1919, but not until a few years later was there any agreement about future supply arrangements.

In December 1917 Mr McCombe was empowered to make such experiments with regard to the through running of cars as he may deem desirable. There is no indication about his thoughts on the matter.

Also in December 1917 the City Engineer referred to his report on 15 April 1915, and stated that the results obtained with the oxy-acetylene welding plant to repair rail joints had been entirely satisfactory, but in recent months dissolved acetate had been in short supply and its price had increased considerably.

He had made enquiries about electric plant and recommended that portable plant be purchased from the Equipment and Engineering Co. This plant could be transported on a light trolley and would cost £313 10s. This would save £300 to £400 a year in gas, but half of this would go towards the overtime payments to staff as the equipment would have to be used at night. If this plant were not bought (and he was reluctant to recommend any additional expenditure at this time) it would be necessary to deal with the joints by cutting off lengths of rail and dropping in a new length which would multiply the number of joints and make expense for the future. His recommendation was approved.

Economies were being sought everywhere, and Mr McCombe was asked to reduce the car mileage as he seemed fit and to report to the next Committee. The need for economy remained uppermost and when asked to run additional Sunday morning cars for munitions workers, the answer was "No" given that only 800 people were likely to be involved. It was also decided to examine the possibilities of through running across the city centre to relieve congestion.

The City Engineer did manage to obtain permission from the Board of Trade to purchase four pairs of points, three open points and seven crossings, but the quotation from Messrs Hadfields Ltd of Sheffield was exactly twice the pre-war price at £60. He recommended the purchase of the points only, whilst admitting that there was a risk in not replacing the crossings even though these should last for another year at least.

An explosion occurred in a section box at Wilton Street on the Holderness Road route at 9 pm on 20 May 1918, delaying the tram service for some time. The emergency gang found gas burning in the box and later, when the cable drawing-in box on the roadway was removed, another explosion took place resulting in the faces and hands of three men being burnt, and flames to a height of between ten and fifteen feet. It was discovered that a cable belonging to the Electric Light Department was laid in contact with the base of the box, and that it was badly burnt and had formed an arc at the point which had burnt away a portion of the tramway section box. Subsequently the Tramways Committee agreed to replace any clothing burnt by the explosion.

The National War Savings Committee asked the Corporation to place a tramcar at its disposal for a week to act as a travelling bank as part of War Weapons Week 8-13 July 1918 or, if not practical, an advertising car to run on all routes. The Committee refused both, but agreed to a reasonable amount of advertising on the cars during that week.

When two former employees, (Messrs D.F. and C.E. Kneeshaw), wrote to say that the Home Office had agreed to their returning home, the Tramways Sub-Committee discovered that they were conscientious objectors who had been arrested as army absentees in 1916. The Hull Branch of the Discharged and Demobilised Sailors and Soldiers objected strongly to their resuming their jobs as motormen, in preference to returning soldiers. After careful consideration the Sub-Committee found that it could not agree to their return.

On 24 June 1918 the price of coal rose by 2s 6d per ton. The Government instructed undertakings to reduce consumption by 15 per cent for 1918. The Tramway Manager reported a deficit of £889 on the first three months of 1918/19, and it was decided that from 5 August all half-penny stages would be abolished, with all passengers being charged 1d except for the Old Town route where the fare remained unchanged.

A special meeting of the Tramways Committee was called on 22 July 1918 by the Chairman. The first three months of the new financial year had revealed a deficit of £889 on the tramway undertaking. After some discussion it was agreed to abolish for the present the half penny stages with 1d being charged on each route, the Old Town route excepted which would be unchanged. Early morning fares were also unchanged. The changes were to be introduced on 5 August.

The Armistice came into force on 11 November 1918 amidst a collective sigh of relief. However, for the tramways the problems were about to get worse.

Chapter 7

POST-WAR PROBLEMS

On 26 November 1918 the Tramways Committee considered the re-instatement process for servicemen. The agreement of July 1915 ordained that the services of women would be dispensed with at the end of the war. There were many temporary male employees, but women would go first and those in last would be the first to go. As demobilised men returned, the equivalent number of women would be given notice. As many temporary employees as possible would be retained on a permanent basis.

Special care would be taken to make returning men feel welcome and to enable them to settle into their former positions. Mr McCombe recorded his appreciation of the men and women in maintaining the tramway service, and he reminded the Committee that conditions of blackout and overcrowding of tramcars were more strenuous than in peace time. Committee members also expressed their appreciation for the way in which services had been run on Armistice Day itself, Monday 11 November. When the tramwaymen's Union asked the Committee to grant women leaving the department having more than six month's service a week's pay in lieu of their annual six days holiday the Committee were less than generous in refusing.

The effect of the influenza epidemic that spread throughout Europe was hard. By late 1918 no fewer than 79 men were absent with the disease. In February 1919 some 50 men were still off duty.

The behaviour of waiting passengers at terminus stops in the city centre had caused concerns. When cars which were late approached the termini they were invaded by crowds of passengers much to their own inconvenience and danger. To prevent this Mr McCombe recommended the provision of a suitable chain for each car entrance to be put in place by either conductor or motorman. The chains were purchased from the Anger Manufacturing and Supply Company at 3s 4d or 3s 7d each according to length.

Although in March 1918 the Tramway Electrical Engineer had obtained approval for new motors for cars nos 1-15, it had been decided not to proceed owing to wartime restrictions. Replacement was now urgent and he was authorised to obtain them once more. He also reported that because he could neither obtain the best materials nor skilled men, it was necessary to institute a thorough overhaul of trucks, electrical equipment and overhead line equipment, and he proposed to use de-mobilised men for this work.

On 5 February 1919 The Chairman, Councillor Hakes, and Deputy-Chairman, Councillor Raine, submitted a paper to the Tramways Committee entitled "Reconstruction, Re-organisation and Extension". This pointed out that the war had naturally put a stop to intended developments in Hull which was now confronted with drastic changes, internally and externally. Running costs had increased enormously and were not likely to decrease in the near future, and it was time for the Committee to put its own house in order.

It was necessary to carry out suggested extensions and develop lines already in existence. Additionally, it must look at other means of tramway development so that revenue might be increased to the furthest possible extent. All schemes including some already suggested were placed before the Committee to be discussed from all points of view and, if approved, to be carried into operation with the least possible delay.

The extension to Newland Park was almost complete and would open shortly. Previously approved extensions to Lees Rest Homes on Anlaby Road, to Inglemire Lane on Beverley Road and the Waterworks Street loop should go ahead. Other possibilities included Pickering Park to Hessle (an echo of previous schemes), Newland Park to Cottingham, and Holderness Road to Sutton. These would require careful consideration as they would cross the city boundary. A light railway might be built into the Holderness district east of the city for both freight and passengers whose transport links were antiquated. A riverfront tramway was suggested linking all the quays, docks and associated ship repairing and building facilities. No mention was made of the Spring Bank West extension to Alliance Avenue or of the Stoneferry project.

The tramway management structure had been in force for 19 years, and it was thought that the time was opportune for a full review of the organisation to be conducted by a tramway "expert" (consultant). This would compare the performance and costs of the tramways' own Power Station with the Corporation's main Power Station at Sculcoates. Car repairs and maintenance facilities, staffing responsibilities and the current fares system would also be reviewed thoroughly. The advisability of having the repairs connected with all tramway work such as the workshops at Liverpool Street and in the car sheds under one management should be considered. Mr J.M. Hamilton of Leeds was asked to carry out the review but before any work could start the City Council on 6 March referred the decision back to the Committee by which time it had more serious matters to consider.

Some form of public transport, either motor bus or trackless car, was required to serve heavily populated areas that lay between the main tramway routes – from Worship Street (H) through Charles Street to Beverley Road (B) and Spring Bank (S); between Hessle Road (D) and Anlaby Road (A), and Cleveland Street via Stoneferry Road and Clough Road to Beverley Road which effectively killed off hopes of trams to Stoneferry.

Approval for the Anlaby Road extension and the Waterworks Street loop was given, but a decision on the Inglemire Lane extension was deferred pending a visit by the Committee members. Powers would be sought to extend tramway services beyond the city boundary to Hessle, Anlaby, Kirkella and Willerby, Sutton, Preston and Hedon. The City Engineer was asked to prepare a rough sketch of the river front tramway.

The Anlaby Road extension would take the trams across the Newington level crossing, and the City Engineer tried in vain to dissuade the North Eastern Railway Company from insisting on catch points and signals. The cost was £5000 plus £2000 for a new set of crossing gates. In addition he obtained approval to purchase land for road widening to 100 feet, in order to allow tracks to be laid on a reservation on the south side of the road beyond the railway bridge.

Later that month Mr McCombe suggested linking routes across Queen Victoria Square to eliminate the daily city centre congestion. Owing to the heavy increase in traffic and the fact that additional cars would soon be necessary on all routes the question of city centre termini should be considered. The method to date had been to have a terminus at the end of each line and a central terminus in Queen Victoria Square, the reason being the delays caused by level crossings were confined to one route. But public demands must bring about changes and the Committee had already sanctioned a combined Hessle Road and Holderness Road which would shortly be introduced. He suggested that the Anlaby Road and Spring Bank routes could be run in combination. It would be an experiment to see whether city centre congestion could be reduced and whether Victoria Square could be done away with as a central terminus.

The Committee should remember that there were two services on Hessle Road to Dairycoates and to Pickering Park, and there was an auxiliary route to Holderness Road via the Old Town which was presently suspended. Dairycoates cars would run via North Bridge to Aberdeen Street whilst Pickering Park trams would operate along Alfred Gelder Street and Salthouse Lane Bridge. Hedon Road cars would be in the way of the through cars, and it might be well to consider extending the track along the eastern part of Jameson Street to Paragon Square. The Old Town service would run once more to the station. Mr McCombe estimated that through running of "D" and "H" cars would save £2500 yearly and a similar saving would accrue from the other through route. His recommendations were agreed.

On 26 November 1918 the Tramways Committee was informed that a subsidiary company of the British Oil and Cake Mills Ltd was planning a garden village on the south side of Holderness Road within the city boundary. A new road was to be built from Holderness Road opposite Ings Lane (Road) (beyond the present tram terminus) which would connect Marfleet Lane at the sharp bend near Bilton Clough. The City Engineer thought it might be advantageous to contribute to the cost of the road being 100 feet wide so as to provide space for a separate double tram track. He was authorised to negotiate but nothing became of the tramway idea.

Both the Tramways Manager and the Tramways Electrical Engineer submitted requests for a review of their salaries. The Tramways Electrical Engineer's salary of £500 per annum had not been reviewed since 1908. Mr McCombe's salary was £600 per annum and this had fallen behind. It was agreed to increase his salary to £800 but Mr Wilkinson's application was deferred. The McCombe decision was referred back by the City Council, by which time Mr McCombe was the subject of an investigation over an "irregular procedure with reference to certain receipts and payments which passed through his hands". An investigation by the City Accountant (Mr William H. Smith) into "Business methods in the Manager's Department" was initiated. Mr McCombe continued with his duties although one of the City Accountant's clerks was lodged in the Tramway offices.

Another fares revision was agreed on 16 April 1919. With the exception of the Old Town route the fare for any distance was to be 1d, the other exceptions being members of His Majesty's forces in uniform (not commissioned officers) and school children up to and including 14 years, who would be charged one half-penny. Wounded soldiers in uniform would be carried free, as would the blind.

To add to the Committee's problems the Overhead Line Superintendent, Stephen William Tarr, was arrested on 13 April when driving away from the Osborne Street Power Station in a motor car. He was convicted of stealing petrol from the Corporation and fined £15 or 51 days' imprisonment. The investigation revealed irregularities in the Tramway Electrical Engineer's Department, and he was asked to make new arrangements for hiring motor cars, and to obtain a refund for driver hire charges from Messrs Lockeys when Mr Tarr had been driving the hired car. Mr Tarr asked the Committee on 26 April for his job back but, having received no encouragement, he submitted his resignation. This episode also revealed shortcomings in the Tramway Electrical Engineer's Department's financial practices, and the City Accountant was asked to examine them. The stage was set for another upheaval.

On 16 April 1919 the Tramways Committee had a long discussion about fare levels and decided that with effect from 5 May the existing morning fares would be abolished and that, the Old Town route excepted, a single fare of one penny be charged. Members of the armed forces, in uniform, officers excepted, and school children up to and including the age of 14 years be charged ½d. Wounded soldiers in hospital uniform and the blind would be carried free.

The Tramways Committee received the City Accountant's Interim Report regarding the Tramway Manager's Administration on 23 April 1919. It revealed a multitude of shortcomings regarding cash handling, conductors' change money, traffic receipts and lost property. The City Accountant revealed that some matters had been raised with Mr McCombe by the Chairman and Deputy-Chairman as long ago as November 1917, but his explanation had been accepted. He was unaware of this until December 1918 when he acquainted them both with a rumour that had reached him about petty cash. Consequently his staff had interrogated (his word) many staff (platform, depot and office) and had conducted searches of the tramway offices, sometimes discovering papers which it was claimed had been destroyed. A record was made of each interview.

There were seven principal areas investigated. The first involved a shortage of traffic cash which had been the source of the Chairman and Deputy-Chairman's concern on November 1917. The Tramway Manager had claimed that the shortage had occurred because the money had been used to settle compensation claims without delay. This was supposed to have ceased, but a surprise test on 10 March revealed a shortage of £19 10s 6d. Mr McCombe stated that the money was for special claims that arose after 5 pm, but he agreed that he did not have the authority to settle a claim without the Chairman or Deputy Chairman's authority, and no such claims had been made. Two days after the test the money was paid in by Mr McCombe.

Authority had been given to dispose of articles found in cars (lost property) to the sum of £65 8s 4d in February 1918, but the last auction had occurred in July 1918 and the proceeds handed to the manager. Again he was unable to provide a satisfactory explanation. A further £24 0s 3d from cash found in cars and unclaimed passengers' change money was discovered. Mr McCombe stated that these were paid in at regular intervals but the last such payment had occurred in August 1913! The City Accountant also found that many receipts for transactions had been destroyed as had some day books pre-1914.

The City Treasurer paid the manager each year a sum that was to be handed over to conductors on a daily basis for change money. The manager had provided a certificate giving the names of conductors who had received this money but, when asked, he could not provide a receipt book to back up the certificates.

Recovery of the cost of damage to tramcars by third parties was the personal responsibility of Mr McCombe, but when the City Accountant requested some official record showing claims made and the sums concerned none could be provided. The copy letter books were of no help and it was the practice for the manager to type such letters. The Chief Cashier of the Tramways Department had no knowledge of what claims had been made but had only occasionally received payments for such claims. Car accident reports in excess of 1000 completed by drivers revealed that little or no action had been taken to recover the costs of damage. Not all damage to cars was reported by drivers,

Car no. 61 is at Liverpool Street and looks a little careworn. (MJW)

and it was recommended that disciplinary action be taken where this was the case.

The Chairman stated that on a visit to the Manager's office on 31 March he had noted a great mass of burnt paper in the fireplace.

Mr Smith in conclusion stated that owing to the inadequate methods within the Tramway Manager's Department it had proved impossible to conduct an exhaustive investigation.

Mr McCombe asked for time to consider the report and was given until 4pm the following day. He chose to make a verbal response (the précis of his reply in the minutes ran to four pages). He admitted that there were shortcomings in the system of taking moneys out of gross receipts, but this had ceased after objections from the Chairman and Vice-Chairman in November 1917. This had been used only for emergencies (unspecified) and not for meeting compensation claims on the Corporation. The proceeds from the auction sale had been retained over a dispute with the Auctioneers regarding some property which it was considered that they had mislaid. He could not explain why he had retained this for such a long time but said it would have been paid in before the year end.

He was at a loss to understand the situation regarding the cash found in cars, said that he knew nothing about it and asked for an opportunity to look at this personally. He refuted some information given by staff regarding the conductors' change money but was unable to account for the state of the records. With regard to the retention of money received for damage to the cars he remembered some situations but said he had been in a hurry, had issued a receipt and put the money in a drawer to be paid in later. He considered that he had the power to settle such claims and that the Chairman and Deputy Chairman understood this, something which they denied at the meeting. Some papers had been burned but these were of no effect on the Corporation and were merely an accumulation of old papers. The department had always worked on a minimum of staff having some of the lowest

administration in the country. He himself had had no holiday since 1914 since when the strain had been intolerable. The sums involved were very insignificant given the large sums of money that had passed through the department's hands. Under examination he admitted that, in general, the City Accountant's report was accurate.

Members were not impressed by his defence and, although they were prepared to take the most lenient view of the situation, they felt that they had no alternative but to request his resignation. Three days later his resignation letter was accepted, but the Committee asked the Council whether, given the strain under which his work had been carried out during the war, he could be re-instated or allocated some similar position. His response was printed and circulated as confidential to all members of the City Council.

The Council with a full public gallery debated the City Accountant's report on 1 May. Some members attacked the Tramways Committee, some were sympathetic to Mr McCombe but eventually declined to re-employ him and he left the Corporation. In June he paid a sum of £87 12s 7d to the Corporation and the matter was closed.

The Tramways Committee was informed of the decision on the following day. The Chairman had asked Mr Tarbet, the Chief Cashier, to take charge of the department until a successor was appointed and he had also seen the majority of the inspectors about the subject. However, there were more problems, and the Committee decided, without giving a reason, to ask the City Accountant to investigate the business methods adopted in the Tramway and Electrical Engineer's Department and to report back to the Committee.

But the McCombe situation rumbled on. A new Sub-Committee to consider claims against and for damage to the cars was created. There were calls for the Tramways Committee to resign en masse and a special Council meeting was called for 12 May to consider a motion from Councillor Willoughby to remove the Committee. At various packed public meetings the "confidential" report was read out and the Tramways Committee was virulently attacked.

The subsequent Council meeting (again with a packed public gallery) was long and gladiatorial. Willoughby's motion was approved with less than half the Council voting. A new Committee of twelve was formed which included seven of the old Committee.

Meanwhile McCombe was made bankrupt with debts of more than £3,000 owing to moneylenders, friends and even members of the Committee. The City Accountant's final report was considered on 31 July and many of his recommendations were accepted. Most of the missing money had been recovered but Mr McCombe did not have all of it.

A radical revision of timetables and running times was submitted to the May Traffic Sub-Committee. A full list is included in Appendix 4. All eight routes would receive an improved service as a result of allocating additional cars to a route or through quicker running. The new timetables had been prepared by three inspectors (Walters, Draffin and Dixon) who attended the meeting. The busiest routes were Anlaby Road whose morning peak service comprised a tram every one and two minutes, and Holderness Road where the lunch time headway was one minute. Additional workmen's specials ran on Hedon Road between 7am and 9am and 4.40pm and 5.30pm including cars from other routes. The last car from Queen Victoria Square would leave at 11pm.

The timetables were in response to recent pay and hours reduction agreements, and would eliminate some 1600 hours of overtime, as well as fully utilise men who had previously worked all day. The Committee asked for proposals for a 30-minute all night service from Dairycoates to Hedon Road to operate from 11pm until 5.30am. This was approved at the following Committee meeting with a fare of 3d for the whole journey and 2d for either route. In addition members requested proposals for the through running of both services.

A Mr John Emerson asked if the Corporation would grant him running powers from Marfleet to the city boundary at Saltend as he intended to seek approval for tram powers to Hedon. The matter was referred to the Parliamentary Committee but no action resulted.

A list of cars which had been damaged and reported and not reported was submitted to the June 1919 Committee. The Staff Sub-Committee was asked to deal with those drivers who had not reported damage. Unfortunately, the list was not attached to the minutes.

On 26 June 1919 the Tramways Committee interviewed seven candidates (Messrs Chamberlain, Fitzpayne, Harvey, Rayner, Richardson, Stokes and Simpson) for the General Manager's post, the decision having been taken to concentrate all tramway matters, permanent way excepted, in a single post. An eighth (Mr Stanley) did not turn up. Mr Rayner received six votes, Mr Chamberlain (who subsequently withdrew) two, and Mr Stokes one. Therefore Mr Edgar Sturdee Rayner A.M.I.E.E. was appointed at a salary of £800 per annum to take responsibility for all matters except the laying, repair and maintenance of the track. He was currently Borough Electrical Engineer and Tramway Manager at Doncaster which used the same track as Hull. He was unable to take up his duties until October 1919.

On 2 July the Tramway Electrical Engineer (Mr J. Wilkinson) submitted his resignation saying that his health after the strain of the war was not very good. He would retire at the end of September.

The Cottingham Road extension to Newland Park opened on 7 July 1919 with a frequency of every seven and eight minutes. Designated BC, the cars worked via Beverley Road. An addi-tional 1037 car miles were operated on the extension per week at an estimated cost per mile of 1s making a total of £51 17s. Some sources state that Service SC (the Newland Avenue route) started at the same time but there is no mention in the minutes. A temporary fare of ½d was fixed for the length of the new extension.

Saturday 19 July 1919 was the nation's official peace celebration day and a restricted service was operated. A separate memorial service was held on Sunday 27 July at the Holy Trinity Church. The start of normal service was put back to 2pm and special cars were provided for tramway employees and their families. Fifteen cars were decorated in connection with the celebrations.

A deficit of £13,495 was recorded for 1918/9 of which £3000 resulted from the coal crisis which had forced up prices. Costs were rising and many were outside the Corporation's control. £1,000 had been spent on canopies for cars and £9,451 on car renewals all from the reserve fund which had also borne the cost of £2,000 of permanent way work. A 12s per week rise for 1000 men would cost £32,448 per annum. The coal strike led to service reductions to save fuel. When further supplies of coal were received at the end of July, the service was extended to operate from 7am until 7pm. The all-night service between Hessle Road and Hedon Road was withdrawn despite some members wanting it to continue.

Mr Tarbert submitted a schedule of annual receipts on the Hessle Road, Beverley Road, Spring Bank and Spring Bank West routes to the July meeting. Between 5am and 6am on Monday 2 June 1919 17 cars were in service, 26 between 6am and 7am, whilst between 7am and 9am 69 cars were in service on these four routes. Total receipts for the four hours amounted to £71 0s 6d but this was £65 1s 2d short of the cost of running the cars, thereby highlighting the financial consequences of providing workmens' fares. Receipts per mile between 8am and 9am were 4s 9d whereas the highest receipts per mile of 11s 8d were earned between 6pm and 7pm. A full schedule is included in Appendix 6.

The report on the management of the Tramway Electrical Engineer's Department was presented on 31 July 1919. Numerous incidents of financial inefficiency were recorded in the 25-page report, which recommended a complete re-organisation. Competitive prices were not sought when ordering goods; some prices were exorbitant; goods were ordered even when stocks were high; orders above £10 were placed without Committee authority; car damage repair books were wrongly priced and understated, and they were not based on actual costs.

The Tramways Electrical Engineer (unlike Mr McCombe who had twenty-four hours) was given fourteen days in which to reply but was suspended in the meantime. He submitted a 15-page rebuttal (on 2 September) which allotted blame on his staff acting without his authority and a shortage of staff (the death of the chief storekeeper and resignation of the Chief Clerk at the same time was a particular burden). The Committee declared its dissatisfaction with his reply and decided that as he had already stated his desire to resign from the end of September, it would be best if he did not return to work. This was not contested.

Thus ended the careers of two of the three senior figures of the tramway management, Clearly neither were good administrators as some of their processes and procedures were a shambles but the financial authorities, which did not suffer any criticism in the reports, were also at fault in that, if there were any audits they failed to discover any problems. It seems unlikely that Mr McCombe would have been appointed as General Manager over a unified tramways organisation. Undoubtedly both suffered from the strain imposed by the war but so did many others in the industry. Contemporary accounts claim that Mr Wilkinson had a drink problem but to what extent, if any, this affected his work is

This is a unique view of cars working routes "SC" and "B" negotiating a fountain on Princes Avenue. The date is between 1919 and 1923 when the Beverley Road and Newland Avenue routes operated as circular services and other Newland Avenue cars were extended along Cottingham Road to Newland Park. (PG)

unclear. He has been accused of not keeping up to date with tramway technology, but he had started to replace car equipment before the war and had attempted to purchase equipment after the conflict when supplies were limited and expensive.

Meanwhile the City Engineer had completed survey work in connection with proposed extensions to surrounding villages. He had concluded that the route to Anlaby should follow the line of the proposed "by-pass road", rather than through the village. Although the City Council had resolved to ask the Ministry of Health to extend the city boundaries, no action had been taken by December 1919. Given that this had an impact on plans for expanding the tramway system, it was decided to defer proposals for extensions for the moment.

Mr Rayner who commenced work in October 1919 was required to restructure the Tramways Department, restore staff morale and discipline and address the worsening finances of the tramways. His first year included a trade depression and a coal strike during which he maintained services by using oil. The local Trades Council accused him of undermining the trades unions and the miners by using oil, reducing services and increasing fares.

In November 1919 Alderman Willoughby was appointed Chairman of the Tramways Committee, a reign that was to last for a decade.

On 19 November 1919 the General Manager described the new system of car service on the Beverley Road and Spring Bank routes and the associated circular service. He also proposed a new tram line west of the statue in Queen Victoria Square.

It will be recalled that in February Mr McCombe had received authority to link the Hessle Road services with the Holderness Road services and the Anlaby Road and Spring Bank

services. Not until 1 December 1919 were the cross town services introduced, but in June the scheme had been altered with the result that the Hessle Road and Hedon Road routes formed one through service, and the Anlaby Road and Holderness Road routes formed another. Their introduction immediately aroused criticism regarding punctuality. On 3 December the Hull Daily Mail contained the first of two advertisements by Mr Rayner which mentioned difficulties from river crossings and rail crossings. There would be some dislocation at first, but it was hoped to overcome these, and he asked the public to bear any slight inconvenience until the innovation had a reasonable trial.

However, letters to the press did not display such patience. Correspondents described a foggy and cold City Square without trams, but with hundreds of freezing expectant passengers who started to walk home. Gaps of thirty minutes on Anlaby Road were experienced, as was the lack of cars after a Hull City game. When a correspondent complained about a late running last car going straight to the Wheeler Street depot, a motorman's wife reminded everyone that the crews had no last car and were arriving home much later than before. Some accepted that the level crossings were partly to blame and advocated their abolition and the end of the trial, both sentiments echoed by an editorial.

At first Mr Rayner spoke with the Mail and asked for patience, but his ran out very quickly and on 18 December he reported to the Tramways Committee. He had spent some time personally observing the operation both in the city centre and in outlying sections. He concluded that it was impossible to run a satisfactory through service from east to west due to differences in the class of traffic, and the delays caused by level crossings and bridges. It was agreed that the cross-city links should be withdrawn from the following Saturday.

However, existing track arrangements in the city centre

were at their limit, and he proposed a series of terminal loops to avoid the shunting of cars that was sometimes necessary. It would accelerate and improve the services. He undertook to submit proposals for loop lines as soon as possible. It was also decided, without his agreement, to abandon the proposed line in Waterworks Street and in front of the City Hall. However, the withdrawal of through services did not affect the night service between Dairycoates and Hedon Road. The Committee agreed to increase fares on this service in that workmen should pay 2½d on either route or 4d for the whole distance. Tickets had to be obtained from the Tramway Offices and presented to the conductor. Anyone else travelling had to pay 3d on both routes.

Approval was given for the purchase of capes for motormen who drove open type cars, such capes to be returned when motormen were allocated to vestibuled cars.

When the General Manager suggested that a deficit of £14,022 would result for the first six months of the financial year, some fare revisions were agreed. The Old Town route fare was fixed as one penny and, after 9am a flat fare of 1½d was charged on all routes (the Beverley Road and Spring Bank routes to be treated as separate routes). Children under 14 would be charged one halfpenny, and 14- to 16-year-olds attending secondary schools would also be charged one penny on school days. The fares came into effect on 12 January 1920. Letters to the press attacked the decision, several writers calling for passengers to pay according to the length of their journey.

During December 1919 the Stores, Depots and Workshops Sub-Committee members carried out their usual rota visits to the Power Station, Liverpool Street Workshops and Cottingham Road Car Shed. They called for improvements in the supply of radiator sand at the workshops and the car shed, repairs to the hearth and floor (including provision of a kerb) of the Mess Room at Cottingham Road, and boxes for the storage and carriage of punches between the shed and the office.

When on 29 December Mr Rayner submitted his thoughts for loop lines, the Committee called for larger scale plans and more information regarding loading and unloading arrangements. Subsequently it was agreed to arrange a joint meeting with the Works Committee to consider the proposals.

A Miss Hume wrote to the Committee suggesting a name change for the "BC" cars but no action was taken. At the same Committee the General Manager was authorised to increase the length of single rail at various termini.

The Tramways Committee on 29 December 1919 considered a report from the Watch Committee of 20 December. The new system of forming queues in the City Square had resulted in two constables devoting their whole time to this, one from 10am to 6pm and the other from 3pm to 11pm. Police Reservists were being used at a cost of 72 shillings per week for each man. It suggested that the Tramways Committee might wish to contribute. It was left to the Chairman, Deputy-Chairman and General Manager to resolve the situation.

Thus ended a busy two-year period of "peace". The following decade was to prove very volatile.

Chapter 8

THE TURBULENT TWENTIES

When Mr Rayner described problems in dispersing large crowds of spectators after a game at the Boulevard or the Hull City ground, approval to spend £200 for a new crossover at the West Park Gates was given.

In February 1920 City centre loop lines were considered again. Mr Rayner's proposal for an anti-clockwise loop via Chariot Street, Waterworks Street and Carr Lane was rejected, as were proposals for termini in Brook Street and Jameson Street. However, the plan to allow the Holderness Road and Hedon Road cars to run into City Square around a loop via Jameson Street and King Edward Street into Savile Street was authorised. The Bridges Committee had asked the Tramways Committee to operate part of the Hedon Road and Holderness Road cars across the Salthouse Lane Bridge at peak times to relieve congestion. It was agreed to assist as much as possible. Councillor Gould advocated the removal of all tram lines from City Square but was told that this was totally impractical.

The department was very short of joiners despite attempts to recruit more. A rota visit to Liverpool Street Workshops revealed that only seven joiners were employed which was delaying the fitting of vestibules. Only two cars had recently been completed whilst another four were in hand. Repair work on damaged cars meant that the plan to turn out two cars a week was not feasible. The paint shop's four car capacity prevented faster work, and over 100 cars were still without vestibules.

Proposed new duties arose again in March. The Union's Executive recommended acceptance, on the basis of a two-month trial after which a review would take place. A mass meeting rejected the duties as men wanted a full eight-hour shift without a break, something prohibited by the National Agreement. The Committee ignored the vote, and agreed to introduce the new duties for two months during which the men could prepare their proposals with a half-hour break. After this the Committee would consider a straight eight-hour duty roster, but only if no extra costs were incurred and that no extra staff were taken on.

Mr Rayner reported that he proposed to alter the seating on the upper deck of tramcars by covering in the seating area outside the saloon at each end thereby increasing the seating from 38 to 44. Members asked to inspect the first such car, which they did in June when they authorised more conversions.

In May the operation over the Salthouse Lane Bridge through the Old Town was again discussed. The "TH" route ran every ten minutes and it was intended to introduce at an early date a service of cars from Hedon Road over the bridge. No further reference was made in the minutes and it is unclear if this was ever introduced.

Mr Rayner reported a deficit of £8726 for 1919/20, despite carrying 78,432,643 passengers, the highest number ever, and he attached a financial review of the undertaking. He warned members that no account had been taken of a possible wage increase of 10s. Car miles totalled 5 million, with average weekly receipts being £6,366 (16.07d per mile) which would need to be increased to 20.02d per mile (£1.730).

He provided three options for fares revisions of which only one, an increase from 1d to 1½d per stage, together with 2d for the whole journey with no increase in workmen's or children's fares, was realistic and likely to generate sufficient income. He

rejected 1d for the first mile with 2d for the whole journey and three 1d stages, whilst the other option of 1d for the first mile, 2d for the second mile or part thereof, and 3d for the third mile or part thereof, mainly because it would cause considerable difficulty in fare collection and the possibility of much overriding. The Old Town fare should be increased to 1d, night services after 1 am should cease, and the half-fare concession for able-bodied soldiers should also cease.

Discussion was intense before Mr Rayner's preferred option of the Old Town fare increase, and the ending of the able-bodied soldiers' concession were approved. Councillor Wheeldon proposed restricting night services to a single car after 1am but an amendment by Councillor Beal that all night cars cease after 2am was carried. The new fares were introduced on 24 May.

Revised byelaws came into effect in May 1920 which prohibited any passenger or person other than an authorised officer of the Corporation from travelling on the platforms or steps, stand on the top deck, or sit on the outside rail on the top deck on any car! Passengers must on demand or before leaving the car (whichever was the sooner), pay to the conductor the fare legally demandable for his journey and accept a ticket therefor.

Rush hour traffic was so heavy that Mr Rayner proposed to run additional cars to intermediate points only. He obtained approval to install new crossovers on Hessle Road near West Dock Avenue, Holderness Road near Durham Street, and on Beverley Road at Queen's Road. He was instructed to report on means of relieving waiting times in rush hours on the section between King Edward Street and the junction of Beverley Road and Spring Bank. The Beverley Road short workings reputedly were designated "QB", but it does not appear that the other two received any designation. In June approval was given to install an additional crossover at Pickering Park.

Passenger numbers boarding the "TH" route between Dansom Lane and Monument Bridge were studied by the Committee, which decided it should continue as at present from 7.30am until 6.30pm on Mondays to Fridays and from 7.30am until 1.30pm on Saturdays.

Members of the Claims Sub-Committee were used to dealing with claims for damage and injury, but even they must have been surprised on 20 May 1920 when not one but two claims were considered which involved a conductor allegedly dropping the trolley rod (pole) on a pedestrian's head! A Mrs Staggimeier of Ebor Terrace, Norwood Street was crossing the City Square when this was alleged to have happened. In this case the Town Clerk was instructed to repudiate all liability. The other claim came from Mrs Connie Swales of Pulman Street who alleged that the same occurred in Savile Street. In this instance the Town Clerk was instructed to proceed along the lines suggested but these were not recorded! Such a situation was apparently not unique since there were other claims including one from a Mrs Annie Elizabeth Thomason on 17 October 1921.

On 26 May Mr Rayner said the Chief Constable could not recommend that the Pier cars be allowed to operate over the Whitefriargate Bridge, as the obstruction to traffic would be too great. From the report it would seem that the Pier cars had not been crossing the bridge for some time, although when this started does not appear to have been before the Committee. This

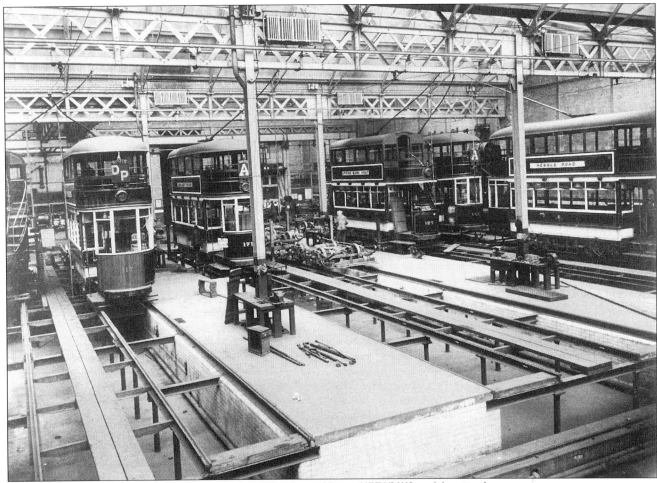

Two photographs chronicle the interior of Liverpool Street Workshops with cars 117/71/24/43 receiving attention. The date is probably March 1923. (PM/MJW)

A final decision about a service to Stoneferry was also taken, with petrol buses being selected with the proviso that if the route required extension trackless type vehicles would be employed and the buses used to open up other routes. This was despite an estimated annual loss of between £5,400 and £7,800 depending on the type of vehicle used.

On 1 July the City Council asked the Tramways Committee to consider the question of free passes for old age pensioners. Mr Rayner discovered that there were no less than 5,000 within Hull, who he calculated would make, on average, three return journeys a week. This would involve an income of £200 per week (£10,400 per annum), approximately 70 full cars daily (500 a year). Existing services could not carry this additional load even in certain slack times during the day. The cost would not be covered by income without increasing fares again. Some 500 blind persons and legless ex-servicemen were already carried free of charge, and he predicted that its introduction could open the door to further claims from workhouse inmates and other charitable institutions. A decision was deferred, but when it was considered again in July a proposed flat fare of ½d for old age

asks the questions as to where the cars were turned back, why were the "TH" cars not obstructive, and when did the cars cease to cross the bridge? Plans show a crossover at the western end of Alfred Gelder Street near Whitefriargate, but can it be assumed that cars terminated here? It is difficult to see that cars reversing here were any less obstructive than operating across the bridge. It is surprising that the Old Town associations had not objected.

No. 101 was designed by Mr Rayner and entered service in March 1923. It was shown to the Yorkshire Area Meeting and delegates were able to sample its riding abilities as shown here on Cottingham Road. (MJW)

pensioners was rejected, and approval given to free rides, on production of a pass, between 9.30am and 11.30am, between 2.30pm and 4pm and after 7pm.

Mr Rayner expressed concern about the cost of laying lines in Osborne Street, citing the reduction of 15 per cent in tram passengers (not according to his own statistics), and the cost of free passes as requiring some reduction in expenditure. Members agreed and decided not to proceed, citing dangers arising from the narrowness of Waterhouse Lane between Carr Lane and Osborne Street as one reason.

Concern was also expressed about increased expenditure on permanent way maintenance, and the City Engineer was instructed, pending submission of a report, to limit monthly expenditure to £2500.

In August, extensions to the tramways and additional bus routes were discussed, and the Parliamentary Committee was instructed to obtain a Provisional Order for tramway extensions to Hessle, from Cottingham Road to the village of Cottingham, and between Anlaby Road and Hessle Road along Hawthorn Avenue, a long densely populated street that was just short of both the "A" and "D" termini, whose residents "enjoyed" a long walk to access public transport. Four bus routes were also included: from the Anlaby Road terminus to Anlaby and Kirkella, to Hedon and Preston, to Stoneferry and Sutton, and from Newland Avenue to Hessle Road via Walton Street, Anlaby Road and Hawthorn Avenue.

Gipsyville residents complained about the loss of the through running at an unrecorded date of the Pickering Park cars. Passengers were apparently having to transfer between cars at Dairycoates, and this was disliked. It was decided to reinstate the through service which would be so arranged as to be run independently of the Dairycoates service.

Mr Rayner reported that the installation of a crossover had proved to be very satisfactory.

Previously unnoticed in the minutes was the purchase of GE 52 motors from Sheffield Tramways at a cost of £45. The General Manager had written to Hull to say that the cost would now be £55. Despite this Mr Rayner was authorised to purchase further motors (number unspecified). Unfortunately it has not been possible to obtain any further information.

Mr Rayner submitted revised loop line proposals in October 1920. The B/S/BC/SC/SW cars would turn left into Jameson Street from Prospect Street, right into Savile Street and right into King Edward Street where loading would take place. "H" and "M" cars would enter Jameson Street from George Street before turning left into King Edward Street, and left again into Savile Street for loading to take place. This would reduce shunting movements, eliminate two lines of cars in the middle of the road, and accelerate the service. Approval was given for the laying of requisite lines in Jameson Street. Subsequently, the Chairman,

Councillor Willoughby, circulated a letter about the changes to all Council members and invited any observations or suggestions. A meeting to discuss the changes was arranged for 10 February 1921.

The Committee considered the effects of another coal strike and a notice from the Coal Mines Department to conserve fuel. The all night service and the "TH" route were suspended, cars altered to start at 6am (outer terminus), and the last cars would leave City Square at 8.30pm (9pm on Saturdays). One car would be run on the Pier route (two on market days (TU/F/S). In January 1921 it was agreed that a compassionate allowance equal to fifty per cent of wages for the lost time be paid to crews.

At the General Manager's suggestion the Tramways Committee agreed to insert weekly advertisements about the tramway service in the *Hull Daily Mail* and the *Hull Daily News* at an average cost of £4 10s for each paper.

These normally appeared on Mondays and were entitled "Tramway Talk" and covered a wide range of subjects. One explained why, when badly delayed, the first car would not stop to pick up passengers; others informed passengers about impending track works; telling cyclists not to hang on to tram stanchions and be pulled by a car; used ticket bins; how to board and alight, and how to queue.

At an unrecorded date (possibly when the circular service was introduced in November 1919), alterations had been made to the Cottingham Road service to Newland Park with the "BC" trams being withdrawn and replaced by "SC" trams which ran via Newland Avenue. Many residents (some of whom were prominent citizens) objected, and submitted a petition to the Traffic and Complaints Sub-Committee calling for the "BC" service to be reinstated. A deputation attended the Committee. Mr Rayner compared traffic levels on the two routes before and after the alteration. A ten minute service was to be provided comprising alternate "BC" and "SC" cars, and other (unspecified) improvements to the Cottingham Road service were being considered.

The City Engineer reported on permanent way maintenance in February 1921. He described the original track laying methods and improvements made since then. He also described the major defects, and increased costs of materials and labour required to carry out remedial work. It was decided to hold another meeting to discuss the matter further. (A fuller summary of the report which includes a description of the original track works can be found in Appendix 3).

No fewer than eleven Tramways Committee members and twenty-two other councillors were present on 10 February to discuss the city centre loops. Six schemes were set before them as follows:

Scheme No. 1
- Beverley Road cars to run along Albion Street, Charles Street and Wright Street.
- Spring Bank cars to run along Jameson Street, George Street, Grimston Street, Jarratt Street and Albion Street,
- Holderness Road and Hedon Road cars to run along Jameson Street, King Edward Street and Savile Street

Scheme No. 2
- Holderness Road cars to run into Jameson Street up to a certain point and turn there
- Hedon Road cars to run into Savile Street as at present

Scheme No. 3
- Hedon Road cars to run into Jameson Street up to a certain point and turn there (if necessary, these lines could be extended to join with the line at Chariot Street, with the present line running to Paragon Street, Brook Street and Carr Lane for through services)

Scheme No. 3A
- Alternate cars from Holderness Road and Hedon Road to run via the Old Town and George Street or via George Street and the Old Town

Scheme No. 4
- The previously agreed (but rejected by Council) loops for the northern routes and the eastern routes

Scheme No. 5
- The loop around the City Square for the "H" and "M" cars

In retrospect, Scheme no. 1 seems illogical and costly since it would increase mileage for little or no additional income, and it would deny passengers the close access to the centre and Whitefriargate that they had enjoyed since horse tram days. Scheme no. 3A seemed to have some merit however. But the meeting overwhelmingly rejected Schemes 1 to 3A along with scheme no. 5 and approved Scheme no. 4.

However, the exercise was a total waste of time as on 3 March 1921 the City Council overturned the decision made by just under half its membership and adopted Scheme No. 2 in lieu of Scheme No. 4! This was a poor decision, with a lost opportunity to relieve congestion and speed up the service, together with a simplified track arrangement in the centre. It was even more annoying for the Chairman had arranged the meeting so that Council members who were not on the Tramways Committee could be informed of the reasons for the proposals, but only served to emphasise how the full Council made life difficult for members and management alike.

The Tramways Committee bowed to the inevitable and instructed Mr Rayner (who must have been upset that so much work had been thrown away) to obtain any necessary powers for the scheme. A single curve from King Edward Street into Savile Street could have allowed the northern trams to return to Prospect Street via Savile Street and Jameson Street.

At the same time authority was given to relay track in George Street and Charlotte Street immediately adjoining North Bridge, and arrangements were made for inward cars from Holderness Road and Hedon Road to run via the Old Town to leave track completely at the disposal of the City Engineer. No mention was made of the arrangement for the other track, but it is assumed that the trams operated the other way round.

Councillor Mackenzie suggested revisions to the Newland Park service. One car should work between Newland Park and Newland Avenue where passengers could transfer between cars. This would save three cars and men. Members were mindful of the Pickering Park transfer experience, the recent complaints from Newland Park residents, and rejected the suggestion as not meeting the wishes of the public.

In 1923 two cars (unidentified) were decorated for the Andrew Marvel Tercentenary by students from Hull's College of Art. The location is the Anlaby Road terminus. (MJW)

150 men were employed, of whom 33 would have to be paid off unless more assistance could be obtained. He was authorised to seek a further grant to the sum of £3,000 for repairs to the permanent way.

The De la Pole and Andrew Marvel statues which were on the line of the proposed works City centre caused problems. Alterations to the Jameson Street lines were made to avoid relocating the De la Pole statue but the Andrew Marvel was moved to a position nearer Bond Street at a cost of £55.

In October 1921 Councillor Webster submitted a scheme for fixing letter boxes to cars leaving the outer termini at 9.30pm to arrive in the City centre before 10pm, where they would be met by postal staff for transfer to the General Post Office in Alfred Gelder Street. One such car on each route could carry a distinguishing light. The Committee would incur little expense. It was agreed to investigate further and to negotiate with the Postmaster-General.

However, in March 1922 the General Manager reported that the Post Office could not afford the expenditure, even though the service could be improved, unless the Corporation could contribute a small sum. Eventually, the Secretary of State for the Post Office instructed the local officials not to proceed with the scheme.

After the Ministry of Transport had written to the Corporation describing the procedure for extending the trams to Hessle, it was agreed to seek a Light Railway Order from Pickering Park to the western end of the Hull Road in Hessle. It was also agreed to seek funding to widen the road at the same time as the tramway was extended. A ten-minute service was proposed with fares set at 1d per mile giving a fare of 4d to Hessle. Half fares would be available before 9am. One million passengers a year would be required to make the service pay.

When the Committee wrote to the East Riding County Council regarding widening Hessle Road, the Council passed a resolution stating that the time was not right. Other objectors included Hessle Urban District Council, The NER and J.B. McMaster & Sons, the operators of a Hull-Hessle bus service. Subsequently it was decided not to proceed after the Minister of Transport had stated that any such order was unlikely to be granted for lines outside the boundary.

Mr Rayner was anxious to reduce congestion in Midland Street, and proposed that the outward route be diverted from Carr Lane along Anne Street to Osborne Street, and thence to Porter Street and the existing route. The cost would be £5,000 and it was agreed to obtain Ministry of Transport approval.

The matter was referred back by the Council and Mr Rayner submitted five alternatives to the Sub-Committee. Scheme no. 1 involved the widening of Midland Street to the same width as Porter Street (minimum cost estimated at £80,000).

Scheme no. 2 covered purchasing and demolishing the Punch Hotel at the corner of Waterhouse Lane and Carr Lane (cost £45,000), but the street was too narrow and the terminus would

Although the Midland Street Signal Cabin had existed since 1899 no lavatory accommodation had been provided. The City Engineer's estimate of £40 to £50 for the installation of such facilities was approved.

The Chairman submitted a report on the state of the Tramways Department in May 1921. It had been a trying year with coal strikes, demands for improved services and free fares, and the problems of city centre congestion which had not been resolved to the Committee's satisfaction. A deficit of £9,646 had been converted into a surplus of £10,857, despite a fall in passenger levels and an increase in costs particularly for the permanent way. The October miners' strike had cost the undertaking over £5,000, whilst the effects of the present strike were unknown. However, the use of oil had gone a long way to mitigating its effects.

Most of the debt of the original system, including purchase of the horse and steam companies, had been paid for, and there was a Reserve Fund of £137, 900 to meet the cost of any renewals. (He might have added that if the undertaking had not been required to allocate sums for the relief of rates, the fund would have doubled in size.)

The Committee had expected much criticism given the scale of its task, and it had not been disappointed in this expectation. He did not mention the constant sniping by Councillor Stark at his own efforts, and those of the Manager who found many of his recommendations opposed by Stark who also criticised Willoughby for creating an expensive office for himself in the Tramways Offices.

He described the free pass system for the blind and pensioners, the low fares for children (of which he was especially proud), and the fact that the average fare paid per passenger per mile was much lower than elsewhere. The minimum fare was 1½d, although a workmen's fare of 1d was available until 9am.

The undertaking had required reorganisation to move from multiple to single control, whilst day-to-day operations had carried on. He thanked the General Manager and his staff for their support as well as his fellow Committee members.

By June 1921 the George Street and Charlotte Street repairs had been completed at a cost of £8,992 of which £3,300 could be recovered from the Highways Account for paving outside the tramways area, and £1,458 would be received as a grant towards labour costs. The City Engineer had received a grant from an Unemployment Grant Scheme which targeted schemes which involved the employment of unemployed men. The City Engineer reported his stock of rails was now fairly limited. Over

Two balcony cars stand at the new Osborne Street terminus in December 1923. The move was not popular with passengers who had to walk to connect with other routes in Queen Victoria Square. The nearest car is a Brush car of 1912 (possibly no. 148). (MJW)

block the Princes Dock entrance. In any case the area for the terminus could only accommodate a single car, which was totally inadequate. As widening Waterhouse Lane was out of the question the scheme had little to commend it.

The next Scheme (no. 3) would be to continue the track in Brook Street and into Osborne Street at a cost of £40,000. Scheme no. 4 was to lay rails to the east end of Osborne Street which would be convenient for the centre (but not much), but without a physical link to the other tracks. Midland Street would have to be retained for workmen's services and cars travelling to and from Liverpool Street Workshops. The cost was £12,000 plus the cost of paving at the eastern end of the street. By far the cheapest scheme at £6,000 was the already agreed Anne Street scheme, which would eliminate the delays at Midland Street and accelerate the service. It was agreed to lay tracks down the east end of Osborne Street, and to construct the Anne Street line. Midland Street would be retained for inward Hessle Road cars only.

In October 1921 the first fully enclosed car, no 56, entered service followed by no. 87 in November and no. 67 in December.

On 21 December 1921 Messrs Amos & Smith Ltd wrote to the Corporation asking it to extend the Hedon Road tramway a distance of approximately one mile long to the east end of King George Dock. The Traffic and Complaints Sub-Committee was reluctant to do so since there was little housing in the area and traffic would be mainly at rush hours. In May 1922 it decided not to extend the tramways, but to run buses from the tram terminus to the dock entrance. This started on 21 February 1923 after prolonged discussions with the London and North Eastern Railway Company about the continued opening of the dock entrance gateway. Despite a promise that this would remain open so that buses could convey workers on to the dock, the gate was in fact closed and the service ceased in March 1923.

It was agreed on 23 January 1922 to charge the Electricity Committee 2s 6d for each tram standard that was being used for street lighting. The Tramways Committee would accept no responsibility for any damage to lamps caused by wayward trolley poles. The Committee also rejected a proposal from Messrs J.C. Francis & Co., Advertising Agents, to rent a large number of these standards to carry special advertising lamps thereon.

Councillor Mackenzie stated that he had received several complaints about the Spring Bank and Beverley Road circular system, and suggested reverting to the old system. Mr Rayner replied that some new systems were to be introduced whereby cars, by means of an indicator (several of which were on order), would be despatched from King Edward Street according to the requirements of each route, and it was agreed to await the experiences from this system.

Old age pensioners' passes were intended for the retired, but when a Mr James Allenby was caught using his pass for the delivery of sugar bags to various local shops he was instructed not to do so or lose the pass.

In March 1922 The Transport and General Workers Union complained that the Tramways Department had broken a verbal arrangement whereby as trams received vestibules each route would be converted starting with Hessle Road, Anlaby Road, Holderness Road and Beverley Road etc. It asked that the Holderness Road route be converted as agreed to avoid motormen having to drive both vestibuled and open trams. Mr Rayner confirmed the verbal promise, and stated that six more cars were required to convert the Holderness Road, which would take three months.

It is worth considering the training given to crews in the 1920s. Mr Henry Sellers joined the City Tramways in the early 1920s. He was put with a conductor, Alf Hargreaves, on the Hessle Road route in order to learn the ropes. After a short time, usually about two weeks, conductors were allocated to permanent jobs. He was allocated to the Spring Bank West route which was being worked by open balcony and non-vestibuled cars. His driver was Albert McWilliams who had fought in the Boer War and The Great War. He wore two or three capes and two pairs of gloves. He was with him for a few years which reflected the way in which crews even within depots were kept to certain routes and did not swap. To an extent the allocation of tramcars to specific routes (especially at Cottingham Road depot) followed a similar pattern.

He was then instructed to learn driving which entailed going out with another driver after his normal shift. He received a card which had to be shown to the motorman authorising him to drive a tram under supervision. The usual motorman stood behind him and watched to ensure that he did everything correctly. After a set number of hours he was examined by Chief Inspector Crawford. This involved driving a tram along the Anlaby Road route and return. The Chief Inspector also stood behind him all the way. Trainees were then simply told if they had passed or not. Mr Sellers was successful but not until the holiday season was he allocated his first tram. Once he had driven a tram he received the motorman's wage whether he conducted or drove. Eventually he became a permanent motorman and later a bus driver.

In April 1922 the Tramways Committee discovered that Mr Rayner was one of a short list of three for the General Manager post with Manchester Corporation and, Councillor Mell dissenting, it was agreed that Mr Rayner be offered a revised salary of £1,200 per annum rising to £1,500 in yearly increments of £100.

In July 1922 the City Engineer discovered a large number of cracked rails on the Hessle Road and Holderness Road routes which had been laid between 1898 and 1902. He recommended tackling the Hessle Road track first at a cost of £29,000, which included 75 per cent new paving wood. As an experiment the City Engineer intended to asphalt the portion of track between the rails from the Boulevard to West Dock Avenue. The eventual contract cost £8300 (less rails). It was decided to ask the Ministry of Transport for authority to borrow the £29,000, and to seek funds from the Unemployment Grants Committee. At the same time it was agreed to replace the centre poles from the Boulevard to West Dock Avenue with side poles and span wire construction. These poles cost £9 6s 6d each to purchase. Finally, the City Engineer was authorised to obtain prices for the supply of 500 to 1,000 tons of rail.

Cars now worked regularly to Durham Street only on the Holderness Road route, but the General Manager had been unable to find a suitable site for a lavatory, so he had arranged for drivers and conductors to change with their colleagues on the through cars when required.

Mr Rayner referred to a meeting of the Municipal Tramways Association at Newcastle upon Tyne when the questions of wear and tear on the track had been discussed. He was of the opinion that if the weight of the cars could be reduced it would prolong the life of the track (he ignored that the fully enclosed cars were heavier than previously). He wished to reconstruct two cars (not identified) along these lines to test the question. This was approved. Which two cars? Not nos 26 and 113 for it is probably much too early.

Thoughts turned to fares revision once more, particularly the penny fare. Mr Rayner informed members that if a penny fare was adopted an additional 90,000 penny fare passengers would be required to break even. Bearing in mind that passengers numbers had fallen by 1,579,000 (revenue decrease of £9,466), as a result of unemployment and wage reductions, it would entail some risk to introduce a penny fare since he could not estimate with any certainty what the effect would be. Recent reductions in tramwaymen's wages would help but not much. However it would be possible to divide each route into three penny stages with two stages at 1½d and three for 2d, and he

NOVEL HULL TRAMCAR: MANAGER DESIGNS SPECIAL CAR FOR QUICK LOADING.

An exclusive series of "Mail" photographs illustrating the various points of improvement in the new tramcar designed by Mr E. S. Rayner (the Hull tramways manager). The car has just been completed and promises to be a great success.
Above (left): A view of the platform of the car, showing the revolving door which the driver adjusts before each journey. By the use of this, the public can gain access to the upper deck by both the front and the back steps; (right), a general view of the car.
Below (left): An interior view, showing the large space at the end of the car and the front steps, which can be used by the public, the driver being partitioned off by the folding door; (right), a close view of the new style of route indicator, which can be lit up at night. The new style of ventilation is also seen. The car has a worm-drive and uses about half the usual current.

A description of no. 101 appeared in the local press and it was accompanied by this page which illustrated the various unique design aspects of the car. (MJW)

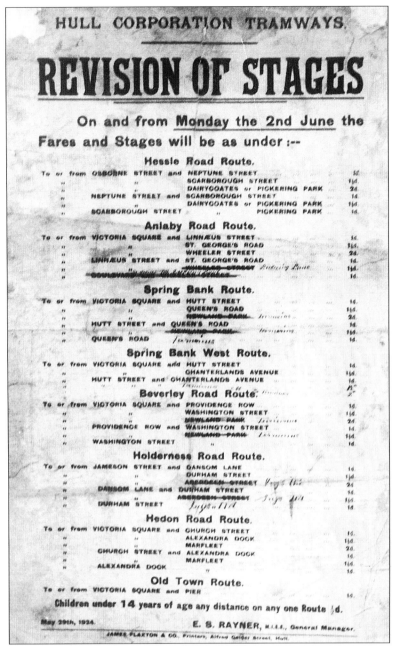

Copy of a notice of the fares revisions of 1924. (MJW)

recommended a trial period starting in November of two months, which was agreed.

At the same meeting the General Manager was instructed to take action to stop tramway employees getting on to the roof of the Holderness Road tram sheds to watch rugby league matches on the Craven Park ground of Hull Kingston Rovers!

On 22 November 1922 the General Manager reported that, as instructed by the Committee, he had fitted roller blinds in the side windows of cars on the Spring Bank and Beverley Road routes as an experiment and that he considered this a success. He asked for 300 more to be ordered to equip the remaining cars at a cost of £2 7s 6d each but the Committee would only authorise 80.

An Enquiry (Special) Committee had been formed by the City Council to look at every department to assess efficiency and to see where possible economies could be made. Mr Rayner (entitled the Tramway Manager) went before this Committee. He stated that the Traffic section had 100 less staff than in 1920 and the numbers could not be further reduced.

Cars were now running 1,000 miles a week less than in 1920 and as the repairs which had been hung up during the war had now been carried out, he said that a considerable reduction could

be effected at the Liverpool Street Car Repair shops, and that 35 men could be dispensed with immediately. The Committee agreed and instructed the Tramways Committee to enquire into this and arrange the reduction of 35 staff at an annual saving of £6,000 in wages. Mr Rayner thought that a further reduction in materials could be made totalling £4,000.

The Committee discussed the question of tram track repairs with the Manager and the City Engineer. The year's estimate for track repairs was £35,100 of which £4,000 had been spent. It was agreed that repairs should not exceed £500 per mile of track per annum which would reduce the remaining expenditure to £18,000 and make a saving of £17,100. (During the past three years £125,000 (£1,100 per mile) had been spent on track repairs, presumably to make up for the neglect of the war years, not that this was admitted.)

No economies could be found in the Distribution and Generating Station but one clerk in the stores could be dispensed with (a favourite term in the minutes) to save £80. It was proposed to transfer the Tramways offices to the Guildhall at a saving of £800. A total saving of £27,980 was involved compared with savings of £800 in the Town Clerk's Department, £186 in the Art Gallery and £158 in the Museums Department!

A more serious subject was the question of staff at Liverpool Street Workshops. A Council-wide Enquiry (Special) Committee, which was examining the efficiency of every department, had cast its eye over the tramways undertaking. It recommended that a number of staff be dispensed with. Some members wanted to defer consideration of that part of the report for six months, but after some discussion (i.e. argument) it was decided (agreed is too strong a word), that the Staff Sub-Committee should consider it at its next meeting.

Approved track repairs (not described in the minutes) were already being carried out according to the City Engineer. Mr Rayner agreed to reduce the Traffic and Stores Section by one clerk but stated that he could be employed in the office handling the additional work created by discount ticket sales and the penny fare!

It proved to be a busy meeting as Mr Rayner's proposals for a two-year track renewal programme at a cost of £88,155 were agreed, and an application to borrow £100,000 to cover the cost was to be made to the Ministry of Transport. The programme was:

1.	Holderness Road from Witham to Summergangs Road (1,983 yards)	£29,120
2.	Beverley Road from Melwood Grove to Cottingham Road (893 yards)	£13,000
3.	Savile Street (165 yards)	£2,435
4.	Witham (165 yards)	£6,600
5.	Beverley Road (1,470 yards)	£22,000
6.	Spring Bank (1,000 yards)	£15,000
		£88,155

To this should be added some £29,000 already agreed for Hessle Road.

made. The Tramways Committee was reminded that if the contract was to receive financial assistance from the Unemployment Grants Committee, local labour must be used. A reply to the application for a grant was still awaited. It was decided that if no grant was forthcoming the reduced price offer would be accepted.

The Unemployment Grants Committee in March 1923 informed the Tramways Committee that if it continued to purchase rails from abroad no grant would be forthcoming. The Tramways Committee was unaware of any such condition and had already entered into a contract for 1,000 tons. The Town Clerk was instructed to take the matter up with the UGC and to communicate with the city's Members of Parliament if no satisfaction was obtained.

On 28 March 1923 it was decided to run further bus services using buses originally purchased for the abortive King George Dock service. The first was to run from Paragon Station along George Street, North Bridge, Witham and Dansom Lane (duplicating the "TH") to the Garden Village. However as two ex-service men were already running buses to this area (Blue Bus Service) the Corporation route was delayed until March after the Council had purchased the company for £975.

The Corporation also bought the Hull to Hessle service of J.B. McMaster, partly to prevent a takeover but also to control services along Hessle Road. The cost was £8,000 for six buses which provided a ten-minute service, but central government would not give powers to run outside the city boundary so it was sold to H.C.Motors for £5,000.

Two more routes were introduced – the first, on 15 October, a semi-circular route that took in English Street and Goulton Street to the south of Hessle Road and St George's Road, Albert Avenue, Chanterlands Avenue, Park Avenue (later rerouted via Newstead Street and Belvoir Street), Princes Avenue, Queens Road, Sculcoates Lane to Air Street in industrial Bankside. The second ran to Southcoates Lane via Alfred Gelder Street, Craven Street and Newbridge Road.

Pressure for external advertising was increasing as several companies were advertising on competing buses. Mr Thomas Bell, who had the advertising rights, wrote to the Corporation appraising it of the situation and was invited to address the Committee.

He showed photographs of advertising on Newcastle Corporation cars, which limited advertising to the outside of the side of the car between the upper deck and lower saloon windows or decency boards on older trams. He was willing to pay £2,000 for the rights if these locations were adopted and he assured the Committee that the enamel plates to be used would not disfigure or damage the cars.

He offered £8 per annum per car but the Committee wanted £10 per annum for 50 of the oldest cars without vestibules, in addition to the existing rent for interiors, on the understanding

In December 1922 the North Eastern Railway's District Engineer informed the City Engineer that certain of the special castings at the Anlaby road crossing were broken and required immediate replacement. The City Engineer estimated that this would cost £500, including a new half-crossing from Messrs Hadfields costing £415 7s 6d. He had discussed the possibility of adopting a built-up crossing at Botanic Gardens but the acuteness of the angled crossing precluded this. However, a built-up crossing was provided at a cost of £710 when the Holderness Road crossing was discussed at the next meeting.

In January 1923 the Tramways Committee asked the Watch and Licensing Committee to consult with it before considering applications to run bus services within the city, or running into the city from outside. When an application was received to run buses from the village of Sutton (immediately outside the city), along Holderness Road, the Tramways Committee advocated refusal as there was an intensive service along the road, and buses would only add to the congestion. It further suggested that all applications to run into the city along tram routes (all roads excepting Stoneferry Road/New Cleveland Street) should be refused unless they were to run to and from the tram terminus.

At the Traffic and Complaints Sub-Committee Mr Rayner informed councillors that he had abandoned the circular working on the Spring Bank and Beverley Road routes. The reversion to the old system was working very well but it was costing more than £1,250 per annum in wages plus extra running and maintenance costs. No one seemed to ask why, but it did seem a popular move.

Mr Rayner was elected a member of the Tramway Rolling Stock Joint Committee of the Tramways and Light Railways Association. He received the congratulations of the Tramways Committee and authority to attend any meetings. In March he informed members that the annual meeting of Tramway Managers would be held in Hull in June and he and the Chairman and Deputy-Chairman were authorised to make any necessary arrangements. Alderman Willoughby was later elected to the Municipal Tramways Association.

A condition of contracts placed for labour intensive work such as track renewal, was that any additional labour should be taken from the local Labour Exchange. The contractors for the Beverley Road and Spring Bank renewals stated that if relieved of this restriction, a price reduction of 7½ per cent could be that such cars would be withdrawn as and when required for vestibuling, and subject to the design approval of the General Manager. Mr Bell accepted the offer.

In March the General Manager submitted a new design for a car body which would permit quicker loading and unloading as well as a considerable reduction in weight. An offer of the English Electric Company, Preston, to construct the car at a cost of £1,045 was accepted. This, of course, was the new number 101, of which more later.

When the Ministry of Transport considered the Corporation's application for a loan in May 1923, it suggested that in view of the fact that the overall width of Hull's tramcars was 7' 2", the minimum interval between track centres was 8' 5" to provide the required clearance of 15 inches between cars, and therefore that the centre poles on Beverly Road between Melwood Grove and Epworth Street be removed.

Councillor Ombler had suggested certain developments for the tram service. These were discussed at the Traffic and Complaints Sub-Committee on 19 June. His suggestion that some cars on the Anlaby Road and Holderness Road routes should be labelled "Football Cars" was accepted, and a minimum fare of 2d for Holderness Road and 1½d on Anlaby Road was also agreed. The installation of a loop line at the top of Boulevard on Anlaby Road for such cars was not approved, although this could have proved useful in turning cars without reaching the level crossing. Nor was there any support for lines to be laid along Queen's Road between Beverley Road and Princes Avenue for a circular service. Consideration of replacing the interlaced track near North Bridge was deferred.

The Sub-Committee looked on with favour a proposal from the Anlaby Motor Bus Company to run a bus between the Holderness Road tram terminus and Aldborough in the east outside the city boundary. It was agreed to introduce through fares.

By July 1923 vestibuling of the cars had almost been completed, and the step risers eliminated as a means of advertising, and it was agreed to discuss a revised contract with Mr Bell.

Mr Rayner's new car arrived in June 1923. It was shown to the annual meeting of the Managers' Section of the Municipal Tramways Association held during the third week of June 1923. The design reflected the principles laid out in his paper at the MTA Annual Conference at Newcastle-on-Tyne in September 1922. The trip taken by the managers proved to be very successful according to the Tramway and Railway World of 19 July

1923. Its silent running was said to be remarkable, little being heard beyond the rolling of wheels on the rails and it was considered that some of the defects of existing designs had been overcome. Seating capacity was 60 compared with 78 of the latest bogie cars, and 56 for normal single truck cars.

His principles that were set down in his paper included:

1. Split back axle with a double worm drive
2. Two high speed motors suspended clear of the axles
3. Wheels other than the driver's free (sic)
4. Drum brakes
5. Ball and roller bearings throughout
6. Low body with no cantilevers
7. Continuous frame carrying the body
8. Springing as easy as possible with the weight reduced to the lowest possible amount compatible with safety and stability

He saw the need for flexibility rather than rigidity and to improve the ride of a tramcar so that it compared favourably with a railway carriage, despite tramcars not having a resilient track on which to run. Given a length of respectably corrugated tramlines, unwelded joints and an average car, individuals could experience a dose of vibro-massage second to none, unfortunately applied to the wrong place! He considered springing to be a neglected science in tramcars and motor vehicles. Motor vehicles had a small amount of unsprung weight compared with a tramcar truck owing to the adoption of propeller shaft with its bevel or worm gearing.

A worm drive permitted the use of an increased gear ratio with an increased motor speed. A smooth start was obtained with a comparatively low starting current. The size of the gears was much reduced and provided an improved road clearance. Previous designs had not exploited the use of roller and ball bearings. His car saved about twenty percent in friction but he anticipated savings to accrue from reduced costs of lubrication, attention, inspection and renewal.

No. 101 was 29ft 8in. long over the collision fenders, the length over platforms being 28ft 8in. The wheelbase was 7ft with body length being 16ft 8in. and vestibules were 6ft long. The car's width was 6ft 10½in. Wheels were 26 inches in diameter. The car weighed 10 tons but had specially designed gears been used, this could have been reduced to 8 tons 10cwt. Propulsion was by two high speed motors (Dick Kerr 85A of 42 hp) giving 1,150 revolutions per minutes, the gear ratio being 4/25. Each motor was separately suspended at each end of the tram, the worm drive enabling the motor at either end to operate the opposite pair of wheels thus reducing the weight on the axle to about 200 lb. Mr Rayner estimated that the worm drive could reduce energy consumption by as much as fifty per cent.

The stairs from the top deck were taken into the lower saloon which was level throughout the lower deck. The driver had a separate cab,

A deserted Jameson Street plays host to car no. 106 which is awaiting departure time before setting off for Ings Road. (MJW)

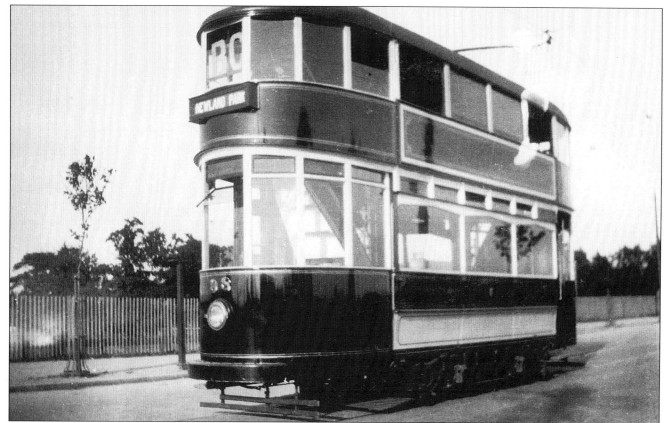

Hurst Nelson car no. 98 stands in a very deserted part of Cottingham Road near Newland Park. The section between Newland Avenue and Chanterlands Avenue was sparsely populated at this point. No. 98 was an early withdrawal in April 1933 its upper deck going to another car. (PM/LRS)

and the vestibule had a revolving folding door making exit and entrance of the lower saloon as easy as possible. This would also reduce the need for passengers to stand on the platform at the conductor's end. Lower deck seating was longitudinal and the top deck had garden seats with swing backs, the arrangement being staggered to give more space when passengers were moving simultaneously to the gangway from both ends.

When the reintroduction of all-night services was raised, Mr Rayner recommended a half-hourly service of motorbuses for the six tram routes. It was agreed to use buses until 2.30am from Queen Victoria Square with a minimum fare of 3d.

Also in July 1923 the Tramways Committee agreed to provide a ten-minute frequency on service "TH" and run it via King Edward Street and Jameson Street for a trial period of two months. This started in September 1923 but was not a success and ceased in December.

In July 1923 the Tramways Committee visited existing routes and the proposed extensions before deciding that eight extensions should be carried out over the next five years at a total cost of £145,000 as follows:

1. From the existing Anlaby Road terminus along Anlaby Road to Pickering Lane (also known as Pickering Road which it became – in 1915 powers had been obtained to extend to Calvert Lane but this was a longer extension)
2. From the Anlaby Road extension along Calvert Lane to Spring Bank West to meet the proposed Spring Bank extension
3. From the Spring Bank West terminus near Walton Street along Spring Bank West to Calvert Lane (powers existed for Walton Street to Alliance Avenue)
4. From Park Avenue along Chanterlands Avenue to Cottingham Road to meet the extended Cottingham Road route
5. From the Pickering Park terminus along Hessle Road to the city boundary near the south end of Pickering Road
6. Along Cottingham Road to the city boundary
7. From Newland along Beverley Road to Endyke Lane
8. From Anlaby Road along Hawthorn Avenue to Hessle Road

No.1 would serve populated areas between the Newington crossing and Calvert Lane and partly built housing developments near Pickering Lane. The Calvert Lane tracks would, presumably, have been for depot access as Calvert Lane possessed only a few houses on the eastern side and the former Hull and Barnsley Railway land on the other. The Spring Bank West extension would have served the northern end of many streets that led to Anlaby Road, and would have enabled residents to avoid a long walk. The proposal to go only as far as Calvert Lane must surely have been a temporary solution as a new large Corporation housing estate immediately west of the terminus was planned to grow shortly.

The Chanterlands Avenue decision was surprising. Beyond Goddard Avenue housing was (and still is) sparse. It would extract traffic from the extended Cottingham Road route. The Cottingham Road route ran alongside a planned Corporation estate on its northern side but did not go into it. The short Hessle Road extension to the City boundary would not serve housing in any quantity. The Beverley Road extension would serve a moderately populated area immediately beyond the existing terminus and a growing area near the terminus. Again, this fell short of a planned Corporation estate along Greenwood Avenue. Councillors asked that the widening of Beverley Road should allow for tram extensions on reservations at the side of the road rather than in the centre, and that all future extensions in such circumstances should be to the side of the road.

The final proposal would link two major routes, the "A" and "D" near their respective termini. Hawthorn Avenue was a long and heavily populated street whose residents had to choose which long walk to make to either of the two routes, a decision familiar to many citizens who lived in large areas between tram routes.

129

Photographs of the Anlaby Road extension, which kept to the southern side of the highway, are very rare so it is fortunate to have this shot of a car at the Pickering Road terminus on an unknown date. Behind the car are the Lees Rest Homes whilst the lack of housing on the right can be seen. (MJW/HC)

Another view of the Anlaby Road extension shows a car crossing the junction with Calvert Lane on the right. Proposals for a tramway along Calvert Lane were thwarted by objections by the LNER. (MJW/HC)

A surprising omission was a potentially more remunerative link from Holderness Road along Southcoates Lane to Preston Road and the large Council housing estate that was being built. This was served by a bus route via Newbridge Road which started on 23 October 1923. This followed the "TH" route as far as Craven Street. Newbridge Road lay at the end of several streets that ran through to Holderness Road. Inevitably it extracted traffic from the trams but not until the late 1920s was it profitable when it became a candidate for trolleybus operation.

After the transfer of the terminus of the Holderness Road cars to Jameson Street the Savile Street traders complained about a reduction in business and a consequent devaluation of their properties. They wanted the trams to revert to Savile Street, or to travel in an anti-clockwise loop around Jameson Street, King Edward Street and Savile Street.

Councillor Hall also attended the Traffic and Complaints Sub-Committee on 20 November 1923 and suggested that compulsory stopping places should be introduced. He claimed that many cars, although not full, did not always stop for passengers who wished to board. It was agreed to investigate specific instances but not to take any other action since delays caused by bridges and crossings made it impossible to impose a rigid stopping system.

The same meeting heard that the Newbridge Road and Fish Dock bus services were running at a loss. As a result the Fish Dock service was divided into two (City-Witty Street and Fish Dock-Air Street) and the Air Street-Stoneferry portion was abandoned except at meal times. The City-Witty Street ran along English Street parallel to Hessle Road. Although the service was not frequent there was some abstraction from the Hessle Road trams since residents could avoid the long walk to the tram. One has the feeling that Mr Rayner did not want the Newbridge Road service but that it was foisted on him by the Committee.

Meanwhile he had conducted a census of passengers boarding the "TH" cars which had been extended to the railway station. Only an average of four passengers travelled to the station, and an average of five passengers boarded there, whilst the extension required two cars from the Holderness Road and also upset (his word) the Durham Street short service running. It was agreed to cut the route back to Jameson Street.

Mr Rayner offered two suggestions for the position of track when the Spring Bank was reconstructed. The tracks could continue along the centre of the roadway or be located at the side. It was decided to retain the central location.

City-centre routings were discussed (again!) and Mr Rayner's suggestion that the Holderness Road trams operate a loop via Jameson Street, King Edward Street and Savile Street as an experiment on four Sundays was agreed, with the addition of the Hedon Road cars. Members also agreed to replace the centre poles in King Edward Street by span wires attached to buildings.

Mr Rayner recommended that the "SC" cars be discontinued and that the whole Beverley Road service be run through to Newland Park. A three- or four-minute service would be provided with additional cars at peak hours to and from Queens Road. School children along Spring Bank would still have special cars, and anyone using the Spring Bank service could transfer with the help of the conductor to Cottingham Road.

Mr Rayner sought permission to acquire a strip of land on the north side of Spring Bank between Vane Street and the Botanic crossing to enable two tracks to be provided for "fast" traffic between the tracks. This was referred to the Housing and Town Planning Committee but no action appears to have ensued.

The planned renewal of track in Witham resulted in Holderness cars being diverted via Drypool Bridge, but concern about the delays incurred from the closure of that bridge for river

traffic led Mr Rayner to arrange the work so that the track could be used at tide times if necessary.

The Osborne Street tramway finally opened on 3 December 1923 when services "D" and "DP" were transferred from Waterworks Street to a new terminus just short of Waterhouse Lane, a minute's walk from Carr Lane and Queen Victoria Square.

Mr Rayner undertook a three-day survey of delays at the Botanic Gardens crossing using a recording clock. On 28 January 1924 he reported to the Tramways Committee. Three separate days were chosen, Thursday 10 January, Saturday 12 January and Monday 14 January. There were 395 cars on the Thursday of which 154 were delayed for more than 3 minutes. The busiest time was between 8am and 9am on each morning when 34 cars were scheduled to work over the crossing. In that hour the gates were closed for a total of 20 minutes (Thursday), 27 minutes (Saturday) but only 12 minutes on the Monday. On Saturdays between 12 noon and 5 pm the number of cars was deliberately reduced so that they could be used for specials on the Anlaby Road route for a Hull City AFC cup-tie. Delays were evenly spread throughout the day there being no let up in the evening. Although not mentioned in the report many of the trains (goods trains in particular) would also cross the Hessle Road, Anlaby Road, Beverley Road and Holderness Road routes with corresponding delays.

The Department had spent between £2,000 and £3,000 a year in providing additional cars to alleviate the delays but without much effect, except for additional congestion in the city centre. Compared with 1913 the situation had deteriorated in that stoppages were only 17½% compared with 26-30% in 1924. (A full schedule can be seen in Appendix 6.)

A meeting with LNER officials at York revealed that they were not unfavourable to proceeding with the abolition of some level crossings. It was agreed to maintain contacts with the LNER.

The Committee declined to comment on a letter from the Hull and District Chamber of Trade stating that no more tramway extensions should be considered since the system was out of date and new routes should be bus operated.

The LNER objected to the provision of a line along Calvert Lane that was included in a Bill then before Parliament, and the Tramways Committee decided that unless a satisfactory agreement could be made with the LNER, section 11 which contained the proposal should be deleted.

In March 1924 approval was given to relay the Anlaby Road track at a cost of £44,000 which included asphalting the areas between the rails and substituting span wires for centre poles.

A special meeting of the Tramways Committee was called by the Chairman on 14 April 1924 to discuss car fares and to see if any fare reduction were possible. He had visited Mr Wilkinson the General Manager of Bradford Corporation on 20 March to discuss the latter's pass system. This had been in operation for 18 weeks and had increased takings by an average of £170 per week. Unlike Hull, unemployment levels in Bradford had decreased from 13,000 to 5,000.

On Bradford's 1½d stages a pass cost 2s per week whilst passes for 3d stages cost 3s 6d. A pass was issued for 1½d routes (13 of them) for 3s 6d, a saving of 1s. The number of passes issued was 9,396 (2s), 1,042 (3s 6d) and 147 (4s 6d). Nearly 12% of the total passengers had purchased passes. Bradford's 1½d ticket carried passengers an average of 1¾ miles. Mr Wilkinson thought that the use of a 1d fare would prohibit the pass system from working.

Mr Rayner stated that in Hull a 1½d stage pass would cost 2s and a 2d stage pass would cost 2s 6d, whilst on all routes the first 1½d stage would cost 4s 6d and a system-wide pass 5s 6d. He proposed the introduction of a 1d fare stage for a minimum of six furlongs. Where that already existed there would be no change necessary but the other routes would require alterations. He submitted a schedule of proposed stages and the number of passengers on each stage. By far the greatest number of passengers was carried on the 1½d stages (between 74% on Hedon Road and 87% on Anlaby Road), so that any alteration to introduce a 1d stage would affect the greatest number of passengers. The proposed 1d fare would cost at least £7,200 per annum.

After a long discussion it was agreed to introduce a weekly pass system similar to Bradford's from 1 June 1924. The passes would be available from conductors and would be transferable and cost:

1½d stages on any one route	2s
2d stages on any one route	2s 6d
The first 1½d stage from the city centre on all routes	4s
Passes over the whole system	5s

The tables circulated by Mr Rayner can be seen at Appendix 6.

The financial results for 1923/4 showed a profit of £24,460 on the trams and a deficit of £5,475 on the buses.

In May 1924 it was agreed to print 20,000 timetables, 16 pages long, by the Goddard Advertising Agency with a map of two colours, all advertising rights to lie with the company.

It was agreed in June to present employees who attained 20 years service with a suitable gift to the value of £5. A presentation evening was arranged for all employees with more than 21 years' service.

In October the contract for the Chanterlands Avenue extension was awarded to Sangwin, Ltd. of Hull, despite this being over £200 more than the City Engineer's estimate. The decision was not unanimous, and when the South-West Hull Labour Party complained about not accepting the lowest tender it was informed that the lowest tender had, indeed, been accepted as the City Engineer could only submit an estimate!

Mr Rayner informed the Traffic and Complaints Sub-Committee on 18 November 1924 that the number of passes sold had risen from 2,453 in the first week to 4,600 in the previous week. Although overall patronage had increased, the annual cost of the concession had risen to £10,000, some £3,000 more than his previous estimate. By October 1925 the number of weekly passes had risen to 4,955 on weekdays and 34 on Sundays (over 100 in the summer) providing an income of £566.

It was agreed to display the model tramcar which had been part of the Corporation's stand at the Wembley Empire Exhibition at the Pickering Museum.

Mr Rayner obtained approval for two more tramcars to be reconstructed along the same lines as the recently rebuilt car.

To meet increased traffic on the Pickering Park route Mr Rayner had allocated another car to increase the frequency from 6¼ minutes to 5 minutes. He was looking at ways in which the "DP" riders could be confined to the "DP" cars. Mr W. Elliot, a "DP" user, wrote proposing that during the hours of 12 noon to 2pm, 5pm to 7pm and 8.30pm to 10.30pm a minimum fare of 2d be charged on "DP" cars. Consideration was deferred to see the results of the increased frequency. Subsequently, a further car (taken from the "D" route) was allocated to the route and this seemed to prove satisfactory.

Approval was given in March 1925 to extend the Chanterlands Avenue route from the original terminus just beyond the railway bridge to the bend near Goddard Avenue, some 250 yards.

In July 1924 it was agreed to alter the four corner windows in the top saloon and the front and back windows on the top of the

vestibules to enable them to be opened. Drivers and conductors were instructed to have the doors in the bottom saloon closed unless a passenger asked for the door to be open.

The vexed question of private omnibuses operating on tramway routes was considered by the Committee. The Ministry of Transport thought that the imposition of a higher fare on such routes was only in the public interest if it were not exorbitant. The Committee asked the Watch Committee to obtain, before issuing or renewing a licence, route details where paralleled by a tramway, and to require the bus operator to charge not less than 1d in excess of the tramway fare for the same route.

Finally, it was resolved, as an experiment, to issue a shilling ticket on Sundays entitling the purchaser to travel by tram or bus on any route, the experiment to last until the end of the year.

As no mains were available beyond Calvert Lane the new Pickering Lane terminus of the Anlaby Road route could not be lit. Lighting was provided as far as Calvert Lane and the City Engineer ordered reflective signs for the route between there and the terminus.

The extensions along Chanterlands Avenue to Park Avenue "SW", along Cottingham Road to Hall Road "BC", and along Anlaby Road to Pickering Lane (later Road), "AP", were opened on 5 October 1925. The Chanterlands Avenue frequency of four minutes would be retained but would require two additional cars, eight men and cost £24 per week. The Anlaby Road frequency of 2⅔ (!) minutes would become every 7½ minutes to Pickering Lane, and three minutes to Wheeler Street, requiring 3 more cars, 16 men and cost £48 per week. Hall Road would enjoy a 7½-minute headway in addition to the 3¾ minute service to Newland.

Plans for the Beverley Road extension were agreed at the same meeting, including a triangular junction at the Haworth Arms crossroads to permit cars to proceed to the depot from the extension.

With increasing traffic and the additional cars on the "AP" route, the "A" terminus was obstructing the flow of traffic and it was decided to construct a short siding at the entrance to the new Boothferry Road in a central reservation.

Whilst the receipts for the trams were falling due to the adverse employment situation, the newly introduced motor bus services were not performing very well either. In November 1925 Mr Rayner revealed that in October and the first two weeks of November only the night buses made a profit (£89 16s 6d). Losses on the other routes ranged from £11 15s 1d on the Newbridge Road services, to £125 13s 11d on the Garden Village route. Income and passenger numbers were remarkably stable.

The additional cars on the "BC" and "SW" routes added to the congestion in the city centre. Mr Rayner sought to cut the Gordian Knot once more by proposing changes to the northern and eastern route termini, only for the matter to be referred to the Traffic and Complaints Sub-Committee. He had five proposals: "BC" and "B" cars to terminate in the west side of Jameson Street, "SW" and "SWC" cars continue to use King Edward Street, Marfleet cars terminate at the east end of Jameson Street, Holderness Road cars "H" terminate in Savile Street, and the "TH" cars terminate opposite the Dock Office.

Delays in King Edward Street at peak times ranged from 5 to 7 minutes and were disrupting the Beverley Road cars more than anything else. Passengers were confused about where they could catch their cars in King Edward Street, there being no definitive stopping place. The eastern services posed different problems since the Holderness Road cars carried twice as many passengers as the Hedon Road cars. Despite some traffic abstraction on Holderness Road by the Newbridge Road bus service, traffic had risen to the extent that the crossover at Durham Street would need improving or moving to Summergangs Road. Traffic

Both views show the effect on car interiors of the use of route letters and route boards. The interior of the car with just a route letter is much lighter. (MJW)

remained heavy as far as the depot (which is why some cars still terminated there) but was, at present, very light thereafter. The revised arrangement for the "TH" service would avoid the need for travel along King Edward Street to reach its terminus in Jameson Street, thus adding to the delays.

Dock traffic on Hedon Road was all one way to the docks between 7am and 8am Mondays to Saturdays, from the docks on Monday to Friday from 4.30pm to 5.30pm and 11.30am to 12.30pm on Saturdays. Through workmen's cars from the northern routes would run via Jameson Street, and from the western routes via Savile Street. It was essential to reduce the number of additional cars provided to obviate delays and to reduce costs, since the granting of various fare concessions was having an adverse effect on the system. A three month trial period commencing 15 February 1926 was agreed.

Mr Rayner also obtained approval to equip two cars with slipper brakes as an experiment in order to improve braking performance, especially on greasy rails and also to accelerate the service.

1925 had also seen the extension of the Wheeler Street Depot opened with a new entrance in Wheeler Street itself (cars continued to leave by the existing single track into Anlaby Road). A new running shed was provided at Liverpool Street Depot.

In 1925 the department moved into the former Education Department offices in Albion Street. It had been accepted that the Albion Street offices were inadequate and several attempts had been made to find new premises.

In January 1926 it was decided to take up the rails that had been laid on Stoneferry Bridge, thus bringing the tram scheme saga to an end.

Councillor Toogood proposed a motion at the Council meeting on 4 February asking the Tramways Committee to abandon the use of route letters, and to introduce a route numbering system. Mr Rayner pointed out that roller indicators were gradually being fitted to cars below the route board which showed the full destination. It was resolved that only a single route letter be used on any route since the blinds would show the actual destination. Photographs taken after this date and in the early thirties show that double letters to show short workings were still in use. As late as July 1938 cars running along Beverley Road to Cottingham Road showed "BN". The decision

was ignored to the extent that the extended Holderness Road cars to Ings Road showed "IRH" or "IRTH" for a while! Tram route letters continued unchanged, even when motor bus routes were given numbers in 1931.

In February 1926 it was also decided that, in addition to the red and white bands painted on tramway standards that were stopping places, a notice indicating a stopping place should be painted.

The City centre termini issue was referred back by the full Council meeting on 25 January. Councillor Wheeldon suggested that the northern routes should follow an anti-clockwise loop around Chariot Street, Waterworks Street and King Edward Street, but he had no support. Councillor Stark suggested installing two crossovers in King Edward Street to enable cars to come in and cross over on to the outgoing track, and it was agreed to look at this and to route the "TH" cars through Savile Street into Jameson Street and return. But consideration of any other termini alterations was deferred until the Beverley Road extension was opened. Meanwhile congestion continued and the loops which might have reduced it were rejected.

Another proposal from Councillor Stark that a "TH" car be run at 10.30pm on Saturdays was agreed for a month's trial period.

A special meeting of the Tramways Committee on 2 March 1926 considered fares. The total surplus after deducting the bus deficit was £4,500 from an income of £326,575 which Mr Rayner considered far too small for the service provided. The

133

situation would be worse for the next year with additional capital expenditure and additional contributions to the Widows' and Orphans' Pension Fund, so that an overall loss was likely. Either some fares should go up or concessions awarded recently should be withdrawn.

Withdrawal of the weekly passes would bring in an extra £18,000. Increases to the pass purchase price as an alternative would accrue some £8,000. Abolition of discount tickets would increase revenue by £1200. Making workmen's fares available to 8am only would create £4800 of increased revenue. The adoption of a universal fare of 1½d (workmen's morning fare excepted) would raise £6,500. Further amendments to the sale of passes could raise £15,000.

Mr Rayner overwhelmed the meeting with six schedules about ridership of each category. A census during week ending 30 January 1926 revealed 1,118,497 paying passengers using the trams, with a further 217,248 (19.4%) journeys made by 6789 pass holders. A further census two weeks later revealed 2154 old age pension pass holders using the trams on a Tuesday (possibly chosen because it was a market day). The previous Tuesday had seen 25,226 workmen using the cars compared with 158,271 passengers paying the full 1d, 1½d and 2d fares. Of the workmen's fares 16,186 were issued between 5am and 8am and 9,040 were issued between 8am and 9am. Although the Chairman wanted to retain the weekly passes, albeit at increased purchase costs of 6d per week for the 2s and 2s 6d passes, 1s per week for the 4s pass and 2s for the 5s pass, he was defeated and it was decided to withdraw the weekly passes from 3 May 1926 and to increase the rate of discount from 14 to 16 tickets for the price of 12.

Mr Rayner was unhappy with this and took the matter back to the Tramways Committee on 22 March 1926. Over a year the number of persons who could take advantage of the discount tickets is 31,300,000 which would affect £212,000 of revenue. He anticipated a reduction in revenue of £51,000 if everyone took advantage of the proposal. In practice he considered that between 40 per cent and 50 percent would do so with income losses of £20,000 to £25,000. The abolition of passes would increase revenue by £10,000 leaving a revised loss of £15,000 at most. He estimated that rising costs in all areas meant that a surplus of £25,000 each year was the most that the tramways could achieve. He wished to continue with modernising cars costing £35,000 which might not be possible otherwise. He recommended that the discount tickets be continued, but at 14 for the cost of 12, and that they become non-transferable. He did not get all that he wanted. The Committee agreed to the passes being non-transferable, and being signed on purchase, but approved the Chairman's previously defeated scheme to continue weekly passes but at increased prices.

At a previous meeting Councillor Stark had suggested running express buses over each tram route. Mr Rayner was not very keen, considering it almost impossible to operate, and to be highly expensive. It might only work if there were sufficient numbers within the area of the terminus, since continual stopping would eliminate the express element. No action was taken.

Perusal of the minutes reveals a great number of suggested amendments to motions made by Councillor Stark, often seconded by Councillor Mell. Every move to alter the Manager's salary was opposed by Councillor Stark! Criticism was directed at both manager and chairman, whose previous cordial relationship was breaking down as a result of the former's ego, it is said. His interference in day to day management had been raised by other councillors in the City Council, but other members of the Committee said that they knew as much about it as the Manager! The Committee minutes abound with decisions being referred back or overturned at the City Council meetings. Mr Rayner had applied unsuccessfully for vacancies, including the Leeds post, so he must have been unhappy with the way in which his recommendations were ignored often at some cost (literally) to the undertaking's finances. His predictions about the Committee's detrimental financial policies were invariably correct.

In March 1926 when the Works Committee enquired about a start date for the Hessle Road extension, it was informed that work would commence in February 1927, but the extension was not approved until 28 March 1927.

On 20 April 1926 some discussion took place at the Tramways Committee regarding the new type of car no. 101, and the General Manager was given certain instructions with regard to it. These instructions were not minuted and we are left to speculate about their content.

The model of Rayner's car no. 101 was built by apprentices at Liverpool Street Workshops in time for the city's exhibition stand at the Wembley Empire Exhibition in 1922. (MJW)

Chapter 9

THE GENERAL STRIKE AND AFTERMATH

On 2 May 1926 the Trades Union Congress instructed transport workers to strike with immediate effect in support of the miners' dispute. Tramway staff (with very few exceptions) ceased work on Monday 3 May. A special meeting of the Tramways Committee held on 4 May deplored the fact that staff had not followed the national agreement whereby one week's notice of any stoppage should be given. The tramwaymen's statement that their strike was not anti-Tramways Department, but was supportive of the miners, did little to alter the Committee's attitude. Mr Henson, the Secretary of the Transport Workers' Union (a future chairman of the Transport Committee), was

By the late 1920s the North Bridge had become very inadequate for the amount of traffic on Hull's roads. This view shows how narrow it was and why a new one was built. (PG)

asked why the required notice had not been given. He stated that the Union had been instructed by the Trades' Union Council to come out on strike and had done so.

A Sub-Committee with full power to act and deal with the situation was appointed, Councillor Stark dissenting. It was decided, Councillor Stark again dissenting, to insert a notice in the local papers instructing staff to report for work by 9am on Thursday 6 May, or return any uniforms and other equipment, thereby ceasing to be employed by the Corporation. As events unfolded they revealed personality clashes between Manager and Chairman, and between members of the Transport Committee, which rumbled on long after the strike ended. What follows is taken from the various Sub-Committee minutes, reports in the *Hull Daily Mail* and the report of the official inquiry.

Before the next meeting Councillor Stark was involved in an incident outside the Holderness Road Depot involving a Binnington's bus from Hornsea, which ended with the bus turning back and passengers alighting. What actually happened is unclear, but on 26 May Councillor Stark was convicted of an act to prevent the proper use of the Binnington bus during the emergency. For this he was jailed for 3½ months and fined £20. Several buses received similar treatment, and they carried notices saying "No Tram Passengers", so that any thoughts of rich pickings for private operators were dashed.

The press notice had no effect, and when the Sub-Committee met on Thursday 6 May the Town Clerk read the section of the Emergency Powers Order that dealt with interference in running the tramcars, and stated that such persons could be fined £100 or

given three months in prison or both. Mr Rayner, who was given Road Transport Officer status by the Military Authorities, stated that he could not put any trams or buses on the road on that day since only two or three men had experience of driving cars, but that he expected to be able to run 14 buses on the Friday 7 May. He was instructed to advertise for drivers and conductors on the usual terms and conditions in permanent jobs. The Sub-Committee agreed to meet daily at 11.15am. It enlarged its membership, but did not include Councillors Mell and Stark (both Labour members).

On 7 May Mr Rayner reported that he had obtained volunteers to act as guards at the various depots, but that he had been unable to run a service without police protection. He had been informed that a large number of Oxford and Cambridge undergraduates were available and a large number of local people had volunteered.

Only four inspectors, three motormen, and three conductors were available on Saturday 8 May. No overhead staff or fitters were on duty, and the repair work fell on the shoulders of Mr Bruce and Mr Ingham. However, the Deputy Chief Constable provided guards for the depots, and a uniformed man for each bus, and Mr Rayner obtained the services of Marines from the light cruiser HMS Enterprise, which had recently arrived in Hull, to provide a service of seven buses on both Spring Bank and Beverley Road, which ran without incident. Mr Rayner drove the first bus with the Chairman and a policeman on board, whilst friends of the Chairman arrived at Cottingham Road to drive other buses.

The military authorities urged Mr Rayner to run trams to

On 5 October 1925 route "BC" was extended along Cottingham Road to the junction with Hall Road where there was newly-built private housing on three sides and on the other (northern side of Cottingham Road) side a Corporation estate all of which afforded additional passengers. The car is no. 113, a "new" car which "emerged" from Liverpool Street Workshops in 1927 and was similar externally to Mr Rayner's no. 101 with a wide entrance but was of more orthodox construction. No. 113 became Leeds no. 483 in July 1945. (PM)

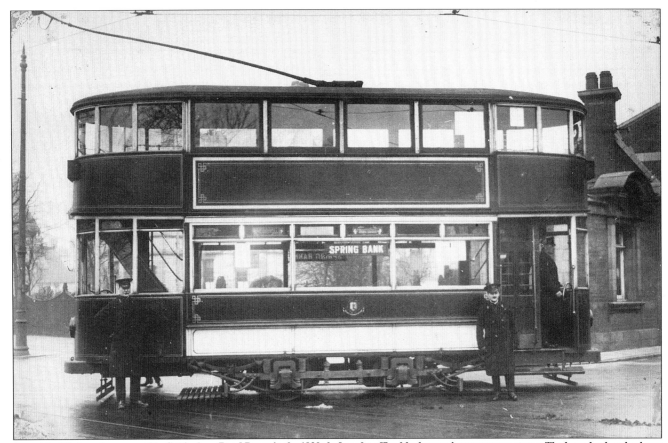

An unidentified car is seen outside Cottingham Road Depot in the 1920s before the office block was given an upper storey. The large brake wheel was the reason that cars which were fitted with these were christened "Mangles" by some employees can be clearly seen. (PM)

Hull had a tradition of decorating cars for special anniversaries and civic occasions. This shows one such car (possibly no. 82) in October 1929 which is celebrating Civic Week and is on the forecourt of Liverpool Street Depot. Behind is Mr Rayner's car no. 101. No. 101 was an early casualty in April 1933. (PM)

restore public morale and some semblance of normality. Staff at the power station had allowed the steam pressure to drop, and an immediate resumption was delayed until the Supervisor (Elliott) was found to feed the boilers.

At 3.10pm on the Saturday the first car left Cottingham Road Depot driven by Mr Eric Johnson. This caused problems since overhead line supervisors were working on the overhead on the assumption that there was no power switched on, when a tram was seen heading for the town. On arrival at Cottingham Road Mr Rayner found, much to his annoyance, the Chairman organising matters. He accused the Chairman of switching the power on, which the latter denied, truthfully as it turned out, for Elliott was the culprit. Rayner as Road Transport Officer was the person responsible, but the Chairman was taking an increasingly "hands on" role to the confusion of many.

Some trams and buses were damaged and the overhead was also targeted. When the first tram arrived in King Edward Street a crowd gathered and obstructed people trying to board. Missiles were thrown and one driver abandoned a car. A pitched battle ensued when the police arrived in force ending with 22 arrests and 40 people in hospital.

More volunteers came forward, so that on Sunday seven cars ran on both Spring Bank and Beverley Road. Trams also operated on the Spring Bank West route, and buses were diverted to other routes. Wire netting was fixed to the windows to prevent further damage and injury to passengers and crews. Volunteers were instructed in driving techniques and ran cars along the tracks within Cottingham Road Depot.

The Chairman and Rayner arranged to meet the students at 7.30am the following day. Rayner was furious that the Chairman was taking all the credit for the work so far, stating that Rayner could not do his job properly. He offered his resignation as RTO to the Military Authorities but this was refused. Having slept in his office all week he went home to Hornsea.

When he arrived at Cottingham Road at 7.30am he learned that the Chairman had put back the meeting to 8.30am. Willoughby had met the undergraduates the previous evening, and he and friends arranged accommodation and blankets for them, criticising Rayner's lack of foresight. (It is uncertain whether Rayner knew when they would arrive.) Rayner dashed to Willoughby's office in the Guildhall, where a violent argument took place, which was stopped only by the intervention of the Town Clerk.

On Monday 10 May it was possible to start operations on Beverley Road and Spring Bank (23 cars); Anlaby Road (7) and Spring Bank West (7), along with buses on Holderness Road, Hessle Road, Anlaby Road and Spring Bank West. During the day more undergraduates reported for duty and it was decided to open Liverpool Street Depot on Tuesday (11 May).

On Tuesday power station workers were called out by the TUC, but volunteers took over and kept it running. The number now employed was between 850 and 900 (only twenty were tramway employees), three-quarters of the normal staff numbers. Liverpool Street Depot opened as planned at 9am initially with eight cars, which rose to 13 by the end of the day. Buses were transferred to Holderness Road, Hedon Road, Garden Village and Stoneferry Road. At noon Holderness Road Depot opened with 12 cars. It was agreed that Anlaby Road and Hedon Road Depots would open on the Wednesday when, despite considerable damage to the overhead, trams ran on all routes. All bus routes were operated apart from the Fish Dock route.

Stoning of buses and trams continued, for which several people were charged and given two or three months prison terms. According to legend, but totally untrue, at least one car was overturned and burnt. This was reported in the national press and later found its way into histories of the strike.

The Sub-Committee decided those at present employed would be retained if they were satisfactory and wished to continue. Anyone who had left the service (ie, gone on strike) would be re-instated only upon individual application and approval in each case by the Tramways Committee. This was to cause great difficulties and resentment in the months to come. Mr Rayner posted notices in all depots informing everyone who wished to obtain regular employment to make an application in writing. In future no foreman, inspector or timekeeper should be a member of the same Union as the men whom he controlled.

When the Sub-Committee was informed that the General Strike was to be called off, Mr Rayner was instructed to carry on with the agreed levels of service, and to prepare a list of vacant posts and a list of applications from former employees, as they applied for re-instatement.

On the Thursday the Town Clerk made it quite clear in the local press that the Tramways Committee was determined to give employment to those volunteers who wanted a permanent job, even if many former employees were not re-engaged.

The Tramwaymen's Union asked for an interview with the Committee, who instructed the Town Clerk to give them a copy of the decision about the terms of return, and to ask the Union to submit its case in writing. A meeting was fixed for 6pm on the Saturday 15 May. This began at 6pm and lasted until 3.30am on Sunday morning! Since the men had broken an agreement to give notice of any action, the Sub-Committee was not in a conciliatory mood.

The Union was prepared to negotiate on being given a list of the men involved. It accused the Corporation of not acting like other tramway undertakings which had taken back the striking men, and of not following the usual practice at the end of such action. Nor did they think that a man's return should be considered by the Sub-Committee, as they had already proved their efficiency in service. Not taking back employees would penalise individuals in regard to the friendly benefits of their association, and was in direct contrast to the Prime Minister's pledge. The Union was prepared to agree that supervisory staff should be in a separate branch from men under their control. During the meeting the men's representatives withdrew on occasions to address the men outside, but the Committee remained resolute.

The Terms of Settlement confirmed that men at present in the Corporation's employ would be retained if they so wished and if satisfactory. Men who had left the service must complete an agreed form supplied by the Committee. Only men approved by the Committee would be re-instated. A period of three months would be given for foremen and timekeepers to find a different Union for the men. Future vacancies would be filled in the first instance by employees who had left, provided that they were suitable. Finally, the union undertook that there would be no interference by men who were taken back with the volunteers who had been taken on by the Committee. The full story was reported to the Tramways Committee on 22 May 1926.

The matter was not concluded satisfactorily whilst relations between the two groups of employees were strained, and continued to be so for many years when some staff would still not talk to one another. Only Hull did not take back the men immediately once the strike ended.

Meanwhile the service continued using volunteers of varying standards, ability and attitude. A daily free bottle of beer was provided, sometimes supplemented by free ale from local public houses. Driving standards were mixed with at least two head-on collisions between tramcars. Damage to the overhead was common, as many were unable to maintain smooth acceleration or braking. Undergraduates were paid 7s 6d per day, whilst volunteers received 10 shillings. Despite a continuing police presence, some volunteers had to endure assaults. It is estimated that 230 of the volunteers became permanent employees.

Treatment of the volunteers was mixed, with complaints about strikers' wives attacking them with needles in sensitive areas, and injuries from cars being attacked. Mr Albert Royle remembered that on Holderness Road near Newbridge Road strike-affected residents resented comparatively wealthy students running the trams and threw stones at passing cars.

A different picture is painted by Henry Sellers, who said that some students passed the contents of fare bags to strikers. Mr A. Fellows didn't think that the tramway men caused any trouble, and were amused at their amateurish efforts. Derailments and dewirements were common, a particular problem spot being Blundells Corner at the junction of the Beverley road and Spring Bank routes. Fortunately the weather was good so volunteers did not have to cope with wet rails.

The effect on the department's finances was catastrophic. Before the strike, income for 1926/7 was up by an average of nearly £250 per week on the trams alone. By 12 June income was £10,463 below the previous year on the trams, and £420 on the buses. Since the strike had ended income remained consistently below the previous levels. With many strikers (not just tramway men) still not back in work, the possibility of a return to "normal" patronage was slim.

On 12 July 1926 the long-awaited Beverley Road extension to Endike Lane was opened. Still designated "B" (not "BE"

Views of trams on the final extension along Hessle Road (or Hessle High Road as locals called it) are very rare so it is a bonus to see this unidentified car nearing the end of its journey at Pickering Road with St Nicholas Church to the left. Hull's "reserved" extensions were leafy affairs. (MJW)

given the practice for previous extensions) the route utilised a central reservation between Inglemire Lane and Endike Lane.

Before Mr Rayner could mend fences, the Tramways Committee decided to hold an enquiry into the department's (ie, his) performance. But the City Council decided (perhaps sensibly) to appoint its own Committee of Chairmen of Standing Committees, of which Councillor Willoughby was a member. However, this body was considered too large and on 5 August a smaller, six man Tramways Inquiry (Special) Committee was formed under the chairmanship of the Lord Mayor, Alderman Boyes. Willoughby was excluded (again sensibly), but one Labour member (Councillor Ceeley) was included. Less sensible, perhaps, was the decision to admit the press and to hold public sessions.

It was not a dignified exercise. Eight meetings were held of which six were public sessions that were fully reported in the following day's papers, whose sales increased as revelation and accusation followed revelation and accusation. In all no fewer than twenty-nine witnesses were heard at various meetings including councillors, tramway employees, police and other Council officials. The first session was held on Tuesday 21 September 1926, and on the Wednesday the front of the *Hull Daily Mail* (all seven columns) was devoted to the proceedings. At the bottom of the rightmost column was a short piece that stated that a further 15 labourers, fitters and blacksmiths had been re-instated, and that between 900 and 1000 men had now been returned to work.

Councillor Willoughby circulated a rough copy of his allegations to members and Mr Rayner, whilst the General Manager relied on the diary which he had kept throughout the strike. The Chairman accused Mr Rayner of never wanting to run a service, whilst the latter complained of undue stress and interference from the Chairman and his friends. Willoughby said that the students and other volunteers had complained of receiving little support from Mr Rayner and other tramways staff.

One of Willoughby's friends claimed credit for starting the bus service, a claim ridiculed by tramways staff. Some of the volunteers in the early part of the strike were friends of the Chairman, being members of various clubs and organisations. Elliot was cross-examined by Rayner about his duties at the Power Station, and alleged misleading information regarding the Power Station steam raising. The Town Clerk described the argument between Willoughby and Rayner. Previous allegations regarding Willoughby's "spies" within the department were confirmed with the admission from Brooker, Liverpool Street Workshops Foreman, that he had written to the Chairman during the strike, and the later revelation that Elliot had also been in contact with him. Councillor Wheeldon claimed to have been responsible for deciding to nail wire netting over the windows, and for the wedges at the King Edward Street points. Rayner's performance as Road Transport Officer was defended by Colonel Oldfield of the Military Authorities.

There was the unedifying sight of Willoughby and Rayner cross-examining each other, with witnesses siding with one or the other. Neutrals appeared to be in short supply. The most damning evidence against the Chairman came from the Chief Clerk (Shearman), and the Chief Cashier (Tarbert). Tarbert stated that Willoughby had returned an account for bottled beer supplied to volunteers with the beverage altered to ginger beer. Shearman alleged that Willoughby had told him that he had spies on the tramways. A Labour councillor alleged that Willoughby had said in March 1926 that he wanted to be rid of Rayner. Willoughby stormed out of the last public session, leaving Rayner to make the final statement and emphasise that he considered it the business of elected members to make policy, and not to interfere in the management of the department. The

This is the only other view of the Hessle Road extension that has been found and shows Milnes car no. 81 on the reservation in Gipsyville en route for Pickering Park approaching the stop. Traffic looks sparse as the fields on the left reveal that the council housing estate has yet to be built. (MJW)

UEC car no. 126 has just left Cottingham Road Depot to make the short journey to Newland Avenue terminus. (MJW)

sight of manager and chairman trading accusations and insults in public must have been unique in British tramway annals.

Willoughby needed police protection for another six months. His meetings were infiltrated by tramway staff and friends who shouted him down. He was sued, unsuccessfully, for slander, after enquiring if a woman who had sworn at him was a "lady of the town". Meetings of the Committee were, following a motion from Councillor Stark, now back in circulation, moved from the Tramways offices to the Guildhall.

The report of the inquiry was presented to a packed (61 members) City Council meeting on 28 January 1927. The following sixteen points were made, and, as will be seen, neither party escaped some criticism although more was directed at Willoughby than Rayner (who in the list of participants was described as the "Tramways Manager").

The conductor of this car braves the downpour on a truly dreadful day to operate the time clock at the Mile House end of the Holderness Road reservation. (MJW)

(1) The long running dispute previous to the Strike between the two men had forced responsible members of staff into taking sides, and there had been a lack of discipline and cohesion in the working of the Undertaking to the detriment of the entire service.

(2) No attempt or arrangements were made to cope with the Strike by the Management before Tuesday 4 May – all parties failing to realise that a strike of tramwaymen was probable.

(3) No instructions were given to the Manager to make arrangements previous to 4 May by his Committee and, therefore, he was not disobeying or neglecting any orders.

(4) No attempt had been made on the morning of the strike, 4 May at 6am to run a service with sixty men remaining on duty.

(5) Although it was probably inexpedient to commence a service with those 60 men, preliminary organisation should have been begun by the Management to run a service at the earliest opportunity.

(6) No proper or adequate attempt was made on the Tuesday, Wednesday or Thursday to organise the forces at the disposal of the Management to run the trams on Friday, probably because the Tramways Committee had given the men until Thursday to resume their duties. An attempt to run buses on the Friday failed on account of inadequate police protection.

(7) When the organisation commenced on the Saturday and succeeding two days, better use might have been made by the Management of their permanent staff who continued at their duties in controlling and directing the men who volunteered for service.

(8) The inquiry considered that the alteration of the day for commencing service from Monday to Saturday after the Committee had given instructions to start on the Monday, led to confusion at the depot and that such confusion could not have been avoided by the Management

This is Chanterlands Avenue North in the late 1920s. The lack of housing illustrates why Mr Rayner was against this extension (receipts were 5d per mile compared with a system average of 14d). Car no. 127 is working on route SWC which as an all day facility did not last long although some peak hour journeys may have continued into the 1930s. (PG)

(9) The Manager was not called upon to resign either his position as Road Transport Officer or temporarily as Tramway Manager, either by the Tramways Committee or the Sub-Committee.

(10) Having regard to the national importance and all the circumstances, it would not have been in the best interest of the community for the Tramway Manager to have insisted in giving up the post of Road Transport Manager as he intimated his willingness to do so.

(11) Having regard to all the evidence the inquiry considered that there was justification for the Manager's complaint of undue interference with his staff and of his duties as Tramway Manager. This was arrived at having taken into consideration the period preceding, during and after the Strike.

(12) With regard to the Chairman's complaint that the Manager was absent when the undergraduates arrived, the evidence shows that other arrangements had been made for the men to be met and, therefore, it was not imperative for the Manager to be present, though it would have been desirable, if possible.

(13) Regarding the second complaint of the Manager leaving the Guildhall on the night of Saturday/Sunday, whilst negotiations with the men's representatives were in progress, the inquiry was of the opinion that the Manager was wrong in asking permission to go, and that the Chairman was equally wrong in giving that permission, and having given that permission, he could uphold his complaint.

(14) The Manager's conduct before, during or after the Strike did not warrant censure, because not having the confidence of his Chairman before the dispute he was at a great disadvantage when the trouble came.

(15) The inquiry members were unanimous that the Tramway Manager should reside in the City so that his services should be available at all times.

(16) The Chairman committed a grave error when he took the account of Messrs Powolny's out of the Tramway offices

This is a rare view of "Rayner" car no. 101 at work near Park Avenue on Chanterlands Avenue (route SW). The date is sometime between 1927 and 1933 when no. 101 was withdrawn. The "SW" may have been cut back to Park Avenue and no. 101 may be standing at the terminus. (PG)

An enlargement showing no. 101 at Park Avenue. (PG)

and returned it to the firm to have the details altered whilst the total remained the same as in the original account. Such action merits the strongest condemnation.

Two Labour members tabled a motion at the Council meeting to replace the entire Tramways Committee, but it was defeated. Politics aside, there was considerable merit in a change. Given the lows to which relationships had fallen, was it reasonable to expect Committee, Chairman, Manager and staff to proceed as though nothing had happened? A new Committee and chairman might have prevented future strife, perhaps. One wonders why Rayner stayed on. Several Committee members were antagonis-

tic, especially Councillor Stark, and it cannot have been very pleasant to attend Committee meetings. A reading of Committee minutes provides a sense that if Mr Rayner recommended something, it was automatically opposed by certain members. The Council emerged from the conflict with little or no credit. One also senses that perhaps Mr Rayner was not the man for the crisis, although his position was difficult given the lack of support from some members of the Council and some of his own staff. Several did support him at the inquiry but some were later the victims of Committee persecution.

The conflict came at a time when key policy questions needed to be resolved. Much track needed relaying, with centre overhead running installed to accelerate journey times, to compete with private buses (and the Corporation's buses). New cars were required, or at the very least an expensive modernisation programme. Extensions into new housing areas (mainly planned council estates), would need consideration, and the ever controversial question of fare levels would require addressing.

Mr Rayner's thoughts were turning to the acquisition of more trams whether for replacement of existing trams, or to increase the size of the fleet, he didn't say. He obtained approval from the Stores, Depots and Workshops Sub-Committee on 18 January 1927 for the purchase of a new 8ft 6in. pendulum truck for trial purposes. There is speculation that this was used for the "new" car no. 26. This appeared in (it is thought) November 1928. No authority was given to construct a car, so its origins remain a mystery. No. 26 did match outwardly Rayner cars nos 101 and 113. When in Leeds it did not have this truck, nor did it have the smaller wheels of the "original" no. 26.

Mr Rayner reported that the Chanterlands Avenue extension would open on 3 January 1927, but that he did not intend to operate the circular service. As no previous mention had been made of any circular service we are left to speculate about what

Brill car no. 28 is caught in Spring Bank. The position of the motorman can be seen as he waits the starting signal. The Brill cars were withdrawn in 1931 in this condition having never received enclosed balconies or fully enclosed upper decks (no. 26 excepted?). (PG)

Four trams display four different route boards (QS/SWC/B/2) in King Edward Street. The leading car is no. 108 which is followed by "Hull Corporation" car no. 127. (MJW)

form this might have taken. A ten-minute headway was provided at a 2d fare over the extension. Cars running via Chanterlands Avenue North were designated "SWC"

The routes in operation at 3 January 1927 are thought to be as follows:

A	Waterworks Street – Carr Lane – Anlaby Road (Boothferry Road)
AP	Waterworks Street – Carr Lane – Anlaby Road – Pickering Road North
---	Waterworks Street – Carr Lane – Anlaby Road – Walton Street (peaks, Hull Fair Week and football matches)
---	Waterworks Street – Carr lane – Anlaby Road – West Park Gates (football matches)
---	Waterworks Street – Carr lane – Anlaby Road – Boulevard (rugby matches)
D	Osborne Street – Porter Street – Hessle Road – Dairycoates
DP	Osborne Street – Porter Street – Hessle Road – Pickering Park Gates
---	Osborne Street – Porter Street – Hessle Road – West Dock Avenue (peak periods)

North Hull

B	King Edward Street – Beverley Road – Endike Lane
BC	King Edward Street – Beverley Road – Cottingham Road (Hall Road)
QB	King Edward Street – Beverley Road – Queens Road
S	King Edward Street – Spring Bank – Princes Avenue – Newland Avenue (Cottingham Road)
QS	King Edward Street – Spring Bank – Princes Avenue (Queens Road) (peak periods)
SW	King Edward Street – Spring Bank – Spring Bank West – Chanterlands Avenue (Park Avenue)
SWC	King Edward Street – Spring Bank – Spring Bank West – Chanterlands Avenue North – Cottingham Road (Hall Road)

SW	King Edward Street – Spring Bank – Spring Bank West (Walton Street) (Peak periods and Hull Fair Week)
---	Newland Avenue – Princes Avenue – Spring Bank West (Walton Street) (Hull Fair Week)

East Hull

IRH	Jameson Street – George Street – North Bridge – Witham – Holderness Road – Ings Road
IRTH	Jameson Street – Alfred Gelder Street – Drypool Bridge – Holderness Road – Ings Road
H	Jameson Street – George Street – North Bridge – Witham – Holderness Road (Depot or Aberdeen Street)
---	Jameson Street – George Street – North Bridge – Witham – Holderness Road (Durham Street) (all day short workings)
M	Savile Street – George Street – Great Union Street – Hedon Road – Marfleet
P	Queen Victoria Square – Monument Bridge – Alfred Gelder Street – Lowgate – Market Place – Pier

There were additional through cars in each direction in the morning and evening between Alexandra Dock and other tram termini.

At the end of January 1927 Mr Rayner reported on the first month of the Chanterlands Avenue extension. Fare income on the "BC" and "S" routes had decreased, and it appeared that passengers had transferred to the Chanterlands Avenue service from these two routes. This is perhaps surprising since the "BC" route was shorter and had a more frequent headway. The reference to the "S" route is interesting. Given the distance from Chanterlands Avenue to Newland Avenue, it is difficult to see how this route could be affected unless the cars had also been extended to Hall Road. The minutes reveal nothing.

In February it was suggested that the vestibuling of tramcars should be stopped, but the Tramways Committee decided to continue with it.

At the Tramways Committee of 28 March 1927 a chart

Regular peak hour journeys and some works journeys worked only as far as Queens Road on the Spring Bank route and carried the letters "QS". Brush car no. 47 is returning to the city centre after working such a duty and is about to enter Prospect Street from Spring Bank, the junction being known as Blundells Corner. (PM/RFM)

showing comparative costs of trams and motorbuses over certain specified distances was considered. Unfortunately the details were not minuted, and do not appear to have survived.

It was agreed to renew the track on Newland Avenue at £11,300. The work could be achieved in a shorter time if a temporary crossover was placed in Newland Avenue at a location to be agreed (possibly Sharp Street), which would permit the service to be maintained and save £1,000. The short extension of the Hessle Road route to Pickering Road was approved at a cost of £3,300. The same Committee agreed to sell the stock of wire netting to Mr J. Baimbridge for £9 2s 6d.

In June Councillor Stark complained to the Tramways Committee that passengers on the upper deck of open top buses on the Garden Village route were at risk from decorative work on tram standards. He also complained that crews were being careless with the changing of illuminated route indicators on the front of the cars, making it impossible to ascertain the destination of a car. The General Manager was asked to deal with these matters.

In June 1927 the Tramways Committee considered the financial situation of the tramways. Mr Rayner compared 1925/6 with 1919/20, there being little point in any comparison with the year of the General Strike. The population of Hull in 1920 was 284,357 and 297,300 in 1926. Other comparisons were:

	1920	1926
Passengers carried (trams)	78,432,643	63,975,265
Passengers carried (buses)		4,647,493
Journeys per head of population	282.14	215.58
Car mileage	4,731,398	4,690.169
Bus mileage		608,536

Mr Rayner laid the drop in passengers to the current situation whereby the numbers out of work had increased, and those who were in work had suffered reductions in wages, and there was not the money to spend. Receipts had been bolstered to some

extent by the profitable all-night bus services, and the minimum 2d fare on both trams and buses. Hull's running costs were within the six lowest in the country, so that there was little room to manoeuvre in terms of cost reductions. He did not consider the surplus on bus routes to be high enough.

He submitted a map (not discovered) showing housing development in relation to existing tram routes. A large proportion of people who lived within the centre of the city had moved to the outskirts.

A further schedule revealed the earnings on the tram routes for a single "typical" week:

	Miles	Receipts			Per car mile
		£	s	d	d
D and DP Hessle Road	17,647	1201	18	10	16.33
A and AP Anlaby Road	13,382	911	7	11½	16.32
H and IR Holderness Road	16,470½	1101	0	6½	16.00
S Spring Bank	12,889	786	0	6	14.64
SW and SWC Spring Bank West	9,383½	495	10	0½	12.65
B and BC Beverley Road	14,970	965	17	1	14.64
M Marfleet	10,511½	507	9	2½	11.55
P Pier	1,330	50	5	1½	9.05
	96,592½	6019	9	3½	14.94

These are the actual figures used in the report which do not accurately compute. Note that he used IR for Ings Road, not IRH as is often portrayed. The use of more than one route letter was still in use despite the decision of 4 February 1926. The Pier service compared poorly with the others, and the figures hid some poor results in that the earnings beyond Park Avenue on the SWC were only 5.1d per car mile. It would appear that the SWC was working all the way to Hall Road, for Mr Rayner recommended that a crossover be put in at the Cemetery Gates

This car is displaying "QS" but is pictured in George Street so it seems likely that it is working an afternoon peak hour journey from Hedon Road (probably Alexandra Dock). It will enter Jameson Street East before turning right into Prospect Street, thus avoiding the congestion in King Edward Street. (PM)

at the northern end of Chanterlands Avenue, and that cars terminate here, thus saving £5,000 a year. He also recommended abandoning the discount tickets in order to increase revenue by a further £9,600.

Reading between the lines (no pun), he really wanted to increase fares, but he recognised the Committee's wish to encourage people to live on the outskirts without unduly increasing the cost of doing so. Since much new development in North Hull, Hessle Road (Gipsyville), and Preston Road, as well as proposed estates at Derringham Bank were council estates whose residents were being re-housed away from the city centre, and whose income was among the lowest in the city, it was

Car no 122 is shown in Queen Victoria Square on 15 March 1931 not long before the Pier route was withdrawn. The Pier route had several different central termini during its twenty-eight year life. Compare the condition of no. 122 with photograph on page 166. (PM/SLS)

This is "sprinkling" car no 2 and its driver. (PM)

unspoken Council policy that fares were to be low. Shorter distance passengers subsidised the longer distance ones. This was often forgotten when the department was criticised for its financial performance, not just in tramway days but also in trolleybus and motorbus days. The wonder is that Managers did as well as they did. A quid pro quo might have been in return for this fares policy not to relieve the tramways of a contribution to the rate fund each year, but such sacrilege was not contemplated.

Mr Rayner reminded the Committee that 1,300,000 passengers rode free of charge each year (he didn't say so, but at a

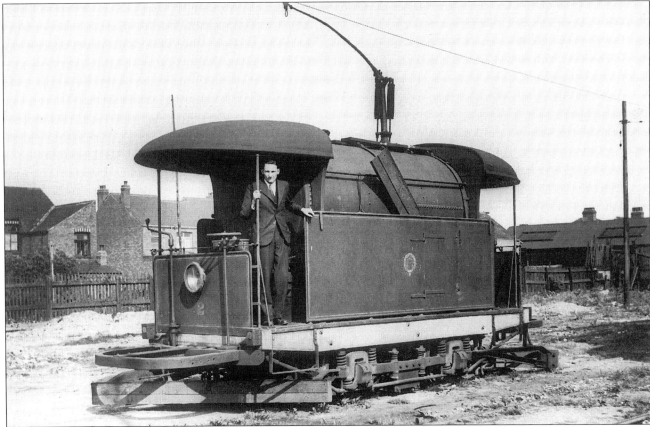

This view of the water car was taken at Holderness Road probably in the mid 1930s. (MJW)

minimum of 1d per ride this was equivalent to an annual income of £5,400). This would rise considerably when on 1 January 1928 the age for old age pensions (and free passes) would reduce from 70 to 65, and that as means testing would cease, those who were presently disqualified would be entitled to a pass. The outcome was the abolition of the discount ticket system from 18 July, the position to be reviewed in one year's time.

Hull's final extension from Pickering Park Gates to Pickering Road opened on 14 July 1927, cars retaining the "DP" route letter.

The first indication that the future of the trams was not secure came on 25 July 1928 when the Chairman moved a motion, seconded by the Deputy Chairman, that buses replace trams on the Old Town route. After some discussion about running trams to the Pier from Beverley Road, Mr Rayner was instructed to report on the proposal to the next Committee.

The same meeting agreed to renew the Holderness Road sleeper tracks, and to pay the contractor renewing the Newland Avenue track an additional sum to cover the arrangements to enable trams to use a single line during the work.

Mr Rayner reported to the next meeting that he had considered the use of one-man buses on the Old Town route, and other bus routes, but difficulties had arisen regarding licences for such operation. He recommended no action be taken until this was resolved.

Was the Old Town proposal the thin end of the wedge? It remained an expensive luxury, and its receipts dragged down the trams in cost comparison with buses, but it would be wrong to assume that a general wish to eliminate the trams prevailed. The Chanterlands Avenue extension against Mr Rayner's advice had proved a mistake. The Spring Bank West route to Calvert Lane, and perhaps Derringham Bank, would have been a much better investment. Nothing had been heard of new car proposals for Mr Rayner had other problems as we shall see.

Workmen's fares were discussed at the same meeting with Councillor Stark, seconded by Councillor Wheeldon (again), proposing the issue of Workmen's at 2d return tickets on any route up to 9am, and between 11.45am and 1.15pm on workdays, for a six month trial period. An amendment by Councillor Woodliffe that the matter wait until discussions about the next year's estimates was passed.

The Sutton Ings Ratepayers' Association asked for a better service to the Ings Road terminus where the "IRH" and the "IRTH" cars enjoyed an equal service. The Association also asked for better timekeeping, and the provision of a shelter at the terminus. Note that the letters denoting the two routes were still in use along with "H" and "TH" for cars terminating at the depot.

When Mr Rayner was appointed he was permitted to reside outside the city boundary, and he chose the small seaside town of Hornsea some 15½ miles (by rail) north east of Hull. Subsequently, he built a house there.

His residence location had been mentioned in the Inquiry report and there must have been other references for, on 21 November 1927, he wrote to the Chairman who submitted it to that day's Tramways Committee. It was clear to him that many people desired him in Hull or nearer the city, and as he was anxious to remove any matter that could cause any strife he was

Hurst Nelson No. 91 is seen in Jameson Street when working on route "TH" and showing "Ings Lane" rather than "Ings Road". It was fully enclosed in 1925 before route "TH" was "temporarily" suspended in 1932. No. 91 was withdrawn in April 1933. This carries a very simplified version of the older livery unlike no. 172 in the previous view. (MJW)

willing to move. However, if it was the Corporation's wish, he thought it right that any financial loss should be borne by it. Living outside the city had not prevented him from reorganising the department, nor had it stopped him from improving its finances until the recent economic depression had materially affected its performance. The introduction of fares concessions (often against his advice), had also affected the finances. Faced with this the Committee did a very local government thing – it passed the buck to the Staff Sub-Committee.

The City Council meeting on 14 February 1928 overturned the decision to defer consideration of a workmen's return fare of 2d, and instructed the General Manager to introduce it before 9 am, with the return at any time of the day for a three month trial period. But Mr Rayner was not happy, and raised it at the Tramways Committee on 20 February 1928. This was probably courageous (or rash), given the apparent strength of support for the measure, but he felt that the Committee should be aware of the loss of revenue that the instruction entailed.

His message was stark. The loss would be £314 10s per week, £16,500 per annum. It was a fallacy (his word), that any reduction in fares would increase passenger levels and income. He came to the Committee armed with his usual detailed analyses. The abolition of the Workmen's ½d fare in August 1919 had increased income by £43,511 a year, despite a passenger reduction of 1,756,313. The abolition of the 1d fare after 9am produced an increase of £58,630 in revenue and a decrease of 10,334,402 passengers per annum. Tramway services before 9am were not profitable where low fares existed. The Committee merely agreed to enter the report on the minutes which meant that the return fares had to be introduced.

The question of tramway operation in Waterworks Street arose once more. The Watch Committee questioned the department's plan to re-arrange the service around the City Hall. The matter was deferred once more and continued to rumble on until the end of the year. After the Watch Committee had requested that all Anlaby Road trams terminate in Carr Lane, a joint meeting was arranged in October. Mr Rayner considered it totally impossible to operate the normal service plus Hull Fair cars (just two weeks away), and football cars, and reaffirmed his wish to use Waterworks Street. The Tramways Committee agreed and instructed him to proceed.

To complete a torrid meeting, Mr Rayner's recommendation to fit upholstered seats to one tramcar as an experiment for £130 was defeated, despite Councillor Stark, for once, being supportive.

Approval for the renewal of the Alfred Gelder Street track from Whitefriargate to Lowgate was forthcoming in May 1928, despite the uncertainty about the Old Town service. Also approved was the purchase of nine moveable points from Messrs Hadfields at a cost of £425.

At the same meeting Mr Rayner reported on the three months operation of the 2d return fares. It confirmed his warning to the Committee. He compared the last eight weeks before its introduction with the first eight weeks of operation. The loss was £1,747 8s 0½d, despite an increase in passengers of 3.371. He didn't say so, but this represented an accumulative loss of £11,268 for the year. A proposal by the Deputy-Chairman that the experiment cease after the three months was lost, because voting was equal, so the 2d fare continued.

A significant event was receipt of a letter dated 11 October 1928 from East Yorkshire Motor Services Ltd. suggesting that the Corporation might consider entering into an agreement under which the firm would operate all omnibus services in the City under the supervision of the Council. If required, the company would submit a detailed scheme which would guarantee a certain profit to the Council, and would in no way compete with the tramways. A motion not to entertain the offer was rejected, and it was agreed to ask EYMS for further details. The company had been formed from several local companies in 1926, and ran buses to villages, suburbs and towns in the East Riding.

In December 1928 a suggestion from Councillors Brett and Smith that the "A" trams be extended along the new Boothferry Road to Askew Avenue was considered. The 500 yard extension on reservation would cost £6,000, and a seven-minute service would be provided. This extension would have been more attractive than the "AP" extension, in that housing density was higher with the northern part of the Gipsyville Corporation Housing Estate on one side, and newly built semi-detached house-lined streets on the other. It was resolved to run a bus service from Newington Crossing (near the "A" terminus) to Askew Avenue as a temporary measure. This inferred that trams would be provided but, perhaps significantly, no instruction was given to obtain powers or tenders.

Another letter from EYMS was considered in December. EYMS said it was not making a bid to run the City's omnibus

No. 112 looks in fine form on Cottingham Road when working route "BC". Fully enclosed in October 1927 it lasted until September 1938 when the Beverley Road route closed. (MJW)

services, but was asking for financial information to enable it to do so. A special Sub-Committee was formed to approach EYMS, members being understandably reluctant to provide such information in the first instance. This proved a stumbling block, since EYMS refused to attend without any information that would enable them to table a definite offer at that meeting, and it was resolved to take no further action, although discussions were resumed.

The first six months of 1928/29 would see a small profit on both trams and buses (£422 and £438 respectively). No doubt Mr Rayner pointed out that if his advice about discount fares had been heeded the tram profit would, using his figures, have been nearer £7,000, since the 2d fare was discussed once more. Predictably the whole question was deferred until November (by which time the distortion of tram finances would be even greater), although the issue of 2d return and workmen's fares was to be discontinued at 9am prompt.

Instead the General Manager was left to arrange transport for 3,000 poor children who were to attend a dinner on Christmas Day provided by the British Legion. If that were not enough, he had to deal with a letter from the Secretary of Hull Kingston

Rovers Football (Rugby League) Club, asking for sufficient transport facilities to take supporters to the Derby games at the Boulevard on Christmas day morning.

Discussions about the Electricity Department taking over the Power Station had by now been agreed, but the question of any displaced staff not taken on by that department was discussed in the December meeting, and it was agreed that such staff should have priority in any suitable vacancies throughout the council.

In January 1929 the Committee discussed the running of tram services, and instructed the General Manager, against his advice, to ensure that a tram standing at a terminus would leave immediately on the arrival of a second tram irrespective of the timetable. Mr Rayner finally received authority to fit upholstered seating in two trams as an experiment at a cost of £130 each. He was also requested to make arrangements for the lighting of stopping places on the portions of tram routes where sleeper tracks are laid. Relationships with certain Committee members were beginning to become very strained.

In another effort to accelerate tram services his recommendations to reduce the number of stopping places still further was approved. This reduced the number on Anlaby Road from 21 to 16, from 24 to 18 on Spring Bank, from 19 to 15 on Beverley Road and from 28 to 23 on Holderness Road. However, the full Council again thought that it knew better, and referred this and the question of upholstered seating back to the Tramways Committee.

An enigmatic entry in the February minutes read that in connection with the proposed revision of the style of the route indicators, the General Manager be requested to arrange for the indicators to show the direction of the city in which trams were travelling. It is unclear which revisions were involved.

Another resolution (from Councillors Stark (of course) and Mell), instructed Mr Rayner to place an adequate tram service on all routes to seat the travelling public at normal times of the day. Since all timetables were approved by members, it was a bit much to suggest that an adequate service was not being provided. It did not define what "adequate" meant, and given the parlous financial nature of the trams due to the Committee's policies (and the full Council's interference), it seemed to bear little relationship with reality. Councillor Stark also tried to get a decision to force men to take all their holidays between 1 April and 30 September, but the Chairman vacated the chair and the meeting terminated.

The proposals for the reduction of stopping places and the fitting of upholstered seating were sent back by the City Council, so that on 25 February Mr Rayner submitted a long list of current and proposed stopping places, containing some amendments from the last version, and these were duly approved. The upholstery proposals were defeated, despite Councillor Stark's motion to fit at least one car with leather upholstery.

In March it was agreed to extend the Boothferry Road bus route (by now working from the city centre), into Askew Avenue and no more was heard about a tram route.

With another increase in the cost of petrol Mr Rayner suggested that some motor bus routes might be replaced by trolleybuses whose operating costs were much less. The Committee agreed to use the new Committee bus to visit Rotherham and Doncaster on 3 April to inspect their trolleybuses. It was decided to delay opening tenders for a new bus garage at Barnsley Street until after the visits.

The visit proved a success, and the Committee agreed to introduce trolleybuses on such routes as may be expedient, and that the General Manager provide them with detailed estimates and proposals. At this stage the reports refer only to bus substitution, not tram replacement, although nothing more had been heard of new trams.

The new North Bridge opened on 31 August 1931 and one of the first trams to cross it was a diverted "TH" car. The new bridge was located at the side of the old bridge and the new short length of roadway was equipped with double track, thus eliminating the interlaced section in Charlotte Street that dated from the Great War. (PG)

The quiet Marfleet terminus is the scene for this view – there were some houses on the left but the area to the right comprises docks and associated industries. (MJW)

Later that month it was agreed to purchase twelve trolley-buses to replace buses on the Newbridge Road route, after consideration of Mr Rayner's cost comparisons of 12.824d per car mile for trolleybuses, and 14.644d per car mile for buses, based on 400,000 miles per annum. The Town Clerk was instructed to obtain the necessary powers, either in addition to or in substitution for existing motor bus or tram routes. This provided an option but did not necessarily condemn the trams. As a result Mr Rayner stated that the Barnsley Street land for a bus garage would not be required.

Once again the minute regarding trolleybuses was taken back at the Council on 11 November. Councillor Stark tried without support to defeat the Newbridge Road proposals, whilst Councillor Finn suggested using them on another route, both for no apparent discernible reasons.

Tramway developments continued to be approved with permission granted for the installation of a crossover on Newland Avenue opposite Sharp Street. Why this was needed is unclear as Mr Rayner stated that it was required "in order to facilitate the service on the Spring Bank route". It is not certain that it was installed.

In July a motion from Councillor Wheeldon supported by Councillor Finn asking the General Manager to report on the desirability of running petrol buses or trolleybuses in place of trams on any of the existing tram routes was defeated.

However fate was on Councillor Stark's side. Legislation then in force required a town's meeting of ratepayers to endorse a Corporation's proposed Bill before submission to Parliament. If the meeting rejected proposals then a poll of electors needed to be called. The latter's decision was final. On 6 January 1930 such a Town's meeting (which was very well attended) defeated Part 5 of the proposed Parliamentary Bill which included the trolleybus clause, as well as proposals to abolish several principal level crossings. A subsequent poll of electors confirmed the result. Local opinion was that a separate trolleybus proposal would have been approved, but it was defeated because it was linked with the unpopular level crossing proposals which many

prominent citizens considered the cost to the Corporation to be far too high.

Tram car services ended at 11pm, but in October it was decided to continue tram services after this hour until the night buses commenced operation, but that night bus fares should be charged. The first quarter of 1928/9 showed an upturn in tram receipts for the first time in two years.

Mr Rayner submitted a major report on tram and bus services to the Traffic and Complaints Sub-Committee on 15 October 1929. He proposed to reduce the Spring Bank (SW) service from 3 minutes to 4 minutes, which saved 1½ cars a day(!), Saturdays excepted. The Chanterlands Avenue service to run only to Goddard Avenue at a saving of £24 per week. Two cars to be taken from the "TH" route and allocated to the "H" route, as passengers could use the Newbridge Road bus service instead. During bad weather there would be 3 extra cars on all routes and stage points would be illuminated at night. Finally, he wanted to increase the 1½d stage for return tickets to 2d, and the 2d tickets to 2½d. The service reductions were referred to councillors whose wards would be affected, but the additional cars and illuminated stages were approved, with the return tickets proposal deferred to another meeting.

Whilst all this was happening a special Sub-Committee was looking at reorganising the department. Its deliberations were not detailed in the minutes, but much concern and resentment among staff from the General Manager downwards was fermenting.

In November 1929 permission was finally given to upholster two trams at £130 each, and for heaters to be fitted to those cars.

To round off the year on a discordant note, some members led by Councillor Stark tried to rescind the 1919 decision that the General Manager could use his own car on Corporation business with petrol supplied by the department, and instead instruct him to use a Corporation car. This failed, but the matter was referred to the Staff Sub-Committee. Finally, when the vote of thanks (at the end of the Civic Year in October) for the Chairman and Deputy-Chairman was passed, Councillor Stark was recorded as dissenting. The clouds were gathering.

Chapter 10

CONTRACTION

In March 1930 Mr Rayner submitted his thoughts on extending and reorganising services. Tram and bus mileage had increased by 1,500,000 since 1926, but passengers carried had fallen by 100,000. The previous year's profit for the cars was only £1,136, and although it would be around £10,900 in the current year, this was the result of a rate reduction and the fact that no income tax was payable. Petrol prices had increased from £4,000 to £6,000 annually (hence the trolleybus interest) and although a profit of £6,362 was expected, this could not last and many bus routes were unremunerative. However, the extension of the city boundary would broaden the scope of operations.

Several tram proposals were included. The first was a half-mile extension northward along Halls (Hall) Road from the existing Cottingham Road terminus. A bus route would abstract passengers from the BC trams (which were competing with EYMS's Cottingham service), and would mean that the investment in track along Cottingham Road and Chanterlands Avenue would be wasted. If the trams were brought up to date and upholstered, much of the advantages of the bus competition would be removed, quoting London Transport's upholstering programme in support. An option was a bus link from Hall Road tram terminus into the estate. Mr Rayner also recommended that the Anlaby Road route be extended from Pickering Road to the City Boundary at Anlaby Common.

He proposed a fast service to Goddard Avenue and a 15-minute service between there and Cottingham Road. He was not keen to run trams after 11pm since demand was low. No mention was made of an extension along Spring Bank West. Instead a one-man operated bus was to run between the estate and the Anlaby Road tram route at the junction of Anlaby Road and Calvert Lane.

Locally assembled car no. 125 of 1909 prepares to turn left into Spring Bank at Botanic Gardens. It was fully enclosed resembling no. 26 in 1929. (MJW)

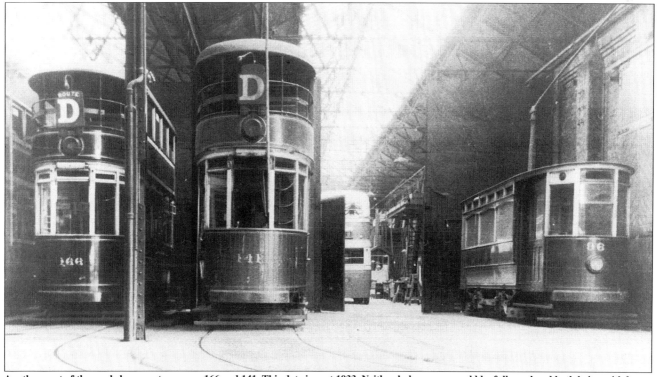

Another part of the workshops captures cars 166 and 141. This date is post 1933. Neither balcony car would be fully enclosed both being withdrawn in this state in September 1938. Also present is a cut-down no. 96. (PM)

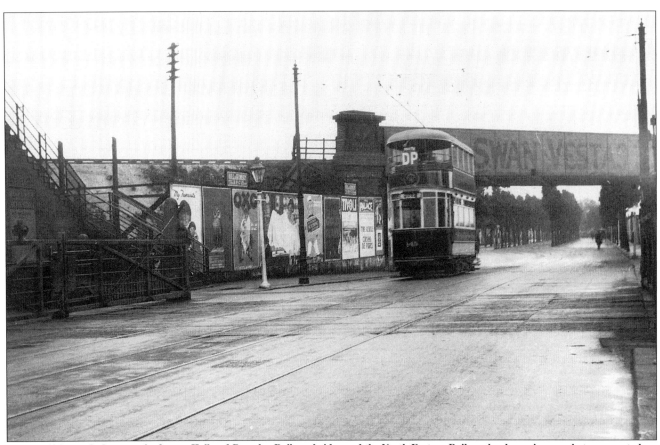

Car no 149 is caught between the former Hull and Barnsley Railway bridge and the North Eastern Railway level crossing on what appears to be a Sunday in 1931. (MJW)

When the Anlaby Road route was cut back to Wheeler Street in July 1934 "A" cars terminated at the crossover in the middle of the main A63 road adjoining the level crossing. Concerns about congestion and safety resulted in East Yorkshire Motor Services agreeing that trams could terminate at the start of the Boothferry Road central reservation. This lay within the "B" area of the Coordination Scheme so no passengers could be carried beyond Wheeler Street. The cars (nos. 20 and 162) possess different route letter and destination arrangements. (PM/HBP. Reproduced courtesy of the National Tramway Museum)

The tram extensions were deferred to a future meeting, but were not raised again, whilst Mr Rayner was asked to draw up plans for a bus service between the tram routes at Chanterlands Avenue South and Calvert Lane (Anlaby Road).

His city-centre proposals were adopted in full. All Beverley Road cars were to terminate in the west end of Jameson Street; Spring Bank and Spring Bank West cars would continue to use King Edward Street; Marfleet cars would terminate in the east end of Jameson Street, and the Holderness Road cars would terminate in Savile Street.

Members inspected the first car to be upholstered, and were so impressed that they authorised ten additional cars to be fitted, all to run on the "BC" route.

In June came a threat to the trams with the agreement to introduce a bus route from Paragon Square along the Chanterlands Avenue route to Hall Road, and to coordinate its headway with that of the trams. The service started on 1 July 1930.

The City Engineer had experimented with the use of a night gang for tramway track repairs but found it no quicker than day gangs, It was more expensive, being carried out at time and a quarter, and cost of additional adequate lighting was high. He recommended a return to the day gang system.

A profit on tram operations of £9,123 (twice the expected surplus) was achieved in 1929/30 compared with a bus surplus of just £380.

In July 1930 Mr Rayner was taken ill and underwent an emergency operation. The Tramways Committee (three days later) wished him well and the Chairman (by now Alderman Mell) took over the management in conjunction with Mr Shearsmith and Mr Bruce until he returned.

His previous recommendation that tram lines be placed on the new North Bridge was accepted as were his alternative proposals (in his absence) for the new Monument Bridge.

In October 1930 a storm broke around Mr Rayner. This arose from the Tramways Enquiry that had been meeting since December 1929. The verbatim transcript runs to 328 pages, and it is evident that whilst there was a genuine concern about the efficiency of the department (much of which was justified as the enquiry progressed) the real target of some members was Mr Rayner due in part to his role in 1926. This time the sessions were held in private but a large number of staff was called before the Committee. Some staff were reluctant to say anything; others were happy to comment and to criticise/accuse superiors and colleagues. Allegations, mainly from Alderman Stark, were made about improper use of petrol for his car whilst he was ill and against other officials for the mis-use of petrol. It was claimed that new spares were put into cars and the used ones added to stock. Examples included dynamos, lights, horns and brake linings. He was accused of having work done at his home in Hornsea using redundant materials and departmental staff. In many cases Mr Rayner was able to produce receipted invoices for the materials (which it transpired had already been brought to the notice of some Committee members).

Accusations were also laid against other members of the department, particularly Messrs Booth, Ingram and Bruce. Aldermen Stark wanted these three and Rayner suspended during the life of the enquiry, but there was little support mainly because a solicitor from the Town Clerk's Department who attended all the sessions advised against it. Mr Rayner's view that any accusations against individuals should be heard by those individuals was supported by the solicitor and was implemented. This probably took the sting out of some accusations and undoubtedly created a reluctance of some witnesses to talk freely. Even so more than twenty were called with varying results. There were even accusations of holes drilled into office walls at Liverpool Street which would enable conversations to

be overheard! It was also alleged that holes were used elsewhere to give advance warning of someone's approach. A secret knock had to be used to gain immediate entry to part of the workshops at Liverpool Street! It was also clear that, like Willoughby before him, Alderman Stark maintained close links with some employees and he ensured that they were called to the enquiry. It was evident that he spoke with employees on the trams, on the road and in the depots and workshops. He was particularly critical of staff's inability to work short when faced with heavy delays or crowds. Yet should staff take orders from him? He gave several examples including the crowds after an event at East Park

The enquiry took nine months and its report was presented to the Tramways Committee. The Town Clerk on the grounds (possibly convenient) of heavy workloads, engaged Mr W.H. Owen, a Barrister-at-law (Alderman Stark dissenting), to comment on the report of the inquiry. His summary and observations were read to the Tramways Committee on 14 October 1930 (Alderman Stark dissenting again, wanting only the summary read out). The Committee "fully considered the matter" and resolved that the General Manager had answered the charges made against him to the Committee's satisfaction and as far as his motor car was concerned, having regard to the original terms of reference, he be paid a suitable allowance or an increase in salary equivalent to such an allowance for the upkeep of his car. Mr Rayner was present. Alderman Stark's amendment calling for his resignation was not seconded and therefore was lost. Mr Owen's report was not entered into the minutes and the contents are unknown.

More was to follow with Mr Bruce (who had strongly supported Mr Rayner during the General Strike) and Mr Ingram being asked to tender their resignations as a result of two motions by Alderman Stark. Two members of staff were to be reprimanded, one of whom was also to be docked 5s a week from his wages for a year.

Seven days later the Council Meeting overturned the decision regarding Mr Rayner and called for him to resign along with Messrs Bruce and Ingram. All three declined to do so, but a letter from Mr Rayner was not entered into the minutes despite the Committee agreeing to do so. The Committee passed a motion deferring consideration for twelve months and an amendment that all three be given six month's notice was defeated.

All to no avail, for the City Council disregarded the Committee's decision (again), and gave notice to all three men. The Committee had no choice but to agree but all three men still refused to resign and on 4 December the Council gave them three months' notice. This was reported to the Tramways Committee on 29 December 1930 by the Town Clerk, but the Committee made no comment. Subsequently, in February 1931, Mr Bruce was reinstated.

Another significant part of the Committee's proceedings was a decision not to lay tram lines over the new Monument Bridge (replacement for the Whitefriargate bridge), thus sealing the fate of the "P" and "TH" trams. Mr Rayner continued to attend the meetings until his notice ran out on 4 March 1931 – a strange state of affairs. In addition to the return of his superannuation payments he was granted a gratuity of £500 (Alderman Stark, of course, and Councillor Finn dissenting). Mr Shearsmith, the Chief Clerk, assumed control of the department although non-routine matters were to be referred to the Chairman and Deputy-Chairman.

Thus ended another chapter of tramways history which showed the Council in a poor light. Undoubtedly the case resulted from the campaign waged by certain members to settle "old scores" arising from the General Strike. At least the

Car no. 170 dating from March 1912 but with the upper deck from no. 152 (1935) is pictured on the short terminus stub for the truncated Anlaby Road route. (MJW)

On 7 July 1937 Milnes car no. 105 passes the Hull and East Riding Institute for the Blind on Beverley Road en route for "town". No. 105 was scrapped in March 1940. (PM/HBP. Reproduced courtesy of the National Tramway Museum)

Tramways Committee emerged with some credit having looked at the evidence over a nine-month period and decided that there was no case to answer but could do nothing with a council determined to have its way. However, it is clear from the transcripts that some reorganisation and tightening up of systems, especially in the workshops, was essential and that matters had drifted for too long. It was also clear that staff relationships between supervisors and men and between individual sections were poor (at best) and downright hostile (at worst). In many ways Mr Rayner was his own worst enemy and should have been aware that his every move would be subject to scrutiny by some Council members and even his own staff. It was also clear that re-instated employees would not speak with former volunteers, and even refused to collect contributions to a hospital/health fund. Retaining a large proportion of volunteers was not Mr Rayner's decision but it saddled him with a great many problems.

A special Sub-Committee which was authorised to deal with traffic matters met on 23 March. It decided that the Pier service should be reduced to a single car running without a timetable (!) which would terminate on the eastern side of Whitefriargate Bridge. (Photographs dated March 1931 show the Pier cars terminating on the southern side of Queen Victoria Square, so for how long did the cars terminate on the eastern side of the bridge?) All cars on the Spring Bank West service would terminate at Park Avenue for a trial period (thus confirming that Mr Rayner's advice was correct). "TH" cars were to operate at peak hours only and "H" cars were not to be diverted via Drypool Bridge when North Bridge was closed to road traffic. The latter is surprising since there were enough delays without adding to them. Another proposal to remove all punch clocks was deferred until a new General Manager was in post.

Members heard that the instruction of 15 January 1929 whereby a tram standing at the terminus should leave immediately on the arrival of a second car irrespective of the timetable, had not been implemented, so the Traffic and Complaints Sub-Committee told the Traffic Manager to do so immediately.

A report on the condition and equipment of the tram cars was submitted to the Traffic and Complaints Sub-Committee on 21 April 1931. No further details have been found but it was agreed to withdraw Brill cars 27/8/9 and advertise the bodies for sale but to defer the rest of the report until the new General Manager arrived.

The new manager was Duncan P. Morrison, the General Manager and Engineer at Dundee. He was appointed in March 1931 from a shortlist of six which included Ben England of St Helens, the managers at York, Halifax and Oldham, and the Works Manager at Bishop Auckland for United Automobile Services Ltd.

The Yorkshire Show was held in Hull in the summer of 1930 and temporary shelters were erected at the Anlaby Road end of Calvert Lane, and another on Spring Bank West, with buses running between these two to connect with the Anlaby Road tram service.

In July it was agreed to change the name of the undertaking to "Hull Corporation Transport Department" and the Committee became the Transport Committee.

The Pier route was withdrawn on 5 September 1931. The circumstances are unclear as no report, either before or after the event, was submitted to the Transport Committee. It may have been in connection with the forthcoming reconstruction of Whitefriargate Bridge since it had already been decided that rails would not be laid over the new road.

On 28 October 1931 the fate of the trams was sealed when the new manager recommended that future expenditure on the tramway section be kept to an absolute minimum, and that

general powers be obtained to abandon the tramways at the earliest opportunity. No details of the reasoning behind this recommendation were minuted nor have any reports been found.

In April 1932 he submitted his thoughts on restructuring the department to the Transport Committee. The Engineering Department would be totally reorganised with the workshops at Liverpool Street under a new Tramway Maintenance Engineer, assisted by an Assistant Maintenance Engineer, a Depot Foremen, a Foreman Painter and Foreman Bodybuilder. The Maintenance Engineer would control all the depots as well as stores.

As there was no one with direct responsibility for permanent way equipment he advocated the appointment of a Track Superintendent with that responsibility. Whilst authority was given for the Tramway Maintenance Engineer to be appointed the post of Track Superintendent was deferred until the City Engineer had been consulted since the permanent way remained his responsibility. Mr Morrison was keen to assume all responsibility for track repairs but the City Engineer contested this and won. Matters came to a head in September 1934 as described in Appendix 3.

Both appointments were long overdue and came too late in the life of the tramways. Their absence was a consequence of the three-way split in responsibilities until 1919. Tucked away in the report was approval for a new post of Chief Assistant, a move which was to be significant for the future. The Car-shed Foreman at Liverpool Street was given one month's notice.

When, at the same meeting, the City Engineer (unintentionally making Mr Morrison's point) asked for authority to spend £920 on renewing three-quarters of the Stepney crossing, he was instructed to ask the LNER if the work could be deferred. The reply was very definite in that the crossing should be replaced or removed. It was left to the General Manager and the City Engineer to determine if the work was necessary and, if so, to go ahead.

Another fares revision was agreed at the April 1932 Transport Committee meeting in that the 2d return tickets were to be available up to 8am, and that between 8am and 9am the fare was to be one penny for a single journey.

The trams recorded a deficit of £4230 for 1931/2 whilst the buses also suffered a loss of £1651, which was a disappointment since it had been forecast they would have a surplus.

On 27 June 1932 the General Manager informed the Transport Committee that, pursuant to a request from the City Engineer, he had suspended the TH tram service as a temporary measure with effect from that date. He did not define "temporary" but a new 1d stage fare was agreed for buses running between Dansom Lane and Whitefriargate Bridge for a three month period. Not that it mattered, for the route never ran again.

At a Committee meeting it was decided to merge the new Traffic Superintendent and Chief Assistant posts, and the first occupant was Mr R.C. Moore. The same meeting (a busy one) decided to appoint Mr H.W. Ashby of Sheffield Corporation to the post of Tramways Maintenance Engineer at a salary of £500, despite an attempt by some councillors to re-advertise the post at £375!

Meanwhile discussions had been continuing with EYMS regarding a coordination agreement, and Mr A.R. Fearnley, the General Manager of Sheffield Corporation Tramways had been retained to advise the Transport Committee. On 13 September a revised heads of agreement was approved and a copy circulated to all Councillors.

In July 1932 a junior clerk, Mr J. Wright, was given a salary increase on his 19th birthday, the first of many in a career that would see him become the Chief Clerk in the Transport Department in the 1950s.

Despite the decision not to spend money on the tramways,

Car no. 130 displays another "standard" configuration with a high destination box as it passes Beverley Road Baths on 4 June 1938. No. 130 dated from 1910 but had been fully enclosed in 1930 and became Leeds no. 448 in February 1942. (PM/HBP. Reproduced courtesy of the National Tramway Museum)

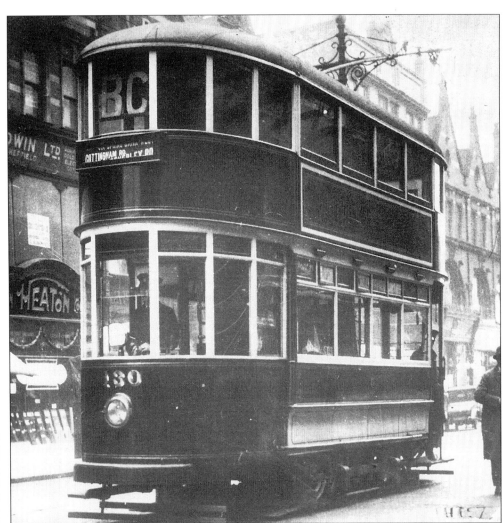

Another view of no. 130 here awaiting departure in King Edward Street on a "BC" working sometime between 1930 and July 1934. Note the unusual destination blind display and the older version of the livery. (PM/RFM)

authority was given in October 1932 to purchase three or four sets of second-hand semi-modern traction equipment, but no details were given.

Arguments about workmen's fares raged at the Claims, Finance and General Purposes Sub-Committee on 3 October 1932. Mr Morrison recommended that the 2d return fare be available on all cars leaving either the outer termini or city termini on each route, up to and including 8am, and that the 1d single fare be available on the same condition up to and including 9am. Like his predecessors he did not succeed, and no changes to the existing system were made. However, this time he was fortunate because the full Council Meeting on 13 October overturned the decision and approved his recommendation.

Further repairs to level crossings were considered in November 1932, and after some discussion the City Engineer was given authority to purchase two Double Star Crossings and four Single Star Crossings for use at the Anlaby Road and Dairycoates crossings.

On 17 January 1933 the General Manager reported to the Stores, Depots and Workshops Sub-Committee on the purchase of 15 tramcar trucks fitted with motors, controllers etc. for the sum of £780.

The City Engineer was asked to report on the cost per yard to take up the tram tracks on Drypool Bridge, Pier route, Jameson Street West to Brook Street and Stoneferry. He was also asked to repair the Osborne Street tracks at the least possible cost.

On 13 February 1933 Mr Morrison sought permission to scrap 15 tramcars, but a decision was deferred until the following meeting. This is interesting as only some Brill cars had been officially withdrawn at this stage, but 15 (nos 1/30/8/69/71/4/7/85/91/6/8/101/2/8/10) cars were withdrawn in April. No. 96 was converted to a single-deck works car. The upper decks from fourteen of the cars including Rayner's 101 were re-used on other cars (see Appendix 1 for full details). There seems to have been no formal authority for the transfer of upper decks, although members must have been aware of the work. The transfers which continued until 1935 all involved fully enclosed bodies. From now on the fleet size quoted in reports does not always agree with Geoff O'Connell's withdrawal dates. There may be good reasons for this, but apparent inconsistencies that might occur from now on cannot be explained!

On the same day an offer from Harvey's Advertising Agency to supply, free of cost, 29,000 copies of the official timetable was accepted for one year with all advertising rights belonging to the Agency, subject to Mr Morrison's approval.

Later that month authority was given to introduce between 9 April and 7 October 6d evening tickets for any bus or tram between 4.30pm and the last ordinary service departure. A 1s Sunday ticket was approved to be available from the start of Sunday morning services until the close of ordinary services.

Discussions about a coordination agreement were resolved in June 1933 with receipt of approval from the Traffic Commissioners. A Special Sub-Committee was formed to consider the detailed proposals. The Chairman and Deputy-Chairman were appointed to a Joint Coordination Committee, which with two EYMS representatives would supervise the coordination agreement.

Two timekeepers were promoted to Inspector in June 1933, one being Mr O'Connell, the father of future Transport Department employee and transport enthusiast Geoff O'Connell.

More track repairs were deferred in July including the section from Queen Victoria Square to South Street, which had not been treated since relaying in 1912. The City Engineer

stated that the rails were seriously cracked at the joints and were worn to such an extent that they could not be re-laid. A cost of £3,800 was involved. It was considered again in July, when it was decided to delay the works with only emergency works being carried out and at the lowest cost. This turned out to be £500 2s 3d and involved 400 feet of rail, the cost being met from the Reserve Fund.

In 1932/3 the department incurred a deficit £6,866 for the trams, an improvement on the anticipated deficit of £8,616, whereas the buses lost £9,186 against an estimated surplus of £17,860. No explanation was given for such a variation between estimates and the actual results.

The Coordination Agreement was never described in the minutes in detail, and indeed even at such a distance little can be found about it. Essentially it was a mileage sharing arrangement, which was balanced from time to time by an operator working a joint licensed service normally operated by the other. It is also claimed that it provided mutual protection for both operators.

It divided Hull and the surrounding areas into three parts or "areas". The "A" area was more or the less the inner city area bounded by the Hull and Barnsley Railway line in the west, Cottingham Road in the north apart from the Beverley Road tram route and the Sutton Road – Leads Road – Ings Road – Maybury Road axis in the east. Within this area all income went to the Corporation. Outside this area was the "B" area in which income and mileage was shared out on an annual basis. Small discs were fixed to traction poles and lamp standards to inform conductors when they crossed from one to the other. The final area was the exclusive preserve of EYMS. Willebrew tickets with separate tickets for the different areas were used by EYMS, whilst the Corporation also had separate tickets for the "A" and "B" areas but using the Setright system.

In October 1933 the special Sub-Committee reported to the Transport Committee which approved their recommendations. The proposals involved the abandonment of three parts of the tramway system, all being replaced by KHCT motor buses. The section between Dairycoates and Pickering Road would be replaced by service 3, that between Wheeler Street and Pickering Road service 9, and the Cottingham Road section from Newland Avenue to Hall Road by service 21. Operation over the crossings at Dairycoates and Newington would cease. It was also decided to replace the Spring Bank West tram route "SWC" when the Coordination Agreement was introduced. No reasons were given, but as duplication of motorbus services along Spring Bank West and Chanterlands Avenue was already high, it was a candidate for substitution.

The City Engineer reminded councillors that expenditure on the permanent way until 30 September 1933 was £9,753 against an estimated expenditure of £13,000. When the estimates were prepared it was expected that the Coordination Agreement would be in force by June 1933, and that ten miles of double track would have been abandoned. If the Spring Bank West, Beverley Road and Cottingham Road tracks were abandoned within the next few weeks the estimate might not be exceeded. Any delays would mean an overspend. It was to be July 1934 before the routes were replaced and the Agreement commenced.

In November Mr Morrison received authority to purchase more equipment for the tramcars (Alderman Stark dissenting, of course), and to dispose of ten cars. The equipment comprised two S.H. trucks at £25 each (source unknown) and 21 trucks complete with traction equipment from Messrs A. Devey & Co., Birmingham at a cost of £70 each. According to Geoff O'Connell's notes only nine cars were withdrawn in November 1933 (nos. 19/23/32/7/42/5/50/2/9), the upper decks being re-used.

In 1934 not long before the closure of route "BC" Milnes no. 115 is about to turn left into Cottingham Road from Beverley Road en route for Hall Road. The Haworth Arms is prominent. Compare this view with the same location in the photograph on page 91. (PM/RFM)

When the BC service closed additional short workings (designated BN) were introduced on the main Beverley Road route as shown on cars 148 and 116. Note the different route board arrangements on the two cars. (PM/RFM)

Another bus route which duplicated a tram route was opened in 1933. This ran along Beverley Road beyond the Endike Lane terminus for a quarter of a mile, where it turned left into Greenwood Avenue within the North Hull Estate. Eventually, a five minute frequency was provided.

Track renewals continued with repairs to the permanent way in George Street (£228 15s 5d) and Hedon Road (£56 5s 3d) during January 1934, followed by Beverley Road (Stepney Lane) at a cost of £118 0s 10d.

In April 1934 Mr Morrison reported that he had been offered traction equipment similar to that recently purchased by the Committee, and that it would be advantageous if he were allowed to tender for any further items that were offered. He was given the approval and duly bought 14 controllers at £105 and 36 controllers with reversing keys at £252.

It is hard to ascertain what the official attitude towards the tramways was at this time. Three years had elapsed since his recommendation to seek powers for abandonment but there appeared to be no conversion plan. Track still needed replacing or repairing and £204 had been spent on spare parts from Hadfields of Sheffield. Other spending included a new mains changeover point in Carr Lane. The Corporation seemed mesmerised by the Coordination Agreement, which was still moving at a slow pace with new buses in store for over a year. Even after its introduction, about 120 trams would remain on six routes and it may have been the capital tied up in the system, together with the income for the power station, that deterred them. Tram services continued to be slower than buses due in part to the areas where side running still existed.

In July Mr Morrison was authorised to provide boxes on tramcars on one route for passengers to deposit uncollected fares, as an experiment. This later became standard, with the red boxes fitted under the saloon window on all buses and trolley-buses and, as far as is known, tramcars.

In the last meeting before the Coordination Agreement was introduced the Annual Accounts for 1933/4 showed a tram profit of £982 against an anticipated loss of £9199 whilst the forecast motorbus surplus of £10,380 turned out to be a loss of £15,653! How much this was due to the expectation that buses would have replaced some trams, and that income would have been affected by the agreement, is unclear.

Tram routes "AP", "BC", "DP", "SW" and "SWC" ran for the last time on 28 July 1934, resulting in the abandonment of track along Chanterlands Avenue, between Hall Road and Newland Avenue, between Dairycoates and Pickering Road and between Newington and Pickering Road. According to Mr Turner's notes, 4.003 miles of track were discontinued. Some but not all of the reserved track sections were discontinued.

The section between Botanic Gardens and Walton Street remained in situ and with the overhead intact. Trams continued to run during Hull Fair week, a fact confirmed in a report to the Transport Committee in October 1935. When the Ministry of Transport's Inspector was inspecting the new Chanterlands Avenue trolleybus route in July 1937, he was informed that it was the intention to run trams for Hull Fair in October. After some hesitation the inspector agreed but in the event trams did not run.

When Mr Morrison recommended the disposal of 22 tram-cars to the September Committee the decision was deferred without any explanation by members. Sixteen trams were withdrawn in November 1934, these being nos 4/7/31/3/5/48/51/5/6/7/72/6/8/9/80/2).

Despite a reluctance to spend money on the tramways the October Stores, Depots and Workshops Sub-Committee agreed to weld rail joints at a cost of £5 per rail joint, apart from that portion of Prospect Street that was to be reconditioned.

Permission was given to replace a number of poles on various routes.

In November 1934 the General Manager reported that he considered the present arrangements for washing and cleaning the upper roofs of tramcars to be unsatisfactory, as they could only be used for one car at a time. A section of an improved type had been erected at Liverpool Street. It was suspended from the roof and ran the whole length of each pit so that the cleaning of the upper saloons could be carried out at the same time. So far two gantries, each 60 yards long had been erected, one fixed to the wall the other suspended between two rows of tramcars. This was a considerable improvement on the former practice and he suggested that Liverpool Street be fully equipped, and that Anlaby Road and Holderness Road be dealt with in a similar manner. The total cost would be around £400. However, the Committee agreed only to fully equip Liverpool Street.

Neither Cottingham Road nor Hedon Road was mentioned. Agreement had been given to fill and cover the tram inspection pits at Cottingham Road which was being used as the work-shops for the bus fleet, but trams were still housed there. In an October 1935 report it was stated that only Liverpool Street, Anlaby Road, Cottingham Road and Holderness Road were in use. Permission had been given to invite tenders for renting Hedon Road which was being used to store surplus trams and motorbuses, but there is no mention of formal closure in the minutes and supporting papers. Permission to equip Holderness Road was given in January 1935, and Anlaby Road in March 1935, but Cottingham Road seems not to have been equipped.

When the Transport Committee considered further track renewals, it decided that before any expenditure was sanctioned the General Manager should prepare a report on the introduction of the electric trackless trolleybus as an alternative to trams or petrol buses.

Revised charges and arrangements were agreed for the use of tram standards for street lighting by the Corporation's Electricity Department. The annual charge was to be 2s 6d per standard. Permission to use 87 standards near Salt Ings Lane to the junction of Cottingham Road and Beverley Road was granted. A similar agreement was reached two months later which allowed the Transport Department to use Electricity poles on the same basis.

At the same meeting a letter from the former General Manager, Mr E.S. Rayner, was read to the Committee which decided to take no action. There is no indication of the contents and no copy has been found in the archives.

In December the Beverley Road, Chanterlands Avenue and Spring Bank West bus services were diverted inward via Prospect Street, Jameson Street and Ferensway, and outward via Ferensway. This led to a daily march of passengers between the east side of Monument Bridge to Ferensway (later to the coach station), something that lasted for thirty years – unless you lived near a tram terminus, in which case you caught the tram and walked the shorter distance thereafter. A by-product was all the fares went to the Corporation!

Also in December 1934 it was decided to discontinue the use of discount tickets with effect from 31 March 1935. The ghosts of McCombe and Rayner must have cheered.

In February 1935 a new Chief Assistant to the General Manager was appointed. This was Jack Lawson who had experience at South Lancashire Tramways.

A quantity of new steel tyres that were urgently needed for the trams was purchased in February 1935. The following month saw permission given to fit one tram with Dunlop Latex cushion and moquette covers, and for that to be inspected by councillors before extending the scheme. Mr Morrison sought permission to erect centre running trolley wire over the whole

Former trailer car no. 66 approaches the policeman on point duty at the George Street/Saville Street junction. (MJW)

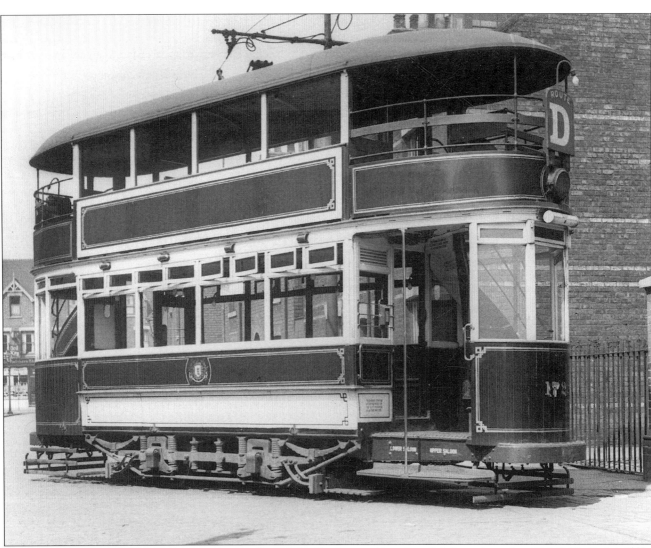

The area outside Liverpool Street depot and works was a favourite location for a small number of photographers who visited Hull in the late 1930s. This is car no. 172. (AG/WAC. Reproduced courtesy of the National Tramway Museum)

tramway system at a cost of £6,500, but the matter was deferred for "the time being". Essential work on the Holderness Road feeder system and renewal of cables was approved at a cost of £150.

This was Mr Morrison's swansong, as he tendered his resignation having obtained the General Manager and Engineer's post at Bournemouth. He had probably had enough of Hull, for the February Transport Committee had appointed a Sub-Committee to "enquire fully into the undertaking and report". The newly-arrived Mr Lawson found himself appointed Acting General Manager, one of the most rapid promotions ever! He was to prove a worthy appointment.

Deficits on both trams (£14,004) and buses (£13,580) were recorded for 1934/5, although income on the trams was up by 2%, but this was offset by increased traffic and increased power costs.

Ten cars were withdrawn in 1935, in March (nos 5/13/4/5/7/22/4/5/34/41) and ten in July (nos 3/6/9/10/47/54/93/5/7/9) reducing the fleet size to 116 cars. The reconditioning of tramcars was halted in July 1935, whilst a special meeting was called to discuss the situation. Any decision was deferred but the meeting did not resume despite some of the newest cars dating from 1915 still retaining open balconies. The oldest cars in service were nos 2/8/11 of 1898 all with fully enclosed bodies.

On 23 August 1935 Mr Lawson recommended trolleybuses in place of tramcars. This was accepted (Alderman Stark dissenting!), and moves were started to obtain the necessary powers. As a result an order for eight sets of tramcar parts from the Lancashire Steel Corporation Ltd was cancelled, and a sum of £12 10s was paid in lieu of the order.

The inquiry Sub-Committee had met six times before reporting on 14 October 1935. It had considered Mr Morrison's report on Administration, Organisation and Personnel, the City Treasurer's Special Report on Finance, the Town Clerk's Report on Free Travelling Facilities, and Mr Lawson's reports on the future operation of transport services in the city and staffing.

It did not make for pleasant reading, not just for the trams but for the department as a whole. It admitted that the permanent way, despite continuous work thereon (which was stretching it a bit), was in a very bad state, and that the overhead was completely out of date. Requests from Mr Morrison to convert to centre running wires had been deferred, and decisions about the permanent way were based on the least cost required. However, Mr Lawson considered that neither the track nor the overhead could stand the strain of increased speeds necessary to compete with buses. The cost of maintaining the permanent way considerably exceeded the costs in other towns.

Although the reconditioned cars were capable of a few more years' satisfactory service, they were totally out-of-date and unsuitable for modern conditions. Only two cars had been purchased since 1914, and both these had been scrapped whilst others dated from 1900 (question – which two? Certainly not 26 and 113 which were still going strong; Rayner's no. 101 had gone but what was the other one?). All the motors of the present stock were reconditioned second-hand equipment discarded by other undertakings. Of the 115 cars in stock 65 had been reconditioned. 83 were in daily service but all were used when Hull Fair took place, at large sporting events and at Christmas. If the system were to be retained for any length of time the remaining cars would have to be reconditioned. At present they were fit to run, but could not produce the necessary speed, acceleration or comfort for the present day.

The reconditioning of cars had been achieved at the expense of any regular regime of docking tramcars, but a system had been introduced for complete overhaul every 14 months, whilst

a routine inspection of all cars was being carried out every second day.

The motorbus side comprised six different makes and sixteen types of vehicle. A significant number (120 vehicles) were hired and this was not viewed with any satisfaction.

All the "A" area services were too slow to attract additional passengers. Unless they could be accelerated further and made more attractive, passengers would use either Corporation or Company services within the "A" area. It was important to retain and if possible increase the revenue from "A" area services. Some accelerated services had been introduced in September, with a reduction of 1,800 miles a week. This had stemmed that loss of revenue and had increased receipts per mile from 13½d to 18½d. An annual saving of £2,000 would result. It was recommended that each route be surveyed to reduce the number of stopping places to aid a further acceleration.

The number of free passes was rising annually; in 1930/1 4961 passes were issued, whilst in 1934/5 this had risen to 5602. Old Age Pensioners passes were 4786 and there were also 80 free passes issued to Members of the Council. Use of passes was not subject to as many restrictions as elsewhere.

A financial report was provided by the City Treasurer which stated that annual receipts on the trams had fallen considerably. In 1921 the income was £372,000, in 1928 it was £325,302, and in 1935 it was £199,512.

The following chart showing how receipts had varied was included:

	Year Ended				
	1921	**1925**	**1930**	**1934**	**1935**
	£	**£**	**£**	**£**	**£**
Hessle Road	80,890	64,076	65,588	54,604	39,790
Anlaby Road	56,271	44,406	51,280	40,339	30,843
Holderness Road	73,868	56,848	53,577	42,650	41,959
Spring Bank and Newland Avenue	72,733	61,886	38,374	30,068	28,234
Beverley Road and Cottingham Road	56,591	45,197	53,075	49,835	38,076
Hedon Road	38,579	30,309	23,229	17,817	17,336
Old Town	3,336	3,234	3,051		
Night Services	1,572				
Spring Bank West			27,000	11,227	3,707
Weekly Passes		19,831			
Gross	383,840	325,787	315,174	246,540	199,943
Less Discount		1,371	1,718	1,590	1,244
	383,840	324,416	313,456	244,950	198,701

This is a remarkable chart. The impression has always been that trams lost passengers to buses, but the evidence of a long decline can be seen as factors such as unemployment and reduced wages took their toll. However, a reduction in receipts did not necessarily mean fewer passengers, given the various discounts and fare policies pursued by the Corporation, often against its Manager's advice. Until recently little had been done to reduce costs. The trams' need to reduce costs came at a time when the permanent way and the cars themselves required investment. Most bus routes extracted passengers from the trams, but they did not necessarily make money. The passenger benefitted but the department did not. Longer distance passengers did not pay a "true" fare and they were subsidised by the many short distance riders.

The extensions of 1924-1928 had added £12,000 per annum in loan charges, whilst permanent way maintenance costs were exceeding £15,000 a year, and an annual contribution to street

Also at Liverpool Street is no. 119 in July 1935. Note how the upper deck does not extend the whole length of the lower deck. Later in that year no. 119 would become fully enclosed with the transfer of the upper deck from no. 55. This would extend its life to the close of tram operation in July 1945 but, unlike many contemporaries, it would be scrapped. (PM)

widening of £2,846 was being incurred. Annual loan charges equivalent to 0.58d per mile were being paid out for abandoned track. (No one seemed to have suggested that the replacement buses should be charged with this – if they had been the trams would have almost broken even, and the buses would have been in deficit). If the trams did not have to pay maintenance for the unused track, they would be in surplus. Some £29,259 of the cost of the abandoned Chanterlands Avenue North extension was outstanding for the permanent way cost, and £6,003 for electrical equipment, (an extension built against the advice of Mr Rayner not mentioned by the report!)

Outstanding debt for the trams exceeded £186,000, of which some (North Bridge) would not be repaid until 1958! The trams had given some £277,627 to the relief of rates. Mr Lawson also pointed out the cost of the free pass scheme, the lack of a uniform fares structure, the duplication of buses and trams over certain sections of route, the cost of retaining redundant staff, and the delay in introducing the Coordination Scheme, which had left some 20 buses unused for over a year and incurred unnecessary expenditure. He was less sanguine about hiring buses, since the charge would cease once the hire ceased, but if the buses had been bought there would still be outstanding loan payments.

The question of free passes was considered at length. With regards to passes for blind persons, limbless ex-servicemen and old age pensioners, it was recommended that a means test be instituted. Passes for retired transport department staff should be withdrawn, and a payment of £10 per councillor should be made by the Council out of the General Rates Fund. The Care of the Blind Committee would be asked to take on the cost of providing passes, and the Health and Public Assistance Committee should be asked to fund the passes for Jubilee Nurses.

The department was seriously overstaffed. Twenty-four men were medically unfit, and it carried 40 redundant staff, to which would be added another thirty when the tramcar reconditioning

ceased. Another batch of men would not be needed when the central bus garage opened and when services were accelerated. The report criticised past recruitment practice, which appeared to take no account of age, physical fitness and general suitability. Mr Morrison had stated that transport was becoming more specialised, and the department should not be looked upon as a dumping ground. There was a need to reduce the average age of the workforce. However, the Corporation was bound by an agreement that promotion was based upon seniority coupled with ability.

Whilst Mr Morrison did not favour trolleybuses, Mr Lawson did (ironic given Mr Morrison's role at Bournemouth). Both agreed that the future did not lie with trams. Renewing the tram system as a whole was financially out of the question, but the agreement with the Corporation's Electricity Department could not be ignored. The Sub-Committee agreed with Mr Lawson's recommendation that trolleybuses should replace the trams over a four year period once powers had been obtained. However, their investigations had shown that the department paid more for the electricity than did comparative undertakings, and it was agreed that the Chairman and Mr Lawson should seek a reduction for the trams and for the trolleybuses.

Mr Lawson recommended the purchase of eighty trolleybuses to replace the trams on each route apart from Hedon Road, for which he wanted to substitute buses that could link with the Newbridge Road route (to form a circular route which never materialised), the conversions to take four years to complete. The project would cost £184,000. Nevertheless the margin was tight, with anticipated profits of £24,404 being reduced to £1,418 after loan charges. All the existing tramway loan charges (including those converted to motorbuses!) were to be charged against the trolleybuses. The Committee sealed the fate of the trams by approving his recommendations.

The female passenger grips her bag
as, with caution, she approaches car
no. 106 near the Dairycoates
terminus on 3 June 1938. (PM)

On the same day no. 106 is on its way to Dairycoates in Porter Street. This
is a good example of how far the trolley boom is from the centre of the
tram. (PM/HBP. Reproduced courtesy of the National Tramway Museum)

Mr Turner whose notes are quoted on many occasions in the text, described no. 144 as a "new type" tram car and it is easy to understand why he might do so. No. 144 has just received a new upper deck (from no. 35) and looks in pristine condition complete with side destination blind in Liverpool Street on 7 February 1935. Withdrawal would come surprisingly early in March 1940. (PM)

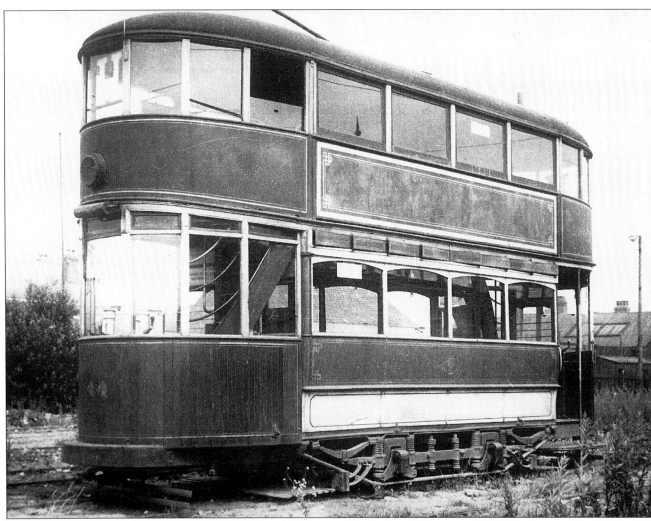

The substantial yard behind Holderness Road Depot appears to have been used for storing withdrawn cars. This is Brush car no. 44 on 17 July 1937. It was withdrawn in July 1937 so it may have already made its last journey. (PM/HBP. Reproduced courtesy of the National Tramway Museum)

Also in the depot yard on that day were several other cars including another Brush car no 46 (also withdrawn in July 1937) and no. 86 which lasted until April 1938. (PM/HBP. Reproduced courtesy of the National Tramway Museum)

Despite many different proposals the Holderness Road cars continued to terminate in Jameson Street East, the location becoming less convenient and more dangerous for passengers as the years passed. Hurst Nelson Car no. 100 stands uncomfortably in the centre of the street. (PM/WAC. Reproduced courtesy of the National Tramway Museum)

This photograph shows the trolley reverser which no. 140 will use when leaving the terminus in place at Ings Road. Its upper deck formerly belonged to no. 59. (PM/HBP. Reproduced courtesy of the National Tramway Museum)

Car no. 122 is pictured at the Newland Avenue terminus complete with a top deck that may have come from no. 96 and high level destination box. This displays "Spring Bank" but the side blind shows "Newland Avenue". (PM/LRS)

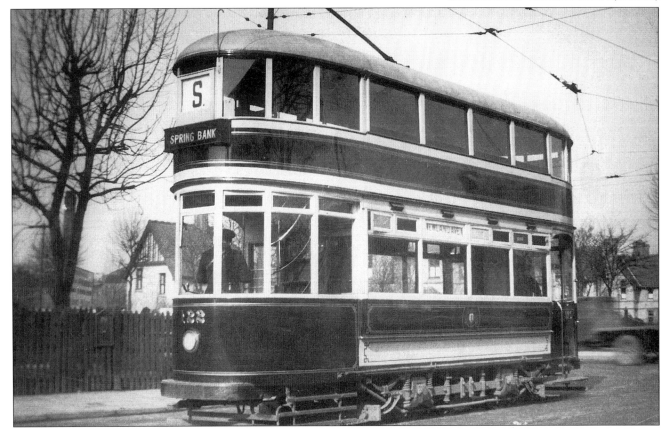

This photograph also shows Newland Avenue but looks towards the terminus with two cars in residence. Note the manner in which the street lights are attached to the bracket arm. This was followed in several places on the system for which the Electricity Department paid an appropriate amount. (PM)

This is close up view of the trucks under car no. 144 at Newland Avenue. (MJW)

These two cars are at the Endike Lane
terminus shortly before trolleybuses
replaced the trams in 1938. (MJW)

This line of cars in Wheeler Street Depot includes
nos 117/164/174 all of which had received upper
decks from withdrawn cars, that of no. 174 being
from Rayner car no. 101. (PM/WAC. Reproduced
courtesy of the National Tramway Museum)

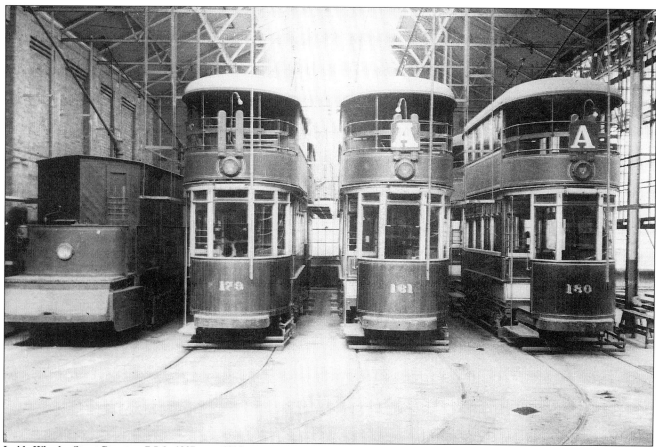

Inside Wheeler Street Depot on 7 July 1937 were 1915
cars 179/61/80 and a works car. All three would be
withdrawn in this condition in September 1938 (nos
161/80) and March 1940 (no. 179). (PM/HBP.
Reproduced courtesy of the National Tramway Museum)

Brush car no. 142 is shown at the Osborne Street
terminus outside the rear of the Willis Department
store some time after 1935 when it received its fully
enclosed upper deck from no. 48. (MJW/HC)

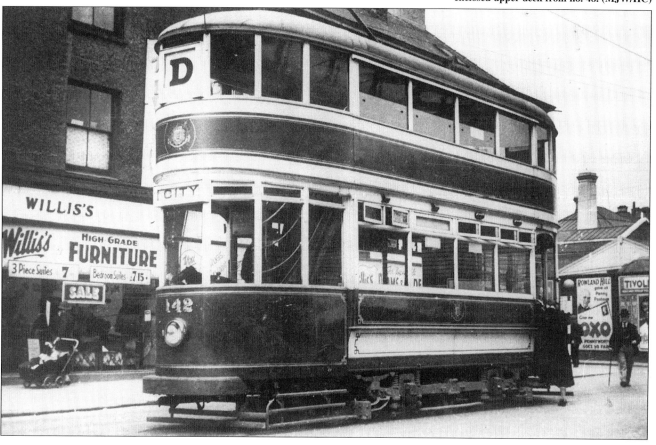

Sometime in the late 1930s car no. 172 waits patiently for the conductor to adjust the trolley pole. Although the destination plate reads "Anlaby Road" it is possible that no. 172 is about to return to Wheeler Street Depot after working on Holderness Road as Wheeler Street provided trams for that route in its last months. No. 172 would be withdrawn upon closure of the Holderness Road route. It carries a full version of the older livery. (MJW)

This shows no. 100 opposite the exit from Wheeler Street Depot on 6 August 1939 at the time when the depot was providing cars for the Holderness Road route. No. 100 has less than six months to live despite receiving a top deck from another car as it was withdrawn in March 1940 shortly after the route closed. (MJW)

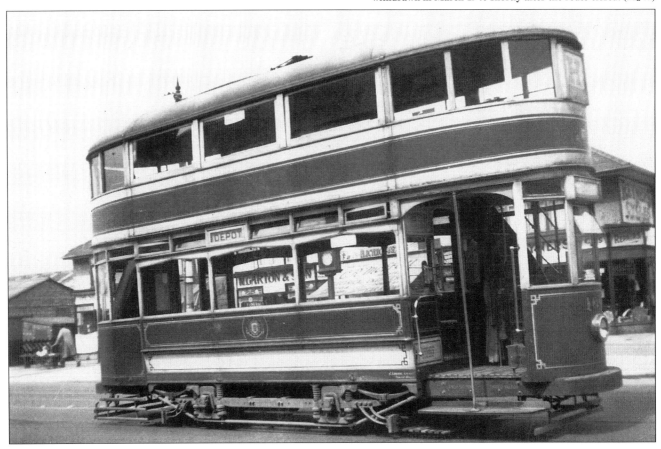

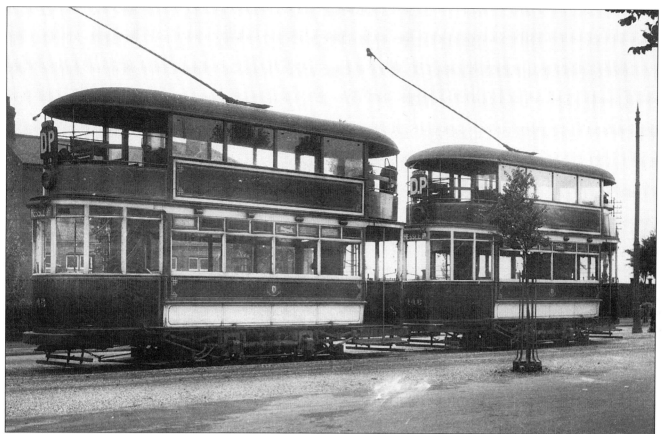

In later years the open balcony cars were, for some reason, allocated to the western routes. Nos 175/6 keep each other company at the Pickering Road "DP" terminus. Both received covered tops in 1935 and 1934 respectively. (MJW)

On 4 June 1938 car no. 145 was pictured inside Liverpool Street Depot. It carries an upper deck from a withdrawn car (fitted in 1934) and remained in service until June 1945 when it was scrapped. (MJW)

The enigma that is no. 26. Was this a completely new car or a substantially rebuilt car dating from 1928? We may never know for certain. This photograph was taken on Cottingham Road in 1933. It was sold to Leeds CT in February 1942 as no. 449. (MJW)

Car no. 160 rests at Endike Lane in the late 1930s. By this time no. 160 had been modernised with Peckham P22 trucks, magnetic track brakes and a transferred upper deck, possibly from car no. 85. It became Leeds CT no. 486 in 1945. (PM/LRS)

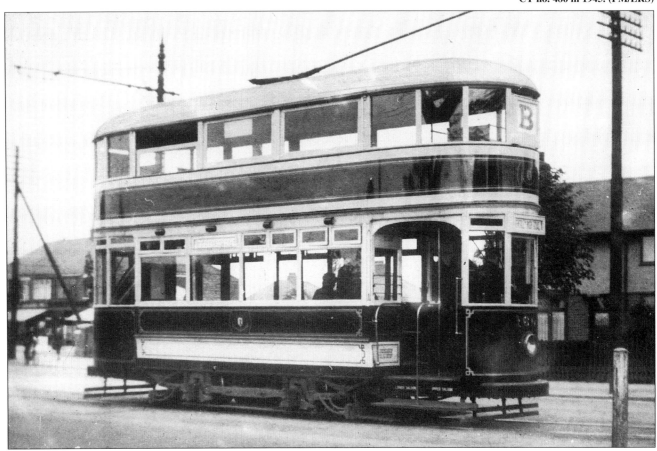

Milnes car no. 103 negotiates the roadworks on Beverley Road closely
trailed by an East Yorkshire Motor Service's single decker no.203. No. 106
would outlast the bus, being withdrawn in March 1940, whilst the bus's six
year life ended in 1935. (MJW)

Former Milnes car no. 81 pauses outside the majestic façade of
Holderness Road Depot. Despite seeming to be in good condition no.
81 was withdrawn in March 1940 after the Holderness Road closure.
(MJW/WAC. Reproduced courtesy of the National Tramway Museum)

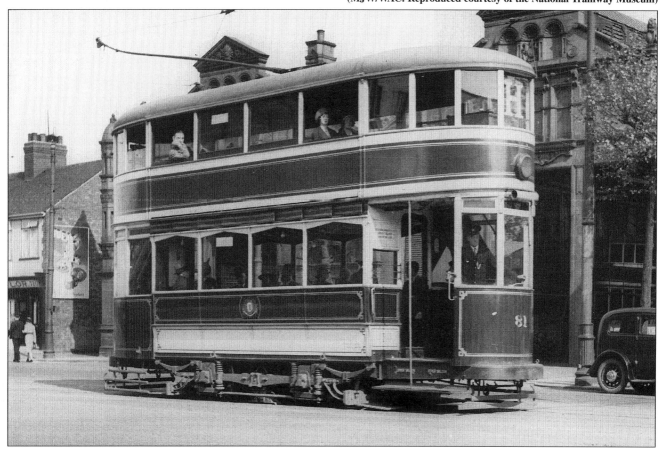

In the winter of 1939/1940 shortly before the closure of the route car no. 68 arrives at Ings Road; it was withdrawn in March 1940. (MJW/LRS)

Three cars led by no. 176 congregate at the Osborne Street terminus in the late 1930s. (MJW/WAC. Reproduced courtesy of the National Tramway Museum)

Former trailer car no. 89 is seen at the Marfleet terminus. The nearest traction pole seems to be leaning somewhat! (PG)

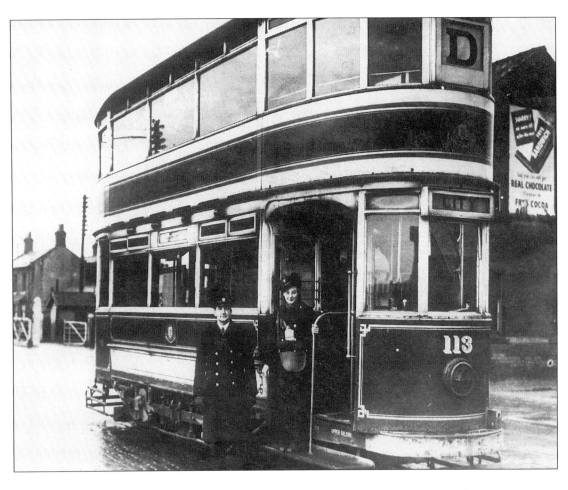

With less than seven months of tram operation remaining no. 113 and crew await departure time at Dairycoates on 1 December 1944. It became Leeds no. 453. (PM)

In the last days of the Second World War no. 117 waits at the Dairycoates terminus. This car was built in 1912 and received a "new" upper deck in 1935. It became Leeds CT no. 485 in July 1945. (PM)

This is Brush car no. 158 in Waterworks Street possibly early in the Second World War as it appears to possess a white bumper, albeit somewhat faded. All the buildings behind no. 158 were destroyed by bombing in 1941/2. (MJW)

Milnes car no. 105 is seen in Osborne Street on the final day of tramway operation on 30 June 1945. The buildings behind the car were once part of the generating station complex. (MJW)

A former Hull car begins its journey to Leeds in 1942 probably following the Anlaby Road conversion in September 1942. It has just passed under the former Hull and Barnsley Railway on Boothferry Road. Mr Rayner suggested that trams be provided along this road but no action resulted. (MJW)

No. 132 is seen in Cottingham Road Depot before transfer to the museum. The colour scheme is attractive. (MJW)

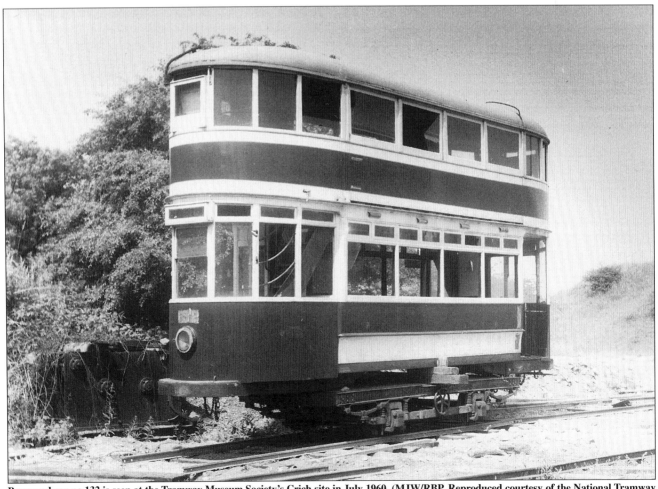

Preserved car no.132 is seen at the Tramway Museum Society's Crich site in July 1960. (MJW/RBP. Reproduced courtesy of the National Tramway Museum)

Chapter 11

THE FINAL YEARS

On 27 January 1936 Mr Lawson was appointed General Manager of the Tramways and Omnibus Undertaking at a salary of £1,000 per annum. He was paid the difference between his salary as Chief Assistant and his new salary whilst he was Acting General Manager.

The Corporation was still contributing to the cost of safety measures at level crossings, and in February the Town Clerk was authorised to pay the sum of £400 per annum for this.

The withdrawal of route "AP" had resulted in the "A" terminus being located outside Wheeler Street Depot immediately before the Newington crossing. Growing congestion led the Watch Committee to suggest that trams should continue over the crossing to the crossover at the junction with Boothferry Road. This lay within the "B" area and it was necessary to seek the Joint Committee (and EYMS) approval, which was given in June 1936 on the understanding that the Corporation would not pick up or set down beyond the Wheeler Street terminus.

Results for 1935/6 revealed a loss on the tramways of £6,782 (estimated loss of £9,636), and a loss on the buses of £1,339. Tram operating costs per mile fell from 12.58d to 12.35d, and the number of miles operated fell by 538,889.

When another enquiry about renting or buying the closed Hedon Road depot was made in January 1937, Mr Lawson stated that he would require the depot in the near future (although he did not state for what purpose) and the offer was refused.

In April the overhead line staff were reorganised and employees were placed in one of three grades – Linesmen, Overhead Drivers, and Assistant Linesmen, and each shift was altered to comprise one of each, with the Linesman to be responsible for the shift. Previously there had been but one grade for all, but Mr Lawson recommended that Linesmen be paid £3 6s 6d, Overhead Drivers £3 1s 0d, and Assistant Linesmen £2 19s 0d, all for a 47 hour week.

For 1936/7 (their last year of full "A" area operation), the trams returned a profit of £3,985 (estimated loss of £3,000), the buses a profit of £10,931, and the trolleybuses which had not yet started had a loss of £496! Again, fares were increased and costs reduced. Tram costs per mile had once again been reduced from 12.35d to 11.47d. Painting of trams continued, some 15 being dealt with in the year whilst 115 cars remained in stock.

The tramway conversion programme resumed on 24 July 1937 when the Newland Avenue service was replaced by motorbuses displaced from the Chanterlands Avenue by new trolleybus services 61 and 61A. This was to avoid mixed operation of trolleybuses and trams along Spring Bank, and to facilitate the conversion of the Newland Avenue route to trolleybus operation (which took place on 3 October 1937). The original intention to run trams in October for Hull Fair was not carried out.

Twelve cars (nos 36/9/44/6/9/61/2/4/5/73/84/9 all dating from 1900, except no.89 (1901), were withdrawn, reducing the fleet size to 104. These were fully enclosed except nos 61/2/4/5 which retained open balconies. The fleet comprised nos 2/8/11/2/6/8/20/1/6/40/3/53/6/7/8/63/8/70/5/81/3/6/7/8/90/2/4/100/3/4/5/6/7/9/111-180. All were fully enclosed apart from nos 136/41/3/57/9/61/2/65-8/70-2/77-80

The Hedon Road route succumbed on 1 January 1938, somewhat later than the anticipated date of October 1937. It was replaced by motorbus route 47 which followed exactly the same route from Savile Street. No trams were immediately withdrawn but, in April eighteen were condemned (nos 2/8/11/6/8/21/40/3/53/6/7/70/5/83/6/7/8/90.

Car no. 142 in 1942 looking in reasonable condition (the faded white bumper excepted) despite the depredations of the Second World War. No. 142 had received the upper deck from car no. 48 in 1935 and was sold to Leeds in July 1945 becoming no 478. (AG)

The offer of the Electricity Department to purchase the Hedon Road poles for lighting purposes at £2 10s per pole was accepted.

In January 1938 a Temporary Draughtsman, Mr J.W. Dent, was appointed to a permanent post with the Department, a career that was to end with him becoming the Chief Engineering Assistant of the undertaking in the early 1960s.

On 24 January Mr Lawson was requested to consider accelerating the conversion programme. The original plan covered Beverley Road in 1938, Holderness Road in 1939, Anlaby Road in 1940, and Hessle Road in 1941. Mr Lawson was not keen to expedite the process. Additional capital charges would be incurred. Also taken into account were prolonged delivery times for trolleybuses, as the first Leylands had been delayed by a shortage of materials, the low operating cost of the remaining trams and the minimum requirement for spares, as these could be obtained from withdrawn cars and, what was for him the most important reason, the need for a gradual driver training programme.

The age of the remaining tram motormen was high and their training required time (and according to a later Chief Driving Instructor, Teddy Mulligan, lots of patience). Motormen opted for conducting rather than becoming trolleybus drivers. His recommendation not to accelerate the programme was accepted.

Tramway operations showed another surplus in 1937/8, this time one of £3,012, again in relation to an anticipated deficit. 103 cars were in stock at the start of the financial year. Another 16 trams were repainted during the year.

When Mr Lawson was called for interview to Bolton in May 1938 the Transport Committee, on condition he withdrew his application, increased his salary from £1,200 to £1,500 per annum plus three annual increments of £100. He withdrew his application.

In October 1938 trolleybus route 63 replaced trams on the Beverley Road route resulting in another fourteen trams being taken out of service, reducing the fleet size to 72. Withdrawn were nos 12/112/37/41/3/62/5/6/7/8/71/7/8/80.

The year 1938/9 saw the undertaking in profit once more but the trams lost £8,181. Tramcar mileage was reduced from 2,340,179 to 1,553,969 whilst passengers fell from 27,475,149 to 18,971,459. Only three trams were repainted during the year but twenty-seven cars were scrapped. Seventy cars remained in stock at 31 March 1939, more than sufficient for the three remaining routes.

Delivery of the twenty trolleybuses for the Holderness Road route began in July 1939 and it was anticipated that conversion would take place in September. During 1939 cars had ceased to use Holderness Road Depot and had migrated to Wheeler Street Depot.

On 3 September 1939 war between Great Britain and Germany was declared. For the trams this meant a slight stay of execution, with the receipt of a letter from the Ministry of Transport informing the Corporation that no trolleybus route inspections would be carried out in the foreseeable future, and that authority to commence any such route would be vested in an undertaking's General Manager. The Committee declined to sanction the conversion at that time.

Bumpers, footboard edges and trolley cane holders were painted white to make them conspicuous in the Blackout. Later roofs were painted dark grey to render them less likely to be seen from the air. Unlike trolleybuses and buses, none of the livery needed to be painted out. Masking plates were placed over frogs to reduce the possibility of electrical arcing being seen from the air. Interior lighting was reduced and headlights were masked to show a reduced beam of light.

The Corporation were advised by the Ministry of War Transport not to dispose of surplus trams and buses, in case severe air raids so incapacitated an undertaking that the acquisition of vehicles was needed to cover for destroyed or damaged vehicles.

Mr Lawson died suddenly as the result of a heart attack whilst hurrying from a theatre to the central Air Raids Precaution point at the start of an air raid. This was a sad and premature end for someone who appeared to have been the only Manager to have the ability to solve the department's problems, and to be able to cope with the vagaries of the Transport Committee. The November Transport Committee expressed condolences to his family but declined to advertise for a successor for the moment. Instead, Mr D. Bellamy, the Manager of the Electricity Department, assumed the Manager's duties.

One of his first tasks was to recommend the conversion, but not until January 1940 was permission granted. Accordingly, trolleybuses replaced trams on 18 February, the city terminus being an anticlockwise loop around Jameson Street, King Edward Street and Savile Street, the terminus being near the Hedon Road bus route terminus. The route was extended in a clockwise circle via Savile Street, Carr Lane, Paragon Square and Jameson Street, in August 1940, in order to serve the station and alleviate the effects of the blackout.

Twenty-one cars were withdrawn including the last open balcony cars. The full list was nos 20/58/63/8/81/92/4/100/6/7/18/20/1/1/44/9/51/7/61/72/9).

No. 96 is preserved at the Heaton Park Tramway in Manchester – seen here whilst still in the Hull Tramways livery.

Fifty-one cars remained in stock for the last two routes.

The cost of track removals would push the department into the red – a sum of £50,000 was estimated to be the 1939/40 deficit. Mr Bellamy recommended that with the reduction of tramway work at Liverpool Street the Ferensway workshops be transferred to there.

The outstanding debt on disused tramway track was £55,800, with a further liability of £71,250 for track removal. The estimated deficit for the current year was £10,418 and for the next year £49,926. He estimated that service reductions on all three modes would reduce revenues by £28,000, to which should be added a £6,800 increase in petrol costs and an increase in the wage bill by £12,800.

He recommended a complete overhaul of the fares system apart from the retention of a minimum fare for buses operating over sections of tram and trolleybus routes. Fares would be on the basis of a maximum 1d per mile with an overall maximum of 3d. Return 5d fares were abolished together with the Workmen's 4d return fares and Workmen's fares between 8am and 9am.

He proposed a transfer system whereby buses from outer areas would feed into trams and trolleybuses during off peak hours to save petrol, and to exploit the frequency of the tram and trolleybus services. Trams ran every three minutes with some duplication at peak periods. There would be some inconvenience to passengers, but the precarious position of the system warranted drastic action. Most of his fare proposals

This was taken at a caravan site in Skipsea, East Yorkshire. Assuming it was sold at the end of the war this will be the lower deck from Milnes car no. 103. (Paul Derrick)

were deferred and considered again on two occasions, the last being in April, when some changes were agreed but not the increase in the maximum fare. The proposal to adopt a feeder system for trams and trolleybuses was confirmed.

The initial proposal was to turn service 48 buses at Holderness Road to feed into trolleybus service 64, which would be followed by service 15 and 16 buses feeding into the northern trolleybus routes. No specific proposals for the two tram routes were made, but this might have involved service 3 and "D" and services 7/7A and 9 with "A". All would require approval from the Joint Coordination Committee and the Regional Commissioners (Ministry of Transport).

The North Hull proposals did not last long. Normal services were soon resumed so the trams were denied a last fling.

Mr Bellamy reported that the pavilion at the Department's recreation ground had burnt down of 14 April 1940, and that it had not been insured. His recommendation that one or two tramcar bodies be given to the Recreation Club, and that the Department erect and fit the bodies for the Recreation Club was agreed. It has not been possible to discover more about this.

He also reported that the last tramcar and trolleybus departure at 10.20pm was being extended to 10.45 on Sundays in order to ease the pressure on the buses.

Between the summer of 1940 and the beginning of March 1941 the city of Hull was subjected to over forty air raids. On 19/20 March a parachute mine fell through the roof of the paintshop at Liverpool Street. This adjoined the tram running shed, and it was fortunate that it failed to explode as, unlike buses and trolleybuses, trams were not parked outside the depots at night.

Also in March 1941 the new General Manager, Mr G.H. Pulfrey, formerly manager at St Helens, started work.

On 7/8 May 1941 an air raid devastated the city centre. No overhead remained in situ within a quarter mile radius of Queen Victoria Square. The Ferensway garage was heavily bombed and 44 buses were destroyed and others damaged. The head office in Baker Street was also destroyed. Staff were transferred to two houses at the entrance to Cottingham Road Depot, only for these to be destroyed almost immediately. Many of the Department's records were destroyed in the attacks.

It appears that the trams were able to operate to as near the city centre as possible, although they were not able to use Waterworks Street for a time. The Hessle Road terminus in Osborne Street was transformed by the destruction of part of the adjoining Willis's department store.

The Department had a surplus of trolleybuses and after failing to arrange an exchange for motorbuses, Mr Pulfrey obtained permission to replace the Anlaby Road trams. Had the war not intervened the sixty-six trolleybuses in stock would have been deemed sufficient to convert this route. Former tramway traction poles which had been used for electric lighting on the Pickering Road (DP) route were re-used, as the reduced amount of illumination permitted the removal of alternate poles. These were used between Walton Street and Wheeler Street to permit span wires to be erected.

A boost to ridership on all "A" area routes came from the decision to introduce on 15 December 1941 a limited stop system on all outward bound peak bus services. The first stop at which passengers were permitted to alight was the first beyond the trolley-bus or tram terminus. This forced short distance riders within the "A" area to use the trams or trolleybuses.

Twelve cars (nos 26/124-33/6) were sold to Leeds Corporation followed by six more in May (nos 115/34/5/53/9).

Erection of trolleybus overhead proceeded slowly, and not until 6 September 1942 did service 69 replace the trams. The route was exactly the same as the trams except that trolleybuses turned at the roundabout at the junction of Anlaby Road and Boothferry Road. Amongst the track that was abandoned was the Midland Street connection.

Fourteen more trams were sold to Leeds (nos 104/9/14/6/38/47/52/4/5/6/8/63/4/74).

As it would be some time before the last route (Dairycoates) could be replaced, the remaining cars were given mechanical and electrical overhauls and received "varnish" treatment to the paintwork.

During the war women were employed as conductresses, this time without any major outcry. Several worked on the trams.

Work started on convert-ing the Hessle Road route in late 1944, and it was envis-aged that the trams would cease in April 1945. Delivery of trolleybuses was delayed and the conversion was post-poned until 1 July 1945.

It was decided to mark the occasion with a decorated and illuminated car (no. 169 complete with a very white bumper). A formal supper was held at the Guildhall starting at 8.15pm on Saturday 30 June 1945.

To mark the passing of the tramways, Brush car no. 169 was suitably decorated and illuminated. It is seen in all its glory at Liverpool Street Depot.

Supper was served at 8.30pm and included toasts to "The King", "The Corporation Transport" and the "The Ministry of War Transport". That latter toast was given by a certain Alderman A. Stark O.B.E who was still a member of the Transport Committee.

At 10.30pm the official party proceeded to Osborne Street where no. 169 awaited them. At 10.45pm (or thereabouts) the tram driven by the Chairman, Alderman J. G. Hewet, JP set off for Liverpool Street.

To the surprise of many, Osborne Street and Hessle Road were lined with thousands of residents wishing to say farewell to the trams. No. 169 entered the central shed and brought 45 years and 10 months of electric tramcar operation along Hessle Road and in the City of Hull to a close.

The remaining cars were sold to Leeds but only nos 105/11/3/7/23/39/40/2/60/73 entered service there.

The final act as no. 169 awaits departure time in Osborne Street at 10 45 pm on Saturday 30 June 1945. Sadly, no. 169 was not preserved and it is rumoured that both decks were sold to a caravan site on the east coast a few miles away. (PM)

Chapter 12

EPITAPH

Thus ended seventy-two years of tramway operation within the city of Kingston upon Hull, years with many highs and lows, managerial upheavals, and uneven management standards.

Hull's horse tramways had little local business and commercial support, and the London based owners seemed to have little interest in developing the service. Its remote management moved painfully slowly at times, and often with such inefficiency that the first lines had to be re-laid within five years. Inconsistent management at local level did not help either. Had Alderman Bannister survived to provide that local focus, things might have improved.

Another hindrance was the 1870 Tramways Act, which provided for the compulsory acquisition of tramways after twenty-one years by the local authority which eventually discouraged investment and improvements. The requirement that tramway companies should maintain the highway between the tramlines and eighteen inches on either side proved a costly burden which competing horse buses and waggonettes did not experience, despite contributing to the wear and tear of the road surfaces.

Yet the company constructed a more than adequate system along the main radial roads (Hedon Road apart – a serious omission) and, in some instances, went beyond the built-up area to cater for anticipated construction.

Its fares and operating costs were amongst the lowest in the United Kingdom. It required fewer horses than most thanks to the level terrain of the town. Yet, almost uniquely, the horse trams succumbed to waggonette competition due mainly to the suicidal fare increases of 1889 which decimated ridership and caused much local ill-feeling.

Labour relations were always poor although it paid very well at first. A fifty-four page rule book gives an indication of the culture of the organisation as did its taking a conductor to court in September 1893 for embezzling one penny! There were bitter labour disputes in 1881 and 1882. As wages fell and labour relations worsened, former employees migrated to the steam trams, horse buses, waggonettes, and even started up their own services. Poor working conditions were the focus of reform campaigns in the local press.

The company suffered from a lack of capital, rendering it almost impossible to maintain and re-lay the tracks, leading to disputes within the Corporation. Complaints about a poor service and the state of the track fuelled pressure for municipal control, and there were few tears when it occurred.

It was with some justification that the Drypool and Marfleet Street Tramways Company Limited was called "a line from nowhere to nowhere". Fatally flawed from the start, having no direct access to the town centre, it effectively conceded the through (and lucrative) traffic to the buses and waggonettes. Although there were several attempts to secure through running, management seemed to lack the will (and possibly the means), to take the final step to achieve it. It seemed doomed to eke out a miserable secondary existence.

It seemed to be better managed than the horse trams, with more continuity than the HST. Its directors were local, and aware of local conditions. Anecdotal evidence from employees and contemporary records indicate much better staff relations, and its drivers were encouraged to develop their skills to ensure that the steam trams were operated correctly and without much in the way of incident.

But it could not continue, even after improvements in the local economy, and the provision of more residential areas and municipal acquisition was inevitable.

Electric tramway operation was, the first decade excepted, a minefield for managers and a battleground for councillors. Even the birth of electrical operations split the town's rulers between direct operation or leasing the tramways to a private company. Visits to other towns and cities (and the poor record of the two city tramways) swung the balance and Alderman Larard who was the principal proponent of leasing bowed to direct operation.

The initial management arrangements were deeply flawed. The division of work and responsibilities had no logical foundation, and divided responsibilities with the workshops was strange, to say the least, and only increased costs. There was no single officer to provide consistency and an overview of the tramways. The three officers did not always agree in Committee especially when considering extensions. Within the Corporation there was no single person whose job was to superintend track matters. It took the motor bus-minded Duncan Morrison to redress this in the early 1930s. To have separated track, electrical and operational functions was bad enough but, when Alderman Larard was forced to give up the chair of the Tramways Committee, no equivalent commanding figure emerged, and not until the early 1920s were all functions merged, at a time when Mr Rayner had other post-war problems to deal with.

It has been argued that because Hull paid lower than average salaries it did not attract the required level of managerial expertise, but perusal of the short lists refutes this. However, it often took the appearance of the chief officials on other undertakings' shortlists to generate pay increases, as happened with McCombe, Rayner, Lawson and Pulfrey. It is possible that attempts to update the equipment of the trams after the First World War failed because of difficulties that might not have been experienced in a unified department.

After the Great War friction, within the Tramways (Transport) Committee and between that Committee and other council members (both personal and political), adversely affected operations and finances. Large sums were abstracted for rate relief, sums that could have been invested on renewals and developments. There were disagreements about fares between Manager and Committee, and between Committee and Council, with the two organisations regularly overturning a Manager's recommendations, often to the detriment of tramway finances. The desire for cheap transport for workers was laudable, but warnings about the effect on finances were ignored. Short riding passengers were often discriminated against in fare proposals.

Officers took to ignoring Committee decisions, never a healthy sign. In the 1920s particularly they had to endure personal and intense attacks (from which Chairmen were not immune), and were given no credit for their professionalism. The wonder is that they stayed so long in Hull. How many organisations would have permitted the public feud between Rayner and Willoughby not only to take place, but to drag on? Not until the mid 1930s did Jack Lawson and Councillor Hurley inject some consistency and harmony into public transport affairs.

The treatment of strikers after the General Strike was unusually harsh and long-lived, and was not replicated elsewhere. Until that date staff relations had been relatively good but it took many years to retrieve the situation. At least four major inquiries were carried out into the operations of various departments during the life of the electrical tramways. These were not necessarily unbiased and independent.

Hindsight tells us that the decision to have a separate generating station was flawed. There was some debate about it before the decision was made (although contemporary opinion seemed to support the decision), but the responsibility for it was a distraction and from about 1910 the main Corporation station was cheaper.

Many cars enjoyed a long life thanks to a combination of rebuilding and re-equipping with second-hand trucks and motors. A possible re-equipment programme in 1918/9 was stillborn. The existence in places of overhead lines that required side running (and these were not as numerous as legend has it), did not permit increased speeds, and the additional weight from rebuilding also militated against higher speeds. A fleet replacement programme was necessary in the 1920s, and might have prolonged the system's life, but whether Hull's divided and unpredictable management would have sanctioned it is another matter. Attempts by Duncan Morrison and Jack Lawson to convert all overhead to centre running were refused.

Hull kept its trams to the long and mainly straight radial roads which permitted the installation of double track throughout (North Bridge and Midland Street excepted), and permitted intense frequencies to be provided. However, there were large areas between the roads which had no facilities (including the Hull and Barnsley Railway's Cannon Street terminus), and where passengers had long walks to reach a tram. The first bus services entered these areas and abstracted traffic from the trams, especially the Newbridge Road service.

Despite the extensions of the late 1920s there appeared to be no strategic vision for the trams (or for the buses). Corporation housing policies which involved the relocation of residents who lived near the city centre to areas at the end of the tracks, or even beyond, had an adverse effect on tram earnings, the unspoken (and understandable) Council wish that such residents should not be penalised in terms of high fares meant that outer sections did not necessarily pay their way. Workmen's fares were very uneconomic, but proved difficult to discard and were still extant when the trams finished.

The final extensions to Pickering Road were not successful and probably not essential. A more lucrative extension might have been along Boothferry Road to serve the Council estate. The Spring Bank West proposals would have been productive, but the Chanterlands Avenue North extension was a disaster (and was built against Rayner's advice). The Beverley Road and Cottingham Road extensions did not penetrate the relevant Council estates. Similarly, a branch off the Holderness Road route along Southcoates Lane to Preston Road would have tapped the large estate that was constructed.

By 1930 the trams were ageing, slow and obsolete. Track renewals were not always to the standard of the original. The city was growing beyond the limits of the trams, and large scale investment was required if they were to continue. It is difficult to see how even a tram-tolerant management could have prevented their demise. Their continued existence would have probably prevented the coordination agreement with East Yorkshire Motor Services being realised, at least in the agreed form.

Often it seems that in spite of its management the tramway system moved large numbers of passengers for work, leisure and shopping at cheap fares and returned for many years handsome profits. Not a bad legacy.

Appendix 1

Rolling Stock including Fleet List and Car Body Details

1. HORSE TRAMS

1.1 Introduction

From September 1878 horse cars were licensed annually in September by Hull's Hackney Coach Sub-Committee. The first licence covered three single-deck cars and twelve double-deck cars. The number of cars in stock as recorded for Board of Trade purposes did not always agree with the number licensed by the Council.

1.2 The Tramcar Fleet

The following list of cars was provided by Richard Buckley. According to Lee one bus was converted into a tram but no further details have been discovered. Double-decked cars were, of course, open top. It is possible that the seating capacity varied from time to time as the Hackney Coach Etc Sub-Committee did vary the maximum on occasions (see below)

New No.	Old No.	Type	Seats	Delivered	Notes
1-2	11-12	Single-deck	16	1875	J
3	13	Single-deck	16	1878	J
4-9	5/6/7/9/10/4	Small Double-deck	16/16	1878	A
10-15	51-56	Large Double-deck	22/22	1875-8	B
16-18		Small Double-deck	16/16	1879	C D
19		Single-deck	16	1879	D E J
20-22		Small Double-deck	16/16	1879	D F
1-3/19		Small Double-deck	16/16	1879/1882	G H
23-25		Small Double-deck	16/16	1882	I
26-31		Double-deck	18/18	1882	

Notes
A. May have been 16/18 seats
B. May have been 24/24 seats
C. May have been 16/18 seats
D. Nos 16-22 may have also had old numbers
E. No. 19 may have been renumbered 24 at one stage
F. May have been 16/18 seats
G. May have been 16/18 seats
H. May have been 16/18 seats
I. May have been 16/18 seats
J. Single-deckers thought to have been withdrawn in 1882

A full fleet list was given to the Hackney Coach Sub-Committee on 15 September 1879. 22 cars were in stock as follows:

No. of Carriage	Number Inside	Number Outside
1, 2, 3, 19	16	0
4 to 9	16	16
10 to 15	22	22
16 to 18	16	16
20 to 22	16	16

All were in sufficiently good condition to be licensed.

At some point the cars may have been provided with additional seating since the full list reported to The Hackney Coach Sub-Committee on September 1880 contained the following information:

No. of Carriage	Number Inside	Number Outside
1, 2, 3, 19	18	0
4 to 9	18	18
10 to 15	24	24
17, 18	18	18
20 to 23	18	18
24	18	0

There is no mention of car no.16 and no car is shown as missing so had this been withdrawn? Were cars 23 and 24 newly delivered somewhat earlier than previously thought? However in September 1882 cars 16 (resurrected?), 19, 20, 22, 24 are shown as 16/16 and 26-29 were 18/18. There is no reference to cars 30/31. Car no 21 was in such a bad state that the Company was told to stop running it at once and both the Company and driver (Thomas Carter) and conductor (Edward A Cook) were prosecuted. Car 24 is a mystery and could not have been a renumbered 19. Was there a mistake in the inspection report?

A further report in November 1882 revealed the existence of cars 30 and 31 and car 21 back in service.

The fleet at 1 November 1882 was probably:

No. of Carriage	Number Inside	Number Outside
1, 2, 3, 19	16	16
4 to 9	16	16
10 to 15	24	24
17, 18	18	18
20 to 25	18	18
26 to 31	18	18

The regular inspections of the cars produced extremes in respect of the condition of each car. In September 1889 no fewer than 17 cars had one defect or another whilst at other times such as August 1887 all but two were reported in fair condition.

A more intriguing report to the Hackney Carriage Committee on 26 August 1891 includes references to cars 32 and 33. No cars are missing from the report so they were not re-numbered cars. The Liquidator, Mr Burkinshaw, in his initial stock survey stated that 33 cars were owned and 33 sets of reins etc. No further information has yet been discovered. However, ensuing reports make no mention of cars 32 and 33 and nor does car 31 feature again.

On 5 October 1892 the Hackney carriage Committee decided that the number of passengers to be carried inside on cars nos 10 to 16 should be reduced from 24 to 22 whilst a month later the numbers permitted outside on cars1 to 9 and 16 to 20/23/4 could be increased by 2.

An article in the *Hull Times* on 10 November 1923 said the original cars seated 22 and were pulled by a single horse. However the reporter, who had assistance from Mr Rayner himself, claimed that these were later converted to double-deck cars seating 44 (the capacity of nos 10-15 (51-56)). At the same time the Old Town route was converted to two-horse operation followed by the remaining routes although some former employees said that the Spring Bank route retained a single horse and the smallest cars to the end.

Single-deck cars and the smaller double-deck cars had six windows at each side whilst the large double-deckers had eight. The double-deck cars had knifeboard seats on the upper deck. The livery was white and dark reddish brown with "HULL STREET TRAMWAYS" on the lower side panels.

Between 1892 and 1896 30 cars were licensed but this fell to 29 in 1897 and to 27 in 1898. The period 1892-4 saw the number of licensed horse tram drivers to be fewer than the number of trailers indicating, perhaps, that not all thirty cars were in service at any one time. After 1895 the number of drivers and conductors exceeded the car numbers. Each car was inspected twice annually at least and the licence issued depending on the condition of the car. Sometimes all passed but at other times several would have licences refused for a while. Drivers and conductors who were the subject of complaints could find themselves before the Committee and be reprimanded or even suspended for a while.

The Company's regulations infer that lower deck passengers were provided with a cushion which is surprising given the expense of cleaning. Standing passengers were not allowed, in theory, and passengers were not permitted to ride on the external roof rail. In practice overcrowding was very prevalent at certain times of the day and despite many prosecutions the practice was not stopped.

Cars carried large white wooden boards at both ends displaying both termini in black capital letters often askew as shown in several photographs. A narrow white rectangular board was fitted above the lower saloon windows which displayed intermediate points along the route. Large advertisements were carried at modesty panel level. Fleet numbers were carried in the middle of the panel under the lower deck windows and at the ends of each car, this in later days being very large. Each tram carried a clock that was synchronised daily with the time shown on the Town Hall clock.

1.3 Horses
Horses were normally changed over at four or four and a half hourly intervals but, as numbers fluctuated, this does not always seem likely. Two were used for each double-decker so that a minimum of four horses per day was required. As a rule the same pair of horses was harnessed to a car together since it was considered that they worked better by being used to each other which made it much easier for the driver. The need for "spares" to cover sickness, accidents and rest days meant at least five horses per tram were required but it varied enormously from nearly seven in 1878 to 3.49 in 1885 although it reached 4.25 in 1888. This is much less than in other undertakings but probably reflected the flatness of the Hull terrain.

In 1878 there were 93 horses for 15 cars. Between 1883 and 1889 the 31 cars were worked by a minimum of 136 (1886) and a maximum of 166 (1890) horses. Between 1885 and 1889 the number of replacement horses was just over twenty-five but only three were replaced in 1890. Replacement costs peaked in 1885 at £1,002 for 33 horses and fell to £81 in 1890. From 1885 to 1889 the average working life of a horse varied from 6.48 years to 4.58 years.

2. THE STEAM TRAMWAYS

2.1 Steam Engines
The Drypool and Marfleet Steam Tramways Company possessed seven steam engines numbered 1-7. They were four-coupled compound steam locomotives built by Thomas Green and Sons of Leeds and London (works nos 128/9/30/1/7/48/9) whose steam trams enjoyed a popular reputation especially in the North. The use of compound locomotives on steam tramways was fairly rare. All seven were delivered in 1889, four in time for the opening, the remainder by the end of the year. They cost between £500 and £600 each.

On compounds the steam passed through two high pressure cylinders (9in. diameter) being exhausted to two low pressure cylinders (14in.) in order to obtain a more expansive and effective use of steam than was achieved in simple operation, the outcome being a saving on fuel. As exhaust steam was emitted at a lower pressure condensation was made easier. The fuel saving was critical for steam operation because Board of Trade regulations prohibiting the issue of smoke resulted in the use of expensive but good quality gas coke. It is debatable whether that economy was achieved in practice on the DMST.

The engines' four-coupled wheels were of 2ft 6in. diameter with 5ft between axle centres, with an 11ft 6in. long and 6ft wide body. Height from rail to the roof was 9ft and to the roof of the condenser 10ft 4in. The condenser fitted by Greens came from the Falcon (now Brush) works. This comprised several hundred copper tubes which were arched over the roof and connected on each side, the air passing over these tubes causing the condensation.

Locomotives had to be driven from either end so all controls were duplicated in order to comply with BOT regulations that ensured drivers had a clear view of the road ahead. All moving parts had to be enclosed from 4in. above rail level achieved by fitting a cab designed, it is claimed, to resemble a horse car. A bonus from the design was that moving parts were protected from dirt and dust, an important consideration given the road conditions of the day. Of course some of the bodywork had to be hinged for access for repairs and maintenance.

The company appeared to maintain its engines in good condition. However, a Board of Trade inspection in 1896 found that none of the engines had speed governors or indicators in working order. The steam brakes on the engines were not connected to the cars.

Twelve drivers were licensed between 1892 and 1894 but this fell to eight in the following two years rising to ten in 1897 before dropping to nine in 1898. Conductor numbers showed a similar trend.

2.2 Trailer Cars
The company purchased eight double-deck trailers (called "carriages") from Messrs G.F. Milnes of Birkenhead at a cost of £240 each. They had rolled steel channel underframes and plate frame bogies. All were fully enclosed apart from platforms and stairs and had a seating capacity of 74. The *Hull News* said that there were longitudinal seats for 32 downstairs and comfortable transverse seats for 42 on the upper deck which were reversible. Hinged doors opened outwards (a not very safe practice given the small space) at either end of the upper deck whilst a lamp in the middle of the bulkhead gave illumination inside and outside the car. Some of the upper deck windows were sliding ones so that they could be opened on hot days to let air in. Eight trailers were licensed from 1892 to 1896 but only seven thereafter.

Route boards were carried above the lower saloon windows. One set states "Alexandra Dock-Hedon Road-North Bridge" and it is thought that another set was used for Clarence Street workings. Later in an attempt to tempt passengers away from the waggonnettes and on to a combination of steam and horse trams another board substituted "Witham for Savile Street" for North Bridge. Originally, some cars carried a "via" board beneath the main board with the legend "Alexandra Dock Entrance"

Like their horse-drawn brethren these trailers were subject to regular inspection and they were consistently rated as in good order.

3. ELECTRIC TRAMCARS

3.1 Introduction
This section owes much to work carried out for members of the Leeds Transport Historical Society and Mr Noel Proudlock who has diligently checked the fleet details and attempted to reconcile inconsistencies. Much material came from the late Geoff O'Connell, Traffic Officer at Hull Corporation Transport whose father was an inspector who had commenced work with the steam tramways company. His researches were incomplete and some of his notes have apparent contradictions and gaps probably because so much rebuilding and modernisation was carried out on the tramcars and possibly because Liverpool Street staff did not always record what they did. Little official information is available, owing to the destruction of the head offices in Baker Street in May 1941 and the temporary head office adjoining Cottingham Road depot shortly afterwards. Without Geoff's efforts we would have only minimum information available so we are very indebted to him. However, the final responsibility is mine.

Another source is a note book of Mr Albert Turner, Rolling Stock Engineer. Mr Turner had been appointed Assistant Omnibus Maintenance Engineer in April 1936, later becoming Chief Engineering Assistant. Some of his notes appear to be at odds with published information and it is possible but not certain that his are the more accurate. I have included his descriptive names for each class.

Some information is gained from photographs and even this depends to a degree on the date in question. There are uncertainties regarding trucks fitted, seating capacity, types of seating and even the origin of certain trams.

All upper decks rebuilt or built in Hull had opening saloon windows mounted in wooden frames. Two exceptions were nos 101 (of 1923) and 113 (of 1925) which possessed top light ventilators. Brush top covers had glass opening windows which were retained in the cases where Hull standard end parts were used to enclose the balconies. As part of the 1933 equipment improvements, lifeguard side gates were fitted to all the re-equipped cars and a number of unrebuilt cars too.

On 24 June 1924 the Tramways Committee agreed that the four corner windows in the top saloon and front and back windows on the top of the vestibuled cars should be altered so that they could be opened.

Were cars 26 and 113 new or substantially rebuilt cars? The Tramways Committee minutes after 1923 (no. 101) contain no approvals for new cars or permission to rebuild any cars in a significant way. Nor does a withdrawal date for either car feature in Geoff O'Connell's fleet lists. Such rebuildings were likely to be costly and it is hard to think that no one knew about them since councillors made regular inspections of the depots and workshops. Is it possible that Mr Rayner was experimenting before considering the purchase of new cars? He did inform the January 1927 Tramways Committee meeting that new cars would be needed in the near future but events overtook him and the trams. Geoff O'Connell speculated that no.26 in the 1930s was not the same as the original as there were fundamental differences in construction. He considered that a new body had been built for

no.26 that was generally similar to Hull built cars 123-136. Official references in the minutes sometimes refer to two new cars since 1920 (but there were "three" - nos 26/101/113).

Neither 101 nor 113 were particularly handsome cars although they do seem imposing but some of the rebuilt cars looked better. The photograph of no.144 in Liverpool Street fresh from rebuilding and with the upper deck from a withdrawn car (either no.66 or no.4) in February 1935 shows a more handsome car with clean lines.

In June 1932 H.W. Ashby from Sheffield Corporation was appointed Tramway Maintenance Engineer. Shortly after his arrival he wrote to his previous manager, A.R. Fearnley, stating that the Hull fleet was outdated technically and possessed slow service speeds. He expressed surprise that the newest cars still retained open balconies and that the oldest cars had the newest enclosed upper decks.

He was constrained by a previous decision to reduce spending on trams to an absolute minimum but he managed to institute a modernisation programme involving the purchase of second hand but more modern equipment and transferring of upper decks from older trams to newer ones although the newest cars were the last to be dealt with. Mr Ashby followed Mr Morrison to Bournemouth in the Spring of 1941.

3.2 Electrical Equipment for the First Cars

3.2.1
The electrical equipment on these cars was by Siemens. The motors were enclosed with the armatures having toothed cores and being wound with "formed" coils. Each field had four poles each having an interchangeable wound coil. The magnet case was in two halves, hinged together, and being easy to open and inspect. It was claimed that when all doors were closed the installation was "practically" watertight!

The whole case was suspended at two bearings from the car axle at one end and at the other end by a "nose" supported through springs from the bogie framing in the usual manner. These motors were rated at 1100 lb pull at eight miles an hour without any excessive heating. Gearing (ratio 4.74 to 1) was of the single reduction spur type and was enclosed in an oil-tight casing.

The Siemens controllers regulated a car's speed by cutting out the starting resistances and grouping the motors in either series or parallel which enabled the motors also to be used as generators to act as a brake. There were four steps with the motor in series, three in parallel and four brake steps. With the controller handle on the latter the motors acted as generators in parallel with each other through a part of the starting resistance. The various circuits were made or opened by carbon tipped switches by a series of cams threaded on the main spindle and activated as the spindle rotated. This was described as "novel" in contemporary accounts.

Efforts had been made to make each position of the controller sensitive to the motorman's touch and the main and reversing spindles were geared together so that both operated simultaneously in going on to the brake positions, whilst the reversing barrel was immoveable except when the main handle was in the "off" position. Each controller weighed about 2½cwt.

Each complete resistance comprised three steps with two steps in one frame and one step in another. The resistances were built up of narrow iron spirals or German silver strip, turns being insulated by thin asbestos strip. Spirals were mounted on a hollow mandril, insulated by porcelain bushes and tightened by nuts on the mandril. The latter was secured at either end in cast iron discs which were bolted to the car body. Terminals were carried on a strip between the discs and were easily accessible for inspection via a hinged cover.

The *Railway World* considered that the Siemens trolley standard, as supplied, was used for the first time on any tram system. It was made of wrought iron and was compact if heavy in appearance. The tension spring was fitted inside the tube and this reduced the likelihood of any injury to passengers. In addition the trolley pole was of the finest taper steel tube and pivoted to enable it to be easily removed. The head of the standard to which the pole was attached rotated on ball bearings to allow lateral movement of the pole within a radius of 8 feet from the standard which itself was fixed 2ft 8in. from the car's centreline. Trolleyheads were of the swivelling kind and were attached in such a way that it would slip off should it be caught in the overhead line in order to avoid damage to the overhead or the car.

Each motor car had two lighting circuits of six 16 candle power lamps in series but only five of these lamps were in use at any one time, the two lights in the canopy headlight at the rear end of the car being short circuited by a special plug switch.

The lamps on vertical standards attached to the roof with half opal globes were a special feature of the cars. The remaining lamps were used for interior lighting and as signal lights with coloured glasses to indicate the route of the car (which did not last long, route boards being introduced at an early date). One Siemens cut-out (which could be used as a switch) and one main switch were located below the driver's canopy, a lightning arrester and a slate panel with the necessary switches and fuses for the lighting circuits were also provided.

3.2.2 Trailer Cars nos 101-105
Each trailer possessed an electric lighting circuit comprising eight 16 candle-power 60 volts lamps in series current being fed through a flexible connection with a motor car.

3.2.3 Motor Cars 16-60
The second contract for cars was awarded to the Westinghouse Electrical Company in September 1898 and comprised forty-five motor cars, fifteen trail cars and two sprinkler cars. Much of the work was sub-contracted the bodies being supplied by Brush (nos 31-60), G.F. Milnes (nos 16-25) and J.G. Brill (nos 26-30). Milnes also constructed the bodies for the trail cars (nos 106-120) whilst Brill built the bodywork of the sprinkler cars.

The motor cars were broadly similar to nos 1-15 but the Brill cars were provided with twin sliding doors which opened simultaneously whilst their interior was described as "particularly attractive" and they appeared to be more spacious than the other cars although the dimensions were not much greater.

Each motor car possessed two no.46 single reduction Westinghouse motors and two series parallel controllers. The motors including field coils, armature, commutator and brushes were totally enclosed by the upper and lower field castings which in turn formed the frame. A large opening covered with a spring lid was provided in the upper casting directly over the commutator and brushes and another opening for hands was placed under the commutator in the lower casting. This had a watertight covering.

The field consisted of four poles projecting radially inwards from the cast steel frame which was split in a horizontal plane through the armature shaft. Pole pieces were a mixture of thin soft steel plates firmly secured. This construction ensured a powerful magnet field and eliminated losses from eddy currents. Field coils were wound on moulds in a winding lathe which were thoroughly insulated. When completed one coil is slipped on each pole and held in place with a cast brass plate bolted to the yoke. The ends of each of the windings of the two coils in the upper half of the field were soldered directly to long insulated conductors which were connected to the car wiring. The lower fields had metallic terminals.

A drum type armature had a laminated core and contained three air passages parallel to the shaft to permit rapid radiation of any heat generated. Air spaces were provided to provide sufficient ventilation. Wires of each coil were insulated separately and the two coils were wound together and enclosed in a protective insulated cell. By treating the coils in this way it was hoped to reduce maintenance and repair time to a minimum. The commutator was composed of hard-drawn segments each being insulated by mica sheets partly to reduce or eliminate the possibility of short circuits. Standard carbon brushes were used.

The gears and pinions were of ample strength to meet the severe demands made by operations. The gear casing was securely fastened to the motor. Gear and pinions were totally enclosed to protect them from any damage. Blackwell trolley standards were fitted.

Westinghouse also provided their motors for the two sprinkling cars which weighed approximately ten tons. Powerful jets were installed which could direct small jets directly into the rail grooves but could also be amended to sprinkle the pavement.

3.3 Trucks and Motors
All the cars (apart from the two motor cars numbered 101) were mounted on four-wheel trucks with a wheel base of 6' and of Brill 21 E pattern. The first deviation from this was the purchase of a 7' 6" wheel base pendulum truck in 1927 as an experiment pending the possible acquisition of new cars. There is speculation that it was meant for the "new" no.26 but it appears to have gone to no.109. It would seem to have been disposed of by 1935.

Much criticism has been levelled at the obsolescence of the equipment fitted to the Hull tramcars but attempts were made to commence a programme of replacement motors at least. On 27 March 1918 the Tramways Electrical Engineer reported that the motors in cars 1-15 were now obsolete and it was necessary to purchase 30 new ones. Approval was given but in November he reported that because of wartime restrictions it had not been possible to proceed but that he now wished to try once more to obtain the motors. In May 1919 he further reported that some more delays had been encountered in obtaining further prices.

He had found that the motors that were being offered to the Corporation were the now standard type manufactured by the companies concerned and that these were a departure from Hull's present standards (meaning better). With a view of future standardisation of motors and renewable parts he was in negotiation with several suppliers to obtain prices and he asked for the matter to be delegated to the Chairman of the Stores, Depots and Workshops Sub-Committee, the Chairman and Deputy Chairman of the Tramways Committee and himself. This was agreed but the trail goes cold perhaps, as related in chapter 7, because the Tramway Electrical Engineer retired under a cloud in July 1919. At the same time the Tramway Manager also left and it seems possible that the matter was dropped. Mr Rayner had his own thoughts about tramway design.

However, four GE 52 motors were purchased from Sheffield Corporation for £220 in September 1920 with a hint that more had been bought previously.

Between October 1932 and May 1934 a great deal of second-hand equipment was bought to modernise cars as follows:

Brill 21E 7' 6" wheelbase, magnetic track brakes, Dick Kerr 40 hp motors from Rochdale CT distributed to cars nos 104/5/6/7/11/2/3/4/5/6/8/20/2/47/52/55/56.
Brill 21E 7' 6" wheelbase to car no. 63 (ex Rochdale).
Magnetic track brakes, Dick Kerr 40 hp motors from Rochdale to car No. 103

Brill 7' 6" truck, magnetic track brakes, BTH 40hp motors ex Sheffield CT to car nos 137/40/3/4/5/6/9/51/4/60 (but photographs of nos 140/3/4 show different trucks fitted).

Peckham P22 7' 3" wheel base, magnetic track brakes, Dick Kerr 40hp motors from Dearne District Tramways to cars nos 26/119/21/3/4/5/6/7/8/9/30/1/2/3/4/5/6/41/8/50/3.

As the previous configuration but source unknown – cars nos 138/9/42/58/9/61/2/5/8/78.

Peckham P22 7' 3" wheel base trucks – source unknown to cars nos 100/67/73/4/9/80.

Peckham P22 7' 6" wheel base trucks – source unknown to cars nos 163/4.

Cravens 7' 0" wheelbase trucks , magnetic track brakes, Dick Kerr 40 hp motors from Sheffield CT to nos 94 and 157(later154).

Original trucks fitted with Dick Kerr 40 hp motors – nos 20/58/166/9/70/1/2/5/6/7.

Subsequent changes included nos 81/140/60 which received Peckham P22 7' 3" wheel base trucks; nos 146/8/51 reverted to 6' wheelbase trucks and Dick Kerr 40hp motors.

A total of eighty trucks were acquired but not all seemed to have been reported to the appropriate Committee although they would have been mentioned in the monthly requisition book report. According to a report by Mr Lawson in October 1935 some 65 cars had been modernised from a stock of 115. He also said that all the 115 cars had received reconditioned second hand motors. In addition he stated that the overhead was not up to increased speeds.

The official list of acquisitions is:

November 1933 – 21 trucks complete with traction equipment from A. Devey of Birmingham at £70 each, possibly P22 trucks originally of Dearne District Tramways with DK30B motors, split frame type.

November 1932 – 15 sets of Brill 21E trucks from Rochdale Corporation when its tramway system closed all with DK30B motors, box frame type.

May 1934 50 controllers, from Rochdale Corporation and Dearne District (the majority).

Date unknown – possible acquisition of trucks from Doncaster Corporation and 3 or 4 sets of BTH RGE 20 motors (40hp) from Sheffield, one of which is still fitted to no.96).

Most sources state that all the cars had 32" diameter wheels but a table in Mr Turner's notebook suggests otherwise. This table also gives the height of the motor and gear case from the rail and the horse power of the motors:

Type	**Wheel Diameter (All in inches)**	**Motor**	**Gear Case**	**Horse Power**
Westinghouse	32	$3\frac{1}{8}$	$3\frac{1}{4}$	25
Westinghouse	28	$1\frac{1}{8}$	$1\frac{1}{4}$	25
B T H	32	$5\frac{1}{2}$	$3\frac{1}{2}$	25
B T H	28	$3\frac{1}{2}$	$1\frac{1}{2}$	
Siemens 250 C.T.	32	$3\frac{3}{16}$	$3\frac{7}{8}$	33
250 C.T.	28	$11\frac{3}{16}$	$1\frac{7}{8}$	33
250 19.C.T.	32	$3\frac{3}{16}$	$3\frac{9}{16}$	33
250 19.C.T.	28	$1\frac{3}{16}$	$1\frac{9}{16}$	33
Dick Kerr	32	4	$3\frac{3}{18}$	40
Dick Kerr	28	2	$1\frac{3}{18}$	
Dick Kerr (car no. 101)			38	
Siemens D53			33	
Siemens D55WG			35	
B T H (Sheffield)			30	

The existence of 28" wheels is interesting since this size of wheel is generally associated with smaller higher speed motors introduced in the mid 1920s after which large wheels were unusual for new designs. Rayner's car had 28" from new according to a drawing in *The Tramway and Railway World.* From photographs and from inferences in Mr Turner's list it seems that the Brill cars might have been fitted with the smaller wheels from new, an unusual state of affairs. In later days they possessed a "block" above the fender which may have been fitted to prevent another car with a higher profile "overriding". But there were only five American cars which would not account for the number of motor types that he listed. Therefore were other cars fitted with smaller wheels or were they subsequently re-wheeled in the modernisation programme of the early thirties? We may never know. No cars with smaller wheels went to Leeds.

An article in *The Railway World* in August 1899 stated that the first sixty cars and twenty trailers had wheels of 30" diameter! Even primary and contemporary sources cannot agree on wheel size!

Mr Turner also listed the types of gears and pinions in use:

Siemens Old Type	G90	P19
Westinghouse	G68	P14
B.T.H.	G67	P14
Siemens D53W	G97	P19
Dick Kerr	G64	P19
Siemens 250 CT	G100	P16
Rayworth	G69	P16
Standardised	G68	P14
Siemens 250.19. C.T	G68	P14

In Leeds all Hull cars were 66.18 except 147 which was 70.14.

There is some uncertainty regarding the re-equipment years when several second hand trucks were purchased. Seven types were bought from Dearne District Tramways, Rochdale Corporation and Sheffield Corporation. The Dearne ones at least are thought to have been obtained through a second hand dealer, A. Devey of Birmingham who in November 1933 supplied 21 trucks each with four magnetic shoes and traction equipment at a cost of £70 each. One source states that fifty-four sets of magnetic brakes were purchased in total. Forty-two cars were re-equipped with the Dearne Valley magnetic shoes, easily identified by the shape of the clamp on the truck frame but it does appear that sixty-two cars were so treated, all having two centrally located magnetic shoes. Not all 42 cars in Leeds possessed magnetic shoes from the Dearne Valley.

Mr Turner records the arrival of second hand trucks from Sheffield (purchase price £25 each) at Liverpool Street Works from 29 May to 2 June 1933 but does not give any further details. It is possible that they were Brill trucks with large axle boxes and BTH motors. A photograph of no. 160 at Holderness Road Depot would seem to confirm thus. He also states that the weight of a truck with Westinghouse motors (minus the brake gear and life guards) was 3 tons 14cwt and 2qrs.

According to research carried out by Mr A.K. Terry the 42 cars which went to Leeds were mounted on the following trucks:

Brill 21E of 7' 6" wheelbase (15)
104/5/9/11/3/4/5/6/7/42/7/52/5/6/8

Peckham P.22 of 7' 6" wheel base (2)
163/4

Peckham P.22 of 7' 3" wheelbase (24)
26/123-136/8/9/40/50/3/5/60/73/4

Cravens of 7' 0" wheelbase (1)
154 (ex 94)

It is thought that nos 102 to 180 were given 40hp motors, mainly DK30B1, but ten sets of BTH motors and DB1K3 controllers were also purchased. Eight of the Brush cars had their higher powered motors fitted in Brill 6' wheelbase trucks. According to Geoff O'Connell the cars in stock in 1945 that were not taken by Leeds (nos 103/46/8/51/69/70/5/6) had short 6' wheel base trucks by Brill. The exception was no.119.

Geoff O'Connell also stated that his photographic collection revealed that a certain amount of truck exchanges took place. Nos 81/96/100/19/20/42/3/4/5/8/58/80 are shown with P22 trucks whilst nos 106/7/18/22 have Brill 21E 7' 6" trucks. Cars 142/58 were mounted on three separate trucks during their career, Brill 6' 6", Peckham P22 and Brill 7' 6"!

The remaining 1903 Milnes cars (103 excepted) were given Brill 7' 6" trucks, some with magnetic brakes. Consistency in approach was not always evident, probably a result of the financial and political restraints on the tramways. Nos 20/58/63/94/100 received "new" electrical equipment, nos 68/81/92 received the same but also received P22 trucks from cars withdrawn in 1938.

No evidence has been found to support the claim that some trucks that were replaced by these acquisitions were sold to operators in Recife in Brazil. Some of the trucks of cars sold to Leeds were, in turn, sold to Calcutta (cars 451/2/63/9/75/7 former Hull cars 126/29/53/52/64/04).

In his efforts to modernise the equipment Mr Ashby visited Sheffield and Barnsley on 9 November 1933, Middlesbrough and Darlington on 27/28 April 1934 and Nottingham on 6/7 September 1934. Invoices laid before the City Council on the following dates show the following purchases:

1 February 1934	£59 0s 0d
Sheffield Corporation	Tramcar trucks
11 October 1934	£30 0s 0d
Sheffield Corporation	Truck side frames
7 March 1935	£29 7s 0d
Sheffield Corporation	Tramway materials
4 April 1935	£52 10s 0d
Sheffield Corporation	Tramway materials
	£24 6s 10d
Steel Nut & Hampton	Tramway materials

3.4 Bodywork

The dates used are based on the research by Mr Proudlock and Mr O'Connell. There remain inconsistencies and uncertainties which will probably never be solved at this late stage. On some cars only parts of the transferred upper decks were used, usually the balcony sections.

By 1928 all cars except nos 26-30/123-136 had received vestibules on the lower deck.

The upper decks on the Brush cars were extended by using recovered upper deck vestibules and roof sections whilst retaining the original pillars and all-glass windows. In 1934/5 twenty cars were rebuilt but retained their unframed windows (nos 138-40/2/4-7/9/51/4/64/9/70/5/6). A good example of this is the February 1935 photograph of no. 144 (new in 1912) fresh from works (see page 163). Mr Turner described this as a "new type" tramcar and it doesn't look like a twenty-three year old car.

No.163 received a balcony vestibule that was fitted under its original roof which gave it a different roof profile at the front. An unusual feature of Hull's cars was the use of matchwood platform dashes which also featured on the upper deck of Rayner's no 101. The upper deck seats in Hull cars were not fixed to the upper deck sides and, as all the cars, as canopied, enjoyed the same length between bulkheads and over canopies it was not difficult to fix upper decks from withdrawn cars to the UEC and Brush cars

without disturbing the seats on both donor and recipient cars.

Cars 91/6/8/102/8/10 possessed an internal layout similar to no. 101 but Geoff O'Connell considered the loading arrangements to be unsatisfactory, a factor which accounted for their early withdrawal.

3.5 Seating Capacity

Sources and records differ (widely in some cases) regarding capacity both before and after rebuilding or the fitting of covered tops. The capacity quoted for cars when new is believed to be as close as can be determined at such a long distance from their operation.

As upper decks were switched about all the cars, in theory, should have had the same body length and, therefore, with longitudinal seating, should have had the same lower deck capacity of 22 for a 16 foot body. With transverse 2+1 seating in the lower saloon (nos 26/124-33/6) it became 20.

Mr Turner compiled the following schedule in his notebook which seems to date from around 1926. It reads as follows:

Cars	Vestibule Type		Semi Vestibule Type		Open	
	Inside	Outside	Inside	Outside	Inside	Outside
1 - 25	22	42				
26 - 30					22	34
31 - 59	22	42				
61 - 65			22	40		
66 - 90	22	42				
91 - 100	22	42	22	40 (no. 94)		
101	24	42				
102 - 116	22	42				
117 - 122	22	42				
123 - 136					22	36
137 - 160			22	40		
161 - 180			22	40		

Mr Turner notes that nos 91/3/5/6/7/8/9/102/8/10/13 had a 101 type body although it is unclear what he actually means by this since nos 101 and 113 differed in several respects from the others, externally at least. He may have been referring to the internal layout and wide doorways. Nos 91/6/8/102/8/10 were "Mangles" which were withdrawn earlier than the others.

The late Donald Wilson made several sketches of the Hull car interiors when in Leeds. He recorded five upper deck layouts, two with half turn stairs (180 degrees) and two with quarter turn stairs (90 degrees). The accompanying drawings show the various upper deck layouts. No car sold to Leeds seems to have had an upper deck of 44 seats. The 1909 cars had quarter turn stairs and their upper decks had six rows of transverse seats, five seat benches outside the balconies and a single seat backing the stairs giving a total of 36. The other cars did not appear to have standard seating layouts on the balconies. Those with 180 degree stairs (Leeds 485/79/61/9/3/6/5/2/86/7, Hull nos 117/40/50/2/3/5/6/9/60/78) had seven pairs of seats, capacity 28, in total in the centre and those with 90 degree stairs had six pairs, 24 in all. These had two benches for up to four passengers on each balcony giving a total of 40 seats. Some of those cars with 180 degree stairs had a bench backing the stairs whilst some did not giving variations in seating up to a maximum of 40. The official upper deck capacity in Leeds for some cars was:

32 seats car no. 164
35 seats car no. 159
36 seats car nos 153/60
38 seats car nos 138/52/4/8/63

Geoff O'Connell considered that stair types may have also

been altered during various stages of rebuilding but had not been recorded which could explain the diverse nature of the arrangements.

Contradicting all these is a report by Mr Rayner to the Stores, Depots and Workshops Sub-Committee on 21 April 1920 stating that he was to cover the seating accommodation outside the saloons of cars at both ends and increase seating capacity on the upper deck from 38 to 44! Perhaps experience showed that this was too many and the number was reduced.

No. 113 was shown in Leeds as having 40 seats on the upper deck whereas some published lists show 44. Car no.101 is shown in some lists as 42 upper and 24 lower but an article in *The Tramway and Railway World* in July 1923 quoted an overall seating capacity of sixty.

According to Mr Turner the first upholstered cars (nos 26-30 excepted) went into service on 20 March 1930. They were sample cars fitted with Longford seats and the inside seating capacity was reduced to 20. Ten cars were subsequently equipped especially for the BC route. The twelve cars were nos 26/124-33/6. However, according to a short history produced by KHCT in 1984 twenty cars were fitted with upholstered seating, a move which reduced the capacity from 62 to 56 but Mr Turner shows the cars to be 58 seaters! However, cars nos 147/155 (Leeds 464/6) were recorded as having longitudinal upholstered seats whilst Geoff O'Connell shows cars 155 and 169 also as having upholstered seating.

G.A. Lee states that because tram wheelbases were only 6ft the length of Hull cars was restricted to 28ft with a saloon length of 16ft. This was not so since nos 161 to 180 were 29 feet in length and no. 101 was 29' 8", but with a 7' wheelbase). He also states that that the first cars had two long benches down the sides in the lower saloon and two long benches back to back on the upper, open deck but were converted to transverse seats on the upper deck in 1903. However, photographs of the cars on the opening day and other contemporary official photographs do not support this at least for the Brill cars and the first Milnes cars but as not all the first cars are portrayed we do not know if this is so.

3.6 Destination Indicators, Boxes and Blinds

When the electric system opened in 1899 all cars carried route boards along each side of the car between the lower saloon windows and the upper deck. Some carried black letters on a white background but others had white lettering on black with no apparent consistency of approach. The following combinations appear on photographs but it is possible that there were others:

Route Details	Colour of lettering
ANLABY ROAD	black on white
ANLABY ROAD	white on black
ANLABY ROAD & ST JOHN STREET	white on black
BEVERLEY ROAD	white on black
BEVERLEY ROAD	black on white
HEDON ROAD	black on white
HESSLE ROAD	white on black
HESSLE ROAD	black on white
HOLDERNESS ROAD AND	
SAVILE STREET	white on black
PIER & WHITEFRIARGATE BRIDGE	black on white
SPRING BANK	black on white
SPRING BANK	white on black
SPRING BANK & SAVILE STREET	white on black
VICTORIA SQUARE & PIER	black on white

It had been accepted that route letters at the ends of cars were introduced in 1902 but in July 1899 the City Engineer was authorised to purchase more route letter boards similar to some already in service. Letters were received from local companies including a horse-drawn rully operator in 1901 asking that all cars be fitted with the route boards at each end as had already occurred with some cars so that other road users could discern which route a car would take at a junction. The boards carried white letters on a black background although there are one or two instances (in photographs) of black on white. Some boards also had "ROUTE" above the letter.

When cars began to be fully enclosed the route letters were hung inside the end upper window which remained glazed and capable of keeping the upper saloon fairly light although some cars possessed horizontal slots into which letters could be placed. Open balcony cars had vertical external slots placed above the headlight. Others appeared to have provision for a full board. It was not uncommon for cars not to display a board.

It is not known when destinations were first displayed at the ends of the cars. These do not appear to have been provided before 1914 if photographs are to be believed. Starting in the 1920s some enclosed cars appear to have had a horizontal metal destination plate in a slot above the motorman's window that was lit by an external light, (see photographs of nos 20 and 119).

Roller destination blinds were not introduced until 1923 when car no. 101 appeared. This carried them in the upper front deck panelling immediately beneath the windows. No.113 had its destination blinds immediately above the motorman's window.

Cars rebuilt to the Rayner "style" received blinds similar to no.101. Some of the 123-136 batch (nos 123/4/31 excepted) and the "new" no. 26 also received the high position. In Leeds nos 26/126/7/30/3/6 still had the high position blinds. When the seven Rayner cars were withdrawn their top decks were used to fully enclose some of the remaining open balcony cars but the high position indicators were not retained in every case. The three Kennington covers from nos 91/6/8 all retained theirs and nos 152/6 retained them whilst in Leeds.

Of the three Magrini covers from nos 102/8/10, those on no.118 retained the high position; nos 150/73 in Leeds had blinds above the motorman's window, as did the top deck from no. 101 which had been fitted to no.174. It would appear that all cars numbered above 101 in service after 1934 had blinds positioned above the motorman's front window. Older car no. 100 had both route and destination blinds, but nos 20 and 81 did not have roller blinds.

Roller blinds for route letters first appeared on car no.122 which was fully enclosed using a Kennington four-window top deck. They were positioned in the upper saloon front window which reduced the forward view of passengers and the amount of light in the car. There seemed to be no systematic provision. Of the cars sold to Leeds it would appear that cars 26/109/11/3/4/5/26/7/8/9/32/4/5/6/8/9/40/2/7/50/4/5/60/3/4/73/4 had them as did nos 100/6/20/1/2/44/5/6/8/69/70/5/6. No.122's blind had black lettering on a white background but many subsequent fittings had white lettering on a black background. A definitive list of which car had what configuration is impossible.

Roller blind side destination indicators were introduced initially for cars on the Spring Bank and Beverley Road routes during 1922 and were extended to many other cars but authority to equip the whole fleet was not forthcoming. A total of eighty was approved but it is not certain that all were fitted. The blinds (and boxes) were of three sizes. No.105 in February 1935 possessed a small version in place of one of the opening windows along the side of the lower deck whilst no.144 in the same month (ex works) had a longer version in place of two of the small opening windows. No.116 which possessed just three side windows had the longer version which occupied about three-quarters of the window's length. Photographic evidence shows the longer version (four windows) fitted to nos 2/122/23/38/40/2/4/8/52/60/70 and the short version fitted to car nos 100/5. No. 113 also had the long version in one of its three windows but this was positioned centrally unlike no.116. It appears that cars 109/20 also received side blinds as did most of the enclosed Brush cars (nos 150/3/9 excepted). The difference may result from the fact that the three window Milnes cars were not alike, some having two opening windows above each main window whilst others had three.

Some cars (at least nos 4/41/84/130) possessed boards in a side window on each side which hung from brackets above the window. These carried the destination but their use like that of the side blinds was not necessarily synchronised with the destination blind at the end of the car. A 1938 photograph of car no 122 at Newland Avenue shows "SPRING BANK" in the front box but "NEWLAND AVENUE" in the side box.

Similarly, the use of destination blinds was anything but consistent. Photographs show three different destinations for the "BC" route: "COTTINGHAM ROAD", "COTTINGHAM ROAD VIA BEVERLEY ROAD" and "NEWLAND PARK". There were complaints at Committee meetings about the wrong destination being shown but to no avail it would seem. There was a committee instruction to use only one letter for each route with the destination box to show the ultimate destination but this appears to have been ignored. Given that not all short workings had a letter anyway there was a great inconsistency in the Department's approach (as was the case in many things!). When the bus routes received numbers starting with no.1 in the west and finishing with no 49 in the east in 1931 the tram route letter system was unchanged. As far as is known short workings to Durham Street (Holderness Road), West Dock Avenue (Hessle Road) and Boulevard (Anlaby Road) for example, do not appear to been allocated separate letters.

It has not proved possible to discover a Hull blind to show what destinations were shown. In the 1920s it was agreed that cars for football and rugby matches should display "FOOT-BALL CAR" to separate ordinary travellers from supporters but we don't know if they ever did.

Photographic evidence shows that nos 103/9/13/5/6/24/6/43/78 had black destination blinds with white lettering whilst nos 100/5/6/14/6/7/23/8/32/4/5/8/40/2/4/5/8/52/8/60/3/4/70/4 had white blinds with black lettering. At some point no. 103 also had a white blind.

To add to this is the existence of photographs showing some cars including no. 88, with a board in the lower dash of the lower deck windows displaying "TO AND FROM MARFLEET AVENUE". It is possible that these were used when the Hedon road route was extended to Marfleet Avenue but this can not be confirmed.

3.7 Tramcar Suppliers

Unusually, early tram orders were placed with equipment suppliers rather than body makers due in part to the adoption by the City Engineer of an all-embracing single contract of which the cars were just one part. In many cases the manufacturers supplied the bodies, trucks and motors but the cars were assembled at Hull. It was always thought that this was done at Liverpool Street Works but some assembly was undertaken at Wheeler Street Depot. Similarly, it was assumed that Hull built cars were built by Tramways Department staff but they were actually built (or assembled) by the City Engineer's staff with assistance from the Tramway Electrical Engineer's staff, not necessarily within a tramway depot or works confines.

3.8 Miscellaneous

Mr Turner's notebook shows the average weight of upholstered cars to be 10 tons 6cwt 5qrs 7¾ lb and the average weight of vestibule cars to be:

	Tons	Cwt	Qtrs	lb
Average Car				
Truck	4	6	2	18
Lower deck	4	10	1	18 ¾
Upper deck	1	17	2	27
Total	10	14	3	7 ¾
Individual Cars				
Car no. 104	10	13	1	0 (14 January 1910)
Car no. 122	10	5	2	0 (14 January 1910)
Car no. 160	9	19	1	0 (May 1914)

4. THE ELECTRIC TRAM CAR CLASSES

4.1 Motor Cars

1-15
Builders: Milnes. Motors: Siemens 4D15/8
Seating (as built): 29/22. Trucks: Brill 21E
In Service: 1898
Notes:
1. The original specification for motors was 4D15/12 but these were changed before delivery at the suggestion of Siemens to 4D15/8
2. Open top uncanopied cars from new, the lower decks having four Tudor arched windows.
3. Fitted with Hull built top covers with four fixed windows between November 1905 and December 1906, seating becoming 30/22.
4. Eight cars fitted with British Thomson-Houston controllers in 1906.
5. Fully enclosed between August 1923 and January 1927 and reseated to 40/22.
6. Withdrawn April 1933 to April 1938.
7. "Milnes".
8. Overall length 27' 6" – body 15' 4" – width over side pillars 6' 6", inside height 6' 6", wheelbase 6'.

16-25
Builders: Milnes. Motors: Westinghouse 25hp
Seating (as built): 29/22. Trucks: Brill 21E
In Service: 1899
Notes:
1. Open top uncanopied cars from new with four Tudor arched windows each side on lower deck and Westinghouse 90 controllers.
2. Fitted with Hull built four fixed window top covers from November 1905 to January 1907, seating becoming 30/22.
3. Rebuilt with canopies, vestibuled platforms and full length enclosed top covers from January 1921 to October 1926 being re-seated to 40/22.
4. No. 20 received more modern Brill 6' 0" wheelbase truck 1933 – 1935, Dick Kerr DK30B1 motors and DBIK3 controllers.
5. Withdrawn November 1933 to April 1938 (except no. 20 withdrawn in March 1940).
6. "Milnes".
7. Overall length 27' 6" – body 15' 4" – width over side pillars 6' 6", inside height 6' 6", wheelbase 6'.

26-30
Builders: Brill. (Pittsburgh USA). Motors: Westinghouse 25hp
Seating (as built): 29/22. Trucks: Brill 21E
In Service: 1899

Notes:

1. Open top cars with four round arched windows on lower deck, uncanopied with Westinghouse controllers
2. Equipped with upholstered seats (later removed) and linen window blinds from new in lower saloon– seats replaced in 1914 with wooden seats and original seats sold to a local firm, Edward Dawson.
3. Fitted with Hull built fixed four window top covers July 1906 to September 1906, becoming 30/22.
4. Withdrawn in 1927 (no. 26?), 1931 (nos 27/8/9) and April 1933 (no.30).
5. None received canopied vestibules or roofed balconies.
6. "Americans".
7. All possessed a much wider saloon doorway with two doors, one opening to the left and the other to the right.
8. May have been fitted with 28" wheels giving a much lower profile than the rest of the fleet – see photograph of no.28 at the Pier which has a block presumably to prevent other higher cars overriding.
9. The Westinghouse Electric Company Ltd was the principal contractor but the complete cars were built in Pittsburgh and delivered to Hull via sea.
10. The Railway World in August 1899 stated that the Brill cars were designed to carry 52 passengers whilst Mr Turner quotes 34/22 in his notebook.
11. Overall length 27' 6" – body 15' 4" – width over side pillars 6' 6", inside height 6' 6".

31-60
Builders: Brush. Motors: Westinghouse 25hp
Seating (as built): 29/22. Trucks: Brill 21E
In Service: 1900
Notes:

1. Open top uncanopied from new, four window round arched lower deck design – Westinghouse controllers.
2. August 1905 no.48 fitted with prototype Hull designed fixed four window top cover – provided a halfway point between the Kennington and Magrini types in depth – adopted as standard domed roof and fitted to the rest of the fleet.
3. Rest of class fitted with this design November 1905 to December 1906.
4. June 1919 – No.35 rebuilt with platform canopies, vestibuled platforms and full length roofed top cover but retaining open balconies – seating capacity 40/22.
5. June 1920 – No.36 first car to be rebuilt as fully enclosed to same design as no. 35 but fully enclosed apparently as 40/22 but the approved design was to have had 44 seats in the upper saloon.
6. Nos 31/2/3/4/7-59 fully enclosed March 1921 to July 1924 becoming 40/22.
7. No. 58 received more modern trucks, Dick Kerr DK30B1 40 hp motors and DB1 K3 controllers 1933-1935.
8. No.60 withdrawn circa 1919 (accident), remainder April 1933 to April 1938 except no.58 (March 1940).
9. "Loughboroughs".
10. Overall length 27' 6" – body 15' 4" – width over side pillars 6' 6", inside height 6' 6".

61-65
Builders: E.R & T.C.W (Preston). Motors: Westinghouse 25 hp
Seating (as built): 31/22. Trucks: Brill 21E
In Service: 1900
Notes:

1. Six-window lower deck with opening top lights above, open top canopied (first cars with canopies) unvestibuled cars with reversed stairs – Westinghouse controllers.
2. September 1903 No.61 fitted with the prototype Kennington four bay adjustable top cover with a deep roof curvature with open balconies.
3. September 1903 No.64 fitted with the prototype Magrini four bay adjustable top cover with a flatter roof profile than the Kennington version. Retained open balconies.
4. Nos 62/3/5 fitted with Kennington type top covers May 1904.
5. All except no. 61 which retained the Magrini profile, altered to fixed top covers with deep roof profile 1907-1909.
6. Full length roof fitted June 1915 to June 1916 with enclosed vestibules but retaining open balconies becoming 40/223.
7. No.63 fully enclosed with top cover (Kennington three-window top deck from a withdrawn former trailer car) in 1934 – later fitted with DK30B1 motors and DB1K3 controllers and a 7' 6" Brill 21E truck.
8. Nos 61/2/4/5 withdrawn July 1937, no. 63 (March 1940).
9. "Old Prestons".

66-85
Builders: Milnes. Motors: British Thompson Houston GE52-6T 25hp
Seating (as built): 29/22. Trucks: Brill 21E
In Service: 1900/1
Notes:

1. Originally trailer cars (nos 106-125) new in 1899 - cars not renumbered in same order.
2. Open top uncanopied four window Tudor arched lower deck design.
3. Bodies mounted on trucks in 1900/1 by Hull City Engineer's Department staff.
4. October 1904 – February 1905 all except nos 66/73/81/2 fitted with Kennington three bay adjustable top covers seating capacity becoming 30/22
5. June 1906 – 1909 All fitted with fixed top covers retaining the Kennington roof profile – nos 66/73//81/2 (see above) which had remained as open toppers received Hull standard 4 window top covers.
6. December 1916 – December 1919 nos 66/70/6/82 reconstructed with canopies, platform vestibules and full length open balcony top covers which retained their former roof profiles – seating became 40/22.
7. November 1921 to September 1923 reconstructed with canopies, vestibules and full length fully enclosed upper decks (nos 76/82 excepted).
8. In 1938 No.81 received a new Peckham truck (P22A) with magnetic track brakes, DK30B1 motors and DB1K3 controllers and no. 68 received DK30B1 motors and DB1K3 controllers the equipment coming from newer cars withdrawn.
9. Withdrawals – All except nos 68 and 81 (March 1940) withdrawn April 1933 to April 1938.
10. "Trailers"

86-90
Builders: Milnes. Motors: British Thompson Houston GE52-6T 25hp
Seating (as built): 29/22. Trucks: Brill 21E
In Service: 1900-1
Notes:

1. Originally trailer cars (nos 101-105) and converted to motor cars by the City Engineer's Department 1900/1 – cars not renumbered in numerical order.
2. Open top four window Tudor arched uncanopied cars.
3. February 1905 – April 1905 all fitted with Kennington 3 bay adjustable top covers, seating becoming 30/22.

4. 1908-1909 Top covers rebuilt in fixed form retaining Kennington roof profile and three windows.
5. November 1921 – July 1924 reconstructed with canopies, vestibuled platforms and full length enclosed top covers, seating capacity being increased to 40/22.
6. All withdrawn July 1937 to April 1938 without any further alteration or upper deck transfers.
7. "Trailers".

91-100
Builders: Hurst Nelson. Motors: British Thompson Houston GE52-6T 25 hp
Seating (as built): 31/22. Trucks: Brill 21E
In Service: 1901
Notes:
1. Three window Tudor arched with opening top lights above, open topped canopied vestibuled cars with reversed stairs and BTH controllers.
2. June 1904 to August 1904 fitted with Kennington four bay adjustable top covers with open balconies.
3. All modified to fixed top cover, retaining Kennington roof profile and unroofed balconies 1908-1909.
4. No.94 (January 1920) and no. 100 (December 1918) fitted with balcony roofs and vestibuled platforms.
5. Remainder fitted with full length top covers and enclosed balconies retaining the Kennington roof profile – platforms also vestibuled (except nos 91/6/8 stairs altered to normal) August 1925 to December 1926.
6. Date unknown but probably at the same time, nos 91/6/8 were converted to the "Rayner" internal standard involving widened entrance to lower saloon to provide a folding door arrangement to close off the front platform from the lower saloon and the reversed stairs. This reduced the space for the motorman and left no room for the traditional hand brake which was replaced by a vertical wheel – received the nickname "Mangle"! These were the first to be withdrawn.
7. 1933 Nos 94 and 100 fitted with fully enclosed three window Kennington top covers from withdrawn former trailer cars – also given DK30B1 motors, DB1K3 controllers, no. 94 given a 7' Cravens truck with magnetic track brakes and no. 100 given a Peckham P22 truck without magnetic track brakes.
8. No. 92 fitted with three window fully enclosed Kennington upper deck from no. 72 in 1934.
9. No.96 was withdrawn from passenger service in 1933, the upper deck removed for re-use and converted into a single-deck service car.
10. No.96 finally withdrawn in Hull in April 1942 and sold to Leeds CT but did not reach there until 1945. Now preserved in Manchester for use on the Heaton Park Tramways.
11. Withdrawal dates – Nos 91/6/8 April 1933, Nos 93/5/7/9 July 1935, nos 92/4/100 (March 1940).
12. "Motherwells".

101
Builders: Milnes. Motors: Westinghouse
Seating (as built): 39/30. Trucks: Brill 22E bogie
In Service: 1900
Notes:
1. Tudor arched six window uncanopied car, Westinghouse controllers.
2. Received a Hull profile six window fixed short top cover in January 1907, becoming 40/30.
3. Received new DK9A 40 hp motors in 1909.
4. Sold to Erith Urban District Council 1916 (no. 19).
5. Overall length 33' 6", wheelbase 14' 0", body 22' 0", plat-

forms 5' 3", ends 6".
6. Height 16' 2" to trolley base.
7. Wheels 39" diameter.
8. Width, upper deck 7' 0", lower saloon 6' 7", platform 6' 1".

102 -116
Builders: Milnes. Motors: Westinghouse 25 hp
Seating (as built): 36/22   Trucks: Brill 21E
In Service: 1903/4
Notes:
1. Delivered as open top cars with three windows and top light ventilators above on lower deck, canopied, unvestibuled and reversed stairs but fitted with Magrini adjustable four bay top covers before entering service from December 1903 to May 1904.
2. All converted to fixed top covers in 1907.
3. April 1921 – No. 114 given Hull standard top deck from car no. 60 (withdrawn after an accident) and reconstructed with full length roof and enclosed balconies, vestibuled platforms and stairs converted to normal – seating capacity became 40/22.
4. All except nos 113 and 114 fitted with enclosed balconies and vestibuled platforms, standard stairs (not nos 102/8/10) retaining flat roof profile with eaves – seating capacity 40/22.
5. Nos 102/8/10 modified to the Rayner type (see nos 91/6/8) seating capacity 40/22 with vertical handbrakes ("Mangles").
6. Nos 103/4/5/6/7/9/11/2/4/5/6 re-equipped with DK30B1 motors, DB1K3 controllers and, except for no. 103, 7' 6" Brill 21E trucks with magnetic track brakes. No. 103 probably received a fresh Brill 6' 0" wide wing truck with magnetic track brakes.
7. Withdrawal dates:
   1925: 113
   April 1933: 102/8/10
   September 1938: 112
   March 1940: 106/7
   May 1942: 115 (Leeds CT no. 459)
   October 1942: 104/9/14/6 (Leeds CT nos 477/67/71/0)
   June 1945: 103
   July 1945: 105/11 (Leeds CT nos 480/4)
8. No. 104 never repainted in revised livery and retained high level headlamp – probably not in service for several years before withdrawal and transfer to Leeds.
9. "New Milnes".
10. Magrini upper decks from no 102/8/10 fitted to nos 173/118/150
11. No. 113 reappeared in 1925 rebuilt externally to match Rayner's car no.101 – some doubt about whether it was a "rebuild" or a new car.
12. When cars rebuilt in 1925-7 the reversed stairs replaced with 90 degree stairs.

117-122
Builders: U. E. C (Preston). Motors: Dick Kerr DK9A 40 hp (except no. 119 – Siemens)
Seating (as built): 36/22. Trucks: Mountain and Gibson 21 EM
In Service: 1909
Notes:
1. Four window with top light ventilators above canopied but unvestibuled cars with Hull style covered top decks but with unroofed balconies, 180 degree direct staircases and BTH B18 controllers.
2. Fitted with roofed balconies and vestibuled platforms in June to August 1917, but roof and panelling did not match the

extent of the lower deck canopy – these and 1912 cars altered similarly were known as "uglies"

3. Reconstructed in 1933-35 to fully enclosed using upper decks from withdrawn cars; 118 from 108, 119 from 55, 121 from 45 and 122 from 96. It has not been possible to identify the donor car for 120.

4. More modern trucks fitted in 1933-1935, nos 117/8/22 being Brill 21E 7' 6" trucks, nos119/20/1 being Peckham P22A 7' 3", all with magnetic track brakes, DKB 30B1 40hp motors and DB1K3 controllers.

5. Withdrawal dates:
   March 1940: 118/20/1/2
   July 1945: 117 (to Leeds as no.485) and 119

6. "New Prestons".

7. No. 122 reportedly the first car to be fitted with a roller blind route letter box in the upper deck window at either end – featured black letters on a white background.

123-136
Builders: Hull Corporation. Motors: Siemens 38hp
Seating (as built): 36/22. Trucks: Mountain and Gibson 21 EM
In Service: 1909-1910
Notes:

1. Four window lower deck with top light ventilator above canopied but unvestibuled cars with Hull standard covered upper decks but unroofed balconies, Siemens Type S controllers

2. Fully enclosed and fitted with vestibuled platforms March 1928 to December 1931 – similar in appearance to the "new" no.26.

3. All except nos 123/35/6 fitted with upholstered transverse 2 + 1 seats in the lower saloon becoming 36/20 (nos 123/35/6 being 36/22 as delivered).

4. All received more modern Peckham P22 trucks ex Dearne District with magnetic track brakes 1933-1935, DK30B1 40hp motors and DB1 K3 controllers.

5. Withdrawal dates
   April 1942: 124-133/6 (all to Leeds C T nos 53/6/51/47/54/2/48/57/46/55/50)
   May 1942: 134/5 (to Leeds C T nos 460/58)
   July 1945: 123 (to Leeds C T no 482)

6. "Hull Corps" – built by City Engineer's staff in CE workshops and completed at Liverpool Street Workshops

7. None appear to have received upper decks from other cars.

8. Six more cars were to have been constructed but the cost of construction forced a decision to revert to purchasing cars outright (which became nos 117-122 (above).

137-160
Builders: Brush. Motors: Siemens 33hp
Seating (as built): 34/22. Trucks: Mountain and Gibson 21 EM?
In Service: 1912
Notes:

1. Four side window in lower deck with top light ventilators above cars, canopied unvestibuled with four window upper deck having unroofed balconies – built to Hull "standard" according to a letter from the City Engineer to the Board of Trade in July 1911.

2. The upper deck windows that were not fixed and could be lowered were of all glass rather than being set in wooden frames.

3. August 1915 to January 1919 platforms vestibuled and top deck roof extended over the balconies with roof and panelling not matching the extent of the lower deck canopy

– more "uglies". According to Mr Turner the seating was 36/22 in the mid 1920s.

4. Nos 138-40/2/4-52/4/5/6/8/60 fitted with fully enclosed top covers from withdrawn cars 1933-1935, becoming 40/22 – nos 137/41/3/57 withdrawn with open balconies (see section 4.4 for details).

5. Ten cars received DK30B1 motors and all received DB1K3B (or K4) controllers and also replacement trucks during 1933-1935:
   Nos 137/40/3-6/9/51/4/60 – Brill 21E 7' 0" with magnetic track brakes and BTH 40hp motors
   Nos 138/9/41/2/8/50/3/8/9 – Peckham P22 7' 3" with magnetic track brakes
   Nos 147/52/5/6 - Brill 21E 7' 6" with magnetic track brakes
   No.157 – Cravens 7' 0" with magnetic track brakes

6. Subsequent changes:
   Nos 140/160 received Peckham P22 7' 3" trucks with magnetic track brakes and DK30B1 motors
   Nos 146/8/51 reverted to Brill 21E 6' 0" trucks, wide wing with DK 30 B1 motors from withdrawn cars nos 166/71/5 in September 1938 (part of policy to eliminate all motors other than DK 30 B1 after March 1940).
   No. 154 received Cravens truck from no. 157.
   Nos 142/158 later had Brill 21E trucks with magnetic track brakes.

6. Withdrawal dates:
   September 1938: Balcony cars 137/41/3
   March 1940: Balcony car 157 and 144/5/9
   May 1942: 150/3/9 to Leeds C T (461/3/2)
   October 1942: 138/47/52/4/5/6/8 to Leeds CT (472/64/9/73/66/5/76)
   July 1945: 139/140/2/60 to Leeds CT (481/79/78/86) and146/8/51

7. "New Loughboroughs".

8. Mr Turner, Engineer, described the rebuilt no.144 as a new "Rayner" car in March 1935 (see page 164). This photograph taken when ex works shows no.144 looking every inch like a new car.

9. Cars were reconstructed in reverse order but were not identical as the approach was not consistent.

10. Some cars had 180 degree staircases replaced with quarter turn stairs.

11. Non Hull upper deck covers were used only from the first batch of withdrawals in April 1933. Complete Hull style top covers were used for the next cars and their own centre sections with Hull's "standard" parts for the last ones except as individually noted.

12. Cars still carried Brush transfers inside when sold to Leeds.

13. Overall length 28' 0" (body 16', platforms 5' 6", ends 6", height 16', width 6' 9" (6' 7" over pillars), height 16' 0" to top of roof.

161-180
Builders: Brush. Motors: Siemens 35hp
Seating (as built): 40/22. Trucks: Brill 21E
In Service: 1915
Notes:

1. Four window lower deck with top light ventilators above, canopied platform, vestibuled cars with four window upper saloon fully roofed but with open balconies – top deck roof and panelling matched the length of the canopies – top deck windows (full drop) were all glass type, Siemens type S controller, direct staircases when built but some were given quarter turn stairs, possibly in the mid 1930s

2. Seven cars (nos 163/4/9/74/4/5/6) altered to fully enclosed.

3. All received DK30B1 40 h.p. motors and DB1 K3B

controllers 1933-1935.
4. Some received new trucks as follows:
Nos 161/2/5/8/78 Peckham P22 7' 3" with magnetic track brakes
Nos 163/4 Peckham P22 7' 6" trucks no magnetic track brakes
Nos 167/73/4/9/80 Peckham P22 7' 3" no magnetic track brakes
Nos 166/9/70/1/2/5/6/7 Brill "wide wing" 6' 0" 21E without magnetic track brakes
5. Withdrawal dates:
September 1938: Balcony cars 162/5-8/71/7/8/80
March 1940 : Balcony cars 161/72/9
October 1942 : 163/4/74 (to Leeds C T (474/5/68) (note that by this time nos 163/4 had received magnetic track brakes)
July 1945 : 169/170/3/5/6, 173 to Leeds C T (487)
6. "New Loughboroughs".
7. Overall length 29' 0" (body 16' 0", platforms 6' 0", ends 6"), height 16', width 6' 9" (6' 7"over pillars) wheelbase 6', height 16' 0" to top of roof.

101
Builders: E.E.C. Motors: Dick Kerr DK85A 42hp
Seating (as built): 40/20. Trucks: E.E.C. /E.S. Rayner
In Service: 1923
Notes:
1. Built to design of the Tramways Manager Mr E.S. Rayner – "Rayner's Car"
2. Fully enclosed with three window upper and lower decks both with top light ventilation – no truck as such but powered by 42hp trolleybus motor driving through cardan shafts with universal joints to differentials on split axles – DK DB1 K3B controllers and Vertical Handbrake.
3. Withdrawn in April 1933 and top deck fitted to car no.174.
4. Full description appeared in *The Tramway and Railway World* on 19 July 1923.
5. Seating described as 60, 64 and 66 by different authors.
6. 28" wheels fitted – length 29' 8", body 16' 8", vestibules 6' each, ends 6" each, width of upper saloon 6' 10½" – dimensions provided in articles but how did the upper deck from no.101 fit on the 16' 0" body of no. 174?
7. Several features ahead of their time – many later became standard such as platform doors, high speed motors, separate driver's cab with seats, internal staircases and level floors throughout the saloon and platforms
8. Mr Rayner used some of the principles from the design of no.101 such as reversed stairs closed off with folding (pivoting) doors on the platforms and wider doors to the lower deck saloon – also used a vertical handbrake wheel which sired the nickname "Mangle" being similar to the wheels used to turn rollers on mangles used for squeezing water from clothes that had just been washed before airing or ironing, see page 136.
9. Six cars converted in this way probably when they were fully enclosed (nos 91/6/8/102/8/110).

26
Builders: Hull Corporation. Motors: not known
Seating (as built): 36/22. Trucks: not known
In Service: 1927 or 1928(?)
Notes:
1. Some doubt about origins of this tramcar – rebuilt or new?
2. Four window lower deck with ventilating top lights above and standard Hull upper deck with typical wooden-framed drop windows. Fitted with enclosed balconies and vestibuled platforms – cars nos 123 – 136 were rebuilt in almost identi-

cal fashion – later had 2+1 upholstered transverse seating.
3. Received Peckham P22 truck with magnetic track brakes, DK30B1 40 h.p. motors 1933-1935 and DK DB1 K3 controllers.
4. Withdrawn February 1942 and sold to Leeds C.T. (449)

113
Builders: Hull Corporation. Motors: Westinghouse
Seating (as built): 44/22. Trucks: Brill 21 E
In Service: 1925
Notes:
1. Rayner car similar externally to no. 101 but with traditional internal layout and equipment – some doubt as to whether it was a new car or a substantially rebuilt no. 113
2. Re-equipped with DK30B1 motors and DK DB1 K3 controllers and Brill 21E 7' 6" truck with magnetic track brakes 1933 -35
3. Withdrawn July 1945 and sold to Leeds C T (483)

4.2 Trailers
101-105
Builders: Milnes
Seating: 22/29
In Service: 1899
Notes:
1. Open top completed in 1898 but not in service until system opened in July 1899.
2. Converted to electric operation in 1900/1 as nos. 86-90 but not in matching numerical order.

106-125
Builders: Milnes
Seating: 22/29
In Service: 1899
Notes:
1. Open top
2. Converted to electric operation in 1900/1 as nos 66-85 but not in matching numerical order.

5. LIVERIES

5.1 The Horse Trams
Cars were painted a dark reddish brown broken by white around the windows and a white rocker panel bearing the legend "HULL STREET TRAMWAYS". The ends of the cars were also painted white and bore the car number in large numerals.

Some cars, at least, had what appears to be white lining out in squares that were aligned with the window lines at the side and at each end.

Advertisements were carried in profusion along the side of the upper deck and on the curved staircase.

5.2 The Steam Engines and Cars
A single livery for both engines and cars was adopted comprising deep crimson and white with the addition that the engines possessed a black skirting. The white area on the engines was mainly around the windows whilst the area of white on the cars was around the lower deck windows at the side and immediately above the frame of the cars. Unlike electric days advertisements were carried in profusion on both engines and cars. They were positioned on the side panels and end panels below the engine windows and above the windows on all four sides. The cars carried them along the white painted panels and between the lower and upper deck windows and at both ends. One unforeseen result was that the route boards above the lower deck windows were almost invisible.

5.3 The Electric Cars

The initial livery was as follows:

Main colours: crimson lake, panels edged black, lined gold with elaborate corner decorations. Window pillars, rails and canopy were broken white, lined in crimson lake. An elaborate coat of arms was carried centred on the side panel, a less elaborate version being used from an unknown date. Trucks were black, roof matt crimson. Until 1919 the rocker panels carried the legend "CITY OF HULL TRAMWAYS" in gold shaded black to right and below.

When top covers were first fitted the area around the windows at both ends was painted white on some cars but not on others.

From 1933 most of the enclosed cars that were not to suffer early withdrawal received a modified livery comprising two horizontal bands of broken white around the upper saloon panels (at first and on a few cars the bands were pale lilac) together with a white roof whilst the trucks were painted bauxite red. Panels were edged in umber with black completely deleted from the livery. Where possible the coat of arms also appeared on the ends of the upper saloon. However, the old livery remained in service until the last open balcony cars were withdrawn in March 1940 (nos 161/72/9) but also on enclosed cars. As late as 1938 car no.130 retained the old style livery whilst no.20 carried it in 1937. No.104 which was sold to Leeds in 1925 still carried the old livery but it is thought to have been stored for many years.

During the Second World War the bumpers were painted white to enable them to be seen in the blackout conditions although photographs show them to be grey and not very clear. It is possible that the white was not varnished and deteriorated in wartime conditions. Roofs were painted grey to prevent them from being seen from the air at night.

6. CAR BODY TYPES

6.1 Introduction

Such was the diversity of alterations to Hull's car profiles that there were at least eighteen different kinds of configuration! Anyone, therefore, who wishes to produce a completely accurate list of the permutations, has problems due to the lack of official records. This is especially difficult with the reconstruction programme of 1933 to 1935. What follows is the detailed history of conversions to the various profiles and the transfer between cars. Several cars will feature more than once. It is as accurate as possible and photographs do not always confirm the content of the lists. This section should be read in conjunction with the fleet list.

Given that one of Mr Morrison's first recommendations in 1931 was that expenditure on tramcars should be kept to an absolute minimum it is perhaps surprising that so much time and money was expended in later years on the re-equipment, reconstruction and upper deck transfers. However, some of the work was undoubtedly value for money.

6.2 The Changes

There were six main phases and these are covered below. The classification was not used by the Tramways Department but is used here for ease of referral. These can be classed as follows:

1 Open Top
1 Open top without canopy
The original trams nos 1 to 60 and the bogie car (no.101) were delivered without canopies as were trailers nos 101 to 125. These were later converted to full electric operation as nos 66 to 90 still without canopies.

1C Open top with canopy
Cars nos 61 to 65 and 91 to 100 and 102 to 116 were delivered with canopies. Nos 102 to 116 received canopies before entering service

2 Moveable Top Cover
The Corporation soon recognised that upper deck passengers needed some form of protection against the elements and Hull was an early convert to providing this although it required some experimentation before deciding upon a standard approach.
The first conversions involved the fitting of moveable top covers which came in three types:

2H Moveable short top cover/high profile without canopy
These were Kennington roll-top covers fitted by A. Leckonby of Hull
October 1905 to April 1906 67 to 72 plus 74 to 80 and 83, 84 to 90

2HC Moveable short top cover/high profile with canopy
These were Kennington roll-top covers fitted by A Leckonby of Hull

September 1903	61
May 1904	62, 63 & 65
June 1904 to August 1904	91 to 100

2L Moveable short top cover/low profile with canopy
These comprised Magrini canvas top cover made by Milnes Voss

September 1903	64
December 1903	109, 112
January 1904	107, 108, 110, 113, 115
February 1904	102, 103, 105, 106, 111, 114, 116
May 1904	104

3 Fixed Top Cover
There were five types of profiles for cars which received fixed top covers. The 3H, 3HC and 3LC conversions used the pillars and roof sticks provided in the type 2 conversions

3H High profile without canopy

During 1907	71, 75
During 1908	67, 69, 70, 72, 77, 78, 79, 80, 83, 84, 86, 87, 88, 90
During 1909	68, 74, 76, 78, 79

3HC High profile with canopy

During 1908	61, 62, 65, 91, 92, 93, 94, 95, 96, 97, 100
During 1909	63, 98, 99

3M Mid profile without canopy

August 1905	48
November 1905	8, 18, 20, 40, 59
December 1905	3, 12, 25, 35
January 1906	7, 21, 31, 56
February 1906	2, 14, 23, 46
March 1906	17, 24, 36, 53, 54
April 1906	1, 10, 34, 45
May 1906	4, 6, 19, 51
June 1906	9, 37, 42, 81
July 1906	5, 26, 28, 49
August 1906	13, 22, 38, 73
September 1906	27, 29, 30, 47
October 1906	11, 41, 44, 58, 66
November 1906	32, 52, 55
December 1906	15, 39, 50, 60
January 1907	16, 33, 43, 57, 82, 101

3MC   Mid profile with canopy
3LC   Low profile with canopy

During 1907	64, 102 to 116

4 Open balcony/vestibuled
Once more there were a few versions as can be seen here

4H Extended top cover (high)/open balcony/vestibuled

June 1915	61
July 1915	63, 65
June 1916	62
December 1918	100
January 1920	84

4M Extended top cover (mid)/open balcony/vestibuled

August 1915	141
September 1915	158, 160
October 1915 to March 1916	159, 157, 156, 155, 154, 153, 152, 151, 150, 149, 148, 147, 146, 145, 144, 143, 142, 141, 140, 139, 138, 137 (in that order)
June 1917	117, 118
July 1917	119, 120
August 1917	121
June 1918	66
July 1918	122
June 1919	35, 36
December 1919	82

4L Extended top cover (low)/open balcony/vestibuled

June 1916	64

5 Fully Enclosed Upper Deck

There were five permutations but it is difficult to state with certainty that cars within each category possessed exactly the same features.

5H High profile roof

January 1920	92
November 1921	67, 87
January 1922	74
June 1922	69
July 1922	90
September 1922	72, 85
October 1922	78, 89
December 1922	71
January 1923	77
March 1923	79, 80
April 1923	75
August 1923	68
September 1923	84
December 1923	88
July 1924	86
February 1925	83
March 1925	93
August 1925	91
January 1926	95
June 1926	96
July 1926	97
August 1926	98
December 1926	99
August 1929	70

5M Mid profile roof

June 1920	36
February 1921	22
April 1921	114
May 1921	48
June 1921	40
July 1921	34
August 1921	47
September 1921	49
October 1921	31, 56
February 1922	45, 50
March 1922	37, 53
April 1922	43, 57
May 1922	42
June 1922	38, 58

July 1922	46
August 1922	32
October 1922	73
November 1922	18, 23
February 1923	39, 52
March 1923	59
May 1923	51, 81
June 1923	44
July 1923	55
August 1923	7, 33
September 1923	17
October 1923	19
November 1923	4, 12
December 1923	3, 9
January 1924	1
February 1924	54
March 1924	6, 10
April 1924	8
May 1924	2
June 1924	5
July 1924	41
September 1924	14
October 1924	15
April 1925	16, 21
May 1925	25
July 1926	11
September 1926	20
October 1924	24
January 1927	13
October 1928	123
August 1931	134
December 1931	135

5MU Mid profile roof with upholstered seats

March 1928	124
April 1928	131
November 1928	26(?)
January 1929	125
May 1929	126
September 1929	127
November 1929	128
January 1930	129
March 1930	130
September 1930	133, 136
July 1931	132

5L Low profile roof

December 1924	116
January 1925	108
November 1925	102
January 1926	110
January 1927	104
April 1927	115
May 1927	106
August 1927	105, 111
October 1927	112
December 1927	103
January 1928	107
May 1928	109

5S Domed roof with quarter lights

November 1925	113(?)

6.3 Reconstructed Cars 1933-1935

After the reconstruction of the Hull built cars no.123 to 136 (see above) a new programme commenced in 1933. The previous programme had included wooden dashes as standard but had not included route indicators.

Between April 1933 and July 1935 the upper decks from over

thirty withdrawn tramcars were transferred to other cars some of which remained in service in Hull until June 1945 and in Leeds until October 1951. The exact number is unclear since official records are unavailable and what information we do have comes from Geoff O'Connell.

This is where the real difficulty begins. There are two lists provided by him which do not agree. Some detective work which compares withdrawal dates of suitable "donor cars" with conversion dates and numbers has not entirely resolved the situation.

The upper saloon shells were only secured by bolts, there being no continuous vertical pillars and the seats were bolted to the floors rather than the sides. Therefore it was a relatively straightforward task to transfer the upper "decks" from one car to another.

The following list covers the cars which were reconstructed in some form. However, the lists in this section and section 7 need to be treated with caution!

	5H	5M	5MU	5L	5S
During 1933	156	158		150	174
		117		118	
		159		173	
		153			
During 1934					
	152	145	155		
	122	148	169		
	160	176			
	63	140			
	94	121			
		164			
		170			
		175			
		163			
During 1935					
	120	154	144		
	100	146	147		
		151			
		142			
		119			
		138			
		139			
		149			

Subsequent alterations made to cars after type 5 conversions during 1933-1935 (no. 103 in 1932):

114 e	124 g	103 k	113 e k
123 g	131 g	109 e k	174 e
134 g		116 k	150 e
135 g			173 e

Notes
e Roller blind letter indicator fitted
g Headlamp transferred to dash
k Stairway trap replaced with vestibule and door

In addition nos 125/8/32/4/5 had their high level destination repositioned above the motorman's window.

These alterations did not alter the shape of the car roof.

6.4 Car Body Transfers

Noel Proudlock and I have revisited the dates shown in Geoff O'Connell's papers and compared these with known withdrawal dates of the "donor" cars.

The following list represents which upper deck transfers are thought to have occurred:

Recons-tructed Car	Date	Upper Deck	Upper Deck Type
63	1934	from 69, 71, 74, 77, 85	Kennington 3
92	1934	72	Kennington 3
94	1934	from 69, 71, 74, 77, 85	Kennington 3
100	1934	from 69, 71, 74, 77, 85	Kennington 3
117(485)	1933	12, 19, 23	
118	1933	108	Magrini
119	1935	55	
120	1934	from 69, 71, 74, 77, 85	Kennington 3
121	1935	45	
122	1934	96	Kennington 4
138(472)	1935	15	
139(481)	1935	17	
140(479)	1934	59	
142(478)	1934	48	
144		4	
145	1934	not known	
146		31	
147(464)	1935	51	
148	1934	from 12, 19, 23	
149	1935	22	
150(461)	1933	110	Magrini
151		33	
152(469)	1934	from 91, 96, 98	Kennington 4 (probably no.98)
153(463)	1933	from 1 or 38	
154(473)	1934	7	
155(466)	1934	from 12, 19, 23	
156(465)	1933	from 91, 96, 98	Kennington 4 (probably no.91)
158(476)	1933	from 1 or 38	
159(462)	1933	from 12, 19, 23	
160(486)	1934	from 69, 71, 74, 77, 85	Kennington 3
164(475)	1934	50	
169	1934	37	
170	1934	52	
173(487)	1933	from 102, 108, 110	Magrini (probably no.102)
174(468)	1933	101	
175	1934	42	
176	1934	32	

6.5. Notes on the variations

There were many subsequent variations to car profiles and equipment whilst some cars retained existing equipment when other members of the same batch were altered. This list is intended to describe these changes and is based on information gathered from observation (when in Leeds), notes from Geoff O'Connell and Mr Turner and photographs which result in cars being on this list and not in theirs. It may not be complete. Several cars appear in more than one list but it is not assumed that any changes were implemented at the same time. I have not attempted to date such changes.

A summary of the various configurations is:

1. Roller blind destination boxes fitted below the upper deck windows at both ends of the car.
26, 70, 91, 93, 95, 96, 97, 98, 99, 102, 108, 110, 118, 122, 123, 124, 125, 126, 127, 128, 129, 130, 132, 133, 134, 135, 136, 152, 156

2. Roller blind destination boxes fitted above the cab

windows at both ends of the car.

63. 94, 100, 103, 104, 105, 106, 107, 109, 111, 112, 113, 114, 115, 116, 117, 119, 120, 121, 131, 138, 139, 140, 142, 144, 145, 146, 147, 148, 149, 150, 151, 153, 154, 155, 158, 160, 163, 164, 169, 170, 173, 175, 174, 176

3. Roller Blind Route letter boxes fitted at upper deck window at both ends of the car

26, 63, 94, 100, 106, 109, 111, 113, 114, 115, 119, 120, 121, 122, 124, 126, 127, 128, 129, 132, 134, 135, 136, 138, 139, 140, 142, 144, 145, 146, 147, 148, 150, 151, 154, 155, 160, 163, 164, 169, 170, 173, 174, 175, 176

4. Fitted with metal dashes

63, 94, 100, 117, 119, 120, 121, 122, 138, 139, 140, 142, 144, 145, 146, 147, 148, 149, 151, 155, 154, 159, 163, 164, 169, 170, 175, 176

5. Headlamp transferred from below upper deck windows to dash at both ends of the car.

26, 58, 63, 70, 91.93, 94, 96, 97, 98, 99, 100, 102, 103, 104, 105, 106, 107, 108, 109, 110, 111, 112, 114, 115, 116, 117, 118, 119, 120, 121, 122, 123, 124, 125, 126, 127, 128, 129, 130, 131, 132, 133, 134, 135, 136, 138, 139, 140, 142, 144, 145, 146, 147, 148, 149, 150, 151, 152, 153, 154, 155, 156, 158, 159, 160, 163, 164, 169, 170, 173, 174, 175, 176

6. Retained Reversed Staircases

91.93.95, 96, 97, 98, 99, 102, 108, 110

7. Retained 180 degree Staircases

117, 140, 152, 153, 155, 159, 160, 164

7. Stairway trap replaced with upper saloon bulkhead and full height door

100, 103, 109, 113, 116, 158, 174, 179

8. Cars having original 180 degree staircase replaced with normal 90 degree type

92, 100, 102

6.6 Service Records

Hull's electric cars experienced long and useful lives. The car with the most continuous service was no. 96 from 25 April 1901 to September 1942 (41 years 4 months) although it lost its upper deck in 1935. The longest life for a motorcar was had by car no. 20 from February 1899 to March 1940 (41 years and 1 month). The trail cars had long lives but some were idle pending conversion to motor cars. Nos 68 and 81 entered service as trail cars in 1899 and lasted until March 1940.

Withdrawal of the cars that received new top decks between 1933 and 1935 began in March 1940 but many lasted until the end in 1945.

Milnes car no.105 was the longest serving car in passenger service being new in Hull on 2 February 1904 being finally withdrawn in Leeds (as 480) on 23 November 1950 (46 years and 9 months) outlasting no. 111 (Leeds 484) which also clocked up 46 years and 9 months by 14 days! Nos 115 and 116 also passed the 46 year mark.

But the former no. 96 outlasted them all being withdrawn in November 1959, 58 years and 7 months in service.

6.7 Hull Cars in Leeds

W.D. Wilson recorded the layout and details of some of the cars that were sold to Leeds:

1. Nos 26, 124 to 133 and 136 were as the diagrams opposite giving a 36/20 arrangement. All others had longitudinal seating and the same length so 36/22 seating.
2. In Leeds former Hull cars 117, 140, 150, 152, 153, 155, 156, 159, 160, 173 (Leeds nos 485, 479, 461, 469, 463, 466, 465, 462, 486, 487) had 180 degree stairs but Geoff O'Connell's list shows no. 164 (475) with this and with 32/22 seating. But at some point

no. 475 may have had no end benches giving seating of 24/22! Other seating arrangements:

462	35/22
469, 472, 473, 474, 476	38/22
463, 485, 486	36/22
446 to 457 (transverse)	36/20
458, 460, 482	36/22
464, 478, 481	40/22
459, 467, 470, 471, 477, 480, 484	40/22
468 and 483	40/22

3. Nos 467, 468, 470, 471, 477, 480, 483, 484 had a stairhead door.

6.8 Hull City Tramways Fleet Totals

Tramcar Withdrawals – Summary	Fleet Total
1915	
101(1)	179
1919	
60	178
1923	
101(2)	179
By 1931	
26, 113 (new or rebuilt)	179
1931	
27, 28, 29	176
April 1933	
1, 30, 38, 69, 71, 74, 77, 85, 91, 96, 98, 101(2), 102, 108,110	161
November 1933	
19, 23, 32, 37, 42, 45, 50, 52, 59	152
November 1934	
4, 7, 31, 33, 35, 48, 51, 55, 66, 67, 72, 76, 78, 79, 80, 82	136
March 1935	
5, 13, 14, 15, 17, 22, 24, 25, 34, 41	126
July 1935	
3, 6, 9, 10, 47, 54, 93, 95, 97, 99	116
July 1937	
36, 39, 44, 46, 49, 61, 62, 64, 65, 73, 84, 89	104
April 1938	
2, 8, 11, 16, 18, 21, 40, 43, 53, 56, 57, 70, 75, 83, 86, 87, 88, 90	86
September 1938	
12, 112, 137, 141, 143, 162, 165, 166, 167, 168, 171, 177, 178, 180	72
March 1940	
20, 58, 63, 68, 81, 92, 94, 100, 106, 107, 118, 120, 121, 122, 144, 149, 151, 157, 161, 172, 179	51
February 1942	
26, 124, 125, 126, 127, 128, 129, 130, 131, 132, 133, 136.	39
May1942	
115, 134, 135, 150, 153, 159	33
October 1942	
104, 109, 114, 116, 138, 147, 152, 154, 155, 156, 158, 163, 164, 174	19
June 1945	
103	18
July 1945	
105, 111, 113, 117, 119, 123, 139, 140, 142, 145, 146, 148, 160, 169, 170, 173, 175, 176	0

Notes

The number of cars reported to the Tramways/Transport Committee as being in stock at various times does not always

HULL CARS
Seat layouts as runnings in Leeds
by W.D.Wilson

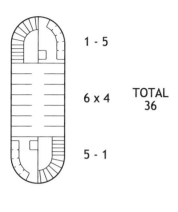

1 - 5

6 x 4   TOTAL
36

5 - 1

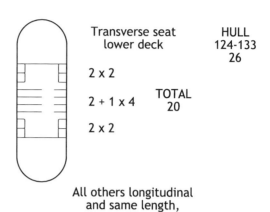

Transverse seat
lower deck

HULL
124-133
26

2 x 2

2 + 1 x 4   TOTAL
20

2 x 2

All others longitudinal
and same length,
hence 22 seats.

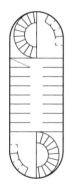

3 or 4

7 x 4   TOTAL
34 or 36

3 or 4

According to Keith Terry, in Leeds the following
Hull cars had 180° stairs:-
Hull No.s   117, 140, 150, 152, 153, 155, 156, 159, 160, 173.
Leeds No.s 485, 479, 461, 469, 463, 466, 465, 462, 486, 487.

According to G.M.O'Connell, the following Hull cars also
had 180° stairs in Leeds:-
164/475; in Leeds shown as 32/22 = 54

Also 446 - 457 (transverse) : 36/20 = 56
     458, 460, 482   : 36/22 = 58
     459, 467, 470, 471, 477, 480, 484 : 40/22 = 62
     462   : 35/22 = 57 (balconies different?)
     463, 485, 486   : 36/22 = 58
     464, 478, 481   : 40/22 = 62
     468, 483   : 40/22 = 62
     469, 472, 473, 474, 476 : 38/22 = 60

467, 468, 470, 476 and 483 with stairhead door.

? 475 2+1 top deck or no end benches ?

3 - 3

7 x 4   TOTAL
40

3 - 3

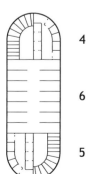

4 - 5 or 3

6 x 4   TOTAL
38 or 44
or even
4 - 4 = 40

5 or 3 - 4

agree with those above and the available evidence does not support one or the other. The above information is based on Geoff O'Connell's overall fleet list.

6.9 Tramcar Working
July 1899 to October 1902

It has not been possible to obtain a car allocation list for the early years but it has been possible, using the surviving accident reports, to compile a list of workings.

Date	Car Number	Route
8 July 1899	1	D
11 June 1900	20	A
12 June 1900	29	S
14 June 1900	30	A
20 June 1900	34	S
21 June 1900	42	H
23 June 1900	27	S
27 June 1900	7	D
22 September 1900	55	H
6 October 1900	58	H
14 October 1900	53	H
15 October 1900	29	S
25 October 1900	40	A
14 November 1900	43	H
17 November 1900	4	D
17 November 1900	12	D
18 November 1900	81	S
19 November 1900	13	D
26 November 1900	30	D
6 December 1900	51	S
10 December 1900	42	H
17 December 1900	16	B
22 December 1900	16	B
29 December 1900	3	D
7 January 1901	52	B
14 January 1901	38	A
15 January 1901	43	H
17 January 1901	101	B
18 January 1901	65	S
19 January 1901	80	B
29 January 1901	38	D
31 January 1901	69	D
3 February 1901	17	D
5 February 1901	43	H
5 February 1901	50	H
6 March 1901	25	D
13 March 1901	59	B
24 March 1901	19	D
29 Match 1901	12	D
3 April 1901	65	S
3 April 1901	53	H
4 April 1901	33	D
10 April 1901	76	B
10 April 1901	112	B (trailer)
11 April 1901	61	B
13 April 1901	47	H
15 April 1901	115	S (trailer)
19 April 1901	15	D
19 April 1901	64	A
22 April 1901	22	D
23 April 1901	51	H
23 April 1901	87	S
4 May 1901	32	D
6 May 1901	115	S (trailer)
1 June 1901	59	H
3 June 1901	32	D
21 June 1901	98	H
5 August 1901	40	H
27 August 1901	92	B
4 September 1901	37	D
6 September 1901	19	H
16 September 1901	15	D
23 September 1901	1	(A) Water Cart
24 September 1901	85	S
7 October 1901	43	H
7 October 1901	39	D
28 October 1901	15	D
9 November 1901	47	H
14 December 1901	29	A
24 December 1901	42	H
24 June 1902	83	D
13 October 1902	47	H
15 October 1902	47	H

6.10 Allocation of cars at 1 September 1938

Geoff O'Connell compiled a list of allocations at the beginning of September 1938 immediately before the Beverley Road conversion. The list is given below but only 69 cars appear on the list against some 84 which were thought to have been in stock. Nevertheless, it shows something of the distribution of cars at that time.

Cottingham Road: (routes B, BN)
26, 105, 109, 113, 114, 115, 116, 123, 124, 125, 127, 128, 129, 131, 132, 134, 135, 147 (18)

Holderness Road: (route H)
58, 68, 81, 92, 100, 107, 119, 120, 121, 140, 145, 149, 150, 152, 153, 156, 158, 159, 160 (19)

Anlaby Road: (route A)
20, 117, 122, 126, 130, 133, 136, 154, 155, 163, 164, 169, 170, 173, 174, 180 (16)

Liverpool Street: (route D)
94, 103, 104, 106, 111, 118, 138, 139, 142, 144, 146, 148, 151, 172, 175, 176 (16)

Fleet No.	First Available	Moveable Top Cover Fitted	Fixed Top Cover Open Balcony Open Platform	Fixed Top Cover Covered Balcony Vest Platform	Fully Enclosed	Withdrawn	Disposal
1	1898		4/1906		1/1924	4/1933	Scrapped
2	1898		2/1906		5/1924	4/1938	Scrapped
3	1898		12/1905		12/1923	7/1935	Scrapped
4	1898		5/1906		11/1923	11/1934	Scrapped
5	1898		7/1906		6/1924	3/1935	Scrapped
6	1898		5/1906		3/1924	7/1935	Scrapped
7	1898		1/1906		8/1929	11/1934	Scrapped
8	1898		11/1905		4/1924	4/1938	Scrapped
9	1898		6/1906		11/1923	7/1935	Scrapped
10	1898		4/1906		3/1924	7/1935	Scrapped
11	1898		10/1906		7/1926	4/1938	Scrapped
12	1898		11/1905		11/1923	11/1938	Scrapped
13	1898		8/1906		1/1927	3/1935	Scrapped
14	1898		2/1906		9/1924	3/1935	Scrapped
15	1898		12/1906		10/1924	3/1935	Scrapped
16	1/1899		1/1907		4/1925	4/1938	Scrapped
17	1/1899		3/1906		9/1923	3/1935	Scrapped
18	1/1899		11/1906		11/1922	4/1938	Scrapped
19	2/1899		5/1906		10/1923	11/1933	Scrapped
20	2/1899		11/1905		9/1926	3/1940	Scrapped
21	2/1899		1/1906		4/1925	4/1938	Scrapped
22	2/1899		8/1906		1/1921	3/1935	Scrapped
23	2/1899		2/1906		11/1922	11/1933	Scrapped
24	2/1899		5/1906		10/1926	3/1935	Scrapped
25	2/1899		12/1905		5/1928	3/1935	Scrapped
26	4/1899		7/1906			1927	Scrapped?
27	4/1899		9/1906			1931	Scrapped
28	4/1899		7/1906			1931	Scrapped
29	4/1899		9/1906			1931	Scrapped
30	4/1899		9/1906			4/1933	Scrapped
31	3/1900		1/1906		10/1921	11/1934	Scrapped
32	3/1900		11/1906		8/1922	11/1933	Scrapped
33	3/1900		1/1907		8/1923	11/1934	Scrapped
34	4/1900		4/1905		7/1921	3/1935	Scrapped
35	4/1900		12/1905	4/19		11/1934	Scrapped
36	10/4/1900		3/1906	5/19	6/1920	7/1937	Scrapped
37	4/1900		6/1906		3/1922	11/1933	Scrapped
38	3/1900		8/1906		6/1922	4/1933	Scrapped
39	3/1900		1219/06		2/1923	7/1937	Scrapped
40	11/4/1900		11/1905		6/1921	4/1938	Scrapped
41	10/4/1900		10/1906		7/1924	3/1935	Scrapped
42	13/4/1900		6/1906		3/1922	11/1933	Scrapped
43	10/4/1900		1/1907		4/1922	4/1938	Scrapped
44	4/1900		10/1906		6/1923	7/1937	Scrapped
45	4/1900		4/1906		2/1922	11/1933	Scrapped
46	11/4/1900		2/1906		7/1922	7/1937	Scrapped
47	11/4/1900		9/1906		8/1921	7/1935	Scrapped
48	13/4/1900		8/1905		5/1921	11/1934	Scrapped
49	14/4/1900		7/1906		9/1921	7/1937	Scrapped
50	4/1900		12/1906		2/1922	11/1933	Scrapped
51	4/1900		5/1906		5/1923	11/1934	Scrapped
52	4/1900		11/1906		2/1923	11/1933	Scrapped
53	11/4/1900		3/1906		3/1922	4/1938	Scrapped
54	4/1900		3/1906		2/1924	7/1935	Scrapped
55	14/4/1900		11/1906		7/1923	11/1934	Scrapped
56	10/4/1900		1/1906		10/1921	4/1938	Scrapped
57	11/4/1900		1/1907		4/1922	4/1938	Scrapped
58	10/4/1900		10/1906		7/1922	3/1940	Scrapped
59	14/4/1900		11/1905		3/1923	11/1933	Scrapped
60	13/4/1900		12/1906			1919	Scrapped
61	22/9/1900	9/3	191908	6/15		7/1937	Scrapped

Fleet No.	First Available	Moveable Top Cover Fitted	Fixed Top Cover Open Balcony Open Platform	Fixed Top Cover Covered Balcony Vest Platform	Fully Enclosed	Withdrawn	Disposal
62	11/8/1900	5/1904	1908	6/16		7/37	Scrapped
63	2/9/1900	5/1904	1909	7/15	1934	3/40	Scrapped
64	10/9/1900	8/1903	1907	6/16		7/37	Scrapped
65	10/8/1900	5/1904	1908	6/15		7/37	Scrapped
66	8/12/1900		10/06	6/18	1119/23	11/34	Scrapped
67	8/12/1900	10/1904	1908		11/1921	11/34	Scrapped
68	8/12/1900	11/1904	1909		8/1923	3/40	Scrapped
69	8/12/1900	11/1904	1908		6/1922	4/33	Scrapped
70	8/12/1900	11/1904	1908	12/16	8/1929	4/38	Scrapped
71	8/12/1900	11/1904	1907		12/1922	4/33	Scrapped
72	8/12/1900	12/1904	1908		9/1922	11/34	Scrapped
73	8/12/1900		8/06		10/1922	7/37	Scrapped
74	8/12/1900	12/1904	1909		1/1922	4/33	Scrapped
75	20/2/1901	12/1904	1907		4/1923	4/38	Scrapped
76	8/12/1900	1/1905	1909	12/16		11/34	Scrapped
77	8/12/1900	1/1905	1908		1/1923	4/33	Scrapped
78	8/12/1900	1/1905	1908		10/1922	11/34	Scrapped
79	8/12/1900	1/1905	1908		3/1923	11/34	Scrapped
80	8/12/1900	2/1905	1908		3/1923	11/34	Scrapped
81	8/12/1900		6/06		3/1923	3/40	Scrapped
82	28/12/1900		1/07	12/19		11/34	Scrapped
83	28/12/1900	2/1905	1908		2/1923	4/38	Scrapped
84	28/12/1900	2/1905	1908		9/1923	7/37	Scrapped
85	28/12/1900	2/1905	1909		9/1922	4/33	Scrapped
86	5/4/1901	3/1905	1908		7/1924	4/38	Scrapped
87	5/4/1901	3/1905	1908		11/1921	4/38	Scrapped
88	8/4/1901	3/1905	1908		12/1923	4/38	Scrapped
89	6/4/1901	3/1905	1909		10/1922	7/37	Scrapped
90	3/4/1901	4/1905	1908		7/1922	4/38	Scrapped
91	25/4/1901	6/1904	1908		8/1925	4/33	Scrapped
92	24/5/1901	6/1904	1908		12/1920	3/40	Scrapped
93	17/5/1901	6/1904	1908		3/1925	7/35	Scrapped
94	25/4/1901	6/1904	1908	1/20	1934	3/40	Scrapped
95	18/4/1901	7/1904	1908		1/1926	7/35	Scrapped
96	25/4/1901	719/04	1908		6/1926	9/42	LeedsCT
97	11/4/1901	7/1904	1908		7/1926	7/35	Scrapped
98	11/4/1901	7/1904	1908		8/1926	4/33	Scrapped
99	18/4/1901	8/1904	1909		12/1926	7/35	Scrapped
100	4/4/1901	8/1904	1908	12/18	1934	3/40	Scrapped
101	1900		1/07			1916	ErithUDC
102	13/2/1904	from new	1907		3/1926	4/33	Scrapped
103	13/2/1904	from new	1907		12/1927	6/45	Scrapped
104	26/5/1904	from new	1907		1/1927	10/42	LeedsCT(477)
105	2/2/1904	from new	1907		8/1927	7/45	LeedsCT(480)
106	7/2/1904	from new	1907		5/1927	3/40	Scrapped
107	10/1/1904	from new	1907		1/1928	3/40	Scrapped
108	14/1/1904	from new	1907		1/1925	4/33	Scrapped
109	23/12/1903	from new	1907		5/1928	10/42	LeedsCT(467)
110	10/1/1904	from new	1907		4/1926	4/33	Scrapped
111	13/2/1904	from new	1907		8/1927	7/45	LeedsCT(484)
112	24/12/1903	from new	1907		10/1927	9/38	Scrapped
113	19/1/1904	from new	1907		11/1925	7/45	LeedsCT(483)
114	5/2/1904	from new	1907		4/1921	10/42	LeedsCT(471)
115	10/1/1904	from new	1907		4/1927	5/42	LeedsCT(459)
116	14/2/1904	from new	1907		12/1924	10/42	LeedsCT(470)
117	22/5/1909		from new	6/17	1933	7/45	LeedsCT(485)
118	22/5/1909		from new	6/17	1933	3/40	Dscrapped
119	2/6/1909		from new	7/17	1935	7/45	Scrapped
120	21/6/1909		from new	7/17	1935	3/40	Scrapped
121	14/6/1909		from new	8/17	1934	3/40	Scrapped
122	1/6/1909		from new	7/18	1934	3/40	Scrapped

Fleet No.	First Available	Moveable Top Cover Fitted	Fixed Top Cover Open Balcony Open Platform	Fixed Top Cover Covered Balcony Vest Platform	Fully Enclosed	Withdrawn	Disposal
123	13/11/1909		from new		10/1928	7/1945	LeedsCT(482)
124	14/12/1909		from new		3/1928	2/1942	LeedsCT(453)
125	18/12/1909		from new		1/1929	2/1942	LeedsCT(456)
126	27/12/1909		from new		5/1929	2/1942	LeedsCT(451)
127	15/2/1910		from new		9/1929	2/1942	LeedsCT(457)
128	13/7/1910		from new		11/1929	2/1942	LeedsCT(454)
129	17/7/1910		from new		1/1930	2/1942	LeedsCT(452)
130	11/6/1910		from new		3/1930	2/1942	LeedsCT(448)
131	26/6/1910		from new		4/1928	2/1942	LeedsCT(457)
132	6/7/1910		from new		7/1931	2/1942	LeedsCT(446)
133	14/10/1910		from new		9/1930	2/1942	LeedsCT(455)
134	23/10/1910		from new		8/1931	5/1942	LeedsCT(460)
135	23/10/1910		from new		12/1931	5/1942	LeedsCT(458)
136	21/11/1910		from new		9/1930	2/1942	LeedsCT(450)
137	14/5/1912		from new	8/1917		9/1938	Scrapped
138	8/3/1912		from new	5/1916	1935	10/1942	LeedsCT(472)
139	8/3/1912		from new	11/1916	1935	7/1945	LeedsCT(481)
140	4/4/1912		from new	1/1919	1934	7/1945	LeedsCT(479)
141	23/3/1912		from new	8/1915		9/1938	Scrapped
142	27/3/1912		from new	7/1917	1935	7/1945	LeedsCT(478)
143	2/5/1912		from new	12/1916		9/1938	Scrapped
144	1/4/1912		from new	11/1918	1935	3/1940	Scrapped
145	6/4/1912		from new	5/1918	1934	7/1945	Scrapped
146	12/4/1912		from new	9/1916	1935	7/1945	Scrapped
147	6/7/1912		from new	11/1915	1935	10/1942	LeedsCT(464)
148	5/4/1912		from new	3/1917	1934	7/1945	Scrapped
149	8/5/1912		from new	10/1917	1935	3/1940	Scrapped
150	5/7/1912		from new	6/1916	1933	5/1942	LeedsCT(461)
151	7/5/1912		from new	2/1915	1935	3/1940	Scrapped
152	27/7/1912		from new	12/1915	1933	10/1942	LeedsCT(469)
153	11/5/1942		from new	10/1916	1934	5/1942	LeedsCT(463)
154	20/5/1912		from new	1/1917	1935	10/1942	LeedsCT(473)
155	1/11/1912		from new	10/1915	1934	10/1942	LeedsCT(466)
156	31/12/1912		from new	2/1917	1933	10/1942	LeedsCT(465)
157	23/11/1912		from new	2/1916		3/1940	Scrapped
158	22/11/1912		from new	9/1915	1933	10/1942	LeedsCT(476)
159	4/12/1912		from new	3/1916		5/1942	LeedsCT(462)
160	8/12/1912		from new	9/1915	1934	7/1945	LeedsCT(486)
161	3/15			from new		3/1940	Scrapped
162	3/15			from new		9/1938	Scrapped
163	4/15			from new	1934	10/1942	LeedsCT(474)
164	2/15			from new	1934	10/1942	LeedsCT(475)
165	3/15			from new		9/1938	Scrapped
166	2/15			from new		9/1938	Scrapped
167	2/15			from new		9/1938	Scrapped
168	2/15			from new		9/1938	Scrapped
169	3/15			from new	1934	7/1945	Scrapped
170	3/15			from new		7/1945	Scrapped
171	4/15			from new		9/1938	Scrapped
172	3/15			from new		3/1940	Scrapped
173	4/15			from new	1933	7/1945	LeedsCT(487)
174	5/15			from new	1933	10/1942	LeedsCT(468)
175	5/15			from new	1935	7/1945	Scrapped
176	4/15			from new	1934	719/45	Scrapped
177	5/15			from new		9/1938	Scrapped
178	6/15			from new		9/1938	Scrapped
179	5/15			from new		3/1940	Scrapped
180	6/15			from new		9/1938	Scrapped
101	3/25				from new	4/1933	Scrapped
26	11/28				from new	2/1942	LeedsCT(449)
113					from new	10/1942	LeedsCT(483)

Appendix 2

Routes, Frequencies & Fares

Information for this section comes from a variety of sources the principal one being reports to the Tramways (later Transport) Committee. These are not always reliable owing to the fact that General Managers sometimes ignored Committee instructions completely and that changes were not always reported.

Other information has come from G.A. Lee and R.J. Buckley, timetables and the files of the Board of Trade at the National Archives at Kew and local newspapers. Any inaccuracies are mine.

1. THE ROUTES – OPENING AND CLOSING DATES

1.1 Horse Tramways Routes – Opening and Closing Dates

Route	Opened	Closed	Note
Beverley Road (Lambert Street)	9 January 1875	30 September 1899	D
Spring Bank (Botanic Gardens)	12 December 1876	30 September 1899	D
Pier	12 March 1877	30 September 1899	D F G
Hessle Road (West Dock Avenue)	7 April 1877	May 1898	A
Anlaby Road (Boulevard)	9 June 1877	November 1898	B
Holderness Road (Mile House)	7 July 1877	June 1899	C
Hessle Road (Dairycoates)	30 March 1878	May 1898	A
Anlaby Road (Wheeler Street)	30 March 1878	November 1898	B
Beverley Road (Newland)	30 March 1878	30 September 1899	D
Pier – Carr Lane – Osborne Street – Pier	August 1879	November 1879	E

NOTES

A   Thought to have been withdrawn by May 1898
B   Thought to have been withdrawn by November 1898
C   Thought to have been withdrawn by June 1899
D   Dyson quotes the closing date as November 1899 but the relevant Committee report by the Town Clerk states very clearly 30 September 1899
E   August date thought to be correct
F   Initially the Pier route was linked with the Spring Bank route until 1879 when the town circular was introduced after which cars ran to the Old Town from Anlaby Road until May 1885 and from Beverley Road thereafter.
G   Originally ran from the eastern side of Whitefriargate Bridge to the Pier, and not until July did it work over the bridge into St John Street

1.2 Steam Tramways Routes – Opening and Closing Dates

Route	Opened	Closed	Note
North Bridge – Hedon Road	21 May 1889	13 January 1901	A
Drypool Bridge – Hedon Road	21 May 1889	13 January 1901	A B

NOTES

A   Official opening day – public service began on 22 May 1889
B   Ran only intermittently in later years

1.3 Electric Tramway Routes - Opening and Withdrawal Dates

Route Letter	Route	Commenced	Withdrawn	Note
A	Anlaby Road (Wheeler Street)	5 July 1899	5 September 1942	A V
D	Hessle Road (Dairycoates)	5 July 1899	30 June 1945	B
H	Holderness Road (Mile House)	10 April 1900	17 February 1940	
S	Spring Bank (Botanic Gardens)	2 June 1900	24 July 1937	
S	Botanic Gardens – Queens Road	8 October 1900	24 July 1937	C
B	Beverley Road (Cottingham Road)	8 December 1900	3 September 1938	D P

S	Queens Road – Newland Avenue End	19 January 1903	24 July 1937	J O
H	Mile House – Aberdeen Street	27 March 1903	17 February 1940	V
P	Old Town (Pier)	20 October 1903	5 September 1931	E U
M	Hedon Road (Drain Bridge)	17 December 1903	1 January 1938	
TH	Aberdeen Street via Town Hall	29 July 1907	27 June 1932	F I
MA	Hedon Road (Marfleet Avenue)	29 April 1912	1 January 1938	G B
SW	Spring Bank West (Walton Street)	9 October 1913	28 July 1934	H
DP	Dairycoates – Pickering Park Gates	16 February 1914	28 July 1934	R B
----	Paragon Station Loop	May 1914		I
BC	Cottingham Road (Newland Park)	14 July 1919	28 July 1934	O S
SC	Cottingham Road (Newland Park)	1919	6 December 1922	S T
B/S	Circular Service	1919	6 December 1922	S T
S/B	Circular Service	1919	6 December 1922	S T
IRH	Aberdeen Street – Ings Lane	7 September 1925	17 February 1940	K L M
IRTH	Aberdeen Street – Ings Lane	September 1925	27 June 1932	L M
AP	Wheeler Street – Pickering Road	5 October 1925	28 July 1934	X
SW	Spring Bank West – Park Avenue	5 October 1925	28 July 1934	N
BC	Newland Park – Goodfellowship Inn	5 October 1925	28 July 1934	
B	Cottingham Road – Endike Lane	12 July 1926	3 September 1938	P
SWC	Park Avenue – Chanterlands Ave North - Cottingham Road (Goodfellowship Inn)	3 January 1927	28 July 1934	N Q
DP	Pickering Park Gates – Pickering Road	14 July 1927	28 July 1934	W
BN	Beverley Road (Haworth Arms)	29 July 1934	3 September 1938	P

NOTES

A Extended across the Newington crossing in 1926 to a short siding in Boothferry Road. Cut back to Wheelers Street on 28 July 1934 when route AP was abandoned, but reverted to the spur owing to traffic problems later in 1936. No passengers were carried as the spur was in the "B" area of the Coordination Agreement

B Formed a cross-city route for a short time in December 1919 but not successful. Late night journeys continued for some time thereafter

C Opened as two independent sections on 8 October 1900 as level crossing equipment was not ready. Through service commenced on 26 October 1900

D Opened as two independent sections on 8 December 1900 as level crossing equipment was not ready. Through service commenced on 25 February 1901

E On opening cars may have terminated in Alfred Gelder Street at a crossover just short of Princes Dock Side

F May not have been extended to Ings Road when track extension first opened

G Use of MA ceased and M used for all journeys at an unknown date

H Regular operation ceased on 28 July 1934 but trams used this section for Hull Fair and other specials until October 1936 at least. Wiring dismantled in July/August 1937

I Thought to have opened in May 1914 (Board of Trade inspection date was 12 May 1914). Used for a short time by route P tramcars but also there is evidence to suggest that TH cars also used the loop before the start of The Great War. Not thought to be used regularly after this time apart from an experimental period from July 1923 to November 1923 by TH cars

J From 1912 to 1922 B and S combined to provide a circular service – may have been designated SB and BS

K IRH replaced with H after a short time – some official minute references to the use of IR with H reserved for cars to Aberdeen Street

L Original destination was Ings Lane (as carried on some destination blinds) but later changed to Ings Road

M IRTH reverted to original designation of TH at a later date

N Terminus reverted to Park Avenue in March 1930

O Originally cars ran via Beverley Road but later another service operated via Newland Avenue

P When route BC was replaced in 1934 short workings to Cottingham Road were designated BN – the June 1938 Hull railway Guide lists BN as a separate service with different start and finish times Monday to Saturday, which infers that some journeys other than peak hour journeys may have worked only to Haworth Arms

Q Opened in two stages – first to Goddard Avenue, then to Cottingham Road (Goodfellowship Inn) – cut back to Chanterlands Avenue North after January 1927 and later to Goddard Avenue (possible peak extras to Cottingham Road remained)

R Opened as two independent sections on 16 February 1914 as level crossing equipment was not ready. Through service commenced on 6 June 1915

S Actual start date unknown

T When the S/B and B/S service ceased all Beverley Road cars worked to Newland Park with Peak hour extras to Queens Road and, it is thought, to Newland.

U May have operated between Alfred Gelder Street and Pier only from 20 October 1903 until 29 July 1907 – references are unclear

V Formed a cross-city route for a short time in December 1919 but not successful

W KHCT and other sources say this opened on 5 October 1925 but the decision to construct the extension was not taken until 28 March 1927

X Various sources quote the extension terminating at Anlaby Park, Pickering Park and Anlaby Park Road, all of which are incorrect.

2. FREQUENCIES

2.1 Horse Tramways

When the Beverley Road route opened two cars provided a thirty-minute headway, but with the arrival of new double-deck cars this was increased to a twenty-minute headway from 6 April 1875. The service on the Pier route when it opened was a ten-minute one. Two cars provided a thirty-minute service on the opening of the Hessle Road route. Services ran from 8am until 9pm on Mondays to Saturdays. Sunday services were introduced on 6 May 1877 running from 2pm until 9pm.

When the system was complete a twenty-minute service was provided on all the routes. On 7 April 1879 the frequency on the Beverley Road, Spring Bank and Old Town routes was increased to fifteen minutes.

In August 1879 early morning workmen's cars were introduced at 6.15am but these were withdrawn in May 1880. Thereafter, cars ran from 8.15am until 9pm to 9.45pm, and an hour later on Saturdays. The level of service varied from route to route but a common ten-minute headway was provided over the more densely populated areas, but the outer areas on Anlaby Road and Holderness Road could only receive a thirty-minute service.

Changes in the 1880s included a 10-minute service over parts of Anlaby Road, Spring Bank and Beverley Roads, and 15 minutes on Holderness Road and Hessle Road. A thirty-minute bus service was operated from Savile Street to the Pier for a time, but it is unclear if this was an additional service or a replacement.

At one point, according to the Hull Times in November 1923, an eight minute service was provided on Hessle Road, but this proved unremunerative and the ten minute service was restored (note that this conflicts with the reference to fifteen minute headway above).

2.2 Steam Tramways

The original service provided workmen's cars every 15 minutes from North Bridge to Lee Smith Street between 5.30am and 8am. From then until 10.15pm a thirty-minute headway served North Bridge or Drypool Bridge to give a fifteen-minute service to Lee Smith Street.

In January 1890 a five-minute service was introduced, but in 1894 this was replaced with a 7/8-minute service between North Bridge and Lee Smith Street with only occasional workings to Drypool Bridge.

Sunday services ran every half hour from 1pm until 9pm.

The Corporation, in 1900, ran every 10 minutes from 5.10am to 8am and then every 7/8 minutes until 6.30pm followed by a 15-minute frequency until 10.12pm (one hour later on Saturdays). These ran only between North Bridge and Lee Smith Street.

2.3 Electric Tramways

1 Sample Frequencies

It would seem that after 8am a three-minute headway was operated when each of the original six electric routes was opened. When the Hedon Road route was extended on 29 April 1912, alternate cars continued to work only as far as the depot giving a six-minute service to Marfleet, and a combined three minute headway to the depot.

An unusually detailed set of timetables was placed before the Traffic Sub-Committee on Wednesday 21 May 1919 showing the current and the proposed frequencies for each route. It was anticipated that they would operate from 2 June 1919, subject to approval by the Trades Union on 25 May. No proposals were made for the Pier service, nor for the TH service (it is not known when this re-started after the war).

	Present frequency (minutes)		Proposed frequency (minutes)
D – Hessle Road			
5.00am to 7.00am	5 and 6	5.00am to 6.40am	6 and 7
7.00am to 11.32am	2 and 3	6.40am to 9.04am	2 and 3
11.32am to 4.15pm	3 and 4	9.04am to 10.10am	4 and 5
4.15pm to 11.00pm	3	10.10am to 11.20pm	2
Increased frequency results from provision of five extra cars and quicker running			
DP – Hessle Road			
5.00am to 7.30am	14 and 15	5.00am to 7.30am	6 and 7
7.30am to 8.08am	7 and 8	7.30am to 12.05pm	7
8.08am to 3.09pm	7 and 8	12.05pm to 11.20pm	7 and 8
3.09pm to 11.00pm	8		
Increased service by quicker running			
A – Anlaby Road			
5.00am to 6.56am	5 and 6	5.00am to 6.40am	6
6.56am to 7.40am	4	6.40am to 9.15am	2 and 1
7.40am to 9.34am	2	9.15am to 10.02am	4
9.34am to 11.23am	3	10.02am to 11.45am	3
11.23am to 5.43pm	2	11.45am to 11.20pm	2
5.43pm to 11.00pm	2 and 3		

B – Beverley Road

5.00am to 7.00am	6 and 7	5.00am to 6.42am	7
7.00am to 7.45am	3 and 4	6.42am to 7.00am	3 and 4
7.45am to 9.00am	2	7.00am to 9.00am	2
9.00am to 1.45pm	3	9.00am to 11.30am	3
1.45pm to 6.30pm	2 and 3	11.30am to 11.20pm	2
6.30pm to 11.00pm	3		

S – Spring Bank

5.00am to 7.00am	5 and 6	5.00am to 6.44am	6 and 7
7.00am to 7.30am	4	6.44am to 7.00am	3 and 4
7.30am to 9.00am	2	7.00am to 9.35am	2
9.00am to 12 noon	4 and 5	9.35am to 11.10am	3
12 noon to 6.15pm	2 and 3	11.10am to 12 noon	2 and 3
6.15pm to 11.00pm	3	12 noon to 11.30pm	2

SW – Spring Bank West

5.00am to 7.40am	10	5.00am to 7.30am	10
7.40am to 10.55pm	5	7.30am to 9.00am	5
		9.00am to 11.30am	6
		11.30am to 11.12pm	4 and 5

H – Holderness Road

5.00am to 7.30am	5	5.00am to 7.00am	6
7.30am to 8.08am	4	7.00am to 11.20pm	2
8.08am to 3.09pm	2		
3.09pm to 11.00pm	2 and 3		

Increased service from 8am to 9am by six cars giving a one-minute service in some places (hint that this is a short working to Durham Street perhaps?)
Increased service from 11.30am to 1.30pm by six cars (dinner hour) making a one-minute service in some places (see above)

MA – Marfleet

5.00am to 7.30am	5	5.00am to 7.00am	6
7.30am to 8.06am	6	7.00am to 11.20pm	3
8.06am to 6.30pm	3		
6.30pm to 11.00pm	5 and 6		

Special cars from Holderness Road and other routes 7am to 8am and 6.10pm until 10.00pm when spare men available. Special cars from Holderness Road and other routes from 7am to 9am.
Service improved 11.30am to 1.30pm (dinner time) by six cars; also special cars from 4.40pm to 5.30pm

The new timetable would absorb 54 men who were employed by the department but not working full time, and would do away with 1,600 hours which the Corporation had been paying since the new award came into force on 26 March 1919.
It will be seen that there were no afternoon additional peak workings other than special cars on Hedon Road (for dockers, ship-builders, etc).
According to a schedule submitted to the Tramways Committee in July 1919 the most profitable time per car (based on a survey on Monday 2 June) was between 6pm and 7pm when 64 cars were in service on the western routes (D, DP, A, S, SW, B) and returned 11s 8d per car. Receipts for every individual hour from 12 noon to 11.0pm were higher than any hour between 5.0am and 12 noon. Early morning workmen's services returned the lowest sum. A loss of £65 1s 2d was made on morning services between 5am and 9am.

The number of passengers carried on each route between 5am and 9am on Tuesday 22 July 1919 was as follows:

Hessle Road	7757
Anlaby Road	4038
Holderness Road	5428
Spring Bank	5726
Beverley Road	4598
Hedon Road	3967

	31514

Old Town	465

This shows the relative importance of each route and also how small the loadings on the Old Town were outside shopping hours.

2. Short Workings

Over the life of the system there were scheduled and special event short workings (often, but not always, called "short running" in the minutes). Some received designated letters, others did not. It is impossible to state with any certainty when and for how long some short workings existed, but the following list gives an indication of what was available and used. Also, it is not known how short workings could have been identified by passengers. It can not be assumed that short workings retained the route letter for the whole route. No destination blind or plate has survived so this remains unsolved. There were, of course, crossovers near or outside depots which could be used. The list is probably not definitive!

Route		Letter	Notes
A	**Anlaby Road**		
	Boulevard		A
	West Park		B
	Walton Street		C
AP	**Pickering Road**		
	Boothferry Road	A	D
D	**Dairycoates**		
	West Dock Avenue		W
DP	**Pickering Road**		
	Pickering Park		X
B	**Beverley Road**		
	Newland (Haworth Arms)		E
	Newland (Haworth Arms)	BN	F
	Queens Road	(QB)	G
BC	**Hall Road (via Beverley Road/Cottingham Rd)**		
	Cottingham Road Depot		H
S	**Newland Avenue**	S	
	Derringham Street		I
	Queen's Road	QS	J
	Sharp Street		K
	Welbeck Street		L
SW	**Spring Bank West**		
	None		
SWC	**Hall Road**		
	Chanterlands Avenue North		M
	Goddard Avenue		N
	Park Street		O
H	**Holderness Road (Ings Road)**		
	Aberdeen Street		P
	Durham Street		R
	Southcoates Railway Station		S
TH	**Holderness Road (Ings Road)**		
	None		
M	**Hedon Road (Marfleet)**		
	Depot		T
	Alexandra Dock		U
P	**Pier (Old Town)**		
	Alfred Gelder Street		V

Notes

Letter	Notes
A	Rugby (Hull RLFC) specials
B	Football specials (Hull City AFC) Cricket specials (Yorkshire CCC) Also used at Hull Fair times
C	Hull Fair specials Also used for football specials
D	A terminus from some time in 1926
E	Short workings after extension to Endike Lane
F	Introduced after "BC" withdrawn in July 1934
G	Peak hours – may have been designated "QB"
H	Depot workings
I	Original "S" terminus – peak workings after extension to Queens Road and beyond – also used to turn cars back when service suffering severe delays
J	"S" terminus from 8 October 1900 to 19 January 1903 used for peak extras and works journeys to and from Hedon Road (Alexandra Dock)
K	No details of use
L	No details of use
M	"SWC" terminus after SWC cut back from Cottingham Road/Hall Road – used for a short time only as service cut back to Goddard Avenue and Park Avenue – possible peak journeys?
N	"SWC" terminus after "SWC" cut back from Cottingham Road – used for a short time only as service cut back to Park Avenue – possible peak journeys?
O	Terminus of "SW" service from 5 October 1925 – all day terminus from 1931
P	Rugby specials (Hull Kingston Rovers Rugby League Football Club)
R	Regular all day short workings – no designated latter
S	Used for turning back cars when service disrupted by bridges and railway crossing
T	Alternative cars terminated here when extension to Marfleet opened on 29 April 1912 – during WW1 all cars extended to Marfleet
U	Workmen's journeys to and from Alexandra Dock and Shipyard on all routes
V	Used as the terminus for various periods of time
W	Peak hours
X	Summer/Special events

3. Other Crossovers for short workings or emergencies

Crossovers were provided in strategic locations to enable cars to turn back or to divert to another route

Route	Location
D - Hessle Road	Liverpool Street (depot workings) Porter Street/William Street (use unknown)
A – Anlaby Road	Wheeler Street (depot workings but original terminus from 5 July 1899) – replaced by Boothferry Road spur
B – Beverley Road	Stepney Station – originally used for access to Temple Street Depot
B.S.SW.SWC	Blundells Corner in Prospect Street (use unknown)
BC – Cottingham Road	Newland Park – originally the BC terminus
H – Holderness Road	North Bridge (western side) – used when bridge closed to road traffic to turn cars back Witham - used when bridge closed to road traffic to turn cars back Lee Street – use unknown
TH – Holderness Road	Clarence Street - used when bridge closed to road traffic to turn cars back
M – Hedon Road	Great Union Street - used when bridge closed to road traffic to turn cars back

3. FARES

3.1 Horse Tramways

The following dates chronicle changes to fares which were sometimes reduced for periods in winter but no actual dates have been discovered. The greater part of the town's population lived within the 1d stages from the town centre, and they enjoyed fares that were amongst the lowest in Great Britain. There may have been other variations in fares that went unrecorded.

1877	2d any distance apart from old Town which was 1d
July 1877	Spring Bank route divided into two 1d stages, the stage point being Blundells Corner at the junction of Spring Bank and Beverley Road
30 March 1878	3d the full distance on the five main roads, the three extensions being a 1d stage
19 June 1879	1d stages on all five main routes became standard – first stage from town centre to Porter Street/Hessle Road, Fountain Street on Anlaby Road, Blundells Corner on Beverley Road/Spring Bank routes and North Bridge on Holderness Road route. Blundells Corner – Spring Bank stage 2d, the rest having two 1d stages. Transfers to the Old Town were at no extra cost
18 August 1879	Workmen's through fare of 1d introduced
December 1887	Through fares reduced to 1d with no real effect
21 October 1889	All inside fares raised to 2d – outside remained at 1d
1 November 1889	Inside fares reduced to 1d on inner stages and outer stages but 1½d for two stages – 2d fare from Pier to and from any other termini
15 November 1889	1d fares for inside passengers re-instated – no further changes

3.2 Steam Tramways

Being such a short tramway fares were simple, being 1d for any journey, ½d for workmen. Such was the dependence on workers that over 90% of the fares were at ½d.

3.3 Electric Tramways

1. Introduction

A simple flat fare system of 1d for any journey was introduced when the electric tramways system opened in 1899. Children were charged at two for 1d. This remained unchanged for a decade before the expansion of the system enforced revised thinking on the subject.

On 6 January 1914 Mr McCombe submitted a report about revision of fares to the Tramways Sub-Committee. Although the flat fare of 1d for any distance (½d before 9am) was very popular, there was a feeling that fares should reflect the distance travelled now that several extensions to the system had been opened. Members had rejected the proposal to charge an additional half-penny fare for the Marfleet extension but he wanted them to review the present system and to create a new fares structure that would apply in Hull for years to come.

He recommended that a 1d flat fare for a whole route should continue and should also apply to any subsequent extension. The transfer system should be discontinued and replaced with a half-

penny fare on the Old Town route, which should be retained when the extension to Paragon Station was opened. He also recommended that the half-penny fare before 9 am should continue.

His next proposal was for the introduction of a large number of half-penny stages on each route apart from the Old Town. This would be more equitable and would reflect the distance travelled. He also predicted that there would be an increase in the number of passengers carried which would offset any possible reduction in income.

He then listed the stages to be introduced.

Hessle Road: Queen Victoria Square and Coltman Street; Dairycoates and Coltman Street; Dairycoates and Terminus

Anlaby Road: Queen Victoria Square and Lansdowne Street; Walton Street and Lansdowne Street; Walton Street and Terminus

Spring Bank: King Edward Street and Cemetery Gates; Queen's Road and Cemetery Gates; Queen's Road and Terminus

Spring Bank West: King Edward Street and Cemetery Gates; Cemetery Gates and Terminus

Holderness Road (both routes): Savile Street and Dansom Lane; Jalland Street and Dansom Lane; Jalland Street and Terminus

Beverley Road: King Edward Street and Wellington Lane; Wellington Lane and Melwood Grove; Melwood Grove and Terminus

Hedon Road: Savile Street and Thomas Street; Thomas Street and Southcoates Lane; Southcoates Lane and Terminus

Old Town: Dock Offices and Pier

Despite his intentions an unbalanced fare system remained in use. The Hessle Road extension was nearly ready and would add three quarters of a mile to the route, yet passengers would pay the same as those travelling only as far as Dairycoates, whilst anyone travelling from there to the new terminus would be able to travel a longer distance than the other two stages. Short distance passengers always lost out in Hull whether travelling by tram, trolleybus or motor bus.

Members were reluctant to introduce the new system but instructed Mr McCombe to conduct a trial on the Hessle Road route as soon as possible. On 25 March 1914 he reported the results, comparing the five weeks with the first five weeks under the old system. Overall, revenue was down by just £3. There was an increase of 377,715 passengers paying the ½d fare but a decrease of 189,693 paying the full fare, a net increase of 188,022 passengers.

Mr McCombe was authorised to introduce the full system but there were several "adjustments" to the stage locations.

2. Penny Fares

These were discussed on 20 September 1922 at the Traffic and Complaints Sub-Committee. Several councillors were keen to introduce a penny fare to alleviate the wage cuts that so many workers had suffered in the previous months. Given the state of the tramways finances Mr Rayner was not really in favour but he recognised that "it was necessary to make a very serious effort towards reducing the fares". Nevertheless he wanted Councillors to be acquainted with the difficulties and costs involved.

In May 1922 he had conducted a very careful census of passengers boarding the cars within a mile radius from the city centre which revealed that, on this stage alone were one penny fares to be introduced, rather more than 90,000 additional 1d passengers would be required per week (!) to maintain the revenue then enjoyed from the existing 1½d minimum fare. Since the census was taken the number of passengers on the cars had fallen further as unemployment and wage cuts took their toll. In fact the cars were carrying 1,579,000 fewer passengers since April 1922, which equated to a revenue loss of £9,466. For the week in which the census was taken revenue was £7,422 but this had now fallen to £6,499.

Another factor was that a reduction in tramwaymen's wages was proposed, which together with already introduced cuts in engineering wages would amount to £425 per week. This gave the sub-committee some freedom of movement should it wish to proceed with the penny fares.

He stated it was absolutely impossible to say with any certainty what the effect of the penny fare would be. Previous increases had generated an additional 20% income (£1,400 a week) despite passenger numbers being reduced by 10%! His proposals were slightly different, being an intention to divide each route into three 1d stages whilst retaining the overall 1½d and 2d fares. It would be almost impossible for conductors to collect fares unless the 1d and 1½d stages coincided, as the sections would be comparatively short. Therefore, he proposed that each route would have two stages apart from Holderness Road (three) and the Old Town which would involve slight changes to those in existence. He was sympathetic to the need to reduce travel costs and thought that the proposed reduction in tramwaymen's wages gave the Committee some room to manoeuvre. A recent reduction in the engineering side wages had saved £300 per week, whilst the saving on traffic wages could be £425 a week.

After some discussion it was agreed to introduce a penny fare for a single stage, and the 1½d for two stages, and 2d for three stages, but for an initial trial period of two months commencing 1 November 1922, after which the situation would be reviewed.

Some key dates regarding fare alterations are:

FARES

Date	Full	Children	Workmen	Stages	Note
		d	d	d	d
5 July 1899	1	2 for 1d			
1 July 1908	1	2 for 1d	½		a
20 April 1911	1	½	½		
18 May 1914	1	½	½	½	c
15 January 1917	1	½	½	½	b
5 August 1918	1	½	½	withdrawn	b
11 August 1919	1½	½	1	1	b
24 May 1920	2	½	1	1½	
1 November 1922	2	½	1	1 and 1½	d

Notes

a ½d "all the way" fare before 9am
b From 15 January 1917 to 24 May 1919 servicemen were charged ½d for any distance.
c Hessle Road fare stage trial started on 15 February 1914
d Trial period commenced

3 Other Tickets

1. Pre-paid Discount Tickets
These were introduced on 4 September 1922. Prices were 1s 6d for 14 (1½d) and 2s for 14 (2d) tickets.

2. Weekly Passes

Commenced Monday 2 June 1924 and discontinued on 17 July 1927. They were available on tram routes only:

Distance	Prices From 2 June 1924	Prices From 3 May 1926
1st or 2nd stage on one route	2s	2s 6d
One whole route	2s 6d	3s
Ist stage on all routes	4s	5s
Through journey on all routes	5s	7s

3. Sunday Passes

Commenced on 9 August 1925 and suspended on 25 October 1925, these were re-started on 8 May 1927, only to be discontinued completely on 2 October 1927. Transfer tickets between routes S and BC were introduced on 3 December 1923.

4. Free Passes

The following passes were introduced:

Old Age Pensioners	October 1920
Legless ex-servicemen	August 1920
Blind Persons	April 1911
Councillors	November 1924
Hull Jubilee District Nursing Association	August 1928

5. Fares in use during Electric Tramways operations

Fare From / To	1899 1908	1901 1919	1920 1921	1922 1923	1924	1925	1926 1927	1928	1929	1930	1931	1932	1933 1934
1d	*	*	*	*	*	*	*	*	*	*	*	*	*
½d		*	*	*	*	*	*	*	*	*	*	*	*
1½d			*	*	*	*	*	*	*	*	*	*	*
2d (single)			*	*	*	*	*	*	*	*	*	*	*
2½d							*	*	*	*	*	*	*
3d			*		*	*				*		*	
Passes						*	*	*					
2½d (tram/bus transfer)								*		*	*	*	*
2d return									*	*	*	*	*
2d exchange									*	*	*	*	*
4d											*	*	
6d (evening)													*
1/- (Sunday)													*

Fares grew in complexity and were subject to many changes in the late 1920s, some of which were against the advice of the current Manager and even the Tramways Committee.

6. Fares in use 2 March 1926

This table was submitted to the Tramways Committee on 2 March 1926 as part of what Mr Rayner hoped would be a major review of the fares structure, in order to address the deteriorating financial health of not only the tramways but the buses as well.

Routes divided into three stages	s	d
Any one stage		1
Two stages		1½
Any distance		2
Children under 14 years any distance		½
School Children 14 to 16 years		1

Discount Tickets		
7 x 1½d		9
14 x 1½d	1	6
7 x 2d	1	0
14 x 2d	2	0

Weekly passes		
1½d stages	2	0
All the way	2	6
First 1½d stage on all routes	4	0
All routes, any distance	5	0

Old Age Pensioners (over 70 years)	5327
Legless Ex-servicemen	193
Blind Persons	316
Corporation Passes	64

7. Illuminated Fare Stage Signs

A number of these signs were provided at various places on the system. Some could be illuminated at any hour (*) whilst others were dependent on the overhead. All were rated at 550 volts. They were situated as follows:

Route	Stage	No.	Stage	No.
Hessle Road	Neptune Street	1	Scarborough Street	1*
Anlaby Road	Linnaeus Street	2	St George's Road	1
Holderness Road	Dansom Lane	1	Durham Street	1
Hedon Road	Popple Street	1	Alexandra Dock	1*
Spring Bank	Sutton Street	2	Chanterlands Avenue	2
Princes Avenue	Queen's Road	1		
Beverley Road	Somerscales Street	1	Washington Street	1

There were proposals for more but it is not known if these were installed.

8. "Tramway Passes" paper presented by Councillor Digby Willoughby (Chairman, Hull Tramways Committee) to the Municipal Tramways Association 13 September 1922

Councillor Digby stated that he knew that tramway managers approached the question with a great deal of reluctance, including Mr Rayner but he hoped to convey the reasoning behind Hull's adoption of the pass system.

The Council considered that those riders who used the system daily and were the backbone of passenger numbers should benefit from the same treatment given to regular passengers by suburban railways. It was accepted that such a system would involve some loss but it was felt that regular passengers should be treated more advantageously than those who used the trams only in an emergency. A particular example was the tens of thousands of bicycle riders who took to the cars in snow and heavy showers. These riders received the same treatment as the year round rider.

The original tramway outlay of £762,000 had been reduced to £280,000, a profit of £60,000 had been made and the reserve fund was £112,500. Therefore the Corporation wished to either reduce fares, or extend stages to provide regular users with some benefit. Current fares were 1d for a minimum of 1,320 yards and 1½d for a minimum of 2,640 yards and 3d thereafter. Of total revenue of £332,000 some £180 was collected in 1½d fares. The Tramway Committee was desirous of giving anything between £20,000 and £30,000 in relief of riders. It was mindful that housing clearance schemes were moving people from sub-standard homes at 4s to 5s a week's rent to new homes at 9s per week and over near the ends of four of the main routes. Also taken into account was the situation whereby some people went home for lunch and were, therefore, making four trips a day. (Author's

note – this was never stated in such terms in meetings of the Tramways Committee).

First it was decided not to grant passes on the central 1d stages, the most congested part of the undertaking. Until 9am the system carried all passengers at a maximum of 1d per person. Therefore it was agreed to issue on the first or second 1½ stages, a weekly pass, transferable for 2/- per week or a pass for the full stage at 2/6 per week and a pass on the six outward stages for 4/- and, finally, one for the whole system at 5/- per week transferrable. 28,182 passes were sold over the first ten weeks worth £3214 9s 0d some 5.34 per cent of all receipts.

However, before commencing the scheme it was revealed that owing to a downturn in business receipts were £200 per week less than the previous year resulting in an amendment to the scheme so that instead of £250 per week being lost by the passes this was reduced to £124. The take up of passes was disappointing with less than half the anticipated number being sold. This was put down to the Discount Ticket scheme still in operation. On Anlaby Road it was found that there were 4.84 rides per pass with an average of 551 passes issued. The morning and evening peak periods showed little change but the dinner period (lunchtime) showed an increased in ridership.

He criticised the attitude of tramway managers (which presumably included Mr Rayner) to passes as obsolete and obtuse. Undertakings must change. In Hull there were three bus companies operating which took a percentage of suburban passengers because they could reach the city centre faster as they did not cater for residents nearer the centre. It was in the interest of the trams to get the passenger either as a weekly, monthly or yearly passenger. After all, the Corporation's electricity policy was to give concessions based on the number of units consumed.

In addition some 4,143 free passes were issued to Old Age Pensioners to ride on the cars between 9.30am and 11am, 2pm to 4pm and 7pm to 11pm. 249 passes were for blind persons and another 200 for war injured servicemen and 64 for councillor members.

It was the intention to make Hull's trams as attractive to passengers as possible so that it would be the "thing" to do.

The discussions revealed a range of opinions with some delegates stating that ratepayers (i.e. passengers) ought to benefit directly on the cars from yearly profits (stable fares or investment in cars) rather than profits being used to keep rate demands down, as this tended to benefit businesses rather than individual ratepayers. Others considered that all passengers should pay the same fare irrespective of distance. Some criticised the easy availability of transfer and thought that this was a mistake. Mr Mattinson of Manchester Corporation Tramways thought that the cost of passes for blind persons and old age pensioners should be borne by the ratepayers not the tramways so that the tramways were not deprived of the income lost by their issue.

Enter Councillor Stark. He accused tramway managers who, having enjoyed a transport monopoly for so long, were unable to cope and were against discounted tickets and passes. Normally he disagreed with Councillor Willoughby on most things but he supported his presentation wholeheartedly. Trams must compete with omnibuses – he did not consider trams obsolete but they must modernise and challenge for passengers. Any benefits from profits must go to passengers – the rate relief payments made by the trams actually benefitted the competition since omnibuses and the railways paid less rates thereby reducing their costs.

Mr Rayner agreed that the passes were an excellent way of dissipating profits. He was not against discounts but his research considered that, based on Councillor Willoughby's figures, pass holders who purchase a 2/- pass for 1½d stages undertake 29 journeys a week compared with the 16 possible if paying for each individual journey, a gift of 1/9 to the passenger. This represented a loss on 3000 passes of £9,076 annually.

The debate was lengthy and heated but Councillor Willoughby's paper at least described Hull Corporation's thinking behind the passes and discount schemes, a policy that was accepted by all shades of political opinion, if not by every individual. But was it wise for Mr Rayner to publically be at odds with two members of his own Tramways Committee? In opposing the passes he did not offer any alternative which would have achieved their objectives.

Appendix 3

Overhead Lines and Permanent Way

1. OVERHEAD LINES

1.1 Traction Poles and Overhead Line

The original tender document specified poles to be wrought iron or steel welded tubes each in one piece, and tapered in the upper part with neat collars at the joints and approved ornamental finish. Side poles were to be of ample strength but not unnecessarily heavy. Any poles which were found to be perceptibly out of line or more out of vertical than specified must be re-set, if straight, or replaced with stringer poles to the satisfaction of the Engineers, if bent, at the contractor's expense. Side poles were to be set so that, when fully loaded, they should not have such an inclination as to be in the Engineer's opinion unsightly. Centre poles were to be set and maintained truly vertical.

Centre poles on the Anlaby Road route were to be so arranged that arc lamps could be readily affixed above them in future. For that purpose they were to be provided with hollow cast iron bases of ample size to accommodate switches and cut-outs whilst each base was to be fitted with a strong door having brass hinges and a railway lock and key.

Mr Turner listed the types of poles that were in use on the system as supplied by the British Mannesmann Tube Company Limited. These were weldless steel poles and were as follows:

Diameter	Length	Thickness
Standard Heavy Type (weight 1158 lb)		
9½	17' 0"	13/32"
8½	7' 0"	13/32"
7½	7' 0"	13/32"

	31' 0"	

Standard Medium Type (weight 872 lb)		
8½	17' 0"	11/32"
7½	7' 0"	11/32"
6½	7' 0"	11/32"

	31' 0"	

Standard Light Type (weight not stated)		
7½	17' 0"	unknown
6½	7' 0"	unknown
5½	7' 0"	unknown

	31' 0"	

The estimated cost in 1931 of excavating a "tram pole" was £1 15s compared with £1 10s for burning off a pole. Burning down an existing pole and erecting a replacement by the City Engineer cost £5 13s 11d. The heaviest pole (called type "C" in some references) cost £22 12s 5d in 1919 whilst the lightest (type" A") cost £16 13s each.

Brackets were to be of wrought iron and of an ornamental design to be approved by the Corporation. It expected to use a radial trolley which would permit the use of comparatively short brackets and whatever lengths were adopted the design was to be of a pleasing and artistic character without being florid or obtrusive. Examples were the brackets employed in Bristol and Leeds.

Trolley wire was to be of hard drawn copper, 3/24 of an inch in diameter and 98% conductivity. Trolley wires were to be supported by span wires or wall brackets in Whitefriargate and Silver Street, centre poles for 100 yards in Market Place, St John Street, on Anlaby Road between Park Street and Walton Street, in the new street (King Edward Street), Beverley Road between Stepney Lane and Sculcoates Lane, and for 270 yards from the terminus, in Spring Bank between Vane Street and Princes Avenue, the wide part of Witham, and side poles and brackets elsewhere except in special cases where span wires might be desirable.

Span wires in Whitefriargate and Silver Street were to be supported from house walls by means of approved ornamental rosettes and wall plates, but if this was impossible the contractor had to supply and fit a pole (at an extra cost). In the event no wires were erected in these two streets. Extensive use of wall plates was made in George Street and Charlotte Street as well as others such as Savile Street.

Contractors were to provide the necessary trolley wires, frogs, switches and accessories for six branches into car depots, the aggregate length of such branches being about 260 yards. Work inside the depots would be the subject of separate contracts.

Contractors would have to provide such additional works as may be necessary or reasonably required by the North Eastern Railway at the four level crossings. This should include special protection for the feeders so that they would not be injured by the weight or vibration of trains. Additionally, special care would be needed to carry the trolley wire under the two bridges of the Hull and Barnsley railway, and any such attachments must be to the satisfaction of that company.

Messrs Siemens Brothers Ltd. constructed the overhead until 1902 when the Tramways Electrical Engineer took over.

1.2 Electrical Supply

A schedule of the current that would be required at 500 volts pressure on the several sections of line in ordinary service was provided. The current density of the feeders was not to exceed 750 ampères to the square inch sectional area of copper and, in the case of those feeders that supplied sections 1, 2 and 3 of the Anlaby Road route, the current density must not exceed 550 ampères per square inch so that, on special occasions 100% more current might be required on the Anlaby Road route and 33% on other routes.

The Corporation enclosed plans indicating where cars would usually stop to load and unload, as well as the level crossings where four or more cars might accumulate and be required to start almost simultaneously.

The schedule was:

	Section	Ampère
Hessle Road	1. (Porter Street)	105
	2.	105
	3.	85
	4. (Terminal section)	85
Anlaby Road	1. (Carr Lane)	130
	2.	130
	3.	100
	4. (Terminal section)	100
Beverley Road	1. (Prospect Street)	130
	2.	130
	3.	100
	4. (Newland)	100
Spring Bank	1.	120
Holderness Road	1. (West of North Bridge)	100
	2. (Witham)	100
	3.	130
	4.	130
	5. (Terminal section)	130
Old Town	1.	85

The Old Town reference was another written insertion!

Contractors were warned that the tramways would cross the bascule bridge at Whitefriargate and the draw bridge at North Bridge, and that the feeders would be carried across the river under the water in both places, although an existing iron pipe at Whitefriargate could be used. Special arrangements were required for disconnecting and reconnecting the trolley wires. However, Whitefriargate Bridge might be reconstructed before the tramways opened for traffic. At both bridges the electrical connection should be made and broken automatically with the closing and opening of the bridge.

1.3 The Original Overhead Line Construction Described

Double trolley wire of No. 0B and S gauge was used throughout and supported by double insulation. Centre poles were used where the road width exceeded 40 feet; otherwise side brackets mounted on poles erected inside the kerb were employed. All the poles were provided with an ornamental finial and a cast iron base on which the city's coat of arms was embossed. Brackets were decorated with ornamental scroll work also of wrought iron.

Trolley wire was divided into half-mile lengths by means of section insulators, connection between the sections being made by means of switch fuses mounted on marble board inside a cast iron pillar box. Provision was also made inside the boxes for feeder connections with the trolley wire protected from lightning by a Garton type arrester. Protection for overhead telegraph and telephone wires was given by guard wires of No. 8 S.W.G. galvanised steel suspended above the overhead.

Feeder cables comprised copper strand insulated with Siemens impregnated fibrous material, lead sheathed and covered with tape and preservative compound. They ran through Doulton conduits with a cast iron watertight disconnecting box every 100 yards. Connection was made between the generating station and several points of the rails by return feeders of 0.75 square inch section similar to the positive feeders.

To meet Board of Trade conditions an insulated test wire was carried to each terminus, and to every point of connection between the rails and return feeders, to estimate the drop of potential along the uninsulated parts of the "return" path of the current. This test wire was looped into each of the previously mentioned section boxes in which an earthed terminal was installed in order to localise any abnormal drop of potential in

the rails. Separate tests could be made of each half-mile sections. Test wires formed part of an air space cable which also contained conductors for the telephone circuits. Two or more sets of telephone apparatus were provided at convenient places on each route, the central exchange being located at the tramway power station.

2. PERMANENT WAY

2.1 Horse Tramways

In December 1874 the HST submitted plans of track work to the Board of Trade. These included a section through a length of rail. Rails would be laid on a 16" cover base. Setts would be laid on ashes. Overall width was 8'. Another plan revealed that the Beverley Road line would have only one passing place at the Sculcoates Union Workhouse opposite Margaret Street. Only a single line was shown in Savile Street, but the terminus near Sculcoates Lane would have two stub tracks.

Mr Dyson considered the rails to be lighter than those in use on the electric tramways. The arrangements in Hull have been described by R.J. Buckley and D.K. Clark. The road was excavated to a depth of 8 inches and a further 7 inches where the chairs were to be placed. The chairs were cast-iron and measured 14 inches by 12 inches at the base tapering to 3½in. square at the top and were embedded in concrete. The tops were secured by metal driven through the rail into hardwood blocks in the chairs placed at a distance of 3ft. They weighed 43 lb per yard and were 24ft long. Concrete was carried along beneath the rails mainly to exclude moisture. Points and crossings were cast iron with wrought iron tongues. The track was paved with wood or stone blocks or with macadam.

This type of track was not really robust enough for Hull's watery sub-soil and it needed good and frequent maintenance costing money that the company rarely possessed. The quality of workmanship on the original Beverley Road line was poor and in 1879 it had to be re-laid on the instructions of Hull's Works Committee.

In 1885/6 track with more modern and robust girder rail was laid in Albion, Prospect and Osborne Streets. They were paved with a line of alternate granite and chilled iron blocks intended to prevent other road traffic making "grooves" in the road surface. Track across the North Bridge was laid at the same time although it appears that the surface of the bridge was not beyond criticism.

But the company continued to incur criticism for the standard of track and roadway. In 1877 the company stated that forty men were working at night to relay the northern part of the Beverley Road line. On 7 April 1887 Mr A.E. White, the Borough Engineer, submitted a highly critical report to the Works Committee. Of 23 streets which possessed tram track only three of those re-laid were in good condition. Five were in "fair" condition but the others were "generally" bad or "very" bad, the Witham track and pavements being poor.

Mr White recommended that all the rails and pavement be re-laid or renewed and that a proper camber be established on all roads. The company disagreed about the condition of the lines and blamed bad weather for delays in carrying out repairs. The Corporation withdrew its notice to give the company time to redress the problem. This was to little avail, although some relaying was done on Spring Bank, Beverley Road, Witham and Beverley Road but the company refused to lay the rails to form a higher camber.

2.2 Steam Tramways

The DMST submitted two plans to the Board of Trade on 18 May 1888. The first showed a longitudinal section of the tramway, a plan of the chilled point and chilled crossing. Also shown were a plan of the permanent way and a cross section of the tramway. The roadway between the rails and for a distance of 18 inches to each side were formed of granite pavements on a bed of concrete, 8" thick.

A second plan gave elevations of the fishplates and rails, bolts and nuts, section of a fishplate, a section and plan of girder rail. Steel rails, 24' long at 79 lb to the yard would be laid. Fishplates would be wrought iron, 19½ lb per pair. Width of the groove in the rail would be one inch whilst the depth would be five-eighths of an inch.

On 25 May the Board approved the proposals subject to the outer edges of the paving being serrated where they adjoined the macadam, and the provision of tie rods between the rails. The company objected saying that many undertakings did not use tie rods and used the same specially made rails. The Board would not change its mind.

The lines which were designed by the City Engineer, Mr Alfred Edward White, were laid by a local company, Messrs Simpson and Malone. A concrete base was laid followed with a seared layer of fine concrete on which the rails were placed and paved with setts. The line into Hotham Street and the depot had the rails bedded directly on to the concrete base before it had the chance to set. This was in place of the proposed use of Welsh setts as the Corporation had instructed the company to provide a non-slippery surface.

In July 1896 the company wrote to the Board about additional passing places, and its intention to use Marshall's automatic points made by Askham Brothers & Wilson of Sheffield. These were designed for single tramway lines with passing places. They were secured by a strong buffer securely protected against dust and water.

Their action was very simple – engine and car coming off a loop opened the tongue the width of the flange of the engine and car wheels and this blocked the right hand road on entering the passing loop. Manufacturers claimed that no single failure had occurred – in cases of breakdown in a loop the points could be wedged and used as moveable points. There was no drop off or jerk when clearing the points and there was very little wear on the tongue due to an "ingenious contrivance" (not defined).

Hull is always regarded as flat but the DSMT plans refuted this to the extent that the "gradient" from Drypool to Lee Smith Street was 1 in 1080!

The final piece of steam tramway track was removed from Hotham Street in late 1960. Lengths were offered to the Transport Museum Society (Mr J.H. Price), Mr S.M. Swift (who really wanted the electrical tramways version) and the Curator of Historic Relics (Mr John Scholes). The TMS only wanted a shim but Mr Scholes wanted a 6 foot length (which cost him the princely sum of £1!) and Mr Swift took a smaller piece at ten shillings. The cost of removing the rail was £7 10s per ton by Messrs Midgley & Sons Ltd of Reservoir Road, Hull.

2.3 Original Specification – Electric Tramways
The lines for the electric tramways were also designed by the City Engineer. The rails were of centre groove section and weighed 96 lb per yard. Rail joints were at an angle of 45 degrees which meant that, when running over a joint, first one bearing surface followed by the other passed from rail to rail which involved less bumping and less noise than with a conventional rail joint. They were laid on stringers. The base foundation laid on the Humber clays was a layer of chalk, then an eight inch layer of broken stones and cement in which the ties for stringers were laid, the whole being toped with blocks of wood or stone.

The specification included information about the lines to be constructed:

	Single track	Double track
Old Town Route	695 linear yards	191 linear yards
Hessle Road Route		2830 linear yards
Anlaby Road Route		3430 linear yards
Beverley Road Route		3188 linear yards
Spring Bank Route		2163 linear yards
Holderness Road Route		3474 linear yards

The length of double track included about 91 linear yards of interlaced track. Cars on two or more routes would work over the Beverley Road section for 762 linear yards (Spring Bank cars) and the Anlaby Road section for 600 linear yards (Hessle Road cars). Note that the Hedon Road route was not included.

A handwritten insertion in the tender document that went to the Board of Trade stated that the gauge of the tramways was 4' 8½"!

Rails were to be bonded at every joint by at least two copper bonds, each having an area of not less than 0.25 square inch and to be cross-bonded at frequent intervals to comply with clauses 32 and 34 of the specification.

Also featured in Mr Turner's notebook were some details about the rails in use. Most were 60-foot lengths. Old sections of rails had a groove depth of 1 3/16" and were 96 lb per yard. Newer sections were of a 1½" depth and were 112 lb per yard. Sole plates were 20" x 8" and weighed 25 lb, fish plates on average were 42 lb per pair whilst the bolts for them weighed 1 lb 1¼oz, sole plates 1 lb 1oz and the holding down bolts were 2 lb 1oz.

2.4 The First Installation
The Railway World in August 1899 described the permanent way. It was the intention of the City Engineer, Mr A.E. White, "to secure not only a durable form of construction but also exceptionally smooth riding". He eschewed the usual way of laying rails directly on a concrete foundation opting instead to rest the rails upon longitudinal sleepers of creosoted redwood 4 inches deep by 7 inches wide. The concrete foundation on which the paving was laid was carried under the sleepers and the rails were bolted down through the sleepers to the underside of the concrete at 3ft 6in. intervals. The roadway was excavated to a depth of 12 inches which under the rails was increased to 17 inches to accommodate the sleepers.

On completion of the evacuations the sleepers were packed on bricks at the right level and clamped tight under the rails and secured to them. Holding down bolts and washers were put into position and, once the rails were carefully in place the foundation concrete was poured in. Care was taken to ensure that the foundation was tight under the sleepers. After the concrete had set the holding down bolts (14 inches long) were tightened up leaving the rail, sleepers and concrete as one.

The rails weighed 94 lb per yard and were 60 feet long with a centre groove of 15/16 of an inch wide, the head being 3¼ inches overall. It was anticipated that this would lead to even wear on both sides of the rails and avoid a projecting lip which became pronounced as the rails wore down. It was also to obtain continuous support for the car wheels when passing over joints that were splayed, when negotiating points and crossovers, and to increase the wearing surface of the head to increase the life of the rail.

Dimensions of the rail were:

• Depth 6 inches
• Width 3¼ inches
• Width of base 7 inches
• Width of groove ¹⁵⁄₁₆th of an inch
• Depth of groove 1¹⁄₁₆th inches

• Fishplates 24 inches long secured by six ⅞th of an inch bolts with square heads.

Additional support was given by a sole plate 20in. by 7in. by 5/8th of an inch at each joint. Rails were held in position by tie bars (1½in. by ½in.) at 6-foot intervals the tie bars being secured by a double nut at each end.

A foundation of 7 inches deep concrete extended over the whole of the width of the roadway. This was faced with cement composition, on which rested the wood pavement, which brought the surface of the road flush with the tread of the rails. The original proposal was to pave only a small part of the streets with wood, but the use of granite sets was abandoned so that tramways in the principal streets were to be all paved with wood.

The majority of the wood was by Jarrah and Karri but where traffic was lighter Baltic redwood was used. Some of this was "Haskinised" (application of liquid similar to creosate), but the greater part was creosoted. The hard wood was imported directly into Hull in planks, mostly 3in. by 9in. and then sawn into blocks 4 3/8th of an inch deep.

Did the design and performance meet its objectives? We can decide after reading the following report.

2.5 Track Maintenance Problems

On 16 February 1921 the City Engineer, Mr F.W. Bricknell, described the state of the permanent way after councillors had expressed concern with rising maintenance costs that were being experienced. His report began with a description of the original method of construction.

Most of the tracks coming under extensive repair were laid between 1898 and 1902 and the rails were on longitudinal creosoted timber stringers, which in turn rested on a concrete foundation, seven inches thick (later nine inches), and were anchored to the underside of the concrete by bolts 3ft 6in. apart. Rails were supported at the joints by sole plates, and were connected by heavy fish plates, the section of rails being such as enabled the fish plates to give exceptionally good support.

When the tramways were laid anchorage of the rails was exceptional and not normal practice, but experience found it be absolutely necessary. Indeed, several towns which laid rails without such an anchorage had to relay the rails to incorporate it at some expense. It was, however, recognised that renewal or heavy repairs would cause serious trouble, and many attempts to alleviate this had been made in Hull but without much material improvement. Nothing better had been devised in the way of bolted joints and he considered that nowhere had enjoyed as long a life as in Hull due in part to the centre groove and the diagonal cutting of the rail.

The ordinary wear of the rails had been beyond all expectation, and only about 100 straight rails had been renewed and although the car wheels, in many places, were running on the bottom of the groove it was found to be permissible until very considerable wear had taken place.

The first defects which developed were naturally at the joints where "hammering" took place. In the early stages this was remedied by wedging up the rail until the deepest indentation was at the correct level of the rail head and then dressed off the projecting portion. Eventually this weakened the rail and split at the bottom of the groove so that it became necessary to cut off the damaged ends of rails and replace with short lengths of new rail, which was expensive and also introduced additional joints.

Oxy-acetylene welding was introduced in 1916 and produced good results, but the durability of the repairs left something to be desired, and when additional plant became necessary an electric welder was purchased. This gave better results but could not be used when the cars were running, and men could be not kept continually on night work, with the result that both methods were being used at that time.

As time passed structural defects occurred at an increasing rate and all involved work at the concrete foundations. These were generally as follows:

1. The heads of the anchor bolts rusted off and created a "pumping" action, which let in water to the three bearing surfaces, and destroyed the carrying capacity of the subsoil. Later construction saw the heads surrounded by concrete
2. Under the vibratory action of traffic the concrete foundation had deteriorated or fractured, and even where the rails had remained fairly rigid the paving blocks had been displaced
3. As the clay subsoil had been deprived of its moisture, formerly received from the street surface, some shrinkage had occurred resulting in the concrete foundation losing its support. Where this process was uniform there was no great harm, but where it was not uniform not only the track but the paving and buildings had also been affected
4. In addition, the wood paving had become worn out. The hardwood had, in fact, reached the end of its working life and needed to be replaced with creosoted deal which would have double the life of the hardwood.

Mr Bricknell emphasised that once defects occurred it was essential to act quickly otherwise the track would deteriorate. With frequent price rises since the war delay in remedying any defects could be (and had been) costly. For the period ending December 1919 total cost on maintenance was £23,692 of which £5,800 was spent on paving blocks. The comparable period to December 1920 was £34,442 (£6,271 on paving). Some prices had stabilised but labour costs were still rising.

He asked councillors to consider carefully whether renewal was preferable to repair. The present cost of rail was £25 to £30, and the cost of replacing it was considerably more than repairs. Renewals were charged to the Reserve Fund which was shrinking in real terms. He had considered ways of reducing costs and had inspected Ingersoll compressed air equipment in Birmingham which had reduced repairs by 50% and A. Dorman's wave transmission apparatus. Either would be useful for Hull, and he favoured a trial to decide the most suitable. Purchase costs were £1,150 and £9,509 respectively.

Not until July 1922 was the City Engineer authorised to renew the Hessle Road track from Walker Street to Dairycoates at a cost of £29,000. In April 1924 a sum of £44,000 was approved for replacing track on Anlaby Road.

In 1923 Messrs Abraham Graham & Sons were awarded a contract for renewal work on Holderness Road, but there were many problems with the result that when the company tendered for renewal work on Princes Avenue and Spring Bank the City Engineer wrote the following on 10 December 1923:

"As I told you at our last interview I do not think there is the slightest prospect of your tender being accepted whatever the amount may be, and, after visiting Holderness Road this morning, I am more impressed than ever by the bad management and the disregard for the convenience of the practices".

This gives an idea of the difficulties faced by many tramway undertakings as the original track work became due for renewal. It also revealed advantages accruing from the use of centre grooved track, and showed that those who designed and laid the first tracks for electric tramways were in advance of the majority of undertakings. However, the trams had to be very healthy financially to bear the cost of renewals.

2.6 Special Track Work

Two pieces of special track work were fitted. Messrs Askham Brothers and Wilson of Sheffield supplied the point work for the Midland Street – Anlaby Road junction and for the level crossing at Boulevard on Anlaby Road. Special patterns had to be made for both railway and tramway rails. Owing to irregular construction these were difficult to manufacture and great care was necessary. Some of the pieces weighed 800 lb and they were bolted down on timber plates and concrete to create a thoroughly substantial structure capable of carrying the railway's heavy traffic. A spare set of crossings was provided in case of emergency. An angle of one in four was adopted for the crossovers. Marshall's patent joint strips were used in laying the points, the strips being laid on top of the rail and point flanges and bolted down.

The rails all over the lines were bonded at the joints with two or more Neptune bonds of 0.25 square inch section and were cross-bonded with bonds of 0.116 square inch sectional area. Bonding was carried out by Messrs Siemens Brothers and Company.

2.7 Track Maintenance Problems of the 1930s

A. Track Condition

The early 1930s saw the arrival of a new manager, Duncan Morrison, who in 1931 decided that expenditure on tramways must be kept to the absolute minimum. All expenditure on track work by the City Engineer was closely questioned by both councillors and Mr Morrison, who also wanted to assume responsibility for all track repairs, something that the City Engineer resisted. Matters came to a head in 1934 when Mr Morrison criticised track expenditure to the Transport Committee. This led to a number of meetings involving the two officers and the respective Chairmen of the Transport and Works Committees to resolve the situation.

The first meeting was held on 21 September 1934 and considered Mr Morrison's complaint that unnecessary expenditure had been incurred. When challenged by the City Engineer to say where this had occurred Mr Morrison referred to areas in Spring Bank where the service had had to be interrupted whilst works were carried out, something he considered was not necessary. The rail depressions could have been filled in using electric welding to save major expense in repairing joints. When haunches in the road were being repaired and the rail side exposed, thermit welding should be employed. In addition he said the cost of using electrolysis was prohibitive and suggested proper bonding of the rails in its place. He complained bitterly that the tramways gang's general practice to file bosses at the ends of a bond left a carbon deposit which prevented conductivity of the current taking place.

The City Engineer said that Mr Morrison should expect an increase in cost per car mileage owing to the reduction in car mileage (remember that routes AP, BC, DP and SWC had been withdrawn in July 1934). The normal working life of much of the permanent way was fast approaching its end and repairs would be necessarily higher. The City Engineer undertook to look at various ways of carrying out track repairs for another meeting.

Three days later the Highways Surveyor, W. H. Goldsmith sent a report which examined the various options to the City Engineer. It contained the following:

1(a) Welding of joints

Electric surface welding was used in every case where the joint was less than ½-inch down – if lower than that the joint had to be uncovered and packed, then surface welded to the spot and welded at the side.

1 (b) Thermit Welding

He had asked Murex Co. Ltd (now taken over Thermit Welding) for a price for joints at so much per joint as to buy plant would be prohibitive. The great danger of thermit welding was the liability of breaking in the rails themselves. It would be more successful when applied to a new job but he was not convinced that it was the right solution here.

2. Electrolysis

Bonding of rails had always been done by the City Engineer's staff. Bridging bonds were put in at the instructions of the Electrical Overhead Equipment Section – if the bonds had been omitted that was their fault!

3. Bonding

Bonding and packing of rails were always done at the same time but the Manager's claim that the bonding generally was bad was true. This is due to the fact that the rails were old. The suggestion that scrap overhead wires be used for bonding was futile as the department possessed enough new bonds for a year or two. He would not rule out the use of scrap wire after this time.

He agreed that bosses at the end of bosses were being filed (sic) but was necessary due to the use of old bonds in new holes. As only new bonds were being used, the complaint no longer held. The use of old bonds was an economy measure. It was impossible to knock out the bosses of a bond without damaging the ends to some extent. Before being put back they had to be filed into shape, but this would make a good electrical contact.

If any bond were knocked out of a rail which had been in position for three months a carbon deposit would be found even with a new bond.

4. Bitu-Grout

He had tried various forms of this but none were successful, as after a few months the bitumen grout had entirely disintegrated by the action of water and rail vibration. The only packing that had been successful had been cement and granite chips. This was only possible where traffic had been diverted in that particular section.

On 26 September 1934 the City Engineer wrote to Murex Welding Process Ltd for a quotation and informed them of the Corporation's centre groove rail where the angle of joint was 45 degrees, requiring a bigger weld than normal. The Corporation would open out to give Murex access and he asked that the Company should assume that 6 joints a day would be possible. Representatives from Murex visited Hull on 9 October to discuss the process and approach.

Murex said with the joints in the condition that they were, it would be essential to cut each joint square and insert a 15" to 16" closure, and if the rail was carried on wood stringers these would need to be replaced with concrete. The price was likely to be between £5 and £6 per joint as each would entail a double weld.

The company needed time to consider its approach to Hull's non-standard rails, but it immediately put in hand some experiments to decide what size of Thermit portion would be required. For this they were using pieces of Hull rail obtained on the visit. An example was posted to the Corporation.

Whilst in Hull its representatives had made a rapid examination of Hull's tracks and submitted an unsolicited report on their condition. It was evident that the diagonal joint had not prevented the effects of pounding in the joint, and the company representatives found joints where the dishing was over an eighth of an inch, and where the wear and tear of the running face of the joint were unequal. The effect of maintenance must be serious and this would, no doubt, reduce practicable car speeds. Many rails had developed longitudinal cracks in the web at the joints owing to the infiltration of water running into the rail groove.

The situation needed a radical solution. The Corporation could Thermit weld existing diagonal joints, and at the same time give a slight lift to the rail ends to make up the dishes. This would involve much grinding to restore a uniform rail level but this might prove impracticable in some cases and might not eliminate the cracks in the rail webs or at the groove bottom. Indeed the welding might extend the cracks.

Instead it recommended cutting off the ends of the rails in situ by means of a burner – a cut of about 9 inches on either side of the joint centre and therefore clear all fishplates and anchor bolt holes. The plate and rail ends would be removed plus the corresponding short length of timber stringer (which would have proved to have decayed anyway). A piece of rail about 18 inches long would be inserted and Thermit welded at both ends to give a continuous jointless track This length could be cut or burned out of any disused rails in stock.

A six-page quote arrived on 18 October 1934 which confirmed the need for a closer Thermit welding, and as the work was to be done at night between 11pm and 5am a trained welder could do six welds or three "closures" which would require the preparatory work to be undertaken the previous night by Corporation staff. The price was 35 shillings for 200 "closures" (400 welds). If the number rose above 500 welds in 12 months a rebate of 9d each would apply, whilst 750 welds would incur an additional 6d rebate. The cost in other towns had been just under £5 per weld. If the Corporation wanted to do its own work plant hire would be 25/- per week, rail planes 37/- per dozen, hand files 23/- per dozen, and magnesia thimbles 7/9 per dozen.

Meanwhile the City Engineer and Mr Morrison had agreed to experiment with Thermit welding in Carr lane after Christmas 1934, and Princes Avenue (and later on parts of Anlaby Road). It was also agreed to hire plant from Murex and to train men in the process, but the City Engineer refused to allow these to be Transport department staff. Murex complied reluctantly claiming that on its visit it had been guaranteed much more work. Subsequently two men were trained by Murex and later inspection by its senior staff of work carried out in Witham showed them to be very competent.

The City Engineer wrote to Murex in March 1935 to state that the welders were getting 2½ to 3 reactions from the thimbles as Murex had claimed that 3 would be the norm. Murex undertook to look at this.

However, in October 1935 the City Engineer wrote to Murex to inform them that the Transport Committee had decided to replace the tramways with trolleybuses and that, in view of the probable limited life of the rails it would discontinue Thermit welding. The company agreed to take back the equipment and any remaining stocks of materials, and thanked the Corporation for the work and the courtesy and willing assistance extended to its employees by the Corporation.

B. Costs

Mr Morrison's criticism of the costs of repairs and the high stock of material held by the City Engineer had been addressed. The Stores and Workshops Sub-Committee visited Stepney Lane Depot to view the material and to decide, given the change in policy, what might be surplus and therefore sold off. The result was submitted to the Transport Committee on 23 July 1934.

The report listed every piece of stock at 31 March 1934. The stock was valued at £5268 14s 8d and included:

- 28 points worth £512 0s 3d
- 8 crossings worth £255 10s 3d
- 3137 fishplates at £632

- 1729 sole plates worth £345 and rails as described below worth £2953 16s

The rails comprised the following:

- 190 tons 12cwt of new section 112 lb @ £12 10s per ton = £2377 10s 0d
- 31 tons 0cwt of new section 112 lb (undrilled) at £12 per ton = £372 0s 0d
- 15 tons 18cwt of new section (various lengths) at £9 10s 0d per ton = £151 3s 0d
- 6 tons 13cwt old section (various lengths) at £8 0s 0d per ton = £53 3s 0d

Such a large stock was a result of the necessity of having to place a minimum order of 500 tons of rail with Messrs Bolcker, Vaughan & Co in August 1927. Some were intended for the Spring Bank West extension (6 furlongs 5.30 chains), and Calvert Lane tramway between Anlaby Road and Spring Bank West (3 furlongs 1.30 chains), which were never built but would have required 396 tons. Subsequently 145 tons had been used on the Holderness Road extension (unlikely as this opened in September 1925), Alfred Gelder Street renewals (72 tons), the new North Bridge (72 tons), and a new siding at Holderness Road Car Shed (18 tons). It was agreed to invite tenders for any surplus material and this was sold to F. W. Ward of Sheffield.

The City Engineer turned his attention to costs and provided to a meeting involving the chairmen and officials the following costs:

Year ending 31 March	£
1930	16,937
1931	17,350
1932	17,795
1933	14,022
1934	14,937
Period ending 15/8/34	4,068 (corresponding period in 1933 was £7,336)

The current track comprised 19 miles 1 furlong 0.54 chains of double track, 1 mile 2 furlongs 7.10 chains of depot track, and 2 furlongs of single track, amounting to 20.65 miles at a cost of £630 per mile.

Very little track had been lifted so some repairs were still necessary to maintain the track in a safe condition, and the reduction in car mileage did not affect permanent way costs. Staff employed on permanent way work had been reduced as follows:

	April 1924	September 1928	September 1934
Foreman	1	1	1
Platelayers/gangers	10	7	7
Welders	4	1	1
Paviors	13	9	4
Labourers	24	21	15
	52	39	28

If any of these men worked on non-tramway work the cost was debited to the appropriate Committee. The Transport Manager's impression that withdrawn track incurred an immediate reduction in permanent way expenses was unfounded, since not until the track was removed would expenditure cease. P.W. costs would actually rise as track got older and reached the end of its working life. The City Engineer provided a weekly

222

programme of proposed track repairs for the Transport Manager, and he or his staff could ask about any of the work on the list that was considered unnecessary. This had not taken place. No estimate of cost was provided because it wouldn't help him! (Very patronising and perhaps defensive and not wanting to show the cost in case he had to justify it.)

Despite Mr Morrison's recommendation in 1931 to keep expenditure to a minimum, very little was done to replace the trams. It took three years to replace the outer routes and it was another two years before trolleybus substitution was agreed, by which time he had gone to Bournemouth. Not until July 1937 did trolleybus operation commence. Even if the original trolley-bus conversion programme's timescale had been carried out it would have been late 1941 before the last tram ran. Was it reasonable to think that expenditure on track could be minimised for such a long period? On the other hand his strictures did result in some changes in practice that might not otherwise have occurred.

2.8 Track Mileages

For many years the annual report and accounts contained details of the mileage for each route. The following table is taken from the 1914-1915 version and shows the track statistics at 31 March 1915.

Actual length of tramways			Route	Route letter	Normal length of run		
M	Fur	Ch			M	Fur	Ch
			Anlaby Road route				
0	2	5.11	Victoria Square to Midland Street Jcn				
1	4	7.45	Midland Street to Terminus	A	1	7	2.56
0	1	2.39	Extra lengths *				
2	0	4.95					
			Hessle Road Route				
0	2	5.11	Victoria Square to Midland Street Jcn				
1	5	3.11	Midland Street to Terminus	D	1	7	8.22
(0	0	1.11)	(less half length single line Midland St)				
0	0	4.17	Extra lengths				
1	5	6.17					
0	5	8.68	**D terminus to Pickering Park**	DP	2	3	6.50
0	0	4.17	Extra lengths		(0	5	8.28)
			Holderness Road Route via North Br.				
0	4	2.50	Savile Street to Great Union Street				
0	2	4.99	Great Union Street to Dansom Lane	H	2	3	4.81
1	4	7.32	Dansom Lane to Terminus				
0	0	9.37	Extra lengths				
2	4	4.36					
			Spring Bank Route				
0	3	3.16	King Edward St to Prospect St Jcn				
1	7	2.73	Prospect St to Terminus	S	2	2	5.80
0	0	9.37	Extra lengths				
2	3	5.26	#				
			Spring Bank West Route				
1	0	3.60	King Edward St to Botanic Crossing				
0	4	5.23	Botanic Crossing to terminus	S/W	1	4	8.83
0	0	0.21	Extra Lengths				
0	4	5.44					
			Beverley Road Route				
0	3	3.16	King Edward St to Prospect Street Jcn				
1	3	2.37	Prospect Street Jcn to Newland	B	1	6	5.53
0	1	8.41	Newland to terminus Cottingham Road				
0	1	1.27	Extra lengths				
1	6	2.05					
			Hedon Road Route				
0	4	2.50	Savile Street to Great Union St Jcn				
2	2	3.49	Great Union Street to Marfleet Avenue	M and M/A	2	6	5.99
0	0	5.94	Extra lengths				
2	2	9.43					
			Old Town Route				
0	2	0.68	Junction Street to Lowgate				
0	3	6.96	Lowgate to Nelson Street	P	0	5	7.64
0	0	5.18	Extra lengths				
0	6	2.82					
			Holderness Road via Old Town				
0	2	0.38	Victoria Square to Lowgate				
0	4	6.83	Lowgate to Dansom Lane Jcn	T/H	2	3	4.53
1	4	7.32	Dansom Lane Jcn to Terminus				
0	0	2.47	Extra lengths				
0	4	9.30					

Actual length of tramways			Route	Route letter	Normal length of run		
M	Fur	Ch			M	Fur	Ch
			Total length of runs		18	6	2.28
15	4	8.46	**Total length of double track**				
31	1	6.92	Total length of tramways in street measured as single track				
1	7	4.97	Length of single track at car sheds				
33	1	1.89	**Grand total of single track**				

Key = * extra length in crossovers, connection to car shed (where applicable) etc
# Length from Botanic Crossing to Walton Street
M = Miles
Fur = Furlongs
Ch = Chains
Jcn = Junction

2.9 International Road Congress in Seville – Spring 1923

In July 1922 the City Engineer of Liverpool wrote to Mr Bricknell (City Engineer), and informed him that he had been invited to present a paper on different methods of constructing and locating permanent way for tramways, and asking Mr Bricknell if he would kindly assist with his comments.

Mr Bricknell's reply, which including drawings of Hull's rails and routes, was interesting. If any further tramways were made in paved streets he would alter the anchorage and probably discontinue the use of wooden stringers. He considered that the continued use of welding would lead to a new design of joint. He mentioned that Hull's track was based on developments by Mr Deacon in Liverpool. He would modify track to use a flat sole-plate instead of a channel bar, as flanges were found to interfere with the tightening of the fish bolts.

He had not laid any tracks away from the road but had prepared plans for an extension beyond the city boundary where the City Council was not prepared to widen the road. On any further extensions he would place the extensions alongside the highway rather than in the centre. (Subsequently, the Anlaby Road extension was laid along the southern side of the road but, despite a Committee resolution to continue in this vein, further extensions clung to the middle of the road).

In addition he considered Hull's rails had been very successful, with over six million car miles per mile of track having gone over them before any significant renewal. Only a very few rails had been re-laid before 1921, despite the fact that most dated back to 1898 and carried trams at three minute headways. Much importance attached to wooden stringers, but he considered the life of rails was due entirely to the secure anchorage which the centre groove and diagonal joints had prolonged the life of the joints. One 1911 mile of track had had nothing spent on it until June 1921. He considered that track laid in paving was cheaper and better than being laid on ballast.

3. THE BRIDGE INDICATORS IN QUEEN VICTORIA SQUARE AND HOLDERNESS ROAD

As mentioned in chapter 6 – bridge indicators were installed to permit Holderness Road (and to a lesser degree) Hedon Road trams to cope with the closures of North Bridge and Drypool (Saltshouse Lane) Bridge, and to avoid long delays. Various suggestions about turning short and transferring passengers by foot across the bridge had been rejected and the new indicators were the result.

The installation comprised two controllers and four double indicators, the controllers being a multiple-contact, sector shaped switch which was worked by a double handle on its axis and was connected by steel rods to an oil dashpot, to a cut-off switch and a lever with an adjustable counterweight. This switch had six contacts that made and broke circuit with suitable spring controlled fingers, that gave a quick break, this being assisted by a magnetic blow-out system.

The dashpot had a cylinder totally immersed in an oil-filled copper tank, the lower half of the cylinder having a valve to regulate the flow of oil. The piston had cup leathers and an internal foot-valve of a mushroom type which allowed the easy flow of oil through the piston on the downward stroke, but closing on the upstroke when oil could only gain admission to the lower part of the cylinder. A gauze filter was fitted so that the oil delivered over the top edge of the cylinder on the upstroke was filtering before entry to the lower part of the tank to avoid any chance of blocking the valve.

The cut-off switch was of a drum type operated by a loose lever attached to the main switch which closed the circuit when the main handle was turned on to its full extent in a clockwise direction. The cut-off switch was held in this closed position during the slow return stroke of the main switch by a gravity controlled device. When the return stroke of the main switch was completed the device was raised and the cut-off switch opened.

In order to operate the indicators before the opening or closing of a bridge, the controller handle was merely turned as far as it would travel in a clockwise direction, and released. This raised the counterweight, forced the dashpot piston to the bottom of its cylinder, and closed the cut-off switch.

A series of three 200-volt 16 candle-power lamps was fitted inside each controller case which were lit up whilst the cut-off switch was closed. This indicated to the operator that the equipment was working. One such controller was fitted in a polished wood case in the bridge master's office at North Bridge, with another in a cast-iron street pillar on Drypool Bridge close to the hydraulic gear of each bridge. Four double indicators were fixed at points where the alternative bridge routes converged. These comprised a watertight wooden case secured to tramway poles, each having an indicator to Drypool Bridge and one for North Bridge. The front of each indicator was of plate glass, the upper part of which had the name of the bridge written in white on an opaque back ground. Below this a clear space through a moveable blind could be shown, and the lower part of the panel carried the words "to land traffic" inscribed.

Each indicator had two aluminium rollers upon which was fitted a translucent blind with a series of phrases which were visible through the glass, and were read in context with the fixed lettering to indicate the availability or otherwise of the bridge concerned.

The wording on the blinds contained the following information:

Normally the indicator read "Bridge OPEN to land traffic".
When the controller was operated the reading changed to "bridge OPEN, will close in 3 minutes to land traffic".

This would change at successive half-minutes intervals until "will close in 1 minute" was shown.

After the one minute expired the indicator changed to "bridge CLOSED to land traffic", the word CLOSED having red letters.

When the bridge was to be thrown open to land traffic a similar series of indicator readings was displayed but substituting "Closed" and "will open" for "Open" and "will close", the blind running back to its original position.

The operating gear comprised an electromagnet with a moveable core which activated a pawl engaging a twelve-toothed ratchet wheel which was rotated through 30 degrees at each current impulse from the controller. This wheel was mounted on a shaft at the other end of which was a gear wheel with 150 teeth, the wheel being mounted on ball bearings on the shaft with a pawl fitted to it through which the drive was transmitted to the wheel by a cam upon the shaft.

This wheel engaged a 25-tooth pinion fixed to the upper blind roller so that the roller made half a turn for each stroke of the magnet. The blind was wound upon the upper roller about seven inches for each controller impulse in order to show the relevant part of the blind. The lower roller had a small drum at one end from which a cord was fastened to a counterweight to keep the blind taut.

It is believed that the system was still in operation in the late twenties but was rendered redundant by a Committee decision not to allow the diversions to continue, a curious decision (not unusual in Hull) that did little to improve punctuality and consequential late running.

Appendix 4

Depots, Workshops and Power Station

1. INTRODUCTION

Information regarding depots and workshops is taken from The Directory of British Tram Depots by K. Turner, S. Smith and P. Smith, from various Committee minutes, maps produced for publications, R.J. Buckley, Ordnance Survey sheets for Hull and, where appropriate, from photographs. Additional information has come from the local archives in the History Centre and Streetlife Museum.

I have not covered the subsequent history of those premises that were sold or rented out after ceasing to be used in a tramways capacity other than to record any demolition or disposal dates (where known).

2. THE HULL STREET TRAMWAYS COMPANY LTD

2.1 Hessle Road

Opened in 1877 this was located on the north side of Hessle Road near the junction with Regent Street. It is thought that it comprised, originally, two timber built sheds and stables with four roads. This was the largest depot on the system and was also the location for the main stores. Buckley gives a capacity of 61 horses after extensions in September 1879 which included building over the former open yard at the front. The site included a granary and store as well as space for saddles and a blacksmith's shop and shoeing area.

Further extensions took place in 1882 when the original car shed was extended into the stables. A fifth road was added at the side, a new 30ft inspection pit was installed and a disagreement with the Works Committee about the building line was weathered.

Fire destroyed the premises in December 1887 but, fortunately, all the cars and animals were saved. Not until mid-1888 was rebuilding completed. The new building contained four roads with space for around 20 cars and there was an inspection pit, workshops and a two-storey stable (52 horses on the first floor and 45 on the ground floor).

It was closed in May 1898 when work was in progress on converting the Hessle Road route to electric traction. No longer extant.

2.2 Holderness Road

This opened in 1882 and was situated on the southern side of Holderness Road opposite Jalland Street. When first constructed Jesmond Gardens was not made up and the entrance was through a door in the side wall. However, when the street was brought up to highway standards a new door was formed at the end of the side wall. The tracks within the shed ran parallel with the street, perhaps a legacy of the original entrance arrangements but also in the same way as Temple Street was laid out. Behind the tracks were the stables and office.

Closure came in 1900 when the Holderness Road route was being reconstructed.

2.3 Scarborough Street

R.J. Buckley refers to temporary stables being located on the west side of Scarborough Street when the Hessle Road route opened in 1877. The stables were situated beyond the original terminus at West Dock Avenue. No further details are known.

2.4 Temple Street

Located on the north side of Temple Street (off Beverley Road) this depot replaced the Terry Street depot in 1882. It was a brick built 3 road straight shed with one doorway that served as entrance and exit. It closed on 30 October 1899 when Hull's last horse tram entered its doors, although Charles Dyson claims that date to be November. The roads ran parallel with the walls in the same way as Holderness Road Depot. It was demolished on an unknown date.

2.5 Terry Street

This was located on the northern corner of Beverley Road and Terry Street on land owned by the North Eastern Railway and was a timber built building dating from 1877. The Beverley Road trams had started in 1875 and it is not known where cars and horses were housed at that time. It is not certain whether it possessed one or two roads but it was a straight shed with access and exit at the front. Closure came in 1882 when it was replaced by Temple Street Depot.

2.6 Witham

This was located on the southern side of Witham west of the Dansom Lane/Clarence Street junction. When opened on 7 May 1877 there was no track connection with the street tramway and trams had to be hauled across the road and pavement until the Corporation instructed the company to stop! Originally timber, it was rebuilt in brick in 1880. There was space for only two cars and sixteen horses. It was replaced by Jesmond Gardens in 1882. No longer extant.

3. THE DRYPOOL AND MARFLEET STEAM TRAMWAYS COMPANY LTD

3.1 Hotham Street

The depot was located on the west side of Hotham Street off Hedon Road and opened on 21 May 1889 although it had been completed before that date. It comprised two sheds, one with two roads and the other with three roads and workshops both being brick built and large enough to accommodate the entire fleet under cover. As Hotham Street was very narrow the curve from the street swung outwards before turning inwards to the depot fans.

The manager's house adjoined the entrance on Hotham Street in front of the shed access tracks. In addition there were stores and repair facilities since the majority of work would have to be carried out on site. As a ground rent of £72 was paid it would appear that the company did not own the land.

Closure came on 13 January 1901. The City Engineer decided that it was unsuitable for conversion for electric trams.

It was used by Messrs Ellison, Cordingley & Co. (who were given two months to complete the work) for scrapping cars and engines before being let to commercial users. Some of the track remained in situ until road works in 1960.

4. CITY OF HULL TRAMWAYS
It was decided at an early date that depots should be constructed on four of the six proposed routes (Hedon Road was a later addition). This would greatly facilitate traffic arrangements and reduce to a minimum any waste mileages.

4.1 Cottingham Road
Construction by Joseph Fenwick started in late 1908. Opened on 13 March 1909 on the north side of Cottingham Road, it replaced Stepney Lane Depot. It comprised an eight road straight shed with access and exit via a narrow opening (16 feet wide by 18 feet six inches high) on Cottingham Road. The two centre roads ran through the shed before terminating in the open outside the rear of the shed. Two long repair pits were provided, one along the two westernmost roads, the other along the two easternmost roads. A large clock was located above the staff entrance facing Cottingham Road. Large ornamental gates were provided on the Cottingham Road frontage, the middle two for trams being 12' 4½" wide (inward opening) which were flanked by two gates for crews each 3' wide. Extensions for motorbuses were added in 1925. The original shed was 347' 10" long and the extension was 152' 1" long on the western side but only 124' 11" long on the eastern side, the angular connecting wall being 104' long. Pits were located on the eastern wall. Trams ceased to use it after 3 September 1938. The original single storey office block became a two storey one in 1925. The depot was demolished in the 1990s and replaced with housing but the office block continues to exist as an office in 2010.

4.2 Hedon Road
This opened on 17 December 1903 on the northern side of Hedon Road adjoining the original terminus. It had four roads and one through road along with an external through road alongside the eastern wall. In many respects both in layout and design it matched the earlier Holderness Road depot. It measured 340' long by 47' wide. Closure came on 31 December 1937 although it did not appear to have been operational for some time and had been used for storing withdrawn trams and buses. About 100' at the front was damaged by bombing in World War II. A scheme exists (dated 1947) showing plans to demolish the damaged front portion, rebuild and use it (capacity 20 vehicles) but no further information has come to light. It is still in use for caravan manufacturing in 2009.

4.3 Holderness Road (temporary)
When it was realised that the depot for the Holderness Road route would not be ready in time a temporary timber depot was erected near Summergangs Road on the northern side of the road. It opened on 10 April 1900 but its short life ended on 27 March 1903 when the new depot near Aberdeen Street opened and the site reverted to the Parks Department,

4.4 Holderness Road
The original depot was constructed by local builder Geo Houlton Ltd and opened on 27 March 1903 on the southern side of Holderness Road near Aberdeen Street. It had a single line narrow entrance from Holderness Road which passed, just inside the shed, between offices and stores on the right and the men's room on the left before fanning out into four through roads all of which became a single track at the rear of the shed. This single line left the shed at the rear and was connected to another single line which ran alongside the depot's external wall to join the tracks in Holderness Road itself. The two westernmost roads were carried over inspection pits approximately two-thirds of the length of the shed. The original shed was 280 feet long and 47 feet wide and had an elegant and elaborate façade. The extension which was built alongside the original was shorter at 197 feet in length and was 40 feet wide. This had three roads with a single entrance from Holderness Road and a rear single exit track which was also connected to the exit track from the original.

At some point, date unknown, extensive sidings comprising eight roads were installed at the rear of the depot. Photographs from the 1930s show several trams apparently withdrawn and with windows and other equipment removed and a general air of neglect with grass growing through the sleepers. It is thought that trams ceased to use the depot some time in 1939 as cars were being provided by Anlaby Road Depot by the summer at least. After use as a trolleybus and motorbus depot it was closed in 1986 and was subsequently demolished being replaced with a supermarket.

4.5 Liverpool Street
The first building at Liverpool Street was 236 ft long by 66' 6" wide and 22' high. There were six tracks with pits extending clear across the depot at each end. Rails were carried over the pits on cast-iron columns which provided plenty of room and permitted free movement from car to car. It was spacious and well lit with large windows at the rear end and sky lights in the roof. Space for forty five cars was available. The original shed was set back from Liverpool Street itself. Cars used an S-shaped single line to enter and leave the shed through ornate double gates and to pass a single storey office block comprising stores, an office and a "workmen's room" access to all three being through a shared entrance on Liverpool Street itself. A small toilet block with external access only was provided at the rear of the office building. There was no physical connection with the running shed. A separate gate was provided for staff. Pointwork for the first two internal tracks started outside the wide main doors giving two sharp curves at least.

At an unknown date the toilet block was demolished and relocated to the south of the office block in preparation for an extension in the area between the original shed and Liverpool Street. The line into the extension passed around the back of offices and fanned into three paralleled lines into the Blacksmith's Shop and then into the paint shop. The end wall extended beyond the line of the original shed.

In 1915 an additional building was constructed between the original shed and Manchester Street on its western side. This became the main workshops with one entrance/exit track but there were two other paralleled tracks within the shed with access via a traverser. An overhead platform at the rear of the shed was also provided.

The original running depot retained the tram rails well into the 1980s. The original workshop constructed later became a fitting shop and the overhead crane in the workshops also lasted into the 1980s. Temporary sheds were erected when the first cars were delivered during 1898 as Anlaby Road was not ready.

A reporter from the Hull Times visited Liverpool Street in November 1923 and wrote a short piece about the workshops. The 138 men were in the charge of Mr Brooker who had worked on the Bombay electric car system. The shops contained a moulding shop and a small well-equipped brass foundry which had opened after Mr Rayner became the general manager. The foundry contained ordinary drop furnaces with forced draught and coke fuel. Only two people worked in there of which one was an apprentice. Previously everything (including brass thrusts, trolley wheels, insulators, double pull-offs and other overhead line parts) had been purchased locally or from a specialist firm in Bristol at twice the cost. Scrap brass was no longer sold but was melted down and moulded into new material. Nothing was made at Liverpool Street if it could be bought cheaper elsewhere. The electrical department undertook repairs to coils, re-winding motors etc and re-wiring cars.

He considered the premises to be bright, healthy and hygienic. There were five fires in the blacksmith's shop under the foreman, Mr Bratley who oversaw three other smiths and four strikers. Stanchions for the trams cost 6s 6d to make in the workshops compared with 15s from private companies. Other items included trolley cord eye-bolts and star-fish clips, the latter taking no more than six minutes to manufacture. The clips were used for clamping down on the car springs instead of old-fashioned pins where were constantly wearing out. It is believed that they were Foreman Bratley's idea.

In the joiners' shop he saw old cars (some a quarter of a century old) being fitted with handsome and modern vestibules with all service cars soon to be modernised in this way. An immense quantity of teak was used for the heavier parts of the cars. As much work as possible was carried out using machinery with only the fitting together being done by hand. Eleven fitters, two drillers, three turners and two sheet metal workers were employed on this work.

Trams ceased to use it operationally after 30 June 1945 although some cars were in residence until collected by Leeds CT or removed for scrap or delivery to a local holiday camp. The entire building was demolished in the late 1990s and a large supermarket and access road now occupies the site.

4.6 Stepney Lane

Opened in 1900 this was always viewed as a temporary/short term shed which served the Beverley Road and Spring Bank routes until replaced with the larger Cottingham Road depot in March 1909. The City Engineer's Department used it until the 1980s.

4.7 Anlaby Road

This was situated on the south side of Anlaby Road between the railway line and Wheeler Street. It was thought that this opened on 5 July 1899 but contemporary accounts show that it was not completed in time although some cars were assembled there earlier in the year. It was originally an L-shaped dead-end shed with access and exit via a single line of track from Anlaby Road which passed the offices, stores and mess room. It was 228 feet long on the western side and 182 feet on the eastern side and contained three tracks but four in the base of the "L" where the inspection pits were located. Access to the four inspection tracks was from the track which ran along the inside of the western road that paralleled the railway line. The side of the "L" was 46 feet long whilst the end wall was 116 feet wide. Double wooden doors were fitted but I have found no record of any gates that might have been fitted at the entry from Anlaby Road.

It was extended in 1910 when a further 24 places were provided and a new entrance was provided from Wheeler Street, the track work costing just over £1,000. There was one through road (the westernmost track being extended to run the length of the extended depot) with a fan of sidings. The additional capacity involved relocating the stores and offices. The City Engineer suggested entry by Wheeler Street and exit by the existing doorway to ensure that trams were turned round each day to reduce wear on their tyres. Trams ceased to use it after 5 September 1942. Most of the depot was demolished in 2007 although one wall remains in situ as does a short stretch of track from the depot exit to Anlaby Road.

Early references in official minutes and reports refer to Anlaby Road Depot. When the extension was built with the entrance in Wheeler Street some reports referred to Wheeler Street Depot but the majority of references (including Mr Turner) used Anlaby Road Car Shed.

5. ELECTRIC TRAMWAYS DEPOT CAPACITY AND USE. THIS LIST COMES FROM MR TURNER'S NOTEBOOK

Depot	Capacity	Monday-Friday	Saturday	Sunday
		Cars in Use		
Cottingham Road	78	44	51	33
Hedon Road	40	12	12	10
Holderness Road	48	23	29	20
Liverpool Street	38	24	30	21
Wheeler Street	50	33	39	25
	254	136	161	109

Notes

1. Hedon Road's capacity far exceeded any possible service provision – it is possible that the workmen's cars that served the shipyards and docks were stabled here during the day but no definite evidence of this has come to light
2. Holderness Road comprised the Old Shed (30) and Extension (18)
3. Liverpool Street comprised Running Depot (28) and Old Shed (10) plus the workshops and paintshop
4. Fleet size was 179 in the mid 1920s
5. Wheeler Street was used for stabling football and rugby special cars during the game
6. Capacity at Liverpool Street is lower than the capacity of the original running shed.

6. THE GENERATING STATION

1. Introduction

The decision to build a separate power station (or generating station as it was officially entitled) was not a foregone conclusion. Indeed the combination of a lighting and traction station was considered and the specifications for electrical equipment allowed for the submission of tenders for the provision of a new and independent station or the development of the existing municipal electricity works at Sculcoates.

In the event the decision was based partly on the unfavourable location of the city's existing station at Sculcoates alongside the River Hull whereas the tramways' own station could be built in Osborne Street in the centre of the city near the hub of the system.

A plain but imposing brick building with stone dressings was designed by the City Engineer. Inside the walls were lined with white glazed bricks to a height of six feet. It is thought that the original dimension of the station were 107 feet by 83 feet. The boiler room of 83 feet by 63 feet contained four Lancashire boilers of 360 horse power supplied By Messrs E. Danks Ltd of Oldbury. They were fired by Vicars' mechanical stokers driven from a shaft connected by worm gear to a 4½ brake horse power electric motor made by Thomas Parker Ltd.

Feed water was taken from the city mains, softened and filtered into a storage tank of 7,000-gallon capacity or delivered through an economiser (from Messrs Greens with 256 pipes) or direct to the boilers by pumps which were activated by an 8 horse power Parker electric motor. Speed of the motor could range from 250 to 800 revolutions per minute. Boiler working pressure was 150 lb and against this pressure the pump could deliver 1,700 gallons of water per hour.

Steam piping from the main steam range, the cast-iron exhaust piping to the condenser and the alternative discharge to the atmosphere were supplied by the Hull firm of Messrs Rose, Downs and Thompson who also supplied water tanks, water softener and feed water filter.

The engine and dynamo room measured 83 feet by 44 feet and contained three generating sets consisting of a Siemens bi polar traction dynamo (H.B.30/40) coupled to a Belliss patent three crank self-lubricating compound engine. Each dynamo gave 550 ampères at 500-550 volts. Dynamos and engines were capable of carrying a full load to a maximum of 50 per cent in excess of the normal for short periods. The engines were of the ordinary double-acting type to which every driver (in a power station) was accustomed and were distinguished by having few working parts. Self-lubrication provided a constant supply of oil under pressure to prevent knocking and to ensure quiet running. This was a particular requirement as the Corporation wished not to intrude on what was a crowded business centre within the city.

Messrs Belliss and Morcom also supplied a motor-driven condensing plant comprising a surface condenser with 2,000 square feet of cooling surface and two single acting air pumps driven by Siemens enclosed type motors through worm reducing gear. Condensing water was taken from the almost adjacent Princes Dock and after use was returned to the dock.

Some writers have questioned the decision to construct and operate a separate power station for the tramways but contemporary reports and articles were in favour. Indeed the Railway World in August 1899 said the provision of "what is now conceded to be the preferable plan of providing a separate station for the tramways" was the right decision. It also stated that running costs would probably compare very favourably with any other station in the country.

Whilst the location seemed advantageous for the power station the owner of the Grosvenor Hotel on Carr Lane whose rear boundary ran alongside the installation was less than enthusiastic. There appears to have been a continuing exchange of letters between the owner, Mr J. E. Foster, and the City Engineer regarding noise and smoke from the station.

In October 1910 Mr Foster claimed that it was becoming increasingly difficult to let back rooms to all but the most deepest of sleepers. Dirt from the chimney was adding considerably to the cleaning bill and the back rooms had to be cleaned more often and thoroughly than those at the front. He complained on 14 October about excessive vibration from 4am on the previous morning which had lasted for an hour. No one was able to sleep. One guest had told him that if he had an enemy or someone to whom he would do a real bad turn he would put him in room 51!

The City Engineer said that the recent nuisance was the result of some special emergency work during the night. He contended that the station's own chimney was innocent and that the hotel's back chimney (which perhaps Mr Foster could not see!) frequently "vomits more smoke than the power station"! He also stated that he had instructed the men that no hammering should take place during the night except in an emergency.

Apparently, the hotel and other businesses had complained of some subsidence as a result of the vibration but it is not clear if this was resolved.

Accidents within the power station were not unknown, some being serious. In April 1906 Fireman A. Smith was closing a damper when the balancing weight became dislodged and dropped on his left foot resulting in the amputation of his big toe. On 4 November 1907 a blacksmith experienced a crushed finger but, after attention, continued at work!

At some point before November 1912 a workshop area at the western end of the Osborne Street frontage was converted into a depot for two tower wagons with some adjoining small rooms allocated to the overhead line department.

Various alterations and additions were undertaken during its life. New boilers (6 and 7) were added in 1906 and a new engine condensing plant was installed by G. Jackson and Sons in 1909 as was a new pump house. The amount of glazing was increased and improved in 1906 also. Various improvements took place in 1912.

Although the station was coal fired there were several occasions when supplies were interrupted by disputes in the coal industry. One such occasion was January 1912 and in order to maintain tramway services the City Engineer decided to convert 2/3 boilers with liquid fuel burners on the Holden System. He obtained a supply of 600 gallons of oil tar from the British Gas Light Company on Sculcoates Lane in Hull. The use of this fuel continued until 17 March 1912.

Appendix 5

Level Crossings and Bridges

1. INTRODUCTION

At its peak in 1870 Hull endured twenty-three railway (level) crossings, a legacy in many ways of Hull's flat landscape location. As early as 1867 the Corporation tried to persuade the NER to replace them with bridges and, indeed, in 1871 work started on replacing the Park Street crossing just outside Paragon Station. In 1887 a bridge replaced the crossing in Argyle Street. Today, just three crossings remain at Walton Street, St George's Road and Hawthorn Avenue.

Horse trams crossed the rails at Stepney (Beverley Road), Southcoates (Holderness Road) and Boulevard (Anlaby Road) but stopped short at Dairycoates (Hessle Road), the little used Newington (Anlaby Road) and Botanic Gardens (Spring Bank) crossings. Steam trams were confronted by just one level crossing on Hedon Road. However, the steam trams were affected by the lifting of both North Bridge and Salthouse Lane Bridge even though they crossed neither. Complaints regarding the time taken by trains to negotiate the crossings were rife in both horse and steam tram days. There was no legal restriction on the time that the crossing gates could be closed to road traffic.

Other obstacles were the lifting bridges at Whitefriargate between Queens Dock and Princes Dock and North Bridge over the River Hull. Whitefriargate Bridge was operated by the NER and was not usually to be opened between the hours of 9am and 6pm except to pass vessels to or from the sea and then could only be lifted so as to allow ten clear minutes from the time when the bridge was lowered to the departure of a train from Paragon Station. In July 1907, in the electric era another, Drypool Bridge (Salthouse Lane Bridge as it was then described) was crossed by the "TH" route from Holderness Road via Clarence Street and Alfred Gelder Street.

Electric tram extensions took the Anlaby Road cars across Newington crossing, the Hessle Road cars across Dairycoates, and the Spring Bank route across Botanic Gardens and up to the Walton Street crossing. The proposed Spring Bank West extensions would have crossed the Walton Street and Waterworks crossings, whilst the proposed Hawthorn Avenue extension would have also crossed the railway. The LNER placed an order for equipment for the Waterworks crossing, some of which was to be financed by Hull Corporation for the provision of gates and signals. It is not known if these were installed. The initial Stoneferry proposals might have involved a level crossing as well as a lifting bridge at Clough Road, depending on the timing of the construction.

When the First World War broke out in August 1914 the Corporation had commenced discussions with the North Eastern Railway regarding the abolition of the Dairycoates crossing. These were suspended and it was to be another decade before any serious attempts were made to consider the level crossing issue.

In the late 1920s discussions with the London and North Eastern Railway (successor to the North Eastern) reached such an advanced stage that a Parliamentary Bill was proposed which would lead to the replacement of the main road crossings. Unfortunately a Town's Meeting in January 1930 rejected the proposals, as did a poll of electors shortly thereafter. Not until the early 1960s were the Dairycoates and Boulevard crossings replaced with bridges ("flyovers" in local parlance)

2. THE LEVEL CROSSINGS

The electric trams had to negotiate six crossings and were affected by a seventh at Walton Street. Special crossings of crucible cast steel were manufactured by Messrs Askham Brothers & Wilson of Sheffield. Tram signals were worked mechanically in the lower quadrant with a vertical operating rod placed inside a hollow post for safety reasons (mischief is not new!). Signals were electrically lit, an innovation for the time. The rod connected with an angle crank in the base of the signal post, below road level, from which ran conventional wire to the signal box. Catch points in the tram rails were worked by rodding as on the railway.

2.1 Dairycoates

Until 16 February 1914 the Hessle Road route terminated a few yards before the crossing. On the 16th it was extended over the crossing to Pickering Park. As the necessary signalling equipment had not been installed, passengers had to walk across the crossing and transfer to a car until 2 June 1915 when through services commenced. Cars were allowed to cross but the actual regulations for such manoeuvres are not known. It is not known if a separate tram frame was installed in the Hessle Road signal box or if spare levers were used. A window was fitted to enable signal men to see trams approaching from both directions, important because the view to the west was slightly affected by the Hull and Barnsley Railway bridge which crossed the road just a few yards from the road crossing. A footbridge was erected in the early part of the Great War, the cost being £550 of which the Corporation paid half. The Corporation also purchased 32 square yards of land for road widening at that point. The crossing ceased to be used by trams on 29 July 1934 when route DP was withdrawn, but "D" trams continued to be affected by it.

2.2 Anlaby Road (Boulevard)

This was crossed by horse trams from 9 June 1877 and electric trams from 5 July 1899 until 5 September 1942. No protective scheme was ever installed despite being a busy crossing, and several attempts by the NER to persuade the Corporation to install it. It is said that there were 310 tram journeys in each direction over a period of eighteen hours. The Tramway and Railway World was enthusiastic about the crossing in August 1899, stating that it was an excellent example of special work of a very difficult kind. Great care had needed to be exercised to obtain straight and level castings. Some pieces weighed 800 lb each and were bolted down on timber plates and concrete.

2.3 Anlaby Road (Newington)

Until 5 October 1925 the Anlaby Road trams terminated just short of the crossing at the entrance to Wheeler Street Depot. On that date the route was extended to Pickering Road, becoming the only tram route to traverse two crossings. The LNER equipped the signal box with a further frame comprising 14 levers from the Westinghouse Brake and Saxby Signalling Co to operate the catch points and semaphores.

The route was cut back on 29 July 1934 to Wheeler Street, but to avoid congestion the "A" cars were allowed to cross the tracks and continue to use the terminal spur at the entrance to Boothferry Road. However, as the terminus was now within the "B" operating area, trams had to unload and load on the eastern side and cross the line empty. No one was permitted to board at the new terminus. It was last used by trams on 5 September 1942 but the crossing remained in use until May 1965.

2.4 Botanic Gardens.

Horse trams terminated just short of the crossing on Spring Bank (previously known as "Cemetery" and later "Cemetery Gates"). Tram route "S" originally terminated here but was extended into Princes Avenue on 2 June 1900. As the requisite signalling equipment was not in place, passengers had to dismount and walk over the crossing, and not until 8 October 1900 was a through service instituted. A separate four-lever frame was installed at right angles to the main frame.

The arrangement was altered when another extension along Spring Bank was opened in October 1913. The full Spring Bank West tram service closed on 29 July 1934 but trams continued to run to Walton Street for Hull Fair until October 1936. The Newland Avenue route was replaced with trolleybuses in October 1937.

2.5 Walton Street

When the trams were extended along Spring Bank West the new terminus was located a few yards short of the Walton Street crossing, which meant that trams were still affected by the crossing being closed for railway traffic, although this was not as busy as other crossings. Powers to extend the trams along Spring Bank West, initially to Alliance Avenue, and later under the bridge to Calvert Lane, were obtained.

In 1924 the LNER closed the former HBR terminus at Cannon Street and installed a new curve from the line to join the line to Paragon Street just north of the crossing. At the same time in anticipation of the extension some spare capacity was provided in the signal box for tramway equipment. The line was never built and no trams ever ran over the crossing.

2.6 Stepney

Horse trams on the Beverley Road service had first traversed the crossing in 1877, and it was not until 8 December 1900 that electric trams replaced them. Again the service was split as the equipment was not in place, and because the new tramway/railway crossing had not been installed. This was carried out in January 1901 but the new gates were not complete until 14 February 1901. A through service commenced on 25 February 1901. As with other boxes a new bay window was provided to give the signalmen a better view of road traffic. The signals were in use until the last tram ran in September 1938. An Occurrence Book for the early dates at Stepney survives and extracts are to be found in the next section (4).

2.7 Southcoates

The Holderness Road horse tram route travelled over this crossing from July 1877. In April 1900 it was used by electric trams. The box received a large bay window to aid visibility. Unusually, the signals were situated behind the catch points, the reverse of the normal situation. Both catch points could be worked independently but the signals could only work at the same time. Trams ceased to use the crossing on 18 February 1940 when trolleybuses took over.

2.8 Hedon Road

This was a goods only line to Victoria Dock and was used by the Hedon Road steam trams from May 1889 until January 1901. When it was proposed to operate electric trams over the crossing, the House of Lords refused to sanction it and, after long discussions between the Corporation and the NER, the crossing was replaced by a bridge, work being completed in December 1903. As Hull is, on average, only seven feet above sea level, flooding was not an unusual occurrence, a feature of the HBR bridge on Chanterlands Avenue.

3. BRIDGES

Hull's trams had to cope with bridges of various types from those across the River Hull at North Bridge (original plus new one in 1931) and Saltshouse Lane, and that between Queens Dock and Princes Dock, all requiring special equipment to be installed.

Both horse trams and electric trams crossed railway lines between Princess Dock Side and Queens Dock before crossing the Whitefriargate Bridge. This was lifted for boat traffic to enter or leave Queens Dock. No signals appear to have been provided over the railway, with regulation of road and rail traffic being left to a "man with a red flag" whose job it was to ensure safe passage of occasional wagon movements to and from Queens Dock. Electric trams started to use the bridge and cross the rails from October 1903, but ceased to do so on 27 June 1932 when the "TH" route was suspended on "a temporary basis".

Electric trams encountered Hull and Barnsley Railway Bridges in seven places, and the North Eastern Railway (one), all requiring work to enable trams to get under them safely and discussions with the Board of Trade. This work was completed by May 1904 when the City Engineer informed the Tramway Manager that following the lowering of the road way under the Hull and Barnsley Railway bridge on Holderness Road, cars with top covers could now travel under all the bridges on the routes.

4. STEPNEY CROSSING OCCURRENCE BOOKS

Not all delays were the fault of the NER, as we shall see when we examine extracts from the Occurrence Books from the Stepney level crossings. Culprits included the trams themselves, private rulleys, motorcars and animals and the NER.

What follows are extracts from the Ocurance Book (the original spelling!) of the signal box at Stepney on Beverley Road which were provided by Mick Nicholson. The extracts are as found in the book. Only the typeface has been changed to fall in line with this history whilst no attempt has been made to correct spelling mistakes. Any delays to westbound freight trains would in turn be experienced at Botanic Gardens, Anlaby Road (Boulevard) and Dairycoates. One train could delay several cars on four or five routes. Delays to eastbound freight trains might have affected those crossings already mentioned and some (but not all) would cross Holderness Road at Southcoates.

It is not known how typical the entries in the book are, but it is likely that they are fairly typical of the busiest crossings at least.

The tram route in question is the "B" to Newland via Beverley Road, and is not to be confused with the "S" which ran to Newland Avenue via Spring Bank. Trams ran every three minutes, so a six minute delay whilst a freight train passed over the crossing would probably delay two cars in each direction at least.

STEPNEY SIGNAL BOX EXTRACTS FROM OCCURRENCE BOOK

Saturday 8 December 1900 Electric trams commence running from Savile Street to Stepney crossing, and Stepney crossing and Newland.

Sunday 9 December 1900 NERly Co. put a cable across Beverley Road (over tram wires) in place of the telegraph wires.

January 16 1901 Gas meter put in bottom lobby.

January 20-28 New level crossing with double tram lines laid.

February 10 New frame and gate wheels put in.

February 14 New gates connected today.

February 25 First electric tram with passengers crosses the line at 12.42pm.

February 25 Trams stabled at Stepney Lane depot tonight for the first time.

January 2 1901 A Tram from Newland came off ???? end of metals and ran ½way across the crossing at 9.10pm he was on again clear of our gates at 9.12pm nothing detained.

April 1 Tram Signal from Newland stuck off yesterday, Fitter at it today, and made alright.

Stepney Sheet No.4.

May 24 Tram Signal Electric light failed at 9 40pm, it was the signal from the city to Newland, sent word to the Office and told Tram Drivers to report it.

May 24 Towler on duty at Tram Signal 10.0pm to 11.45 pm.

May 31 Tram Signal from Newland Stuck off at 8.30am plate-layers oiled it and made it work.

July 18 Electric Car run off the points at the south side at about 9.41am. No.66.

July 25 Tram Signal from Town went amiss (would not come off) at 9.45am reported and made alright at 11.45am.

Stepney Sheet No.5.

August 3 1901.

August 5 Tram No.91 stopped right on middle of crossing 1.46/2pm, from town.

August 22 After passing of 6.38am Down W/sea Pass at 6.46am I could not get the Home and starting signal levers back the gates and Tram signals and points were all fast I sent for fitters and they came and made alright by 8.0am, Trams transferred passrs till Ganger disconnected tram points and wedged them over, reported.

August 31 At 6.6pm after tram car No.66 had left the signal for Newland he again stopped before getting over the Crossing, his car being foul of the Gates.

September 13 At 7.59pm Tram Car No.66 from Newland stopped at the signal and then again opposite Station Inn to pick passengers up.

November 20 Down Distant signal wire broke 6.55pm, repaired next morning.

November 21 Gateman told the driver of No.93 Tram Car to report the Signal light from Newland very bad, nearly out, also reported to inspector at 7.45pm. The above light made right at 8.35pm.

December 6 Electric of the Tram Signals wouldn't Light this Morning at 4.0am. Lighted up 6.0am.

Stepney Sheet No.6.

January 14 1902 Tram points from Newland not fitting properly reported about 4.0pm. made right same night.

January 31 Tram Car 100 from Newland to City off at Trap points at 4.15pm, he was nowhere near when I opened out for train. Reported.

March 27 Gates open from 9.16 to 9.22pm for York Gds Engine No.973 with a heavy load of 52 wagons on.

March 29 Gates open from 8.24½ to 8.31pm for York Goods Eng No973 coming Independent.

March 30 Reported Tram Signal from Newland stuck off when 4.15pm

Hull to Hsea Pass came out. Made right March 31 1902.

5. LEVEL CROSSING DELAYS 1924

The problem confronting the Tramways Department was illustrated in a report by Mr Rayner to the Tramways Committee on 24 February 1924. He referred to the Beverley Road and Spring Bank routes, and stated that the main cause of delays to the service was stoppage occasioned by the level crossings. A recording clock had been used to record delays at the Botanic Gardens crossing on three separate days (Thursday 10 January, Saturday 12 January and Monday 14 January). It was impossible for any organisation to get over the delays at these crossings, and although between £2,000 and £3,000 a year had been spent on putting additional cars on the routes they had not done away with the delays but had merely added to congestion in King Edward Street. In 1913 the train stoppages at the gates were only 17½% of the time whereas in 1924 they were between 26 and 30 per cent.

This shows the number of crossing closures and the delays of over three minutes on the "S" route:

Time	Cars per hour	Inward Over 3 mins	Outward Gates closed	Mins
Thursday 10 January 1924				
7 – 8	29	5	3	16
8 – 9	34	5	5	20
9 – 10	22	5	7	15
10 – 11	22	5	4	15
11 – 12	22	4	6	12
12 – 1	24	2	5	15
1 – 2	24	3	6	15
2 – 3	24	4	5	12
3 – 4	24	3	6	9
4 – 5	30	5	5	20
5 – 6	30	5	3	17
6 – 7	22	3	5	13
7 – 8	22	4	8	9
8 – 9	22	4	6	15
9 – 10	22	4	6	16
10 – 11	22	7	3	10
	395	68	88	229
Saturday 12 January 1924				
7 – 8	29	2	5	15
8 – 9	34	2	4	27
9 – 10	22	2	5	13
10 – 11	22	5	4	12
11 – 12	29	5	4	15
12 – 1	22*	5	6	23
1 – 2	22*	5	6	15

Time	Cars per hour	Inward Over 3 mins	Outward Gates closed	Mins
2 – 3	22*	7	8	23
3 – 4	22*	5	6	12
4 – 5	22*	6	5	21
5 – 6	26+	3	6	12
6 – 7	26+	3	6	18
7 – 8	26+	6	7	19
8 – 9	26+	3	4	20
9 – 10	26+	4	5	19
10 – 11	26+	4	4	13
	402	67	85	277

Notes * Cars taken for football cup tie specials
+ Four special cars put on for the evening

Monday 14 January 1924

7 – 8	29	3	6	23
8 – 9	34	1	3	12
9 – 10	22	4	4	25
10 – 11	22	7	5	16
11 – 12	22	7	8	10
12 – 1	24	3	6	10
1 – 2	24	6	3	17
2 – 3	24	4	8	12
3 – 4	24	6	6	17
4 – 5	30	6	7	14
5 – 6	30	9	6	12
6 – 7	22	8	6	12
7 – 8	22	7	8	8
8 – 9	22	7	5	9
9 – 10	22	6	8	20
10 – 11	22	3	4	5
	395	87	93	222
Total	1182	222	263	728

For gaps of over 7 to 10 minutes a "spare" car (duty 48) was used to maintain a service with ten runs each way.
Average time gates closed in:

Percentage of 4 hours

7 to 11	69.6	29.0
11 to 3	59.6	24.8
3 to 7	59.0	24.5
7 to 11	54.3	22.6

The above survey tells us much about the number of cars in service and what happened to the normal service when there was an important cup tie at the Hull City ground on Anlaby Road. Assuming four cars on "S" to three on "SW" it means that the Newland Avenue passengers were short of over two hundred seats an hour and that the service was irregular. Cars could be delayed on both inward and outward journeys so that the scheduled headway was not maintained, and waiting for cars to arrive in what was probably a cold January would have done passengers no good at all. The report does not say whether cars were turned short anywhere such as Queens Road or even short of Botanic in Spring Bank, to try to even out the delays. Of course this would have played even more havoc with the crew's duties and scheduled break times.

6. LEVEL CROSSINGS PAYMENTS FOR SIGNALMEN

For the five years from 1 January 1928 the Corporation would pay a flat rate of £800 a year in respect of the working of safety devices at the Botanic, Southcoates, Stepney, Hessle Road and Newington Crossings. The actual cost for these boxes would be paid for 1927 only, whilst £160 would be paid for the Newington Crossing for the period 5 October 1925 to 31 December 1927. An example of a heads of agreement follows. This was provided by the group that is building a model of Botanic Gardens station and the tramways as they were circa 1915.

Heads of Agreement between the Hull Corporation and the North Eastern Railway Company as to the Tramway Level Crossing in Spring Bank, Hull.

"The catch points and signals already arranged to be provided (at the Corporation's cost) to be worked from the Railway Company's signal cabin adjacent to the crossing.

The Corporation to be responsible for the maintenance of the points and signals and for the connections thereto so far as they are off the Company's land. So far as on the railway Company's land, they will be maintained by the Railway Company at the cost to the Corporation.

The catch points and signals to be interlocked with the gates and stops, so that they cannot be set for tramway traffic until the gates are secure across the railway. The catch points and signals to be worked by the Railway Company's signalmen in the adjacent cabin, a proportion of their wages (corresponding with the number of levers working the catch points and signals compared with the total number of working levers in the cabin) being charged to the Corporation. The points and signals to be worked in such a manner as to facilitate as far as reasonably practicable the working of the tramway traffic.

The electric current for the lamps in the signals to be provided by the Corporation, the Company allowing them to place a current meter and a switch in the signal cabin, and the Company's signalmen as part of their service to the Corporation to switch the lamps on and off as required.

The laying in and maintenance of the crossings between the carriage-way gates as altered (both temporarily and permanent) to be done by the Railway Company at the cost of the Corporation, the work of laying in the crossings to be carried out in accordance with plans signed by the Engineers of the Corporation and the Railway Company respectively and attached hereto, and the Corporation at their own cost to maintain the whole roadway between the crossing carriage-way gates as altered in accordance with the attached plan. Provided that the Company shall themselves maintain the covers of the boxing for gate and point rodding.

The Company to substitute for the existing crossing gates enlarged gates in accordance with the attached plan at the cost to the Corporation and the Corporation to be at the expense of any alteration rendered necessary by the carrying of the tramway across the Railway of the gate posts, gearing, gate rodding, point rodding, and any other work incidental thereto and also to bear one-fourth the cost of maintaining such enlarged gates.

The work to be subject to any requirements of the Board of Trade."

The agreement was signed on 23 August 1900 by Mr A.E. White, the City Engineer and Mr J. Cudworth for the North Eastern Railway Company.

7. LEVEL CROSSING DELAYS JANUARY 1879

The horse tramways were also subject to delays at railway crossings although with lower frequencies than the electric cars there would not be as many delays. Following complaints to the

Streets and Lighting Sub-Committee the Borough Engineer carried out a survey of the Beverley Road (Stepney) crossing on 2-4 January 1879 between 6.30am and 7.30pm and reported the results to the next meeting on 9 January 1879.

Although intended to ascertain of how the closures affected pedestrians it provides yet another insight of the crossing problem impinged on tram operations, even the limited Beverley Road service:

Minutes Closed	Times
0 to 1	9
1 to 2	57
2 to 3	66
3 to 4	38
4 to 5	6
5 to 6	5
7 hours 37minutes	181

This averaged more than 2½ hours per day and the North Eastern Railway was asked to explain the reasons for the dealy not only to road traffic but also to foot traffic. Compare these statistics with those in Section 5 when delays were more numerous.

Appendix 6

Statistics

1. Introduction

These statistics come from two main sources – some information gathered by G.A. Lee and the returns submitted to the various Committees and Sub-Committees of the Council between the commencement of the horse trams and the cessation of the electric tramways.

Only a selection of statistics has been included – a full version could warrant a book of its own! The figures are not always complete and different methods of compiling them have had to be overcome. Some returns for example stick to the standard financial year cycle but others particularly the horse trams were compiled to the 30 June. Others referred to a calendar year. A complete record for the entire operational life of the three systems is not available.

From 1901 to 1928 the tramways contributed £267,629 towards the relief of rates a rate saving of 5.49d in 1901 but a lesser amount for each year thereafter with the 1928 figure being 0.46d. No payments were made in 1917 to 1921/3 and payments ceased in 1928.

Whilst the statistics may seem just figures they can provide a snapshot of operations at a certain time and a valuable insight into how and which passengers used the services.

Table 6A Hull Street Tramways Company Passenger Statistics 1878-1890 (years ending 30 June)

Year	Passengers Carried	per car mile	Car Miles	Rides per inhabitant
1878	2,224,187	n/a	n/a	14.4
1879	2,214,109	n/a	n/a	14.1
1880	2.325.714	7.25	316,295	14.4
1881	2,997,164	9.06	330,639	18.2
1882	3,789,949	8.83	429,269	22.4
1883	4.231,561	9.49	446,123	24.6
1884	4,595,189	9.61	478,613	26.3
1885	4.254,646	9.49	448,526	23.9
1886	3,528,439	8.32	423,899	19.5
1887	3,786.525	8.83	428,636	20.5
1888	3,831,555	7.60	504,258	20.4
1889	3,875,888	7.52	515,127	20.2
1890	3,119.075	7.32	426,269	16.0

Notes:
Between 1877 and 1889 the population of Hull increased from an estimated 154,000 to 195,000. Although passenger numbers rose from 1880 to 1889 the number of rides per inhabitant fell, an indication of the horse bus competition and the trend of moving away from the town centre into the suburbs.

Notes for Table 6D (right):
1. The motor buses in 1909 were the three Corporation buses
2. By 1923 there were 111 private motorbuses and 15 Corporation motorbuses

Table 6B Hull Street Tramways Receipts and Profits 1878-1890

Year	Gross Receipts Income £	PCM d	Working Expenses £	Net Receipts £	Net Profit £
1878	14,961	n/a	8,401	6,560	5,714
1879	15,589	n/a	10,762	4.827	4,092
1880	13,516	10.26	11,609	1.907	1,174
1881	14,277	10.36	11.165	3,112	2,379
1882	16.797	9.39	13,202	3,595	2,860
1883	18,465	9.93	13,716	4,749	4,039
1884	19,883	9.97	14,442	5,441	4,731
1885	18,455	9.88	14,152	4.303	3,646
1886	15,443	8.74	13,473	1,970	1,317
1887	16,583	9.29	14,398	2,185	1,531
1888	16,491	7.85	15,070	1,421	764
1889	16,711	7.79	18,551	(1,840)	(2,498)
1890	13,649	7.68	12,608	1,041	383

Notes:
Between 1894 and 1890 the income included an average of £65 per annum from parcels traffic

Table 6C - Drypool and Marfleet Steam Tramways Company Limited

Receipts 1889 – 1899 (all ending 30 June)

Year	Income £	Per Car Mile d	Working Expenses £	Net receipts £
1889	480	9.97	133	347
1890	2,883	4.44	2,833	50
1891	2,999	4.73	3.055	(56)
1892	3.168	4.86	3,242	(74)
1893	2,667	4.12	3.067	(400)
1894	2,436	4.91	2.903	(467)
1895	2,373	6.38	2,385	(12)
1896	2,911	7.57	2,454	457
1897	2,911	7.77	2,/05	251
1898	2,952	7.44	2.596	356
1899	3,112	8.29	2,833	279

Table 6D Waggonettes, Carriages and Double Deck Omnibuses Licence Returns

Selected Years

Year	Wagonnettes				Carriages		Omnibuses	
	5-7	8	9	10	11/12	13+	Horse	Motor
1889	68	28	20	64	43	35	15	0
1894	9	90	5	207	54	22	6	0
1899	1	81	2	288	38	38	29	0
1904	0	22	0	140	12	32	18	0
1909	0	16	0	128	6	48	14	3
1914	0	6	0	87	5	49	7	0
1920	0	1	0	8	1	26	0	18

Table 6E Hull Corporation Tramways Passenger Statistics 1900-1945

Year 31/3	Passengers Total	Car Miles	Passengers Per Car Mile	Car Averages		
				Miles	Hours Per Day	Cars in Use For16-hour Day
1900+	6,218,971	573,420	10.85	n/a	n/a	23.70
1901	17,264,013	1,647,026	10.48	n/a	n/a	48.16
1902	21,956,999	2,218,696	9.49	n/a	n/a	65.87
1903	22,062,703	2,293,282	9.62	n/a	n/a	63.96
1904	24,220,718	2,512,821	9.64	n/a	n/a	64.41
1905	27,102,921	2,910,698	9.31	n/a	n/a	73.22
1906	27,729,356	2,940,815	9.43	109.79	1,174	73.38
1907	29,151,543	2,956,406	9.86	113.68	1,140	71.25
1908	30,964,254	3,022,844	10.24	115.11	1,148	71.75
1909	32,958,883	3,379,117	9.75	119.45	1,240	77.50
1910	35,588,800	3,655,542	9.74	122.14	1,312	82.00
1911	37,415,152	3,695,281	10.13	121.99	1,328	82.99
1912	41,277,202	3,761,809	10.97	123.82	1,328	83.01
1913	42,997,226	4,040,739	10.64	127.10	1,394	87.10
1914	45,679,094	4,229,625	10.80	127.60	1,453	90.82
1915	52,087,770	4,551,125	11.44	123.53	1,566	97.85
1916	53,731,387	4,072,342	13.19	123.27	1,445	90.31
1917	54,125,213	4,200,426	12.89	121.07	1,521	95.05
1918	63,089,709	4,124,851	15.30	120.67	1,498	93.65
1919	69,506,332	4.098,058	16.96	118.40	1,513	94.59
1920	78,432,643	4,731,398	16.58	109.84	1,882	117.69
1921	69,130,674	4,526,316	15.27	108.02	1,837	114.81
1922	62,214,660	4,337,649	14.34	109.38	1,738	108.65
1923	60,276,615	4,413,863	13.66	110.70	1,748	109.24
1924	60.316,860	4,529,379	13.32	113.47	1,745	109.06
1925	62,387,677	4,570,277	13.65	115.92	1,728	108.02
1926	63,975,265	4,690,169	13.64	117.22	1,754	109.63
1927	58,780,560	4,715,449	12.47	121.14	1,699	106.21
1928	60,540,644	4,892,767	12.37	120.30	1,778	111.12
1929	59,692,198	4,842,225	12.33	120.11	1,767	110.45
1930	60,427,001	4,986,871	12.12	121.94	1,793	112.04
1931	57,943,902	4,906,515	12.22	121.34	1,772	110.78
1932	54,528,919	4,605,006	11.84	121.64	1,655	103.44
1933	49,077.631	4,467,352	10.99	124.89	1,568	98.00
1934	47.026,462	4,202,532	11.19	128.00	1,444	90.00
1935	38,342,279	3,434,179	11.16	129.00	1,168	73.00
1936	33,240,389	2,895,240	11.48	130.00	976	61.00
1937	31,902,887	2,764,030	11.54			
1938	27,475,149	2,340,179	11.74			
1939	18,971,459	1,553,969	12.21			
1940	16,066,054	1,297,275	12.38			
1941	10,449,063	750,000	13.93	These figures unavailable after 1936		
1942	10,479,967	605,199	17.32			
1943	9,282,946	460,076	20.18			
1944	7,725,946	327,964	23.55			
1945	8,497,825	346,457	24.52			
1946*	2,191,565	89,350	24.51			

Notes:
+ From 5 July 1899
* To 30 June 1945

Table 6F Financial Statistics Hull City Tramways 1899/1900 to 1945/1946

Year	Income	Traffic	Power	Repairs	General	Loans	Total	Net Surplus
	£	£	£	£	£	£	£	£
1899/1900	26,265	6452	2144	619	1135	5923	16,274	9943
1900/1901	72,381	15,886	6035	4815	4861	13,105	44,702	27,118
1901/1902	88,294	21,134	7378	10,775	7040	17,128	63,455	24,838
1902/1903	92,237	21,541	8240	10,009	7830	19,442	67,062	25,173
1903/1904	101,259	24,254	8649	17,936	10,937	20,462	82,273	18,985
1904/1905	113,326	28,514	7367	22,796	6494	20,935	86,102	27,224
1905/1906	115,832	30,295	9496	21,646	9246	25,997	96,680	19,680
1906/1907	121,679	30,566	9352	11,837	9644	26,222	87,621	25,604
1907/1908	129,278	32,384	11,837	20,212	9201	26,740	100,374	29,895
1908/1909	129,212	37,305	11,722	20,386	9665	26,946	106,024	24,319
1909/1910	136,276	40,503	10,455	24,540	9891	28,227	113,616	22,942
1910/1911	142,750	42,702	10,692	29,527	11,819	29,459	124,119	18,372
1911/1912	151,755	43,701	10,617	30,706	11,889	30,531	127,450	25,504
1912/1913	157,687	47,495	11,245	41,235	12.138	33,549	145,752	13,435
1913/1914	166,650	50,240	11,803	41,556	14,863	34,450	152,942	14,526
1914/1915	162,347	54,429	11,622	31,312	12.547	36,252	146,182	16.076
1915/1916	162,548	54,786	13,336	27,419	12,750	37,807	146,099	12,469
1916/1917	164,810	61,928	14,612	31,529	12,320	40,258	161,667	(1,448)
1917/1918	187,163	69,966	17,503	36,636	13,291	37,040	174,436	8,751
1918/1919	231,078	99,673	23,386	48,320	16,048	37,720	225,147	1,600
1919/1920	308,364	142,996	31,376	82,315	24,109	37,158	317,954	(9,467)
1920/1921	386,651	166,795	36,683	100,634	31,529	39,719	375,315	11,338
1921/1922	364,428	153,700	41.037	105,832	33,094	34.398	368,063	2,208
1922/1923	344,000	137,227	25,257	68,159	35,025	36,685	302,253	43,659
1923/1924	330,505	130,894	24,712	52,210	28,916	41,488	278,220	54,608
1924/1925	326,303	132,579	24.525	58,130	29,837	51,261	296,332	23,033
1925/1926	329,098	140,414	22,617	56,679	30,047	60,744	310,501	15,449
1926/1927	312.771	138,030	33,034	61,021	35,144	53,775	321,004	(14,508)
1927/1928	325,059	146,510	21,356	61,816	33,927	48,845	312,454	3,348
1928/1929	312,715	143,059	21,078	59,026	34,236	45,428	302,821	1,137
1929/1930	314,678	141,937	22,640	65,441	21,902	44,285	296,205	9,123
1930/1931	300,099	139,233	23,279	69,328	21,224	38,764	291,828	(2,246)
1931/1932	282,403	132,412	20,127	68,071	16,772	39,183	276,565	(4,230)
1932/1933	257,190	120,627	16,948	63,001	16,537	37,475	254,570	(6,866)
1933/1934	245,888	111,810	16,193	53,449	16,623	38,303	236,378	982
1934/1935	199,479	97,968	14,988	49,435	8,659	34,378	206,428	(13,674)
1935/1936	172,584	79,635	12,796	40,937	6,982	32,113	172,193	(6,782)
1936/1937	167,017	71,695	13,312	28,639	10,229	31,352	155,227	3,985
1937/1938	144,012	62,239	11,688	25,942	8,538	26,111	134,518	3,012
1938/1939	99,972	43,613	8,580	19,127	5,944	25,607	102,871	(8,181)
1939/1940	85,013	37,729	7,259	17,002	5,589	23,559	91,138	(9,446)
1940/1941	55,278	27,632	4,907	12,724	4,267	22,557	72,087	(20,264)
1941/1942	60,002	22,058	4,229	13,262	4,891	15,211	59651	(3,898)
1942/1943	52,039	17,277	3,237	11,727	3,051	12,761	48,056	1,819
1943/1944	41,953	11,678	2,385	7,372	1,719	9,191	32,345	9,458
1944/1945	45,949	12,872	2,668	7,564	1,886	6,453	31,443	10,967
1945/1946	11,312	3,162	703	5,588	751	21	19,225	219

Table 6G Average Receipts, Monday 2 June 1919
Hessle Road, Beverley Road, Spring Bank, Spring Bank West Routes

	No. of Cars in service	Receipts per car mile s d	No. of runs	Receipts per run s d
a.m.				
5 to 6	17	2 9	60	0 9
6 to 7	26	4 0	78	1 4
7 to 8	69	4 7	223	1 5
8 to 9	69	4 9	241	1 4
9 to 10	59	5 10	171	2 0
10 to 11	50	6 4	144	2 2
11 to 12	57	6 11	179	2 3
12 to 1	87	6 10	209	2 10
1 to 2	72	8 10	217	2 11
2 to 3	84	6 6	204	2 8
3 to 4	65	7 1	193	2 5
4 to 5	79	7 9	208	2 11
5 to 6	85	9 10	221	3 9
6 to 7	64	11 8	217	3 5
7 to 8	66	9 4	217	2 10
8 to 9	65	6 7	220	1 11
9 to 10	64	6 0	219	1 9
10 to 11	64	7 1	194	2 4

This gives a very good illustration of car output on the routes and the times when the most revenue was collected. Car output varied considerably throughout the day, the maximum, perhaps surprisingly, being from noon to 1pm yet the receipts for this period seem not to justify the number of cars employed. However, the strong sense of public service ensured that cars ran when they did. The period from 6pm to 7pm saw the most receipts per car mile and per run of individual cars. The cars worked harder in the morning as the 69 cars in service performed marginally more runs than those at other times, albeit for a reduction in receipts per car run.

Mr McCombe also provided the following table for the morning services on the above routes. The remarkable point is that even an old style Liberal administration was quite willing to accept such a price to provide cheap transport for workers and was willing to let the receipts from the rest of day's operations subsidise this, in effect. As table 6H shows the deficit on morning services was substantial. There was some criticism which claimed that there were few workmen on the cars between 8am and 9am and that the shop workers and office workers who were paid more were not the people for whom workmen's fares were intended.

The table shows the almost hourly fluctuation in the number of cars on the road and begs the question if all the additional cars were necessary. Without even more detailed information it is difficult to comment with any certainty.

Table 6H Receipts and Working Expenses Monday 2 June 1919

Hours	Total Receipts £ s d	Working Expenses £ s d
a.m.		
5 to 6	3 18 2	11 4 1
6 to 7	8 9 5	14 19 0
7 to 8	29 8 9	41 14 7
8 to 9	29 4 2	45 7 11
Total	71 0 6	113 5 7
Deficit	42 5 1	

Table 6I Report by Mr Rayner to the Tramways Committee 14 April 1924.

Schedule 1 – Distances of fares stages present and proposed

Fare d	Stage Number	Present Yards	Proposed Yards	Difference Yards	% Change
Hessle Road					
1	1	1116	1320	+ 204	18.0
1	2	1441	1441	-------	---
1	3	2043	1839	– 204	10.0
1½	1	2557	2761	+ 204	8.2
1½	2	3484	3280	– 204	5.9
2		4600			4.4
Anlaby Road					
1	1	1045	1320	+ 275	26.3
1	2	1450	1430	– 20	-----
1	3	875	1320	+ 445	50.9
1½	1	2475	2750	+ 275	11.1
1½	2	2305	2030	– 275	11.7
2		3350			8.2
Beverley Road					
1	1	1166	1320	+ 154	13.2
1	2	1529	1429	-------	-----
1	3	1905	1751	– 154	8.1
1½	1	2695	2849	+ 154	5.7
1½	2	3434	3280	– 154	4.5
2		4600			3.3
Spring Bank					
1	1	1358			
1	2	1595			
1	3	1197			
1½	1	2053			
1½	2	2792			
2		4150			
Holderness Road					
1	1	1479 (T/H) 1540 (H)			
1	2	1259	1320	+ 61	0.46
1	3	1601			
1½	1	2799	2860	– 61	0.22
1½	2	2860			
2		4400			
Hedon Road					
1	1	1431			
1	2	1390			
1	3	2204			
1½	1	2821			
1½	2	3594			
2		5025			

Schedule 2 – Percentage of Passengers on each stage

Route	1d Stages 1st %	2nd %	3rd %
Hessle Road	44	37	19
Anlaby Road	53	37	10
Beverley Road	50	36	14
Spring Bank	57	27	16
Holderness Road	58	24	18
Hedon Road	38	28	34
Spring Bank West	46	54	---

	1st	1½d stages 2nd
Hessle Road	81	10
Anlaby Road	87	13
Beverley Road	83	13
Spring Bank	76	24
Holderness Road	81	19
Hedon Road	74	26
Spring Bank West	100	---

The following statistics are taken from the Tramways Committee meeting of 2 March 1926 and formed part of a major report by Mr Rayner regarding proposals for significant fares revisions. It shows the ridership trends and the effect of free passes and discount tickets on the receipts of the tramways. The probable surplus for the year 1925/6 was estimated to be a mere £4,500 from an income of £326, 575.

Table 6J – Weekly Passes
Tuesday 9 February 1926

	Passes Issued	Pass Riders	Average Ride Per Pass	Paying Passengers
Hessle Road	1006	6878	6.85	33,855
Anlaby Road	1146	5842	5.10	22,637
Holderness Road	1425	8163	5.73	26,931
Spring Bank	1228	5776	4.70	21,703
Spring Bank West	533	2608	4.90	10.021
Beverley Road	1169	6348	5.42	25,567
Hedon Road	196	1636	8.35	14,989
Old Town	77	116	1.50	1.562
	6780	37,367	5.50	157,355
		Pass Riders		37,367
		Total Riders		194,722
		Proportion of Pass Riders		19.40%

Table 6K – Weekly Passengers
Week ending 30 January 1926

Route	Passes Sold	Estimated Rides	% Pass Riders	Paying Passengers	Total
Hessle Road	1004	32,128	13.0	244,160	276,288
Anlaby Road	1160	37,120	23.0	162,693	199,813
Holderness Rd	1439	46,048	23.2	197,025	243,973
Spring Bank	1228	39,296	26.2	150,004	189,300
Spring Bank W	537	17,184	23.6	72,214	89,394
Beverley Road	1161	37,152	21.0	177,519	214,671
Hedon Road	186	5,952	7.8	102,787	108,739
Old Town	74	2,368	21.2	11,199	13,567
Total	6789	217,248	19.4	1,118,497	1,335,745

Table 6L – Number of Old Age Pensioners Riding on Tuesday 16 February 1916 between 9.30am & 11.30am, 2.30pm & 4pm and 7pm to the finish of services

Hessle Road	445
Anlaby Road	304
Holderness Road	452
Spring Bank	236
Spring Bank West	156
Beverley Road	300
Hedon Road	175
Old Town	86
Total	2154

Appendix 7

Rules, Regulations and Bye-Laws

1. INTRODUCTION

Whilst tramway operators had to make their own rules and regulations they were themselves subject to various statutory provisions and "advice" issued by the Board of Trade. The Board issued guidance to all would be tramway operators "regarding the details of construction and equipment for tramways". These were modified to apply to electric tramways and in the light of experience and what follows is an edited version of an April 1910 memorandum to operators.

1. Clearance
- At least 15 inches between the sides of passing cars and side of a car and any lamp, telegraph or trolley pole in any street
- Bases of side posts inside kerb sufficient to prevent road vehicles coming into contact with them
- At least 15 inches between the side of a car and the kerb whether on a straight or curved road
- The clearance between top decks of cars and the underside of bridges should, if possible, be no less than 6' 6".
- Where special conditions prevail no less than 6' will be accepted with uncovered cars

2. Posts and Brackets
- Centre posts should not be used without consent in every case from the Board
- Stone kerbing around centre poles should not be such as to enable any person to stand upon it, as a refuge, unless the clearance is ample for safety
- Where bracket arms 16' long will not suffice span wire construction should be used
- Overhead conductors must be securely attached to supports; intervals must not exceed 120 feet unless the Board approves
- Between every two poles should be inserted an emergency switch so enclosed to be inaccessible to pedestrians
- Poles supporting gas brackets should be efficiently bonded to the rails

3. Permanent Way
- The weight of rails to be not less than 90 lb per yard, 100 lb being preferred
- The groove of the rail should not exceed one and one-eighth inch in width, but a groove not exceeding one and a quarter inch will be accepted on curves of less than 150' radius
- There shall be no variation to this without BOT approval

4. Cars
- Drawings must be sent to the Board before any orders are placed
- Stairs of the reversed type should be avoided, more especially on lines of less than 4' 8½" gauge
- "Trigger" life guards are the preferred pattern – the hanging gate to be as close to the ground as possible – at least 3' between it and the foot of the guard
- The tray of the guard should be provided with a spring so as to hold the front edge down to the surface of the roadway when a tray is dropped
- Folding steps to be adopted on all new cars to avoid interfering with the efficiency of the guard
- On severe gradients and sharp curves the Board may object to double deck cars
- On 3' 6" gauge or less top covers not to be used without BOT approval
- Sanding gear to be provided at each end of the car
- Top deck railing to be at least 3' 6" high
- All railings connected with earth
- All electrical conductors fixed on cars shall be flexible cables protected with India rubber insulation of the highest quality – additionally protected wherever adjacent to any metal to avoid the risk of metal becoming charged
- Trolley standard to be electrically connected to the wheels of the car in such manner to prevent the standard becoming electrically charged from any defect in the conductors contained within it, or in the event of the standard becoming electrically charged, to give a continuous and distinctive warning signal to the driver or conductor – signal may be a red lamp bridged with a suitable fuse or preferably giving an audible signal
- The signal device to be tested at least once a week
- Emergency cut off switch to be provided and fixed so as to be conveniently reached by the driver in case of any failure of action of the controller itself
- Where trolley ropes can not be dispensed with or tied up, precautions must be taken to prevent the "slack" causing incidents
- To prevent the trolley booms being pulled down or trolley standards being broken, "traps" should be minimised and detachable trolley heads provided – a catch rope should be attached to prevent the trolley head from falling
- No material alteration should be made in cars after inspection nor any fresh types of car adopted without BOT approval.

2. RULES AND REGULATIONS OF HULL'S TRAMWAYS UNDERTAKINGS

Tramway undertakings of any description were required to produce and publish their operating rules and regulations. These had to be posted in the London Gazette and local newspapers before the proposed rules were submitted to the Board of Trade, together with any comments or objections received.

At first they were relatively simple and concise and were often based on the Board's own model regulations, but as systems expanded and operations became more complicated so did the regulations.

Whilst much of the content seems to be negative the rule books provide much information about how the undertakings were organised and how they operated their cars. It does seem that crews from the start needed a high level of both numeracy and literacy.

2.1 Hull Street Tramways Company

It is worth looking at some of the rules to gain an insight into operations and conditions in the 1880s. All Officers and Servants were to abide by, fulfil and comply with the rule book, the Corporation's Bye-Laws, the Police Act and Police Bye-Laws! Did anyone tell them the provisions of these? They were to devote their whole time and attention to the Company's service and business whilst their engagement lasted. An ominous statement at the start of the rule book said that "constant employment will not be guaranteed"!

Reference is made in the text (and in published articles) to the HST whose rule book ran to 54 pages. In fact the 54 pages of the "Rules and Regulations for the Officers and Servants of the Hull Street Tramways Company" of 1 March 1882 comprised 34 pages covering general regulations, inspectors, car cleaners and washers, drivers, conductors, omnibus drivers and all officers and servants. The next ten pages were the agreements (conditions of service) with drivers and conductors which were issued when they started work. Then came four pages that were the bye laws and regulations of the HST under powers of the Tramways Act 1870, whilst the next six were "Byelaws made by the Corporation of the Mayor, Aldermen and Burgesses of the Borough of Kingston upon Hull under the provisions of the 46th section of the Tramways Act 1870." Thus the entire book did not apply to all staff although some were rules that seemed draconian and were couched in harsh terms.

Every servant was required to have a copy when on duty and in his possession when applying for his wages, failing which another copy would be delivered to him and its price deducted from his wages. In case of sickness a timely report was to be sent to the head of department, and an employee was to furnish a proper medical certificate or his post would be filled up. No absence was permitted without prior permission of his manager.

In addition, every Servant of the Company was liable to a reduction in pay for unsatisfactory services, or to instant dismissal by the Company, without any reason being assigned.

Drivers had to report ten minutes before the car was due to leave the yard. They were to check brakes and equipment to ensure all were in good order, and report any defects immediately to the duty inspector. In addition they had to examine the horses to ensure that they were properly harnessed before setting off. If a driver considered a horse unfit for service he must submit a written report to the duty inspector. This is interesting given the complaints about the treatment of horses.

Cars must never leave the yard without being equipped with "pieces of iron suitable for lifting the car on the rails in the event of its getting off." When cars going in opposite directions and meeting near a facing point, drivers were not to pass each other until both were certain that the car approaching such facing point had taken it safely. The car about to take the facing point had precedence. Cars must never stop abreast of each other. Drivers were paid according to that version of the book 3s a day for second class drivers and 3s 5d for first class drivers, the distinction not being described. Rule XIV (2) stated that "it was not the intention of the Company to ensure constant daily employment to the drivers"!

Conductors were to report ten minutes before the car was due to leave the yard and check cushions, tarpaulins, route boards, fare and other plates and report any defects to the duty inspector. Conductors were responsible for the cleanliness of the cushions and where cars were provided with "aprons" they must throw them on the top seats to keep them dry in wet weather. Conductors must see that they were properly cared for. Any defect on a car in the morning must be reported to the Inspector and if the latter did nothing the Conductor must report him in turn to the Manager.

They must also comply with a Borough of Hull Byelaw in that carriages (cars) were to display sufficient lamps which must be lit after 4pm in October, November, December and January of each year.

Inspectors were responsible for the proper and efficient performance of all workings within their respective districts, good conduct of subordinates and cleanliness, efficient and running of the Cars in use. Cars were to be examined every day as well as advertising boards, which should be washed without injury to the adverts thereon. They must ensure the timely departure of the Cars from the yard so as to give them time to reach and leave the terminus at the time stated in the table.

Cars must be supplied with time and fare bills as well as route and destination boards before they left the yard. Any defects were to be reported in writing to the Manager and under no circumstances were they to allow a car to run when in an improper order.

Inspectors had to check their watches by the Town's Clock and personally give the correct time to the Conductors in their respective districts. They were to regulate traffic accordingly and check that the clocks in the Cars are kept in order. (Interesting that all horse cars had internal clocks fitted).

A daily report was required to show that all of the Cars made all their stated journeys, and where they had not give an explanation of the reasons why. Whenever an accident occurred, no matter how trivial, or when a Car broke down Inspectors had to proceed to the spot with "all necessary appliances, and spare neither time nor trouble to arrange for the speedy resumption of traffic". A full investigation must be made at once and the facts reported to the Manager, and at the same time the Conductor's official report should be forwarded.

Inspectors could suspend (but not discharge) any Driver or Conductor in the case of insubordination, drunkenness, neglect of duty, incompetence or improper conduct and report the facts in writing to the Manager. If this were not enough they were to travel a route before noon on each day and submit a written report stating any irregularities occurring during the previous day, whether the rails were clean, the state of the roadway and where platelayers or causewayers were at work They were to check and examine tickets and check conductors' waybills on entering a Car.

Cleaners and washers were to thoroughly clean Cars inside and out, being careful not to tear the linings or scratch the paint, break the glass or injure any part of a Car. Wheel boxes were to be removed and cleaned once a week, but lamps on each car were to be cleaned and trimmed daily. Any property found on a Car was to be handed to the Inspector.

2.2 Hull City Tramways

It is useful to compare this with the late 1900 version issued by Mr McCombe the Tramway Manager. This had 72 sections, nos 1-15 for all staff, nos 16-24 for inspectors, nos 25-40 for motormen and nos 41-71 to conductors plus one for both conductors and motormen.

Rule 40 listed the equipment that each motor car should carry:

2 screw drivers	1 controller handle
1 hammer	1 reverser handle
1 chisel	1 bell knob
1 grease tin	1 sand knob
1 oil can	1 coupling bar
1 pinch bar	2 coupling pins
1 jumping iron	1 head lamp plug
1 piece insulation cable	1 controller case key

2 spanners	1 bulkhead fitting key
1 pair pliers	1 locker key
6 fuses	1 canopy switch key
1 pair rubber gloves	

Where was that lot stored, one wonders?

It also listed rates of pay. Motormen received 4s 8d per day (28 shillings a week of six days) rising to 35s a week by yearly increments of 1s. Conductors received 3s 6d per day (21 shillings a week of six days) rising to 27s a week also by yearly increments of 1s. One day was allowed off for every six days worked.

Page 22 gives instructions to crews about operating the signals at Midland Street box if there was no signalman on duty:

"If signal man absent from sickness, accident or any other cause, points and signals must be worked by the conductor of the car which requires to pass.

The levers are interlocked and it will be necessary to observe the following instructions:

To pass Anlaby Road cars out
      Levers 1.3.4.5 must be in normal position
To pass Hessle Road cars out
      Pull over 1.2.3.4 in the order named
To pass Anlaby Road cars in
      No 5 must be in normal position
To pass Hessle Road cars in
      Pull over no 1
      No 4 must be in normal position
      Pull over no 5

In case of difficulty inward cars may be called on by hand – in such cases the conductor must first go to the crossing and assure himself that the road is clear."

On 18 January 1901 Alderman Larard and Mr McCombe issued a warning to conductors not to change trolleys before the car is at the end of the line. Cars must run with trolleys pointing forward except under special instructions. Breach of the rule would result in instant dismissal of the conductor.

Another notice to staff entitled "Warning to Motormen" was dated 14 March 1904, and advised motormen how to save current by having the controller in the OFF position as much as possible, and to save wear and tear on the brakes. "When approaching a stopping place at a good speed motormen were advised to shut off power at least two poles distant (approximately 80 yards) and allow the car to run on its own impetus. If the conductor rings the bell to stop, apply the brake gradually and stop slowly and gently. Do not "ram" the brake on and stop suddenly".

"When approaching a terminus, the car will move over 200 yards without power.

Any driver not conforming with this instruction will be removed from the service as an inefficient driver".

Two months later on 27 April 1904 Mr McCombe issued a further instruction to demonstrate other ways by which current could be saved but started by expressing satisfaction that motormen generally were carrying out the first instruction.

The advice stated that "When starting move the controller handle smoothly and easily to eliminate a "jerk" or "drag". Do not hurry or slur over notches and the car should gain speed gradually. When approaching a curve let the car go on easy speed until you touch the curve then throw all power off and glide round without power.

When starting from the white mark at a railway crossing do not move the car smartly forward and apply brake (presumably over the railway track) immediately after, but let the car go slowly and the brake will not be needed".

Motormen were to report 15 minutes before departure time and satisfy themselves that the car is in perfect working order and that bearings are properly greased and oiled. The tools were to be checked to ensure a full set was in place (Rule 40 above). Brake, bells and sanding gear were to be checked at each end of the car, as were the controller and reversing handle. These were to be left in the OFF position before placing the trolley on the line and taking care that it was in the right direction before closing the canopy switches.

At each terminus the motorman must check that the trolley on line is in the right direction and that the handbrake is on at the front and off at the rear of the car.

Conductors were also to report 15 minutes before departure, but they had to brush the cushions, polish bright metal parts, clean the windows and see the lamps were in good order (all in 15 minutes!). Cleaning materials were supplied and kept in a box for that purpose.

Every night the conductor had to place in the "Cell" in the depot rack, his duty number, duty card, ticket box, punch, cash bag and brush etc.

The Rayner version of 1926 provides for staff to "exercise and use discretion" when faced with circumstances not covered by the rules" and promises support for such action from the management.

Duties of motormen and conductors and other employees are clearly defined and, at times, difficult to carry out. Rule 72, for instance, informs conductors that if fares are not collected by the time that cars have travelled two stopping places from the point of boarding they will be deemed to have neglected to collect those fares and will be dealt with accordingly.

An important rule was that a distance of 40 yards or the distance between two poles was to be left, wherever possible, between cars. At the Beverley Road end of Spring Bank and at Botanic Gardens, cars from Spring Bank had the right of way and the Holderness Road cars had similar precedence at Great Union Street corner.

The regulations also provided advice about possible technical problems, faults and breakdowns as well as instructions should an accident occur. Reference is also made to various bye-laws which have not been traced. It was important to word them carefully as this could and did cause problems should some one decide to challenge them, as happened in 1913 (and described in chapter 5).

Throughout the day there would be little opportunity for rest for any crew member.

Appendix 8

Life in Leeds

Between 27 March 1942 and 14 March 1946 Leeds Corporation Transport placed some forty-two former Hull cars in service numbered 446 to 487. The first to enter service was Hull car no.132 (as no.446) and it was also the last to be officially withdrawn although no.484 (ex 105) was the last in ordinary passenger service on 23 November 1951.

Leeds paid £83 6s 8d each for the first 32 cars and spent a further £176 18s 8d each on re-tyreing and overhaul. The last cars cost £60 each with another £278 0s 5d on overhauls. Leeds are reputed to have bought the last eighteen cars in stock but only ten went to Leeds.

They were normally allocated to Swinegate Depot and were usually to be seen on routes that possessed no significant gradients to Harehills, Hawksworth Road, Dewsbury Road, Meanwood, Elland Road and Hunslet. They were also used on Leeds United football specials from Swinegate to Elland Road and could be seen in the sidings there after matches. They were not normally used on Sundays.

Because the Hull cars were higher than was usual in Leeds they were prohibited from certain routes which ran under railway bridges such as the Wellington Road.

Leeds found them to be anything but standard although they were considered "fast cars" which, given the accusations about low speeds in Hull, seems ironic. Perhaps the absence of side running gave then an opportunity to show their paces. According to the Leeds history the Hull cars with transverse seating were highly regarded.

Some of the Hull cars had side destination boxes but those that did not were fitted with the Leeds standard side destination boxes. Many cars had full drop windows along the side operated by straps but these were removed in Leeds. Some cars had wooden 2/2 seating in the upper saloon and 2/1 in the lower saloon whereas others possessed longitudinal seating in the lower saloon.

Nos 446 to 477 were repainted in khaki livery on entry into service. All but nos 451/71/6 were repainted in Princess blue livery whilst no.467 received the Matterface royal blue livery (the only Hull car to receive three different liveries). Nos 478 to 487 received the Princess blue livery. Cars 479/81/5/6 were repainted in the Matterface blue livery.

Two cars experienced spectacular accidents. No.458 (ex car no.135) collided with a lorry which overturned and no.473 (ex no.154) fell into the inspection pit at Swinegate in September 1949. It did not run again.

On withdrawal two cars (nos 458/64, ex Hull nos 135/47) lost their upper decks which were used as pavilions at the Department's sports field at Red Hall lasting until 1960. Another car, no.470 (ex car no.116) survived intact in a field on Baildon Moor until June 1950.

Withdrawal took place between 1945 and 1951 as follows:

1945: 451
1946: 471
1949: 447, 448, 450, 452, 459, 460, 461, 463, 466, 468, 469, 473, 475, 476, 477, 483
1950: 449, 453, 454, 457, 458, 462, 464, 465, 467, 470, 472, 474, 480, 484, 487
1951: 446, 455, 456, 478, 479, 481, 482, 485, 486

There are two survivors. No.446 (ex Hull no.132) was with-

A Hull car arrives in Leeds in 1943. (MJW)

drawn on Sunday 21 September 1951 after it worked a Light Railway Transport League tour in Leeds that covered Lawnswood, Whingate, Stanningley and Crossgates. It is thought that it last worked in passenger service during May 1951. It was stored in Swinegate until being sold to the Tramway Museum Society. It was restored to its former Hull livery and can now be seen in the Streetlife Museum in Hull.

The other survivor is the former works car no.96 which was sold to Leeds in 1945 for the princely sum of £35. It was numbered 6. Initially it was used as a snow plough until February when it became a works car until being fitted out as a rail grinder in 1954. It became the last tram to run on the streets of Leeds when it was towed from Sovereign Street Yard to Swinegate Depot on 8 December 1959. Mr A.J. Brown purchased it and it later passed to the Leeds Transport Historical Society and is now kept at the Heaton Park Museum in Manchester. It has been converted internally so that it can carry passengers.

Leeds no. 469 was formerly Hull no. 115. (MJW/LHTS)

This is Leeds car no. 483 which was the last car to enter service in Hull (no. 113). (MJW)

Former Hull car no. 127 became Leeds no. 447. (MJW/LHTS)

Hull car no. 159 of 1912 became Leeds no. 462. (MJW/LHTS)

Another ex Hull car was no. 132 which became Leeds 446 and was subsequently preserved. It is seen here on the farewell tour of Leeds in 1951. (MJW/LHTS)

Appendix 9
Legislation and Proposals

As might be expected for tramways that served the city for over seventy years there were many pieces of legislation that provided the power to operate and regulate tramways, the "Bible" being the 1870 Act.

1. The following major items were enacted for the Hull systems.

Tramways Act 1870

Tramways Orders Confirmation Act 1872

Hull Tramways Order 1872

Hull Street Tramways Act 1875

Tramways Orders Confirmation Act 1877

Hull Street Tramways (Extension) Order 1877

Hull Street Tramways Act 1878

Tramways Orders Confirmation (No. 2) Act 1886

Drypool and Marfleet Steam Tramways Order 1886

Borough of Hull Provisional Order 1889

Tramways Orders Confirmation (No. 1) Act 1890

Drypool and Marfleet Steam Tramways Order 1890

Tramways Orders Confirmation Act 1892

Drypool and Marfleet Steam Tramways Order 1892

Tramways Orders Confirmation (No. 1) Act 1896

Hull Corporation Tramways Order 1896

Tramways Orders Confirmation (No. 3) Act 1900

Hull Corporation Tramways Order 1900

Kingston upon Hull Corporation Act 1901

Kingston upon Hull Corporation Act 1903

Kingston upon Hull Corporation Act 1906

Kingston upon Hull Corporation Act 1911

Tramways Orders Confirmation Act 1915

Kingston upon Hull Corporation Tramways Order 1915

Provisional Orders Confirmation (No. 8) Act 1921

Kingston upon Hull Corporation Act 1926

Kingston upon Hull Corporation Act 1936

Whilst some were exclusively tramway legislation others contained several items. For instance the 1901 Act empowered the Corporation of Kingston upon Hull to make certain works to construct a bridge (Stoneferry Bridge) over the River Hull, to lay down tramways and to confer powers with regard to the water supply, health, local government and improvement of the city and for other purposes.

It contained 65 clauses in 40 pages of which 8 clauses referred to tramways, specifically, the extension from Queens Road on Princes Avenue to Newland Avenue and from the easterly approach to Whitefriargate Bridge along a new street to Lowgate and along Lowgate to join the existing line. It also repealed part of the 1900 Order regarding the Hedon Road tramway. This part of the Act is attached.

The Corporation also had powers to make bye-laws to regulate the horse and steam tramways and these were included in the regulations issued by those companies (see Appendix 7).

2. Board of Trade Regulations and Provisional Orders.

Applications to construct and operate tramways were subject to the provisions of the Tramways Act of 1870. This was administered by the Board of Trade which issued a twelve page set of rules to guide intending applicants both public and private.

A Provisional Order authorizing the construction of tramways in any district could be obtained by the local authority of such a district and any person, persons, corporation or company, with the consent of the local authority (including highway boards and health boards) of such a district. Local authorities required a special council meeting of which one month's notice had to be given and at which two-thirds of the membership must be present and vote on the proposal which then required a simple majority for it to be passed.

The BOT guide contained twenty-one rules that had to be heeded. Certified copies of the notice calling the council meeting, the resolution and the numbers present had to be submitted to the Board by local authorities whilst private applicants had to submit this evidence also. If any organisation wanted to change the motive power of an existing tramway this process had to be followed to obtain approval.

Promoters seeking a Provisional Order must publish their intentions at least once in each of two successive weeks in the local press and in the *London Gazette* (*Edinburgh Gazette* in Scotland) in the months of October and November and submit/deposit documents by 23 December in the same year. These should contain a general description, objects of the application, names of areas in which the proposed works would be made and the location of an office in London or the location of the proposals where the documents may be obtained. In the same months notices must be posted in every street or road along which it was intended to lay a tramway. Notices were also to be given to the owners of any railway bridges, road bridges or canals or rivers. Notices were also to state the gauge of the proposed tramways and the power to be used to move carriages or trucks.

Similar notices were required for an extension of time for the construction of tramways (or the abandonment) approved by Parliament. The advertisements must state that any objections must be submitted to the Railway Department of The Board of Trade by 15 January of the following year. The notices were also to be served by 15 December to the owners or reputed owners of any building which abutted the road to a distance of thirty feet on which tramways were to be laid. Provision was made for depositing proposals before 30 November of each year. All plans were to show the lengths of double and single lines of tramway, the total lengths of streets concerned and distance between centre lines on streets all in miles, furlongs, chains and decimals of a chain and any gradients concerned.

A draft Provisional Order had to be deposited in triplicate and be printed on one side of the paper only. Passing places must be described as a double line in accordance with a Standing Order of the House of Lords which provided that "two lines of tramway running side by side shall be described as a double line". On or before 22 February there must be deposited at the

Board's offices a complete manuscript with all the proposed/agreed clauses.

When a Provisional Order was made it required to be advertised not later than 25 April in much the same way as the application and copies made available for inspection at various public offices. Proof of compliance was required to be deposited at the Board's offices. Most of the orders affecting the Hull tramways were deposited at the Town Hall (later Guildhall) in Hull and at the various board offices in Newington, Sculcoates (when still outside the boundary), Hessle and in Beverley for the East Riding County Council.

Examples of proposals that were deposited in accordance with these regulations but not pursued are:

- West Hull Tramways 1889
- Hull Street Tramways 1891
- West and East Hull Tramways 1892
- Hull Tramways 1892

At least fourteen days' notice in writing had to be given to the BOT of the intention to open any tramway or portion of any tramway and no tramway could open for public traffic until an Inspector appointed by the Board had inspected and certified that the tramway was fit for such traffic. The notice was to be accompanied by a copy of the Act or Order, copy or tracing of the deposited plans, a list of local and road authorities concerned and a diagram of the lines submitted for inspection (scale two inches to a mile).

3. Proposals

In addition to the lines that were constructed the following proposals were planned or discussed:

1. Walton Street Crossing – Spring Bank West to Alliance Avenue, later extended to Calvert lane and along Calvert Lane to its junction with Anlaby Road
2. Cottingham Road (Good Fellowship Inn) – Hall Road (Inglemire Lane End)
3. Junction of Anlaby Road/Boothferry Road – Boothferry Road to its junction with Pickering Road
4. Hessle Road – Askew Avenue to its junction with Boothferry Road (in a letter from Mr Rayner to the City Engineer stating the only reason for a dual carriageway was to provide for a tram reservation.)
5. Anlaby Road – Hawthorn Avenue – Hessle Road
6. Witham – New Cleveland Street – Stoneferry Road – Stoneferry.

G.A. Lee in his dissertation states that there were proposals for the Charles Street area but I have found no evidence of this...

Appendix 10

Bibliography and Sources of Information

1. Introduction

Anyone who attempts to write any articles about municipal transport in Kingston upon Hull is frustrated by the fact that so many records were destroyed in air raids in May 1941 when the head offices in Baker Street were bombed followed a few days later by the temporary head offices alongside Cottingham Road garage.

Nevertheless there are public records at the National Archives at Kew, Hull's History Centre, Hull's Streetlife Museum and the Carnegie Heritage Centre which have been raided as much as possible.

2. Drypool and Marfleet Steam Tramways Company
3. Hull Street Tramways Company

1. Hull Street Tramways Company Prospectus – November 1875
2. Hull's Steam Tramway – R.J. Buckley in *Tramway Review,* volume 111 no. 83 Autumn 1975 and no. 84, Winter 1975
3. *The Kingston upon Hull Steam Tramways: a history of private enterprise in Hull tramway operation 1870-1899* – M. Charlesworth and S.F. Robinson, 1976
4. *Hull Trams – The Early Days* – retitled and revised edition of the Charlesworth and Robinson published by Hull City Museums and Art Galleries 1999
5. Horse Tramways in Hull – R.J. Buckley in *Tramway Review,* volume 14, no. 111 Autumn 1982 and no.112, Winter 1982
6. *"Fares Please!"* – published privately by Charles Dyson in 1922 being his personal memories of working on the horse system
7. *Tramways. their Construction and Working* – D.K. Clark 1894
8. Hull's Steam Tramway – Chris Allan in *Yorkshire History Quarterly,* volume 1, no. 6, May 1996

4. Hull Corporation Tramways (later Hull Corporation Transport)

1. Hull Corporation Electric Tramways – *Railway World* volume 8, 10 August 1899
2. Hull Corporation Tramways – *Light Railway and Tramway Journal,* volume 1 September 1899
3. The City of Hull Tramways – *The Tramway and Railway World* – 10 July 1902
4. Hull's Decorated Cars – *The Tramway and Railway World* – 19 May 1921
5. Oil Fuel on Hull tramways: a comparison with coal consumption by E.S. Rayner – *Electric Railway and Tramway Journal* volume 54, 19 July 1923
6. Improved Tramway Cars – *Electric Railway and Tramway Journal,* volume 49, 13 July 1923
7. Hull Corporation tramway car with worm drive – *Tramway and Railway World* volume no.54, 19 July 1923
8. Modern Tramway – June 1942
9. *A Brief History of Municipal Passenger Transport in Kingston upon Hull* – Diamond Jubilee brochure published by Hull Corporation Transport 1949
10. Urban Transport in Hull – E.N. Osborne in *Omnibus Magazine* volume 13, no.90, 29 September 1954
11. British Bus and Tram Systems No. 19 – Hull – G.M. O'Connell in *Buses* May-June 1957
12. *A Guide to past and present route numbers used by Kingston upon Hull Corporation* – H.C. Goldspink published by the Omnibus Society 1967
13. *The Tramways of Kingston upon Hull: a study in municipal enterprise* – G.A. Lee – Thesis submission to University of Hull 1967
14. The Tramways Of Kingston upon Hull – J.S. Nicholson in *Trams* no.27, October 1967, no.28 January 1968 and no. 29 April 1968
15. *An Illustrated History of Kingston upon Hull City Transport 1899-1979,* Kingston upon Hull Corporation Transport 1979
16. Hull 132 – J.H. Price in *Modern Tramway* volume 47, no.557 May 1984
17. *Kingston upon Hull City Transport 1899 to 1984* – A Short History published by Kingston upon Hull City Transport 1984
18. *Those Infamous Level Crossings – An Illustrated History of Hull's Railways* – Irwell Press 1993
19. The Railway/Electric Tramway Crossings in Hull – in *More Illustrated History of the Railways of Hull* – Challenger Publications 1995
20. Tramway Level Crossings – N. Proudlock in *Tramway Review,* volume 22, Autumn 1997
21. *Directory of British Tram Depots* – K. Turner, S. Smith and P. Smith published by Ian Allan
22. R. Berrieman – *Six Buses and a Tramway to Nowhere* – Hull College Local History Section
23. *Hull Tramways* – Paul Morfitt and Malcolm Wells – Middleton Press 2005
24. *Tramcars of Hull* – N. Proudlock in Tramway Review, volume 26, June 2007
25. *Tramways Developments* by Mr W.J. M'Combe in *Hull Trades and Labour Council Year Book 1903*

5. Other References

1. Light Rapid Transit for Hull – R. J. Buckley in *Modern Tramway and Rapid Transit Review,* volume 38, no.452, August 1975
2. *Light Rail for Hull* – Andy Comfort and Tom Hepworth for Radio Humberside 2003
3. Invitation to Councillor and Mrs Brown to the formal opening of the Electrical Tramways Service on 5 July 1899
4. *Leeds Transport* – Volume 3 (1932 – 1953) – J. Soper, Leeds Transport Historical Society 2003
5. *"A Century of Public Transport in Hull"* – MSC Oral History Project published by the Manpower Services Commission 1988

6. Statutory References and Public Records

1. Files held at the National Archives (Public Record Office) at Kew
2. USA Department of Commerce and Labor – Daily Consular Report no.1995 *"City-owned Street Cars",* published 5 July 1904

7. Newspapers

1. Various editions of the *Hull Daily Mail, Hull Evening News* and *Eastern Morning News* at the History Centre, Hull
2. *New York Times,* 18 July 1897, 25 July 1903, 6 July 1904, 10 December 1904, 25 February 1907 and 6 December 1929
3. Press Cuttings at the Carnegie Heritage Centre, Hull

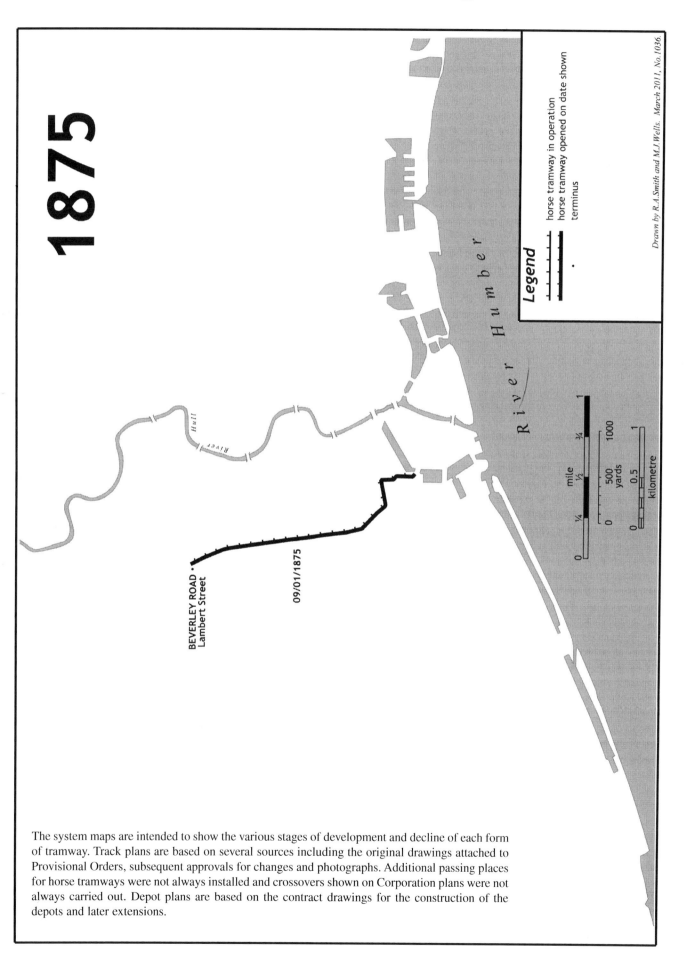

The system maps are intended to show the various stages of development and decline of each form of tramway. Track plans are based on several sources including the original drawings attached to Provisional Orders, subsequent approvals for changes and photographs. Additional passing places for horse tramways were not always installed and crossovers shown on Corporation plans were not always carried out. Depot plans are based on the contract drawings for the construction of the depots and later extensions.

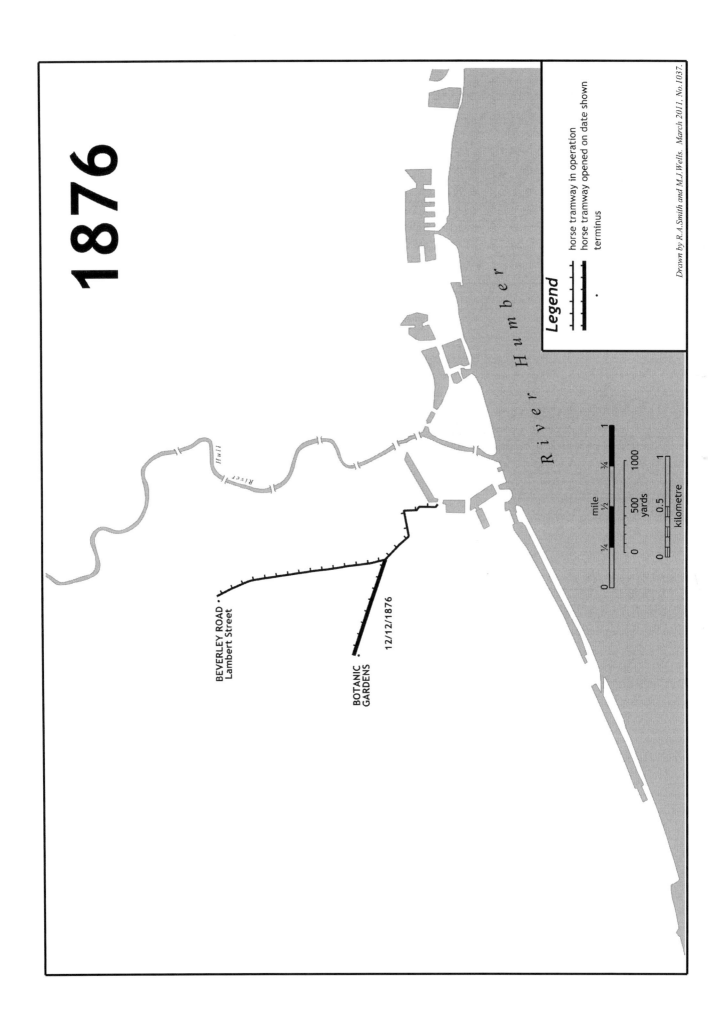

1876

River Humber

River Hull

BEVERLEY ROAD · Lambert Street

BOTANIC GARDENS ·

12/12/1876

Drawn by R.A.Smith and M.J.Wells. March 2011, No.1037.

Legend

— horse tramway in operation

▬ horse tramway opened on date shown

· terminus

mile
¼ ½ ¾ 1
0

0 500 1000
yards

0 0.5 1
kilometre

256

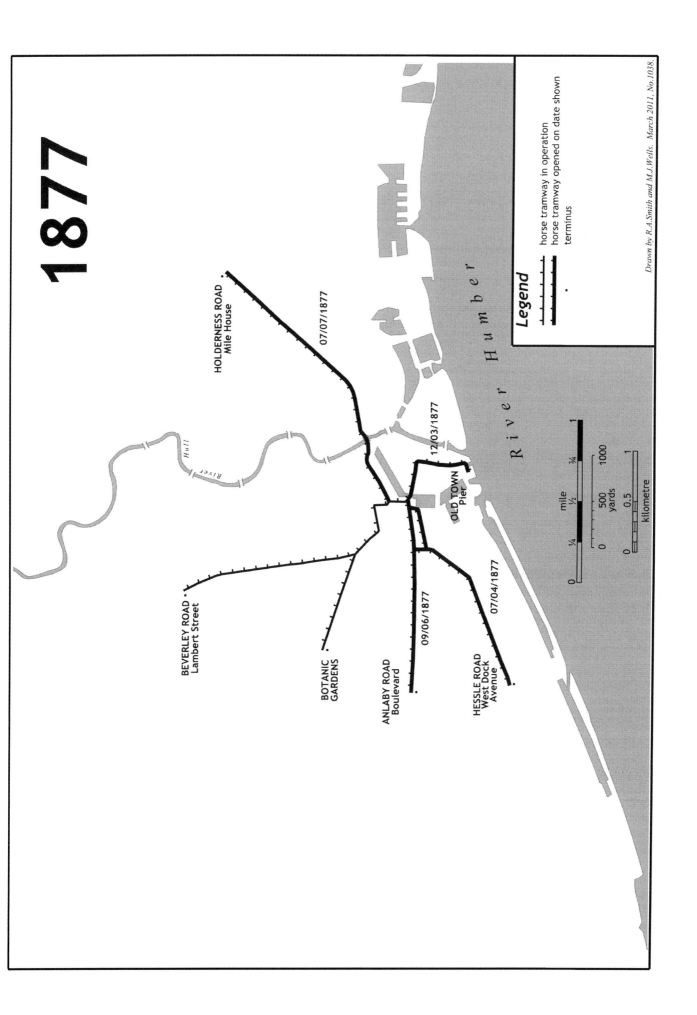

1877

BEVERLEY ROAD
Lambert Street

BOTANIC
GARDENS

ANLABY ROAD
Boulevard

09/06/1877

HESSLE ROAD
West Dock
Avenue

07/04/1877

HOLDERNESS ROAD
Mile House

07/07/1877

12/03/1877

OLD TOWN
Pier

River Humber

River Hull

Legend

horse tramway in operation
horse tramway opened on date shown
terminus

mile
¼   ½   ¾   1

0   500   1000
yards

0   0.5   1
kilometre

Drawn by R.A.Smith and M.J.Wells. March 2011, No.1038.

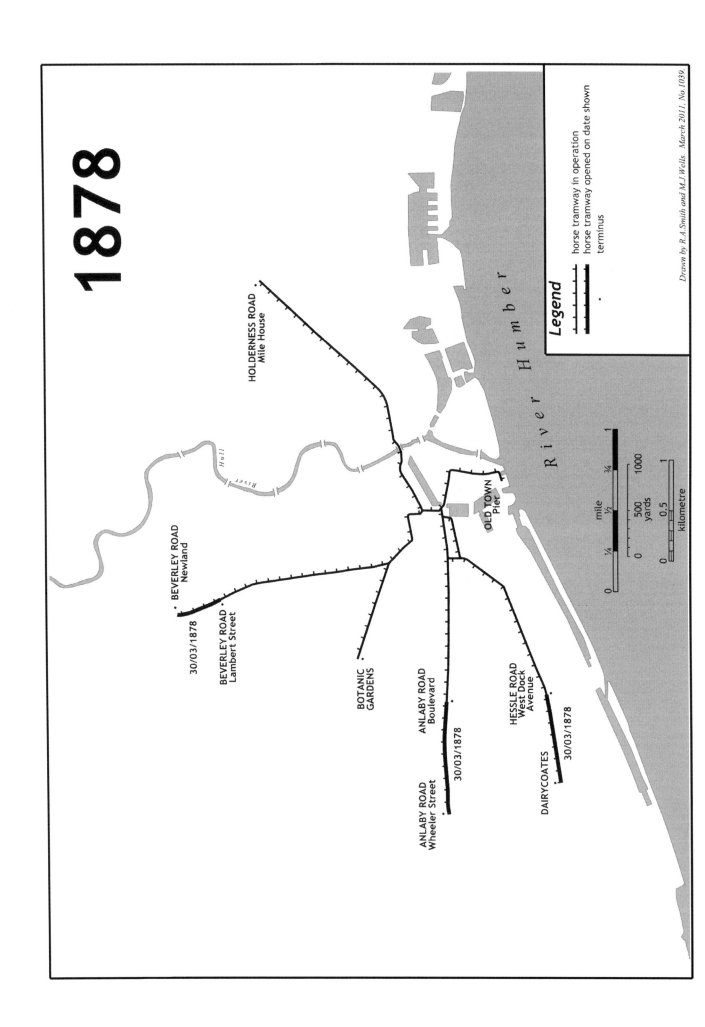

1878

HOLDERNESS ROAD
Mile House

BEVERLEY ROAD
Newland

30/03/1878

BEVERLEY ROAD
Lambert Street

River Hull

BOTANIC
GARDENS

ANLABY ROAD
Boulevard

ANLABY ROAD
Wheeler Street

30/03/1878

HESSLE ROAD
West Dock
Avenue

DAIRYCOATES

30/03/1878

OLD TOWN
Pier

River Humber

Legend

horse tramway in operation
horse tramway opened on date shown
terminus

mile
¼   ½   ¾   1
0   500   1000
yards
0   0.5   1
kilometre

Drawn by R.A.Smith and M.J.Wells. March 2011. No.1039.

258

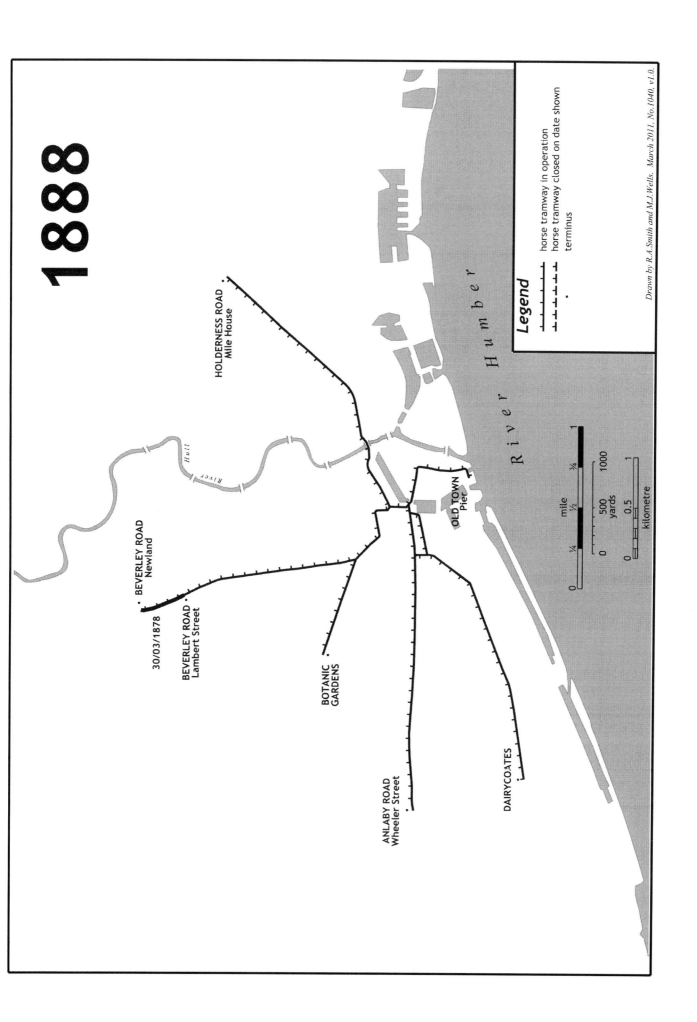

1888

Legend

— horse tramway in operation

–··–··– horse tramway closed on date shown

· terminus

HOLDERNESS ROAD
Mile House

BEVERLEY ROAD
Newland

30/03/1878

BEVERLEY ROAD
Lambert Street

River Hull

BOTANIC
GARDENS

OLD TOWN
Pier

ANLABY ROAD
Wheeler Street

DAIRYCOATES

River Humber

mile

0   ¼   ½   ¾   1

yards

0   500   1000

kilometre

0   0.5   1

Drawn by R.A.Smith and M.J.Wells. March 2011. No.1040, v1.0.

259

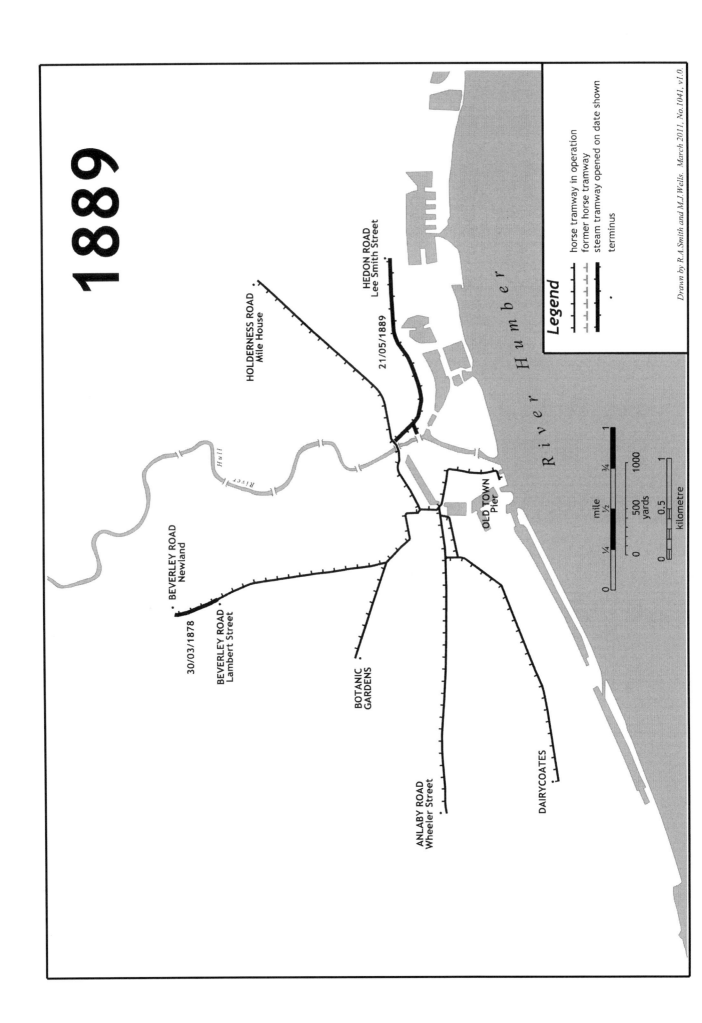

1889

HOLDERNESS ROAD
Mile House

HEDON ROAD
Lee Smith Street

21/05/1889

BEVERLEY ROAD
Newland

30/03/1878

BEVERLEY ROAD
Lambert Street

BOTANIC
GARDENS

ANLABY ROAD
Wheeler Street

DAIRYCOATES

OLD TOWN
Pier

River Humber

River Hull

Legend

horse tramway in operation

former horse tramway

steam tramway opened on date shown

terminus

mile

¼   ½   ¾   1

0

yards

0   500   1000

kilometre

0   0.5   1

Drawn by R.A.Smith and M.J.Wells. March 2011, No.1041, v1.0.

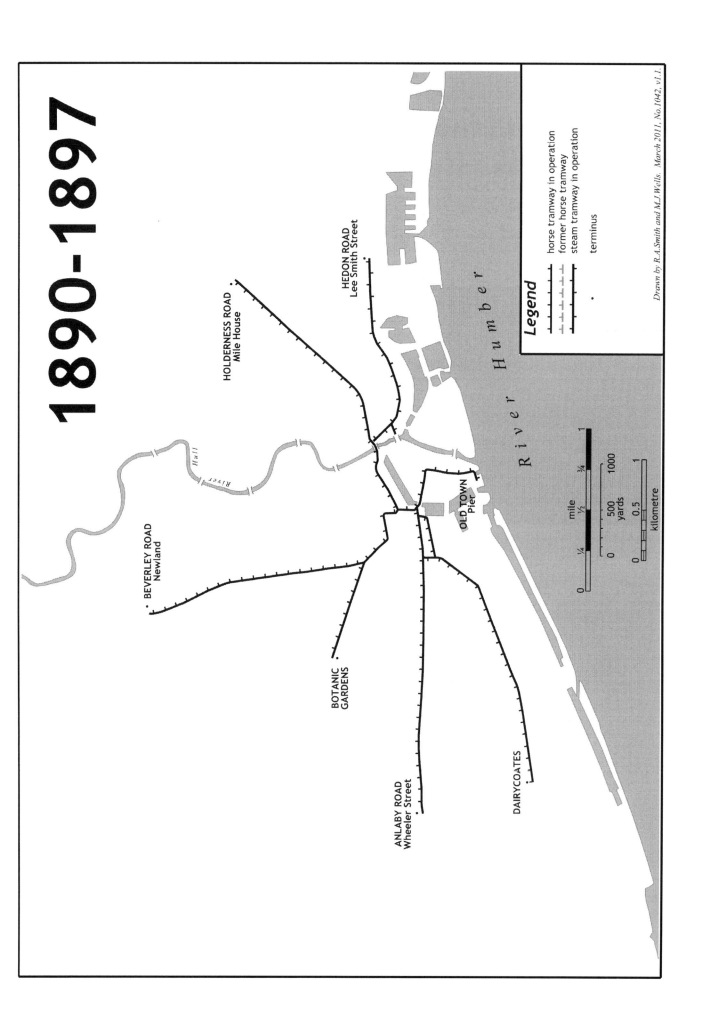

1890-1897

BEVERLEY ROAD
Newland

HOLDERNESS ROAD
Mile House

HEDON ROAD
Lee Smith Street

River Hull

BOTANIC
GARDENS

ANLABY ROAD
Wheeler Street

OLD TOWN
Pier

DAIRYCOATES

River Humber

Drawn by R.A.Smith and M.J.Wells. March 2011, No.1042, v1.1.

Legend

horse tramway in operation
former horse tramway
steam tramway in operation

• terminus

mile
0   ¼   ½   ¾   1

yards
0   500   1000

kilometre
0   0.5   1

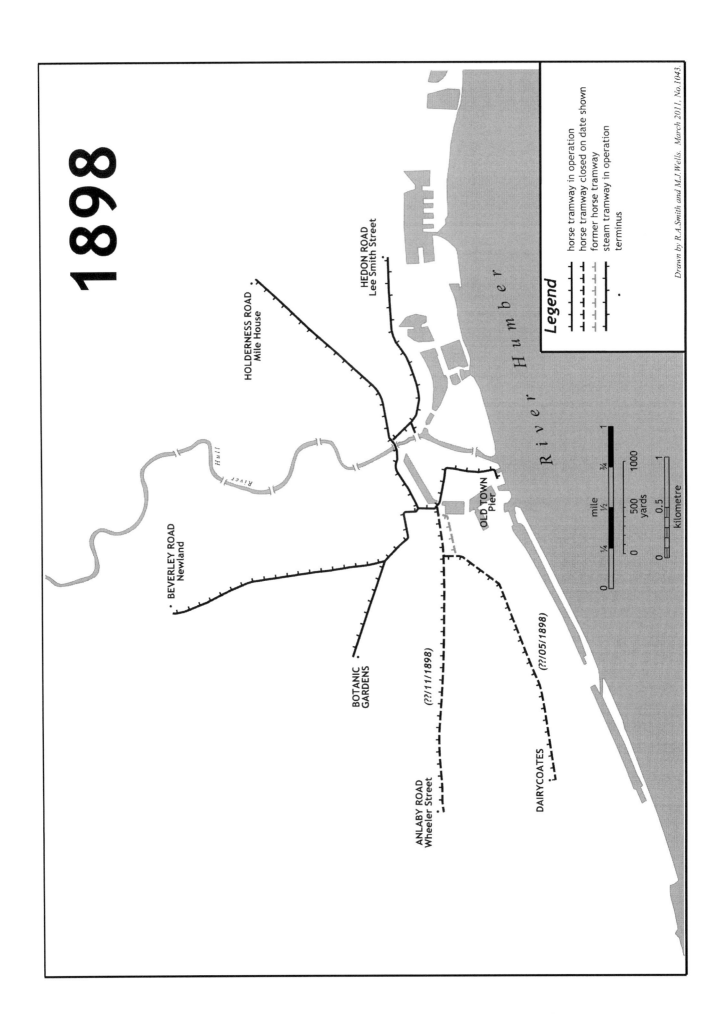

1898

HOLDERNESS ROAD
Mile House

HEDON ROAD
Lee Smith Street

River Hull

BEVERLEY ROAD
Newland

BOTANIC
GARDENS

ANLABY ROAD
Wheeler Street

(??/11/1898)

DAIRYCOATES

(??/05/1898)

OLD TOWN
Pier

R i v e r   H u m b e r

mile
¼   ½   ¾   1
0   500   1000
yards
0   0.5   1
kilometre

Drawn by R.A.Smith and M.J.Wells. March 2011. No.1043.

Legend

horse tramway in operation
horse tramway closed on date shown
former horse tramway
steam tramway in operation
terminus

1899

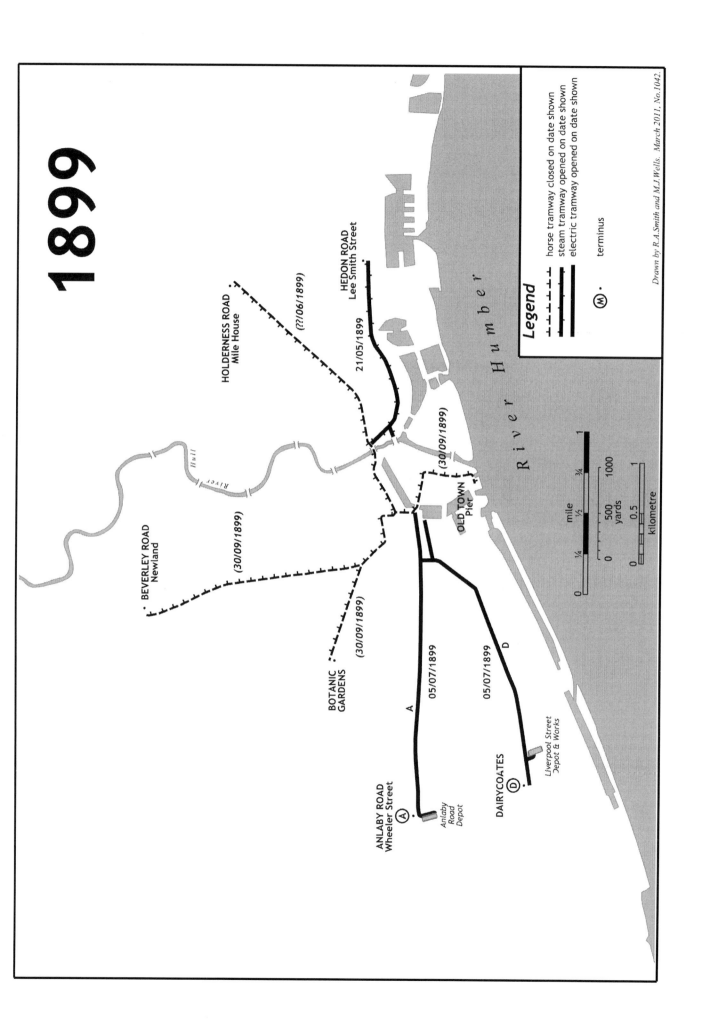

HOLDERNESS ROAD
Mile House
(??/06/1899)

HEDON ROAD
Lee Smith Street
21/05/1899

BEVERLEY ROAD
Newland
(30/09/1899)

BOTANIC
GARDENS
(30/09/1899)

(30/09/1899)

OLD TOWN
Pier

River Hull

River Humber

ANLABY ROAD
Wheeler Street
Ⓐ
Anlaby
Road
Depot

A
05/07/1899

D
05/07/1899

DAIRYCOATES
Ⓓ

Liverpool Street
Depot & Works

Drawn by R.A.Smith and M.J.Wells. March 2011. No.1042.

Legend

- horse tramway closed on date shown
- steam tramway opened on date shown
- electric tramway opened on date shown

Ⓜ · terminus

mile
¼   ½   ¾   1
0
yards
0   500   1000
kilometre
0   0.5   1

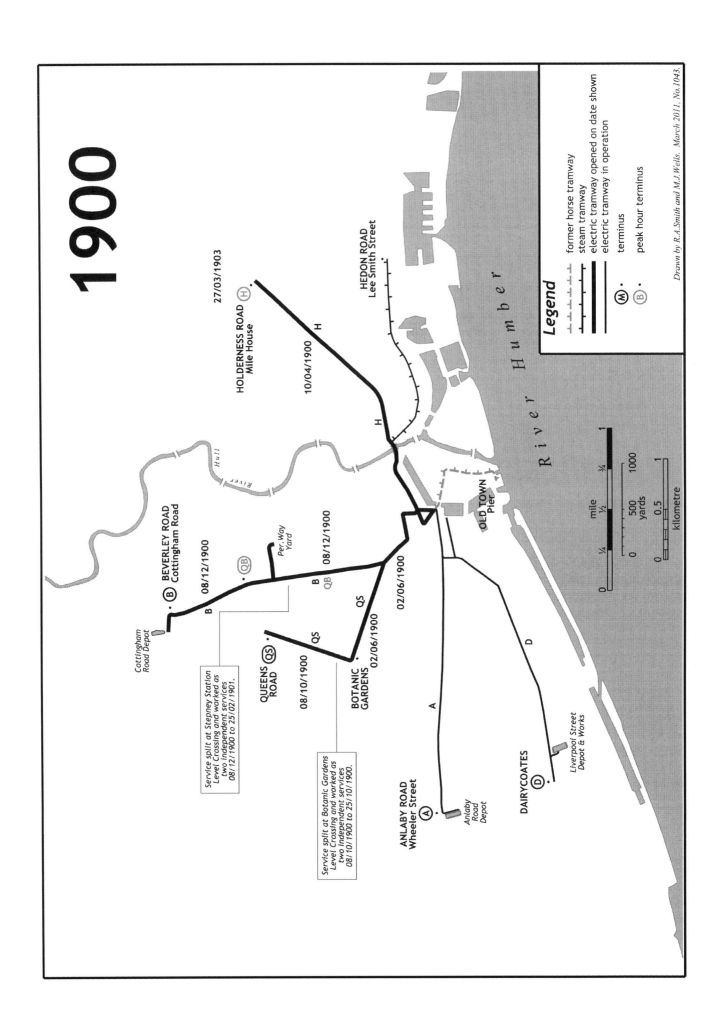

1900

27/03/1903

HOLDERNESS ROAD
Mile House (H) •

H
10/04/1900

HEDON ROAD
Lee Smith Street

H

River Hull

BEVERLEY ROAD
(B) Cottingham Road

08/12/1900

B

(QB) •

Per. Way
Yard

B

QB

08/12/1900

Cottingham
Road Depot

Service split at Stepney Station
Level Crossing and worked as
two independent services
08/12/1900 to 25/02/1901.

QUEENS (QS) •
ROAD

08/10/1900

QS

QS

02/06/1900

BOTANIC
GARDENS •

02/06/1900

OLD TOWN
Pier

River   H u m b e r

Service split at Botanic Gardens
Level Crossing and worked as
two independent services
08/10/1900 to 25/10/1900.

A

ANLABY ROAD
Wheeler Street
(A) •

Antaby
Road
Depot

D

DAIRYCOATES
(D) •

Liverpool Street
Depot & Works

Legend

- - - - former horse tramway
━━━ steam tramway
━━━ electric tramway opened on date shown
─── electric tramway in operation
(M) • terminus
(B) • peak hour terminus

mile
¼   ½   ¾   1
0   500   1000
yards
0   0.5   1
kilometre

Drawn by R.A.Smith and M.J.Wells. March 2011. No.1043.

1901

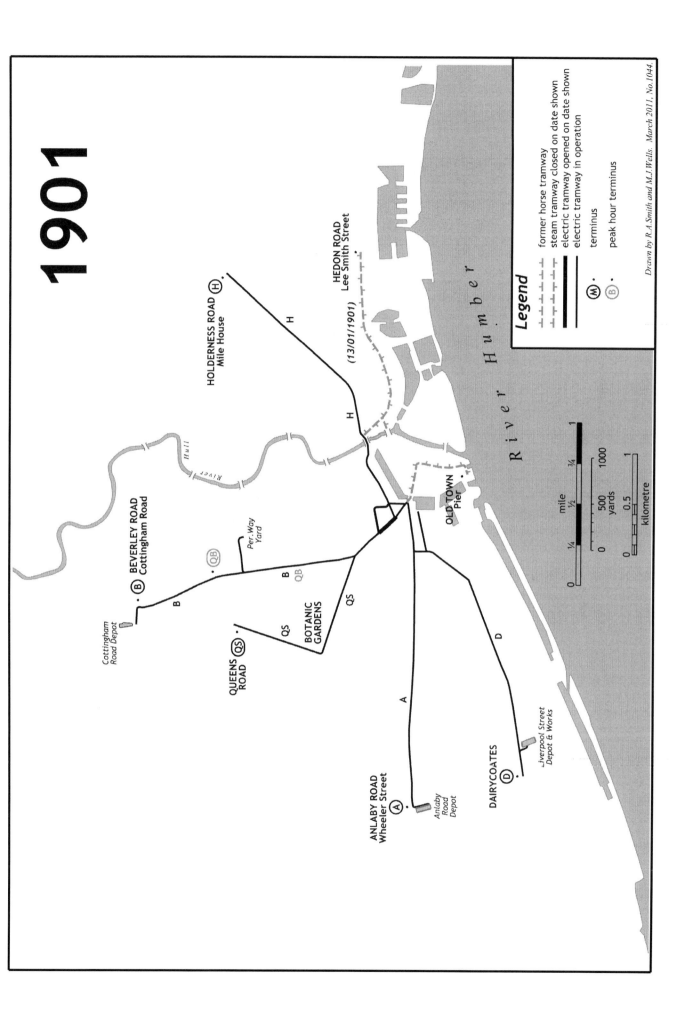

HOLDERNESS ROAD (H) Mile House

HEDON ROAD Lee Smith Street

(13/01/1901)

BEVERLEY ROAD Cottingham Road (B)

Cottingham Road Depot

River Hull

Per. Way Yard

(QB)

QB

B

QS

BOTANIC GARDENS

QUEENS ROAD (QS)

QS

B

A

ANLABY ROAD Wheeler Street (A)

Anlaby Road Depot

DAIRYCOATES (D)

D

Liverpool Street Depot & Works

OLD TOWN Pier

R i v e r   H u m b e r

Legend

	former horse tramway
	steam tramway closed on date shown
	electric tramway opened on date shown
	electric tramway in operation
(M) ·	terminus
(B) ·	peak hour terminus

mile
0   ¼   ½   ¾   1

yards
0   500   1000

kilometre
0   0.5   1

Drawn by R.A.Smith and M.J.Wells. March 2011, No.1044.

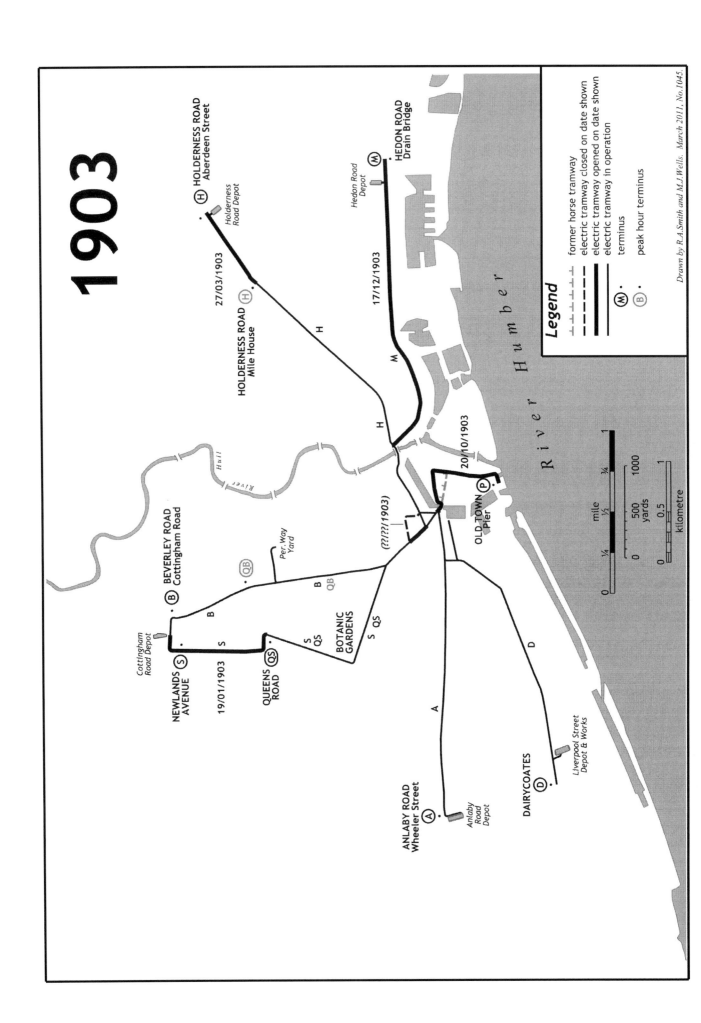

1903

Drawn by R.A.Smith and M.J.Wells, March 2011, No.1045.

Legend

	former horse tramway
	electric tramway closed on date shown
	electric tramway opened on date shown
	electric tramway in operation
·	terminus
·	peak hour terminus
Ⓜ ·	
Ⓑ ·	

HOLDERNESS ROAD
Aberdeen Street Ⓗ

27/03/1903

Holderness
Road Depot

HOLDERNESS ROAD
Mile House Ⓗ

HEDON ROAD
Drain Bridge Ⓜ

Hedon Road
Depot

17/12/1903

BEVERLEY ROAD
Cottingham Road Ⓑ

Cottingham
Road Depot

NEWLANDS
AVENUE Ⓢ

19/01/1903

QUEENS
ROAD Ⓠⓢ

Per. Way
Yard

River Hull

BOTANIC
GARDENS

OLD TOWN
Pier Ⓟ

20/10/1903

(??/??/1903)

River Humber

ANLABY ROAD
Wheeler Street Ⓐ

Anlaby
Road Depot

DAIRYCOATES Ⓓ

Liverpool Street
Depot & Works

mile
¼   ½   ¾
0   1

yards
0   500   1000

kilometre
0   0.5   1

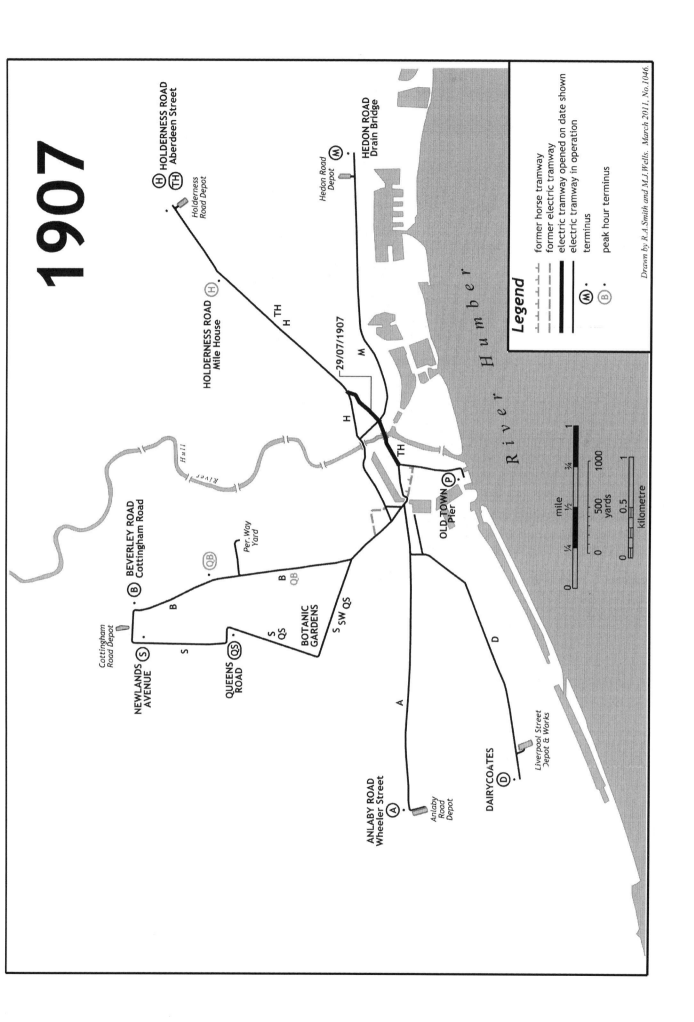

1907

HOLDERNESS ROAD (H) (TH)
Aberdeen Street

Holderness Road Depot

HOLDERNESS ROAD (H)
Mile House

TH
H

29/07/1907

M

H

TH

HEDON ROAD (M)
Drain Bridge

Hedon Road Depot

River Hull

BEVERLEY ROAD (B)
Cottingham Road

QB

Per. Way Yard

B
QB

B

NEWLANDS AVENUE (S)

Cottingham Road Depot

S

S
QS

QUEENS ROAD (QS)

S SW QS

BOTANIC GARDENS

OLD TOWN (P)
Pier

R i v e r   H u m b e r

A

D

ANLABY ROAD
Wheeler Street (A)

Anlaby Road Depot

DAIRYCOATES (D)

Liverpool Street Depot & Works

Legend

— · — · —   former horse tramway
— — — —   former electric tramway
———   electric tramway opened on date shown
━━━   electric tramway in operation
(M) ·   terminus
(B) ·   peak hour terminus

mile
¼ ½ ¾ 1
0

0 500 1000
yards

0 0.5 1
kilometre

Drawn by R.A.Smith and M.J.Wells. March 2011, No.1046.

267

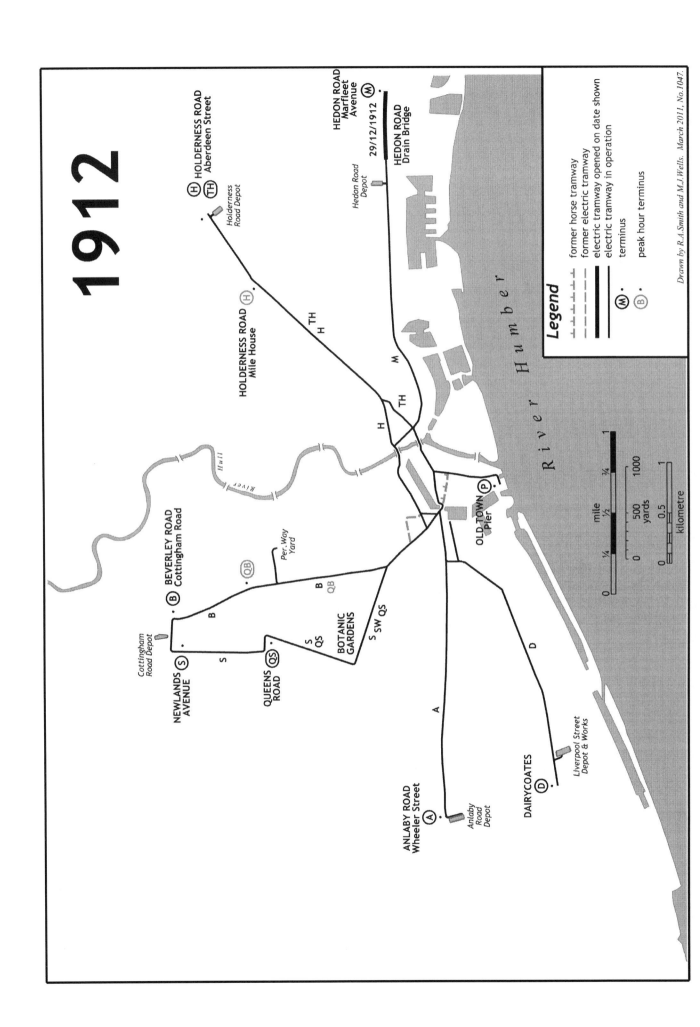

1912

HOLDERNESS ROAD
Aberdeen Street

HEDON ROAD
Marfleet
Avenue

29/12/1912

HEDON ROAD
Drain Bridge

Hedon Road
Depot

Holderness
Road Depot

HOLDERNESS ROAD
Mile House

Per. Way
Yard

BEVERLEY ROAD
Cottingham Road

Cottingham
Road Depot

NEWLANDS
AVENUE

QUEENS
ROAD

BOTANIC
GARDENS

OLD TOWN
Pier

River Humber

River Hull

ANLABY ROAD
Wheeler Street

Anlaby
Road Depot

DAIRYCOATES

Liverpool Street
Depot & Works

Legend

former horse tramway
former electric tramway
electric tramway opened on date shown
electric tramway in operation
terminus
peak hour terminus

Drawn by R.A.Smith and M.J.Wells. March 2011, No.1047.

mile
¼   ½   ¾   1
0   500   1000
yards
0   0.5   1
kilometre

1913

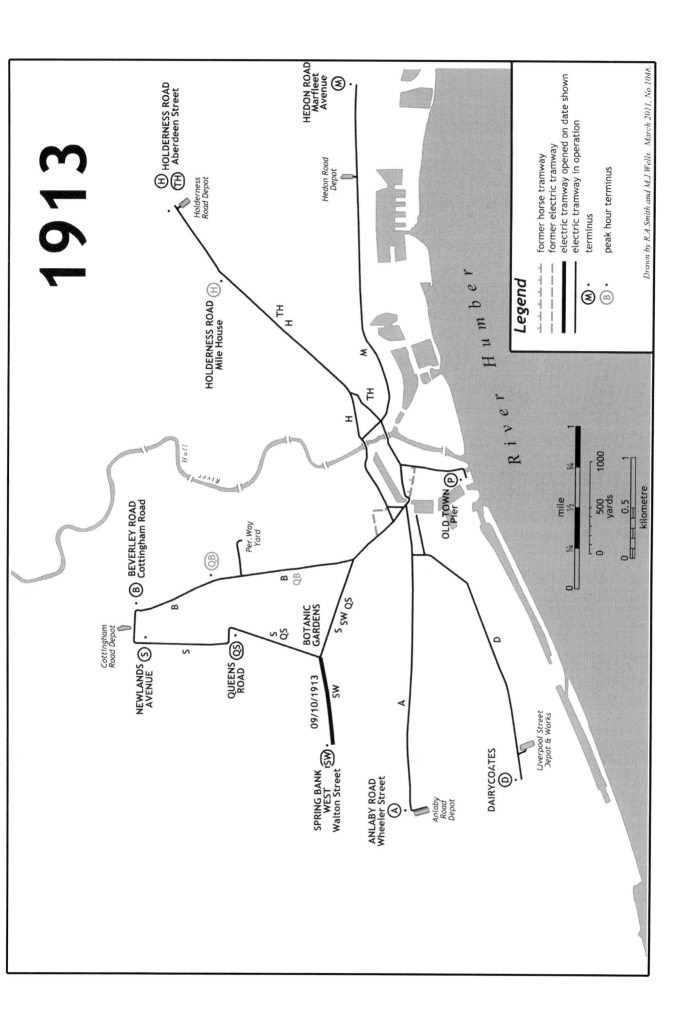

HOLDERNESS ROAD
Aberdeen Street

HOLDERNESS ROAD
Mile House

Holderness
Road Depot

HEDON ROAD
Marfleet Avenue

Hedon Road
Depot

BEVERLEY ROAD
Cottingham Road

River Hull

Per. Way
Yard

Cottingham
Road Depot

NEWLANDS
AVENUE

QUEENS
ROAD

BOTANIC
GARDENS

09/10/1913

SPRING BANK
WEST
Walton Street

ANLABY ROAD
Wheeler Street

Anlaby
Road
Depot

DAIRYCOATES

Liverpool Street
Depot & Works

OLD TOWN
Pier

River Humber

Legend

former horse tramway
former electric tramway
electric tramway opened on date shown
electric tramway in operation
terminus
peak hour terminus

Drawn by R.A.Smith and M.J.Wells. March 2011, No.1048.

mile
0   ¼   ½   ¾   1

yards
0   500   1000

kilometre
0   0.5   1

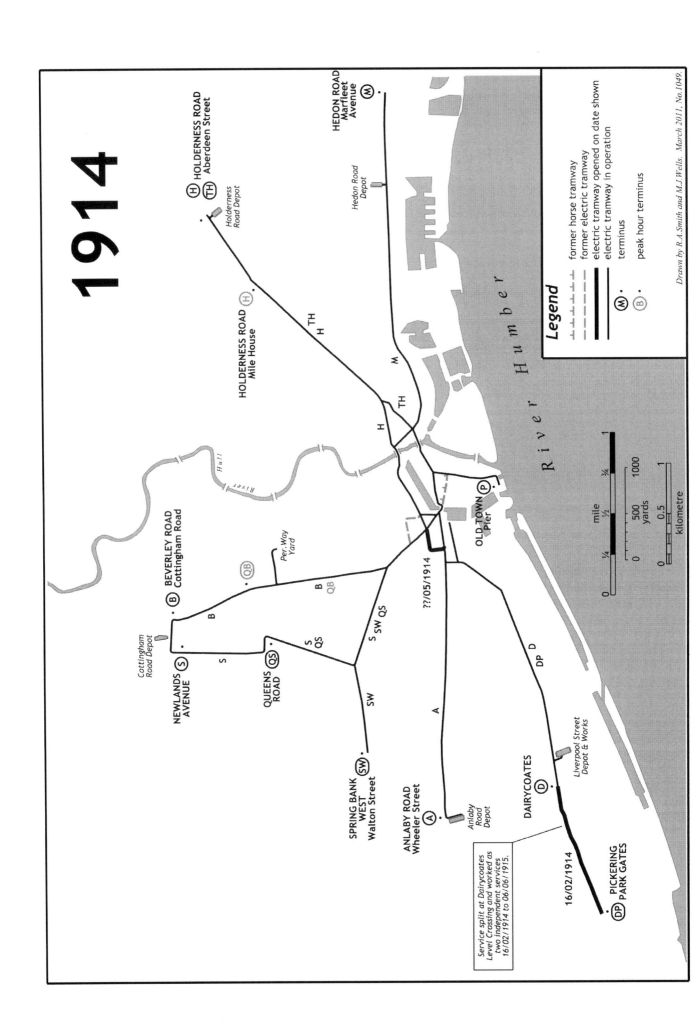

1914

HOLDERNESS ROAD Aberdeen Street (H) (TH)

HEDON ROAD Marfleet Avenue (M)

Holderness Road Depot

Hedon Road Depot

TH
H
H

M

HOLDERNESS ROAD Mile House (H)

TH

H

River Hull

BEVERLEY ROAD Cottingham Road (B)

(QB)

Per. Way Yard

B
QB

Cottingham Road Depot

NEWLANDS AVENUE (S)

S
B

QUEENS ROAD (QS)

S
QS

S SW QS

River Humber

OLD TOWN Pier (P)

SW
S

??/05/1914

SPRING BANK WEST Walton Street (SW)

SW

A

D
D

ANLABY ROAD Wheeler Street (A)

Anlaby Road Depot

DP
D

DAIRYCOATES (D)

Liverpool Street Depot & Works

Service split at Dairycoates Level Crossing and worked as two independent services 16/02/1914 to 06/06/1915.

16/02/1914

PICKERING PARK GATES (DP)

Legend

former horse tramway
former electric tramway
electric tramway opened on date shown
electric tramway in operation
terminus
peak hour terminus

(M) ·
(B) ·

Drawn by R.A.Smith and M.J.Wells. March 2011, No.1049.

mile
¼   ½   ¾   1
0   500   1000
yards
0   0.5   1
kilometre

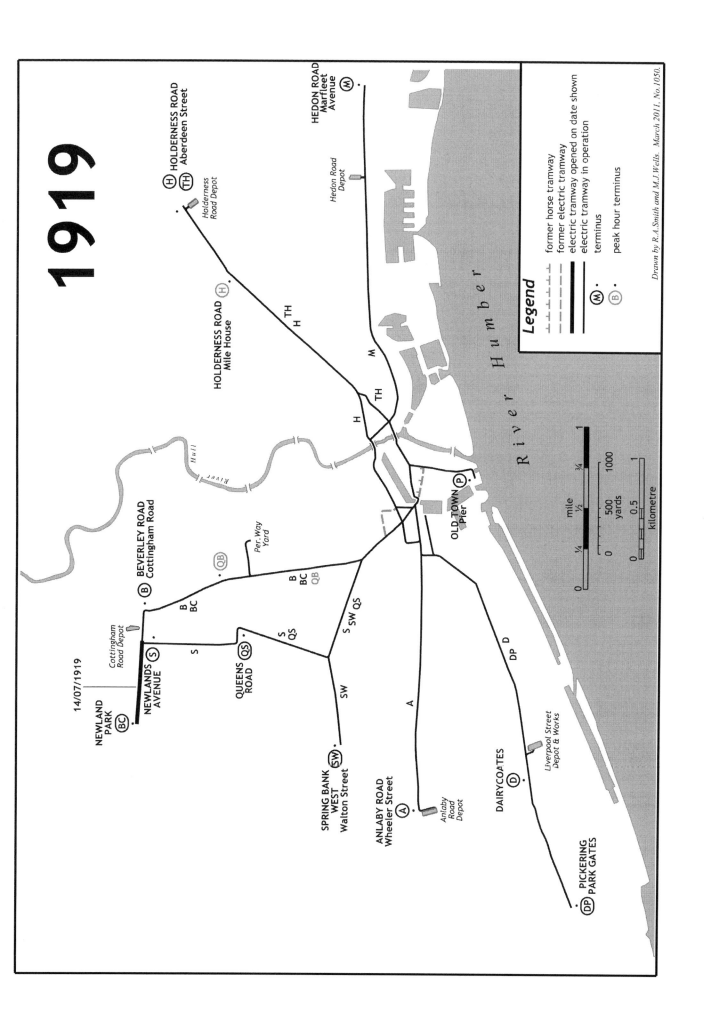

1919

14/07/1919

NEWLAND PARK (BC)

NEWLANDS AVENUE (S)

Cottingham Road Depot

BEVERLEY ROAD (B) Cottingham Road

(QB)

Per. Way Yard

HOLDERNESS ROAD (H) Mile House

HOLDERNESS ROAD (H) Aberdeen Street (TH)

Holderness Road Depot

QUEENS ROAD (QS)

SPRING BANK WEST (SW) Walton Street

ANLABY ROAD (A) Wheeler Street

Anlaby Road Depot

DAIRYCOATES (D)

Liverpool Street Depot & Works

PICKERING PARK GATES (DP)

OLD TOWN (P) Pier

HEDON ROAD (M) Marfleet Avenue

Hedon Road Depot

River Humber

River Hull

Drawn by R.A.Smith and M.J.Wells. March 2011. No.1050.

Legend

former horse tramway
former electric tramway
electric tramway opened on date shown
electric tramway in operation

(M) terminus
(B) peak hour terminus

mile
¼ ½ ¾ 1
0   500   1000
yards
0   0.5   1
kilometre

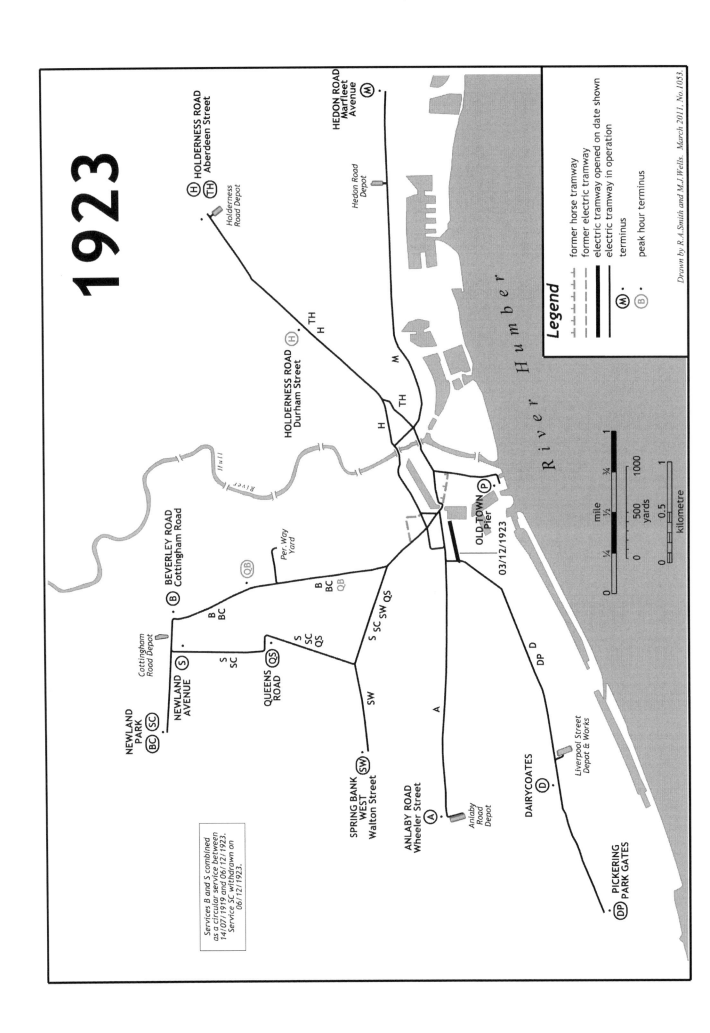

1923

NEWLAND PARK (BC) (SC)

NEWLAND AVENUE (S)

Cottingham Road Depot

BEVERLEY ROAD Cottingham Road (B)

(QB)

Per. Way Yard

HOLDERNESS ROAD Durham Street (H)

HOLDERNESS ROAD Aberdeen Street (H) (TH)

Holderness Road Depot

TH
H

B
BC

B
BC
QB

QUEENS ROAD (QS)

S
SC

S
SC
QS

S SC SW QS

TH

H

M

HEDON ROAD Marfleet Avenue (M)

Hedon Road Depot

SPRING BANK WEST Walton Street (SW)

SW

ANLABY ROAD Wheeler Street (A)

Anlaby Road Depot

A

OLD TOWN Pier (P)

03/12/1923

R i v e r   H u m b e r

Liverpool Street Depot & Works

DAIRYCOATES (D)

D

DP

PICKERING PARK GATES (DP)

Services B and S combined as a circular service between 14/07/1919 and 06/12/1923. Service SC withdrawn on 06/12/1923.

River Hull

Legend

- former horse tramway
- former electric tramway
- electric tramway opened on date shown
- electric tramway in operation
- (M) terminus
- (B) peak hour terminus

mile
¼   ½   ¾   1
0

0   500   1000
yards

0   0.5   1
kilometre

Drawn by R.A.Smith and M.J.Wells. March 2011. No.1053.

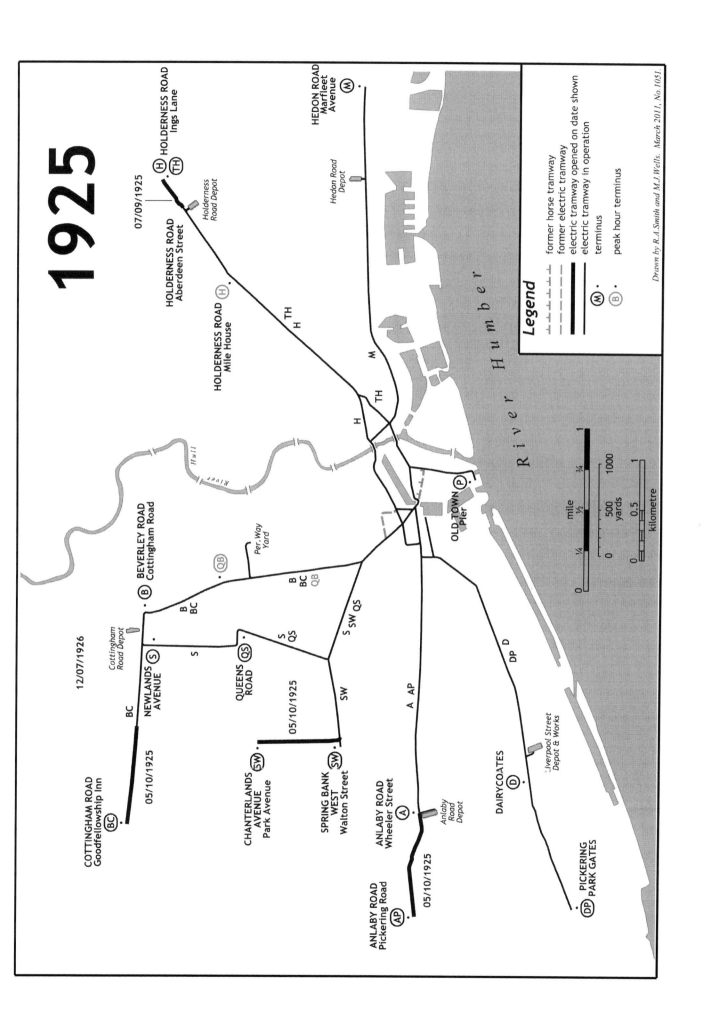

1925

COTTINGHAM ROAD
Goodfellowship Inn
(BC)

12/07/1926

05/10/1925
BC

*Cottingham
Road Depot*

**NEWLANDS
AVENUE** (S)

**CHANTERLANDS
AVENUE**
Park Avenue (SW)

05/10/1925

**SPRING BANK
WEST**
Walton Street (SW)

ANLABY ROAD
Wheeler Street (A)

*Anlaby
Road Depot*

ANLABY ROAD
Pickering Road (AP)

05/10/1925

**QUEENS
ROAD** (QS)

S

SW

S
QS

SW

A AP

DAIRYCOATES (D)

*Liverpool Street
Depot & Works*

DP D

**PICKERING
PARK GATES** (DP)

BEVERLEY ROAD
Cottingham Road (B)

B
BC

(QB)

*Per. Way
Yard*

B
BC
QB

S SW QS

OLD TOWN
Pier (P)

HOLDERNESS ROAD
Ings Lane (H) (TH)

07/09/1925

*Holderness
Road Depot*

TH

HOLDERNESS ROAD
Aberdeen Street (H)

HOLDERNESS ROAD
Mile House

TH
H

M

TH

H

HEDON ROAD
Marfleet
Avenue (M)

*Hedon Road
Depot*

R i v e r   H u m b e r

R i v e r   *Hull*

mile
¼   ½   ¾   1

0   500   1000
yards

0   0.5   1
kilometre

Drawn by R.A.Smith and M.J.Wells. March 2011. No.1051.

Legend

— — — former horse tramway
– – – former electric tramway
▬▬▬ electric tramway opened on date shown
——— electric tramway in operation
(M) • terminus
(B) • peak hour terminus

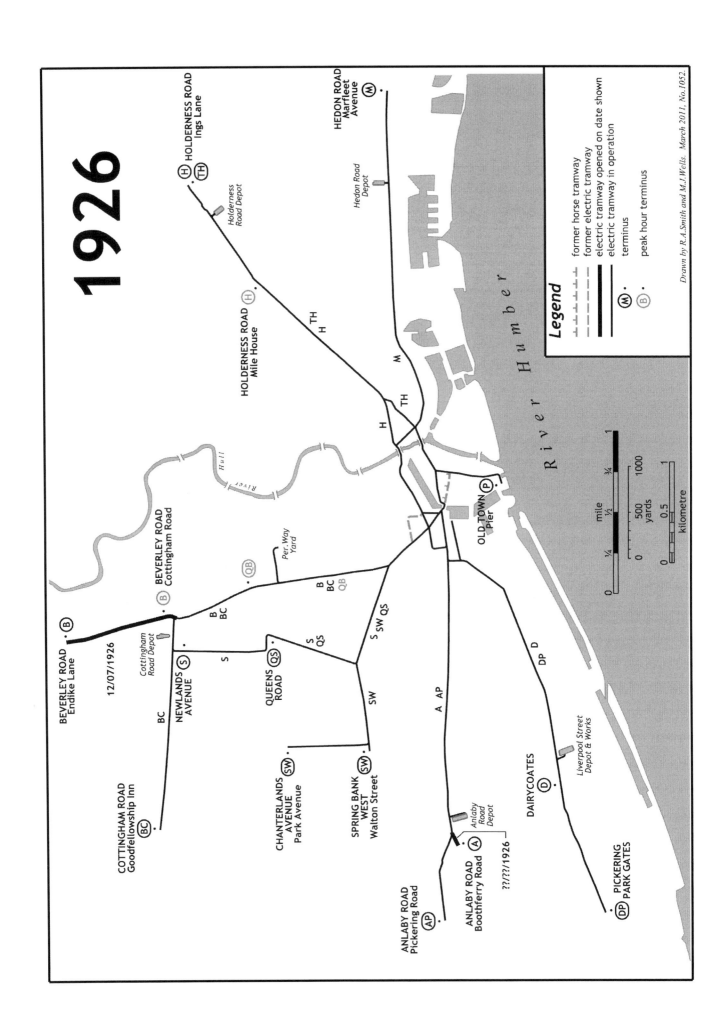

1926

BEVERLEY ROAD
Endike Lane Ⓑ •

12/07/1926

COTTINGHAM ROAD
Goodfellowship Inn (BC) •

NEWLANDS
AVENUE Ⓢ •

CHANTERLANDS
AVENUE (SW) •
Park Avenue

SPRING BANK
WEST (SW) •
Walton Street

DAIRYCOATES
Ⓓ •

ANLABY ROAD
Pickering Road (AP)

ANLABY ROAD
Boothferry Road Ⓐ •
??/??/1926

PICKERING
PARK GATES (DP) •

BC

*Cottingham
Road Depot*

BC

S

S

SW

A AP

DP D

*Anlaby
Road Depot*

*Liverpool Street
Depot & Works*

B
BC

B
BC
QB

S
QS

S SW QS

D

BEVERLEY ROAD Ⓑ
Cottingham Road

(QB)

*Per. Way
Yard*

QUEENS
ROAD (QS) •

HOLDERNESS ROAD Ⓗ
Mile House

HOLDERNESS ROAD Ⓗ (TH)
Ings Lane

TH
H

H

TH

H

M

*Holderness
Road Depot*

HEDON ROAD Ⓜ •
Marfleet
Avenue

*Hedon Road
Depot*

OLD TOWN Ⓟ
Pier

R i v e r   H u m b e r

H u l l
R i v e r

Legend

- – – former horse tramway
- – – – former electric tramway
- ▬▬ electric tramway opened on date shown
- ─── electric tramway in operation
- Ⓜ terminus
- Ⓑ peak hour terminus

mile
¼ ½ ¾ 1
0 500 1000
yards
0 0.5 1
kilometre

Drawn by R.A.Smith and M.J.Wells. March 2011, No.1052.

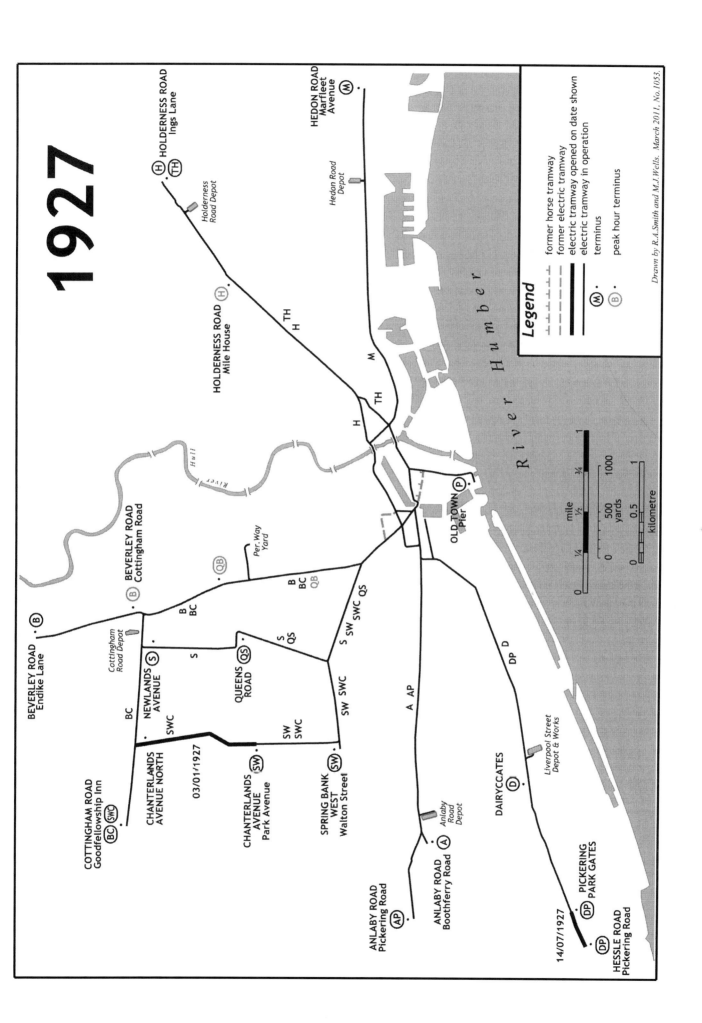

1927

COTTINGHAM ROAD
Goodfellowship Inn (BC) (SWC)

BEVERLEY ROAD
Endike Lane • (B)

CHANTERLANDS AVENUE NORTH
03/01/1927

CHANTERLANDS AVENUE
Park Avenue (SW)

SPRING BANK WEST
Walton Street (SW)

ANLABY ROAD
Pickering Road (AP)

ANLABY ROAD
Bootferry Road (A)

DAIRYCCATES
(D)

PICKERING PARK GATES
14/07/1927 (DP)

HESSLE ROAD
Pickering Road (DP)

BEVERLEY ROAD
Cottingham Road (B)

NEWLANDS AVENUE (S)

QUEENS ROAD (QS)

HOLDERNESS ROAD
Mile House (H)

HOLDERNESS ROAD
Ings Lane (H) (TH)

HEDON ROAD
Marfleet Avenue (M)

Holderness Road Depot

Hedon Road Depot

Cottingham Road Depot

Per. Way Yard

Anlaby Road Depot

Liverpool Street Depot & Works

OLD TOWN
Pier (P)

River Hull

River Humber

BC
B
BC
BC
SWC
S
S
SW
SWC
SW
SWC
SW
SWC
S
QS
S
SW
SWC
QS
A
AP
D
DP
B
BC
QB
(QB)
TH
H
TH
M
H

Legend

- former horse tramway
- former electric tramway
- electric tramway opened on date shown
- electric tramway in operation
- (M) terminus
- (B) peak hour terminus

Drawn by R.A.Smith and M.J.Wells. March 2011, No.1053.

mile
¼   ½   ¾   1
0   500   1000
yards
0   0.5   1
kilometre

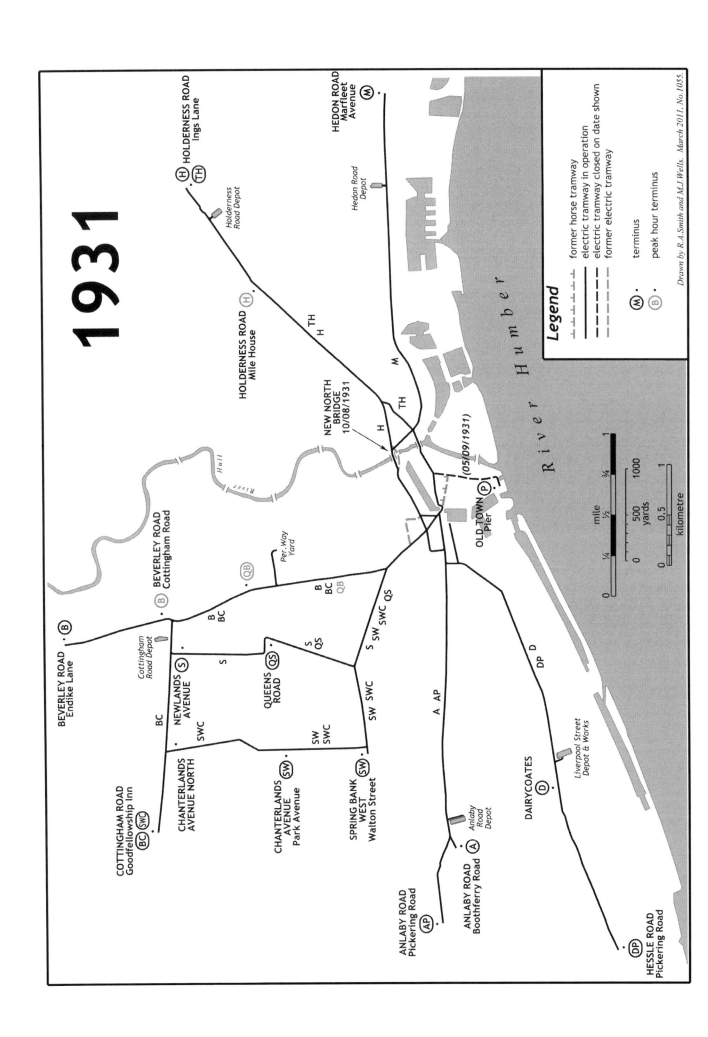

1931

COTTINGHAM ROAD
Goodfellowship Inn
(BC) (SWC)

BEVERLEY ROAD
Endike Lane
(B)

CHANTERLANDS
AVENUE NORTH

NEWLANDS
AVENUE (S)

Cottingham
Road Depot

CHANTERLANDS
AVENUE (SW)
Park Avenue

QUEENS
ROAD (QS)

SPRING BANK
WEST (SW)
Walton Street

BEVERLEY ROAD (B)
Cottingham Road
(QB)

ANLABY ROAD
Pickering Road
(AP)

ANLABY ROAD (A)
Boothferry Road

Anlaby
Road
Depot

DAIRYCOATES (D)

Liverpool Street
Depot & Works

HESSLE ROAD
Pickering Road
(DP)

HOLDERNESS ROAD
Ings Lane
(H) (TH)

Holderness
Road Depot

HOLDERNESS ROAD (H)
Mile House

NEW NORTH
BRIDGE
10/08/1931

Per. Way
Yard

OLD TOWN (P)
Pier

(05/09/1931)

HEDON ROAD (M)
Marfleet
Avenue

Hedon Road
Depot

River Hull

R i v e r   H u m b e r

Drawn by R.A.Smith and M.J.Wells. March 2011. No.1055.

Legend

— former horse tramway

── electric tramway in operation

─ ─ electric tramway closed on date shown

─ ─ former electric tramway

(M) • terminus

(B) • peak hour terminus

mile
¼   ½   ¾   1
0
0   500   1000
yards
0   0.5   1
kilometre

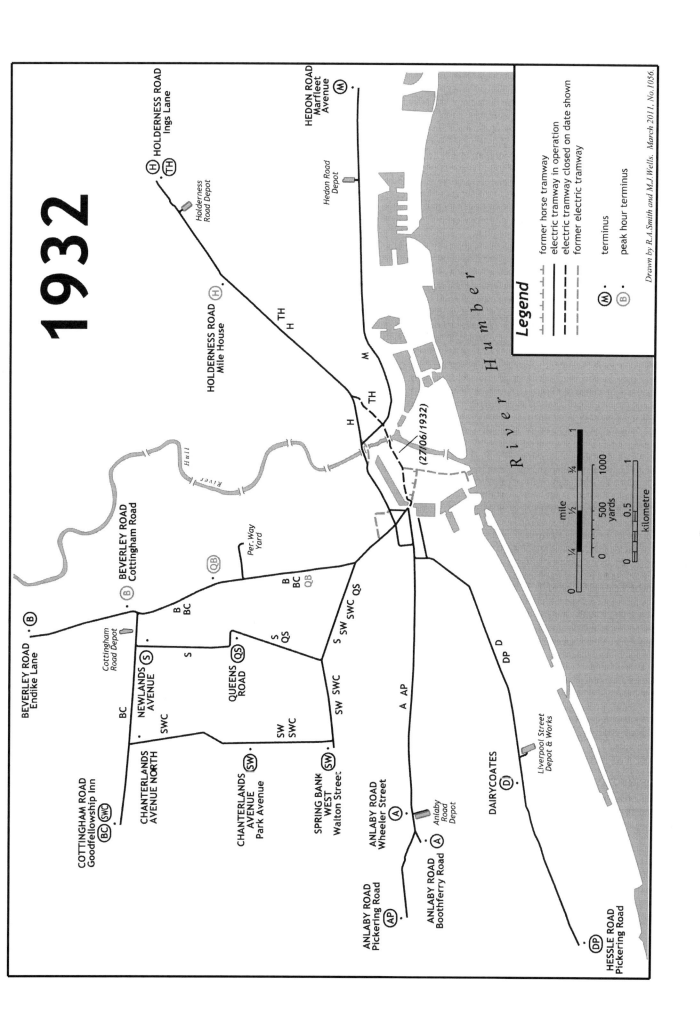

1932

Legend

- former horse tramway
- electric tramway in operation
- electric tramway closed on date shown
- former electric tramway

- Ⓜ terminus
- ⓑ peak hour terminus

Drawn by R.A.Smith and M.J.Wells. March 2011. No.1056.

mile
¼ ½ ¾ 1
0 500 1000 yards
0 0.5 1 kilometre

River Humber

River Hull

COTTINGHAM ROAD
Goodfellowship Inn
ⒷⒸ ⓈⓌⒸ

BEVERLEY ROAD
Endike Lane
Ⓑ

CHANTERLANDS
AVENUE NORTH

BEVERLEY ROAD
Cottingham Road
ⓑ

*Cottingham
Road Depot*

ⓆⒷ

NEWLANDS
AVENUE
Ⓢ

*Per. Way
Yard*

CHANTERLANDS
AVENUE
Park Avenue
ⓈⓌ

QUEENS
ROAD
ⓆⓈ

HOLDERNESS ROAD
Mile House
Ⓗ

HOLDERNESS ROAD
Ings Lane
Ⓗ ⓉⒽ

*Holderness
Road Depot*

HEDON ROAD
Marfleet
Avenue
Ⓜ

*Hedon Road
Depot*

(27/06/1932)

SPRING BANK
WEST
Walton Street
ⓈⓌ

ANLABY ROAD
Wheeler Street
Ⓐ

*Anlaby
Road
Depot*

ANLABY ROAD
Pickering Road
ⒶⓅ

ANLABY ROAD
Bootferry Road
Ⓐ

DAIRYCOATES
Ⓓ

*Liverpool Street
Depot & Works*

HESSLE ROAD
Pickering Road
ⒹⓅ

277

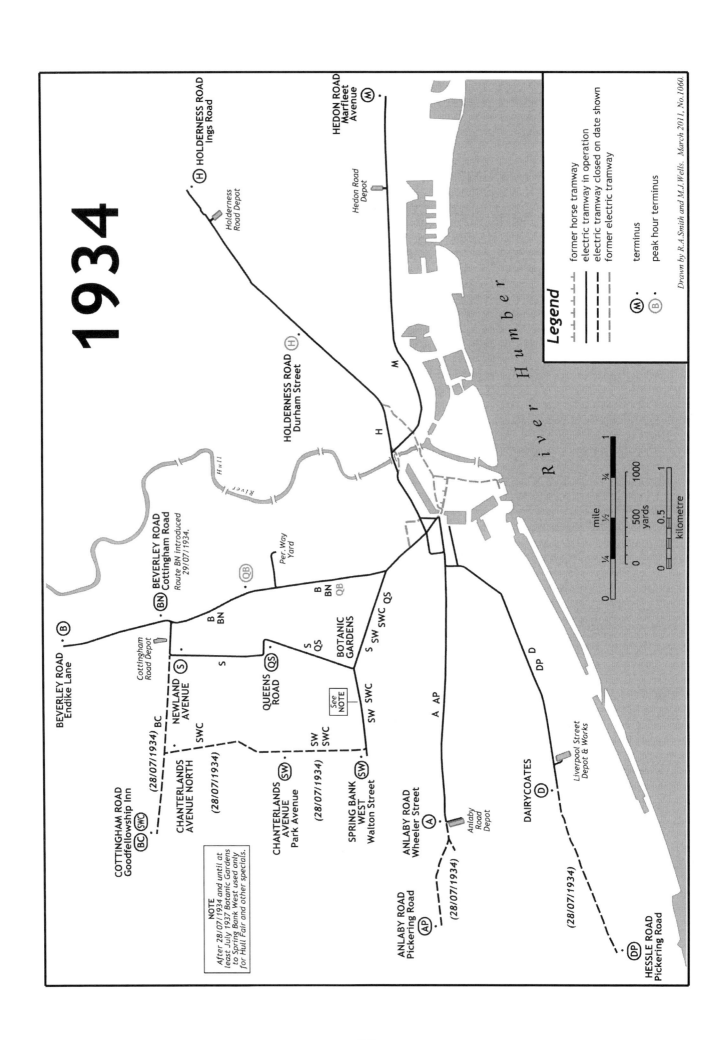

1934

BEVERLEY ROAD
Cottingham Road
Route BN introduced
29/07/1934.

HOLDERNESS ROAD
Ings Road
(H)

HOLDERNESS ROAD
Durham Street
(H)

*Holderness
Road Depot*

HEDON ROAD
Marfleet Avenue
(M)

*Hedon Road
Depot*

M

H

River Hull

River Humber

BEVERLEY ROAD
Endike Lane
(B)

COTTINGHAM ROAD
Goodfellowship Inn
(BC) (SWC)

*Cottingham
Road Depot*

(28/07/1934) BC

*Per. Way
Yard*

(BN)

B
BN

QB

B
BN
QB

**CHANTERLANDS
AVENUE NORTH**
SWC

(28/07/1934)

**NEWLAND
AVENUE**
(S)

S

**QUEENS
ROAD**
(QS)

S
QS

BOTANIC
GARDENS

S
QS

S SW
SWC QS

*See
NOTE*

SW SWC

S SW SWC

**CHANTERLANDS
AVENUE**
Park Avenue
(SW)

SW
SWC

(28/07/1934)

**SPRING BANK
WEST**
Walton Street
(SW)

SW
SWC

A AP

ANLABY ROAD
Wheeler Street
(A)

*Anlaby
Road Depot*

D

DP D

DAIRYCOATES
(D)

*Liverpool Street
Depot & Works*

ANLABY ROAD
Pickering Road
(AP)

(28/07/1934)

(28/07/1934)

HESSLE ROAD
Pickering Road
(DP)

NOTE
*After 28/07/1934 and until at
least July 1937 Botanic Gardens
to Spring Bank West used only
for Hull Fair and other specials.*

Legend

—— former horse tramway
—— electric tramway in operation
– – – electric tramway closed on date shown
- - - former electric tramway

(M) • terminus
(B) • peak hour terminus

Drawn by R.A.Smith and M.J.Wells. March 2011, No.1060.

mile
0 ¼ ½ ¾ 1
yards
0 500 1000
kilometre
0 0.5 1

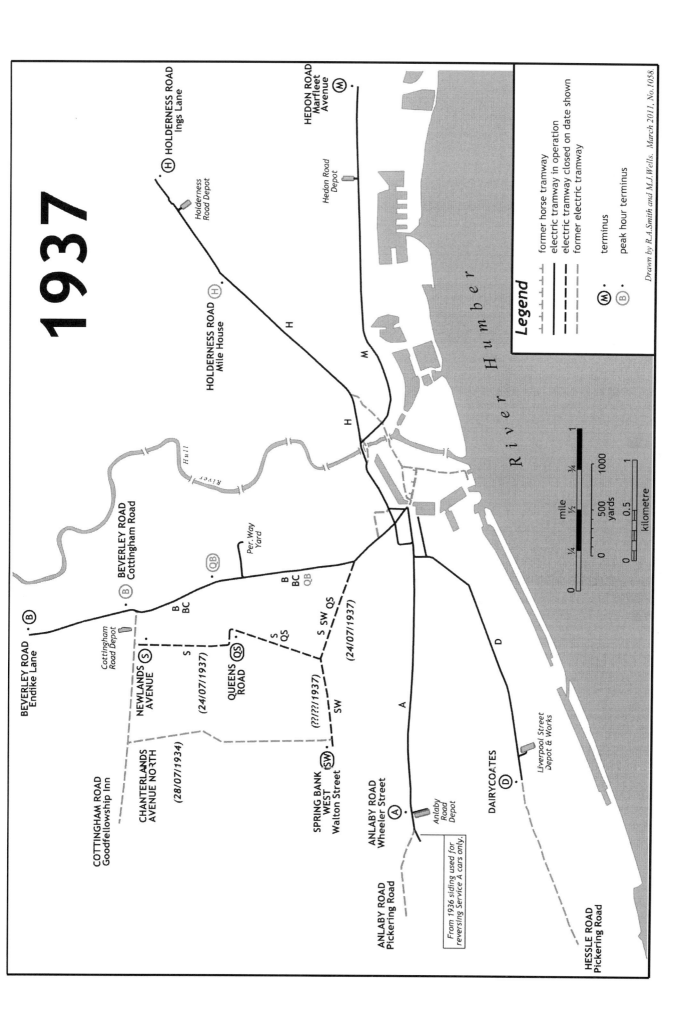

1937

COTTINGHAM ROAD
Goodfellowship Inn

BEVERLEY ROAD
Endike Lane
(B)

HOLDERNESS ROAD
Ings Lane
(H)

BEVERLEY ROAD
Cottingham Road
(B)

HOLDERNESS ROAD
Mile House
(H)

HEDON ROAD
Marfleet Avenue
(M)

Holderness
Road Depot

Hedon Road
Depot

Hull

River

H

M

H

Per. Way
Yard

Cottingham
Road Depot

B
BC

B
BC
QB

(QB)

**CHANTERLANDS
AVENUE NORTH**
(28/07/1934)

**NEWLANDS
AVENUE**
(S)

S

(24/07/1937)

**QUEENS
ROAD**
(QS)

S
QS

(24/07/1937)

(??/??/1937)

SW

S SW QS

S SW QS

**SPRING BANK
WEST**
Walton Street
(SW)

ANLABY ROAD
Wheeler Street
(A)

A

Anlaby
Road Depot

D

ANLABY ROAD
Pickering Road

From 1936 siding used for
reversing Service A cars only.

DAIRYCOATES
(D)

Liverpool Street
Depot & Works

HESSLE ROAD
Pickering Road

R i v e r   H u m b e r

Drawn by R.A.Smith and M.J.Wells. March 2011. No.1058.

Legend

	former horse tramway
	electric tramway in operation
	electric tramway closed on date shown
	former electric tramway
(M) ·	terminus
(B) ·	peak hour terminus

mile
¼   ½   ¾   1
0

yards
0   500   1000

kilometre
0   0.5   1

279

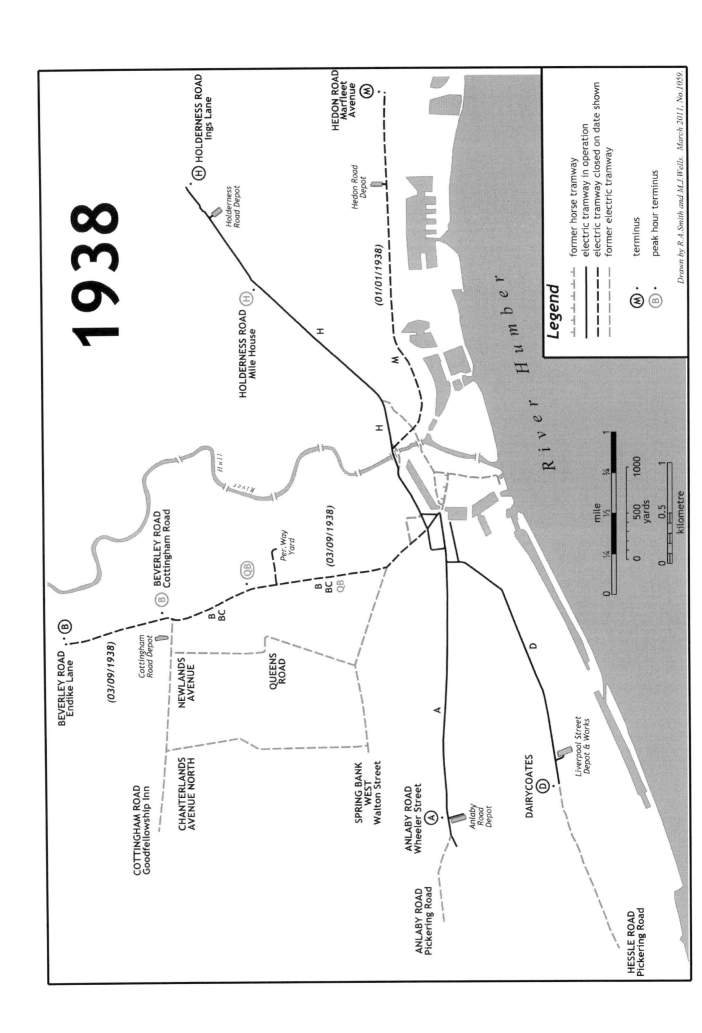

1938

COTTINGHAM ROAD
Goodfellowship Inn

BEVERLEY ROAD
Endike Lane (B)

(03/09/1938)

CHANTERLANDS
AVENUE NORTH

NEWLANDS
AVENUE

BEVERLEY ROAD
Cottingham Road

QUEENS
ROAD

SPRING BANK
WEST
Walton Street

ANLABY ROAD
Wheeler Street (A)

ANLABY ROAD
Pickering Road

DAIRYCOATES (D)

HESSLE ROAD
Pickering Road

HOLDERNESS ROAD
Ings Lane (H)

HOLDERNESS ROAD
Mile House (H)

HEDON ROAD
Marfleet Avenue (M)

(01/01/1938)

Holderness
Road Depot

Hedon Road
Depot

Cottingham
Road Depot

Per. Way
Yard

B
BC

QB

(03/09/1938)

B
BC
QB

H

H

M

River Hull

River Humber

Anlaby
Road Depot

Liverpool Street
Depot & Works

Legend

- former horse tramway
- electric tramway in operation
- electric tramway closed on date shown
- former electric tramway

(M) • terminus

(B) • peak hour terminus

mile
¼   ½   ¾   1

0   500   1000
yards

0   0.5   1
kilometre

Drawn by R.A.Smith and M.J.Wells. March 2011. No.1059.

280

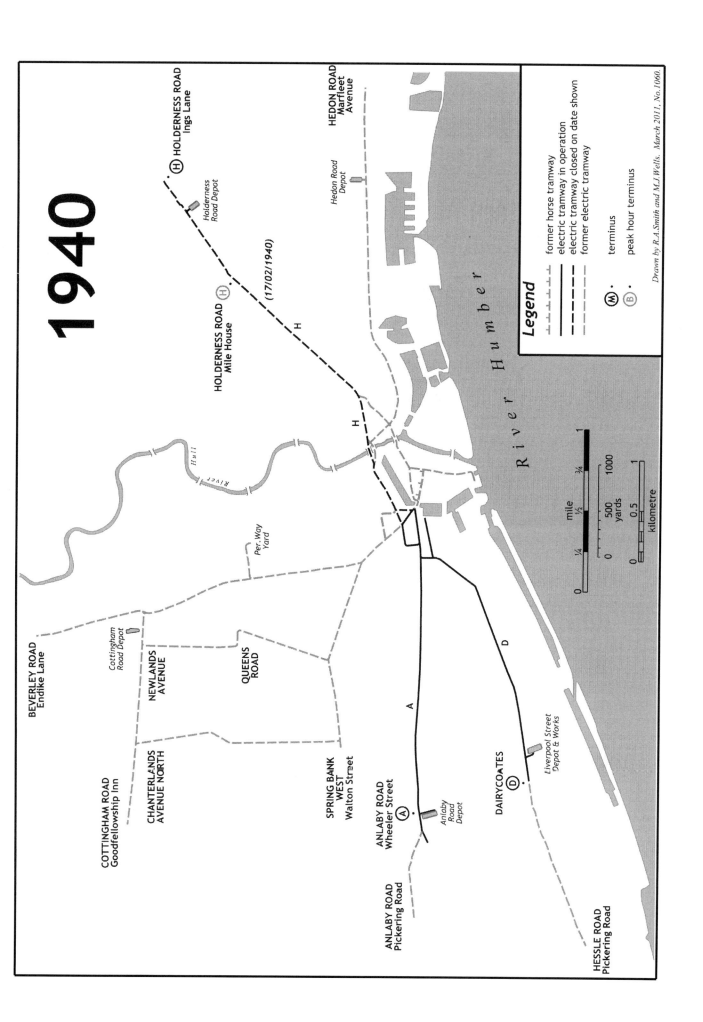

1940

Legend

- former horse tramway
- electric tramway in operation
- electric tramway closed on date shown
- former electric tramway

- Ⓜ · terminus
- Ⓑ · peak hour terminus

Drawn by R.A.Smith and M.J.Wells. March 2011. No.1060.

Ⓗ HOLDERNESS ROAD
Ings Lane

HEDON ROAD
Marfleet Avenue

Holderness
Road Depot

HOLDERNESS ROAD Ⓗ
Mile House

(17/02/1940)

H

Hedon Road
Depot

H

River Hull

River Humber

BEVERLEY ROAD
Endike Lane

COTTINGHAM ROAD
Goodfellowship Inn

Cottingham
Road Depot

NEWLANDS
AVENUE

CHANTERLANDS
AVENUE NORTH

QUEENS
ROAD

Per. Way
Yard

SPRING BANK
WEST
Walton Street

ANLABY ROAD
Wheeler Street

Ⓐ

Anlaby
Road Depot

A

ANLABY ROAD
Pickering Road

DAIRYCOATES

Ⓓ

D

Liverpool Street
Depot & Works

HESSLE ROAD
Pickering Road

mile
¼   ½   ¾   1
0

yards
0   500   1000

kilometre
0   0.5   1

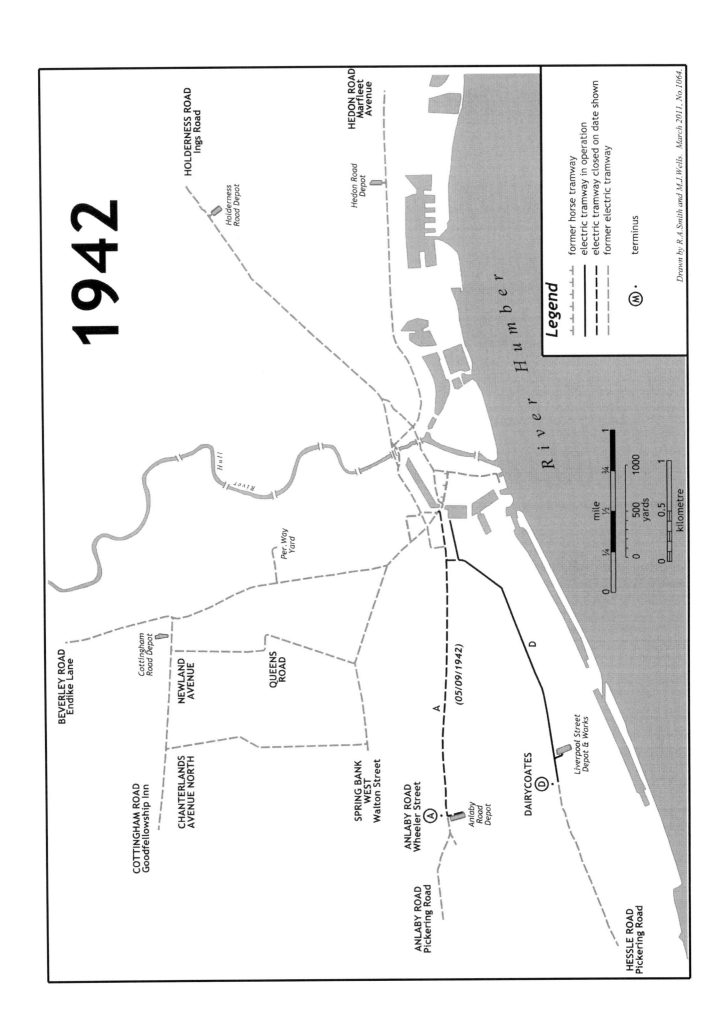

1942

COTTINGHAM ROAD
Goodfellowship Inn

BEVERLEY ROAD
Endike Lane

HOLDERNESS ROAD
Ings Road

*Cottingham
Road Depot*

*Holderness
Road Depot*

CHANTERLANDS
AVENUE NORTH

NEWLAND
AVENUE

*Per. Way
Yard*

QUEENS
ROAD

River Hull

HEDON ROAD
Marfleet
Avenue

*Hedon Road
Depot*

SPRING BANK
WEST
Walton Street

A

(05/09/1942)

ANLABY ROAD
Wheeler Street Ⓐ

*Anlaby
Road Depot*

ANLABY ROAD
Pickering Road

DAIRYCOATES Ⓓ

D

*Liverpool Street
Depot & Works*

HESSLE ROAD
Pickering Road

River Humber

Legend

	former horse tramway
	electric tramway in operation
	electric tramway closed on date shown
	former electric tramway
Ⓜ •	terminus

mile
¼   ½   ¾   1

yards
0   500   1000

kilometre
0   0.5   1

Drawn by R.A.Smith and M.J.Wells. March 2011. No.1064.

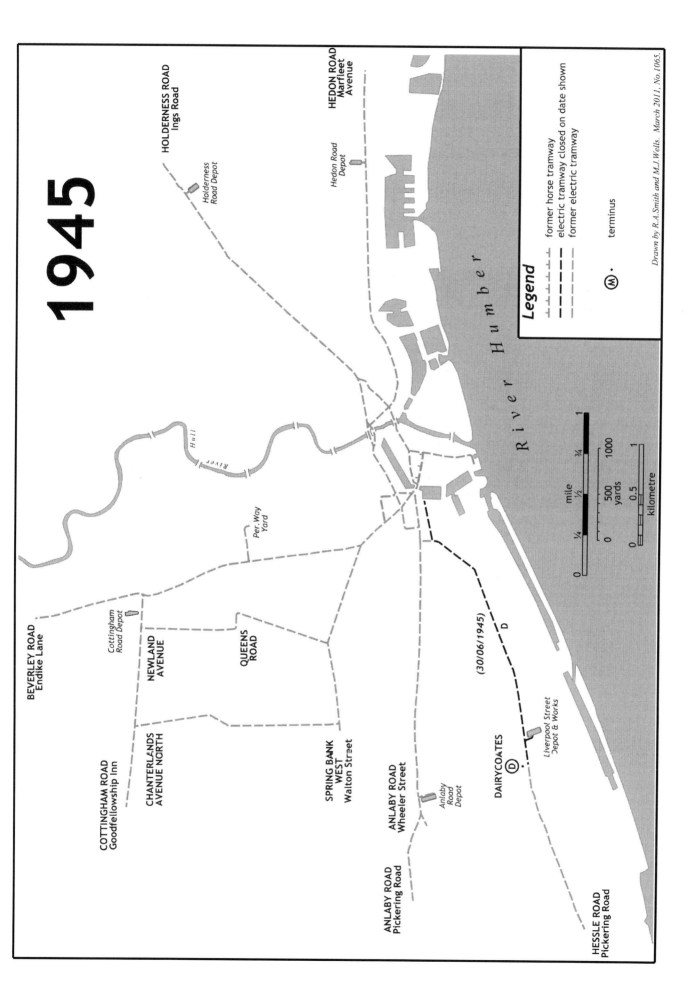

1945

COTTINGHAM ROAD
Goodfellowship Inn

BEVERLEY ROAD
Endike Lane

*Cottingham
Road Depot*

**CHANTERLANDS
AVENUE NORTH**

**NEWLAND
AVENUE**

**QUEENS
ROAD**

*Per. Way
Yard*

HOLDERNESS ROAD
Ings Road

*Holderness
Road Depot*

**HEDON ROAD
Marfleet
Avenue**

*Hedon Road
Depot*

**SPRING BANK
WEST**
Walton Street

ANLABY ROAD
Wheeler Street

*Anlaby
Road Depot*

ANLABY ROAD
Pickering Road

DAIRYCOATES
(Ⓓ)

(30/06/1945)

D

*Liverpool Street
Depot & Works*

HESSLE ROAD
Pickering Road

River Hull

River Humber

Legend

— former horse tramway

— — electric tramway closed on date shown

- - - former electric tramway

Ⓜ · terminus

Drawn by R.A.Smith and M.J.Wells. March 2011. No.1065.

mile
¼ ½ ¾ 1
0

500 1000
yards
0

0.5 1
kilometre
0

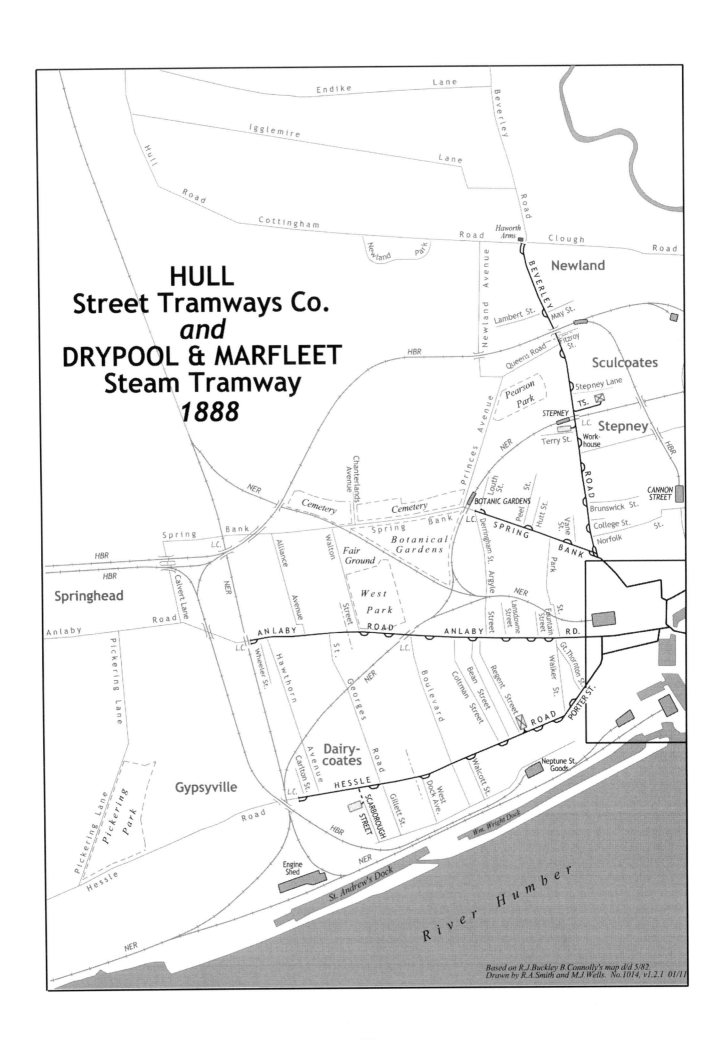

HULL
Street Tramways Co.
and
DRYPOOL & MARFLEET
Steam Tramway
1888

Endike Lane

Igglemire Lane

Beverley Road

Hull Road

Cottingham Road

Haworth Arms

Clough Road

Newland

Newland Avenue

BEVERLEY ROAD

Lambert St.

May St.

Sculcoates

Queens Road

Fitzroy St.

HBR

Pearson Park

Stepney Lane

TS.

STEPNEY

L.C.

Stepney

Princes Avenue

NER

Terry St.

Work-house

Chanterlands Avenue

Cemetery

Cemetery

Louth St.

Peel St.

BOTANIC GARDENS

Hutt St.

Vane St.

CANNON STREET

Brunswick St.

College St.

Norfolk St.

Spring Bank

Spring Bank

L.C.

Derningham St.

SPRING BANK

Spring Bank

L.C.

Botanical Gardens

Alliance Avenue

Walton Street

Fair Ground

Argyle Street

Park St.

HBR

West Park

NER

Fountain Street

Lansdowne Street

St.

HBR

Springhead

Calvert Lane

NER

ROAD

ANLABY ROAD

ANLABY

R D.

Anlaby

Road

L.C.

Wheeler St.

Hawthorn Avenue

St. Georges Road

NER

L.C.

Boulevard

Bean Street

Cottman Street

Regent Street

Walker St.

Gt. Thornton St.

PORTER ST.

Pickering Lane

Pickering Lane

Pickering Park

Carlton St.

Dairy-coates

ROAD

West Dock Ave.

Walcott St.

Neptune St. Goods

Gypsyville

L.C.

HESSLE

Gillett St.

Road

SCARBOROUGH STREET

HBR

Wm. Wright Dock

Hessle

NER

Engine Shed

St. Andrew's Dock

River Humber

NER

Based on R.J.Buckley B.Connolly's map d/d 5/82.
Drawn by R.A.Smith and M.J.Wells. No.1014, v1.2.1 01/11

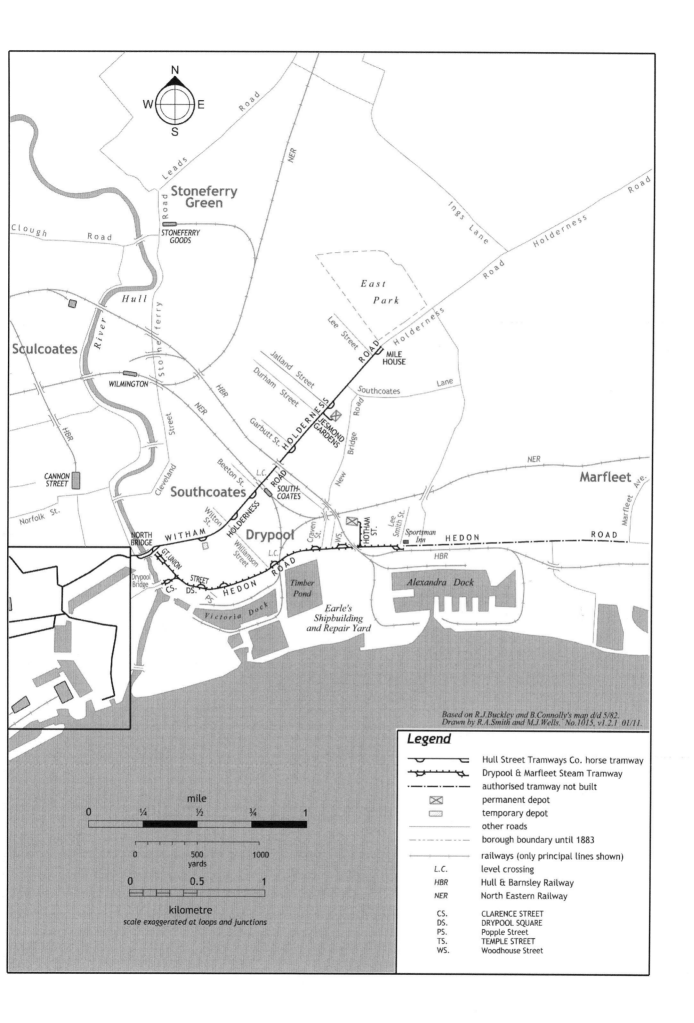

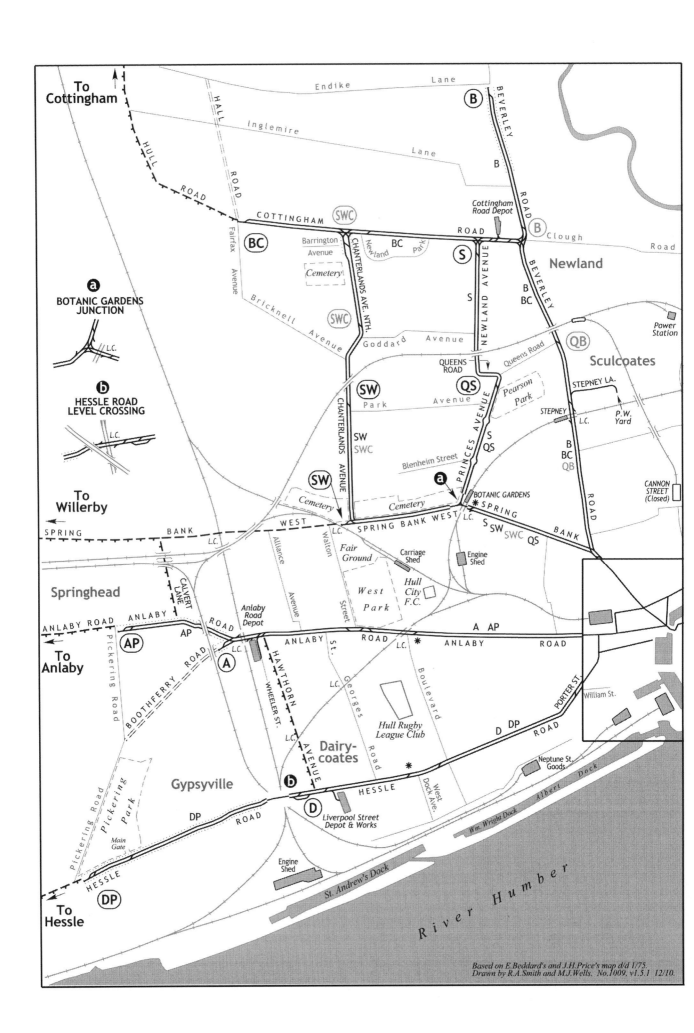

To Cottingham

Endike Lane

Inglemire Lane

Hull Road

Hall Road

COTTINGHAM ROAD

Beverley Road

(B)

Cottingham Road Depot

(B) Clough Road

(SWC)

(BC)

Fairfax Avenue

Barrington Avenue

Cemetery

Newland Park

BC

(S)

S

Newland

Bricknell Avenue

Chanterlands Ave. Nth.

Newland Avenue

B
BC

a
BOTANIC GARDENS JUNCTION

L.C.

(SWC)

Goddard Avenue

QUEENS ROAD

Queens Road

(QB)

Power Station

Sculcoates

STEPNEY LA.

P.W. Yard

b
HESSLE ROAD LEVEL CROSSING

L.C.

(SW)

Park Avenue

(QS)

S
QS

Pearson Park

STEPNEY

L.C.

B
BC
QB

Chanterlands

SW
SWC

Blenheim Street

PRINCES AVENUE

a

BOTANIC GARDENS

CANNON STREET (Closed)

To Willerby

(SW)

AVENUE

Cemetery

Cemetery

SPRING BANK WEST

L.C.

SPRING

S SW
SWC QS

BANK

SPRING BANK

L.C.

WEST

Walton Street

Fair Ground

Carriage Shed

Engine Shed

Springhead

Alliance Avenue

West Park

Hull City F.C.

ANLABY ROAD

Calvert Lane

ANLABY ROAD

ROAD

AP

A AP

(AP)

AP

(A)

L.C.

Hawthorn Avenue

WHEELER ST.

ANLABY

St. Georges Road

ROAD

L.C.

*

ANLABY

ROAD

Boulevard

PORTER ST.

William St.

To Anlaby

BOOTHFERRY ROAD

Pickering Road

L.C.

Hull Rugby League Club

D DP

ROAD

Gypsyville

Pickering Park

b

AVENUE

Dairy-coates

HESSLE

West Dock Ave.

*

Neptune St. Goods

Albert Dock

(D)

Liverpool Street Depot & Works

DP

ROAD

Main Gate

HESSLE

(DP)

Engine Shed

St. Andrew's Dock

Wm. Wright Dock

To Hessle

River Humber

Based on E.Beddard's and J.H.Price's map d/d 1/75.
Drawn by R.A.Smith and M.J.Wells. No.1009. v1.5.1 12/10.

286

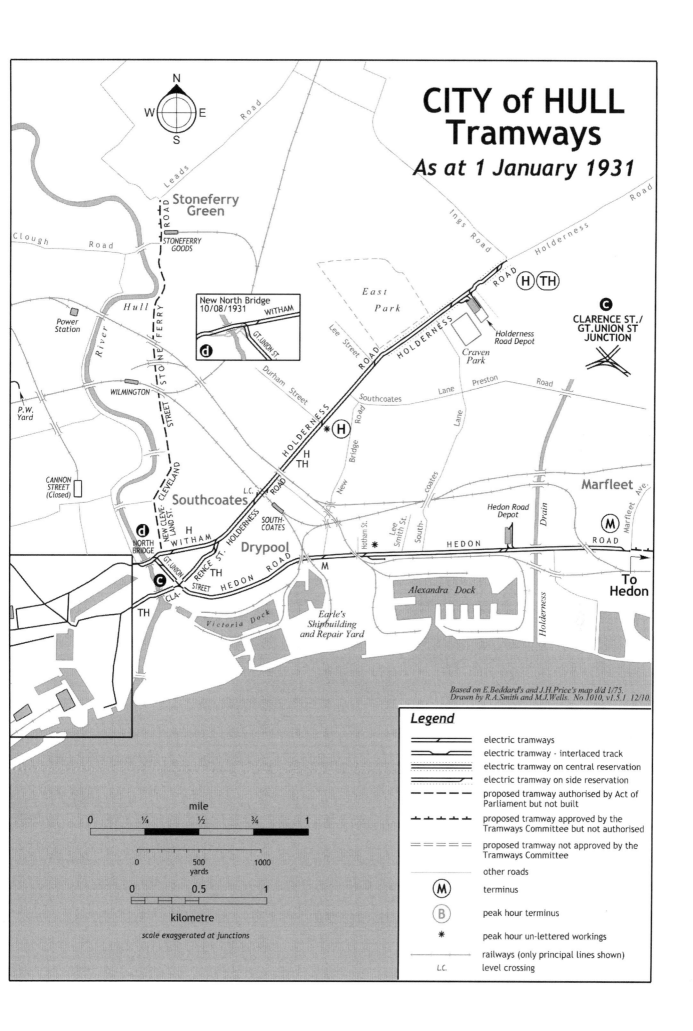

CITY of HULL
Tramways
As at 1 January 1931

Stoneferry
Green

Leads

Road

Clough

Road

STONEFERRY
GOODS

Hull

Power
Station

River

P. W.
Yard

WILMINGTON

CANNON
STREET
(Closed)

STONE·FERRY STREET

NEW CLEVE-
LAND ST.

CLEVELAND STREET

North Bridge 10/08/1931
WITHAM
GT. UNION ST.

d

Durham   Street

*East
Park*

Lee Street

ROAD

HOLDERNESS

HOLDERNESS ROAD

Southcoates   Lane   Preston   Road

Southcoates

New   Bridge   Road

South-   coates   Lane

Ings Road

Holderness   Road

H **TH**

C
CLARENCE ST. /
GT. UNION ST
JUNCTION

Holderness
Road Depot

*Craven
Park*

H
✳

H
TH

L.C.

d
NORTH
BRIDGE

Southcoates

C

H
WITHAM

RENCE ST.

GT. UNION
STREET

CLA-

TH

SOUTH-
COATES

HOLDERNESS

ROAD

Drypool

TH
HEDON   ROAD

M

Hotham St.

Lee   Smith St.

✳

HEDON

Hedon Road
Depot

Alexandra   Dock

Drain

Holderness

M

Marfleet
Marfleet   Ave.

ROAD

**To
Hedon**

Victoria Dock

*Earle's
Shipbuilding
and Repair Yard*

Based on E.Beddard's and J.H.Price's map d/d 1/75.
Drawn by R.A.Smith and M.J.Wells. No.1010, v1.5.1 12/10.

Legend

≡≡≡	electric tramways
≡≡≡	electric tramway - interlaced track
≡≡≡	electric tramway on central reservation
⋯⋯	electric tramway on side reservation
– – –	proposed tramway authorised by Act of Parliament but not built
–·–·–	proposed tramway approved by the Tramways Committee but not authorised
=====	proposed tramway not approved by the Tramways Committee
——	other roads
M	terminus
B	peak hour terminus
✳	peak hour un-lettered workings
——	railways (only principal lines shown)
L.C.	level crossing

Scale

mile
0   ¼   ½   ¾   1

0   500   1000
yards

0   0.5   1
kilometre

scale exaggerated at junctions

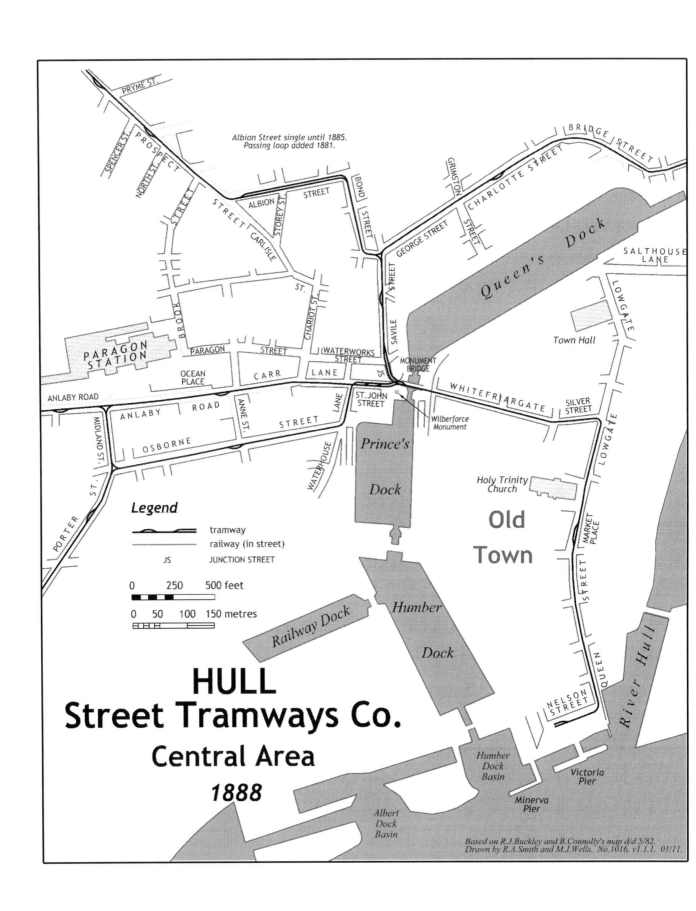

Albion Street single until 1885.
Passing loop added 1881.

PRYME ST.

SPENCER ST.
NORTH ST.
PROSPECT STREET
ALBION STREET
CARLISLE STREET
STOREY ST.
BROOK ST.
CHARIOT ST.
BOND STREET
GEORGE STREET
GRIMSTON STREET
CHARLOTTE STREET
BRIDGE STREET

PARAGON STATION

PARAGON STREET
OCEAN PLACE
CARR LANE
WATERWORKS STREET
SAVILE STREET
JS
MONUMENT BRIDGE

Queen's Dock

SALTHOUSE LANE

LOWGATE

Town Hall

ANLABY ROAD
ANLABY ROAD
OSBORNE STREET
ANNE ST.
MIDLAND ST.
ST.JOHN STREET
JS
Wilberforce Monument

WHITEFRIARGATE
SILVER STREET

LOWGATE

PORTER ST.

WATERHOUSE LANE

Prince's Dock

Holy Trinity Church

Old Town

MARKET PLACE
STREET
QUEEN STREET
NELSON STREET

River Hull

Legend

tramway
railway (in street)
JS   JUNCTION STREET

0   250   500 feet

0   50   100   150 metres

Railway Dock

Humber Dock

HULL
Street Tramways Co.
Central Area
1888

Humber Dock Basin

Victoria Pier

Minerva Pier

Albert Dock Basin

Based on R.J.Buckley and B.Connolly's map d/d 5/82.
Drawn by R.A.Smith and M.J.Wells. No.1016. v1.1.1. 01/11.

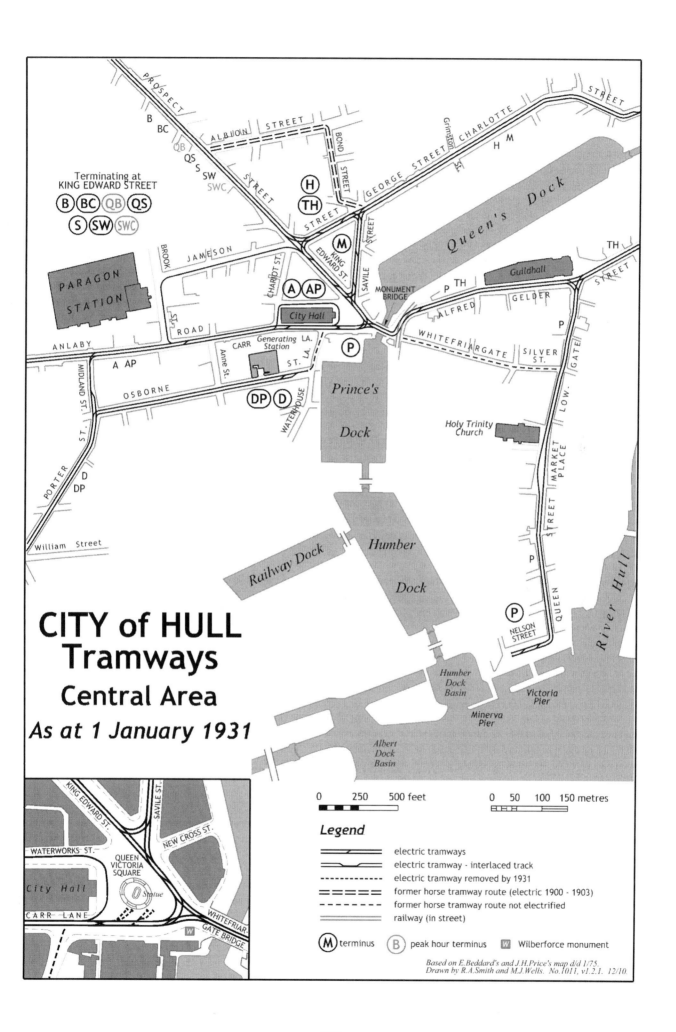

CITY of HULL
Tramways
Central Area
As at 1 January 1931

Terminating at
KING EDWARD STREET
(B) (BC) (QB) (QS)
(S) (SW) (SWC)

PARAGON
STATION

City Hall

Generating
Station

Prince's
Dock

Railway Dock

Humber
Dock

Queen's Dock

Guildhall

Holy Trinity
Church

Monument
Bridge

Humber
Dock
Basin

Minerva
Pier

Victoria
Pier

Albert
Dock
Basin

River Hull

| 0 | 250 | 500 feet |
| 0 | 50 | 100 | 150 metres |

Legend

══════	electric tramways
══════	electric tramway - interlaced track
- - - - - -	electric tramway removed by 1931
═ ═ ═ ═ ═	former horse tramway route (electric 1900 - 1903)
– – – – –	former horse tramway route not electrified
══════	railway (in street)

(M) terminus   (B) peak hour terminus   W Wilberforce monument

*Based on E.Beddard's and J.H.Price's map d/d 1/75.
Drawn by R.A.Smith and M.J.Wells. No.1011, v1.2.1. 12/10.*

KING EDWARD ST.
WATERWORKS ST.
SAVILE ST.
NEW CROSS ST.
QUEEN VICTORIA SQUARE
Statue
City Hall
CARR LANE
WHITEFRIAR GATE BRIDGE

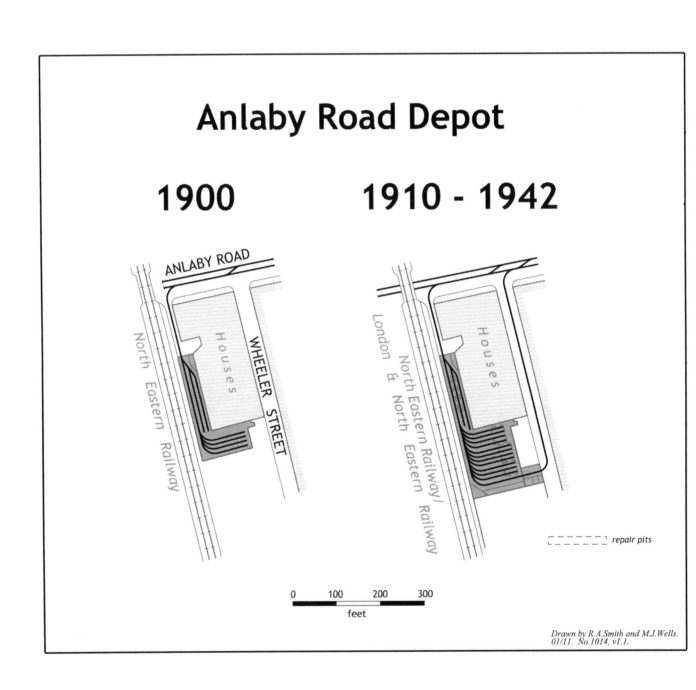

Anlaby Road Depot

1900

1910 - 1942

ANLABY ROAD

Houses

WHEELER STREET

North Eastern Railway

North Eastern Railway/
London & North Eastern Railway

Houses

repair pits

0   100   200   300

feet

Drawn by R.A.Smith and M.J.Wells.
01/11. No.1014, v1.1.

Cottingham Road Depot

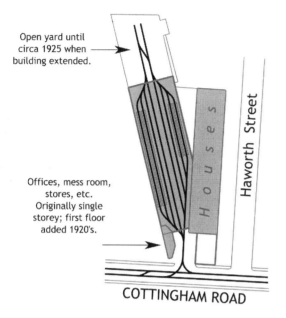

Open yard until circa 1925 when building extended.

Offices, mess room, stores, etc. Originally single storey; first floor added 1920's.

Houses

Haworth Street

COTTINGHAM ROAD

Hedon Road Depot

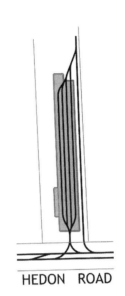

HEDON ROAD

Holderness Road Depot

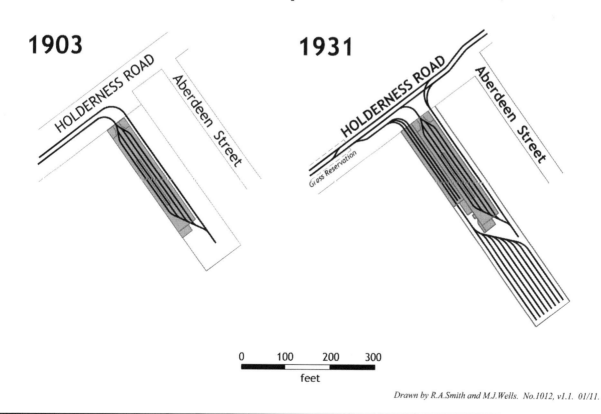

1903

HOLDERNESS ROAD

Aberdeen Street

1931

HOLDERNESS ROAD

Aberdeen Street

Grass Reservation

0   100   200   300
feet

Drawn by R.A.Smith and M.J.Wells. No.1012, v1.1. 01/11.

Liverpool Street
Depot & Works

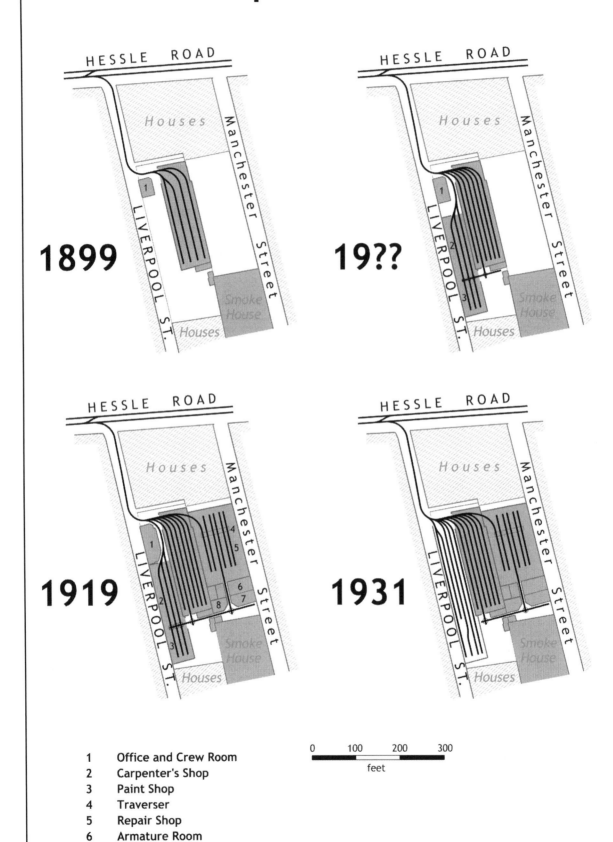

1899

19??

1919

1931

1	Office and Crew Room
2	Carpenter's Shop
3	Paint Shop
4	Traverser
5	Repair Shop
6	Armature Room
7	Smithy
8	Stores

0   100   200   300
feet

1931 plan based on E.Beddard's and J.H.Price's map d/d 1/75,
as anotated by J.C.Gillham, .
Drawn by R.A.Smith and M.J.Wells. No.1013, v1.1. 01/11.

Appendix 12

Hull Tramways Accident Reports 1899 to 1902

Crews who were involved in an accident were required to complete an accident report form giving details and names and addresses of witnesses. It was sent direct to Mr McCombe who would instruct an inspector to investigate and interview crews and witnesses before reporting back to him. Each form asked for the route, duty number, car number, date and the names of motorman and conductor. Forms, showing perhaps a surprising degree of literacy (and imagination on occasion), would be completed by either member of the crew dependent on the nature of the incident. Mr McCombe would write to the other party asking it to accept liability. Sometimes the cost of any remedial work would be included, but this usually came later. In some instances the other party did pay up, albeit reluctantly. Car no.68 was hit by a laundry van belonging to Yorkshire Laundries Ltd on 12 June 1900. The company accepted some liability and offered to pay 6/3, half the cost of repairs. This was accepted. If the other party did not accept liability Mr McCombe would write to the Town Clerk instructing him to obtain the costs.

At first only occasional reports (usually the more serious) were presented to the Tramways Sub-Committee but as the system expanded and the number of accidents increased a special sub-Committee was formed to deal with such matters. The process was not sound by any means and it would be a principal feature of Mr McCombe's dismissal in 1919. Usually the Corporation did not accept responsibility but when one car ran into the back of another the motorman was suspended and compensation was paid.

The following are taken from a batch of accident reports covering the period from July 1899 to March 1902. Not all accidents are there but they are of interest in revealing the perils of newly installed electric trams. As far as possible I have used the words as set down by the crews and some witnesses.

The first recorded incident involved Brill car no.26 on 6 July 1899 just one day after the system's inauguration! The car was driven by C. Nicholson and its conductor was Ernest White. It had left Dairycoates at 5.46pm and had reached Paragon Station gates at 5.58pm when it collided with a waggonette owned by F. Hunter and Son. The car struck the waggonette knocking horse and waggonette completely over. The conductor and witnesses who included the Midland Street junction signalman stated that the waggonette was on the wrong side of the road. Hunters stated the fault lay with the motorman but the Corporation repudiated this. This would not be the last altercation with a waggonette.

Two days later car Milnes no.1 driven by Mr Pearson and conducted by J.E. Wilson had negotiated the junction at Midland Street and was about to pass Brill car no.26 (again). No.26's conductor was on the foot board with the intention of changing the trolley pole at the junction (conductors were having to guide the trolley poles through the curve due to problems with the pole not keeping to the wires). As the rope was loose it swung out and knocked the hat off the head of a passenger on the upper deck of no.1. Both cars stopped and the gentleman concerned was able to retrieve his hat from the road. He did not complain at the time but on 8 July wrote to claim for a new hat which had been entirely spoilt, a claim backed by witnesses who blamed the conductor on no.26. The outcome is not known but Mr McCombe replied refuting the claim!

Brush car no.59 driven by W. Blythe and conducted by E. Parott left the Newland terminus at 9.48am and was approaching Wellington Lane where a waggonette driven by a Mr E. Mainprize was stationary. Mr Blythe rang his bell to warn of his approach but the waggonette deliberately pulled out to overtake a Post Office parcels cart and struck the car making two rather deep scratches. Mr Mainprize stated that he didn't hear the bell. One of the witnesses was a PC 289 who said that Mainprize was known to the police and that he had pulled out deliberately. He also stated that he considered that he was not fit to be in charge of a horse.

Mainprize was a persistent offender having collided with car no.16 on 17 December 1900 causing 7/- damage and again with no.16 on 22 December. Mr McCombe had received several reports about his conduct and asked the Town Clerk to take action.

When the Beverley Road route opened in December 1900 the equipment at the Stepney level crossing was not installed so cars stopped short at the crossing and passengers had to alight and walk across the crossing to another car. On 7 January 1901 car no.52 stopped before the crossing. The conductor, William Arksey got off to change the trolley round at 6.44pm. A pony and trap driven by two men came over the crossing at a furious rate and its shaft struck Mr Arksey between the shoulder blades and knocked him down. The men did not stop but were later arrested at 9.45pm and charged with being drunk at Norfolk Street Police Station. Mr McCombe asked the Town Clerk to obtain damages for Mr Arksey but the outcome is unknown.

There was no crossover on the south side of the crossing so how did trams operate? Did they return on the wrong line with special operating procedures or was a temporary crossover installed? There was a crossover north of Stepney at the end of Stepney Lane so cars on that side could keep to the correct line. Did cars cross the railway empty and cross in order to return?

Hull's only bogie car, no.101, had an altercation with a waggonette at Staniforth Place on Hessle Road on 3 February 1901. Driven by J. Hutchinson it had left Dairycoates at 8.24 and collided with a waggonette driven by a Mr Howland who refused to get off the tracks and out of the way. When he did move he steered the horse towards the side of the car causing the forewheel of the waggonette to catch the step of the car but without any damage. Motorman Hutchinson stated that Howland was a regular problem who was always obstructing the cars.

There appeared to be several waggonette drivers who regularly obstructed the cars, sometime for personal reasons. On 4 April 1901 car no.33 driven by R. Winter had left Dairycoates at 5.30 and had reached Porter Street when a waggonette driven by William Butterill crossed in front of him and wouldn't let him pass so that he had to apply the electric brake to avoid hitting him. Mr Winter said that this man made a practice of such tricks some of which were dangerous. He had cautioned Butterill on 17 March for a similar trick.

In his letter requesting the Town Clerk to take action Mr McCombe said that Butterill was a persistent offender and that he had refused to employ him on the tramways. Another persistent offender was a Mr Holgate of whom the Hull Waggonettes Proprietors Protection Society said was a poor man and a cripple as well.

On 23 April 1901 former trailer no.87 which had started its second life only on 5 April 1901 had an altercation on Spring Bank. It had left the Pearson Park terminus (all crews regarded the Queens Road terminus as Pearson Park) at 11.9am for Savile Street. It was approaching Morpeth Street when the driver perceived a mineral rully coming out. He rang his bell and slowed down. The rully continued to come out and drew in towards the curb and came into line with another vehicle which was drawn up there. Motorman C.H. Simmons, seeing the line was all clear, let off his brake, rang the bell and was proceeding when the rullyman drew out to pass the other cart with the result that the car and rully came into collision with such force that one of the upright bars in the iron gate was bent and the wood rail was split whilst it broke a piece of beading almost four inches off a car window and made three scratches, the longest being about 20 inches.

He asked the rullyman what damage his rully had received and was told only a bent rail. Three witnesses were obtained and were persuaded by Mr Simmons to write down their comments. They confirmed that the rullyman was to blame and that he had taken no notice of the car's bell. Mr McCombe wrote to the owners Hindles Aerated Water Company asking them to accept blame and pay damages. Hindles refuted that and produced their own witnesses stating the opposite of the Corporation's witnesses and wondering if the car's brakes were defective (which they weren't). Eventually Hindles agreed to pay 10 shillings towards the 20 shillings cost of repairs.

The reports that have survived show more accidents on Hessle Road than on any other route. Milnes car no.19 had left Dairycoates at 9.24am. 0n 24 May 1901 and was approaching Wassand Street. The conductor (H. Walshaw) was on the upper deck collecting fares when a woman got up inside the car and walked straight off the car, falling into the roadway, cutting her forehead and hurting her shoulder. The car was going at half speed as the motorman (G. Brumby) was easing the car for the next stopping place.

Witnesses stated that the car was travelling at 4-5 mph, a fact confirmed by Inspector H.R. Harper when he interviewed them. They also confirmed that the conductor was on the upper deck. However, on 1 June a letter was sent from a solicitor Geo S. Jordeson on behalf of Mrs A. Benfield, widow of 52 Goulton Street to the "Chairman, Electric Car Company, Town Hall, Hull"! He accused the conductor of total negligence as the car continued to move as she alighted causing eye damage and a dislocated shoulder. She was still confined to the house and Mr Jordeson said that he would forward Dr Wm Jackson's bill to the Corporation. Councillor Larard passed the letter to Mr McCombe who wrote repudiating the claim and enclosing the conductor's report and witness statements.

A more unusual incident on 5 August 1901 involved Brush car no.40 and a flock of sheep! No.40 had left Savile Street at 10.42 (probably pm) bound for the Mile House driven by Motorman F. Thompson. He stopped the car at Southcoates Lane to permit two passengers to alight and set off. As he approached Westcott Street a flock of sheep came out the street! They were clear of the track at first but the drover started to hurry them and let his dog on them to such an extent that they ran across the track. Four ran right in front of the car. He imme-

diately applied the brake and stopped the car within its length but ended with three sheep on his lifeguard and one underneath.

The drover was under the influence of drink and incapable of action and the motorman had to get the sheep off the lifeguard by himself. The other was dying as it had been caught by the wheel and the drover borrowed a knife from a bystander but was too drunk to put the animal out of its misery. When the motorman offered to do the job the drover threw the knife at him and swore.

When walking home the motorman met the drover who had returned in a cart to collect his sheep. Still drunk, he refused to give his name but the motorman got it from a bystander. Three witnesses were obtained all of whom blamed the drover.

The drover got his claim in first blaming the motorman's reckless speed but Mr McCombe pointed out that the speed could not have been great or the damage would have been more severe. The claim was not paid.

Midland Street with its narrow width and single line was the scene of several incidents and was the location for a collision between Milnes car no.21 and a trap on 13 August 1901. The car, driven by J. Hutchinson had left Dairycoates at 8.48pm and on reaching the single line in Midland Street found a pony and trap on the track. The two men on the trap were, according to conductor W. Tinkler's report, "quite drunk" and made no move to get out of the car's way forcing the driver to stop the car.

Suddenly the man in charge of the trap whipped the pony so that it moved off and collided with the car knocking down a rail and breaking the woodwork at the top. The men in the trap fell into the road and one had to be taken to the infirmary. Witnesses who again included the signalman blamed the driver of the trap. The car lost one journey as a result but the report does not reveal if the car was parked anywhere or if the delay to it and other cars was such to miss a complete run.

When car no.15 collided with a waggonette on 20 September 1901 the repairs amounted to £2 2s 0d made up as follows:

	£	s	d
Painters' time		2	4
Joiner		13	2
Blacksmith		1	4
4 Labourers		16	0
2 brackets		3	0
Timber		2	5
Replacement Wood		2	3
Supervisor's use of tools		1	6
Total	2	2	0

It was not only the cars that had collisions as shown on 23 September 1902 when water cart no.1 collided with a Corporation night soil cart driven by J. Lawton! J. Ingamells was in charge when the cart pulled out on to the lines and ignored the bell so he applied the electric brake which caused the wheels to pick up to counter which he put the car into reverse. All to no avail for he crashed into the back of the cart as the night soil cart was pulling off again so that the buffers of the water cart caught the tyre and the top of the other cart hit the dash of the water cart and bent it. Witnesses said that the other driver appeared to be asleep and was to blame. Lawtons agreed that it was the man's fault but asked the Corporation to be lenient as he had only one arm.

Other collisions involved a ginger beer rulley, various cabs and NER rulleys, the latter involving copious correspondence and often a settlement without recourse to letters from the Town Clerk.

Appendix 13

Report of Councillors Richardson and Wheeldon and the City Accountant upon the Business Methods of the Tramway Electrical Engineer's Department 31 July 1919 and his response

Tramway Electrical Engineer's Department.

REPORT

OF

Councillors Richardson and Wheeldon

AND

The City Accountant

UPON THE

BUSINESS METHODS OF THE TRAMWAY ELECTRICAL ENGINEER'S DEPARTMENT

AND

Reply of the Tramway Electrical Engineer.

1919.

This is described in Chapter 7. It was a very detailed investigation to which the Tramway Electrical Engineer responded in great detail. The exercise uncovered a lack of compliance with the Council's own standing orders and an implied lack of financial auditing at the centre although this was not mentioned in the report. Whilst there were some extenuating circumstances resulting from the Great War the shortcomings could not be ignored.

INQUIRY *re* TRAMWAY ELECTRICAL ENGINEER'S DEPARTMENT.

Referring to the Committee's resolution of the 2nd May last, instructing the City Accountant to report upon the business methods of the Tramway Electrical Engineer's Department, Messrs. R. Richardson and R. W. Wheeldon stated that, in accordance with the Committee's resolution of the 5th ultimo, they had been associated with the City Accountant in his inquiry, and, after examining the information obtained in the course of the investigation and satisfying themselves as to the business procedure generally, they beg to join him in the following report.

PRIVATE AND CONFIDENTIAL.

JOINT REPORT WITH REGARD TO THE BUSINESS METHODS OF THE TRAMWAY ELECTRICAL ENGINEER'S DEPARTMENT.

To the Tramways Committee.

As the result of the investigation conducted in accordance with the resolutions referred to in the preceding statement, we beg to report that, in our opinion, the Tramway Electrical Engineer's Department has not been satisfactorily and economically managed, and a complete re-organisation of the administration is essential.

Our conclusions are mainly based upon the ascertained facts dealt with below :—

(1) *It has not been the general practice to obtain competitive prices when ordering goods.*

In an interview with the Tramway Electrical Engineer (Mr. J. Wilkinson) at the Guildhall on the

23rd instant, he stated that competitive prices were *sometimes* obtained. We accept this statement, but in so far as we can trace, such cases are few in number.

Without having gone exhaustively into the matter, it would appear that a number of orders have been placed with traders in other towns, although, had competitive prices been obtained, it would probably have been found that similar goods could have been obtained from local firms at prices equally satisfactory.

We are of the opinion that, whenever possible, local firms should be invited to tender, and if prices, quality and conditions generally are equal (or more favourable) the orders should be placed accordingly.

(2) *It is found that prices charged for goods supplied to the Department have, in certain cases, been exorbitant.*

We draw attention to the transactions with Mr. Arthur Canty (Turning and Saw Mills, Malton Street, Drypool) for supplies of hardwood, &c. The purchases from this tradesman have been scrutinised for the period selected (February, 1913, to March, 1919) so as to include purchases prior to and during the war.

It is found that the prices charged by Mr. Canty (and certified as correct by the Tramway Electrical Engineer) have been inordinately excessive and several hundred per cent. in excess of the highest quotations obtained during the course of the inquiry from firms of repute for precisely similar articles.

This department's dealings with Mr. Canty disclose a condition of affairs which is serious and disquieting.

In order that the position may be clearly placed before the Committee, the schedule of six years' transactions appended hereto (pages 10 to 17) gives the following information:—

Date of purchase.
Description of articles.
Quantity purchased.
Mr. Canty's charges.
Sample number.
Recent quotations by other firms.
Difference—being excess cost.
Remarks.

We have interviewed the Tramway Electrical Engineer with regard to the above matter, and in reply to questions put, he made statements to the following effect:—

(1) There was no special reason for ordering these goods from Mr. Arthur Canty.

(2) It was probable that orders were placed with this person because he had previously supplied similar goods.

(3) He accepted responsibility for certifying these accounts for payment.

(4) He had no knowlege that the prices charged by Mr. Canty were excessive.

The Engineer added that at such short notice it was impossible for him to adequately deal with the matters upon which he had been questioned, and asked for details to be furnished so that he might report in writing. It was pointed out that the details were obtainable from the records kept in his own department, and to this he agreed.

We subsequently questioned the Assistant (Mr. Bruce) as to his knowledge of the transactions with this tradesman. We have verified the accuracy of Mr. Bruce's statements, and from the evidence before us we are of the opinion that he (Mr. Bruce) is in no way responsible for the matters now reported.

On the 28th instant Mr. Canty was interviewed at the Guildhall by ourselves with the Town Clerk. With samples of the goods supplied before us, he was questioned with regard to his exorbitant charges, as compared with the recent quotations by other firms. He stated that "Lignum Vitæ now costs over five times as much as before the war," but it was pointed out to him that in certain cases even his pre-war charges were 200 and 300 per cent. more than the recent quotations referred to. Instancing other items (appearing in the schedule), his attention was directed to the fact that in some cases his charges during the war period were five times as much as the highest recent quotations.

In reply to various questions, Mr. Canty contended that, notwithstanding the evidence to the contrary, his charges were fair, and that he simply worked out the cost and charged accordingly. He asked that the Corporation should obtain goods on the tenders submitted by the other firms, and said it would, no doubt, prove that the firms had quoted far too low, and that the goods would fail to satisfy the requirements. He was informed that the matter would be reported to the Tramways Committee, and asked whether he would furnish a statement of the actual cost incurred in executing orders for four specific classes of articles supplied during the current year (viz., the last four items of Schedule 1, page 17). Mr. Canty declined to do so. He also declined to permit the City Accountant to refer to his ledger account relating to his dealings with this department.

In the course of our investigation, other cases were observed in which exhaustive inquiry would have been made had time permitted. In view of the desirability of presenting a report before the Recess, we have been unable to do more than make one or two tests which indicate that excessive prices have been paid for articles other than those mentioned above.

(3) *Orders have been given when the Stocks on hand were apparently adequate.*

Independent tests made as to average consumption and quantities of stock held shew that the orders for goods have apparently been placed unnecessarily. Examples are given in Schedule 2 (headed "Excess Stores") attached hereto, page 18.

The Tramway Electrical Engineer informs us that as to quantities ordered he was guided by his subordinate, and on special reference being made to the copper barrel strips supplied by Messrs. Player & Mitchell (Birmingham), he states that the controller "overhaul" had been practically at a standstill for the last two years, and he supposed that orders were placed in anticipation of a much larger quantity of work having to be carried out in the near future. He agreed, however, that the ordinary maintenance of controllers had proceeded during the last two years. He had no recollection of the order for emery blocks supplied in March, 1917, by Messrs. McEwan, Denby, Hart-Briggs & Co., and stated that probably they were obtained at the request of his Assistant (Mr. Bruce).

We have questioned Mr. Bruce, who informs us that during the 18 months which elapsed between the late store-keeper's death and the appointment of a chief store-keeper, he exercised a general supervision over the stores department, and would accept full responsibility as to the necessity for the quantities of stores for which he had signed requisitions. He stated that 1-in. copper barrel strips for controllers were seldom used, and that he had no recollection of requisitioning emery blocks since about 1910, and that not many were used after the late City Engineer (Mr. White) retired.

(4) *Orders have been frequently placed for amounts exceeding £10 in value without the authority of the Committee.*

The Tramway Electrical Engineer stated that this occasionally happened, but he believed that it would be found that orders placed for goods required in an emergency were included in subsequent requisition lists and the Committee's approval thus obtained. He was informed that this statement was not borne out by the records of the Committee's proceedings.

Schedule 3, giving a list of cases in which goods have been ordered without the Committee's authority covering the test period January, 1917, to January, 1918 (inclusive) has been prepared for the Committee's information, see page 21.

(5) *The books and statistical costing records have been unsuitably and unsatisfactorily kept, not giving the information for which they were intended.*

The car damage books (shewing the cost of repairs as the result of collisions, &c.) have been wrongly priced, i.e., they are not based upon the actual cost of the materials used, &c., whilst in other cases the cost of materials has been omitted, with the result that claims made on third parties have been under-stated. Fortunately, however, these claims are comparatively few in number.

The Car Cost Ledger (cost of maintenance of each car) shews the quantities of materials used, but not the values thereof. There are other omissions, and for the period under review the book has not served any useful purpose.

With the authority of the former Chairman and his Deputy, the City Accountant inaugurated a new system as and from 1st April last, which, if properly carried out, will put this matter upon a proper basis.

(6) *There has been an absence of precautionary measures in the collection and storage of Scrap Metals (Copper, Brass, &c.)*

It will be seen from Schedule 4 attached to this report (page 25) that from 17th April to 28th June, 1919, as a result of the new stores system and the more vigilant methods adopted by the recently appointed store-keeper, the accumulation of scrap metals during these two-and-a-half months has been greater than any one year during the period of the war. These metals have recently been placed under lock and key.

(7) *The Clerical Staff is badly organised, and there is a lack of proper discipline.*

The present staff consists of 7 clerks and 1 temporary clerk (female), 1 draughtsman, the chief store-keeper and two boys. This small staff is divided into four small sub-departments, each self-contained.

The principle of dividing so small a staff into independent sections and restricting the responsibilities of the chief clerk is not conducive to the efficient working and discipline of the department, provided that he is a suitable person for the position held.

The chief store-keeper is responsible for the custody of the stores, and at present has control of the stores ledgers, a great amount of his time, as a consequence, being spent in the office. This is not compatible with the duties of a chief store-keeper, and we consider it irregular for any store-keeper to have access to stores ledgers.

Certain of the clerks are handicapped by lack of training, but are very willing, and, under efficient supervision, would soon become competent.

With four exceptions, the members of the office staff are paid either a fixed weekly wage or by the hour through the weekly wages book, which is contrary to the practice followed by the Authority.

The desirability of merging the traffic and electrical office staffs, and generally re-organising is a matter which should receive the early consideration of the new General Manager.

We are of opinion that a thorough and impartial enquiry into the personnel of the department covering the circumstances of appointment and duties performed, is essential in the interests of the undertaking.

In conclusion, we beg to state that, notwithstanding the heavy work which this inquiry has involved on the part of the City Accountant and his staff, and the great amount of time we have personally given to the matter, the investigation could be carried considerably further. It is a question, however, whether in all the circumstances, any useful purpose would be served by so doing.

R. RICHARDSON,
R. W. WHEELDON, } Members of the Committee.
WM. H. SMITH, City Accountant.

Guildhall,
Hull,
30th July, 1919.

SCHEDULES APPENDED HERETO.

No.

1. *Pages 10 to 17*—Comparative statement of prices *actually paid* to Mr. Arthur Canty (Turning and Saw Mills, Malton Street, Hull) and *highest quotations* obtained from other firms.

2. *Pages 18 to 20*—Excess Stores on hand.

3. *Pages 21 to* —Stores ordered (above £10 in value) without the authority of the Committee.

4. *Page 25* —Comparative Statement showing accumulations of scrap metal.

SCHEDULE 1 (see page 4 of Report).

HULL CITY TRAMWAYS.

ELECTRICAL ENGINEER'S DEPARTMENT.

STATEMENT SHEWING THE DIFFERENCE BETWEEN PRICES ACTUALLY PAID FOR GOODS SUPPLIED BY MR. ARTHUR CANTY (TURNING AND SAW MILLS, MALTON STREET, HULL) FROM FEBRUARY, 1913, TO MARCH, 1919, AND HIGHEST QUOTATIONS OBTAINED FROM OTHER FIRMS DURING THE INQUIRY, JULY, 1919.

SUMMARY.

	Actual Cost.				Value based on highest quotatios July, 1919.				DIFFERENCE being excess cost.		
	£	s	d		£	s	d		£	s	d
Page 11	44	8	3	..	16	3	2	..	28	5	1
Do. 12	36	6	9	..	19	18	11	..	16	7	10
Do. 13	54	16	0	..	24	5	0	..	30	11	0
Do. 14	31	4	9	..	17	4	0	..	14	0	9
Do. 15	38	17	10	..	26	6	9	..	12	11	1
Do. 16	133	4	0	..	51	16	0	..	81	8	0
Do. 17	191	12	6	..	47	7	6	..	144	5	0
	£530	10	1	..	£203	1	4	..	£327	8	9

Being 161 per cent. in excess of value based on present prices, which are still at their highest on account of the scarcity of Lignum Vitæ and other hardwoods.

For the purpose of this statement, where more than one quotation has been received, the highest has been used.

If the lowest quotations were used, the " overcharge " would be over 200 per cent., i.e., the prices paid average THREE TIMES the actual value.

							PURCHASES MADE.						HIGHEST QUOTATIONS, July, 1919.			
Item.	Date.	Art. No.	Description.	Quantity.	Rate.	Amount.			Sample No.	Rate.	Value.			Difference, being excess cost.		Remarks.
						£	s	d			£	s	d	£ s d		
	1913.															
I.	Feb. 28	—	Oak section insulators, 11¼ by 1 by ¾ in. distance pieces.	—	—	—			—	—	—			—		P.S.
2.	Mar. 20	C 61	L.V. Auto-point runners ..	51	2/9 each.	7	0	3	2	(1) 9½d. (2) 1/4½ (3) 1/6	3	16	6	3 3 9		P.S.
3.	,, 20	C 62	L. V. aminium cross-runner	56	do.	7	14	0	13	4½d.	1	1	0	6 13 0		P.S.
4.	,, 20	C 76	L.V. Bushes to sample ..	144	12/- doz.	7	4	0	23	4/6 doz.	2	14	0	4 10 0		P.S.
5.	,, 20	C 76	do.	36	do.	1	16	0	23	do.	0	13	6	1 2 6		P.S.
6.	Apr. 19	C 64	L.V. Runners, 17 in. steel plates and rivetted each end.	49	3/6 each.	8	11	6	1	(1) 5½d. (2) 8d. (3) 9¾d. (4) 11d. + 1⅝d.	2	13	1	5 18 5		P.S.—See 16th July, same articles 2/6 each, also bought previously at 2/6.
7.	May 15	—	A.B. Distance pieces 6¼ by 2½ by ⅛ in.	14 doz.	1/6 doz.	—			—	—	—			—		—
8.	,, 28	—	Sawdust (white) ..	6 bags.	—	—			—	—	—			—		P.S.
9.	July 16, 18 & 20	C 64	L.V. Runners, 17 in. steel plates and rivetted each end.	97	2/6 each.	12	2	6	1	1/1 See No. 6.	5	5	1	6 17 5		P.S.
						£44	8	3			16	3	2	28 5 1		

PURCHASES MADE.							HIGHEST QUOTATIONS, July, 1919.				
Item.	Date.	Art. No.	Description.	Quantity.	Rate.	Amount.	Sample No.	July, 1919. Rate.	July, 1919. Value.	**Difference,** being excess cost.	Remarks.
	1913.					£ s d			£ s d	£ s d	
10.	July 26	C 64	L.V. Runners 17 in. steel plates and rivetted each end.	38	2/6 each.	4 15 0	1	1/1 See No. 6	2 1 2	2 13 10	P.S.
11.	Sept. 17	C 65	Oak Distance pieces to sample.	38	7/6 doz.	1 3 9	9	4/6 doz.	0 14 3	0 9 6	P.S.
12.	Oct. 10	—	L.V. Trolley standard insulator blocks, 6 holes in each.	12	4/- each	2 8 0	6	3/6 each	2 2 0	0 6 0	L.S.
13.	,, 10	—	L.V. Trolley standard insulator blocks to pattern	12	do.	2 8 0	7	do.	2 2 0	0 6 0	L.S.
14.	May 14	C 76	L.V. Bushes, 1¼ by 1, ½ hole in two pieces.	24	15/- doz.	1 10 0	23	4/6 doz.	0 9 0	1 1 0	P.S.
	1914.										
15.	Mar. 17	C 61	L.V. Autopoint runners, 7¾ by 1½ by ½ in. to sample.	36	2/9 each	4 19 0	2	(1) 9½d. (2) 1/4½ (3) 1/6 each	2 14 0	2 5 0	P.S.—24 ordered, 36 supplied.
16.	Apr. 7	C 64	L.V. Runners 17 in. steel plates and rivetted each end.	72	2/6 each	9 0 0	1	1/1 See No. 6	3 18 0	5 2 0	P.S.
17.	May 29	C 62	L.V. Cross-runners to sample.	28	2/9 each	3 17 0	13	4½d. each	0 10 6	3 6 6	P.S.
18.	June 30	C 83	W.B. Sleeves 4½ by 2⅞ by 2⅝ in.	72	1/9 each	6 6 0	22	1/6 each	5 8 0	0 18 0	P.S.
						£36 6 9			19 18 11	16 7 10	

Item.	Date.	Art. No.	Description.	Quantity.	Rate.	Amount.	Sample No.	Rate.	Value.	Difference.	Remarks.
19.	July 10	C 76	L.V. Bushes 1¼ by 1 in. ½ hole in 2 pieces.	5 doz.	15/- doz.	3 15 0	23	4/6 doz.	1 2 6	2 12 6	P.S. — 3 doz. ordered, 5 doz. supplied.
20.	,, 13	C 62	L.V. Cross-runners, 6¾ by 1¼ by 5/8ths to sample.	94	2/9 each	12 18 6	13	4½d. each	1 15 3	11 3 3	P.S.—72 ordered 94 supplied.
21.	,, 24	C 83	W.B. Sleeves 4½ by 2 7/8th ⅜ pole to sample.	84	1/9 each	7 7 0	22	1/6 each	6 6 0	1 1 0	P.S.—72 ordered 84 supplied.
22.	Sept. 22	C 71	L.V. Bushes 1½ by 1 in. 7/16ths holes.	86	12/- doz.	4 6 0	3	4/6 doz.	1 12 3	2 13 9	P.S.—72 ordered 86 supplied.
23.	Nov. 23	—	L.V. Bushes 1¼ by 1 in. ¼ in. hole.	18	—	—	—	—	—	—	P.S.
			L.V. Washers 1 by ¼ in. ½ in. hole.	18	—	—	—	—	—	—	P.S.
24.	,, 24	C 61	L.V. Auto-point runners	72 each	2/9	9 18 0	2	(1) 9½d. (2) 1/4½d. (3) 1/6	5 8 0	4 10 0	P.S.
	1915.										
25.	Feb. 24	—	L.V. Runners, 17 in. steel plates and rivetted each end.	54	3/6 each	9 9 0	1	1/1 See No. 6	2 18 6	6 10 6	P.S.—36 ordered 54 supplied.
26.	Apl. 16	A 243	A. Birch Siemen Controller handles and knobs to sample.	24	15/- doz.	1 10 0	26	7/6 doz.	0 15 0	0 15 0	L.S.
27.	May 7	C 73	Hardwood bobbins, 3¼ by 2 in. 5/8ths holes to sample.	30	12/- doz.	—		—	—	—	P.S.
28.	June 17	—	L.V. Controller standards, 4⅛ by 1½ base insulators; 6 holes in each, to sample.	25	4/6 each	5 12 6	6	3/6 each	4 7 6	1 5 0	L.S.
						54 16 0			24 5 0	30 11 0	

			PURCHASES MADE.				HIGHEST QUOTATIONS, July, 1919.				
Item.	Date.	Art. No.	Description.	Quantity.	Rate.	Amount.	Sample No.	Rate.	Value.	Difference, being excess cost.	Remarks.
	1915.					£ s d			£ s d	£ s d	
29.	July 20	—	L.V. Runners 17 in. steel plates and rivetted each end.	40	3/6 each	7 0 0	1	1/1 See No. 6	2 3 4	4 16 8	P.S.
30.	Aug. 5	—	A.B. Controller handles and plugs, 5 in. by 2 in.	25	18/- doz.	1 17 6	5	8/6 doz.	0 17 8	0 19 10	L.S.
31.	,, 5	—	A.B. Controller handles and plugs 4½ in. by 1 5/8ths.	25	18/- doz.	1 17 6	4	7/6 doz.	0 15 8	1 1 10	L.S.
32.	Sept. 7	—	Birch washers 1½ in. diam. by ¾ in. ¾ in. hole.	72	4/- doz.	—	—	—	—	—	L.S.
	1916.										
33.	July 6	C 64	L.V. Runners, 17 in. to sample.	74	2/9 each	10 3 6	—	(1) 5½d. (2) 8d. (3) 9¾d. (4) 11d.	3 7 10	6 15 8	P.S.
34.	Sept. 30	C 73	Hardwood bobbins 3¼ in. 2 in. ⅜ in. hole.	72	12/- doz.	—	—	—	—	—	—
35.	,, 20	C 72	Hardwood bobbins 2 in by 2 in., to sample.	72	11/- doz.	—	—	—	—	—	—
36.	Oct. 4	C 67	Hardwood backs for aluminium cross overs 2 ft. by 2¼ in. by 1⅞ in.	24	5/6 each	6 12 0	25	3/3 each	3 18 0	2 14 0	P.S.
37.	,, 10	—	Sycamore strips 12 in by ⅝ in. by 3/16ths.	324	33/- gross	3 14 3	21	4/6 doz.	6 1 6	Gain 2 7 3	L S.
						31 4 9			17 4 0	14 0 9	

38.	Oct. 10	—	Sycamore Strips 10 by ⅝ in. by ¼ in.	324	30/- gross.	—	—	—	—	—	L.—1 gross ordered 2 gross supplied.
39.	Nov. 20	—	Making patterns and finding wood for same 9¼ in. by 9¼ in. by 3 in.	—	—	—	—	—	—	—	—
	1917.										
40.	Feb. 13	C 64	L.V. Runners 17 in. to sample.	72	3/3 each	11 14 0	1	See 33	3 6 0	8 8 0	P.S.
41.	May 17	—	Sycamore strips 10 in by ⅞ in by 3/16ths in., planed and bevelled.	229	4/- doz.	3 16 4	..	3/6 doz.	3 6 10	0 9 6	1 gross ordered 19 doz. sent.
42.	,, 17	..	Ash strips 9 in. by ¼ in by ⅛ in. planed.	408	2/6 doz.	4 5 0	14	2/6 doz.	4 5 0	..	1 gross ordered 34 doz. sent.
43.	July 5	—	Teak wedges 2½ in. by ½ in. by 3/16ths planed.	1100	10/- 100	5 10 0	16	12/6 100	6 17 6	Gain 1 7 6	L.S.
44.	,, 5	—	Teak blocks ⅝ in by ⅝ in. by 3/16ths planed.	1100	6/3 100	3 8 9	17	1/- doz.	4 11 8	Gain 1 2 11	L.S.
45.	,, 9	B 95	R.W. Motor cable wood, insulators, planed, grooved and bored, 7 in. by 1 13/16ths in. sq.	72	15/- doz.	4 10 0	24	6/6 doz.	1 19 0	2 11 0	L.S.
	1917.										
46.	Sept. 18	B 96	Hardwood motor cable insulators 2¼ in. by 1¾in. diam. 2 7/16ths holes through.	53	15/- doz.	3 6 3	18	6/- doz.	1 6 6	1 19 9	L.–36 ordered 53 supplied.
47.	,, 26	B 96	Hardwood trolley standard cable wood insulators 2 in. by 1⅛.	38	do.	2 7 6	19	4/6 doz.	0 14 3	1 13 3	L.—24 ordered 38 supplied.
						38 17 10			26 6 9	12 11 1	

			PURCHASES MADE.				HIGHEST QUOTATIONS, July, 1919.				
Item.	Date.	Art. No.	Description.	Quantity.	Rate.	Amount.	Sample No.	Rate.	Value.	Difference, being excess cost.	Remarks.
	1917.					£ s d			£ s d	£ s d	
48.	Oct. 27	—	*L.V. top controller standard cable insulators $4\frac{1}{4}$ in by $1\frac{3}{4}$ in., $\frac{7}{8}$ in. hole.	72	9/– each	32 8 0	6	3/6 each	12 12 0	19 16 0	L.—*Order 194 is for 72 top and 72 bottom controller standard insulators.
49.	,, 31	—	*L.V. top controller standards 4 in. by $1\frac{3}{4}$ in. cable insulators. $\frac{7}{8}$ in. sq. hole in each to sample.	36	do.	16 4 0	6	do.	6 6 0	9 18 0	Supplied:—144 top, 152 bottom. Order more than doubled at a price 150 per cent. above present (high) prices.
50.	Nov. 29	—	*L.V. bottom trolley standards $4\frac{1}{8}$ in. by $1\frac{1}{2}$in. 6 holes in each.	72	do.	32 8 0	7	do.	12 12 0	19 16 0	L.S.
51.	,, 30	—	*L.V. top controller standard cable insulators 4 in. by $1\frac{3}{4}$ in., $\frac{7}{8}$ in. sq. hole in bottom.	36	do.	16 4 0	6	do.	6 6 0	9 18 0	L.S.
52.	,, 30	—	*L.V. Bottom controller standards $4\frac{1}{8}$ in. by $1\frac{1}{2}$in. 6 holes in each.	36	do.	16 4 0	7	do.	6 6 0	9 18 0	L.S.
53.	,, 30	—	*L.V. bottom trolley standards $4\frac{1}{8}$. in. by $1\frac{1}{2}$ in., 6 holes in each.	44	9/- each	19 16 0	7	3/6 each	7 14 0	12 2 0	L.S.
						133 4 0			51 16 0	81 8 0	
54.	Nov. 30	C 66	Oak air gap insulator section pieces $8\frac{1}{4}$ in. by $1\frac{1}{4}$ in by $1\frac{1}{4}$ in., planed.	86	12/– doz.	4 6 0	10	4/6 doz.	1 12 3	2 13 9	P.S.
55.	,, 30	C 65	Oak section distance pieces $11\frac{1}{2}$ in. by $1\frac{1}{4}$ in. by 13/16ths, planed.	80	do.	4 0 0	9	do.	1 10 0	2 10 0	P.S.
56.	Dec. 5	C 84	L.V. Auto-point insulators 13 in. by 1 in. by [illegible] in. to sample.	60	4/11 each	14 15 0	8	$7\frac{1}{2}$d. each	1 17 6	12 17 6	P.S.
57.	,, 5	C 64	L.V. 17 in. runners to sample.	168	4/6 each	37 16 0	1	See No. 33	7 14 0	30 2 0	P.S.—144 ordered 168 sent.
	1918.										
58.	Feb. 18	—	Controller handles and plugs 5 in. by 2 in.	48	1/9 each	4 4 0	5	$8\frac{1}{2}$d. each	1 14 0	2 10 0	P.S.
59.	,, 18	—	Controller handles and plugs $4\frac{1}{2}$d. by $1\frac{3}{4}$ in.	45	do.	3 18 9	4	$7\frac{1}{2}$d. each	1 8 2	2 10 7	P.S.
60.	Mar. 4	B 62	L.V. Runners 7 in. by $2\frac{1}{4}$ by $1\frac{1}{4}$ in. to sample.	41	6/3 each	12 16 3	20	$10\frac{1}{2}$d. each	1 15 11	11 0 4	P.S.
	1919.										
61.	Jan. 21	C 64	L.V. 17 in. runners to sample.	120	4/6 each	27 0 0	1	See No. 33	5 10 0	21 10 0	P.S.
62.	,, 25	C 64	L.V. 17 in. Runners to sample.	132	4/6 each	29 14 0	1	See No. 33	6 1 0	23 13 0	P.S.—144 ordered, 252 supplied.
63.	,, 30	C 61	L.V. Under runners $7\frac{3}{4}$ in. by $1\frac{1}{2}$ in. by $\frac{1}{2}$ in. to blue print, A 496.	107	6/3 each	33 8 9 3/6 doz.	2	(1) $9\frac{1}{2}$d. (2) 1/$4\frac{1}{2}$d. (3) 1/6	8 0 6	25 8 3	P.S.—72 ordered, 107 supplied.
64.	Feb. 11	—	Sec. wood strips 10 in. by $\frac{3}{4}$ in. by 3/16ths in. to sample.	550	50/– 100	13 15 0	15	29/2 100	8 0 5	5 14 7	L.S.
65.	Mar. 17	C 81	Hardwood Cable bobbins $1\frac{7}{8}$ in. by $1\frac{1}{2}$ in., $\frac{1}{2}$ in. hole to sample.	150	9/6 doz.	5 18 9	11	3/6 doz.	2 3 9	3 15 0	P.S.
						191 12 6			47 7 6	144 5 0	

SCHEDULE 2 (see page 6 of Report).

EXCESS STORES.

From Tests made, the following particulars are extracted :—

Folio.	Description.	Consumption 1917–1918.	1918–1919.	Stock when last order placed.	Last Order Date.	Order No.	Quantity.	From.	Rate.	Value £ s d	Stock 31/3/19.	Remarks.
A. 1	K. 10 Controller Barrel Strips, 1 in. by 1⅛ in.	17	14	91	4/2/18	529	288	Player and Mitchell.	1/–	14 9 0	353	L.S.
A. 2	K. 10 Controller Barrel Strips, 1 in by 1⅝ in.	54	18	169	4/2/18	529	288	do.	10d.	12 0 10	449	L.S.
A. 128	Westinghouse Controller Barrel Strips, ¾ in. by 10¾ in.	76	20	97	25/1/19	651	576	do.	1/9	50 8 8	653	L.S.
134	Do. 1 in. by 12 in.	11	2	34	25/1/19	651	576	do.	2/3	64 18 3	609	L.S.
54	L.V. Cable Insulators (tops and bottoms).	22	5	117 30th Sept.	10/10/17	194	144	Arthur Canty	9/–	133 4 0	386	L.S. Supplied 296 at 9/–
88	McEwan Emery Blocks.	24	12	307	26/3/17	411	72	McEwan, Denby & Hart-Briggs, Ltd.	12/6	43 17 6	367	P.S.
81	2 ft. 10 in. Bonds and Pins.	109	99	45	17/5/18	14	500	Forest City E/L. Service Co., Ltd.	4/5½ each	111 9 2	502	P.S.—Excessive order.
	Grooved ... ing Ears.	3	—	—		736	144	G. Clark, Jun., & Co.	8/6	61 4 0	139	P.S.
	... 3/0 Splicing Ears.	20	20	22	Sept., 1918	310	144	Fleming, Birkby & Goodall.	7/1	51 0 0	149	P.S.—Size of order.
	L.V. Auto-point Runners.	9	15	73	Jan., 1919	568	107	A. Canty	6/3	33 8 9	180	P.S.
	3 in. Forked Globes.	20	—	33	13/3/18	619	144	Fleming, Birkby & Goodall.	3/4	24 0 0	158	P.S.
	3/0 Bronze Wire.	429	120	No orders lately.				Present stock	6d.	294 5 0	11770	P.S. Excess
6	Section Insulated Brass.	8	8		do.			do.	1/6	49 2 6	655	P.S.
164	Reversing Barrel Contacts.	12	9	76	11/3/19	S/28	144	Player & Mitchell.	—	—	—	L.S.—Not yet received.
15	K. 10¾ in. Barrel Strip Tips.	36+44=80	65	430	11/3/19	S/28	288	do.	6/9	—	430	do.
8	K. 10 Barrel Strip Tips, 1 in by 5¼ in.	7	30	76	11/3/19	S/28	288	do.	1/2	16 16 0	76	292 supplied.
A. 300	T.A. 3 Reversing Barrel Contacts	—	—	1	11/3/19	S/31	72	G. Clark & Sons	6/6	23 8 0	1	Size of order.
A. 291	T.A. 3 Barrel Strips.	5	6	60	11/3/19	S/28	290	Player & Mitchell.	1/6	21 12 0	60	—

Folio.	Description.	Consumption. 1917–1918.	1918–1919.	Stock when last order placed.	Last Order. Date.	Order No.	Quantity.	From.	Rate.	Value. £ s d	Stock 31/3/19.	Remarks.
A. 71	B. 18 Barrel Strips, 1 in. by 6½ in.	15	28	59	25/1/19	652	576	Player & Mitchell	1/2	33 12 0	39	L.S.
A. 66	B. 18 Barrel Strips ¾ in. by 6 in.	13	37	26	25/1/19	652	576	do.	11d.	26 8 0	6	L.S. — Excessive order.
A. 63	B. 18 Barrel Strips 2 in. by ¾ in.	2	8		No orders lately.	—		—		12 10 8	573	L.S.—Dead stock.
A. 24	18 in. Mechanical Ears.	25	9		do.			—		82 0 0	188	P.S. do.
A. 4	24 in. 3/0 Splicing Ears.	2	1		do.			—		12 15 0	85	P.S. do.

SCHEDULE 3 (see page 7 of Report)

HULL CITY TRAMWAYS.

ELECTRICAL ENGINEER'S DEPARTMENT.

LIST OF GOODS ORDERED WITHOUT THE AUTHORITY OF THE COMMITTEE (*i.e.*, PER REQUISITION LIST OF PURCHASES OVER £10 IN VALUE).

1ST JANUARY, 1917, TO 30TH JANUARY, 1918 (1 YEAR 1 MONTH).

Date of order.	Order No.	Description of Goods.	From whom purchased.	Rate.	Value. £ s d	Remarks.
1917. 1 Jan.	162	Petrol, 132 gallons	Anglo-American Oil Co., Ltd.	—	14 0 6	Repeated—30th Jan. (259). March, (418). (then) monthly.
3 „	173	Coke, 12 tons	British Gas Light Co., Ltd.	—	14 5 0	—
10 „	186	1 in. Screwed Tubing, 1,200 ft.	Edison & Swan U.E.L. Co., Ltd	—	23 17 9	—
10 „	190	Compressed Lubricant, 6 barrels	Pollard & Winter	—	42 1 5	—
10 „	191	Trolley Wheels, 144	Fleming, Birkby & Co.	—	41 4 3	—
10 „	199	Siemen's Barrel Strip Tips, 4 gross	Player & Mitchell	—	16 8 8	—
10 „	203	Brake Hangers, 1 gross	Harper, Phillips & Co.	—	29 0 0	—
2 Feb.	270	Traction Lamps, 8 c.p., 4 gross	Edison & Swan U.E.L. Co.	—	16 7 7	—
10 „	291	Soda Ash, 2 tons	W. Carlin, Ltd.	—	17 0 0	—
14 „	310	7/16th Lighting Wire, 220 yards	Callender Cable Co., Ltd.	—	12 10 0	—
14 „	311	do.	W. T. Henley	—	12 10 0	—

Date of order.	Order No.	Description of Goods.	From whom purchased.	Rate.	Value. £ s d	Remarks.
1917.						
3 Mar.	348	100 v. 8 c.p. Lamps, 4 gross	Edison & Swan U.E.L. Co., Ltd	—	16 7 7	—
3 ,,	380	Compressed Lubricant, 6 barrels	Pollard & Winter	—	42 18 3	—
20 ,,	391	Siemen Controller Tips, 2 gross ..	G. Clark & Sons	—	31 13 9	—
20 ,,	392	do.	G. Clark, Junr. & Co.	—	25 8 0	—
20 ,,	434	Soda Ash, 2 tons	W. Carlin, Ltd.	—	17 0 0	—
18 April	469	Compressed Lubricant, 6 barrels	Pollard & Winter	—	45 12 3	—
27 ,,	479	Zinc Plates, 48	G. Clark & Sons	—	23 5 7	—
27 ,,	483	Brake Blocks, 4 gross	Moss & Co.	—	61 2 7	—
2 May	499	Compressed Lubricant, 6 barrels	Pollard & Winter	—	45 12 7	—
15 ,,	526	do.	do. ..	—	42 17 9	—
17 ,,	535	Cup-headed Pins, 2 gross.. .. Brake Lever, 2 ,, .. }	Woodall & Co.	—	25 4 0	—
17 ,,	536	Brake Blocks, 2 gross	Moss & Co.	—	23 17 9	—
17 ,,	544	Oil, 17 barrels	J. L. Seaton & Co., Ltd. ..	—	99 9 10	—
17 ,,	545	Oil, 5 barrels	do.	—	59 13 7	—
19 ,,	546	Siemen's Barrels Strip Tips, 4 gross	G. Clark, Junr., & Co. ..	—	31 4 0	—
18 ,,	547	Siemen's Barrel Strips, 2 gross ..	G. Clark & Co.	—	22 17 3	—
6 June	596	Brake Blocks, 2 gross	Moss & Co.	—	30 0 0	Approx.
13 ,,	622	Lamps, 100 v., 4 gross	Edison & Swan U.E.L. Co. ...	—	21 1 2	—
18 ,,	634	500 pr. Arc Lamp Carbons	Jandus Arc Lamp Co. ..	—	36 14 8	—
27 ,,	670	Compressed Lubricant, 12 barrels	Pollard & Winter	—	96 17 6	—
25 July	735	do.	do. ..	—	93 3 7	—
25 ,,	741	Side Window Glasses, 48 ..	H. Halmshaw..	—	32 14 5	—
28 ,,	749	Soda Ash, 2 tons	W. Carlin, Ltd.	—	17 0 0	—
8 Aug.	15	Gearpaco, 4 casks	J. L. Seaton & Co., Ltd. ..	—	32 12 3	—
15 ,,	31	Oil, 4 barrels	do. ..	—	33 9 0	—
28 ,,	57	Office Linoleum	Anstey's	—	18 0 0	—
12 Sept.	101	Compressed Lubricant, 12 barrels	Pollard & Winter	—	98 11 11	—
3 Oct.	161	Barrel Tips, &c., 18 gross ..	G. Clark, Junr., & Co., Ltd.	—	100 0 0	Approx.
3 ,,	164	Compressed Lubricant, 12 barrels	Pollard & Winter	—	97 18 9	—
17 ,,	215	S.C. Oil, 12 barrels .. .. S H. Cylinder Oil, 6 barrels .. Colza Oil, 10 gallons .. .. }	J. L. Seaton & Co., Ltd. ..	—	111 12 10	—
18 ,,	234	Knife Switch Slate Slabs, 144 ..	Clark & Graham	—	52 12 0	—
22 ,,	240	D. C. C. Wire, 2 cwts.	British Insulator Co... ..	—	18 0 2	—
24 ,,	245	Machine Brush Holders, 36 ..	Siemens Bros.	—	16 4 0	—
7 Nov.	309	Waste, 10 cwts.	Hall & Hamlyn	—	17 10 0	—
9 ,,	312	Arc Lamp Inner Globes, 72 ..	General Electric Co., Ltd. ..	—	11 11 8	—
1 ,,	320	Compressed Lubricant, 12 barrels	Pollard & Winter	—	100 19 10	—
3 ,,	345	Gearpaco, 4 barrels	J. L. Seaton & Co., Ltd. ..	—	39 4 0	—

Date of order.	Order No.	Description of Goods.	From whom purchased.	Rate.	Value.			Remarks.
					£	s	d	
1917.								
8 Dec.	365	C. C. Oil, 4 barrels Car Oil, 2 barrels Gearpaco, 2 barrels	J. L. Seaton & Co., Ltd.	—	59	6	6	—
1918.								
5 Jan.	416	Compressed Lubricant, 12 barrels	Pollard & Winter	—	98	3	1	—
5 ,,	420	19/20ths Lighting Wire, 220 yards	W. T. Henley	—	11	12	10	—
5 ,,	421	3/20ths do. 440 yards 7/22nds do. 440 ,,	Callender's Cable Co.	—	13	19	4	—
5 ,,	432	C. C. Oil, 3 barrels	J. L. Seaton & Co., Ltd.	—	18	14	9	—
9 ,,	444	Cylinder Oil, 3 barrels	do.	—	16	13	10	—
11 ,,	451	Slate Slabs for Fuses, 72	Clark & Graham	—	26	6	6	—
11 ,,	451	Slate Slabs for Automatic Switches, 72	do.	—	26	6	6	—
23 ,,	482	1/16th in. Insulating Fibre, 12 sheets	Bell's United Asbestos Co.	—	12	17	9	—
23 ,,	487	B.T.H. Dust Caps, 72	G. Clark & Sons	—	11	14	0	—
23 ,,	493	Brake Chains, 72	Woodall & Co.	—	27	0	0	—

TRAMWAYS ELECTRICAL ENGINEER'S DEPARTMENT.

SCHEDULE 4 (see page 8 of Report).

COMPARATIVE STATEMENT SHEWING THE ACCUMULATIONS OF SCRAP METALS FROM APRIL, 1912, TO JUNE 1919.

Year.	Quantity.				Proceeds.		
	Tons.	Cwts.	Qrs.	Lbs.	£	s.	d.
1912–13	7	18	1	25	333	5	7
1913–14	7	15	0	23	350	12	5
1914–15	3	1	1	3	158	5	2
1915–16 (average)	3	3	2	17	300	14	8
1916–17 do.	3	3	2	17	300	14	8
1917–18 do.	3	9	1	5	308	16	7
1918–19 do.	3	9	1	5*	308	16	7*
17th April to 28th June, 1919 (2½ months)	3	14	2	20	—		

*Includes stock on hand at 17th April, 1919, 2 tons, 13 cwts. 0qrs. 6 lbs., representing an approximate value of £260.

ENQUIRY *re*

THE TRAMWAY ELECTRICAL ENGINEER'S DEPARTMENT.

———

REPLY TO REPORT

———

To the Chairman and Members of the Tramways Committee.

TRAMWAY POWER STATION BUILDINGS,
Osborne Street, Hull.
12th August, 1919.

ENQUIRY *re* THE TRAMWAY ELECTRICAL ENGINEER'S DEPARTMENT.

With reference to the report which has been submitted to the Chairman and Members of the Tramways Committee with regard to my Business Methods, I respectfully beg to submit herewith a detailed report in my reply thereto.

With regard to the statement that the business of my Department has not been carried out in a satisfactory and economical manner, it is desirable that I point out that the last report on the methods of this Department was embodied in a general report referring to the various departments of the Corporation investigated by Sir Harmood Banner, M.P., in his report, dated 17th April, 1915. This report read as follows:—

"I have examined the accounts of the Tramways Department, and need only refer here to the Stores and Costs Accounts kept by the Electrical Engineer. Neither of these is quite complete, and the system should be revised. The accounts are very well kept so far as they go, and revision will be easy. The Electrical Engineer will co-operate in revision, and agree to Cost and Stores Accounts being kept in the Accountant's Department, relying on it to supply him with any information he requires."

With reference to Stores Accounting, on the death of my Chief Storekeeper, Mr. Rose, on November 4th, 1917, at the request of my Chief Assistant, who stated that in his opinion the work of storekeeping could be carried on between himself and the Chief Clerk, I agreed to his suggestion. At the end of the Financial Year I received a letter from the City Accountant which indicated that more detail with regard to stores was required. I then made a report to my Committee as follows:—

TRAMWAYS COMMITTEE MINUTES, JULY 24TH, 1918.

CHIEF STOREKEEPER, TRAMWAY ELECTRICAL ENGINEER'S DEPARTMENT.

"The Tramway Electrical Engineer reported that to keep up to the requirements of the City Accountant and Government restrictions in connection with the consumption of material, both at the Power Station and Car Sheds, it would be necessary to appoint a Chief Storekeeper to replace Mr. H. Rose, who died on November 4th, 1917. Since Mr. Rose's death the work had been divided between the Assistant Engineer and the Chief Clerk. Unfortunately, the requirements of the Accountant's Department are such that it is impossible to deal with it under the present conditions. The material and goods issued from the Stores of the above Department, during the twelve months, amounts to no less than nine to ten thousand pounds, consisting of thousands of both small and large fittings. It is essential that the man appointed should have some Engineering knowledge in addition to being smart at figures and ledger work."

On the appointment of the Chief Storekeeper and Inspector of Material, I wrote to the City Accountant as follows:—

10th January, 1919.

TRAMWAY STORES.

"As the Committee have now appointed a Chief Storekeeper and Inspector of Material to take over the duties of the late Mr. Rose, it has opened up an opportunity to consider any improvements that might be made in our system of storekeeping and which you think would in any measure facilitate matters for your department. If you could possibly spare a capable assistant who has had some experience in this direction, I should be pleased to go into the matter with him along with our new Storekeeper, Mr. Houston."

On going through the Accountant's report I find that the period covered by it is the War period, with the exception of the item of Mr. Canty, which dates back to the year 1913.

In a great measure owing to the increased responsibility during this period, I had to rely on as much assistance as possible from my staff, particularly in the way of scrutinising delivery notes, advice notes, and accounts,

The members of my committee will no doubt appreciate these difficulties under the following circumstances. At the beginning of hostilities, a number of my staff and men employed on important work at the Repair Sheds were under canvas and were mobilised at once. These were replaced by others who were unfamiliar with the work, and who afterwards volunteered or were called up for service, and changes were again made with female labour, particularly in connection with the Stores Department. Although they did certain work in a creditable manner, their lack of technical knowledge resulted in considerable confusion arising in connection with the requisitioning and serving out of material. This was further developed by firms we were dealing with having to utilise female labour also, with the result that invoices and advice notes were found difficult to deal with by my clerical staff, and in a number of cases in scrutinising these documents I have found that orders for material had been repeated, and put forward. More difficulties arose owing to the death of my Chief Storekeeper and the resignation of my Chief Clerk at a time when their services were badly needed. These difficulties were further accentuated by a serious breakdown in my health in July, 1917.

The following extract from " Electrical Industries " dated 6th August, 1919, may give members of the Committee some idea with regard to the difficulties experienced:—

"TRAMWAY CONGRESS, POST WAR PROBLEMS BY H. ENGLAND.

As regards materials, the position is chaotic. We are paying any prices asked by the manufacturers, and even then have difficulty in obtaining deliveries. I am tempted to ask whether we cannot do a great deal more to help ourselves in this matter. Surely a way can be found to standardise the bulk of our daily stores, and to buy on a co-operative basis."

Item No. 1.

With reference to the statement that it has not been the general practice to obtain competitive prices when ordering goods, it has always been the custom of this Department to purchase certain goods from the tradesmen appointed annually by the Works Committee, and as stated in my interview competitive prices were sometimes obtained for other material. This remark

referred in a great measure to the war period. In the early stages of the Undertaking it was the practice in almost every case to obtain competitive prices. It was, found, however, that the bulk of the material and fittings required for Tramway purposes were more or less manufactured by specialists on Railway and Tramway work, and when tests of material and fittings were made in competition with these firms the practice was to select that material or fitting which gave the best results and the highest efficiency, and the lowest price was not necessarily accepted.

Every facility has been given to local tradesmen, who have been supplied with blue prints and samples of all classes of fittings and material for the Power Station, Overhead Equipment, and Rolling Stock, and all possible assistance has been given to enable them to supply the types of fittings, etc., which had previously been obtained from outside specialists. The result is that the local tradesmen have been supplying us with large quantities of goods for maintenance and renewals.

Where Tramway Equipment has had to be imported from America, I myself have designed special fittings for the manufacture of it in our Workshops at Liverpool Street, and have effected considerable savings. This refers particularly to the repair and renewal of Armatures, etc.

May I state that in my Stores Department at Liverpool Street there are no less than 2304 items, and at the Power Station Stores there are no less than 1369, making a total of 3673 items, and to obtain prices for the whole of my purchases would be almost impossible, especially in the smaller matters. I should first of all require a considerably larger staff than I have at present, and the delay would prevent me from getting along with work of much more importance.

Item No. 2.

With reference to the statement that the prices charged for goods supplied to the Department in certain cases were exorbitant, may I respectfully state that as the matter in question is in the war period between 1914 and 1919, with the exception of that of Mr. Canty, I believe the figures would compare very favourably with prices paid by Engineers of other Undertakings. I have from time to time consulted my Chairman with regard to the difficulty in obtaining material, and I was instructed to do my best. My first duty as Tramway Electrical Engineer to this City was to maintain throughout the war, a service of cars to a high standard of public safety, and prices were a secondary consideration compared with the difficulty in obtaining the necessary material. Not only this but as the war progressed I was informed by most important firms that the Government had secured all their material in stock and they refused to quote, stating that they could not supply. I then had to use every possible means and every opportunity to get a standard quality in any market, without entering too far into details with regard to its increased cost. To have done so at such a crisis would have resulted in the material being lost to this Undertaking.

LIGNUM VITAE FITTINGS.

With reference to the transactions with Mr. Arthur Canty, Turning and Sawmills, Malton Street, Drypool, who has been supplying Hard Wood, etc., for overhead Line Equipment, Feeder Cables and Trolley Standards, on making careful enquiries from men who have been engaged on the Overhead Equipment and Cable work, I find that it was the practice to visit Canty's works, without my knowledge, for the purpose of obtaining fittings of the above description, both in cases of emergency and otherwise. At one time considerable trouble had been experienced in connection with Section Insulator Runners breaking and warping, and Bobbins and smaller fittings for Overhead Work and Pole Work on being screwed up into position giving way at their flanges to such an extent as to reduce our stock of these fittings very rapidly.

At this stage, assistants, without my knowledge, arranged with Mr. Canty, to experiment with Lignum Vitae for the purpose of getting over the trouble, i.e. cutting into the block in such a manner as to get out the best material. It was afterwards verbally reported to me (unfortunately I cannot give the date) that the material supplied after this was giving most satisfactory results. As these fittings were of considerable importance in regard to outside equipment, the report that they were doing well was a great relief to me. On the outbreak of hostilities, as this transaction compared with other matters was a minor one, and in addition to my ordinary business I was overloaded with military matters in connection with the calling up of the men, I was unable

to give the attention to it which I should have been able to have done otherwise, and left it more or less in the hands of my assistants, who were responsible to me for the maintenance and upkeep of the Overhead Line. I must, however, state after carefully looking into the matter that it would appear that this section of my Department has been giving verbal orders to Canty in addition to those sent through the official channel. This is borne out by the figures of delivery of material to the Stores. During the whole of this time various alterations were being made in the staff, including the replacing of called-up men by women workers, and at no time has my attention been called to excess deliveries or exorbitant prices in regard to transactions with this firm.

Suggestions have been made in connection with this case that I must have had some interest in the firm. This I absolutely deny. I have had no interest whatever, neither have I received one farthing nor present from Canty during the whole of the time I have been purchasing material from him. If any neglect has been shewn on my part it has been due to the heavy load I have had during the period of the war, but the suggestion of interest in the firm is both unjust and painful to me.

Item No. 3.

With reference to independent tests with regard to the average consumption and quantity of material held, and the statement that orders have apparently been placed which were unnecessary, this is without foundation, as any tests made during the past four years would be misleading. It has been absolutely impossible to continue the work of keeping up either rolling stock or overhead equipment to the pre-war standard of maintenance, and we have never had such excessive loads as those experienced during this abnormal period. We have also experienced considerable difficulties with regard to labour. There were certain times when men were being rapidly called up for service with H.M. Forces, and they had to be replaced with women with no knowledge of the work. After a few months training and just when they were becoming useful, through an action of the Trades Union, they had to be discharged and replaced by boys.

With regard to the quantities of material ordered, may I mention that on December 18th, 1918, I reported to my Committee as follows :—

"GENERAL OVERHAUL OF ROLLING STOCK AND OVERHEAD EQUIPMENT.

The Tramway Electrical Engineer reported that owing to the severe stress and strain put on rolling stock and overhead equipment during the four years of the war, and the difficulty in obtaining both suitable labour and material, he had been unable to keep up the pre-war standard of maintenance and it will now be necessary to make a thorough overhaul, particularly of Trucks, Electrical Equipment and Fittings, &c., of the Overhead Equipment, and that he is at present engaged in re-adjusting demobilised employees with a view of carrying out this work as quickly as possible."

I had forseen that it would be necessary to make a thorough overhaul at the end of the war, and from my knowledge of the engineering world, I was convinced that there would not only be difficulty in obtaining material, but that prices would be considerably increased during a certain period. I therefore placed orders for further material to follow in the train of the stock in hand, so that the cars could be repaired without any interference with the traffic arrangements, and that whatever the magnitude of these repairs within limits I should still hold a moderate stock of parts for ordinary maintenance. After my report to the Committee re the Overhaul, I had an interview with the Chief Storekeeper and assistants engaged on various sections of the work and instructed them to get out samples of fittings, find what we had in stock, and let me know what would be required to deal with a thorough overhaul of the parts of equipment which they were engaged upon.

With reference to the Copper Barrel Strips supplied by Messrs. Player & Mitchell, Birmingham, this order followed the enquiry held at the Power Station as to what would fill our requirements. May I point out that this portion of the report states that I stated that controller overhaul had practically been at a standstill for two years This is a clerical error, and should read '4 years.' I did not agree that the ordinary maintenance of controllers had proceeded during the last two years.

With reference to Emery Blocks ordered from Messrs. Mc Ewen, Denby and Hart-Briggs, I was not at the time of the interview in a position to state the conditions under which these were ordered. These blocks are used for the purpose of grinding out rail corrugations, and this work was carried on before the war very slowly, although the rails were then in a bad state. The delay in dealing with them was due to us being unable to get on the track for the purpose during the hours of service and the men accustomed to the work being afterwards called up, so that very little progress was made in getting out these corrugations. During the last four years they have developed to an enormous extent, and I learned through engineering channels that the material required for the purpose of grinding these out had been taken over by the Government, and that we were unlikely to be able to get any supplies of material from America for some considerable time. I could foresee that it would be absolutely essential that rail grinding should commence again directly the men who had been engaged on the work were demobilised, and I therefore placed an order with the firm in question for additional blocks. This order was placed on March 26th, 1917, and delivery was not made until March, 1918. In connection with these blocks, I may mention that a considerable number of experiments were carried out and a good number of blocks of various makes were tested for the purpose of rail grinding, and it was some time before we were able to get a mixture which would stand the work it had to do. Messrs. McEwens' spent some time in experimenting to get the desired results, and I was anxious that I should not lose the results of these experiments.

With regard to Mr. Bruce's statement that 1" Copper Barrel Strips for Controllers were seldom used, I find that previous to the war it was decided to order the 1" Barrel Strips in the form of Strips 1" x 12" for the purpose of cutting down to any size required for controller barrels, and this could be done without waste. The advantage in doing so was that greater accuracy could be gained in fitting and drilling out the holes in the strip. This practice of cutting the 1" strip down has been going on for some time, but apparently it was unknown to Mr. Bruce.

With further reference to Mr. Bruce's statement, on looking up the Requisitions of January, 30th 1918, I find that he himself requisitioned 2160 different articles of the 1" class for Controller repair work.

The following is a copy of correspondence between the Tramways (Board of Trade) Committee and myself with reference to surplus material; together with my Chief Assistant's report after his inspection of the Stores, etc. :—

Tramways (Board of Trade) Committee,
No. 8, Buckingham Gate,
London, S.W. 1.
7th May, 1918.

Sir,

During 1917, the Municipal Tramways Association and the Tramways Light Railways Association circulated lists of material of all classes which Tramway Undertakings had for disposal or exchange. It has been found on enquiry that these lists were of considerable assistance and enabled Tramway Undertakings to obtain spare parts for cars and overhead line equipments.

The whole question of the transfer of materials is now being dealt with by the Tramways (Board of Trade) Committee, and it is proposed to revise and circulate detailed lists at an early date.

The Committee would be glad if you will let me have a complete list of any materials which you do not require, or of which you have a surplus stock, and which you consider likely to be of service to other Tramway Undertakings.

In sending this information please give detailed particulars so that the materials can be classified and readily identified by any Tramway authority receiving a list. Where possible it will be advisable to state the price required and whether new or second-hand materials are offered.

I am, Sir,

Your obedient Servant,

(Signed) A. L. C. FELL,
On behalf of Secretary.

COPY OF CHIEF ASSISTANT'S REPORT ON THIS MATTER.
LIST OF MATERIALS FOR DISPOSAL.

Mr. Wilkinson,

The following are the only materials we have for disposal :—

2 second-hand Rayworth Controllers.
Traction Patents, Ltd.
Type T. I. R.
Style 14535.
Serial B150702 B150701.
With spare Finger and strip contacts.
1 New Controller.
Make A. Reyrolle & Co. Ltd.
Hebburn and London.
550 volts.
30 H.P.
No. 2037.
8 stops.
No load and overload release and button release.
*6 New " Solid " Steel Gear Wheels.
Type Westinghouse Standard.
Bore 4"
Face 5"
No. of teeth 68.
Dia. 23.33.

(Signed) B. J. E. BRUCE.

COPY OF MY REPLY TO THE TRAMWAYS (B.O.T.) COMMITTEE.

17th May, 1918.

re Transfer of Material.

The Secretary of the
Tramways (Board of Trade) Committee.
No. 8, Buckingham Gate,
London, S.W. 1.

Dear Sir,

Referring to your circular of the 7th instant, re the transfer of material, spare parts for cars and overhead line equipments. The only material we have for disposal is as follows :—

2 Second-hand Rayworth Controllers.
Traction Patents, Ltd. Serial B150702. B150701.
Style T.I.R. No. 14535.
(and Type)
with spare Finger and strip contacts.
1 New Controller.
Make A. Reyrolle & Co., Ltd., Hebburn, London.
550 volts. 8 stop.
30 H.P. No load and overload release,
2037 No. and button release.

I regret the delay in replying to your circular, but unfortunately owing to the death of my Chief Storekeeper, and members of my Stores Department being called up, some little difficulty has been experienced in dealing with these matters.

I am, Dear Sir,

Yours faithfully,

(Signed) J. WILKINSON.

Tramway Electrical Engineer.

*It was decided to retain these Gear Wheels.

Item No. 4.

With reference to orders having been frequently placed for amounts exceeding £10 in value without the approval of the Committee, I am at a loss to understand how it is that these items have not been entered up on the Requisitions in accordance with usual practice. It was the usual practice for all orders to be scrutinised before the next meeting, and all orders which may have been sent in the case of emergency or for fear of delay in delivery were then placed on the Requisition for the next meeting. Apparently my small staff has been overworked, resulting in these matters being overlooked.

Item No. 5. (CARS DAMAGED BOOKS).

In my opinion these Books have been kept up in a manner which is creditable to those who have been engaged upon the work, although they have passed through several hands during the period of the war. Nearly all repairs to cars damaged are carried out under the headings of Electrical repairs, Carpenters' Repairs and Painters' Repairs, and the two latter of which there have been numerous instances, have been under the control of the City Engineer's Department, from whom prices have had to be obtained. At times owing to various circumstances it has been impossible to obtain the actual cost for some weeks, and claims have had to be put in based on an estimated cost by both departments.

With regard to the Cars Cost Ledger, this has been kept up as far as ever possible and when actual costs of maintenance of cars were required the figures were easily obtained from copies of the accounts for material supplied.

Item No. 6.

With reference to the statement that there has been an absence of precautionary measures in the collection and storage of scrap metals (Copper, Brass, &c.) and to the comparative Statement on Schedule 4, these are incorrect. The scrap accumulated during the period 1918-19 as shown on the Schedule is an average quantity, 3 tons 9 cwts. 1 qr. 5 lbs. In this there is included 2 tons 12 cwts. 3 qrs. 24 lbs., which we have in stock at the present time, being an accumulation of scrap covering the period November, 1918 (which was the last date of sale) to March 31st, 1919, this being a matter of five months.

In addition to the amount of 2 tons 12 cwts. 3 qrs. 24 lbs. aforementioned we have 1 ton, 1 cwt. 2 qrs. 24 lbs., which is an accumulation covering the period April, 1919, to June, 1919, making a total amount of scrap of this type on hand in my stores at the present time of 3 tons 14 cwts. 2 qrs. 20 lbs. This total amount has been shown in the report as an accumulation of only 2½ months, whereas it is actually the recovery for the period from November, 1918, to June, 1919, a matter of eight months. In accordance with the reading of Schedule 4, we should have in stock at the present time 6 tons 7 cwts. 2 qrs. 16 lbs., whereas the actual amount is 3 tons 14 cwts. 2 qrs. 20 lbs. My Department is therefore being credited with about £260 worth of scrap metal, which we do not at the present time hold.

With reference to the statement that these metals have recently been placed under lock and key, may I state that for years it has been the practice to keep metals of this description under lock and key, in addition to having a watchman on the works.

Item No. 7.

With regard to the clerical staff being badly organised, the organisation of the staff has been most difficult owing to the changing over from women to my demobilised men during the last few months, and the principle of dividing the staff into independent sections is brought about for the purpose of the staff engaged on work of a technical nature being in close touch with the assistant engineers.

I think in the interest of the Undertaking generally, a thorough and impartial enquiry into the personnel of the department should be carried out. This refers to the last paragraph of the report submitted to the Committee.

I cannot pass over the reference to my clerical staff without speaking in the highest terms of Mr. Maslin,

Mr. Hyman and the Draughtsman, Mr. Gibson, who have recently been demobilised and who under most difficult circumstances and conditions of working during the last few months, have carried out their duties in a manner which reflects great credit upon them and upon those under whom they served during the time they were engaged in H.M. Forces.

I give below some explanations re the various articles shown on the Schedule of Excess Stores.—

Article No. A. 1. K. 10 Controller Barrel Strips 1" x 1$\frac{7}{8}$"

In the K10 Controllers two of these Barrel strips are used. At the present time we have 80 controllers in use, and they are in such a condition that they require renewing, and the renewing of these strips is now in hand, and will reduce my stock by half, thereby leaving us approximately two spare Barrel strips for each Controller. These strips are also used in the B 18 Controller and were requisitioned by my Chief Assistant on January, 30th, 1918.

Article No. A. 2. K. 10 Controller Barrel Strips 1" x 1$\frac{5}{8}$".

Two of these strips are also used for this class of Controller, and the preceding explanation also covers this item of stock.

Article No. A. 128, Westinghouse Controller Barrel Strips $\frac{3}{4}$" x 10$\frac{3}{4}$"

Two of these strips are used in the Westinghouse Controller, and we have 200 of these Controllers in use. When the Controllers have been overhauled, it will leave us with about 250 strips in stock. These strips are also used for cutting up to make the smaller strips, and the only waste in the cutting is a saw thickness, as the spare parts after cutting form the "tips" at the end of the strips, which of course are being continually renewed.

Article No. A.134, Westinghouse Controller Barrel Strips 1" x 12".

One of these strips is used for controller and to overhaul our controllers completely up to date the stock left on hand would be insufficient, as out of these we cut 200 10" strips, 200 2$\frac{1}{2}$" and smaller sizes, some of which form the tips at the end of these strips.

Article No. F. 54, Lignum Vitae Insulators. Tops and Bottoms.

This class of insulator is used on the cars. Two are used on each car and are in various sizes; we have approximately 77 of each size. This gives us one spare set per car.

Article No. G. 88. McEwen's Emery Blocks.

The consumption of these blocks shown for the years 1917-18-19 is a very unfair test, as from 1916 rail grinding to a certain extent was suspended. Although it was necessary to continue grinding it was impossible to do so owing to the calling up of the men who had been engaged upon this work. Reference to this item is made in my general report.

Article No. G. 81. Bonds and Pins. 2' 10".

This article is now in the City Engineer's Stock.

Article No. A. 1. 18" Grooved Splicing Ears.

On Sheet 1 of Excess stores I have no doubt that a clerical error has been made by the Accountant's Staff engaged on this work. Item "18" Grooved Splicing Ears" stock in hand shown as 139, actual stock in hand as proved by my test is only 7. (This article was shown on Schedule as No. A. 2).

Article No. A. 5. 15" 3/0 Splicing Ears.

This splicing ear is one of our most useful and universal fittings and is carried on our emergency wagon for quick repair of overhead line, some of which has been in use for 15 years. The reason for ordering these ears in such quantities is due to the delay in receiving the goods from the time when they are ordered. They were requisitioned by my Chief Assistant on September, 18th, 1918.

Article No. C. 1. Lignum Vitae Auto Point Runners.

Article C. 1, is an Air Gap Insulator complete. I take it that article C. 61 is the one in question. Under normal conditions I admit that this stock is in excess of our usual requirements. They were requisitioned by my Chief Assistant on 1st January, 1919.

Article No. C. 106. Fork Globes.

By the time the present replacements which we are engaged upon are completed and they are being carried out at every available opportunity this stock of Fork globes will be used up. During the war very little has been done in the way of replacements and after examining the different routes it is found that there are a large number of cracked globes which require replacing at once and for which the present stock is necessary. I should also like to say that these globes take the place of the ordinary shackles. They were requisitioned by my Chief Assistant on March 13th, 1918.

Article No. D. 42.   3/0 Bronze Trolley Wire.

As shown in the report submitted on page 2 of Excess Stores, we had in stock 11,770 feet of wire. This, as I could have explained at the time the stock was taken was by no means excessive. A glance at the stock card shows the following:—

Stock, March 31st, 1919 :—11770 feet.

Issued.	Date.	Route.	Left in Stock.
	Mar. 31st		11770 feet.
2640 feet.	May 5th	Hessle Road,	9130 do.
150 do.	do. 29th	Square,	8980 do.
5180 do.	June 13th	Cottingham Road	3800 do.
615 do.	July 31st	Hessle Road,	3185 do.

As will be seen by the above details, the " excess stock " has now come down to a matter of 3185.

Article No. E. 6.   Section Insulated Brass.

This article known as Section Insulated Bolt with Brass Collar is an article used on the overhead fittings and now that the labour question is to a certain extent solved, we shall be able at a future date to replace the whole of the bolts at present in use, of which quite a number are cracked and in other ways defective.

Article No. A. 164.   Reversing Barrel Contacts.

11 of these contacts are used in each controller and as before stated we have 200 of these controllers and 22 are used to complete a car set. The majority of the controllers are down for overhaul and our present stock is not above normal requirements.

Article Nos.

A. 15.   K. 10   ¾" Barrel Strip Tips.
D. 8.   K. 10   1" x 5¼"   do.
A. 300. T. A. 3.   Reversing Barrel Contacts.
A. 291. T. A. 3.   Barrel Strips.
A. 71.   B. 18 Barrel Strips 1" x 6½".
A. 66.   do.   do. ¾" x 6"
A. 63.   do.   do. 2" x ¾"

These matters can be explained by referring to Car Shed Requisition Book (March, 11th, 1919). The above were ordered for the general overhaul.

Articles Nos.

A. 24.   18"   Mechanical Ears.
A. 4.   24"   Splicing Ears.

These fittings work in conjunction with the 15" Ears, *i.e.,* when the Overhead wire at the points leaving the 15" Ears is worn to such an extent as to become dangerous, the 15" Ears are replaced by 18" Ears, and at a later date when the same trouble occurs 24" Ears are used. As will be seen these Ears are a great saving as regards Overhead Wire.

As mentioned in my General Report the bulk of the above stock has been purchased for general overhaul.

I think, gentlemen, in view of the many items covered by the City Accountant's Report you will agree that it was almost impossible for me to have made a verbal statement at the Committee Meeting, which would have been satisfactory to you or myself.

(Signed) J. WILKINSON.

Appendix 14

Interim Report of the City Accountant on Administration of the Tramway Manager's Department and a Précis of the Tramway Manager's Reply

The circumstances are detailed in Chapter 7. The investigation revealed what can only be described as a shambles within the department and an implied lack of financial audit. The subsequent sacking was surely justified, despite the wartime pressures.

TRAMWAY MANAGER.

INTERIM REPORT
OF
CITY ACCOUNTANT
on Adminstration of Tramway
Manager's Department

AND

PRÉCIS
OF
TRAMWAY MANAGER'S REPLY
upon such report.

TRAMWAYS COMMITTEE'S RESOLUTION OF
27TH MARCH, 1919:—

" That the City Accountant be instructed to report
to this Committee in writing on the matters with full
power to call upon any official or servant of the
Corporation for any information, books or papers,
he may require ; and as to whether there are any,
and, if so, what duties which should be transferred
to the City Treasurer's or City Accountant's
Departments ; also as to what other changes, if any,
he would recommend in the business administration
of the Tramway Manager's Department, and that on
such Report being received, an Inquiry thereon be
held by this Committee."

GUILDHALL, HULL,
    26th April, 1919.

TRAMWAY MANAGER'S ADMINISTRATION.

CITY ACCOUNTANT'S INTERIM REPORT.

To the Chairman and Members of the Tramways Committee.

At a meeting of the Tramways Committee held on the 27th ultimo, I was instructed to report in writing upon certain matters which had been brought to light during an examination into the business methods in the Manager's Department, which I had made at the Chairman's and Deputy-Chairman's request. The Town Clerk verbally reported such matters to the Committee on the 26th ultimo and 7th instant.

My inquiry is not yet completed, for which reason the recommendations to be made with regard to future business administration will be laid before the Committee at a later stage. It appears desirable, however, to present an interim report upon the irregularities referred to.

It is not proposed to deal in this report with the two matters enquired into by the Chairman and Deputy-Chairman in November, 1917, as the Manager's explanations were then accepted. I was unaware of such matters until December, 1918, when I acquainted the Chairman and his Deputy with a rumour which had reached me in connection with Petty Cash, in consequence of which I was desired to undertake an examination of the business methods generally.

The following is a list of the irregularities which have been disclosed by the inquiry up to the present time. The ascertained facts in each case are given later under their respective headings.

		£	s	d
(a)	Shortage, *Traffic Cash*	19	10	6
(b)	*Articles found in Cars—Proceeds of Auction Sale* paid to Manager, 12th July, 1918, not accounted for ..	65	8	4
(c)	*Cash found in Cars and Unclaimed Passengers' Change-Money* as under; handed to Manager and not accounted for:—			
	26th February, 1918 .. .. 4 10 1			
	14th March, 1918 .. .. 19 10 2	24	0	3
(d)	*Allowances to Employees with H.M. Forces—*			
	(1) Overpayment refunded to Manager by employee's dependent (Mrs. Levi) 6th December, 1916, not accounted for .. 18 18 7			
	(2) Amount paid to wrong person (*re* Hatfield), recovered and handed to Manager 2nd May, 1918, not accounted for 9 0 0	27	18	7
(e)	*Petty Cash* drawn by Manager through cashier 14th July, 1911, and still retained.. ..	5	0	0
(f)	*Conductors' Change-Money—* 204 signatures produced by Manager as receipts for change-money		See later notes.	
(g)	*Cost of Damages to Tramcars* recovered by Manager and not brought to account—			
	(1) 23rd Nov., 1918, N.E. Railway Co. .. 5 8 0			
	(2) 17th Dec., 1918, E. B. Burn .. 5 0 0			
	(3) 20th Dec., 1915, Scottish Insurance Corporation, Ltd., Edinburgh 1 6 0	11	14	0

In none of the foregoing cases have official receipts been given, nor have the amounts received been officially recorded.

Certain of the irregularities were disclosed during the examination made at the Tramway Offices on Friday, 7th March. I conferred with the Town Clerk on the following day.

The investigation was resumed on Monday, 10th March. The Manager, who had been away from Hull on business for a few days, returned to his office on the following morning and obtained from his Chief Cashier (Mr. Tarbert) full particulars of the matters enquired into. The Manager thereupon telephoned and asked me for an early appointment, but later in the morning telephonic messages were received to the effect that such appointment could not be kept.

After a consultation between the Chairman, Deputy-Chairman, the Town Clerk and myself held the same day (11th March), a further meeting was held in the Town Clerk's room, when the Manager was asked to explain the matters referred to under (a), (b), (c) and (d) (1). His replies (taken from notes dictated immediately after the interview) are referred to later on in this report.

(a) Shortage, Traffic Cash, £19 10s. 6d.

The system in vogue re Traffic Cash has been that this money is not handled by the Manager personally, but is counted by the traffic cashiers.

I have recently been informed that a meeting was held in November, 1917, at which the Chairman, Deputy-Chairman, Town Clerk and City Treasurer questioned the Manager as to an alleged shortage in the traffic cash, brought about (the Manager explained) in consequence of various sums being required from time to time to settle compensation claims without delay. It was then laid down that this practice must cease at once and that any sums required to meet compensation claims be provided by the City Treasurer direct.

In order to satisfy myself that this arrangement had been adhered to, I carried out a surprise test on the 10th March last and found a shortage of £19 10s. 6d.

The senior traffic cashier (Mr. Summers) states that he had heard that some inquiry had taken place about a year previously, but that the shortage had not been made good, and that all that was done was to discontinue the practice of placing I.O.U.'s in the till, any shortage being styled "claims." According to an unofficial record kept by Mr. Summers, the Manager (since the making of the new arrangement) has drawn sums on 16 occasions, totalling £83 3s. and has made 10 reimbursements, amounting to £82 3s.

At the interview on the 11th March, the Town Clerk asked how it was that the foregoing arrangement had not been carried out and that, according to the City Accountant, there was at that moment a shortage of £19 10s. 6d. The Manager replied the money was required to meet *special* compensation cases which might arise at any time of the day or night : that he (the Manager) was often at the office after his cashiers had gone home and that these matters might crop up at any hour after the City Treasurer's office was closed. On being asked if he would settle any compensation claim without the Chairman or Deputy-Chairman's authority, the Manager replied in the negative. The Chairman and Deputy-Chairman then stated that on no one occasion had they been telephoned or spoken to by the Manager after 5.30 p.m. The Manager observed that " it must have happened with some previous Chairman."

Two days after this interview the Manager paid to his senior traffic cashier the above amount of £19 10s. 6d.

When scrutinising the counterparts of the bank slips, it was observed that frequently cheques (names unstated) had been paid into the bank as forming part of the traffic cash, although in a number of cases these amounts could not be traced in the Manager's books or the office records. The senior traffic cashier explains that it has been the general practice to cash cheques for tramway employees (and occasionally others). I observe that one cheque amounted to £233 15s.

(b) Articles found in Cars—Proceeds of Auction

Sale   £65   8   4

Having in mind the Committee's resolution of 27th February, 1918, authorising a sale of articles found in the cars, I wrote to the Manager on 8th November last asking whether the goods had been disposed of. His reply was " the matter is now in hand."

In the course of my inquiry, however, it was found that the auction sale had taken place on 5th July last and that a cheque for the net proceeds (£65 8s. 4d.) had been received by the Manager on the 12th of that month. On the same day the Manager instructed the senior traffic cashier (Mr. Summers) to hand over cash for this amount in exchange for the cheque, volunteering the information that "the payment was on account," as the auctioneer contented that certain articles included in the schedule had not been delivered to him or else had been lost.

At the interview on the 11th March, the Manager confirmed the accuracy of this statement and said that the cheque was cashed to get it through at the bank and that he had retained the cash so that it could be paid in "with the rest of it." When asked what was meant by the term "the rest of it," he eventually stated that it referred to the cash found in the cars.

The Manager was then reminded that on the 26th July, the auctioneer had written to him explaining the deduction of £1 11s. 11d. referred to in his (the auctioneer's) letter of the 11th July and disclaiming liability; he was asked whether it was not a fact that, on receiving this second letter, the dispute had lapsed, and the Manager replied in the affirmative.

The Manager was questioned as to why the sale proceeds could not be paid in to the City Treasurer until the cash found in cars had been counted. He stated that the one was dependent upon the other, but did not say why, and added that the matter had drifted somewhat and that, owing to being understaffed, they had not been able to settle up. He added that both the sale proceeds and the cash found in the cars would have been paid in before the end of the financial year. To a further question put by the Town Clerk, the Manager replied that the cash found in cars was paid over to the City Treasurer every year regularly. I pointed out the fact that the last payment of such cash was in August, 1913.

The Manager was next asked whether he still held any monies belonging to the Corporation other than traffic cash and proceeds of sale, to which he gave a definite negative. He remarked several times that the cash had been kept in his desk and was there to be seen; further, that he would like those present to go to his office in order that he might produce it. (After the interview the Chairman and Deputy-Chairman decided to accompany the Manager to his office for this purpose).

Two days after this interview the Manager paid over the £65 8s. 4d. to the Chief Cashier, who has given him an official receipt.

Articles found in cars, when periodically transferred from the ticket office to the general office, have been accepted without being checked over with the Found Property Day Book, neither has the inspector been required to produce the receipts obtained by him from claimants on the recovery of their property. He (the inspector) informs me that following his predecessor's practice, he has destroyed the receipts after he has marked off the returns in the day book.

(c) *Cash found in Cars and Unclaimed Passengers' Change-Money, £24 0s. 3d.*

Conductors are required to pay over to the inspector in the Ticket Office (in the City Square) all monies found in the cars and any change which they recollect not having given to passengers, in the same way as they hand in any articles found in the cars. Cash, &c., unclaimed is made up into monthly parcels and subsequently transferred to the Manager's office. It was ascertained that it has not been the practice for any one to compare the contents of these parcels with the Day Book at the Ticket Office, neither was the inspector there required to produce the signatures obtained for the sums marked off by him in that book as "refunded to claimants."

On 7th March it was found that the monthly parcels of cash and what are termed "valuables" found in the cars during the two years 1st January, 1917, to 31st December, 1918, remained in the Chief Cashier's custody. At my request, the cash in these parcels has been counted in the presence of two members of my staff and found to amount to £47 16s. 9d., whereas the abstract of the items recorded in the Found Property Day Book shews a total of £47 0s. 3½d., a difference of 16s. 5½d. Acting on my recommendation, the Chief Cashier (Mr. Tarbert) has paid over the former sum to the City Treasurer.

On examining this official with regard to cash so found prior to January, 1917, he was unable to state definitely what period was covered by the payment of £21 17s. 9d. made to the City Treasurer in August, 1913, but expressed the opinion that such cash would cover some period up to 31st March, 1912.

The Chief Cashier informed me that on 26th February, 1918, he was instructed to hand to the Manager a sum of £4 10s. 1d. out of certain parcels, &c., "made up to about a year previously," and on the 14th March, 1918, he was likewise required to hand over £19 10s. 2d. representing other monies from a similar source (a total of £24 0s. 3d.).

As the current day book was brought into use in June, 1914, the production of the earlier books was called for, but after a search had been made the Chief Cashier and the messenger (the Manager acquiescing), informed me that apparently the books had been sent with waste paper to the paper mills, in compliance with an appeal from the Government for material of this nature. I expressed surprise that a book forming the only record of cash not yet paid over to the City Treasurer should be thus destroyed.

It was ascertained that the cash recorded in the current day book from June, 1914, to December, 1916, exceeded the sum of £24 0s. 3d. handed over to the Manager. The Chief Cashier was questioned as to who would be responsible in the event of any discrepancy between the cash and the amount shewn in the day book. His reply was that it would surprise him to hear that the amount of money found exceeded the cash handed in to the Manager, but that, in such event, "he would personally have to make it up"; that he did not expect there would be a shortage. At a later date Mr. Tarbert qualified this statement by saying that he did not recollect having used these words (N.B., taken down in shorthand at the time by Mr. Blakeley, who accompanied me), and that what he meant to convey was that he supposed that he would be looked to for an explanation.

On the 3rd April, however, the messenger brought to my office the day book in use for the period 1st August, 1912, to 30th June, 1914, and stated that he had found the book in a cupboard in the ticket store when looking for waybills. As the day books used prior to August, 1912, are not forthcoming, I am unable to ascertain the total amount of cash shewn therein as unclaimed for the period 1st April, 1912, to 31st December, 1916. The items appearing, however, in the book commencing August, 1912, to such latter date have been abstracted and amount to £66 2s. 11½d., whereas the cash handed last year to the Manager and not accounted for was

£24 0s. 3d. leaving a difference of £42 2s. 8½d. to be explained, irrespective of the unclaimed cash for the four months for which the day book has not been produced.

At the interview on the 11th March, the Manager was asked who held the cash found in the cars and not yet paid in to the City Treasurer and he first replied, "Mr. Tarbert, all of it," but when further questioned as to whether he himself had not possession of part of such cash, he added "that is so far as I recollect—possibly I may or may not hold some of it; I cannot say, but will look into it."

Two days afterwards, the Manager paid the sum of £24 0s. 3d. (£4 10s. 1d. plus £19 10s. 2d.) to the Chief Cashier, who has handed him an official receipt.

(d) *Allowances to Employees with H.M. Forces.*

(1) re *Levi*, £18 18s. 7d.

It appears that in December, 1916, a money order, value £18 18s. 7d., was received by a Mrs. Levi (an employee's mother) from the Army Authorities in respect of "back pay" for her son.

On 7th March last, the Chief Cashier, when requested to give me information as to monies not brought to account, mentioned this matter and stated that in the first place the Manager handed the cash in question to him but instructed him two days later to return it for the stated purpose of consulting the ex-Chairman as to its disposal. He (the cashier) kept a memo. of the matter (now in my possession), which is in agreement with the following information given by Mrs. Levi, who was subsequently interviewed on my behalf.

Mrs. Levi states that after cashing the Order she proceeded to the office to interview the Manager and told him that she had received the amount from the Army and as it had been overpaid by the Corporation she desired to refund the money. The Manager accepted the cash from her, but did not give a receipt, she did not ask for one as the payment was made to the Manager personally. Her daughter confirmed the above statements and mentioned that upon returning home her mother told her of the result of her interview.

At the interview on the 11th March, the Town Clerk referred to the Manager's first assurance that he held no reference is made to this item in Mr. McCombe's letter quoted on page 17 of this report).

The amount in question is apparently still retained by the Manager, although a special arrangement was made with regard to the payment of compensation claims (see page 4).

(f) Conductors' Change-Money.

For a considerable number of years the Manager has been responsible for cash paid to him by the City Treasurer in order that sums of 5s. could be advanced to conductors for the purpose of change-money. At the end of each financial year the Manager has furnished his certificate giving the names of conductors holding these sums and such certificates have been duly produced to the professional auditors.

At my first interview with the Manager towards the end of February, I asked for the production of any receipts given by the conductors for change-money and was informed that they signed for these amounts in a book kept for the purpose. The Manager promised to hand me this book, but it was not forthcoming.

At one stage of the interview in the Town Clerk's office on the 11th March, the Manager thought that reference was about to be made to conductors' change-money and volunteered the information that certain conductors joined H.M. Forces at such short notice that change-money was not recovered from them and that in all such cases he himself had refunded the Corporation out of his own pocket, in order that advances could be made to the persons temporarily filling the places of conductors on service. (I find that a similar statement was made in a letter addressed to the City Treasurer on 31st July, 1916).

After this latter interview it was arranged that the receipts should be handed to me inspection on the 12th March, on which date the Manager requested that the matter should stand over until the following week as he was much rushed owing to having to proceed to London the next day. I pointed out that these particulars had been asked for two or three weeks previously and that I must press for their production on the following morning.

On calling at the Manager's office early on the 13th March, I was again asked to agree to the matter standing over until the following week, to which request I was

monies other than the proceeds of sale and £19 10s. 6d. belonging to traffic cash and then asked whether it was a fact that the Manager also held the above sum of £18 18s. 7d. Mr. M'Combe replied that he could not remember such a case and several times asked for the date of the occurrence.

At the Committee meeting on the 26th March last the Manager, commenting on the Town Clerk's verbal statement, said that he had not yet looked into this matter. (This item is referred to in the Manager's letter, dated 5th April, appearing on page 17, but he has not yet paid over the amount.)

(2) re Driver Hatfield, £9 0s. 0d.

When the subject of unclaimed wages was enquired into, the Chief Cashier informed me that a certain increase in wages due to a driver named Hatfield on his promotion was overlooked for a considerable time. When the oversight was discovered, the accumulated arrears (£12 4s.) were brought into the Wages Book and the cash was wrongly paid to a Mrs. Rastall (the wife of a conductor in H.M. Forces) instead of to Mrs. Hatfield—whose husband was also in the Army. £9 of this money was subsequently recovered from Mrs. Rastall—part of the balance of £3 4s. having since been deducted from the weekly allowances made.

Mr. Tarbert states that this sum of £9 was handed to the Manager on 2nd May, 1918.

This case was not discussed at the interview, but has since been verbally reported by the Town Clerk to the Committee. (This item also is referred to in the Manager's reply as set out on page 17 but the amount has not yet been paid in).

(e) Petty Cash £5 0s. 0d.

When questioned with regard to petty cash, the Chief Cashier (Mr. Tarbert) informed me that some years ago the Committee increased the Manager's requisition from £5 to £10 and that on the 14th July, 1911, the Manager required him to hand over to him the additional £5, stating that he would retain such sum as a provision to meet compensation claims. The Chief Cashier's statement is further borne out by reference to the Petty Cash Book, in which on one occasion this sum in the Manager's hands is shewn separately as part of the balance. (No

unable to accede. (It transpired that on this morning the messenger was engaged in giving out change-money at the box-office in the City Square). The earliest appointment the Manager said he could make was for 4.30 p.m., when, accompanied by a member of my staff, I again called upon him, and loose sheets bearing various signatures were then produced to me. With one exception these sheets bore a typed heading in the form of a receipt.

The Manager handed me a rough summary which he had written of the sheets handed over for inspection.

No. 1	25
No. 2(a)	32
No. 2	26
No. 3	32
No. 4	33
No. 5	27
No. 6	29
	204

	£	s.	d.
204 @ 5s.	51	0	0
Balance	18	15	0
	£69	15	0

He voluntarily produced several bank and treasury notes which, he stated, represented the balance shewn thereon. I did not consider it necessary to examine these notes as I had not called for the production of such balance.

On the 14th March, when engaged in testing the accuracy of these sheets of signatures by interviewing certain conductors, it came to my knowledge that at a late hour on the 11th March (3 days previously) the office messenger (Hewlett) visited the five depots for the purpose of handing out sums of money (£16 in all). Hewlett subsequently confirmed this, stating that, in accordance with instructions received from the Manager, he had started from his home in a taxi at 9.30 p.m. on Tuesday, 11th March, for the purpose of handing sums of money for immediate distribution by the foremen at the respective depots to the conductors whose names appeared in lists supplied by the Manager. These statements were verified by the foremen, who stated that, in accordance with instructions, they duly reported to the Manager the next morning.

Between 14th March and 8th April, 141 tramway employees (in respect of whom signatures were put forward on these lists as proof of their having received change-money) were interviewed either personally by myself or my representatives with the following result:—

Employees who agree that they hold change-money:—

		No. of Signatures put forward
75	conductors	75
15	do. (two signatures each for one payment)	30
11	motormen (occasionally conductors)	11
	employees who disclaim holding change-money:—	
29	conductors	29
9	motormen	9
2	women as inspectors	2
		40
141		156
42	persons no longer in the tramway service	42
6	doubtful (sick, &c.)	6
		204

With regard to certain of the signatures appearing twice, the office messenger has explained to me that in certain cases women conductors informed him that they had previously received change-money for which they had signed at the time of payment and that he told them to sign a second time. He states that on his return these cases were duly reported to his principal.

Provided that change-money was duly recovered from the 42 persons who have left the service and that the statements made by the 141 employees are correct, there is a sum of £24 5s. still requiring elucidation on the part of the Manager, quite apart from the balance of £18 15s. shewn on his summary previously referred to.

At the meeting of the Committee, held on the 7th instant, the above facts were verbally reported and the Manager when asked to explain, stated that it was possible that the lists were not altogether accurate.

(g) Cost of Damages to Tramcars recovered.

The Manager has personally dealt with claims made for the recovery of the cost of damages to cars by third parties. I have called for the production of some official record shewing what claims have been made and for what sums. No such record can be produced, the Manager stating that he has dealt with these matters by correspondence alone, and that the cases can only be traced by reference to copy letter books.

With regard to outward letters, the Manager informs me that no copy letter books have been used other than those kept in the general office. These letters for nearly three years have been searched by members of my staff.

At my request, a large number of inward letters was likewise deposited at my office for perusal.

I am informed that from time to time, during the period of the war, letters have been personally typed by the Manager, but I cannot say whether these and all other letters have been copied in the official letter books or, for that matter, whether all inward letters and car accident reports not sent to the paper mills have been produced.

The Chief Cashier informs me that he has no knowledge whatever of claims made re car damages excepting when cheques and cash have occasionally been handed out to him by the Manager and official receipts despatched.

The production of drivers' car accident reports has been required. In very few cases do any notes appear on the reports as to what action (if any) has been taken to recover the cost of the damages.

On the afternoon of Saturday, 29th March, I visited the Manager's office with a member of my staff, and with the concurrence of the Manager examined all the papers in his private room relating to Corporation matters. Certain reports were then found which the Manager stated had been overlooked.

On the same occasion the Manager expressed his intention of taking an early opportunity of destroying a considerable number of papers which I observed had accumulated in connection with matters which did not concern the Authority. The Chairman has reported to me that on entering the private room on Monday, 31st March, he noted a great mass of burnt paper in the fireplace.

On the Tuesday (1st April), two heavy parcels of additional reports (relating mainly to 1910) were delivered at my office by the messenger (Hewlett), who stated that such reports must have been placed in the room on the 2nd floor opposite the Manager's between 1.30 p.m. on the previous Saturday and that morning. In view of the assurance given by both the Manager and certain of his staff that all reports not sent to the paper mills had been deposited at my office, enquiry was made as to the responsibility for non-delivery. The Manager, in reply to my letter on the subject, has verbally stated that he had turned out these reports from his private room early in the previous week and that the messenger was under a misapprehension and that he personally had quite forgotten their existence when giving me the assurance referred to.

Of the thousands of car reports perused a considerable number were extracted from which it would appear that the recovery of the cost of repair might have been claimed. These have been investigated and it has been found that in the majority of cases no claims have been made. The Manager points out that in these matters he has had to take into consideration facts which do not necessarily appear in the drivers' reports.

In the cases set out under heading (g) on page 4, the Manager has personally received three amounts totalling £11 14s. for which he has given unofficial receipts. The first two items are referred to in the Manager's reply of the 5th instant and the three sums have not yet been brought to account.

A few more cases are under inquiry at the present time.

Compensation Claims.

Apart from the matters specifically reported upon at the Committee meetings on the 26th ultimo and 7th instant, I have investigated over 30 cases of compensation claims paid by the Manager and reimbursed by the City Treasurer prior to the arrangement made in November, 1917, and have found same to be in order. One case is still under inquiry.

General.

On the 4th instant I wrote the Manager asking him to let me know whether there were then any monies owing by him to the Corporation and if so requesting him to specify all such cases, furnishing me with names, the amounts involved and the dates when such sums were received by him. I give below a copy of his reply of the 5th April :—

" Dear Sir,

" In reply to yours of the 4th instant, I have gone " into the matter with Mr. Tarbert, and have verified " the details from my own notes. The amounts " oustanding are as follows :—

	£	s	d	
H. Levi,	18	18	7	6th December, 1916.
H. Hatfield,	9	0	0	2nd May, 1918.
N. E. Railway	5	8	0	23rd November, 1918.
E. B. Burn	5	0	0	December, 1918.

Yours faithfully,

(Signed) W. J. M'Combe."

The items set out in this letter were reported by the Town Clerk at the Committee's previous meeting on the 26th ultimo.

Whilst I have already stated that my inquiry is not yet completed, it is obvious that many alterations should be made in the office administration of this department, but this question will be dealt with in my final report which will be presented at the earliest date possible. At this stage I express the conviction that owing to the inadequate methods which have obtained and to the conditions prevailing, it is impossible to make an investigation which can be regarded as exhaustive.

In the course of the inquiry I have been given ready assistance by the members of the staff whom it has been necessary to interrogate.

Wm. H. Smith,

City Acco

23rd April, 1919.

PRÉCIS OF
TRAMWAY MANAGER'S REPLY.

The Tramway Manager stated that he preferred to make a verbatim reply to the report of the Accountant, rather than to put what he had to say into writing, and he proceeded to make a long statement dealing with various parts of the report, much of which it is unnecessary to reproduce, but his statements dealing with the particular items of irregularities must be set out.

To take them in the order in which they appear in the Accountant's report, as to—

(a) *Shortage of Traffic Cash.*—He admitted that the system of taking moneys out of gross receipts which had prevailed up to November, 1917, when it was objected to by the Chairman and Deputy-Chairman, had been carried on since, though he stated that this was not done for the purpose of meeting ordinary claims as had been done previously, but only for cases of emergency. He did not, however, exemplify, by any instance, the arising of such cases, and he reminded the Committee that this amount had been paid in.

(b) *Proceeds of Auction Sale.*—The Manager repeated what he had previously said to the Committee, namely, that he had kept this amount in hand because of an outstanding dispute with the Auctioneers as to a small amount of property which had been mislaid or was missing from the Auctioneers' premises, and he also reminded the Committee that this amount also had been paid in. He did not explain why the amount had been kept for so long a time, except by saying that the intention was to pay it in with other sums which would in the ordinary course be accounted for before the end of the financial year.

(c) *Cash found in Cars, &c.*—The Manager stated that he was at a loss to understand these items at all, and that he would like to have an opportunity of going into this matter personally to find out how it stands. Personally, he knew nothing about it, but stated there must be some reason for it which he could not then think of.

(d) (1) *Levy's Repayment, £18 18s. 7d.*—He admitted that he had had this money, and said that he had asked for it to be handed to him because he wished to mention the matter to the then Chairman of the Committee. He said "I tell you frankly I cannot tell you where the money went to," but he admitted that it had never been paid to the Treasurer. When asked why he wanted the money, even if he did want to mention the matter to the Chairman, he was unable to give any satisfactory reply.

(d) (2) *Hatfield's Money, £9.*—In this case too, the Manager admitted having had the money, but said he believed he was going up to London when it was handed to him, and with reference to it, he could only say the same as he had said with regard to the Levy case. When asked whether it was a fact that Mr. Tarbert had mentioned the matter to him since more than once, he stated that he had no recollection of any such occurrence.

(e) *Petty Cash, £5.*—He admitted that he recollected now that Mr. Tarbert had handed to him this sum of money, and stated that he must have overlooked the fact that it had been done.

(f) *Conductors' Change Money.*—The Manager made a lengthy statement on this item, and pointed out the reasons why it was extremely difficult to keep this matter right, owing to the frequent coming and going of the conductors, especially during the war. He was unable to account for the state of things disclosed by the receipts for change money produced, and did not admit that the messenger Hewlett had given to the City Accountant an accurate account of what had taken place on the 11th March, though he desired to add that he believed Hewlett to be a truthful and honest man.

(g) *Damages recovered by Manager.*

(1) *North Eastern Railway.*—He remembered receiving this amount, and believed it was on a Saturday afternoon. He said that he was in a hurry going out, and gave a hurried receipt and put the money in his drawer.

(2) *E. B. Burn.*—He admitted also receiving this amount, and believed that he was going to London that afternoon. He believed that on both these occasions "the official Receipt Book was at the

as to the items was apt to magnify the irregularities in the eyes of the Committee.

Questioned by the Chairman as to whether he admitted the accuracy of the City Accountant's report, he said, "Speaking generally, yes." So far as the items referred to had not been accounted for, he admitted responsibility for them, and offered to pay them in. He pleaded with the Committee to take a lenient view of the position, especially having regard to his 20 years' service, and to acquit him of any intention at any time to do any wrong or any injury to the Corporation.

Guildhall. He was questioned as to what right or power he had to settle cases of damages by compromise or otherwise, even without mentioning them to the Chairman and Deputy-Chairman, and he stated that it was a power that he had always had, and was understood both by him and the Chairman and Deputy-Chairman. The Chairman and Deputy-Chairman disclaimed any knowledge of this, and Alderman Robson stated that he had no such knowledge when he was Chairman. The Manager stated that in the North Eastern case the offer to settle for half came from the North Eastern Railway Company.

(3) *Scottish Insurance Corporation, Limited.*--This case (which, it may be stated, is the only item referred to in the whole of the Accountant's report, which was new since the Town Clerk made his statement to the Committee in the presence of the Manager at their meeting on the 26th March), dates back to 1915, and the Tramway Manager stated that he knew nothing whatever about it.

The Tramway Manager dealt with various other parts of the Accountant's report, such as the question of correspondence, stating that all letters in connection with car accidents had been copied, and he also explained that the papers referred to by the Chairman and the Accountant as having been burnt in his room consisted of a large accumulation of papers which did not affect the Corporation, and which he burnt merely to get rid of them.

The Tramway Manager laid stress on two matters, namely, that the Manager's Department of the Tramway Undertaking had always been worked on a minimum staff and at a rate of expense which was about the cheapest in the country, and that the Tramway concern, ever since he took it in hand 20 years ago, had been a success. Further, that during the war he had had to work under very adverse and trying conditions, and that the strain had been almost intolerable, and that he himself had had no holiday since the outbreak of war. He emphasised the fact of the large amount of moneys which had passed through his office, and pointed out how very insignificant in amount the total of the items referred to in the Accountant's report was, and he thought that the manner of the drawing of the Accountant's report, containing, as it did, reiteration

MINUTES

Of the proceedings of the

TRAMWAYS COMMITTEE.

GUILDHALL, HULL, Thursday, 31st July, 1919.

Present :

Councillor WALKER, in the Chair.

Messrs. WILLOUGHBY (D.C.), GIBSON, GOWER, MELL, RICHARDSON, SHERWOOD, WHEELDON and WOKES.

The Town Clerk, City Accountant, Tramway Electrical Engineer; Mr. Tarbert and Mr. Benson attended.

TRAMWAYS (TRAFFIC) DEPARTMENT.

READ—The following report, viz. :—

To the Chairman and Members of the Tramways Committee.

Referring to the Tramways Committee's resolution of the 27th March last, requesting me to undertake an inquiry into the business methods of the traffic department and to make recommendations with regard thereto, I have already presented an interim report (dated 23rd April last) bringing to the Committee's notice certain irregularities which had been discovered during the investigation. I now submit a final report dealing generally with the business methods in that department.

TRAFFIC CASH.

Cheques, &c., cashed for employees and others.

It was found that cheques passed through the bank were frequently for amounts for which no debits appeared in the official records. The explanation given was that it had been the general practice for traffic cashiers to cash cheques, money orders, &c., for persons in the Committee's employ, and occasionally for members of the outside public. On a recent occasion a cheque for £233 15s. was cashed for an employee in this manner.

It is desirable that this practice should cease.

"Shorts" and "Overs."

Shortages and also surpluses in the cash handed over by conductors are adjusted without passing through the official accounts. Differences between conductors' cash and the amounts represented by the tickets sold are recorded on specially ruled forms kept for the purpose in the Manager's office, but are not shewn in the waybills. Surpluses are returned to the conductors, by whom paid in and shortages are collected from them.

It was observed that "overs" and "shorts" were not necessarily settled the following day, and that, in the first place, "shorts" have been met out of petty cash, although not entered in the petty cash book.

The practice of returning "overs" is open to objection on the ground that it may lend itself to dishonesty on the part of an unscrupulous employee.

If it were decided to alter the practice, "Conductors' shorts and overs books" should be introduced and differences settled weekly, "shorts" being deducted from the conductors' weekly wages and transferred to the credit of traffic revenue. On the other hand, surpluses would automatically fall into the daily receipts. In this event, the said books could be checked, proved with the wages sheets and compared with the total of the waybills, being from time to time tested by my internal audit clerks.

Issue of Tickets, &c.

A general ticket stock book is not in use at the traffic office. A daily record of tickets issued is kept at the Box Office, City Square, and this return is examined daily with the waybills. Each Monday morning numbered tin boxes containing the necessary bundles of tickets are handed out to the conductors, such boxes being returned 7 days later with the unused tickets. Tickets required by the conductors during the course of the week are obtained from the Box Office and recorded on the return above referred to.

A suitable ticket stock book should be kept.

Certain minor suggestions have been made with regard to the collection of monthly accounts *re* tokens.

To avoid floating cash balances, it would be better if monies received from the sales of "prepaid" tickets were paid over daily to the City Treasurer through the "Sundries" cash book.

Counting and Banking of Cash.

The Committee is aware that it is not the practice for the conductors' cash to be counted in their presence. It is understood that to do so has been considered somewhat impracticable. If it were possible, however, to arrange otherwise, the innovation would probably be welcomed by the conductors, who at the present time are required to make good any shortages, as to which, however, they are unable to personally satisfy themselves. In certain towns this practice is followed and found to work satisfactorily. As a general principle, it appears a reasonable thing that the conductors, if they so desire, should see the cash counted in their presence. The mere magnitude of the undertaking does not seem to be a sufficient reason for a departure from ordinary business procedure.

It is for the Committee to consider whether a scheme should be devised by which accommodation could be provided at the inward termini for the purpose stated. Some arrangement of this sort would considerably expedite the banking of cash, but would probably necessitate a re-arrangement of staff duties and hours.

It frequently happens that part of the traffic cash is paid direct into the bank, the balance being handed over to the City Treasurer in the form of silver and copper required for the payment of salaries and the like. When transactions of this sort take place, the cashier at the Guildhall notes and initials the amount on the back of the bank slip counterpart produced daily at the City Treasurer's office. To avoid floating balances, it would be preferable for an official acknowledgment (carbon style) to be given for each sum so received, and for the said amount to be entered as a direct payment in the Manager's traffic cash book and as a direct receipt in the City Treasurer's cash book.

A question recently put to me was whether the traffic cashiers should be placed on the City Treasurer's staff. I am of opinion that this course should not be adopted. The conductors are members of the Manager's staff and responsible to him for the performance of their duties, and it logically follows that they should pay over their takings direct to his representatives.

Verification of Cash.

For years past I have expressed the view that occasional surprise visits should be paid by the professional auditors (or the internal audit staff) for the purpose of testing the accuracy of cash in all Corporation departments. As this general recommendation has not yet been adopted by the Council, the Committee's attention is drawn thereto.

LOST PROPERTY.

The system of dealing with articles found in the cars is capable of improvement. The practice is for conductors to hand in such articles to the inspector in charge of the box-office in the City Square between 9 a.m. and 6 p.m. Articles found in the cars before and after these hours are handed by the conductors to the various depot foremen, by whom they are sent daily to the said inspector. Conductors handing in the articles record the time when the goods were found, car number and route, on a tag label which the inspector (or depot foreman) attaches to each article. Signatures are obtained on the back of such labels for goods returned to owners. Unclaimed articles are periodically handed over in bundles to the Manager's office, Alfred Gelder Street, for storage.

It is found that the inspector at the box office has not been required to produce the receipts which, he states, have invariably been taken from owners recovering lost property, and that, following the practice of his predecessor, such receipts were destroyed after entering in the day book the names and addresses of the persons to whom the goods were returned; neither has it been the practice for the Manager's office staff to check off the unclaimed articles transferred to the general office with the articles appearing as unclaimed in the inspector's day book. The necessary precautionary measures should be taken forthwith.

Coins found in the cars and passengers' unclaimed change-money are placed by the inspector in envelopes on which are written similar particulars to those above mentioned. In the case of "valuables" (watches, &c.), labels are attached. Cash and "valuables" unclaimed are handed over to the Manager's office on the expiration of a few months. At the time of my investigation it was found that the chief cashier had not realised the necessity of checking these monies with the day book.

Every article and item of cash entered in the lost property register could be given a consecutive number which would be recorded on the label (or envelope) for verification purposes. When articles are returned to owners, the officer handing such article over should sign his name on the back of the tag as well as the claimant, the return being duly recorded in the day book. Found articles should be sold by auction or otherwise (as the Committee may determine) at periods not exceeding one year, such articles being checked with the records prior to being sent to the sale room. It would be well for the Committee to view and to consider whether the storage arrangements in the cellars are suitable.

In certain towns a small fee of 2d. or 3d. (for accommodation and custody) is made when returning articles to claimants, a special form of receipt being used. It is suggested that the Committee should consider the advisability of introducing some such charge.

In the future the Manager's office staff should call for the production of all receipts for articles returned to owners and compare same with the day book, and take all requisite steps to ensure regularity in this matter.

Cash and articles should be transferred to the Manager's office at short regular periods and all such items checked off at the time with the day book.

In my interim report, dated 23rd April last (pages 9 and 10), attention was drawn to the fact that, according to the day book, the unclaimed cash found in the cars from 1st April, 1912, to 31st December, 1916, amounted to £66 2s. 11½d., whereas the cash handed last year to the Manager and not accounted for by him until the 12th March, was £24 0s. 3d., leaving a difference of £42 2s. 8½d. to be explained, irrespective of the unclaimed cash for the four months commencing 1st April, 1912, for which period the day book has not been produced. The chief cashier subsequently informed the Committee that he could positively state that the ex-Manager (Mr. McCombe) had not had possession of this money and he could only conclude that the items of cash making up this amount had been repaid and the receipts destroyed. In accordance with the Chairman's instructions, the sum in question has been written off as a bad debt in the accounts for the year ended 31st March last.

WAYBILLS.

If the Committee is likely to require statistics shewing the numbers of passengers carried and fares received during the different hours of running, the form of the waybill could be somewhat altered so that this information could be given without undue labour.

The Committee might also consider the desirability of a space being provided on the waybill in which the conductors could note the articles and cash found in the cars (also passengers' change-money), stating the time when found. Space could then be provided for the receiver's initials.

WAGES.

During the course of the inquiry, the question of the deduction of army pay and allowances made to employees serving with H. M. Forces was probed into. It was found that the increases of pay which took effect from 29th September, 1917, were not taken into account in the Manager's department until the January following—with the result that a considerable amount was dropped without the Committee's authority. The acting-Manager's attention has been drawn to the fact that further increases of pay were made from the 1st February last to men serving with the Army of Occupation and that such increased rates also applied to other soldiers from the 1st May. From his reply, dated 2nd June, it appears that no action had been taken to adjust the differences brought about by such increases.

Separate wages books are in use for drivers, conductors and sundry persons.

In a report, dated October, 1913, dealing with the financial administration as a whole, I recommended (amongst other things) that whilst it is desirable that all wages books should continue to be prepared in the various executive departments, the accuracy of such books should be tested by my staff with the time sheets (including, of course, the rates of pay, &c.) instead of being (as now) little more than an arithmetical check. It is advisable that this course should be generally adopted.

DAY BOOK—

It is recommended that particulars of *all* accounts to be rendered should be entered in a departmental day book, which should be deposited at my office in order that the charges may be debited in the official records in accordance with the general custom and accounts despatched; further, that all such accounts be payable at the City Treasurer's office.

REQUISITION AND ORDER BOOKS—

All goods over a certain specified value should be entered in a requisition book, which should be submitted to the Committee for approval. In case of emergency, it may be necessary to place orders prior to such approval being obtained. In such case items should be entered in the book in, say, red ink in order that the Committee may know what goods have been ordered in anticipation.

All orders should be given on an official form (consecutively numbered). Tradesmen's accounts should be impressed by a rubber stamp somewhat similar to the one used in the Health Department, and shewn below.

```
Goods Received by .............................
Prices and Extensions checked .............
Countersigned ..................................
       MEDICAL OFFICER OF HEALTH.
Reqn. Book.......... Order No. ...............

CHARGE TO

Allowed ..................... Chairman.

Committee ...................
```

These books should be deposited with the accounts at my office at least a day before the Committee meetings in order that tests may be made, as is the practice with certain other Corporation departments.

CONDUCTORS' CHANGE-MONEY.

In the course of the inquiry a considerable number of conductors voluntarily stated that they would prefer change-money being withdrawn. I express no

COMPENSATION CLAIMS BY THIRD PARTIES.

It is desirable that a continuous record should be kept in a suitable book in the Manager's office of all compensation claims received and that such book should be regularly submitted to the Claims Sub-Committee. It is also desirable that the drivers' report forms should be numbered consecutively after completion and filed for purposes of reference.

CLAIMS FOR THE RECOVERY OF COST OF DAMAGES BY THIRD PARTIES.

In the past no satisfactory log has been kept for the purpose of recording all car damages caused by third parties and shewing what action (if any) was taken to recover the cost incurred, with particulars thereof.

The remark with regard to drivers' reports also applies in this matter.

UNIFORMS.

It was observed that notwithstanding the fact that men on service with H.M. Forces were being rapidly demobilised, no action had been taken to cancel the order or arrive at some arrangement with Messrs. H. Lotery & Co., for the supply of women conductors' uniforms, leggings, &c., ordered about a year ago and not delivered until after the inquiry. The outlay incurred represented some £1,000.

I am informed that old uniforms are not generally returned when new clothing is issued, but are regarded as being in the nature of perquisites.

RECEIPT BOOKS.

The "sundries" receipt books have been ordered by the traffic department, each book being numbered 1 to 250. It is recommended that, in accordance with the general practice, all receipt books be ordered and stocked by the City Treasurer and that they be continuously as well as consecutively numbered and on the carbon duplicate system; further, that all old receipt books should be returned to the Treasurer so soon as the last form has been used and recorded (and initialled for), in the register of such books. When a new book is issued, the person to whom it is handed should sign therefor in the register, it was not advisable that the report of the Sub-Committee should go further.

The Tramway Electrical Engineer, at the request of the Committee, retired, and a discussion having taken place, it was

Moved by the Deputy-Chairman,

Seconded by Councillor Gibson,

That the Tramway Electrical Engineer be suspended as from to-day until a reply be received to the report ; that he be given 14 days in which to reply, and for this purpose he be allowed full access to the station and works under such conditions as the Chairman and Deputy-Chairman may think desirable.—Motion carried.

The Tramway Electrical Engineer was then called into the room and the above resolution was read to him by the Chairman.

opinion upon the matter except to mention that the practice of advancing these sums should either be made general or discontinued. If the practice is continued, conductors should sign for sums handed to them, and should be handed an official receipt whenever repayments are made.

It is probable that the recently appointed General Manager, on taking over control of the traffic and engineering departments, will find it necessary to make various alterations in the re-organisation and administration. With regard to certain of the foregoing matters, the Committee, however, may consider it expedient to give instructions forthwith.

WM. H. SMITH,
City Accountant.

Guildhall,
Hull,
30th July, 1919.

RESOLVED—That the report be entered on the minutes.

Moved by Councillor Richardson,

Seconded by Councillor Sherwood,

That the recommendations contained in the report relating to

(1) the cashing of cheques for employees and others ;
(2) the payment in of monies received from the sales of "prepaid" tickets ;
(3) lost property ; and
(4) wages ;

be adopted and immediately brought into operation, and that the remainder of the report be left over for discussion until the arrival of the General Manager.

TRAMWAY ELECTRICAL ENGINEER'S DEPARTMENT.

A report was received from Councillors Richardson and Wheeldon and the City Accountant with reference to the Tramway Electrical Engineer's Department. The Tramway Electrical Engineer was questioned on the report, but the Committee were not satisfied with his replies. He asked for time in which to make a formal written reply to the report, and the Committee decided that until such reply was received

Appendix 15

The first proposals by Messrs England, Saxelby and Sharp for the construction of horse tramways within the town of Hull and subsequent consideration by the Corporation

The papers describe the case made by the applicants in November 1871 and the questions raised by the Corporation. It is probably difficult to appreciate just how radical the proposal was in 1871. Other details can be found in chapter 1.

FACTS

RESPECTING

STREET TRAMWAYS;

THE SUBSTANCE OF

A SERIES OF

OFFICIAL REPORTS,

&c, &c, &c,

ADDRESSED TO THE

MAYOR, CORPORATION, AND INHABITANTS

OF THE

BOROUGH OF HULL.

London:

W. MORRISON & SONS, 44, LIME STREET, E.C.

1871·

THE TRAMWAYS ACT, 1870.

HULL STREET TRAMWAYS.

To the Mayor, Aldermen, and Burgesses of the Borough of Kingston-upon-Hull, acting by the Council of the said Borough as and for the Local Board of Health in and for the said Borough, and to the Dock Company at Kingston-upon-Hull, and to each of them.

GENTLEMEN,

Tramways have for some years past been universally adopted in all the great cities and towns of the United States of America and Canada, and in most of those places have become an absolute necessity. They are in universal favour with the great masses of the people on account of the cheapness of the fares, and the accessibility, ease and comfort of the carriages.

They have been introduced into many of the principal cities and towns on the Continent of Europe, and in South America, viz., Copenhagen, Brussels, St. Petersburg, Madrid, Geneva, Hamburgh, Constantinople, Buenos Ayres, and other places, in all of which they have proved a great public convenience, arrangements have also been made for their construction in several other large cities in Europe and South America.

In the United Kingdom, tramways are working, or have been authorised by the local authorities, in the principal cities and towns, such as Edinburgh, Glasgow, London, Liverpool, Birken-

head, Birmingham, Sheffield, Leeds, Cardiff, Dublin, Cork, and other places.

Tramways have conferred the greatest benefits upon the inhabitants in places where they have been brought into practical operation, and no higher testimony of their character could be afforded than that the success which has attended their adoption at home and abroad has led Parliament to sanction their construction through the principal thoroughfares in London, *including some of the narrowest and most crowded streets, where they have been found to absolutely free instead of impede the traffic.*

Probably no town in the United Kingdom is better adapted for the use of street tramways than Hull. The streets are level, and a system of cheap, capacious, and comfortable locomotion to unite the town with the suburbs is, without doubt, very much required. In the Session of 1870 the Government introduced a general Bill into Parliament for the construction of tramways, on which Bill a committee of the House of Commons heard evidence from a large number of towns, and being satisfied of the public advantage of the system such Bill was passed into law in the same Session under the title of "the Tramways Act, 1870." By clauses 26 to 33 of this Act all the rights and privileges of the local authorities as well as the gas and water companies are preserved intact, and our client, the projector, is prepared, if required, to arrange, with the local authorities for the maintenance of those portions of the streets at the cost of the proprietors of the tramways, *by this means there will be no interference of any sort with the local authorities in maintaining the roads.* Under this Act, a provisional order of the Board of Trade, which can only be made with the consent of the local authority, is necessary for the authorisation of a tramway, and an application for this order must be made in the months of November and December, or one of them.

Our client, Major Trevenen James Holland, C.B., of Tremayne, Upper Norwood, in the County of Surrey, and of No. 15, New

Broad Street, in the City of London, who is the projector of this scheme for supplying Hull with a system of tramways, is prepared and desirous to make application for a provisional order under the Act for authority to construct the tramways in the Borough of Hull, and is ready and willing to arrange for the construction, management and working of such tramways *without any cost whatever to the mayor, aldermen and burgesses of the borough.*

It is proposed to lay tramways along the following routes, that is to say,—

From Suffolk Terrace, on the Beverly Road, down that road, down Prospect Place, Albion Street, Bond Street, George Street, Charlotte Street, North Street, Bridge Street, across the north bridge, Witham, and along the Holdemess Road.

From the cemetery gates, down the Spring Bank, to the junction of the Spring Bank with the Beverley Road.

From St. Matthew's Church on the Anlaby Road, down that road, Midland Street and Osborne Street to Saint John's Street.

On the Hessle Road, down that road and Porter Street, to Osborne Street.

In Savile Street, Junction Street, across Whitefriar Gate Bridge, down Whitefriar Gate, Silver Street, the Market Place, Queen Street, and Nelson Street.

The rails proposed to be laid down are similar to those used in London, Liverpool, and Leeds, and will not cause any interference with the ordinary traffic passing over or across them.

The construction of such tramways will be of the greatest benefit to the public and meet the wants of the traffic which now passes along these thoroughfares, and which is constantly increasing.

It is intended that special tram cars shall run early in the morning, and again in the evening for the convenience of the working classes, at one uniform small charge of 1d. per passenger whatever the distance ; and that the tram cars running during the day shall also have a small fixed charge, in no case exceeding 3d. per journey.

In America and on the Continent it is common to have tickets, which are sold in the towns for the greater convenience of passengers, and it is intended that this plan should be adopted in Hull, as it would save considerable trouble and inconvenience to the public.

The accommodation afforded by the cars running on such tramways will be very superior to the ordinary road omnibuses, in respect of comfort, convenience, speed, and facilities of transit. The outside width of the cars will be considerably less than the present road omnibuses, whereas the inside will be much wider, owing to the wheels of the cars running under the seats instead of outside the body of the vehicle as in omnibuses.

The annexed evidence affords abundant proof of the benefits conferred on the public by the construction of street tramways, and their adaptability to the the most dense population and crowded narrow streets, or the more thinly inhabited suburbs.

By the 4th section of the Tramway Act it is enacted, "That provisional orders authorising the construction of tramways in any district may be obtained by any persons with the consent of the local authorities of such district."

We have, therefore, humbly to request that you will give your consent to Major Hollands' application for a provisional order under the said Act, and authorising him and those with whom he is concerned to construct the lines of tramway above mentioned.

We have the honor to remain, gentlemen,

Your most obedient Servants,

ENGLAND, SAXELBYES & SHARP.

HULL, *6th Nov.,* 1871.

LOCAL BOARD OF HEALTH,
KINGSTON-UPON-HULL,

WORKS COMMITTEE

TOWN-HALL, HULL,

10th NOVEMBER, 1871.

Present :

Mr. Alderman CHAPMAN, in the Chair.

Mr. ABBEY,   Mr. BRYSON,
Mr. DENISON,   Mr. DOWNS,
Mr. DOWSING,   Mr. EASTERBY,
Mr. ELLISON,   Mr. FOUNTAIN,
Mr. HALL,   Mr. SEWARD,
Mr. WITTY,   Mr. WOODHOUSE.

The Mayor (R. JAMESON, Esq.)

STREET TRAMWAYS.

Mr. Saxelbye, with his Client, Major Holland, and Mr. Kincaid, his Engineer, Mr. J. Smith, (High street), and Mr. Smith, the Corporation's Surveyor, attended the Meeting; with reference to the laying down of Street Tramways in the Borough.

Mr. Saxelbye presented a Plan of the various Tramways now proposed to be constructed in the Borough, shewing a slight alteration from those contained in the notice given by Messrs. England, Saxelbyes and Sharp, and dated the 12th October last.

Mr. Saxelbye then made a statement, to the effect that it is proposed to lay Tramways along the following routes, that is to say,— From Suffolk terrace on the Beverley road, down that road, down Prospect street, Albion street, Bond street, George street, Charlotte street, North street, Bridge street, across the North Bridge, Witham, and along the Holderness road. From the Cemetery Gates down the Spring-bank, to the junction of the Spring-bank with the Beverley road. From St. Matthew's Church on the Anlaby road, down that road, Midland street, and Osborne street to St. John's street. On the

WORKS COMMITTEE.

Hessle road, down that road and Porter street, to Osborne Street. In Savile street, Junction street, across Whitefriargate Bridge, down Whitefriargate, Silver street, the Market place, Queen street, and Nelson street.

The rails proposed to be laid down are similar to those used in London, Liverpool, and Leeds, and will not cause any interference with the ordinary traffic passing over or across them.

It is intended that special tram-cars shall run early in the morning, and again in the evening, for the convenience of the working classes, at one uniform small charge of 1d. per passenger, whatever the distance; and that the tram-cars running during the day shall also have a small fixed charge, in no case exceeding 3d. per journey.

The outside width of the cars will be considerably less than the present road omnibuses, whereas the inside will be much wider, owing to the wheels of the cars running under the seats, instead of outside the body of the vehicle, as in omnibuses.

By the 4th section of the Tramway Act it is enacted, "That provisional orders authorising the construction of tramways in any district may be obtained by any persons with the consent of the local authorities of such district."

WORKS COMMITTEE.

Mr. Saxelbye remarked that the original route through Carr lane had been changed to one through Osborne street and Midland street.

In reply to the Mayor, Mr. Saxelbye said it was proposed that working men should be allowed to ride from one extremity of the town to the other for 1d, so far as the Company's tramways went. After some conversation as to the width of busses, the Mayor said he saw that by the the provisions of the Act there was a clause on the point.

The Law Clerk (Mr. Todd) reported that "by section 25, every tramway is to be constructed on the guage prescribed by the special Act; but if no guage is prescribed, then on such guage as will admit of the use upon the tramways of carriages with a guage of four feet eight inches and a half, and maintained in such manner as the uppermost surface of the rail shall be on the level of the road."

The Corporation Surveyor observed that he had measured a cab from centre to centre of tire, and found it only half-an-inch more than what was proposed.

In reply to Mr. Denison, Mr. Kincaid said the tramways did not inconvenience carriages, as they could cross without difficulty, the grooves for the tramway carriages being both

WORKS COMMITTEE.

narrow and shallow. Mr. Sharp, the Board's Surveyor, remarked upon the state of the roads at Leeds where tramways existed. In two miles there was not a distance of 100 yards together where the road was level with the tramways. The roads were in a bad state close by the tramways. Mr. Sharp expressed an opinion that if tramways were allowed in Hull, the construction of the road between the ways and close outside them should be of granite, and not macadam, as the latter could not be kept in repair.

Mr. Denison asked if the intention was to proceed with one tramway ot once, or with them all? Major Holland said they asked for general powers to construct and they intend carrying out all the tramways.

In reply to Mr. Alderman Witty, who said he should like a definite answer as to laying down granite sets, Major Holland said they were bound to put down what the Board insisted upon, and, as had been stated, it would be to the Company's interest to keep the roads in a good state, and thus prevent accidents.

The Mayor said he thought the tramways should be carried on the Anlaby Road, beyond

WORKS COMMITTEE.

St. Matthew's Church, to the limits of the borough.

Major Holland and Mr. Saxelbye said the company would probably consent if there was no opposition from the North Eastern Railway Company.

The Mayor asked if, in the event of running the present 'busses off the road, which would most likely happen, the Company would undertake to run as many 'busses as there were at present.

Major Holland said he should like to see the Company's busses run every quarter of an hour, or even more frequently, if required.

On the question of the Company not being prosperous, and becoming insolvent, being raised, Major Holland said the company could from the first agree not to mortgage their property without the consent of the Corporation; or else make a deposit, which should be invested. The Board could have a condition.

The deputation then withdrew, and the question having been discussed, and it appearing that the rights of the Board could be protected by the insertion of proper clauses in any Provisional Order that was obtained, it was ultimately

LOCAL BOARD OF HEALTH,

KINGSTON-UPON-HULL.

TOWN-HALL, HULL,

13th NOVEMBER, 1871.

At a General Meeting specially convened, for the purpose of considering an application by Messrs. England, Saxelbyes and Sharp, on behalf of Major T. J. Holland, C B., to make Tramways in certain of the Streets and Roads in the Borough, and to pass such Resolution or Resolutions thereon, as such Special Meeting may determine."

Present—

The Mayor (R. JAMESON, Esq.,) in the Chair.
12 ALDERMEN AND 38 COUNCILLORS.

WORKS COMMITTEE

Moved by the Mayor, seconded by
Mr. Alderman Dowsing,

That this Committee, being of opinion that laying down Street Tramways within the Borough, under the "Tramways Act, 1870," will be a great boon and convenience to the inhabitants, recommend the Local Board, at their Special Meeting on Monday next, to consent to Major Holland's application for leave to lay down, maintain, and construct such Street Tramways as are shown upon the Plan thereof, marked "A," now produced to this Committee by Mr. Saxelbye, and signed by the Chairman presiding; subject, nevertheless, to such special regulations and stipulations being introduced into the Provisional Order, consequent upon such consent being passed, as may hereafter be determined upon by a Special Committee, to be appointed by the Board at such Meeting.

Carried.

LOCAL BOARD OF HEALTH.
(GENERAL MEETING)

The Clerk produced the following application by Messrs. England, Saxelbyes and Sharp, viz :—

"HULL STREET TRAMWAYS.

To the Mayor, Aldermen and Burgesses of the Borough of Kingston-upon-Hull, acting by the Council of the said Borough, as and for the Local Board of Health, in and for the said Borough, and to the Dock Company at Kingston-upon-Hull, and to each of them.

We beg to inform you that application is intended to be made to the Board of Trade, in the ensuing Session of Parliament, for a Provisional Order to authorise our Client, MAJOR TREVENEN JAMES HOLLAND, C.B. of Tremayne, Thicket Road, Upper Norwood in the County of Surrey, and of number 15, New Broad Street, in the City of London, to construct and maintain the Street Tramways mentioned in the annexed Schedule, or some of them, with all necessary Approaches, Sidings and Conveniences connected therewith; and as we understand the District in which the Tramways are proposed to be laid, or part or parts thereof, are within the jurisdiction of you, or one of you, it is necessary for us to obtain the consent of you, or one of you, to the intended application. We have, therefore, to request you respectively to obtain such sanction to our application as is required by the provisions of, and pursuant to "The Tramways Act, 1870," and if you will inform us of the time fixed for such Meetings respectively, we shall be happy to attend,

LOCAL BOARD OF HEALTH.
(GENERAL MEETING)

with our Client and the Engineer, and to afford the Meetings every information.

Your most obedient Servants.

ENGLAND, SAXELBYES & SHARP.

Hull, 12th October, 1871."

Also the Schedule referred to in such resolution, viz :—

"HULL STREET TRAMWAYS.
SCHEDULE.

A Tramway (No. 1) from the corner of Junction-street and St. John-street, passing through Junction-street, Savile-street, Bond-street, Albion-street, Prospect-street, and the Beverley-road, to the limits of the Borough of Kingston-upon-Hull on that road.

A Tramway (No. 2) from the corner of Junction-street and Saint John-street, passing through Saint John-street, Carr-lane, Chariot-street, Carlisle-street, Prospect-street, and the Beverley-road, to the limits of the Borough of Kingston-upon-Hull on that road.

A Tramway (No. 3) from the corner of Prospect street and the Beverley-road, passing through and along the Spring-bank to the East side of the Victoria Dock branch of the North-Eastern Railway near the Cemetery Gates Station, within the said Borough.

A Tramway (No. 4) from the corner of Junction-street and Saint John-street, through Saint John-street, Carr-lane and the Anlaby-road, to the East side of the Hull and Selby Branch of the North Eastern Railway, within the said Borough.

LOCAL BOARD OF HEALTH.
(GENERAL MEETING.)

A Tramway (No. 5) from the corner of Junction-street and Saint John-street, through Saint John-street, Carr-lane, Midland-street, Porter-street, and the Hessle-road, to the limits of the said Borough on that Road.

A Tramway (No. 6) from the North-Eastern corner of Savile-street, through George-street, Charlotte-street, North-Street, Bridge-street across the North Bridge, through Witham and the Holderness-road, to Mile House on the said Holderness road, within the said Borough.

A Tramway (No. 7) from the North-End of Great Union-street, through Great Union-street, Popple-street, and the Hedon-road, to the Hull Borough Prison on the said Hedon road, within the said Borough.

Which several Tramways will pass through or into the Parishes of Holy Trinity and Saint Mary, Sculcoates, Sutton, Garrison-side, and Drypool, including the Township of Southcoates, or some of them, in the Town and County of the Town of Kingston-upon-Hull.

ENGLAND, SAXELBYES & SHARP.

The Clerk reported that in order to a thorough understanding of the matter by the Board, he had prepared and forwarded to every Member of the Board an analysis of the "Tramways Act, 1870", upon which the application for the consent of the Board to construct Street Tramways was founded.

The Clerk further reported that Mr. Saxelbye, with his client, Major Holland, and his Engineer, &c., had attended a Meeting of the Works Committee on Friday last,

LOCAL BOARD OF HEALTH
(GENERAL MEETING.)

the 10th instant, and having produced a Plan of the various Street Tramways now proposed to be constructed by his client, in the following Streets of the Borough, viz:—

From Suffolk Terrace, on the Beverley Road, down that Road, down Prospect-Street, Albion-Street, Bond-street, George-street, Charlotte-street, North-street, Bridge-street, across the North Bridge, Witham, and along the Holderness-road.

From the Cemeetry Gates, down the Spring Bank, to the Junction of the Spring Bank with the Beverley Road.

From Saint Matthew's Church on the Anlaby Road, down that Road, Midland-street and Osborne-street, to Saint John-street.

On the Hessle Road down that Road, and Porter-street to Osborne-street.

In Savile-street, Junction-street, across Whitefriar-gate Bridge, down Whitefriar-gate, Silver-street, the Market Place, Queen-street, and Nelson-street.

Showing a slight deviation from the Streets set out in the Notice and Schedule of the 12th October last, the Works Committee, after a full consideration of the whole matter, passed a Resolution recommending the Board to accede to Messrs. England, Saxelbyes and Sharp's application.

The Clerk further reported that a printed Copy of the Minutes and Proceedings of the Works Committee of the 10th instant had been sent to each Member of the Board,

LOCAL BOARD OF HEALTH.
(GENERAL MEETING.)

and it was thereupon

Moved by Mr. Alderman Chapman, seconded by Mr. Alderman Bannister;

That such Minutes and Proceedings of the Committee of Works of the 10th instant, be now received.

Carried unanimously.

The Clerk having produced and read the following further communication from Messrs. England, Saxelbyes and Sharp, viz:—

THE TRAMWAYS ACT, 1870.

HULL STREET TRAMWAYS.

To the Mayor, Aldermen, and Burgesses of the Borough of Kingston-upon-Hull, acting by the Council of the said Borough, as and for the Local Board of Health, in and for the said Borough.

Gentlemen,

Tramways have for some years past been universally adopted, in all the great Cities and Towns of the United States of America and Canada, and in most of those places have become an absolute necessity. They are in universal favor with the great masses of the people, on account of the cheapness of the fares and the accessibility, ease, and comfort of the carriages.

They have been introduced into many of the principal Cities and Town on the Continent of Europe, and in South America, viz:—Copenhagen, Brussels, St. Petersburg, Madrid, Geneva, Hamburg, Constantinople, Buenos Ayres, and other places, in all of which they have proved a great public convenience; arrangements have also been made for their construction in several other large Cities in Europe and South America.

In the United Kingdom Tramways are working, or have been authorised by the Local Authorities in the principal Cities and Towns, such as Edinburgh, Glasgow, London, Liverpool, Birkenhead, Birmingham, Sheffield, Leeds, Cardiff, Dublin, Cork, and other places.

Tramways have conferred the greatest benefits upon the Inhabitants in places where they have been brought into practical operation, and no higher testimony of their character could be afforded than that the success which has attended their adoption at home and abroad, has led Parliament to sanction their construction through the principal thoroughfares in London, including some of the narrowest and most crowded streets, where they have been found to absolutely free, instead of impede the traffic.

Probably no Town in the United Kingdom is better adapted for the use of street Tramways than Hull. The streets are level, and a system of cheap, capacious, and comfortable locomotion to unite the Town with the suburbs, is without doubt, very much required. In the session of 1870 the Government introduced a General Bill into Parliament, for the construction of Tramways, on which Bill a Committee of the House of Commons heard

LOCAL BOARD OF HEALTH.
(GENERAL MEETING)

evidence from a large number of towns, and being satisfied of the public advantage of the system, such Bill was passed into law in the same Session, under the title of "The Tramways Act, 1870. By clauses 26 to 33 of this Act, all the rights and privileges of the Local authorities, as well as the Gas and Water Companies, are preserved intact, and our Client, the Promoter, is prepared, if required, to arrange with the local authorities for the maintenance of those portions of the streets at the cost of the proprietors of the Tramways; by this means there will be no interference of any sort with the Local authorities in maintaining the Roads. Under this Act a Provisional Order of the Board of Trade, which can only be made with the consent of the Local authority, is necessary for the authorization of a Tramway, and an application for this Order must be made in the months of November and December, or one of them.

Our Client, Major Trevenen James Holland, C.B., of Tremayne Upper Norwood, in the County of Surrey, and of No. 15, New Broad-street, in the City of London, who is the Promoter of this Scheme for supplying Hull with a system of Tramways is prepared and desirous to make application for a Provisional Order under the Act for Authority to construct the Tramways in the Borough of Hull, and is ready and willing to arrange for the construction, management and working of such Tramways without any cost whatever to the Mayor, Aldermen and Burgesses of the Borough.

LOCAL BOARD OF HEALTH.
(GENERAL MEETING)

It is proposed to lay Tramways along the following routes, that is to say,—

From Suffolk Terrace on the Beverley Road, down that road, down Prospect Street, Albion Street, Bond Street, George Street, Charlotte Street, North Street, Bridge Street, across the North Bridge, Witham, and along the Holderness Road.

From the Cemetery Gates, down the Spring Bank to the junction of the Spring bank with the Beverley road,

From Saint Matthews Church on the Anlaby road, down that road, Midland street and Osborne street, to Saint John street.

On the Hessle road, down that road and Porter street to Osborne street.

In Savile street, Junction street, across Whitefriargate Bridge, down Whitefriargte, Silver-street, and the Market place, Queen-street, and Nelson-street.

The rails proposed to be laid down are similar to those used in London, Liverpool, and Leeds, and will not cause any interference with the ordinary traffic passing over or across them.

The construction of such Tramways will be of the greatest benefit to the public, and meet the wants of the traffic which now passes along these thoroughfares, and which is constantly increasing.

It is intended that special Tram-Cars shall run early in the morning, and again in the evening for the convenience of the working classes, at one uniform small

LOCAL BOARD OF HEALTH.
(GENERAL MEETING.)

charge of one penny per passenger, whatever the distance; and that the Tram-Cars running during the day shall also have a small fixed charge, in no case exceeding three-pence per journey.

In America, and on the Continent it is common to have Tickets which are sold in the Towns for the greater convenience of passengers, and it is intended that this plan should be adopted in Hull, as it would save considerable trouble and inconvenience to the public.

The accommodation afforded by the Cars running on such Tramways, will be very superior to the ordinary Road Omnibuses, in respect of comfort, convenience, speed and facilities of transit. The outside width of the Cars will be considerably less than the present Road Omnibuses whereas the inside will be much wider, owing to the wheels of the Cars running under the seats, instead of outside the body of the vehicle as in Omnibuses.

The evidence sent herewith affords abundant proof of the benefits conferred on the public by the construction of Street Tramways, and their adaptability to the most dense population, and crowded narrow streets, or the more thinly inhabited suburbs.

By the 4th Section of the Tramway Act it is enacted "that Provisional Orders authorizing the construction of Tramways in any district, may be obtained by any persons with the consent of the Local authorities of such district."

LOCAL BOARD OF HEALTH.
(GENERAL MEETING.)

We have therefore humbly to request that you will give your consent to Major Holland's application for a Provisional Order under the said Act, and authorizing him, and those with whom he is concerned to construct the lines of Tramway above-mentioned.

We have the honour to remain,

Gentlemen,

Your most obedient Servants,

ENGLAND, SAXELBYES, & SHARP.

Hull, 6th November, 1871.

___

And Mr. Saxelbye, with Major Holland, being now present, and the former having handed in an amended Plan showing the extension of the proposed Tramways to the "Crown Inn," on the Holderness Road, and such Plan and a duplicate thereof, having been marked with the letter "B", and signed by the Mayor, as the Chairman of this Meeting; and Major Holland, in answer to an objection to the Tramways being brought into the Old Town, having stated that if the Board's Special Committee, to be appointed to-day, should be of opinion that no Tramway should be introduced into the Old Town, or if introduced, then that the Cars should be worked on Market days under Special Rules and Regulations to be made or approved of by such Special Committee, he, in the event of the Resolution now before the Board being carried, pledged himself and the Promoters, to abide by the Committee's decision in the matter, either way; and such explanation having been considered satisfactory, it was

LOCAL BOARD OF HEALTH.
(GENERAL MEETING.)

Moved by Mr. Alderman Chapman, seconded by Mr. Alderman Bannister,

That in accordance with the recommendation of the Works Committee of the Board, now received, this Board hereby consents to and approves of an application being made, by Major Trevenen James Holland, C.B. of Tremayne Thicket Road, Upper Norwood, in the County of Surrey, and of Number 15, New Broad Street in the City of London, or by such person, persons, or Corporation, or Company, as he may associate with himself, for a Provisional Order, or an Act, authorising the construction of Tramways in the Streets, shewn in the accompanying Plan marked "B," and the duplicate thereof, colored blue, (both signed by the Mayor, as the Chairman of this Meeting; subject nevertheless to such special regulations and stipulations being introduced into the said proposed Provisional Order, or Act, as may be determined upon by this Board.

Motion put and Carried, Messrs. Carlin and Jackson dissenting.

Moved by Mr Alderman Chapman, seconded by Mr. Councillor Bellamy,

That such Special Committee consist of the following Members, viz:—The Mayor (ex officio) and Messrs. Bannister, Chapman, Denison, Dowsing, Glover, Hall, Seaton and Witty.

Motion put and Carried.

The Clerk reported that he had this morning been

LOCAL BOARD OF HEALTH.
(GENERAL MEETING.)

served with two notices, by Messrs. England, Saxelbyes & Sharp, the one notifying intention to apply to Parliament in the next Session for leave to bring in a Bill, under the short title of 'The Hull Tramways Act," to authorise the construction of Tramways in the Borough, and the other notifying their intention to make a similar application to the Board of Trade for a Provisional Order, under the same short title, authorising the construction of such Tramways as aforesaid ; and that as the Standing Orders of Parliament, and the Regulations of the Board of Trade require that notice of these applications should be posted in the Street or Streets along which it is proposed to lay such Tramways, for fourteen consecutive days, before the end of this month, in such manner as the Board shall direct, and requiring to be furnished on or before to morrow with such directions as the Local Board may deem necessary with reference thereto, it was

Moved by Mr. Alderman Chapman, seconded by Mr. Alderman Bannister,

That the Local Board so far as they can or lawfully may, hereby consents to Messrs. England, Saxelbyes & Sharp posting, under the superintendence of the Board's Surveyor, the several notices above referred to.

Motion put and Carried.

Moved by Mr. Alderman Loft, seconded by Mr. Alderman Witty,

TRAMWAYS COMMITTEE.

LOCAL BOARD OF HEALTH,
KINGSTON-UPON-HULL.

TRAMWAYS COMMITTEE.

TOWN-HALL, HULL,
17th NOVEMBER, 1871.

Present :—

The Mayor (R. JAMESON, Esq., in the Chair.

Mr. BANNISTER. Mr. CHAPMAN,
Mr. DENISON, Mr. DOWSING,
Mr. GLOVER, Mr. HALL,
Mr. WITTY.

The business of the Committee being to appoint a Chairman, it was

---

LOCAL BOARD OF HEALTH.
(GENERAL MEETING.)

That the Clerk furnish Major Holland with a copy of the foregoing Minutes and Proceedings, and affix the Common Seal of the Board thereto, and to the Plan marked " B," and the duplicate thereof now produced to this meeting.

Motion put and Carried.

ROBT. JAMESON, Mayor,
Chairman.

LOCAL BOARD OF HEALTH

KINGSTON-UPON-HULL.

TRAMWAYS COMMITTEE.

TOWN-HALL, HULL,

12th DECEMBER, 1871

Present—

The Mayor (R. JAMESON, Esq.,) in the Chair.

Mr. BANNISTER,	Mr. CHAPMAN,
Mr. DENISON,	Mr. DOWSING,
Mr. GLOVER,	Mr. HALL,
Mr. SEATON,	Mr. WITTY.

READ—Resolution passed by the Local Board on the 13th ultimo, appointing this Committee.

The Clerk having produced the Draft of the proposed Provisional Order of the Board of Trade authorising the

---

2   TRAMWAYS COMMITTEE.

Moved by Mr. Alderman Chapman, seconded by Mr. Councillor Glover,

That the Mayor be the Chairman.

Carried unanimously.

Robt. JAMESON, Mayor,

Chairman.

LOCAL BOARD OF HEALTH,
KINGSTON-UPON-HULL.

TRAMWAYS COMMITTEE.

TOWN HALL, HULL,
13th MAY, 1872.

Present :

The Mayor, (R. JAMESON, Esq.,) in the Chair.

Mr. CHAPMAN,	Mr. DENISON,
Mr. DOWSING,	Mr. GLOVER,
Mr. HALL,	Mr. SEATON,
Mr. WITTY.	

The Minutes of the last meeting having been printed and distributed amongst the Members were taken as read.

The Clerk presented the following report. viz :—

---

construction of Tramways within the Borough, as lodged by the Promoters, and also various amendments and alterations therein suggested by the Mayor, himself, and the Surveyor, after several conferences upon the subject; and such Draft and suggested alterations and amendments having been discussed and considered by the Committee, Mr. Saxelbye and Mr. Smith, on behalf of the Promoters having attended the meeting, and after a long discussion upon the whole matter, commencing at 11 a.m, and ending at 5 p.m., it was

Moved by Mr. Alderman Bannister, seconded by
    Mr. Councillor Seaton,

That such Draft Provisional Order, with the several amendments and alterations, now made and agreed to by Mr. Saxelbye, as the Local Solicitor to the Promoters, be approved by this Committee, and a Print of such Draft as so approved be forwarded to each member of the Board.
Carried unanimously.

A letter from Col. Francis and others, requesting the Board to repave Whitefriargate and Silver-street with Val-de-Travers asphalte, was

ORDERED—to stand over for the present, in order to see whether any arrangement can be made with the Tramways Company.

" To THE TRAMWAYS COMMITTEE.

Gentlemen,

On the 12th December last, the Draft Provisional Order, authorizing the construction of Tramways within the Borough, in its then shape, with the several amendments and alterations suggested by you, and agreed to by Mr. Saxelbye, as the Local Solicitor of the promoters, was approved, and such approval was subsequently confirmed by the Local Board.

The Provisional Order so approved, was subsequently submitted to the Board of Trade, and at the request of Mr. Saxelbye, on the 25th day of March last, and agreeably to the directions of the Board, I sent an intimation to the Board of Trade that the Local Board approved the Order in its then form.

Understanding on the 23rd April, that the Draft Order had been much altered by the Board of Trade, I wrote that Department stating that I understood some considerable alterations had been introduced into the Provisional Order herein, altering the complexion of the whole affair, and that no copy of the Order as so altered had been submitted to me, and requiring that they would consider my letter of the 25th March, approving the Provisional Order in its then shape, to be withdrawn, until the Order as it now stands was submitted to me for revision on behalf of the Local Board.

On the 26th ultimo, I received the Order as finally approved by the Board of Trade, and in the discharge of my duty I have now to point out the alterations introduced after its approval by the Local Board.

1st.—In Clause 3 the expression that the " road authority " should mean the Local Board of Health, has been struck out, and the following introduced :—

The expression " road authority " shall, with respect to any roads which are vested in, or which are maintained and repaired by the Dock Company, at Kingston-upon-Hull, include the said Dock Company.

Notwithstanding this alteration, the Board still remains the Road Authority under the " General Tramways Act." The words originally inserted in the Clause, should I think be reinstated, the words as to the Dock Authority, in respect of their Streets being retained.

Clause 7 of the Order, approved by you, limiting the guage to 4 feet 8¼ inches, is struck out. Under the 25th Section of " The General Tramways Act," the guage of any Tramway, if not otherwise prescribed, is to be 4 feet 8¼ inches ; the alteration is not perhaps therefore of much importance.

The 8th Clause inserted by you, and stipulating as to the proper " making, &c.," of the Tramways, seems to me to be one of great importance, and should I think be restored into the Order, "The General Tramways

TRAMWAYS COMMITTEE.

Act" not dealing with the "making," but only with the "renewal, &c.," of Tramways.

The 9th Clause approved by you has been struck out altogether, and a new Clause omitting the words "the Corporation or any other" in the first line substituted in lieu thereof. I think the new Clause may be considered sufficient.

The 10th Clause approved by you, has been amended by substituting the words "road authority" for the word "Corporation" in the former Clause, and by the following proviso, after the word "Promoters" in the 8th line in such Clause, being added, viz:—

"Provided that in the construction of any such works, no rail shall be so laid, that a less space than 9 feet 6 inches shall intervene between the said rail and the outside of the footpath, on either side of the road, if the owner or owners, or occupier or occupiers of the premises, abutting on the place where such rail is proposed to be laid, shall, by writing under their hand, addressed to the promoters, express their objection thereto."

This proviso seems to me only to extend to control all such crossings, passing places, sidings, junctions and other works in addition to those particularly specified in and "authorised by the Order" as may from time to time be necessary or convenient for the efficient working of the Tramways or any of them, or for providing access to any stables or carriage sheds or works of the Promoters.

TRAMWAYS COMMITTEE.

The Committee will consider whether there is any necessity for this proviso therefore remaining part of the proposed Order.

The same Clause has been further altered, the following words, having been struck out, viz:—
"Provided always, that if any alteration should be required in any of the crossings or sidings leading directly into the premises of the Promoters, they shall have the same power of appeal to the Board of Trade as is provided by Section 33 of "The Tramways Act, 1870.""

I can see no sufficient reason for this proviso being struck out.

After Clause 12 of the Order as approved by you, the following additional Clause has been introduced.

11.—In the construction and use of the Tramways over the North Bridge and the Whitefriargate Bridge belonging to the said Dock Company, the Promoters shall be bound by the following conditions:—

1.—The Promoters shall have no ownership or other interest in the said Bridges other than an easement of laying and maintaining the Trams

2.—The laying down of the Trams and all alterations or repairs thereof shall be done under the superintendence and to the reasonable satisfaction of the Surveyor to the Corporation, or the Engineer to the said Dock Company, as the case may require, and at the cost of the Promoters, unless after 7 days notice given by the

Promoters of their intention to commence such works, such superintendence is refused or withheld.

3.—The Corporation as to the North Bridge, and the said Dock Company as to the Whitefriargate Bridge, shall be at liberty to stop the traffic and the passing of the Promoters' Carriages over such Bridges at such times as shall be necessary for the opening and passages of vessels through the said Bridges, and for all repairs thereto or to the approaches or machinery thereof.

4.—That the passing of vessels through the said Bridges shall at all times have precedence of the traffic of the Promoters.

5.—That in the event of any difference between the Corporation or the said Dock Company and the Promoters, the same shall be settled by a Referee to be appointed by the Board of Trade, in the manner prescribed by the 33rd section of "The Tramways Act, 1870."

6.—That the Promoters shall be subject to such Bye-Laws, Rules and Regulations made by the Corporation, as may from time to time be enforced for the regulation of the traffic and passing of carriages over any of the Bridges in the Borough of Kingston-upon-Hull, over or across which the Trams of the Promoters may be laid.

There are no objections to the introduction of this Clause and its various Sections.

The 18th Clause of the Order approved by you, has been altered as follows:—

"The Promoters may demand and take in respect of any articles or things in small parcels conveyed by them from any point on one Tramway to any point either on the same or on any other Tramway, including the tolls for the use of the Tramways and for waggons and motive power, and every other expense incidental to such conveyance, any tolls or charges not exceeding the rates specified in the Schedule to this Order annexed."

I don't see any particular objection to this alteration if the Committee see fit.

The 20th Clause in the approved Order requiring a list of tolls to be exhibited inside and outside of the Promoters' Carriages is struck out altogether, but the Clause, I think, should for the public convenience be reinstated.

The 22nd Clause, relating to the discontinuance of Tramways during execution of certain work and construction of temporary Tramways, has been altered by striking out after the word "Promoters" in the second line on page 19, the following words, viz.:—"shall within 7 days of receiving an order from the Corporation or Road Authority, under the hand of their Clerk or Secretary, discontinue or take up such Tramway for such term as may be necessary for the execution of the said work, provided the Promoters may."

I think the Clause was better adapted as first drawn and should be therefore reinstated.

At the end of the same Clause the following words have been added:—

"If any difference arises between the Promoters and any Road Authority with respect to the reasonableness of any regulation or with respect to the mode of constructing any temporary Tramway or Tramways under the authority of this Section, the same shall be settled in the manner specified in Section 33 of "The Tramways Act, 1870," for the settlement of differences in the said Section mentioned."

I see no objections to these words!

Wherever the word "Corporation" occurs in the 26th, 27th, 28th, 29th 30th and 31st Clauses of the Order approved by you, the words "Road Authority" are substituted in lieu thereof, and looking to the alteration in Clause 3, the substituted words are correct.

Clause 29 of the approved Order, has been altered by the payment of any overcharge by the Road Authority being made out of the revenue of the Dock Company, as well as out of the Board's General Rates, according as the Road Authority be the "Corporation" or the "Dock Company." An alteration from the word "Corporation" to "Local Board," will be all that is requisite to make this alteration correct.

The 30th Clause of the approved Order, relating to the investment of the sum of £2,000 has in like manner been

altered, the amount required to be invested, is to be invested to the satisfaction of "The Mayor of Kingston-upon-Hull and Chairman of the Dock Company" for the time being, in the joint names of the Promoters, the "Treasurer of the Corporation" and the said Chairman of the Dock Company. This alteration will require amendment, and the words "Chairman and Treasurer of the Local Board" introducing, instead of the Chairman and Treasurer of the Corporation.

Saving Clauses protecting the rights and interests of the Corporation, in its Municipal character, and the Dock Company have been inserted, and to these there seems no objection.

I am, Gentlemen,

Your obedient Servant,

C. S. TODD,

Clerk.

The Clerk reported that on the 8th instant, after seeing the Mayor upon the matter, he wrote to Messrs. England & Co., stating that after looking over the Draft Provisional Order as received from the Board of Trade, he was desired to express to them the great surprise of the Mayor that the alterations introduced should have been made without any communication with the Board, or without any copy of the Order having been previously submitted for its consideration, and enquiring, for the information of this Committee, by whose authority these alterations had been introduced; and that to such communication, he (the Clerk) had received the following reply, viz.:—

TRAMWAYS COMMITTEE.

Hull, 10th May, 1872.

Dear Sir,

HULL TRAMWAYS.

We have forwarded copy your of letter of the 8th instant, to Messrs. Durnford & Co.

You are aware that the Corporation and the Dock Company required alterations. We saw the Town Clerk who stated he had received a letter from the Board of Trade and copy of proposed Order with alterations for Dock Company, and after going through clauses with him on behalf of the Corporation he stated he would write you, as Clerk to the Local Board in London, direct with the Draft forwarded by the Board of Trade to him (as altered and approved by him,) and requesting your assent to the alterations.

We understood that he forwarded the alterations to you and asked you after perusing them to forward them to the Board of Trade with your approval. The Town Clerk also stated that he had written direct to the Board of Trade, approving of the Order as altered. We understood afterwards the Town Clerk had received a letter from you stating that you had called on the Secretary of the Board of Trade thereon: there the matter ended so far as we were concerned.

Messrs. Durnford state they were informed by the Board of Trade that the Local Board, the Corporation and the Dock Company had submitted amendments, and that they, Messrs. Durnford, only objected to alterations in one clause in reference to the Dock Company. They considered the matter was then in the hands of the Board of Trade.

The alterations made in the Order must have been made by the Board of Trade.

Yours truly,

ENGLAND, SAXELBYES & SHARP,

C. S. Todd, Esq.,
Local Board of Health.

And such report and correspondence, having been read and the matter discussed, it was

Moved by Mr. Councillor Glover, seconded by Mr Alderman Witty,

That the Clerk's report now read, be received and adopted, and that this Committee require, that the Promoters of the Hull Order for authorising the construction of Tramways within the Board's district, shall restore such Order to the same state, as it was approved of by this Board in December last, with the addition of the Clause proposed by the Municipal Corporation and the Hull Dock Company, and the alterations suggested by the Clerk's report; and that in the event of the promoters refusing, neglecting, or being unable to comply with the terms of this resolution, the Clerk do thereupon prepare a Petition against the confirming Bill, and present same to the House of

TRAMWAYS COMMITTEE.

Commons in due course, and also take such other steps in the matter, as this Committee may hereafter see fit or be advised.

Carried unanimously.

———

354

Appendix 16

Depot Plans

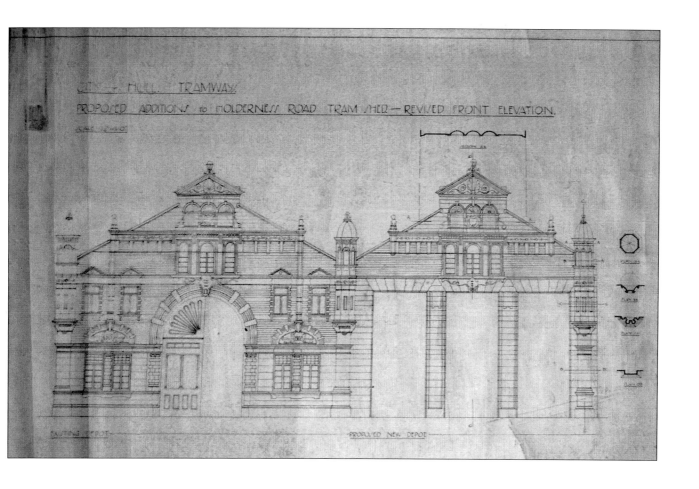

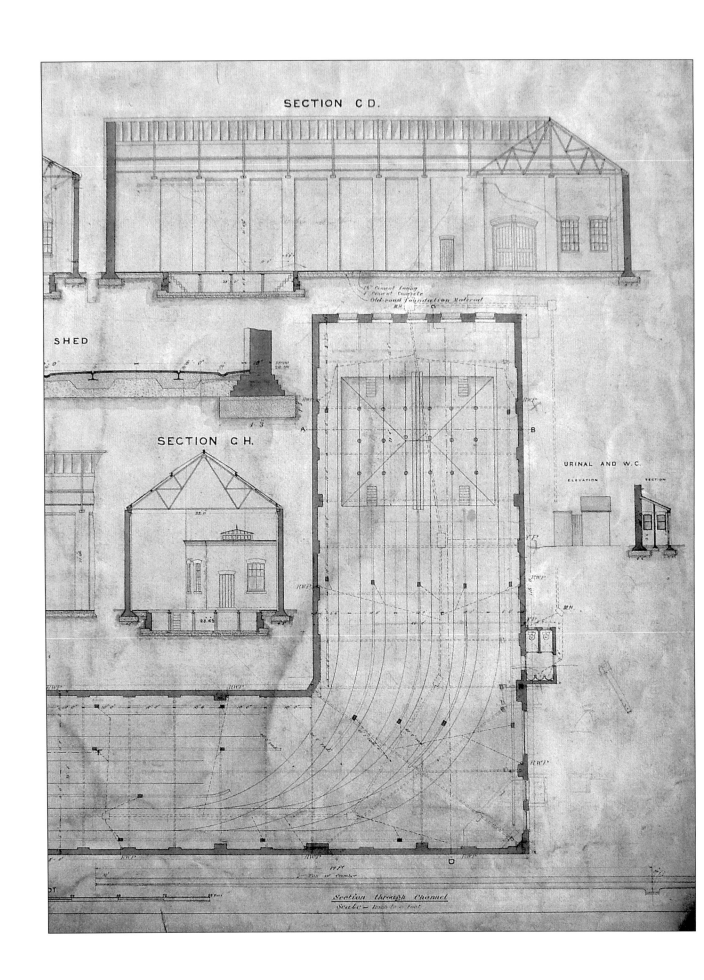

SECTION CD.

SHED

SECTION G.H.

URINAL AND W.C.

ELEVATION   SECTION

Section through Channel
Scale — inch to a foot

Details of Front Elevation

Front Elevation.

Sectional Plan.

357

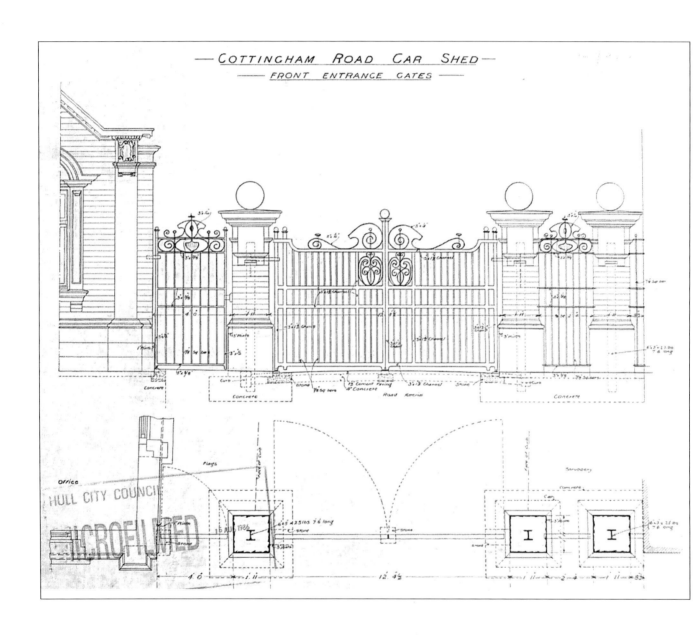

Index

Adam Gordon Books

Battery Trams of the British Isles. David Voice, B5, softback, 56pp, £12

Bibliography of British & Irish Tramways. David Croft & Adam Gordon, A4, softback, 486pp, £35

British Tramcar Manufacturers: British Westinghouse and Metropolitan-Vickers. David Voice, B5, softback, 110pp, £16

British Tramway Accidents. F. Wilson, edited by G. Claydon, laminated hardback, 228pp, £35

The Life of Isambard Kingdom Brunel. By his son, reprint of the 1870 edition, softback, 604pp, £20

Treatise upon Cable or Rope Traction. J.Bucknall Smith plus some other literature on that subject, 434pp., all reprints, card covers, limited print run of 125, £45

The Definitive Guide to Trams (including Funiculars) in the British Isles, 3rd edition. D. Voice, softback, A5, 248pp, £20

The Development of the Modern Tram. Brian Patton, hardbacked, 208pp, profusely illustrated in colour, £40

Double-Deck Trams of the World, Beyond the British Isles. B. Patton, A4 softback, 180pp, £18

Double-Deck Trolleybuses of the World, Beyond the British Isles. B. Patton, A4, softback, 96pp, £16

The Douglas Horse Tramway. K. Pearson, softback, 96pp, £14.50

Edinburgh Street Tramways Co. Rules & Regulations. Reprint of 1883 publication, softback, 56pp, £8

Edinburgh's Transport, Vol. 2, The Corporation Years, 1919-1975. D. Hunter, 192pp, softback, £20

Electric Railway Dictionary, definitions and illustrations of the parts and equipment of electric railway cars and trucks. Reprint of 1911 publication by R. Hitt, huge number of figures including numerous very detailed scale drawings, 350pp; hardbacked in buckram, limited print run of 125, £45

Electric Tramway Traction. A. Greatorex (Borough Engineer and Surveyor, West Bromwich), reprint of 1900 original, 92pp, hardbacked in buckram, limited print run of 125, £25

Fell Mountain Railways. Keith Pearson, A4, hardback, 362pp. £45

The Feltham Car of the Metropolitan Electric and London United Tramways. Reprint of 1931 publication, softback, 18pp, £5

Freight on Street Tramways in the British Isles. David Voice, B5, softback, 66pp, £12

The Age of the Horse Tram. David Voice. A4, laminated hardback, 208pp, £40

Hospital Tramways and Railways, third edition. D. Voice, softback, 108pp, £25

How to Go Tram and Tramway Modelling, third edition. D. Voice, B4, 152pp, completely rewritten, softback, £20

London County Council Tramways, map and guide to car services, February 1915. Reprint, 12" x 17", folding out into 12 sections, £8

Manx Electric Railway Saga. Robert P. Hendry. A4. Full colour. 144 pp, hardback. £38.80.

Metropolitan Electric, London United and South Metropolitan Electric Tramways routes map and guide, summer 1925. Reprint, c.14" x 17", folding out into 15 sections, £8

Modern Tramway, reprint of volumes 1 & 2, 1938-1939. A4 cloth hardback, £38

Monorails of the World. D. Voice, A4 softback, 96pp, colour, £25

My 50 Years in Transport. A.G. Grundy, 54pp, softback, 1997, £10

Next Stop Seaton! – 55 Years of Modern Electric Tramways Ltd. Second revised and enlarged edition, D. Jay & D. Voice, B5 softback, 142pp, coloured covers, £20

Omnibuses & Cabs, Their Origin and History. H.C. Moore, hardback reprint with d/w, 282pp, £25

The Overhaul of Tramcars, reprint of LT publication of 1935. 26pp, softback, £6

The History and Development of Steam Locomotion on Common Roads. W. Fletcher, reprint of 1891 edition, softback, 332pp, £18

The History of the Steam Tram. H. Whitcombe, hardback, over 60pp, £12

A History of the British Steam Tram, Volume 1. D. Gladwin, hardback, coloured covers, 176pp, 312 x 237mm, profusely illustrated, £40

A History of the British Steam Tram, Volume 2. D. Gladwin, hardback, size as above, coloured covers, 256pp, £40

A History of the British Steam Tram, Volume 3. D. Gladwin, hardback, size as above, coloured covers, 240pp, £45

A History of the British Steam Tram, Volume 4. D. Gladwin, hardback, size as above, coloured covers, 256pp, £45

A History of the British Steam Tram, Volume 5. D. Gladwin, hardback, size as above, coloured covers, 256pp, £45

A History of the British Steam Tram, Volume 6. D. Gladwin, hardback, size as above, coloured covers, 256pp, £45

A History of the British Steam Tram, Volume 7. D. Gladwin, Include a complete reprint of Some Remarks on Working Street Tramway Lines by Steam Power with Description of Various Engines. By Leonard J. Todd, May 1874. 1008pp in 2 parts, hardbacked, limited print run of 400, £95

Street Railways, their construction, operation and maintenance C.B. Fairchild, reprint of 1892 publication, 496pp, hardback, profusely illustrated, £40

Toy and Model Trams of the World – Volume 1: Toys, die casts and souvenirs. G. Kuře and D. Voice, A4 softback, all colour, 128pp, £25

Toy and Model Trams of the World – Volume 2: Plastic, white metal and brass models and kits. G. Kuře and D. Voice, A4 softback, all colour, 188pp, £30

Trackless to Trolleybus – Trolleybuses in Britain. By Stephen Lockwood, A4, hardbacked, small colour section. £50

George Francis Train's Banquet, report of 1860 on the opening of the Birkenhead tramway. Reprint, softback, 118pp, £10

My Life in Many States and in Foreign Lands. G.F. Train, reprint of his autobiography, softback, over 350pp, £12

Tram and Bus Tokens of the British Isles. David Voice, B5, colour softback, 66pp, £20

Trams Across the Wear: Remembering Sunderland's Electric Trams. Stephen Lockwood. A4, laminated hardback, 160pp, £35

Trams, Trolleybuses and Buses and the Law before De-regulation M. Yelton, B4, softback, 108pp, £15

The Tram Driver. by David Tudor, hardbacked, 72pp, £20

Tramway Review, reprint of issues 1-16, 1950-1954. A5 cloth hardback, £23

Tramways and Electric Railways in the Nineteenth Century, reprint of Electric Railway Number of Cassier's Magazine, 1899. Cloth hardback, over 250pp, £23

Tramways – Their Construction & Working. D. Kinnear Clark reprint of the 1894 edition, softback, 812pp, £28

Life of Richard Trevithick. two volumes in one, reprint of 1872 edition, softback, 830pp, £25

The Twilight Years of the Trams in Aberdeen & Dundee. All colour A4 softback, introduction and captions by A. Brotchie, 120pp, £25

The Twilight Years of the Edinburgh Tram. A4 softback, includes 152 coloured pics, 112pp, £25

The Twilight Years of the Glasgow Tram. Over 250 coloured views A4, softback, 144 pp, £25

The Wantage Tramway. S.H. Pearce Higgins, with Introduction by John Betjeman, hardback reprint with d/w, over 158pp, £28

The Wearing of the Green, being reminiscences of the Glasgow trams. W. Tollan, softback, 96pp, £12

Works Tramcars of the British Isles. David Voice, B5, softback, 238pp, £25

TERMS OF SALE

RETAIL UK – for post and packing please add 10% of the value of the order. Orders £100 and over post and packing free. I regret that I am not yet equipped to deal with credit/debit cards.

RETAIL OVERSEAS – postage will be charged at printed paper rate via surface mail, unless otherwise requested. Payment please by sterling cash or cheque, UK sterling postage stamps, or direct bank to bank by arrangement.

SOCIETIES, CHARITIES etc. relating to tramways, buses and railway – a special 50% discount for any quantity of purchases for resale is given provided my postal charges are paid.

WHOLESALE (TRADE) DISCOUNTS FOR MULTIPLE COPIES OF THE SAME TITLE post free – details are available from Adam Gordon

ADAM GORDON
Kintradwell Farmhouse, Brora, Sutherland KW9 6LU
Tel: 01408 622660   E-mail: adam@ahg-books.com   Website: www.ahg-books.com